Handbook on Student Development: Advising, Career Development, and Field Placement

edited by
Mark E. Ware
Richard J. Millard
Creighton University

 LAWRENCE ERLBAUM ASSOCIATES, PUBLISHERS
1987   Hillsdale, New Jersey   London

MAR   1989

Lawrence Erlbaum Associates, Inc., Publishers
365 Broadway
Hillsdale, New Jersey 07642

ISBN 0-89859-918-0

Printed in the United States of America
10 9 8 7 6 5 4 3 2 1

Table of Contents

Preface

Each year in the United States, literally millions of individuals return to or begin undergraduate or graduate school. Those students face a variety of academic, occupational, and personal challenges that can affect them for a lifetime. Most who read this will be able to identify at least one college adviser, broadly defined as any significant other, whose influence continues to be felt. The editors of this book are no exception. For one of us, a faculty member elicited respect for and reinforced the value of the teaching profession; he loved what he did and cared about those whom he taught. The other encountered a faculty member who informed him about the relevance of computer skills for succeeding in graduate school and taught him those skills in a tutorial fashion.

Students can encounter a wide variety of advisers during their short or long term tenure in college. Many students make that discovery in the classroom or in a faculty member's office and others in the context of student personnel services. But whatever the context, advisers have the opportunity to make a profound difference in students' lives.

To whom is this book directed? Although the book's objective is to foster and promote student development, the intended audience consists of those dedicated to teaching, service, and scholarship in higher education. That audience can consist of individuals in the academic areas of the behavioral and social sciences, as well as in counseling and student placement. However, the contents of the book are not restricted to those areas. In fact, the book can appeal to anyone working in academe who possesses a commitment to improving undergraduate and graduate students' quality of life.

Readers will find more than 90 articles in this book. The articles are distributed across three significant challenges to students' development; the academic, occupational, and personal. We organized the materials around three approaches to those challenges; advising, career development, and field placement activities.

We found the contents of the three sections of the book both informative and instructive. From wrestling with the design of an advising system to helping students to develop or refine their study, note taking, or test taking skills, readers will find page after page of helpful suggestions. In addition, those who counsel students seeking admission to graduate school and those who promote personal, teaching, and scholarly development among graduate students will find a plethora of valuable data. The growing literature on career development examines major facets about which teachers and advisers need to know. Readers responsible for managing undergraduate and graduate students' field activities can also profit from others' accumulated experiences.

Researchers will discover that the contents of this book provide an inexhaustible source of information. Whether one is searching for provocative problems, relevant literature, or data that are pertinent to a theory, collectively, the articles provide a thorough representation of the last decade's literature on advising, career development, and field placement issues.

The source for the articles in this book is the official journal, *Teaching of Psychology* (*ToP*), of Division Two of the American Psychological Association. In 1974, the Division initiated the publication of this journal. By publishing a dozen volumes, the journal has provided increased visibility to teaching and teaching related activities, has accumulated a wealth of information, and has promoted scholarly activity. In a survey reported in the *American Psychologist, ToP* ranked 30th out of 99 journals based on the frequency of citation. We encourage those who wish to contribute to the literature on the teaching of psychology to send their manuscripts to Charles L. Brewer, Editor; Department of Psychology; Furman University; Greenville, SC 29613.

We are grateful to many individuals. To the many authors whose dedication and persistence contributed to the substance of this book, we extend a hearty thanks. Jack Burton at Lawrence Erlbaum Associates provided us with support and counsel throughout. We also thank Ludy Benjamin whose encouragement and direction as President of Division Two reinforced our tentative behaviors. By providing his experience, guidance, and active support, Bob Daniel, Founding Editor of *ToP*, contributed significantly to producing a quality product on time. Finally, Suzanna Kempf, Bonnie Ware, and two computers named Apple made an otherwise herculean task, possible. For any errors we have made in producing this book, we can only assume responsibility and apologize.

Finally, we want our readers to know that all royalties produced from the sale of this book will be paid directly to the treasury of Division Two of APA. Our hope is that such funds can be reinvested in our students' development.

We further hope that those who read this book will appreciate our broad perspective about teaching that an anonymous source expressed: "Until one has learned to listen, that person has no business teaching: Until one realizes that every person has something of truth and wisdom to offer, that person has not begun to learn."

Mark E. Ware
Richard J. Millard

Section I
Advising

A common complaint among undergraduates is that they often feel anonymous in a college or university system that does not respond to their needs for academic and career advising. At the same time, faculty may feel over worked and/or under rewarded for their advising efforts. Nevertheless, one of the most pressing problems for many departments is to provide adequate academic and career advising for their students. Quality advising not only aids students in adapting to college life and preparing for a career, but it also helps institutions meet their goals for providing a relevant educational experi-ence and retaining students.

The articles in this section contain pertinent informa-tion for the idiosyncrasies of advising undergraduate and graduate students. The first collection of articles provides an overview and perspectives for an advising system. Two groups of articles concentrate on factors affecting academic performance and major considera-tions for students interested in pursuing graduate edu-cation in psychology. The final selection of articles ex-amines and evaluates issues confronting graduate students and their administrators.

1. DEVELOPING STRATEGIES FOR ADVISING

This selection of articles provides a strong rationale for every department of psychology to assign a high priority to advising. The authors provide a model for an advising system and identify numerous suggestions and strategies for improving advising.

Robert Titley has served as a member of the faculty advising staff and Bonnie Titley as Director of Academic Advising at Colorado State University. They identified the "professional obligation" that psychology departments have to provide quality academic advising. They cited evidence to show that students not only need help in choosing a major but also in identifying career options so they are not confused by the familiar question, "What can you do with a degree in psychology?" The authors further demonstrated that high retention of students depends as much on good advising as it does on a sound and marketable curriculum. Finally, the Titleys provided a list of specific suggestions that should guide readers to improving faculty academic advising.

Richard Halgin and Lucille Halgin noted that there is no literature that specifically describes an effective and comprehensive advising program for a large psychology department. Their article described a system used to advise more than 800 majors at the University of Massachusetts. Their system includes compulsory "check-ups" for students at critical periods during their training, workshops on topics of wide interest, and a resource center with a collection of information that undergraduates most commonly seek. The program is a practical option for faculty who feel over worked by advising demands, but who want to meet their responsibilities to students.

John Kremer from Indiana-Purdue University made a disheartening discovery when he found that most students did not seek faculty or advisers' assistance, even though 50% reported that they were experiencing serious study problems. The author elaborated on three obstacles that can account for low rates of academic advising: lack of faculty knowledge about techniques to improve student performance, time and attitude barriers between students and professors, and lack of reinforcement for professors. Kremer provided simple and effective suggestions to aid educators in overcoming those obstacles.

The use of printed materials can reach more students and enhance one on one advising. Uwe Gielen described a handbook he developed at York College. The book, which is available from the author, has an impressive variety of material that is relevant to psychology majors. It contains information about department programs, policies, course sequences, descriptions of faculty, extracurricular activities, and application to graduate school. Advisers may want to examine the author's book and use it as a model to develop one for their own departments.

Academic Advising: The Neglected Dimension In Designs for Undergraduate Education

Robert W. Titley and Bonnie S. Titley
Colorado State University

Quality of academic advising is of continuing importance, and that function impinges upon other aspects of the program.

Psychology majors. Liberal education. Career education. Vocationalism. Needs. Expectations. Diversity. Mobility. Curriculum. Programs.

These were words and phrases that the professor/psychologist half of us (RWT) marked during a perusal of the "challenge" topics embedded in the call for papers for this issue of *Teaching of Psychology*. These words and phrases seemed to key in on the issues which have been of the most concern in my involvement with undergraduates over the past several years at Colorado State University. Facing my fourteenth year as a member of the faculty advising staff of "Preview CSU," our summer orientation program, I was moved to add another topic: the entering freshman. Knowing that fewer than half of the incoming freshman class would complete a degree program and graduate from Colorado State, the "why?" of attrition also came to mind.

My co-author, Director of Academic Advising at CSU, observed that the topics listed were certainly not unique to psychology, but represented a number of the critical issues permeating the university at large. We agreed that one common thread running across the topics was the need for quality academic advising. So this paper is about advising, specifically the necessity of incorporating a commitment to and delivery of effective academic advising in any effort to meet the problems confronting undergraduate psychology in the 1980s.

Academic advising has both a history and a reputation. In 1841, when President Rutherford B. Hayes was a student at Kenyon College, he wrote a letter to his mother describing a new "rule" that had been adopted at Kenyon: Each student must select a faculty member who would become both an advisor and friend "in all matters" and serve as a medium of communication between the faculty and the student (Hardee, 1970). A hundred years later an educator (MacLean, 1953) alluded to both the history and reputation of advising.

Advising is a process with a long and dignified history in college and university. At the same time, involving as it often does tedious clerical work combined with hit-and-run conferences with students on curricula, it is a most cordially hated activity by the majority of college teachers . . ." (p. 357)

Student input will alert one to the reputation of advising Some excerpts from a 1976 student evaluation of academic advising on one campus in response to the sentence stem "Advisors are . . . : friends, helpful, uninformed, doing their best, working overtime, necessary, teachers, counselors, knowledgeable, a drag, problem solvers, nervous, listeners, the ones who have all your information but don't remember your name, too busy," (Cited in Crockett, 1978a). "Too busy' raises the question, "Too busy doing what?" Research and teaching? Expending their time on content, designing curricula, and developing programs to match the faculty's perception of what students need? Trying to keep the administration, legislators, and other sources of dollars believing that what we do for the students is valuable?

Faculties are not unsuccessful at such activities, nor are their efforts born of ill intentions. But beyond course content and programs, what do we convey to students about the assumed wisdom of our plan for them—or their plans for themselves? The reward hierarchy for faculty has possibly become so distorted in the hundred and forty years since President Hayes' college days that an advisor's "rule" in some colleges and universities might now read:

Each faculty member shall be *assigned* a number of undergraduate students as his or her advisees and shall, with a minimum expenditure of time, effort, and caring, answer whatever trivial questions they might have, inform them as to what courses they must take to graduate in whatever major they've chosen (however capricious that choice may be), and be available, if possible, to sign necessary registration forms. The faculty shall also be aware that, for themselves, advising is primarily a perfunctory clerical duty and a minor academic activity relative to teaching, research, and one's own career development, and that there shall be little or no reward or recognition for the performance of advising activities, save for the occasionally expressed appreciation of a grateful, well-advised student.

Is it conceivable that some contemporary college student might apprise his or her mother in a letter home of this "rule"? We believe some students probably already have.

Hardee (1970) summarized the history and reputation of advising in one sentence: "Faculty advising is dignified and derided, much desired but often denigrated, done well and done ill" (p. 27). The process of advising is still with us and students expect to be advised, even those who don't want advice. Faculty, some at least, will continue to offer advising within the many systems that exist, whether their efforts are rewarded or not. Some educators claim an increase in the awareness that advising is an important and critical function

in relation to both the development of curricula and the development of students. In 1979, Crockett stated:

There exists in higher education today a renewed interest in academic advising. Academic advising is recognized as an educational service to be provided by an institution of higher education. Academic advising, properly delivered, can be a powerful influence on student growth and development. It can also interpret, enhance, and enrich the educational development of any college or university. (p. 5.420)

Dressel, in his recently published book *Improving Degree Programs* (1980), writes:

Student advising—especially in relation to teaching and program planning—presents a series of problems and concerns that must be addressed in the curriculum and the programs derived from it are to serve their purposes in preparing students for living, learning, and working . . . If education is indeed to be a continuing lifelong process, the individuals who engage in it must have some sense of the significance and of the sequence to achieve desired goals. In many ways, good advising may be a more critical and a more significant academic function than teaching. (p. 250, p. 261)

Let's be more specific and relate advising to selected areas that present a challenge to undergraduate psychology and its students in the coming decade: (a) the initial choice of major (b) retention and attrition, and (c) vocationalism.

Initial Choice of Major. Large numbers of entering freshmen continue to select psychology as their intended major. They are often unclear as to why they have chosen psychology, although there is some evidence (Titley & Vattano, 1972) that a primary source of interest in psychology is exposure to the topic in high school. In the same study it was found that entry into an applied human service delivery profession was the predominant long-range career goal for the majority (61%) of them. Another 24% were undecided or vague concerning their eventual goal. But an "aura of uncertainty or tentativeness" (p. 136) seemed to prevail when they were asked, "Should you stay in psychology, what is your goal or what do you see yourself doing someday?" A four-month followup confirmed the tenuousness of both major choice and goal. Many, when asked again about their goal, could not recall accurately what they had told the interviewer four months earlier, and several had changed their minds in the interim. After just one year of college, over one-third had changed majors, transferred, or dropped out of school.

In a second followup conducted four and a half years later (Titley & Vattano, 1976) fewer than one-fourth of the original group had completed the degree in psychology, with the remainder having changed majors, withdrawn from college in good standing, transferred to other schools, or left school because of academic difficulties, and none had entered graduate study in psychology. We concluded that for entering freshmen declaring psychology, their choice tended to be tenuous, tentative, unstable and unenduring. While one could ask whether our program matched their abilities, needs, and expectations, it could also be concluded that these students might have benefited from better academic advising.

The authors are near the final stages of another longitudinal study on major choice and major change among undergraduates across all majors at CSU. Some preliminary findings (Titley & Titley, 1980) are worth reporting here. Struck by the high rate of major changing among undergraduates, we are following the major selections and degree progress of 2,451 students who attended our summer orientation program in 1977. After the initial shifting of major selection had occurred (that always occurs) between application to the university and orientation, 942 or about 38% had declared an "undecided" category or had already changed their minds at least once between application and initial contact with the orientation and registration procedure. The remaining 62% were considered the most "decided" behaviorally as a result of having stayed with their original choice during the same period.

Using a self-report measure of "certainty" about choice of major, these 1,509 "decided" freshmen were classed into three categories—"low certainty," "tentative," and "high certainty." It was found in a two-year followup that even among those who had selected a specific major while still in high school, stayed with that choice through the summer, registered for classes in that same major, and who felt "certain" about their choice, there was a fair proportion (17%) who had made a change during the first two years at the university. Among those who had indicated uncertainty or tentativeness about their choice, over one-third had shifted to another major by the end of their second year. Apparently it is not only the "undecided" who are undecided, and our findings dovetail with the results of a recent study at Brigham Young University (Goodson, 1981) which revealed that students with declared specific majors need as much help with career choice and career development as those who are officially in an "undecided" category.

In another few months we will have data on these students at the fifth year point since matriculation. Yet, noting their status after two years, it becomes obvious that we cannot assume that because a student selects a major, his or her major or career choice has crystallized. We believe that colleges and universities are not operating in a manner which fully recognizes the developmental qualities in students and the pressures they are experiencing with respect to choosing a major. These pressures include parental expectations, information from college catalogs which imply that one ought to be able to "pick something," curricula distinguished by inflexibility and designed as though we assume every eighteen-year-old knows what he or she wants to become, and the increasingly powerful force of vocationalism—"Will I be able to get a job when I graduate?"

Psychologists know a great deal about the developmental stages of older adolescents and young adults in terms of personal and vocational growth, yet we sometimes seem to ignore our own knowledge. We especially seem to ignore it when we assume that every beginning psychology major really has his or her mind made up and only the brighter ones who know exactly where they are headed are worth bothering with. Further, are we not sometimes guilty of equating exploratory undecidedness with indecisiveness, immaturity, and academic ineptness? If we are guilty of this, we are no doubt communicating this invalid equation to students.

We would argue that by recognizing the principles of personal and vocational development, and by a greater commitment to the proper delivery of sound academic advising, we might facilitate the growth and progress of the beginning freshmen. This might even lead eventually to better programs and curricula.

Attrition. The negative term is "attrition"; the positive term is "retention." No matter which is used, the issue is how best to create a "staying" atmosphere in academic settings wherein a larger proportion of those entering college complete a degree program.

Maintaining high academic standards will always produce scholastic casualties. Many students at all levels of ability enter college at the wrong time in their lives or for the wrong reasons, reasons which include the inexorable dreams of parents, lack of acceptable alternatives, and unrealistic fantasies about future careers. Once in college, inadequate pre-college preparation, disappointments and frustrations, lack of reinforcements, boredom, inadequate coping or social skills, delayed development of independence, and the realization that college is not what the brochures led them to believe it was, will add to the attrition list.

Trends toward declining enrollments began in the '70s and with the expected decrease in the numbers of high school graduates, there will be a sharper decline in the '80s. Couple declining numbers of high school graduates with increasing costs and predicted cutbacks of financial support for those who want to go to college, and the emerging scenario is one in which, for the '80s, retention will become a salient challenge.

The attrition rate among those who enter college is alarmingly high. About 40% of entering freshmen who enroll in institutions granting the baccalaureate degree never achieve that degee, and it is estimated that of the fifteen million men and women who enter college, some five to six million will never earn degrees of any kind (Cope, 1978). What is killing the educational spirit in so many of these people?

Perhaps there are flaws in the recruiting and admissions process. Often there is little communication between those who are responsible for recruiting and admitting students and those who are responsible for educating them. It is possible that weaknesses exist in the process through which students select the alternative of college, including the guidance systems which direct them our way. Communication boundary walls exist between high schools and colleges, with the only opening in the wall being the admissions "door." Academic departments and admissions offices generally relate only on the basis of numbers. Ott (1978) points out that "the role of admissions in a campus wide retention strategy is too often non-existent. 'We get 'em, you keep 'em' is too often the trend." (p. 73). Academic advising exists primarily as a departmental function and is often limited to interaction between faculty and departmental majors. Occasionally, advising may extend to students in other departments if they are assertive enough to seek it, or to high school seniors on a visitation day. But there is very little interaction between those who "get 'em" and faculty who are asked to "keep 'em," and even less between faculty and the high schools who "send 'em."

James L. Fisher, president of Towson State University, argues that academic soundness is the heart of any academic institution. While recognizing that college is not for everyone, he believes "It is obvious that high retention depends as much on good teaching and advising as it does on sound and marketable curricula" (1978, p. 72). He proposes that faculty should not only meet their responsibilities as advisors to ongoing students, but that they can be

5

effective when involved in the admissions process. James Jose, a dean at Lycoming College who has been addressing the retention issue since 1970, has come forth with this direct challenge to faculty: "You and I may be retention problems" and "the attitude of faculty, administrators is a significant factor in retention" (1978, p. 57). He offers a list of 26 specific ways to attack the retention problem; 11 of his proposals either mention "advising" specifically or describe an approach which involves some facet of the advising process. In summing up Crockett's argument (1978b, p. 29) that academic advising is the "cornerstone of student retention," especially in the area of educational and career goals, Noel concludes that, "A caring, competent advisor can be a powerful retention agent by helping students in these areas" (1978, p. viii). Noel's own position is expressed this way: "How an institution's academic advising measures up to students' needs is the major determinant of whether or not the institution has a 'staying' environment" (p. 96).

In the section on initial major choice, we described the results of our ongoing study on major changing and subjective certainty. In that same study (Titley & Titley, 1980) we found that after two years, students who were either "uncertain" or "tentative" about their major choice were three times more likely to appear on the attrition list than those who expressed a high degree of certainty. We wonder whether those who had doubts and are now gone received the advising they needed and wanted.

Vocationalism.   "What can you do with a bachelor's degree in psychology?"

Whether students direct this question to themselves or others, it can take on an affect-laden quality. If it is self-directed, and the student is a psychology major, it can raise wrenching doubts about the wisdom of his or her choice. If directed toward a psychology faculty member who is unwilling to go beyond the perfunctory "nothing" reply, it can strike at the very existence of the discipline as a degree offering. Many of us have listened to students report the negative reactions they have gotten upon informing parents, spouse, roommate or friends of the fact that they are, or are even considering becoming a psychology major.

Only a very small percentage of graduating seniors in psychology apply for and are accepted into graduate programs in the field and go on to become psychologists. Can we justify the existence of a baccalaureate program which results in only a small proportion of its graduates eventually becoming psychologists? Oh, we have our rationalizations. The purist will restate the concepts of the liberal arts tradition. The pragmatist will offer curricular tracks designed to train students in the skills needed in paraprofessional applied human service delivery. The compromiser will suggest a minor in "something you can use," or state that "psychology can be a good background for many jobs, or for graduate work in other' fields." Many faculty prefer to let the students shift for themselves.

But try to explain to the average undergraduate or to his or her parents the concept of becoming an educated person in and for its own sake, or tell them that college prepares students for "life-long learning." Tell them where the jobs are for the bachelor level paraprofessional, how well those jobs pay, and whether they offer an opportunity for a lifetime career. Tell them exactly what can be paired with psychology to make a person marketable, who the employers are who will be waiting at the end of the commencement platform with a contract, and which areas of graduate study look with favor upon the holder of the psychology baccalaureate degree. Show them a list of jobs obtained upon graduation by last year's graduating seniors. Then observe the look on their faces when they write out the check to pay the tuition bill.

Some students have a career plan at the outset or develop one early in their undergraduate years. Tying back to the retention issue, there is evidence (Tinto, 1975; Astin, 1975; Cope, 1978) that expectations, aspirations, and career plans are related to attrition. Hillery (1978) points out that "The literature consistently documents the fact that postsecondary students who have not made a commitment to a career plan are significantly more dropout prone than those who have a career commitment" (p. 20). It has been our experience that many students who transfer both into and out of CSU can verbalize a connection between career plans and transferring (now apparently called "mobility").

> In a recent conversation with a transfer student, he described this scenario as having occurred at the school of his initial entry:
> Student to faculty member in psychology: "I think I need some career counseling."
> Faculty member: "You should go to the Counseling Center."
> Student to staff member in Counseling Center: "I've been thinking about declaring a major in psychology."
> Counseling Center staff member: "You need to talk to someone in the Psychology Department."
> At a later point in our conversation he was asked: "What made you decide to come to CSU?" His reply: "I have a friend who goes here."

The relationship among career planning, attrition, and mobility is unclear, but each may be related to the quality of academic advising existing in various institutions. Quality academic advising might also help some students who are career casualty cases, the students who had career plans shattered by disillusionment or low academic performance and who must find another path. An example would be the student leaving engineering and wanting to change to psychology as an escape or survival route to a degree in "anything."

Earlier we addressed the marketability of the psychology baccalaureate holder. The limited time perspective of many undergraduates, published job market statistics, and the limited anecdotal information most of us have on recent graduates create the impression that many bachelor graduates are destined forever to settle for jobs they could have gotten with only a high school diploma. Longitudinal studies (Titley, 1978; Davis, 1979) refute this, and there is a wealth of data and information on training and strategies for employment for the psychology major (Woods, 1979). The question is whether these data and information are being communicated to the undergraduate.

More and more students are asking questions about jobs and careers. So are their parents. It is part of what is called "vocationalism," and vocationalism is pervasive on the campuses, whether we like it or not. And there is no excuse for "Nothing" as a reply to the question about what one can do with a degree in psychology.

Conclusions and Recommendations.   Psychology faculty will go on forever building curricula and programs for the psychology majors and will persist in debating liberal arts versus career education and vocationalism. Talk of students' needs and expectations will creep into their considerations. Mobility, diversity and retention have emerged as the big issues for the next decade. But perhaps because of its history and reputation, the critical role of academic advising continues to suffer neglect in our grand designs for undergraduate education in psychology.

It is beyond the scope of this paper to propose or describe comprehensive models of advising and it would be presumptuous of us to think we can offer specific solutions to the advising problems at other colleges and universities. Nevertheless, we would recommend that any department of psychology committed to improving academic advising consider the following:

1. Greater recognition of the educational and vocational development stages in college students, not only in designing curricula and programs, but in the provision of types of advising services.
2. The offering of a special seminar for juniors and seniors on educational and career development. (It is at this stage that undergraduates are the most receptive to advising on "what can I do with a bachelor's degree in psychology?")
3. Establishment of a data base for advising students about the potentials of the degree in psychology, e.g. surveys on the longitudinal career histories of former graduates.
4. Improving the lines of communication among the department faculty, high school personnel, admission and recruiting offices, other institutions, and the parents of incoming freshmen.
5. Better coordination of advising efforts, utilizing a combination of professional academic advisors/counselors from a centralized source, trained peer advisors, and a select group of departmental faculty—faculty who like to advise and who are good at it.
6. Separation of the advising and registration functions and the use of peer advisors during registration time.
7. Adjusting the reward hierarchy in order to foster advising behaviors among faculty and reinforce quality advising.

The major responsibility for providing quality academic advising lies with the departmental faculty. It is our contention that the same people who so eloquently define the issues, who so ably sense the needs of students, and who debate and then create programs and curricula have a professional obligation to interpret these designs to their students—through sound academic advising. After all, the students are the paying consumer in every college and university, and they will continue to be just that in the 1980s, and the 1990s, and . . .

References

Astin, A. W. *Preventing students from dropping out.* San Francisco: Jossey-Bass, 1975.

Cope, R. G. Why students stay, why they leave. In L. Noel (Ed.), *Reducing the dropout rate. New directions for student services* (No. 3). San Francisco: Jossey-Bass, 1978.

Crockett, D. S. (Ed.). *Academic Advising: A resource document.* Iowa City: American College Testing Program, 1978a.

Crockett, D. S. Academic advising: Cornerstone of student retention. In L. Noel (Ed.) *Reducing the dropout rate. New directions for student services* (No. 3). San Francisco: Jossey-Bass, 1978b.

Crockett, D. S. (Ed.). *Academic advising: A resource document* (supplement). Iowa City: American College Testing Program, 1979.

Davis, J. R. Where did they all go? A job survey of BA graduates. In P. Woods (Ed.) *The Psychology Major: Training and strategies.* Washington, DC: American Psychological Association, 1979.

Dressel, P. L. *Improving degree programs.* San Francisco: Jossey-Bass, 1980.

Fisher, J. L. College retention from a presidential perspective. In L. Noel (Ed.). *Reducing the dropout rate. New directions for student services* (No. 3). San Franciso: Jossey-Bass, 1978.

Goodson, W. D. Do career development needs exist for all students entering colleges or just the undecided major students? *Journal of College Student Personnel,* 1981, *22,* 413-417.

Hardee, M. D. *Faculty advising in colleges and universities.* American College Personnel Association Monograph, Student Personnel Services, No. 9, 1970.

Hillery, M. C. Maintaining enrollments through career planning. In L. Noel (Ed.). *Reducing the dropout rate. New directions for student services* (No. 3). San Francisco: Jossey-Bass, 1978.

Jose, J. R. Some plain talk on retention by a college dean. In L. Noel (Ed.). *Reducing the dropout rate. New directions for student services* (No. 3). Jossey-Bass, 1978.

MacLean, M. S. Counseling and the Tower of Babel. *Personnel and Guidance Journal,* 1953, *31,* 357-362.

Noel, L. Editor's notes. In L. Noel (Ed.) *Reducing the dropout rate. New Directions for student services* (No. 3). San Francisco: Jossey-Bass, 1978.

Ott, L. S. Admissions management with the focus on retention. In L. Noel (Ed.) *Reducing the dropout rate. New directions for student services* (No. 3). San Francisco: Jossey-Bass, 1978.

Tinto, V. Dropouts from higher education: A theoretical synthesis of recent research. *Review of Educational Research,* 1975, *45,* 89-125.

Titley, R. W. Whatever happened to the class of 1967? Psychology baccalaureate holders one, five, and ten years after graduation. *American Psychologist,* 1978, *33,* 1094-1098.

Titley, R. W., & Titley, B. S. Initial choice of college major: Are only the "undecided" undecided? *Journal of College Student Personnel,* 1980, *21,* 293-298.

Titley, R. W., & Vattano, F. J. Psychology as a "major" step from high school to college. *Vocational Guidance Quarterly,* 1972, *20,* 133-138.

Titley, R. W., & Vattano, F. J. A case of tentative choice: The freshman psychology major. *Vocational Guidance Quarterly,* 1976, *25,* 126-129.

Woods, P. (Ed.). *The psychology major: Training and employment strategies.* Washington, DC: American Psychological Association, 1979.

An Advising System for a Large Psychology Department

Richard P. Halgin and
Lucille F. Halgin
University of Massachusetts

This department has faced up to its responsibilities to students and to the university by reorganizing advisement.

One of the most common complaints from undergraduates enrolled at large universities is that they feel a sense of being anonymous—lost in a large system which is not typically able to respond to them in a personalized manner. Though a large university often has a correspondingly large faculty, these faculty often devote most of their energies to scholarly pursuits and to the graduate students who are participants in their programs of scholarship. One of the most serious problems for a large psychology department lies in the provision of adequate advising for its majors. This article chronicles some of the unsuccessful attempts to establish effective advising at the University of Massachusetts/Amherst in the past, and then describes the current system, which by all reports is regarded as the first successful advising system in the past fifteen years.

What a Good Advising System Should Do. A departmental advising system has weighty and diverse responsibilities. On the one hand it should be of service to the students, helping them to adjust, plan and prepare. On the other hand, it is an agent of the institution, as it goes about promulgating, and at times enforcing, the standards and practices of the institution. With regard to the former tasks, an advising system should sensitively cater to the needs of students during those tempestuous undergraduate years, when they need help and direction in both personal and professional development. College students have been characterized as feeling alienated (Burbach & Thompson, 1971) and as being in desperate need of help with the resolution of the typical transitional tasks of adolescence and college life (Coons, 1970). Once they are settled into college, students need help becoming familiarized with their department, their major, and future applications of their learning. As they prepare to graduate, they need help in defining a post-baccalaureate direction for their lives.

With regard to institutional needs, an effective advising system should ensure that students are complying with the expectations of the faculty, the department, and the university. Such an advising system should also be sensitive to possible discordance between student goals and curriculum goals (Malin & Timmreck, 1979), and sound the alarm to the department if and when these goals differ markedly.

Relatively little has been written on the establishment of an effective overall psychology advising system, and we have found nothing which specifically describes a system for a large psychology department. Heiney (1977) quite emphatically calls upon psychology departments to assume a more conscientious role in advising; and Kremer (1980) enumerates some of the obstacles to advising, which account for so few students seeking academic consultation. Other than these two articles, most of what has been written pertains to career advising and career preparation concerns (Boltock, Peterson, & Murphy, 1980; Caffrey, Berger, Cole, Marx, & Senn, 1977; Korn & Lewandowski, 1981; Korn & Nodine, 1975; Malin & Timmreck, 1979; McGovern, 1979; Turner, 1974; Ware & Beischel, 1979; Ware & Matthews, 1980).

History of Advising System Failures. The University of Massachusetts/Amherst is an institution that has grown very rapidly during the past three decades. In the early 1950s it was making the transition from being the relatively small Massachusetts Agricultural College with less than 5,000 students to the University of Massachusetts, which currently enrolls more than 25,000 full time students. The Psychology Department grew from a handful of students and faculty to its present size as one of the largest departments in the country with 55 full time faculty, 800 undergraduate majors, 200 graduate students, and 11,000 psychology course enrollees per year. Other major universities have typically grown in steady increments over a period of decades, but at the University of Massachusetts there was an almost overnight growth explosion in the later 1960s. In a three year period the psychology faculty grew from 25 to nearly 60 members. The problem with such sudden and dramatic growth was that the department had not really developed appropriate strategies for dealing effectively with its undergraduates. The department lacked traditions which might serve as the backbone for its growth, and it stumbled in its early attempts to personalize the psychology program for its majors.

In the "old days" (pre-1970), the psychology department used an advising system which is still popular, and probably quite effective, at smaller colleges and universities, namely, each faculty member was randomly assigned a certain number of students who were required to have a specified number of advising sessions each year. Such a system has its merits, the most striking of which is that it ensures that faculty maintain some personal contact with undergraduates, and that the students know precisely to whom to turn with academic questions or concerns. However, at the University of Massachusetts the problems of this system soon began to outweigh the benefits. The major problem had to do with the deficient advising expertise of most of the faculty. At such a large and growing institution faculty members found it difficult to keep up with departmental requirements and programs, to say nothing of university-wide systems; faculty and students alike were reporting frustration. Secondly, there was wide variability in the approaches taken by faculty members; this resulted not only in differing levels of accessibility, but also gross inconsistencies in policy implementation.

Because of the above-mentioned problems the department decided to restructure the advising system in the early 1970s; in fact, the department opted to be concordant with the "do your own thing" era, and it abandoned compulsory advising for its majors altogether. The presumption was that, as adults, undergraduates could be responsible for attending to their own programs of study, and did not need to be monitored by an advising superstructure. The department recognized that some advising system would be needed for the students choosing or needing to seek direction, and so a group of approximately five faculty were appointed by the chair each academic year to constitute an advising corps. One of these individuals served as Chief Advisor; this person was given responsibility for coordinating the efforts of the appointed advisors, and attempted to ensure consistency of policy implementation. These advising faculty worked out of a centally located advising office, which was equipped with all the materials needed for advising, such as student files and departmental and university information.

After a few years under this new system, it was apparent that the department had a fiasco on its hands. Though the advising corps was comprised of five consistent, knowledgeable, and available faculty members, they were being shockingly underutilized . In 1979, less than five percent of the 800 psychology majors chose to speak to an advisor; and the handful of students who did come to the advising office were typically those who were in dire straits. Students complained bitterly about the lack of advising, but continued to stay away from what was available. The kind of student apathy which was being discussed elsewhere (Coffield, 1981) had certainly become quite apparent at our university, and it seemed that our system was colluding with such student passivity.

The major side effect of this underutilized system was that curriculum chaos developed: courses were being taken out of sequence; required courses were being avoided until the last possible moment; and some of the basic courses were being skipped completely. There were cases of students reaching their final semester with many of their departmental core course requirements missing, due to their earlier choices of more esoteric seminars. Professors were complaining about inadequately prepared students in the advanced courses, but it took some time for the department to realize that this was resulting from an inadequate advising structure. Transfer students and incoming freshmen felt hopelessly confused and neglected, and a sense of anonymity and apathy prevailed among our majors. Although majors respected the academic strengths of the department and the prestige of the faculty, they were grossly dissatisfied with our lack of an effective and appealing advising system.

The New Advising System. Following an extensive advising system analysis undertaken in 1980 by the Director of Undergraduate Studies (first author of this paper), and completed in 1981 by Dr. Nancy Myers, the subsequent Director, the Department decided to overhaul the advising structure. The importance of a high quality advising system was recognized, and the financial resources were found to develop one. The second author of this paper (LFH), who at that time was a part-time instructor, was asked to take on the

newly created position of Advising Coordinator. She was commissioned to develop an advising system which would avoid the pitfalls of the previous systems and more satisfactorily address the needs of both students and faculty for more effective and intelligent advising.

The first task was the re-establishment of some form of compulsory advising. Rather than going back to the old system of requiring every student to see an advisor every semester, a new method requiring specified "check-ups" was established. Three "check-up" points were designated: (a) prior to freshman or transfer entry (summer), (b) second semester of sophomore year (spring), and (c) first semester of senior year (fall). These three times were chosen because it was found that these were the most common problem/question periods for students. Incoming students obviously need help; sophomores typically need help establishing a general sense of direction as they begin to think about careers; and seniors need more specific guidance as they work to define their post-baccalaureate plans.

In order to address concerns about consistency, it was decided that all three of these check-ups would be done by the Advising Coordinator. Five faculty advisors would still be available for general advising needs. In addition there would also be a group of five undergraduate volunteers who would be available for peer advising, a procedure which has been documented as being quite successful by others (Brown, Wehe, Zunker, & Haslam, 1971; Gentry, 1974; Heiney, 1977; Wasserman, McCarthy, & Ferree, 1975; Wrenn & Mencke, 1972). All official advising tasks would be done by the advising coordinator.

Once the system was formulated, there remained the formidable tasks of getting it publicized and respected. The compulsory system was initiated in the spring semester of 1981. All second semester sophomores were sent a letter explaining the new system and requesting that they sign up for an advising appointment. They were told that failure to make an appointment would result in denial of pre-registration privileges for the following semester. Sign-up sheets were posted outside the advising center and the 200 sophomores were alphabetically staggered so that those whose last names began with "A" or "B" were asked to sign up for the first week, "C", "D" and "E" the second week, and so on. These students were informed that the purpose of the 15-20 minute meeting was to review the student's academic program and begin a discussion about career planning. Though a negative reaction from students was anticipated following so many years of laissez-faire advising, the response was quite the opposite. Students were really delighted that their needs were finally being addressed. During that semester, 93% of the sophomore majors were seen for required appointments, with many of them subsequently returning for additional consultation.

The shocking concomitant of the success with sophomore advising was the influx of other students who came to the advising center, after having heard via the grapevine about the new system. In fact, not counting the nearly 200 sophomore appointments, more than 300 other student advising contacts were logged. These contacts were with the Advising Coordinator as well as with the faculty and student advisors. In contrast to the minuscule percentage of students utilizing the former advising system, more than half of all majors have come for some form of advising during each of the three semesters with the new system.

Once the task of coordinating the individualized advising program was organized, the Advising Coordinator initiated other endeavors, which were considered part of the advising domain. Attention was focused on group programs which would serve to facilitate the adjustment of incoming students, familiarize current students with departmental and university opportunities, and prepare advanced students for life after graduation. The advising system has become an invaluable resource system for both students and faculty, systematically acquiring and organizing informational materials, coordinating workshops, and arranging events which might personalize an undergraduate's experience in the department.

The advising office was transformed into a resource center with a substantial collection of materials and information most commonly sought by undergraduates, such as handouts on departmental and university programs, and information about the Graduate Record Examination. Information about current opportunities in research, teaching, field work, and employment was solicited from appropriate sources and systematically organized. We purchased relevant publications of the American Psychological Association, such as *Graduate Study in Psychology and Related Fields* (American Psychological Association, 1983), *Preparing For Graduate Study: Not For Seniors Only* (Fretz & Stang, 1980), and *Career Opportunities for Psychologists* (Woods, 1976). Graduate catalogs for all major university psychology departments were ordered and made available to students for reference purposes. The University's Career Development office provided the advising center with materials which might prove useful to the large group of students who were not graduate school bound. Books such as *A Practical Manual for Job Hunters and Career Changers: What Color Is Your Parachute* (Bolles, 1981) and other similar career definition aids were purchased.

Several workshops were organized for each semester. These included (a) Applying to Graduate School; (b) Possible Careers for Psychology Majors; (c) How to Write a Resume; and (d) How to Get Field Experience. Approximately one hundred majors attended each of these workshops.

The Advising Coordinator also arranged less formal gatherings in an attempt to enhance a feeling of affiliation for undergraduates. The most successful of these events has been the reception held each fall for new majors, which gives incoming students an opportunity to meet faculty and other psychology undergraduates. A reception has also been held for Psi Chi installation, and another following commencement for all graduating seniors and their families.

Conclusions and Recommendations. Following three semesters utilizing the new advising system, evaluations by students, faculty, and administrators have been most favorable; and the deficiencies of our former systems are glaringly apparent. What we had failed to recognize with former advising systems was the ripple effect that resulted from inadequate advising; students were not getting direction they needed, and the results were career confusion, academic chaos, and increased alienation. Large departments should undertake objective appraisals of their advising systems, particularly attending to the costs of poor or non-existent advising. Quite often there is so much acclaimed scholarship, grantsmanship, and graduate educa-

tion in large departments that undergraduates' needs are ignored.

Departments with inadequate advising have a professional responsibility to rectify such a situation. Improvement can only come if there is a commitment on the part of the departmental administration, and this commitment must be demonstrated by the allocation of financial and time resources to the establishment of a good advising system. Often a large faculty has an energetic individual capable and willing to undertake such substantial systems reorganization; this person would need a release from other responsibilities so as to devote the extensive amount of time needed. However, many departments find that the good people are already doing everything else, and the not-so-good people would probably do a not-so-good job; the alternative here would be the hiring of a professional, who is not a tenure-track faculty member, as was done in our program at the University of Massachusetts.

The advantage of this latter option is that continuity and consistency are more likely; and these two factors have proven to be the greatest benefits of our system. Realistically speaking, it is unlikely that either administrators or tenure-track faculty members would feel comfortable with an individual's multi-year commitment to advising duties, in lieu of other professional duties such as research or teaching. This unwillingness probably reflects an unstated bias toward scholarship and teaching over service in such departments; that is unfortunate but not easily modifiable. Thus, it would seem optimal to hire a professional who does not have professorial responsibilities. This becomes a financial dilemma, and it may necessitate that a department forfeit a tenure track hiring so as to fill this position with a non-tenure track staff person. Very likely it will be at this specific choice point where the commitment to good advising will be most surely tested. Though it is conceivable that a non-doctoral staff person could be hired for considerably less money than a professional, there would be several problems. Such individuals would have a very limited knowledge of psychology, and would probably also have more difficulty acquiring the respect of students and faculty.

At the University of Massachusetts our advising system is still very much in an experimental stage. There are probably other ways of accomplishing our goals more efficiently, and it is our plan to continue evaluating our system and improving it. We feel that we have made substantial gains in a short period of time in better serving our undergraduates' advising needs; but the more dramatic and surprising results have been the improved functioning of our undergraduate program and the facilitation of interpersonal connectedness in our department as a whole. Significant progress has been made in the war on alienation and apathy and we urge other departments to join with us and share insights and techniques, so that as psychologists we may become better educators.

References

American Psychological Association. *Graduate study in psychology and related fields.* Washington, DC: Author, 1983.

Bolles, R. N. *A practical manual for job hunters and career changers. What color Is Your parachute?* Berkeley, CA: Ten Speed Press, 1981.

Boltock, M. A., Peterson, T. L., & Murphy, R. J. Preparing undergraduate psychology majors for employment in the human service delivery system. *Teaching of Psychology,* 1980, *7,* 75-78.

Brown, W. F., Wehe, N. O., Zunker, V. G., & Haslam, W. L.   Effectiveness of student-to-student counseling on the academic adjustment of potential college dropouts. *Journal of Educational Psychology,* 1971, *62,* 285-289.

Burbach, H. J., & Thompson, M. A., III.   Alienation among college freshmen: A comparison of Puerto Rican, Black and White students. *Journal of College Student Personnel,* 1971, *12,* 248-252.

Caffrey, B., Berger, L., Cole, S., Marx, D., & Senn, D.   Integrating professional programs in a traditional undergraduate psychology program. *Teaching of Psychology,* 1977, *4,* 7-13.

Coffield, K. E.   Student apathy: A comparative study. *Teaching of Psychology,* 1981, *8,* 26-28.

Coons, F. W.   The resolution of adolescence in college. *Personnel and Guidance Journal,* 1970, *48,* 533-541.

Fretz, B. R., & Stang, D. J.   *Preparing for graduate study: Not for seniors only.* Washington, DC: American Psychological Association, 1980.

Gentry, W. D.   Three models of training and utilization. *Professional Psychology,* 1974, *5,* 207-214.

Heiney, W. F., Jr.   "Practicing what you preach:" A plan for helping freshmen psychology majors get off to a good start. *Teaching of Psychology,* 1977, *4,* 73-76.

Korn, J. H., & Lewandowski, M. E.   The clinical bias in the career plans of undergraduates and its impact on students and the profession. *Teaching of Psychology,* 1981, *8,* 149-152.

Korn, J. H., & Nodine, B. F.   Facts and questions concerning career training of the psychology major. *Teaching of Psychology,* 1975, *2,* 117-119.

Kremer, J. F.   Three obstacles to improving academic consultation. *Teaching of Psychology,* 1980, *7,* 117-118.

Malin, J. T., & Timmreck, C.   Student goals and the undergraduate curriculum. *Teaching of Psychology,* 1979, *6,* 136-139.

McGovern, T. V.   Development of a career planning program for undergraduate psychology majors. *Teaching of Psychology,* 1979, *6,* 183-184.

Turner, R. H.   What happens to the liberal arts BA in psychology who doesn't go to graduate school? *Teaching Psychology Newsletter,* Feb. 1974, 3-4.

Ware, M. E., & Beischel, M. L.   Career development: Evaluating a new frontier for teaching and research. *Teaching of Psychology,* 1979, *6,* 210-213.

Ware, M. E., & Matthews, J. R.   Stimulating career exploration and research among undergraduates: A colloquium series. *Teaching of Psychology,* 1980, *7,* 36-38.

Wasserman, C. W., McCarthy, B. W., & Ferree, E. H.   Student paraprofessionals as behavior change agents. *Professional Psychology,* 1975, *6,* 217-223.

Woods. P. J.   *Career opportunities for psychologists.* Washington, DC: American Psychological Association, 1976.

Wrenn, R. L., & Mencke, R.   Students who counsel students. *Personnel and Guidance Journal,* 1972, *50,* 687-689.

Three Obstacles to Improving Academic Consultation

John F. Kremer
Indiana University-Purdue University

Recently, I heard an eminent authority on higher education chastise the college professor for not providing adequate consultation to students for academic problems. His suggestion for alleviating this problem was to have professors make more office hours available to students. However, my experience indicates that listing many office hours may not be the solution. When I have been available at my office from 9 a.m. until 5 p.m., Monday through Friday, fewer than 5% of the students came for consultation. At first I assumed that this figure represented most of the students who wanted consultation. However, since I didn't know the number of students who needed help, I decided to get an estimate. To my surprise, on a survey and on a behavioral measure, 50% of the students indicated that they had a serious study problem for which they could use some consultation.

To reduce the gap between the students' expression of need and their use of my time during office hours, I changed the pattern of talking with students by indicating on numerous occasions that consultation sessions outside of class were part of my responsibility as a teacher; reducing the stigma associated with having a problem by indicating that students at all levels of ability want to change their study habits and by using the neutral word "consultation" to describe sessions with students; meeting at a convenient time (immediately before or after class, or at another agreeable time); talking at a convenient place (in the hall, at an office near the classroom, or at a student lounge). As a result, more students came for consultation than I could adequately handle (approximately 10 to 15 percent of the 250 students enrolled), and they came with academic problems which I could not easily solve. In addition, I was spending a substantial portion of my uncommitted time doing a service which was not enhancing my job stability (promotion and tenure). For me the cost-benefit ratio was high.

An examination of these personal efforts revealed three obstacles to improving academic consultation to students. First, faculty members aren't likely to know the *techniques to improve student performance.* Second, there are many students who could profit from knowledgeable advice, but the *reduction of barriers* (time, place, and attitude) between professors and students is necessary to increase the probability that students will seek out professors for consultation and use their recommendations. Third, attention must be directed to the needs of and *reinforcements for professors* to encourage them to attain the appropriate skills and to reduce barriers. The remainder of this paper will summarize strategies for overcoming these obstacles to academic consultation with students.

Techniques to Improve Student Performance.   Reviews of the literature (Glasgow & Rosen, 1978; Groveman, Richards, & Caple, 1975) on improving students' academic performance suggest that there are two simple steps which a professor can use in consultation sessions. The most important step is to give the student a good study method. Robinson's (1970) SQ3R technique has consistently led to improved performance. This acronym represents the five sequential steps in the process, Survey, Question, Read, Recite, and Review. Using this method students should survey the chapter headings, turn the headings into questions, actively read by answering the questions, stop reading periodically and recite the substance of each major section, and review several times before a test. The second step is to get the student to monitor study time. An accounting of study time provides a student with accurate feedback. Counting and recording of study time is a manipulation which by itself can lead to increases in the amount of time the student studies (Richards, 1975). Other more complicated techniques, e.g., self-reward for increases in study time, have not been found to significantly increase students' test performance (Glasgow & Rosen, 1978). If professors want to further increase their competence by gaining more knowledge of these procedures, they could read one of the general self-help manuals (e.g., Watson & Tharp, 1977), a recent review of self-help programs (Glasgow & Rowen, 1978), a comprehensive book on self-control procedures (Mahoney & Thoresen, 1974), a literature review of study skills counseling (Groveman, Richards, & Caple, 1975), additional references on study methods (Norman & Norman, 1976; Pauk, 1974), and a book describing a complete counseling program (Brown, 1977).

Reduction of Barriers.   There have been two implicit assumptions of research on study skills, needy students will seek advice from knowledgeable persons and students will follow reccomendations. The first section of this article indicated that students in need will not necessarily solicit help from their professor, so strategies for increasing professor-student contacts were presented. Regarding the second assumption, most studies on compliance (Stone, 1979) suggest that professors and researchers should assume that students will not follow through on recommendations. However, based on our studies and on studies of compliance to medical treatments, professors can greatly enhance their effectiveness by adopting a few simple practices: reducing the expert role and adopting a mutual problem solving approach; demonstrating that they listen to students by making specific recommendations which encompass the limitations of each student's unique situation; in very practical ways, telling students that they are worthwhile persons (e.g., by being on time for appointments and giving them undivided attention); making tasks as simple as possible; making sure the students clearly understand what to do; developing a program based on what students will actually do; obtaining their commitment to do it; building rewards into the program for simply doing the tasks (if students think this is necessary); and setting an appointment within a week for a progress report. The above strategies reflect the position that compliance can be enhanced if students are involved in planning and the professor is involved in the post-planning activities.

Reducing barriers for large classes poses additional problems. Individual sessions with professors are not possible. There are also obvious logistic problems in implementing the suggestions presented above. For example, it is impossible to meet immediately before or after class with all students requesting help. In an attempt to implement a program based on these principles for a large number of students, peer consultants have been effectively used to interact with students individually, in groups, or over the phone.

During a regular class session, interested students are given a short lecture on a study method and a pamphlet which presents a study method and a step by step method for monitoring study time. After they are given this material, they are asked to sign a contract to monitor their study time for several weeks, to try the SQ3R method if they are dissatisfied with their own method of studying, and to call in their data to an answering service. They may also call this service at any time for more academic consultation. If a peer consultant is not immediately available, students leave a message with the answering service. A consultant returns the call within 24 hours and either works with them over the phone or arranges a group session with other students who have similar concerns.

Those students who initially monitor their study time generally continue to do it and need little further intervention from a professor or peer consultant. Compliance to the suggestion to monitor can be moderately increased for these motivated students by simply calling them and reinforcing them for their work. Students who initially fail to comply with the contract need a more intense intervention. A reminder phone call does not bring about compliance, but several in-person or phone counseling sessions will gain compliance from a significant portion of these unmotivated students. For most students who need a new study method, individual or group sessions explaining the new method are necessary to achieve compliance.

Reinforcements for Professors.   In order for professors to learn more about consulting skills and/or to develop a program using undergraduate consultants, they must find some time in a busy schedule to read, plan, solve problems, and write. Although successful consulting with students may be its own reward, additional reinforcements will be necessary to initiate and to sustain a substantial investment of time (Tharp & Wetzel, 1969). In order for faculty to implement an adequate consultation program, they must not only learn the skills and reduce the barriers, but also devise ways for this effort to count within the university promotion process. The most important reward may be publishing articles on innovative ways of providing consultation to students.

References
Brown, W. F.   *Student to student counseling; An approach to academic achievement* (2nd ed.). Austin: University of Texas Press, 1977.
Glasgow, R. E., & Rosen, G. M.   Behavioral bibliotherapy: A review of self-help behavior therapy manuals. *Psychological Bulletin*, 1978, *85*, 1-23.
Groveman, A. M., Richards, C. S., & Caple, R. B.   Literature review, treatment manuals, and bibliography for study skills counseling and behavioral self-control approaches to improving study behavior. JSAS *Catalog of Selected Documents in Psychology*, 1975, *5*, 342-343. (MS. No. 1128)
Mahoney, M. J., & Thoresen, C. E.   *Self-control: Power to the person.* Monterey, CA; Brooks/Cole, 1974.
Norman, M. H., & Norman, E. S.   *How to read and study for success in college* (2nd ed.). New York: Holt, Rinehart & Winston, 1976.
Pauk, W.   *How to study in college.* Boston: Houghton Mifflin, 1974.
Richards, C. S.   Behavior modification of studying through study skills advisement and self-control procedures. *Journal of Counseling Psychology*, 1975, *22*, 431-436.
Robinson, F. P.   *Effective study* (Revised ed.). New York: Harper, 1970.

Stone, G. C. Patient compliance and the role of the expert. *Journal of Social Issues,* 1979, *35,* 34-59.

Tharp, R. G., & Wetzel, R. J. *Behavior modification in the natural environment.* New York: Academic Press, 1969.

Watson, D. L., & Tharp, R. G. *Self-directed behavior: Self-modification for personal adjustment* (2nd ed.). Monterey, CA: Brooks/Cole, 1977.

A Helping Hand for the Psychology Major: The Student Handbook

Uwe Gielen
York College

Acclimating into the environment of any university or college is not an easy task. Upon application the student is typically swamped with forms to fill out and deadlines to meet. The consequence of this overload is that many vital pieces of information are neglected or overlooked. Although every school offers some sort of college bulletin to help deal with this dilemma, it is usually an all-inclusive volume. The result is that most bulletins tend to emphasize school-wide procedures and say very little about the nuances of each individual department. The senior psychology major may suddenly realize that explicit requirements for graduation have not been adequately satisfied. This may sound like an extreme example, but any student who has had to spend an extra summer session in college to make up three credits in mathematics or pass an equivalency examination in English will agree that this is not an unrealistic possibility.

At York College it was decided that something should be done to help alleviate the annoying worries associated with college life. It became the job of several faculty members and students to devise a solution. This combined effort resulted in the creation of the "York College Psychology Student Handbook." Departmental handbooks are not a new concept. Since the York Handbook has come into existence, this eighty-two page guide has been evoking favorable comments. Its success has prompted us to recommend the use of a handbook and we are pleased to offer our model for future attempts.

Content. Any busy student will be able to appreciate the convenience of a handbook. This may be especially true at colleges like York where the student body is atypical. York is a commuter's college where the average student is somewhat older. These students, whose responsibilities are divided between their families, work and school, cannot afford the time to drop in on an advisor for every question to be asked. The content of the Handbook is intended to supply answers as they are needed.

The Handbook begins with an introduction describing its purpose and follows with a brief history and some background about the science of psychology. The next sections deal with the various programs available at York and in the Psychology Department itself. It describes procedures for declaring a major in the department and gives a detailed account of the Psychology Program. This includes instru-

mental and area requirements that are needed to satisfy college-wide guidelines, the psychology major requirements, a complete listing of course offerings in the Psychology Department, a guide on how to choose courses and suggested course sequences for the different specialties such as General-Experimental Psychology, Clinical-Personality Psychology, Industrial Applications, and Educational and Social Applications. This section also includes pages to be filled in by the student so that progress can be monitored. These pages are quite an asset since they facilitate advisement proceedings.

The Handbook supplies an extensive bibliography that covers virtually every area in psychology. It offers the best sources available in each area and a place to begin when doing research. The bibliography permits more effective use of library time. The student is able to spend less time rummaging through the card catalogue and more time engaged in productive research. The Handbook provides a handy assessment of faculty members along with areas of interest and research for each. This enables the student to choose a faculty advisor that shares his or her own curiosities. In the case of experimental research, it tells the student which faculty member can best answer questions about a particular topic.

Information is provided in the Student Handbook about departmental resources such as academic advisement, tutoring, student advisement, its research library and the extra-curricular activities available to the student. This would include the Psychology Club and Psi Chi, the National Honor Society. There is a section on how to study and one on how to write a research paper. There are substantial data on graduate school and career opportunities. These sections stress the correct methods of applying to schools and seeking employment. The Handbook gives the proper format for letters of recommendation, resumés and how to approach an interview.

The Handbook closes with a partial listing of recent graduates of the Psychology Program at York along with graduate schools they are attending or jobs they are holding.

Format. Information is important and the purpose of the Handbook is to convey as much information as possible. It should be obvious that if the material at hand is not presented in an effective and interesting manner, no one will pay close attention to it. The solution to this quandary was the inclusion of cartoons and appropriate quotations. The York Student Handbook displays the adventures of Oscar, a typical psychology major, as he muddles through the rigors of college life. Oscar's situations reflect the written material being presented and enhance many salient features. He lets the students know that they are not alone in their plight and allows for some welcomed laughter.

The Psychology Student Handbook has been part of an effort at York to arouse further student activity and interest in the department and its programs. It is proving to be an effective catalyst and it certainly shows that the Psychology Department is concerned for its students.

Note

A copy of the York Handbook may be obtained from the author for $2.00 to cover the cost of postage and handling.

2. IMPROVING ACADEMIC PERFORMANCE

The following collection of articles examines some questions that students frequently ask. We grouped the articles into four areas of academic performance: study techniques, note taking strategies, test taking strate- gies, and changing answers on multiple choice tests. Faculty and advisers will be richly rewarded by research findings that dispel many student and faculty misconceptions about study and test taking techniques.

a. Study Techniques

Some faculty members may not know about techniques for improving student performance. Indeed, many advisers find themselves telling students, who are performing poorly, to study harder. Edward O'Conner, Marilyn Chassie, and Fay Walther obtained data from students at the University of Texas at Dallas and correlated the amount of study time with the grades they achieved. The authors controlled for SAT and high school GPA. They found a negative relationship indicating that those who spent more time studying obtained lower grades in an introductory psychology course. Thus, simply admonishing students to study longer is not the answer to performance problems. Advising should focus on how students use the study time, i.e., the use of effective study techniques.

An issue related to the previous article is whether there are performance differences between students who study regularly and those who study sporadically. P. A. Spiers and R. O. Pihl from McGill University demonstrated that regular study was positively related to test performance. Thus, the data support recommending that students establish a routine study schedule. They also found that the order of questions on the exam did not effect exam performance. The latter finding should settle concerns that some instructors have about a bias that favors those students whose exam questions parallel the presentation order of course material.

Michael Aamodt authored two articles that investigated factors associated with the effectiveness of study sessions preceding a general psychology exam. Students from the University of Arkansas were participants in his research. The results of the first study revealed that students attending the study session obtained higher scores on the exam than those who didn't attend and higher ability students obtained higher scores than did lower ability students. In the second study, Aamodt reported that the type of study session, i.e., organizing text and lecture material versus answering questions, was a relevant variable influencing student performance on the exam. Faculty who teach large classes and provide study sessions may discover from this article how to make the study sessions a useful tool for improving performance.

Mark Dean, Richard Malott, and Barbara Fulton reported on two studies conducted at Western Michigan University. The studies evaluated self-management training interventions designed to improve individual academic performance. The first experiment consisted of a combination of self management procedures, including personal planning and goal setting, performance graphing, and environmental management. Students participated in an "AB" design replicated across subjects. The median quiz score for the nine students increased from "D" to "B" following implementation of the self-management package. Readers will find the results of the second experiment that indicated that the program can be self taught, particularly significant because training costs would be low.

Douglas Hindman invited students to cheat in his abnormal psychology class at Eastern Kentucky University. In a controlled study, the instructor allowed some students to use compact crib notes. The findings indicated that crib notes did not significantly improve academic performance of the group that used them. Faculty may also want to examine more closely the author's conclusion regarding the value of crib notes as study aids.

Expended Effort and Academic Performance

Edward J. O'Connor, Marilyn B. Chassie
University of Texas at Dallas, and
Fay Walther, *NCR Corporation*

With effort defined from student reports, this study shows a negative relationship, even with other variables partialed out.

Prior researchers have presented both theoretical models and empirical evidence supporting a positive association between greater effort and higher performance. Vroom (1964), for example, argued that performance is a function of a multiplicative combination of ability and motivation. In testing Vroom's model, researchers have often operationalized motivation in terms of expenditure of effort or energy. In one such study, Terborg (1977) found that effort was significantly associated with performance on a learning task. A study by Peters (1977), which examined the performance of undergraduates on a spelling task, concluded that performance was highly correlated with skill level and marginally associated with effort. A third study by Terborg and Miller (1978) demonstrated that quantity of output was significantly associated with both self and supervisory perceptions of effort as well as with abilities needed to do the task.

Within educational research, however, empirical evidence supporting a positive association between effort and actual classroom performance has been limited. Carroll (1963), in his model of school learning, suggested that the amount of academic information students acquire is a positive function of the amount of time the students actively engage in learning. Carver (1970), in a study designed to test this hypothesis in a classroom setting, found that the zero order correlation between learning time and amount of learning as assessed by examination performance was non-significant ($r = .07$). However, when a second hypothesized determinant of academic success (i.e., learning ability) was partialled out of the association, the resulting correlation increased to $r = .30$ ($p < .05$) and provided some support for Carroll's (1963) model.

The current research was designed to clarify further the effort-to-performance relationship within a classroom context by first replicating Carver's (1970) study and then extending these findings by examining the cumulative impact of two additional hypothesized correlates of academic effort performance and student grade associations. Specifically, the relationship between effort (time actively spent in learning) and academic performance (grades achieved) was computed and then this association was re-examined after controlling for (a) learning ability (i.e., Scholastic Aptitude Test scores), (b) learning ability and prior academic achievement (i.e., high school grade point average), and (c) learning ability, prior academic achievement, and academic load (i.e., credit hours taken). Based on Carroll's (1963) model and Carver's (1970) findings, it was hypothesized that (1) a non-significant correlation would exist between effort and academic performance and (2) that effort would be positively associated with academic performance after controlling for the three other correlates of academic performance assessed during this investigation (i.e., (a) learning ability, (b) learning ability and prior academic achievement, and (c) learning ability, prior academic achievement and academic load).

Method. Subjects were 90 undergraduates (46 males and 44 females) enrolled in three sections of introductory psychology at a major southeastern university. Approximately 40% of the subjects were freshmen, 40% sophomores, 13% juniors, and 7% seniors. Thirty-two percent of the participants were attending a college class for the first time. Parents of 65% of the students and siblings of over 50% of these subjects had attended a four year college.

At the end of the first third, middle third, and last third of the school term (i.e., quarter), a specially developed, short questionnaire was administered to the subjects. At each administration, participants indicated the average number of hours per week they had studied psychology since either the beginning of the term (first administration) or since the previous administration of the questionnaire. An estimate of total effort was computed by summing the average number of hours subjects reported having studied on each of the three administrations of the questionnaire. During the first administration, participants also provided their Scholastic Aptitude Test (SAT) scores, and on the second administration subjects reported the number of credit hours they were taking at that point in the term. In addition, students' final psychology grades were provided at the end of the term by the course instructors.

The first hypothesis was tested utilizing Pearson Product-Moment Correlations between the effort measures and academic performance. The second hypothesis was investigated by examining the partial correlations between these variables while controlling for SAT scores, high school grade point average, and academic load.

Results. Table 1 presents the zero order correlation between effort and academic performance. Three of the four observed relations are significant and all are negative. Specifically, those students who reported studying psychology the greatest number of hours during the first and final segments of the academic term and the greatest number of total hours during the complete academic term tended to receive the lowest final course grades.

Table 1 also presents the partial correlations of effort with academic performance while controlling for (a) SAT scores, and (b) both SAT scores and high school grade point average. Consistent significant negative associations are again evident between effort and performance indicating that those students who reported studying psychology for the greatest number of hours were typically the same individuals who received the lowest course grades. These partial correlations tended to be slightly larger than the zero order correlations presented in the first column.

Finally, partial correlations were also computed between effort and academic performance while controlling for SAT scores, high school grade point average, and academic load. These partial correlations between effort and academic performance were also significant and negative. Each of these associations was similar in size to the last set of comparable correlations presented in Table 1.

Table 1. Pearson Product-Moment Correlations and Partial Correlations of Effort with Academic Performance

| Effort (third of term) | No Control | Controlled for | |
		SAT Scores	SAT & GPA
First	−.23*	−.29**	−.30**
Second	−.12	−.14	−.18
Third	−.30**	−.30**	−.31**
Total	−.39***	−.45***	−.47***

N varies from 78 to 83 across thirds
Total is the sum of the three efort measures, N = 66
$* p < .05; ** p < .01; *** p < .001$

Discussion. Contrary to our hypotheses and to prior findings, the current results indicate that effort was significantly and negatively associated with academic performance. After statistically controlling for SAT scores, high school grade point average, and academic load, those students who reported spending the greatest number of hours studying psychology still tended to be the individuals who received the lowest grades. The incremental effect of controlling for academic load over and above SAT scores and high school grade point average was negligible. Post hoc analyses conducted to clarify these outcomes revealed that the variances in academic load was small, ($M = 16.01$, $SD = 1.67$) and that the relationship between this variable and academic performance was non-significant. As would be expected, however, academic performance was significantly associated with both SAT scores ($r = .31, p < .01$) and high school grade point average ($r = .21, p < .05$). The correlation between SAT scores and high school grade point average was also significant ($r = .25, p < .05$) within the current sample.

It is not clear why substantive differences exist between the current data and those presented earlier by Carver (1970). One potential explanation may involve sample variations. In the current study, for example, non-significant associations were found between effort and learning ability. In contrast, Carver reported a negative association ($r=-.42$, $p<.05$) between these variables. In these prior data the fact that high effort participants also tended to be those individuals lower in learning ability may have resulted in the non-significant zero order association between effort and amount learned. Under these circumstances, controlling for

learning ability might reasonably be expected to produce a positive association between effort and amount learned.

Further understanding of these across-study differences in results may be gained from an examination of the manner in which effort measures were collected. In Carver's study, students reported during each class period, the number of hours (to the nearest half hour) spent studying psychology during the prior week, whereas data in the current investigation were collected on questionnaires by researchers (not the instructor) at three points during the term. Carver's method of collecting effort data may have produced both predictor and criterion bias. While students were told their grades would not be affected by the number of hours they reported studying psychology, the process of collecting effort data in class may have caused some students to bias the number of hours they reported studying. In addition, if reports of hours studied were available to instructors, this information may have inadvertently resulted in criterion contamination when grades were assigned (Anastasi, 1976). In contrast, during the current study the effort information was collected by researchers other than the class instructors and was not available to those instructors until after grades had been assigned.

Carver's (1970) results differ substantially from those of the present study, but other literature seems potentially consistent with the current findings. Although no association between effort and grades was reported by Henson (1976), other aspects of his data seem to suggest that a negative association may have existed between these variables. For example, Henson reported significant negative associations between SAT scores and effort as well as significant positive relationships between SAT scores and grades. It is not unreasonable, therefore, to assume that the unreported relationship between effort and grades may have been negative in Henson's sample.

One explanation for the present findings is that the individuals who received the lowest grades were handicapped by an inadequate understanding of the intensity and direction of effort necessary to achieve high performance. It could be, for example, that such students tended to study material which was irrelevant or to use their time inefficiently due to their limited knowledge of appropriate study skills. Similarly, subjects may have been aware of effective study skills, but an inadequate application of these techniques may have interfered with the predicted positive effort to academic performance relationship within the current data. Caldwell (1977), for example, has reported that the academically unsuccessful students he studied often did not apply study skills effectively, although they generally possessed knowledge of appropriate study methodology. These interpretations appear to be consistent with Henson's contention that as a measure, the number of hours studied may reflect the presence of non-functional study habits. If such dysfunctional activities did occur, the current data would appear to also be consistent with prior literature which has confirmed a positive association between effective study habits and strategies and grade success (Caldwell, 1977; Cohen, 1977; Lin & McKeachie, 1970).

Finally, it is important to remember that the findings reported in this manuscript may be unique to and constrained by characteristics of the present sample, the research setting, or the operationalization of the variables studied. Students enrolled in introductory psychology at a single institution, for example, may not be representative of the population of university students at large. Nevertheless, the current findings suggest that additional research should be undertaken to examine the effort-academic performance relationship. Replication of these findings across diverse samples would suggest that teachers should focus attention toward conveying and/or encouraging the use of appropriate study habits among low performers early in each academic term. Moreover, research assessing the value of planned interventions which provide training in appropriate methods for the accumulation and retention of information would allow the testing of one viable explanation for the findings reported above. Such research designed to provide appropriate tests of alternative explanations for the current findings and to explore the generality of these findings certainly seems warranted.

References

Anastasi, A. *Psychological testing.* New York: Macmillan, 1976.

Caldwell, J. F. A descriptive study of academically unsuccessful arts and sciences freshmen (Doctoral Dissertation, Oklahoma State University, 1976). *Dissertation Abstracts International,* 1977, *37,* 5597A.

Carroll, J. B. A model of school learning. *Teachers College Record,* 1963, *64,* 723-733.

Carver, R. P. A test of an hypothesized relationship between learning time and amount learned in school learning. *The Journal of Educational Research,* 1970, *64,* 57-58.

Cohen, S. R. Influence of organizing strategies, time, and grade point averages on retention performance. *The Journal of Educational Research,* 1977, *70,* 219-221.

Henson, R. Expectancy beliefs, ability, and personality in predicting academic performance. *The Journal of Educational Research,* 1976, *70,* 41-44.

Lin, Y., & McKeachie, W. J. Aptitude, anxiety, study habits, and academic achievement. *Journal of Counseling Psychology,* 1970, *17,* 306-309.

Peters, L. H. Cognitive models of motivation, expectancy theory and effort: An analysis and empirical test. *Organizational Behavior and Human Performance,* 1977, *20,* 129-148.

Terborg, J. R. Validation and extension of an individual differences model of work performance. *Organizational Behavior and Human Performance,* 1977, *18,* 188-216.

Terborg, J. R., & Miller, H. E. Motivation, behavior, and performance: A closer examination of goal setting and monetary incentives. *Journal of Applied Psychology,* 1978, *63,* 29-39.

Vroom, V. *Work and motivation.* New York: Wiley, 1964.

The Effect of Study Habits, Personality and Order of Presentation on Success in an Open-Book Objective Examination .

P. A. Spiers and R. O. Pihl
McGill University

Multiple-choice, objective examinations are a popular form of testing in university level psychology courses. Very little, however, is known about the actual mechanics of this method of measuring knowledge, its effects on study habits, or if it may offer a particular advantage to one kind of student as opposed to another.

It is a common assumption that the student who works regularly and keeps up with his courses will get better marks. Informal and personal experience with students who get good results, however, often suggests that they may actually do the opposite: concentrating, for example, on one course at a time and cramming just prior to exams, particularly in those courses using the multiple-choice format. Pauker (1974), in examining the effect of practice on open-book objective exams, reported that his only consistent finding in both experimental and control groups was that students who did better on scheduled exams given earlier in the term also did better on the final exam.

A common practice, in order to minimize cheating on objective examinations, is to present two forms: an original, which frequently follows the order of presentation of the course, and a random form, which contains the same questions but in a different order. It is unknown, however, whether this procedure is more advantageous to either group. Memory studies (Tulving 1962, Tulving & Pearlstone 1966, Cohen 1966) would suggest a bias is created in favor of the groups whose questions parallel the presentation of course material.

The following questions are raised. First, do students who do better on multiple-choice, objective exams tend to study regularly or sporadically? Second, are there personality characteristics which correlate with students' performance on the two exam arrangements and are they relevant to patterns of studying? And finally, does the order in which the material is presented for recognition consistently affect the quality of the recall? Two separate studies were used to investigate these questions.

Study I. Students in an undergraduate introductory class in Abnormal Psychology (n = 185) were given the test materials. Student numbers were used for identification in order to preserve anonymity and the research was explained to Ss as an attempt to determine the characteristics of people who register in psychology courses.

Approximately one-third of the way into the term an unannounced closed-book, thirty question, multiple-choice objective exam was administered on the readings and lecture material for which students were responsible up to that time. Immediately following the exam, students were asked to fill out nine subscales from the Jackson Personality

Research Form (1967): achievement, aggression, cognitive structure, dominance, endurance, impulsivity, social recognition, succorance and understanding. It was felt that the results on the exam would indicate who was or was not keeping up with the assigned material and also would provide students with some feedback on their current status in the course.

Results on the final announced exam (a fifty question, open-book objective type), the surprise exam, and the personality research form were analyzed.

An analysis of covariance and correlation matrix revealed very few significant statistics. Results on the final exam correlated significantly with those on the surprise exam, ($r = + .4357$, $p < .001$). Success on the surprise exam correlated significantly, but at very low levels, with the factors Achievement ($r = +.1566$, $p < .01$) and Understanding ($r = +.2286$, $p < .001$) as measured by the personality research form. There was no indication of a relationship between personality and success on the final exam.

Study II.   Data from two undergraduate classes in Abnormal Psychology were analyzed. One was a class of 275 and the other of 325 students. Approximately half of each class wrote either the random order or original form of each exam.

In the case of the first class, students writing the form which followed the presentation structure of the course achieved a mean of 64.1, whereas those writing the random form averaged 61.9. A T-test of this difference was not significant ($p < .15$). Interestingly enough, in the second sample the difference was reversed, with students who took the random form doing very slightly better ($\overline{X} = 64.0$) than those taking the original ($\overline{X} = 63.8$). This difference was also non-significant.

Discussion.   It would seem from the results that the old dictum that regular work leads to good marks is by no means unfounded and that our intuitive hypothesis regarding in- consistent habits of good students is not, in fact, the general case—at least insofar as undergraduates in this abnormal course are concerned.

It was, however, rather surprising to find that personality traits that one would tend to associate with hard-working students did not bear a strong relationship to success on the surprise exam. In fact, although achievement was mildly related to the degree of success on the surprise exam, this relationship was absent on the final, suggesting that personality factors as measured by the Personality Research Form have little predictive power relative to academic success with this material. This finding is both somewhat puzzling and rather disturbing, in light of the importance which guidance services often place on this type of information.

Another interesting outcome is that contrary to expectations from theories of encoding and recognition, the order of presentation of course materials in an exam does not seem to have a consistent effect on students' performance.

In summary, then, none of the factors that we have discussed, with the exception of regular study habits, tends to be either a help or a hindrance to academic success as measured by a multiple-choice, open-book exam.

References

Cohen, B. H.   Some or none characteristics of coding behavior. *Journal of Verbal Learning and Verbal Behavior*, 1966, *5*, 182-187.

Pauker, J. D.   Effect of open-book examinations on test performance in an undergraduate child psychology course. *Teaching of Psychology*, 1974, *1*, 71-73.

Tulving, E.   The effect of alphabetical subjective organization on memorizing unrelated words. *Canadian Journal of Psychology*, 1962, *16*, 185-191.

Tulving, E., & Pearlstone, Z.   Availability versus accessibility of information in memory for words. *Journal of Verbal Learning and Verbal Behavior*, 1966, *5*, 381-391.

Jackson, D. N.   *The Personality Research Form*. New York: Research Psychologists Press, 1967.

The Effect of the Study Session on Test Performance

Michael G. Aamodt
University of Arkansas

A common practice in higher education is for instructors to help their classes prepare for tests by holding study sessions prior to exams. However, the effectiveness of study sessions vis-a-vis test performance has not been empirically demonstrated. Arguments in favor of their usefulness are that study sessions (a) allow the student a chance to ask questions and thus clear up points of confusion and fill in lecture note gaps, (b) provide a repetition of information, and (c) help provide additional framework for the student to organize the material to be covered on the test. This last argument is perhaps the most important in light of studies showing increased memory performance when material is organized (Mandler, Pearlstone, & Koopmans, 1969; D'Ago- stino, 1969). On the other hand, arguments can also be made in opposition to the usefulness of the study session. One argument is that all that the study session does is provide students with information that they would have obtained for themselves by studying harder. Thus, there should be no increase in test performance after attending a study session. Another argument is that the study session works only because the instructor leaks information to the students about the upcoming test items.

One final possibility is that the study session is useful, but only for some types of students. One potentially relevant dimension is that of academic ability. If study sessions are helpful, especially for organizational reasons, they should help the better students more than the poor students. That is, poorer students may either not have the intellectual capacity to organize or use the provided organization of the material. Another issue is that poor students may have delayed preparing for the test until the night before, thus not allowing enough time to prepare, even with the help of the study session.

In order to examine these questions, students enrolled in a general psychology course were tested for academic ability. An optional study session was held and attendance was monitored. It was predicted that students who attended the session would score higher on exams than those who did not. Moveover, for those who attended, it was predicted that those who scored in the high and middle range of ability would show significantly greater test performance improvement than those in the low range.

Method. In order to estimate the students' academic abilities, the Wonderlic Personnel Inventory (Wonderlic, 1978) was administered during the eighth week of the semester to students enrolled in a large general psychology course at the University of Arkansas. The Wonderlic is used in personnel selection, and it measures abilities in math, vocabulary, and logic. The Wonderlic can be administered in 12 minutes and thus is compatible with a group testing situation. Students scoring above 26 (70th percentile) were designated as higher in academic ability, students scoring below 21 (48th percentile) were designated as being lower in academic ability, and those scoring in between were considered medium in academic ability. These cutting lines were used in order to both maximize the sample size in each condition and to maximize the ability differences between the groups.

An optional study session was held the night before the test. The session was conducted by a graduate assistant who was blind to the specific test item content. During the study session, students were allowed to ask questions about material covered in the text and in lecture, and the session leader attempted to outline the major points under each of the broad concept areas. Attendance was taken at the one-hour session.

The exam consisted of 50 multiple-choice items covering three chapters from the *Psychology: Understanding Behavior* text (Baron, Byrne, & Kantowitz, 1978) and were taken from the item pool supplied by the authors. The time allowed for the test was 50 minutes and each correct answer was worth one point.

The scores on the exam were examined in a 3(high, medium, and low Wonderlic score) by 2(attended, not attended) between subjects factorial design using an unweighted means analysis of variance correcting for unequal cell size. The dependent measure was the test score for each individual for the test.

Results. The data were analyzed in a 3 by 2 analysis of variance using the General Linear Model Procedure of the Statistical Analysis System (Barr, Goodnight, Sall, & Helwig, 1976). As predicted, students who attended the study session ($M = 43.86$) performed better on the tests than did those who did not attend ($M = 39.40$, $F(1,79) = 5.89$, $p < .05$) and overall, high ability students performed better than lower

ability students, $F(2,79) = 4.24$, $p < .05$. The interaction between academic ability and study session attendance was not significant, $F(2,79) < 1$. Planned t-tests across the levels of intelligence showed that of the students scoring high on the Wonderlic, those who attended the study session ($M = 46.53$) did better than those who did not attend ($M = 42.36$), $t(19) = 2.52$, $p < .02$. Likewise, of those students scoring in the middle range of the Wonderlic, the students who attended ($M = 44.40$) scored significantly higher than those who did not attend ($M = 38.76$), $t(38) = 2.52$, $p < .01$. The differences in the low range between those who attended ($M = 40.78$) and those who did not ($M = 37.00$) were not significantly different, $t(17) = .69$.

Table 1. Means, Standard Deviations, and n of Test Scores

Attendance		Academic Ability			
		High	Medium	Low	Total
Attended	M	46.54	44.40	40.78	43.86
	SD	3.36	4.31	5.31	4.92
	N	13	15	14	42
Not Attended	M	42.36	38.76	37.00	39.40
	SD	5.08	6.72	8.10	6.69
	N	11	25	7	43
Total	M	44.62	40.88	39.52	
	SD	4.65	6.49	6.43	
	N	24	40	21	

Discussion. The results supported the hypothesis that study sessions held prior to an exam do help students perform better on the exams. However, the reason for the effectiveness of the study session is still not clear. Because the teaching assistant conducting the study session was blind to the specific content of the test, it is unlikely that the effectiveness was due to test content leakage. Another possibility is that the students who attended were more motivated than those who did not. While this is possible, it is not likely because such an explanation would have difficulty accounting for the fact that the study session did not help the poorer students who attended.

It is likely that the effectiveness of the study session was due either to further clarification of the lecture material or to the provision of an organizational framework or perhaps a combination of the two. These possibilities can not be differentiated from the present data. Moreover, either could explain why the review session did not help the poorer students. It could be that those students who score poorly on the Wonderlic have poor organizational skills and are not able to utilize the organization provided by the teaching assistant. It could also be that the poorer students' comprehension of the material was not sufficient for them to obtain acceptable levels of mastery of the material. It might also be that poorer students may be helped by a different type of study session. Perhaps one that moves slower or concentrates on memory aids and/or drill would be more appropriate. These suggestions would of course need further empirical review. Until then, in terms of delivery of teaching services, the current study strongly suggests that pre-exam study sessions are a useful teaching tool in terms of improving test performance, and therefore can be justifiably incorporated into the teacher's armamentarium.

References

Baron, R., Byrne, D., & Kantowitz, B. *Psychology: Understanding Behavior*. Philadelphia: Saunders, 1978.

Barr, A. J., Goodnight, J. H., Sall, J. P., & Helwig, J. T. *A User's Guide to SAS76*. SAS Institute, Raleigh, NC, 1976.

D'Agostino, P.R. The blocked-random effect in recall and recognition. *Journal of Verbal Learning and Verbal Behavior*. 1969, 8, 815-820.

Mandler, G., Pearlstone, Z., & Koopmans, M. H. Effects of organization and semantic similarity on recall and recognition. *Journal of Verbal Learning and Verbal Behavior*, 1969, 8, 410-423.

Wonderlic, E. F. *How to use the Wonderlic Personnel Test*. Northfield, IL: E. F. Wonderlic and Associates, 1978.

Note

The author would like to thank J. Scott Mizes for his useful comments on earlier drafts of this manuscript.

A Closer Look at the Study Session

Michael G. Aamodt
University of Arkansas

In a recent study, Aamodt (1982) found that overall, students who attended a study session prior to an exam performed better on the exam than did those students who did not attend. Moreover, it was found that the study sessions helped the students in the higher and middle academic range but not those in the lower range. However, it was not possible from the experimental design of the earlier study to determine the reason for the success of the study session.

Three possible reasons for the effectiveness of the study session were considered: (a) the repetition of information, (b) the chance to ask questions, or (c) the organization of the material. It was also noted that another possible explanation was that it was not the study session itself that was effective, but rather, that it was only the most motivated students who attended the sessions. Thus, the increased test performance was an artifact of student motivation rather than the result of the study session. Although the motivation hypothesis is possible, the fact that similar proportions of students in all academic levels attended, combined with the fact that the session did not help students in the lower range, made this hypothesis less plausible.

It was the purpose of the present study to investigate the reason for the effectiveness of the study session. To do so, two types of sessions were held; one in which students only asked questions and another in which in addition to asking questions, the major concepts were organized and presented to the students. If both types of sessions were helpful, then the reason for the study session effectiveness would not be due to the increased organization of the material. However, if only the organized sessions were helpful, then the effectiveness of the study session would be due to organization rather than the chance to ask questions or to the motivational effect. In addition, in order to help instructors schedule study sessions in the future, the students were asked to indicate how far in advance of the exam they preferred the study sessions to be held.

Method. Subjects were 277 students enrolled in a large General Psychology course at the University of Arkansas. All students enrolled in the course were allowed to attend optional study sessions held prior to the final exam. The sessions were conducted by one of four graduate assistants and were of one of two types; questions or organization. The questions sessions consisted of a graduate assistant answering questions asked by the students. The organization sessions consisted of a graduate assistant organizing the text and lecture material in outline form and presenting the material to the students via an overhead projector. The graduate assistant went over all of the major concepts from the text and lecture in this manner and also answered any questions asked by the students.

The outcome measure used was a 50 point multiple choice exam covering the Personality, Abnormal, and Therapy chapters from Baron, Byrne, and Kantowitz (1978). Forty-five of the items came from the item pool supplied by the text authors and the remaining five were constructed by the instructor for material covered in the lecture only. On a separate sheet of paper, the students indicated how far in advance of the test they preferred the study sessions to be held.

Results and Discussion. As indicated in Table 1, an analysis of variance using the General Linear Model procedure of the

Table 1. Means and Standard Deviations of Test Scores by Type of Study Session

	Type of Study Session		
	No Session	Questions	Organization
M	39.81	40.30	43.08
SD	7.47	5.44	5.03
n	144	23	108

Note. No attempt was made to equalize *n* by assigning subjects to a particular condition. N = 275

Statistical Analysis System (Barr, Goodnight, Sall, & Helwig, 1976) revealed a significant overall effect for the type of study session attended ($F(2,272) = 7.53$, $p < .001$). Using the Least Significant Difference test, students who attended the organized session ($M = 43.08$) performed better on the exam than did students who did not attend a study session ($M = 39.81$) and better than those who attended the questions session ($M = 40.30$). However, the subjects attending the questions session ($M = 40.30$) did not differ significantly from the students who did not attend. Thus, it appears that for a review session to be effective, some type of organization of the material is essential; merely answering questions is not enough to produce an improvement in exam scores. These results also seem to rule out the motivation hypothesis.

As shown in the lower part of Table 2, students prefer the study sessions to be held within two days of the exam. Furthermore, as depicted in the upper part of Table 2, when students were segmented by their final course grade, it appeared there was a slightly greater preference by the A and B students for the sessions to be held the day before the exam and a slightly greater preference by the D and F students for the sessions to be held at least two days before

Table 2. Percent of Each Grade Category
Indicating Preference for Study Session Times

Grade Category	Number of Days Before Exam						
	1	2	3	4	5	6	7
A	48.00	44.00	8.00	0.0	0.0	0.0	0.0
B	53.16	31.65	12.66	1.27	1.27	0.0	0.0
C	43.55	38.71	11.29	4.84	1.61	0.0	0.0
D/F	32.32	42.42	17.17	3.03	4.04	0.0	1.01
All Students							
N	113	102	36	7	6	0	1
%	42.64	38.49	13.59	2.64	2.26	0.0	.38

N = 265

the exam. Thus, it might be possible for two types of study sessions to be held, one on the night before the exam for the superior students and one or two days before for the others. In the earlier session, the material could be presented at a slower pace with more individualized instruction than would be possible if only one study session were held.

In summary, the present study concerned the effectiveness of two study session methods and student preference for when these sessions should be held. The results indicated that organization, rather than motivation, repetition of material, or the opportunity to ask questions is what makes the study session effective. Furthermore, in order to make the most preferred study session scheduling, a review session should be held one day prior to the exam for the A and B students and two days prior to the exam for the D and F students.

References

Aamodt, M. G.   The effect of the study session on test performance. *Teaching of Psychology,* 1982, 9, 118-120.
Baron, R., Byrne, D., & Kantowitz, B.   *Psychology: Understanding behavior.* Philadelphia: Saunders, 1978.
Barr, A. J., Goodnight, J. H., Sall, J. P., & Helwig, J. T.   *A users guide to SAS76.* Raleigh, NC: SAS Institute, 1976.

The Effects of Self-Management Training On Academic Performance

Mark R. Dean, Richard W. Malott
and Barbara J. Fulton
Western Michigan University

Increases of one letter-grade were obtained, and the majority of the students continued use of the methods.

Each school year in most courses there are usually a few students having academic difficulty, including the courses offered through our own psychology department, and an instructor is pressed to determine an intervention strategy to improve the students' grades. Many factors may be responsible for this poor academic performance. For example, the students may lack the necessary prerequisite skills for current instructional materials (Holland, Soloman, Doran, & Frezza, 1976, pp. 171-185), or they may not be motivated to do well because current contingencies are weak or poorly programmed (Skinner, 1969). Some students may need more time than others to prepare for course examinations and meet mastery standards (Keller, 1968), but academic deficiencies may be prevented by an increase in studying (see Grant & Keenan, Note 1, for a review of study behavior in college).

Insufficient study preparation may occur for several reasons including the following: (a) Reinforcers inherent in the study materials may be weak and infrequent (Michael, 1974). (b) External sources of reinforcement for studying are usually absent (Reese, 1978, pp. 54-58). (c) Test scores are usually too delayed to effectively reward studying or to punish insufficient studying (Malott, Tillema, & Glenn, 1978, pp. 165-184). And, (d) reinforcers for many behaviors incompatible with studying are usually numerous and immediately available (Malott, Note 2). For these reasons, students will often postpone studying to engage in other activities, and some students will obtain low academic grades as a result.

One source of data useful in devising an intervention for students having academic difficulty comes from the area of self-management. In recent years, researchers have demonstrated that an individual may use various self-management techniques to increase the frequency of selected behaviors (see O'Leary & Dubey 1979; Rosenbaum & Drabman, 1979; Jones, Nelson, & Kazdin, 1977, for review). Self-management techniques specifically designed to increase the amount of time a student studies have had positive results. For instance, self-monitoring and self-recording of study time have led to increments in studying (Miller & Gimpl, 1972; Champlin & Karoly, 1975; Tichenor, 1977), and studying also increased when students used self-reinforcement techniques (e.g., money and special privileges) contingent upon a predetermined amount of studying (Richards, McReynolds, Holt, & Sexton, 1976; Greiner & Karoly, 1976).

In many of these experiments, process (i.e., study behavior) measures have been taken, but outcome (i.e., quiz score) measures have not been taken, or if taken, have shown no effects. The present study includes two experiments: The first experiment involves a combination of self-management procedures, including self-monitoring and self-recording, for students having academic difficulty; the second experiment evaluates three self-management procedures, and provides an extension of the literature to include student-constructed rule statements and environmental management as additional self-management techniques. The effectiveness of this program is evaluated on the basis of outcome measures of the students' quiz performance.

Experiment 1.

Method. Nine students elected to participate in the first experiment after an announcement was made in their classroom explaining that, by participating, students could earn five bonus points (out of at least 450 total course points) and could learn useful self-management skills. The subjects were undergraduate students enrolled in one of two psychology courses at Western Michigan University.

Quiz scores served as the dependent variable for all subjects. The eight students enrolled in an intermediate level psychology course took two quizzes per week, with the remaining student enrolled in an introductory psychology course taking three quizzes each week.

Intervention involved six independent variables in the form of self-management procedures taught to students. The experimental sessions followed an "AB" design replicated across subjects. Baseline quiz scores were recorded for each student for an average of seven weeks before self-management training began, with training sessions scheduled across a two-week period.

The students used a notebook, called the *Self-Management Calendar* (Sundberg, 1979), for all self-management activities. A weekly schedule form and standard graph paper were attached to the front and back covers of the notebook for additional self-management purposes. Training occurred during each of six one-to-one meetings with the researcher.[3]

Meeting 1. This meeting served as an opportunity for the students to identify the most important variables that might exert control over their studying. The students developed a list of the following: (a) personal and career goals related to their school work, (b) additional positive outcomes, or rein-

forcers, that might result if they achieved outstanding grades in school, and (c) punishers, or undesirable outcomes, that could result from poor academic performance. To establish a permanent record of these variables, the students listed them as "rule statements" using an "If-then" format, such as "If I do this behavior, then I can expect this consequence to follow," entering the list onto a blank page of their self-management notebook.

Meeting 2. The students received instruction in self-monitoring and recording, performance graphing, and schedule planning. First, for purposes of self-evaluation, the students were instructed to begin self-monitoring on an hourly basis, recording general activities that they engaged in from waking to retiring each day in the appropriate hour block of their self-management notebook. As part of this self-recording procedure, the students totaled the number of hours they studied each day and the number of hours they subjectively evaluated as "wasted" (i.e., behaviors involving neither academics nor important non-academic activities), and listed these amounts at the bottom of each daily column. Second, the students began to graph the number of hours that they studied each day, and also began to graph the socres that they received on their weekly quizzes. Finally, they began to use a schedule form for planning hourly, daily, and weekly activities, with special emphasis on establishing regular and reliable study periods. Both the graph pages and the schedule form were attached to the covers of their self-management notebook.

Meeting 3. In order to establish stimulus surroundings most favorable to studying, the students received instruction in environmental management which involved the manipulation of study room conditions. During this meeting, the students engaged in the following activities: They developed a list of those behaviors and events that interfered with studying, and based on this analysis, developed a list of changes to be made in their study environment, including both the addition of stimuli that might prompt studying and the removal of stimuli that might set the occasion for behaviors incompatible with studying.

Suggested additions to the study room included the strategic posting of the students' rule statements (developed during Meeting 1), weekly schedule form, and quiz or study graphs near their desk, in such a location as to make it most likely that they would be read when studying. Suggested items to remove included magazines, pictures, certain foods or alcohol, televison sets or stereos, and whatever else that the students themselves had identified as discriminative stimuli for their non-studying.

Meeting 4. For general time-organization purposes, the students received training in the self-management technique of constructing and then prioritizing a list of academic and non-academic tasks that they needed to complete on any given day. The area of the self-management notebook labeled "non-recurring tasks" was used for the listing of these tasks.

Meeting 5. No new procedures occurred at this time. The experimenter reviewed previous instructions and answered any new questions the students had.

Meeting 6. Further review and clarification occurred. The students received their earned bonus points, and were informed that all meetings and self-management activities for the remaining weeks of the semester were now optional.

As part of the bonus point policy, during the two-week intervention period, students would lose one bonus point (out of five) each time their self-management notebooks were incomplete when checked by a reliability observer. All checks were unannounced. A student's notebook was categorized as "incomplete" if the student had failed to complete any of the assigned procedures up to 24 hours prior to that check. For example, if the notebook was checked at 1:00 P.M. on Tuesday, a rating of "incomplete" would be scored if the student had failed to complete a self-management procedure prior to 1:00 P.M. on Monday. Hourly recording records, quiz graph, study hours graph, and task-prioritizing lists were included in the assessment of reliability, with each student's notebook being checked a minimum of once a week. For the self-recording component, a student's work was scored as "complete" if at least 60% of the hourly blocks were completed for each day. Interobserver reliability was calculated according to the following formula: reliability = number of agreements/number of agreements plus disagreements, times 100. All reliability figures were above 91%.

Results. Eight of the nine students showed academic improvement as a result of the self-management training, with six demonstrating marked change. Before the training had begun (baseline), the nine students had a median quiz score of 70% (range 58-81); following intervention, they had a median score of 88% (range 72-100, see Figure 1).

From a total possible of 45 bonus points (five points per student), the students lost only three points across all weeks of the study due to the non-completion of any of the various self-management exercises. During the majority of unan-

nounced checks, most students maintained the self-management behaviors consistently.

Follow-up checks conducted at one- and three-month intervals after the termination of the experiment revealed that three students continued all of the self-management procedures: hourly behavior recording, graphing, schedule planning, and list-prioritizing; four other students continued one or more of the self-management procedures, and only two subjects had stopped all self-management activities. Those two were the students who demonstrated the least improvement in quiz performance (i.e., Subjects 6 and 9).

Discussion. Experiment 1 evaluated several self-management procedures as part of the intervention for low-scoring students. The students responded favorably to the self-management program as indicated by their quiz score improvement, their reliable completion of the assigned self-management exercises, and their maintenance of the self-management procedures after the experiment had concluded.

The results support the utility of self-recording and the behaviors involved in "self-organization," that is, schedule-planning and list-prioritizing, for students having academic difficulty. To further assess the contributing influence of individual components of this multiple intervention, Experiment 2 was conducted.

Experiment 2.

A second study evaluated the following individual self-management procedures: (a) hourly self-recording, (b) student-developed rule statements, and (c) environmental management procedures.

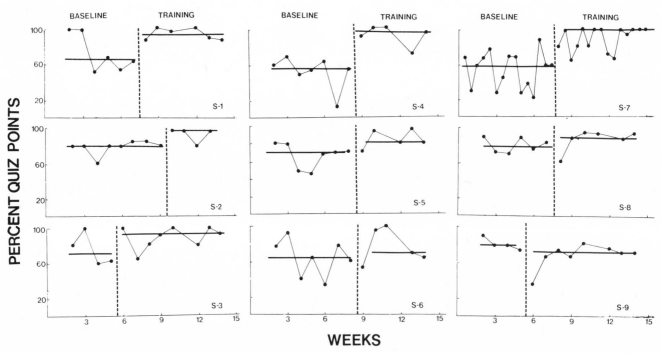

Figure 1. Percentage of quiz points earned for each quiz of the semester across weeks. The horizontal solid lines indicate the median percentage points earned by an individual student in each phase. Experiment 1.

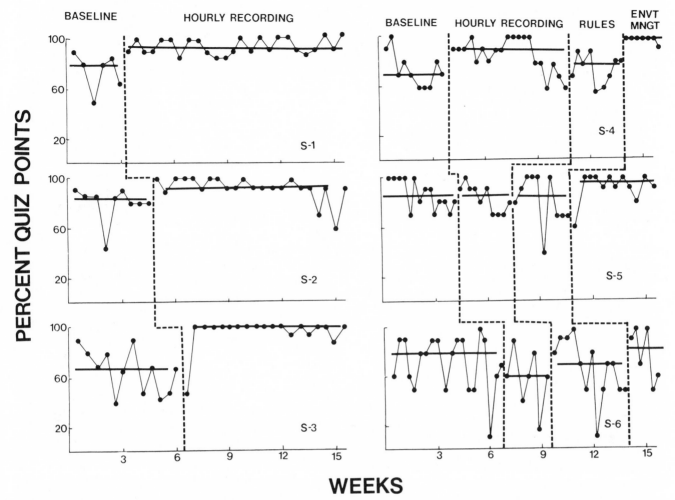

Figure 2. Percentage of quiz points earned for each quiz of the semester across weeks. The horizontal solid lines indicate the median percentage points earned by an individual student in each phase. Experiment 2.

Method. Six low-performing undergraduate psychology students participated in Experiment 2, involving two psychology courses at Western Michigan University. The students were solicited and informed of the study as described in Experiment 1.

Again, quiz scores served as the dependent variable. Three students took three quizzes per week and the remaining three students took two quizzes per week. As in Experiment 1, the Self-Management Calendar (Sundberg, 1979) served as a record for all written products of self-management program.

Based on a multiple-baseline design across subjects with at least one week between intervention dates, the students participated in the training program, as in Experiment 1, through one-to-one meetings.

The procedures of Experiment 2 paralleled those of Experiment 1; however, instructions presented orally to students in the first experiment were administered via standardized, written handouts during Experiment 2.[3] Also, for the duration of the second study, the experimenter explicitly refrained from providing positive or negative feedback contingent upon a subject's quiz performance or self-management behaviors.

During the first meeting, all six subjects received instruc-

tions to begin self-monitoring and self-recording on an hourly basis, totaling at the bottom of each daily column the number of hours they studied each day and the number of hours they evaluated as "wasted." However, the students did not transfer these data to a graphic display during Experiment 2.

Self-management training interventions occurred for the remainder of the experiment as warranted by a visual inspection of the students' quiz scores. That is, additional self-management procedures were implemented for only those students who did not improve satisfactorily as a result of the first self-management procedure, i.e., the hourly self-recording component. Therefore, only three students received the rule-construction training (Component 2) and the environmental management training (Component 3), in addition to the hourly self-recording training.

Results. Three students (i.e., Subjects 1, 2, and 3) improved their academic scores markedly upon implementation of the hourly recording procedure (Component 1), having median scores of 66, 80, and 78 before training and median scores of 100, 91, and 93 respectively after intervention (see Figure 2).

No lasting effects were demonstrated as a result of the

second component, i.e., student-constructed rule statements for studying, when the students were merely asked to develop these rules. During the third self-management component, i.e., environmental management, the remaining three students improved their quiz scores substantially, having median scores of 68, 79, and 84 before intervention and median scores of 82, 100, 95, respectively, following this particular self-management training component.

Reliability was conducted as done in Experiment 1, with all reliability checks above 93%. Six bonus points (out of 30 total) were lost by the students as a result of incomplete self-management exercises.

General Discussion.   Self-management training can be an effective method for improving a student's academic performance. In Experiment 1, the median quiz score for the nine students before implementation of the self-management package was one point above the grade of "D" and following training was a solid "B" grade. In Experiment 2, the six students had a median quiz score of "C" before self-management training. Three of the six students achieved "A" level performance during the self-recording phase, with two students achieving "A" level and one achieving "B" level performance when the environmental management procedures were added.

The results of Experiment 1 support the combined efficacy of graphing, schedule-planning, list-prioritizing, environmental management, and self-recording for self-management purposes; Experiment 2 provided further support for the latter two procedures through an individualized implementation of each. An analysis of the role that these procedures may have played in the improvement of students' grades will now be provided.

Hourly self-recording may be an effective self-management procedure for several reasons. If the student was neglecting or had neglected homework during the day, self-punishing statements might result from the self-recording. The self-recording procedure may have an effect on behavior if, for instance, the student opens a book and begins to study to terminate the punishing self-statements. Self-recording each hour may also, in general, strengthen "self-awareness" and a self-evaluation repertoire as the students monitor their behavior; this monitoring might also increase the likelihood that they will make reinforcing statements contingent upon appropriate responding during the hour. In fact, several students made comments that support these assumptions, reporting that they had not previously realized how little time they actually spent studying, and commenting further that they were now more observant and critical of how they spent the hours of the day.

A somewhat different analysis might apply to the environmental management procedures. Often, prevailing stimulus conditions do not support the behavior we would like to engage in. Exercising, dieting, and studying are three examples; the controlling variables for these activities are often outnumbered by incentives for behaviors incompatible with them. Thus, during the environmental-management training, the students acquired the self-management skill of manipulating the physical conditions of their room for studying purposes. After they identified the variables controlling both their studying and non-studying, appropriate physical

changes were planned. Though reliability on such changes was not determined, unsolicited self-reports from the students indicated that many such changes did take place.

Developing a list of rule statements for studying did not, by itself, produce lasting academic improvement, though the three students receiving this intervention did show higher quiz scores initially. This may have been caused by a loss of contact with the rules after they had been entered into their notebooks. Posting these rules in proximity to their study desk as part of the environmental management procedure (Phase 3 of Experiment 2) may have influenced studying if the students evaluated their behavior with respect to the rule. Again, comments by the students supported the value of this procedure as they reported that a given rule statement (e.g., one identifying parental rewards—such as increased monetary support—contingent upon satisfactory academic performance, or one identifying parental punishment—such as loss of car privileges—contingent upon unacceptable academic performance) did indeed "make them study more." Rule statements, in general, may serve a mediating function, controlling behavior when the usual consequences are certain and powerful but temporarily deferred, when the individual states the rule as a "reminder."

The present research provides further support for the effectiveness of self-monitoring and self-recording as a method to increase the frequency of a selected behavior, and in addition, suggests that extensive environmental management, possibly including student-determined rule statements, could serve a useful function in self-management programs.

Several cautionary statements should be made however. These procedures may not work equally well with all populations, or with all students within a given setting, as was found in the present study. For instance, self-recording was maintained by the college students in this study with external weekly monitoring and the use of a bonus point system. Younger students or students with more serious academic or behavioral problems may not respond as readily to such a procedure. Further research could address these issues by replicating these procedures with different populations, while continuing to experimentally isolate the specific self-management procedures that are the most effective.

The self-management procedures described here seem practical, and the cost of implementing the training is low. Though done on an individual basis for experimental purposes, the entire package could be taught to a group in two to three hours. The procedures appear to have academic generality at the university level, as students in four different psychology courses demonstrated substantial improvement. Also, the procedures appear to lead to durable behavior change, as indicated by the maintenance of self-management procedures by the majority of the students for several months after all training had concluded.

References

Champlin, S. M., & Karoly, P. Role of contract negotiation in self-management of study time: A preliminary investigation. *Psychological Reports*, 1975, *37*, 724-726.

Greiner, J. M., & Karoly, P. Effects of self-control training on study activity and academic performance: An analysis of self-monitoring, self-reward, and systematic-planning components. *Journal of Counseling Psychology*, 1976, *23*, 495-502.

Holland, J. G., Solomon, C., Doran, J., & Frezza, D. A. *The analysis of behavior in planning instruction.* Reading, MA: Addison-Wesley, 1976.

Jones, R. T., Nelson, R. E., & Kazdin, A. E. The role of external variables in self-reinforcement: A review. *Behavior Modification,* 1977, *1,* 147-148.

Keller, F. S. "Goodbye teacher . . ." *Journal of Applied Behavior Analysis,* 1968, *1,* 78-89.

Malott, R. W., Tillema, M., & Glenn, S. *Behavior analysis and behavior modification: An introduction.* Kalamazoo, MI: Behavioradelia, Inc., 1978.

Michael, J. The essential components of effective instruction and why most college teaching is not. In F. Keller and E. Ribes (Eds.), *Behavior modification.* Boston, MA: Academic Press, 1974.

Miller, A., & Gimpl, M. P. Operant verbal self-control of studying. *Psychological Reports,* 1972, *30,* 495-498.

O'Leary, S. G., & Dubey, D. R. Applications of self-control procedures by children: A review. *Journal of Applied Behavior Analysis,* 1979, *12,* 449-465.

Reese, E. P. *Human operant behavior.* Dubuque, IA: Brown, 1978.

Richards, C. S., McReynolds, W. T., Holt, S., & Sexton, T. The effects of information feedback and self-administered consequences on self-monitoring study behavior. *Journal of Counseling Psychology,* 1976, *23,* 316-321.

Rosenbaum, M. S., & Drabman, R. S. Self-control training in the classroom: A review and critique. *Journal of Applied Behavior Analysis,* 1979, *12,* 467-485.

Skinner, B. F. *Contingencies of reinforcement.* Englewood Cliffs, NJ: Prentice-Hall, 1969.

Sundberg, M. L. *Self-management calendar.* Grand Rapids, MI: Behavior Associates, Inc., 1979.

Tichenor, J. L. Self-monitoring and self-reinforcement of studying by college students. *Psychological Reports,* 1977, *40,* 103-108.

Notes

1. Grant, L., & Deenan, J. B. Studying in college: A review. Manuscript submitted for publication, 1981. (Available from L. Grant, Department of Educational Psychology, West Virginia University.)

2. Malott, R. W. Rule-governed behavior and the achievement of evasive goals: A theoretical analysis. Unpublished manuscript, 1980. (Available from R. W. Malott, Department of Psychology, Western Michigan University, Kalamazoo, MI 49008.)

3. This study is based on a thesis submitted to the Department of Psychology, Western Michigan University, by the first author in partial fulfillment of the requirements for the MA degree. It contains all self-management forms and a copy of the standardized instructions administered to students, and is available from University Microfilms International, P.O. Box 1764, Ann Arbor, MI 48106.

Crib Notes in the Classroom: Cheaters Never Win

C. Douglas Hindman
Eastern Kentucky University

Preparation of crib notes may have some value, but their use in the classroom does not significantly improve performance.

Psychologists have long been involved in the study of classroom cheating. The rather extensive literature (see Wildemuth, 1976) can be divided into two general groups. The larger group consists of studies investigating individual differences in cheating propensity using a wide range of personality, attitudinal, and socioeconomic measures. A considerably smaller body of literature exists on cheating prevention using methods ranging from structuring the classroom situation to behavior modification (Flowers, 1972) to moral suasion (Ackerman, 1971).

Throughout the literature there is a general assumption that students who cheat do, in fact, increase their test scores. This assumption is rarely investigated directly.

One form of classroom cheating involves copying answers from another student during a test. This would seem an obvious way to illicitly increase test scores, yet Houston (1977) found that, under some conditions, it may not be effective. In a free-recall task, subjects increased their recall of words "carelessly" left exposed, but correspondingly decreased their recall of the remaining words. Houston argued that the effort involved in surreptitiously looking at the exposed answers interfered with efforts to search internally for other answers. Cheating was effective overall only when the exposed words were conceptually related to unexposed words, thus providing cues for them.

Another form of cheating, bringing crib notes into the test, would also seem to offer ample opportunity to increase test scores. However, there are practical limits to the amount of information a student can place on a concealable note. Not only may efforts to surreptitiously retrieve this information interfere with other test-taking behavior, as Houston suggested, but it is questionable whether one could reduce the amount of material covered in a typical college test to such a small area. In fact it is possible that much of the possible benefit of crib notes comes from the process of reducing information to a compact crib note format. Such a process involves many elements stressed in study systems (see Thomas & Robinson, 1977) such as active organization, identification of key concepts, mnemonics, etc.

In order to investigate this form of cheating, students were invited to "cheat" by being allowed to bring crib notes to the test on standard 3 x 5 cards. To control possible effects of the note-making process, they were allowed to use their cards on only some of the tests.

Method. Fifty-two students in two sections of undergraduate abnormal psychology participated in the study. The students were from a broad cross-section of college interests. Less than 15% were majoring in liberal arts areas. The largest group was in law-enforcement (63%).

Procedures were announced the first day of class and students were offered the opportunity to transfer to another class. No student accepted the offer. Tests were scheduled bi-weekly and covered two chapters each. One third of the tests were given under normal conditions ("No Cards"). On the remaining two thirds, students were invited to bring to the test a 3 x 5 card on which they could write anything they wished. Just before the test a member of the class drew a slip of paper to determine whether or not the cards would be used during the test ("Used" or "Not Used"). In reality the instructor used sleight of hand techniques to balance the order of using or not using cards. When cards were not used, they were collected before the test began. On each test students were asked to indicate if they had made a crib card. Students also completed a course evaluation questionnaire at the end of the semester. No student gave evidence of detecting the sleight of hand procedure during the semester although one student did propose a less fakable procedure on the questionnaire.

Otherwise the classes were conducted in conventional fashion. Class sessions consisted of lecture and discussion. A standard text (Davison & Neale, 1978) was used. Tests consisted of 10 multiple choice and 10 short answer items (5 points each) taken from the text item files. As announced in class, all items were selected to relate to one or more objectives in the text study guide (Hindman, 1978). Two tests were conducted under each of the three conditions ("No Cards", "Not Used", "Used"). An additional test, needed to fill out the course schedule, and two review tests were also given but are not included in the results. Results were analyzed using standard statistical computer programs (SAS, 1979).

Results. Preliminary analysis of the data revealed a significant difference between the sections on short answer items (t = 3.5070, P = .0005). Although the sections did not differ on multiple choice items, it was felt desirable to retain "classes" as a variable in all further analyses.

Because many students had not made cards on one or more occasions, an analysis was also conducted to determine whether better (or worse) students had made cards more often. For this analysis, students were grouped by the number of times they reported making cards and the groups were compared on those tests when no cards were made by the entire class ("No Cards"). One-way analysis of variance revealed that students who made cards more often score significantly higher on short answer items (F = 5.27, P = .0007) and marginally higher on multiple choice items (F = 2.49, P = .0476).

As a result it was necessary to remove the contribution of students who had made cards not only from the two card conditions ("Not Used" and "Used") but also from the control

condition ("No Cards"). The primary analysis, therefore, was run using scores only from those students who had made cards on every opportunity. An analysis using Kirk's (1968) SPFp.q model revealed no significant differences due to the three card conditions, the interaction of cards and classes, nor the classes themselves. In the analysis of short-answer items, "classes" approached significance (F = 3.95, P = .0615).

For illustrative purposes, the means and standard deviations of both measures under the three card conditions are shown in Figure 1. Notice that differences due to the cards are not only statistically nonsignificant but are very minimal

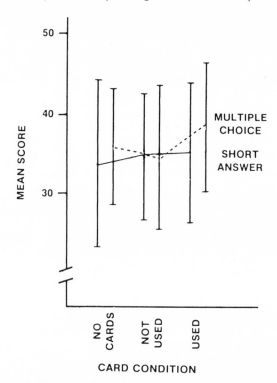

Figure 1. Means and standard deviations of multiple choice (dotted line) and short answer (solid line) scores under the three card conditions by students who made cards on every opportunity.

under these circumstances. Only the multiple choice data show any appreciable difference and this is not consistent across conditions.

The lack of differences raises a question of whether the tests were, in fact, discriminating anything. That is, was the lack of differences in card conditions a result of the ineffectiveness of the crib cards or the inability of the tests to detect the differences? In an attempt to evaluate this question intertest correlations were computed between all six tests for both the multiple-choice and short answer scores. Of the resulting 30 correlations, 26 were significant at or above the .01 level and 28 were significant at or above the .05 level. Using Fisher's Z-transformation average correlations were calculated as .375 and .620 for multiple-choice and short answer items respectively. These correlations are well within the normal range for tests of this type and length.

Additional information on the role of the crib cards was gained by looking at the course evaluation results. On this questionnaire two five-point rating scales asked students to rate how helpful the crib cards were to them when (a) they were able to use the cards and (b) when they prepared but did not use the cards. On a scale from one, ("Useless") to five, (Extremely Helpful") mean ratings were 2.955 and 2.682 respectively. The difference was not significant (t = 1.74, P = .09). Thus students considered the cards only moderately helpful, and, more important, did not consider that using the cards during the test was more helpful than simply making the cards.

General confirmation of this came from an open-ended item on the course evaluation which asked students to describe ways in which the cards had been helpful. The comments were scored for content reflecting utility as a study aid and reflecting utility on the test. Two raters scored the comments with 91% agreement and resolved remaining differences. Of those students responding, 60% commented on the cards as useful study aids and 44% commented on their usefulness on tests. The high percentage of students commenting on the cards as study aids was considered surprising as this possibility was never mentioned during the course. Typical comments mentioned the usefulness of the cards in organizing ideas, recognizing main points, or developing concise answers and the value of writing out information as a general review. On the tests students typically commented on the cards as a memory aid especially on definitions and lists of terms.

Discussion. It is worth noting that the effort students put into their crib cards sometimes bordered on the heroic. Many of the cards collected were works of art painstakingly printed with fine-line pens and using several colors to organize information. Although small print and many abbreviations made accurate word counts impossible, some cards were estimated to contain over 2,000 words.

Despite their efforts, students derived little apparent benefit from their crib cards. Not only were differences between the three card conditions nonsignificant but inspection of Figure 1 reveals that they were no more than about four points in any event. This four point difference held up when scores were compared for all students irrespective of whether they had made cards. The mean test scores (multiple choice and short answer items combined) for all students under the three card conditions were 63.39, 63.69, and 67.43 respectively. Even had such differences been significant, the effect of cheating (crib cards) was only about four points on a 100 point test—and these data were collected under relatively optimal conditions for cheating. Students attempting to peek at slips of paper concealed in their pocket, sleeve, palm, etc. while watching out for an instructor would surely derive even less benefit.

Students themselves may have reached a similar conclusion about the benefits of cheating. The number of students making crib cards declined steadily during the semester and, by the end, only 42% reported that they had even bothered to do so.

Although the number of students making cards fell, all but three students were able to specify some benefit from making the cards. An examination of their comments is enlightening. Psychologists have long distinguished between rote memorization and concept learning. Student comments appeared to reflect a similar understanding. They reported that the cards were primarily helpful during the test in remembering lists and definitions. Such material is essentially memorized, difficult to recall, and one would expect crib notes to be helpful. Crib notes should be much less helpful in concept learning. Concepts and their relationships must be understood before they can be summarized on a crib card and the value of writing them down may be primarily in organizing and clarifying what has been learned. Once this is done there may be little additional value in having the written result available. Student comments also seemed to reflect this recognition.

Classroom cheating raises a number of ethical and social issues not addressed in this study. Still the possibility that cheating (at least in some forms) is ineffective has interesting implications. Most instructors claim (or at least hope) that they teach concepts, not rote memorization. If so, perhaps they might expect that crib notes and similar forms of cheating should not be effective. In fact, judicious use of crib notes might even be a desirable practice since it might relieve students of the time and worry expended in rote memorization, leaving them and the instructor free to concentrate on other, more socially desired, forms of learning. In a word, many test items that a student can answer by looking at a few words on a crib note may simply not be worth asking.

References

Ackerman, P. D. The effects of honor-grading on student's test scores. *American Educational Research Journal,* 1971, *8,* 321-333.

Davison, G. C., & Neale, J. M. *Abnormal psychology: An experimental clinical approach* (2nd ed.). New York: Wiley, 1978.

Flowers, J. V. Behavior modification of cheating in an elementary school student; A brief note. *Behavior Therapy,* 1972, *3,* 311-312.

Hindman, C. D. *Study guide to accompany abnormal psychology.* New York: Wiley, 1978.

Houston, J. P. Cheating: The illusory edge. *Contemporary Educational Psychology,* 1977, *2,* 364-372.

Kirk, R. E. *Experimental design: Procedures for the behavioral sciences.* Belmont CA: Brooks/Cole, 1968.

SAS Institute. *Statistical Analysis System Users Guide; 1979 edition,* Raleigh, NC: Author, 1979.

Thomas, E. L., & Robinson, H. A. *Improving reading in every classroom.* Boston: Allyn & Bacon, 1977.

Wildemuth, B.M. *Cheating: an annotated bibliography.* Princeton, NJ: ERIC Clearinghouse on Tests, Measurement, and Evaluation, 1976. (ERIC Document Reproduction Service No. ED 132 182)

b.   Note Taking Strategies

Virtually all instructors have advised students who are performing poorly. Frequently, discussions center around note taking strategies. Indeed, many individuals presume that note taking skills are essential for academic success and that poor test performance is related to inadequate note taking skills. However, Robin Palkovitz and Richard Lore from Douglass College, Rutgers University reported the results of a study that faculty will find informative. Their results indicated that students did not miss exam questions based upon lecture material primarily because their notes were incorrect or incomplete, but because students failed to review and learn the material in their notes. Those who advise students about academic performance may revise their approach after reading the authors' specific suggestions about note taking and note studying.

Linda Baker and Bruce Lombardi described a naturalistic investigation conducted at the University of Maryland Baltimore County to evaluate the notes students took during lectures; they also examined the relationship between students' notes and their performance on exams. The study provided answers to four important questions about note taking: a) Do some students overrely on instructor provided notes? b) What is the relationship between lecture note quantity and test performance? c) What kinds of information do students include in their notes? d) Is there a relationship between the specific information included in the lecture notes and test performance. The study also indicated that both "remedial" and above average students needed more information about note-taking skills.

Note Taking and Note Review: Why Students Fail Questions Based on Lecture Material

Robin J. Palkovitz and
Richard K. Lore
Douglass College, Rutgers University

Data collected in this study suggest that deficits in note taking ability are not as critical as deficits in studying from notes.

Students at virtually all educational levels spend the bulk of their classroom time taking notes on information presented orally by teachers. Thus, note-taking skills are assumed to be crucial for academic success and most method-oriented books and courses emphasize the mastery of techniques that will help students accurately organize and record verbally presented information. This emphasis suggests that deficits in test performance are due to poor note-taking skills. There is, of course, an alternate explanation as to why students fail test items based upon lecture material: Students may take adequate notes but fail to review and learn the information in their notes.

Experimental evidence regarding the efficacy of note-taking and subsequent review has not yielded consistent conclusions. Several studies have reported facilitative effects of note-taking on the learning of lecture material (DiVesta & Gray, 1972; Fisher & Harris, 1973) whereas others have failed to demonstrate improved performance associated with note taking (Berliner, 1969; Peters, 1972). Carter

and Van Matre (1975) suggest that these conflicting results may be partially explained by the presence or absence of a review and the timing of the review, if any, relative to the test.

Among theoretical models of the function of notes, the "external memory device" position (Miller, Galanter & Pribram, 1960) suggests that the benefits of notes is not in taking them, but rather in having them, in that they provide information necessary for later review and elaboration. Note taking has also been described as an "encoding" process in which the student personalizes information by putting it into his own words (DiVesta & Gray, 1972; Howe, 1970). Although note taking may include transformational and elaborative processes, there is no assurance that this actually occurs (Carter & Van Matre, 1975). According to Anderson (1970), note taking more closely mirrors verbatim transcription than the transformational and elaborative processes involved in efficient learning.

Research by several investigators (e.g., Carter & Van Matre, 1975; Fisher & Harris, 1973) has suggested that the "external memory device" view best characterizes the primary function of notes. In other words, although note taking may be a necessary condition for good test performance, it is not sufficient; good notes must be coupled with intensive review for optimal performance. In the present study, we compared the test performance of students taking a course in introductory psychology with the quality of notes taken during lectures in order to provide more precise information on why students fail test items based upon lecture material.

Method. Ten male and 32 female college students enrolled in an introductory psychology course participated as subjects in the present study. Subjects volunteered for the experiment to partially fulfill course requirements.

Stimulus materials consisted of a series of four 75-minute lectures presented to the entire class as a basis for a portion of an in-class multiple-choice exam. Eight multiple-choice questions from the exam were selected as target questions to be discussed with each of the subjects individually in order to determine the completeness and correctness of their notes in regard to those questions. Criteria for selection of the eight exam questions included: (a) that the question could only be answered by having knowledge of material covered in the lecture (i.e. topic not discussed in the text-book), and (b) that the question was derived directly from the lecture material rather than being a paraphrase of the material or the application of a principle discussed in the lecture.

After the first exam was scored and the results returned to the class, announcements soliciting volunteer subjects for the present study were made. All students who volunteered were individually scheduled for a 30-minute interview and instructed to bring their class notes to the interview. When subjects arrived for their interview, the purpose of the study was explained to them. The subject and the experimenter then examined the subject's lecture notes for material which the subject had recorded pertaining to each of the eight questions selected from the exam. When the subject's notations relevant to each question were found, the experimenter recorded the notes as being in one of the four following categories: (a) Completely correct, (b) Partially correct or incomplete, (c) Missing, or (d) Incorrect. These categories, coupled with the exam performance for each question (correct or incorrect) created a 2x4 matrix for categorizing each response and the notes corresponding to it.

Results. The reliability of the experimenters' ability to classify the lecture material into the four categories was evaluated by having two independent judges classify the lecture material presented by 10 subjects. For these 80 questions, both judges agreed upon the classification of the students' notes 73 times for a percentage agreement of .913.

The overall performance of the 42 subjects on the 8 exam questions is presented in Table 1. One student insisted that her notes for 2 questions had been misplaced after the exam had been taken and thus the results are based upon a total of 334 questions.

A chi-square analysis of the data in Table 1 indicates that test item performance is influenced by the quality of the students' notes, $\chi^2(3) = 12.94$, $p < .01$.

A total of 227 questions were correctly answered. For 82 percent of the correctly answered questions, the appropriate

Table 1. Classification of Lecture Material in Notes as a Function of Test Item Performance

| Performance | Notes | | | | |
	Correct	Incomplete	Missing	Incorrect	Total
Correct	187	17	19	4	227
Incorrect	71	19	16	1	107
Total	258	36	35	5	334

lecture material was judged to be complete and correctly recorded in the students' notes. However, for 66 percent of the 107 questions that were answered incorrectly by the students, the appropriate lecture material had also been judged to be complete and correctly recorded in the students' notes. Obviously, performance on exam questions is not simply determined by the ability of students to take accurate or complete notes: 18% of the questions were answered correctly despite faulty or missing notes and two-thirds of the mistakes were made by students with notes judged both complete and correct.

When one focuses on questions missed by the students, a clear pattern emerges. Incorrect notes were quite rare, with only one question possibly missed because the student distorted the lecture material. Higher percentages of the incorrectly answered questions were based upon notes judged to be either incomplete or missing (18% and 15% respectively) but even these combined categories account for no more than one-third of the student mistakes and a chi-square analysis of the classification of the lecture material for incorrect items only (bottom row of Table 1) is highly significant, $\chi^2(3) = 104.5$, $p < .001$. In other words, students incorrectly answered a disproportionate number of questions for which they had accurate notes.

Further analysis of the data split by overall exam performance indicated that high scorers (those who had over 74% of all exam questions correct) and low scorers (subjects correctly answering less than 60% of all exam questions) did not perform differentially based on the quality of their notes, $\chi^2(3) = 1.62$, n.s. That is, both high and low scorers tended to incorrectly answer exam questions although both groups had complete, correctly recorded notes.

Discussion. The results of the present study indicate that students do not miss exam questions based upon lecture material primarily because their lecture notes are incomplete or incorrect. Rather, most errors are made by students who accurately record the lecture material but then fail to adequately review and learn the information in their notes.

Students tend to focus on inadequate note-taking skills as the primary source of errors on tests and often express surprise when the correct answers to test questions are found to be clearly stated in their notes. Several strategies developed by the second author during 16 years of teaching introductory psychology courses have proven helpful in emphasizing the importance of note studying as well as note taking.

Students who request an office meeting to discuss their performance in the course are required to bring (a) copies of all course tests, (b) their lecture notes, and (c) the textbook. With practice and a little preparation, it is an easy matter to select five or six questions derived directly from lecture material that were missed by the student and then point out the correct answers *in the student's own notes*. Incidentally, viewing students' notes can also provide the instructor with information on lecture topics that were unclear or boring (doodling frequency goes up!). A comparable analysis of questions derived from the textbook is also profitable for students. Often, questions are missed from sections of the text that the student has obviously not read; clean pages and no underlining offer some evidence that the material has not been studied. This procedure invariably provides remarkably graphic information for students with academic problems and can effectively refute the usual student rationalizations (e.g., "But I read the material four times", "I just don't do well on multiple-choice tests").

Typically students do not review their lecture notes until just prior to a test. But, by this time, much of the content of the lectures has been forgotten and their telegraphically written notes are meaningless. The importance of early and regular review of notes can be vividly demonstrated by requesting students to compare their ability to read and interpret their own notes taken during a recent lecture with those taken three-four weeks earlier. The poor performance of most students on the earlier material will convince even the most skeptical student of the benefits of early review.

We each have a tendency to place undue faith in published material and question the authority of information in our own handwriting. In our view, most instructors draw a high percentage of test questions from lecture material (or material covered both in the text and lectures). In such cases, more information which the instructor views as important is contained in 20 pages of lecture notes than in 20 pages of text material. Students should therefore be encouraged to allocate more study time per page to lecture material than to assigned readings.

The notes we examined were virtually always a verbatim copy of the lecture material. Typical students do not appear to employ "encoding" processes to personalize information from lectures (DiVesta & Gray, 1972; Howe, 1970). Finally the results of our study support the "external memory device" (Miller, Galanter, & Pribram, 1960) function of notes in that they provide information necessary for later review.

References

Anderson, R. C. Control of student mediating processes during verbal learning and instruction. *Review of Educational Research*, 1970, *40*, 349-369.

Berliner, D. C. Effects of test-like events and note taking on learning from lecture instruction. *Proceedings of the 77th Annual Convention of the American Psychological Association*, 1969, *4*, 623-624.

Carter, J. F., & Van Matre, N. H. Note taking vs. note having. *Journal of Educational Psychology*, 1975, *67*, 900-904.

DiVesta, F. J., & Gray, G. S. Listening and note taking. *Journal of Educational Psychology*, 1972, *63*, 8-14.

Fisher, J. L., & Harris, M. B. Effect of note taking and review on recall. *Journal of Educational Psychology*, 1973, *65*, 321-325.

Howe, M. J. A. Using students' notes to examine the role of the individual learner in acquiring meaningful subject matter. *Journal of Educational Research*, 1970, *64*, 61-63.

Miller, G. A., Galanter, E., & Pribram, K. H. *Plans and the structure of behavior*. New York: Holt, 1960.

Peters, D. L. Effects of note taking and rate of presentation on short term objective test performance. *Journal of Educational Psychology*, 1972, *63*, 276-280.

Students' Lecture Notes and Their Relation to Test Performance

Linda Baker
Bruce R. Lombardi
University of Maryland Baltimore County

The empirical relations between quantitative and qualitative aspects of students' lecture notes and test performance are not well known. The present study examined these relations naturalistically by analyzing the notes taken by college students during a specially constructed, but otherwise typical, classroom lecture. Key findings were as follows: (a) Most students included in their notes less than 25% of the propositions judged worthy of inclusion and only 50% of the targeted main ideas; (b) The amount and kind of information included in the notes was related to test performance; (c) Inclusion of specific information in the notes was a sufficient but not a necessary condition for correctly answering a question based on that information. These findings suggest a stronger relation between note-taking and test performance than has previously been revealed.

Among the many skills involved in academic success is the ability to take thorough and accurate lecture notes. This skill, like so many others that support academic endeavors, is rarely explicitly taught in the traditional classroom (Baker & Brown, 1984). Students must develop their note-taking skills on their own, deciding for themselves how much and what kinds of information they should include. It would appear, however, that these efforts are often unsuccessful, as any instructor who has ever examined students' lecture notes can attest. Nevertheless, our anecdotal observations have seldom been validated by empirical tests of either the extent of note-taking problems or of the relation between lecture note adequacy and course performance.

Although there have been several studies on the relation of note-taking to test performance, the majority have compared test scores of note-takers and non-note-takers but have not considered the contents of the notes themselves. Some of these studies have shown that note-taking facilitates performance (DiVesta & Gray, 1972; Fisher & Harris, 1973); others have shown no effect (Eisner & Rhodes, 1959; Peters, 1972); and others have shown facilitative effects under some conditions but not others (Carter & Van Matre, 1975; Peper & Mayer, 1978). Efforts to reconcile the inconsistent results have led to two different conceptions of the function of note-taking. Carter and Van Matre (1975) argue that notes are useful only to the extent that they serve as an external storage device for subsequent review. Peper and Mayer (1978) argue that the act of note-taking itself enhances test performance by promoting a richer encoding of the lecture material. Different predictions with respect to the role of note adequacy can be derived from these two perspectives. If note-taking is useful only as a means for review, then if students fail to review their notes before a test, it should not matter whether the notes were adequate or inadequate. On the other hand, if the act of note-taking itself is facilitative, better notes should promote better test performance with or without a subsequent review.

One of the few studies to relate the content of students' lecture notes to their test performance was a naturalistic investigation by Palkovitz and Lore (1980). Introductory psychology students were interviewed after taking an objective exam based on four lectures, and their lecture notes were examined for the presence and accuracy of information needed to answer eight target questions. Most of the students correctly recorded the target information in their notes; 77% of the relevant points were included. Analysis of the relation to test performance indicated that 82% of the correct test responses were associated with the presence of relevant information in the notes. Surprisingly, 66% of the incorrect responses also were! Moreover, students who performed well on the exam and those who performed poorly did not differ in the quality of their notes. These data, supplemented by students' self-reports of study behaviors, led Palkovitz and Lore (1980) to conclude that accurate notes do not ensure good test performance; rather, students must adequately review the notes prior to the exam.

The thoroughness of the students' notes was somewhat surprising, but the target facts may have been signalled as important by Palkovitz and Lore. We know that students are more likely to remember information if the instructor tells them that it is important as opposed to unimportant (Goolkasian, Terry, & Park, 1979); and it is reasonable to assume that such information would also be more frequently included in students' lecture notes. Signals of importance may also be provided if the instructor writes anything on a blackboard or transparency since we know that they both influence note content and test performance.

Locke (1975) examined the notes of nearly 200 college students enrolled in 12 different courses for inclusion of information identified as important by the instructors. Whereas 88% of the ideas that had been presented on the blackboard were included in the notes, only 52% of the non-blackboard ideas were included. Boswell (1980) compared test scores of a class that received critical information on a transparency accompanying a lecture with those of a class that received the lecture alone. Results revealed that the lower third of the class benefitted from having the information presented on a transparency, whereas the upper two-thirds did not. This suggests that more able students can identify the relevant information on their own, and so do not need instructor-provided cues; but the poorer students, who have more difficulty extracting the main ideas, benefit from the additional help. It may be unwise, however, for students to interpret the use of blackboards or transparencies as signals of importance. Teachers may use these devices simply to illustrate the spelling of new terms or to provide a hierarchical overview of the lecture. Under these circumstances, the burden of extracting and recording important information rests with the student, and overreliance on what the teacher has written may be deleterious.

In the present study we examined the aforementioned issues within a naturalistic setting and also examined the kinds of information students include in their notes. Introductory psychology students attended a regularly scheduled class lecture, took a multiple-choice test on the material 3 weeks later as part of a regularly scheduled exam, and submitted their lecture notes for photocopying. The lecture included four different kinds of target information: main ideas, supporting details, logical transitions, and examples. A transparency was prepared and used in order to provide a hierarchical overview of the lecture, but it contained almost none of the target information. We sought answers to the following questions: (a) Is there evidence that some students overrely on instructor-provided notes? (b) Is there a relation between lecture note quantity and test performance? (c) Are students more likely to include some kinds of information in their notes than others? (d) Is there a relation between the specific information included in the lecture notes and test performance?

METHOD

Subjects

The subjects were students enrolled in one section of an introductory psychology course. All students who attended class on the day the target lecture was delivered and who took the test on the material 3 weeks later were eligible to serve as subjects provided they turned in their lecture notes for photocopying. A total of 94 students out of a class of 125 met these criteria. The analyses reported in this paper were based on a randomly selected subsample of 40 students.

Materials

The lecture topic selected for the study dealt with the physiological aspects of emotion. Several factors entered into the selection of this particular topic: (a) The lecture date was midway through the semester so students were familiar with the instructor's style of teaching and testing; (b) The lecture date was 3 weeks prior to the next exam, a sufficiently long interval that students should feel the need to review their notes and not depend solely on memory; and (c) The topic was not covered exhaustively in the text so new information could be presented. As the lecture was being prepared, we incorporated information that would be the basis of the test questions. The target information included six transition points, six main ideas, six supporting details, and two examples.

Because the instructor routinely used a transparency instead of a blackboard, we did so here. Two transparencies were prepared on which key words were written in a rough hierarchical structure. To illustrate, a portion of the lecture was devoted to the disruptive effects of arousal with particular focus on Richter's work in which wild rats were stressed by forcing them to swim for many hours. Seven of the test questions were based on information presented during this part of the lecture, none of which could be answered on the basis of the rough outline alone. The transparency representation was as follows:

> Disruptive effects of arousal
>> Side effects
>> Long-term effects
>> Death
>>> Voodoo
>>> Richter

Procedure

The lecture was presented to the class by their regular instructor, the first author. The students had no reason to believe that there was anything special about this lecture. The lecture was attended by the second author who was unknown to the students. He tape recorded the lecture and also took notes. A transcript of the tape was later checked against the instructor's lecture notes in order to verify that the target information had been clearly presented. The test on the lecture material was given 3 weeks later. Six of the target questions (3 main points, 2 supporting details, and 1 transition) were included on the regularly scheduled 60-item multiple-choice exam, which also covered other lectures and assigned chapters in the text. The remaining 14 questions were incorporated into a separate "quiz" on the emotion lecture. These questions were substantively similar to the questions on the exam, although the "example" questions would be unlikely to appear on an actual exam. Just before taking the exam, students were informed of our interest in the relation between class notes and exam performance and were invited to participate in our study for extra credit. They were asked to remain in the lecture hall after they finished the exam in order to take the quiz. They were also asked to turn in their lecture notes to be photocopied. All students were given the opportunity to participate, regardless of whether they had attended class on the day of the emotion lecture. As long as they took the quiz and handed in *any* set of lecture notes, they received extra credit.

RESULTS

All students' notes were first examined for degree of correspondence with the outline presented on the transparency. With but few exceptions, all sets of notes included all of the information, consisting of 35 propositions. There were vast differences among the students, however, in the amount of additional information they included in their notes. Each set of notes was scored for the number of added propositions; repetitions of the same proposition were not counted twice and propositions were counted without regard to degree of importance. The number of propositions added ranged from a low of 0 to a high of 82, with a mean of 26.6 and a standard deviation of 16.55. In order to evaluate the thoroughness of the notes, we used as our standard lecture notes taken in class by the co-investigator. Although it is true that the co-investigator had an advantage over the students in that he was familiar with the lecture material, his notes reflected what students *could* have recorded in class had they chosen to do so. The co-investigator's notes consisted of 98 propositions in addition to those presented on the transparency. The majority of the students recorded considerably less information than this experienced instructor; in fact, only 7% of the students included even half as many propositions.

Qualitative aspects of the lecture notes were examined by scoring the notes for the presence or absence of the specific information needed to answer each test question. For each type of question, the total number of items included in the notes was calculated. As expected, some kinds of information were more likely to be included than others. For main point questions, 47% of the target information was included in the notes, and for detail questions, 42%. However, some of the detail information was presented on the transparency. If we base the average only on those questions, which required the students to use their own initiative, the percentage decreases to 13. These data suggest that students do differentiate the main points from the supporting details in the process of note-taking. An examination of the example information revealed even more differentiation of importance level: Only 3% of the students included *any* mention of the examples in their notes. Finally, for the transition questions, 29% of the relevant information was included in the lecture notes. What this indicates is that students usually did not explicitly state the logical relations between ideas, perhaps on the assumption that the links would be readily inferable.

Each student's quiz and the relevant portions of the exam were scored for the number of target questions of each type that were answered correctly. Overall, 70% of the main point questions were correct, 59% of the details, 63% of the transitions, and 50% of the examples. (Note that two of the detail questions, unlike all others, were based directly on notes presented on the transparency, and these two questions were answered correctly 90% of the time.)

Intercorrelations among 9 variables of interest were calculated, and the resulting correlation matrix is presented in Table 1, which excludes examples because they were recorded so infrequently in the notes. Of the 36 different correlations, 19 were statistically significant, at least at the .05 level. Only those of particular interest will be discussed later. The number of propositions included in students' notes was significantly related to overall test scores, supporting the intuitively compelling but empirically undocumented expectation that the more information students include in their lecture notes, the better their test performance. Since our primary goal in lecturing is for students to learn the main ideas, it is encouraging that performance on the main point questions was related to note quantity. The correlations were not significant for the less-central detail and transition information. Note also that the total test score was significantly related to the final grade obtained in the course, suggesting that this one test was representative. The correlation between number of propositions in the notes and final course grade was also significant, suggesting that the degree of elaboration in a student's notes is a predictor of overall course performance. Also of interest was the fact that inclusion of main point information and detail information in the notes was correlated with performance on the corresponding types of test questions; for transition information, the correlation was positive but not statistically significant.

Though suggestive, the correlational analysis does not indicate whether the presence of specific propositions in the notes was associated with correct responses to the questions based on those propositions. This issue was addressed by creating 2 × 2 contingency tables for each question based on presence or absence of target information in the notes and correctness or incorrectness of the response on the test. The cell frequencies differed somewhat from item to item, but the patterns were similar for items within question type. Accordingly, for ease of exposition and comparison across question types, the data are reported in Table 2 as average proportions for each type of question. Note that a distinction has been made between detail information that was and was not presented on the transparency. Tests of association were conducted using Yates' Corrected Chi-Square analyses and yielded significant effects for the following question types: main points, $\chi^2(1) = 18.93$, $p < .001$; details (not on transparency), $\chi^2(1) = 11.57$, $p < .001$; and transitions, $\chi^2(1) = 4.96$, $p < .05$. There are several general trends apparent in these data. First, it is clear that inclusion in the notes is not a *necessary* condition for students to answer the question correctly. It was frequently the case that there were more subjects in the notes-absent/response-correct cell than in the notes-present/response-correct cell. However, there is strong evidence that inclusion in the notes is a *sufficient* condition for students to answer the question correctly. There were very few students who fell into the notes-present/response-incorrect cell. Of all the questions answered incorrectly, only on 14% of the occasions was the relevant information included in the notes.[1]

DISCUSSION

The present study was designed as a naturalistic investigation of the notes students take during actual classroom lectures and their relationship to performance on actual classroom exams. Some degree of control must be sacrificed in such a study (e.g., we do not know how much time students spent studying their notes before the exam), but the advantages outweigh the limitations. Because students did not know in advance that the notes taken during this lecture were to be examined, the quality of the notes should be representative of those they usually take. And because the test on the lecture was incorporated into the exam itself or given immediately afterwards, the incentives for studying and the study behaviors should also be representative.

One of our concerns was with the amount of information students included in their notes. Locke (1975) reported that students are more likely to include information presented on the blackboard than information that they must extract on their own. In the present study, virtually *all* students included *all* of the information presented on the transparencies, while recording only 27% of the additional information identified by the investigators as important. A few students were exceptionally thorough note-takers, but most did little more than copy down the key terms and topic headings provided on the transparency. A disconcerting implication is that students might take a more active role in processing the lecture material if they were given *no* assistance. On the other hand, perhaps the students would have nothing at all in their notes without these aids. As Boswell (1980) reported, it was the less successful students who benefitted most by the use of transparencies.

Examination of the content of the notes revealed that students were more likely to include some types of information than others. This suggests that they selected information for recording differentially; they were more likely to include main ideas but omit details and information that could be reconstructed or inferred (transitions and examples). The fact that students did show sensitivity to importance is encouraging; the fact that they recorded less than half of the main ideas is rather less so.

Finally, the study revealed a relation between the content of the students' notes and test performance. The more information students included of a particular type, the better they did on the corresponding questions. Moreover, the presence of target information in the lecture notes appears to be a sufficient, but not a necessary, condition for correctly answering the question based on that information. Although students were able to answer many of the questions without having recorded the relevant information in their notes, they rarely answered the questions incorrectly if the information was present in their notes. This finding conflicts with that reported by Palkovitz and Lore (1980), who found that most students who answered questions in-

---

[1] One additional question we were able to address concerns the relationship between a student's test performance and class attendance on the day of the lecture. If the test was in fact a valid indicator of learning, students who attended class should do better than those who did not attend class. To determine whether this was true, performance on each question was examined on the basis of lecture attendance. Overall, on 16 of the 20 questions, students who attended class were more likely to give the correct response than those who did not attend, with the difference ranging from 3% to 26% (mean = 11.17, standard deviation = 7.63). A matched pairs t-test on the difference scores for the 20 questions proved reliable, $t = 2.82$, $p < .01$; students who attended class had higher test scores than students who did not. These results are reassuring in supporting our belief that lecture attendance *does* matter!

Table 1. Intercorrelations Among the Dependent Measures

	1	2	3	4	5	6	7	8	9
1. Total No. of Propositions in Notes	—								
2. No. of Correct Main Point Questions	.47*	—							
3. No. of Correct Detail Questions	.12	.14	—						
4. No. of Correct Transition Questions	−.14	−.12	−.09	—					
5. Total No. of Correct Test Questions	.35*	.68*	.52*	.33*	—				
6. Final Grade in Course	.30*	.33*	.30*	.13	.55*	—			
7. No. of Main Points in Notes	.73*	.56*	−.07	−.15	.27*	.23	—		
8. No. of Details in Notes	.45*	.17	.32*	.10	.22	.09	.25	—	
9. No. of Transitions in Notes	.60*	.25	.17	.21	.31*	.27*	.51*	.31*	—

*$p < .05$
Note: Measures 1, 7, 8, and 9 are derived from the students' lecture notes; measures 2, 3, 4, and 5 are based on test performance.

Table 2. Relationship between Lecture Note Contents and Responses to Test Questions for each Type of Information[a]

	Main Points		Details (not on transparency)		Details (on transparency)	
	Notes		Notes		Notes	
Test Response	Present	Absent	Present	Absent	Present	Absent
Correct	.39	.31	.11	.38	.94	.01
Incorrect	.07	.23	.02	.49	.05	.00

	Transitions		Examples	
	Notes		Notes	
Test Response	Present	Absent	Present	Absent
Correct	.22	.42	.03	.53
Incorrect	.08	.29	.00	.45

[a]Cell entries are proportions of subjects, averaged across individual items within types.

correctly *did* include the relevant information in their notes. Palkovitz and Lore interpreted their data as support for the view that notes are useful only if they are adequately reviewed. However, the present study shows that the content of the students' notes does indeed make a difference. Nevertheless, we would not argue for a causal link, because it may be that students who take better notes in class *also* engage in more effective study strategies or have higher levels of achievement motivation.

In conclusion, the study has provided a number of important findings regarding the note-taking skills of college students. The paucity of information included in most students' notes implicates a real need for more direct information in note-taking skills, not just for the "remedial" student but for the majority of college freshmen. The frequent failures to record even the main points of the lecture further emphasize the need to help students differentiate the important information from the less important.

REFERENCES

Baker, L., & Brown, A. L. (1984). Metacognitive skills and reading. In P. D. Pearson, M. Kamil, R. Barr, & P. Mosenthal (Eds.), *Handbook of reading research* (pp. 353–394). New York: Longman.

Boswell, D. A. (1980). Evaluation of transparencies for psychology instruction. *Teaching of Psychology, 7,* 171–173.

Carter, J. F., & Van Matre, N. H. (1975). Note taking vs. note having. *Journal of Educational Psychology, 67,* 900–904.

DiVesta, F. J., & Gray, G. S. (1972). Listening and note taking. *Journal of Educational Psychology, 63,* 8–14.

Eisner, S., & Rhodes, K. (1959). Note taking during or after the lecture. *Journal of Educational Psychology, 50,* 301–304.

Fisher, J. L., & Harris, M. B. (1973). Effect of note taking and review on recall. *Journal of Educational Psychology, 65,* 321–325.

Goolkasian, P., Terry, W. S., & Park, D. C. (1979). Memory for lectures: Effects of delay and distractor type. *Journal of Educational Psychology, 71,* 465–470.

Locke, E. A. (1975). *A guide to effective study.* New York: Springer.

Palkovitz, R. J., & Lore, R. K. (1980). Note taking and note review: Why students fail questions based on lecture material. *Teaching of Psychology, 7,* 159–161.

Peper, R. J., & Mayer, R. E. (1978). Note taking as a generative activity. *Journal of Educational Psychology, 70,* 514–522.

Peters, D. L. (1972). Effects of note taking and rate of presentation on short-term objective test performance. *Journal of Educational Psychology, 63,* 276–280.

c.   Test Taking Strategies

Many teachers and students accept the proposition that higher achieving students finish objective exams faster than their lower achieving classmates. But do they? Not according to Clyde Paul and John Rosenkoetter who conducted a study using a large sample of students from four introductory classes at Southwest Missouri State University. In a similar study, James Johnston from the University of Wisconsin at Stevens Point found that those students who were among the first to finish were likely to obtain especially high or especially low grades. Taken together, the results of these two studies provide a body of evidence for advising students. Students should not become anxious and conclude that they are performing poorly because they are taking longer than others to complete an exam.

Lucinda McClain conducted a novel study at Marquette University that provides instructors with a plethora of information to use in advising students about techniques for improving performance on multiple choice exams. Her investigation instructed students to talk into a tape recorder while answering examination questions. The study clarified four aspects of test-taking behavior among "A," "C," and "F" students: a) number of alternatives that students considered, b) number of times that students anticipated answers before reading alternatives, c) number of incorrect alternatives that students dismissed by stating the reasons they were unacceptable, and d) number of questions that students initially skipped. The author recommended that readers share the "A" students' strategies to improve other students' performance.

Gabriel Cirino-Cerena from the University of Puerto Rico evaluated the use of 14 essay test taking strategies by high and low performing students. Strategies such as writing extensively, rephrasing, and expressing a similar opinion to that of the teacher were among those that higher achievers used most often.

The Relationship Between the Time Taken to Complete An Examination and the Test Score Received

Clyde A. Paul and John S. Rosenkoetter
Southwest Missouri State University

Do higher achieving students complete an achievement test faster than lower achievers? Logic would suggest that they do. The higher achievers are probably better at recognizing a correct answer and would more rapidly complete the inferences and decisions needed in order to choose the best answer for complex questions. The reading rate for better students should be faster than that of their less able classmates, thus increasing the prospect of a quicker completion time. Therefore, although other factors, such as motivation and confidence, may influence how long a student works to complete a test, in general, it would seem that better students would tend to finish sooner.

This logic seems to be tacitly accepted by teachers and students. Most of us can remember taking a test and experiencing anxiety when others turned in their papers and we still had a major portion of the examination to complete.

We felt those students must have done well while we were performing poorly because we were slow. It has also been suggested (Burack, 1967) that early studies supported this popular belief.

Several studies (Burack, 1967; Ebel, 1972; Johnston, 1977; Michael & Michael, 1969; Terranova, 1972) have failed to find evidence which would support the hypothesis that higher achieving students tend to finish examinations earlier.

Burack (1967) studied two introductory psychology courses (N = 39, 41), using a test which consisted of one-half multiple choice items and one-half short answer questions. He found that rank-difference correlations between the amount of time taken on the test and the raw scores did not differ significantly from zero. Michael and Michael (1969) used ten sections of varied graduate and undergraduate classes employing tests with objective questions and either an open or close-book format. Only one section produced a significant relationship between total score and the order of completion. Examining four sections of public school pupils, Terranova (1972) also correlated test scores with time. He did not find any significant linear correlations. Ebel (1972, p. 108) reported on a class of 100 students enrolled in a course on educational measurements. Division of the students into groups of ten based on order of finish indicated that performance, as determined by the total number of questions answered by each group, was similar. Johnston (1977) investigated two sections of psychology students. He reported that the mean scores for the groups finishing "early," "late," or "neither" were not significantly different. However, he did discover significant differences between the variances of the three groups. He suggests that the "early" and "late" groups had extremely high and low scores which tended to cancel out and produce means similar to that of the "neither" group. The disparity between the "early" and "late" groups and the "neither" group was apparent when analyzing the group variances.

The participants in the present study were students enrolled in five sections (N = 162, 167, 151, 161, 159) of a university general psychology course. The students were drawn from all four class levels, although a majority were freshmen. The students had a wide variety of academic majors and were approximately equally divided between males and females. The test was an instructor-prepared achievement test covering a unit of study based on the text by Mischel and Mischel (1977). The instrument consisted of either 40 (4 sections) or 50 (1 section) four-alternative, multiple-choice questions. To discourage cheating, 10 forms of the test were prepared. However, while different questions were developed for each section, the two forms used each period contained identical questions which differed only in the arrangement of the alternatives. Post-administration analysis of the tests revealed all 10 forms possessed a Kuder-Richardson reliability of at least .75.

The answer sheets were collected in the order that the students completed the test. After all answer sheets were received, the order of finish was recorded on each one.

For analysis, the two test forms were separated for each section. This procedure provided 10 sets of data. Each set, consisting of approximately 80 scores, was then divided into quartiles according to the rank which had been determined when the examination was completed. The test score mean and variance were computed for each quartile.

A one-tailed t-test indicated that in only one instance did the first quartile group have a mean score significantly higher ($p < .05$) than that of any other quartile group. Computation of F-ratios did not indicate that there was an unexpected number of significant differences between group variances.

It can be concluded that there is no support for Johnston's finding that the variance between groups is significantly different. There is evidence in the analysis to support previous findings that within each section, score performance is not significantly related to the time taken to complete a test.

However, a final observation is in order. It was noted that while the first quartile group did not achieve a significantly higher mean score than the other three groups, there was an apparent trend for that group to have a higher mean score. In particular, on six of the ten forms the first quartile group ranked first. On the remaining four forms the first quartile group tied for first once, ranked second twice, and third once. The sum of these ranks is 14.5, whereas the sums of the remaining quartile group ranks are 32, 29.5 and 24 respectively. This observation prompts speculation that perhaps there is a tendency for better students to finish early on tests. However, because the correlation between test score and order of finish is usually rather weak, it has remained undetected in previous research. Two studies (Johnston, 1977; Ebel, 1972) report their data in a manner to allow further analysis. These studies offer extremely weak support, but no apparent contradiction of our speculations.

References

Burack, B. Relationship between course examination scores and time taken to finish the examination, revisited. *Psychological Reports*, 1967, *20*, 164.

Ebel, R. L. *Essentials of educational measurement* (2nd ed.). Englewood Cliffs, NJ: Prentice-Hall, 1972.

Johnston, J. Exam-taking speed and grades. *Teaching of Psychology*, 1977, *4*, 148-149.

Michael, J. J., & Michael, W. B. The relationship of performance on objective achievement examinations to the order in which students complete them. *Educational and Psychological Measurement*, 1969, *29*, 511-513.

Mischel, W., & Mischel, H. N. *Essentials of psychology.* New York: Random House, 1977.

Terranova, C. Relationship between test scores and test time. *The Journal of Experimental Education*, 1972, *40*, 81-83.

Exam-Taking Speed and Grades

James J. Johnston
University of Wisconsin

Several of my colleagues and I have formed the impression that those students who tend to finish objective exams very quickly, and those who are among the last to finish, are likely to be among *either* the best or the poorest students in the class. A possible rationale for this impression goes something like this: Some top students are conscientious and take a lot of time to make sure they have considered all the possibliities, while others know the material so well that they answer immediately and confidently; some poor students are unsure of their answers (e.g. because several alternative answers look right) and take a lot of time to consider and reconsider their answers, while others realize they don't know the material very well, answer whatever questions they can, take a quick stab at the rest (maybe), and promptly hand in their exams so they can leave.

The present study was conducted to test that impression. It was first tested in an undergraduate course in industrial psychology (n=26) which I taught. An "early" finisher was defined as one who was among the first five in the class to finish one or more of the five objective exams given. A "late" finisher was one who finished among the last five on any of the exams. (No subject finished both early and last on different exams.) Everyone else fell into the category of "neither" early nor late. The mean percentage correct over all exams (not just those on which a person finished early or late—to maintain independence of observations and a constant comparison basis for all subjects) and the variances for each group are given in Table 1.

The difference in means does not approach significance. However, the variances are very different, with the neither group being significantly less variable than both the early group ($F=4.70, p < .05$) and the late group ($F=3.53, p < .05$), even with a rather small sample size. The early and late groups do not have significantly different variances ($F=1.33$). These results support the hypothesis that scores of both early and late finishers tend to differ considerably from the average in both high and low directions, with high and low scores tending to balance out, causing little difference in means for the three groups.

The study was then repeated with a larger sample ($n=97$) from an introductory psychology class. Because the class was larger, "earlies" and "lates" were those who finished among the first or last 10 students on one or more of the five objective exams given. One subject who finished early on one exam and late on another was not included in the analysis. These results are also shown in Table 1.

The pattern of results is similar to that from the first study, with the difference in means not approaching significance and the variances quite different. The early group has a significantly higher variance than the neither group ($F=2.22$ $p < .01$), but the comparison between the variances of the late and neither groups does not reach statistical significance ($F=1.52$).

The results from both classes taken together indicate that those students who are among the first to finish an objective exam are likely to get especially high or especially low scores. (This finding may not apply to essay exams where the best students may generally have too much to say to be among the first to finish). The same may be true for those who are among the last to finish under some conditions, but the present study does not explain the discrepancy between significance in one class but not in the other.

Table 1
Test Performance by Test-Taking Time

	First Study			Second Study		
	Early	Late	Neither	Early	Late	Neither
Number	9	6	11	28	23	46
Mean (%)	80.9	83.2	80.1	85.0	83.7	84.8
Variance	98.6	131.5	28.0	143.7	97.8	64.6

Behavior During Examinations: A Comparison of "A," "C," and "F" Students

Lucinda McClain
Marquette University

In taking objective tests, superior performers use more sophisticated strategies than do poor performers.

Many instructors have been questioned by students wanting to improve their performance on multiple-choice examinations. The "What can I do?" is often followed by well-meaning suggestions about increasing study time, thoroughly reviewing the material, and asking questions to insure understanding. These suggestions are designed to help students arrive at the examination better prepared. Less frequently, instructors offer advice on how to improve performance during the examination itself. Yet, the ways students attempt to answer questions during an exam—their test-taking strategies—may be important determinants of their exam scores. In an effort to provide my students with concrete suggestions for improving their performance, I investigated the exam-taking strategies used by different groups of introductory psychology students and found that "A" students used entirely different strategies than do "C" or "F" students.

Very few investigations of students' behavior during examinations have been reported, and most of the previous research has been concerned with answer-changing on multiple-choice tests (Bath, 1967; Best, 1979; Edwards & Marshall, 1977; Johnston, 1975, 1978; Mueller & Wasser, 1977). These studies consistently found that wrong-to-right changes were more frequent than right-to-wrong changes. In addition, Johnston and Best found that the best students engaged in the least answer changing, but Bath reported that the best and worst students made more changes than average students.

The speed with which students finish exams has also been studied. Paul and Rosenkoetter (1980) reported no significant relationship between the order in which students finished an exam and the scores they earned. Johnston (1977) found that the mean performance of "early" and "late" finishers did not significantly differ, but noted that the variability of these students' scores was greater than the variability of the scores of students who finished neither early nor late. This finding suggested that both good and poor students tended to be among the early and late finishers.

A final test-taking strategy that has been investigated is to skip difficult questions. Rindler (1980) reported that more "middle ability" (GPA = 2.20 to 2.79) students initially skipped questions on a timed verbal aptitude test than did "high ability" (GPA > 2.79) or "low ability" (GPA < 2.20) students. However, any benefit of initially skipping a question and returning to it later depended on the ability level of the students. Among high ability students, those who skipped earned higher final scores than those who did not. Among low and middle ability students, those who did not skip questions earned the higher scores.

The purpose of the present study was to describe the test-taking strategies used by "A," "C," and "F" students during a multiple-choice examination in an introductory psychology course. The strategies employed were revealed by asking student volunteers to talk into a tape recorder while answering their examination questions. Five aspects of test-taking behavior were measured: (a) the number of alternatives read per question, (b) the number of times students anticipated the answer after reading the question, but before reading the alternatives provided, (c) the number of incorrect alternatives that were eliminated by stating the reasons that these answers were unacceptable, (d) the number of questions that were initially skipped, and (e) the total score on the examination. The choice of these performance measures was based on informal conversations with students and on the conviction that optimal performance on a multiple-choice exam depends on carefully considering each answer and systematically eliminating the incorrect alternatives.

Method. One week before the fourth hourly exam was scheduled, my 523 introductory psychology students were invited to participate in this study. Students were informed that the purpose of the project was to investigate how they choose their answers to exam questions, and that they would be asked to "think out loud." Students were further informed that the experimental exam would contain the same questions as the regularly scheduled examination, that the score they earned would count toward their final grade, and that volunteers would receive extra credit points as they did if they participated in other departmental research projects. Students of all performance levels were encouraged to participate. From a list of 129 volunteers, three groups of students were selected based on their average performance on the three previous 70-question multiple-choice exams given in the course. The 20 "A" students had averages greater than 90% ($M = 64.42$, $SD = 1.23$), the 20 "C" students had averages from 70-76% ($M = 51.52$, $SD = 1.24$), and the 20 "F" students had averages below 60% ($M = 37.15$, $SD = 2.06$). Each group contained 12 females and 8 males.

Volunteers took their exams individually in small private rooms on the same day as the regularly scheduled exam or on the day after. A student experimenter not enrolled in the course was present to operate the tape recorder and to insure that the subject kept talking. Each of the five experimenters tested 12 randomly assigned subjects. The subjects were instructed to read each question aloud and then to answer it while verbalizing their thoughts. Subjects were not specifically instructed to read each of the four alternative answers for each question aloud. The experimenter stated that he or she would not provide feedback on the correctness of the student's answer, but that questions of clarification would be answered as they were at regular examinations. Students were allowed as much time as they needed to complete the 70-question exam, and all required more time ($M = 105$ min, range $= 79$-120 min) than the 60 min allotted on regular examinations. Many students expressed some apprehension about the procedure, but none withdrew from the study, and most expressed surprise at the ease with which they could comply with the instructions.

Results and Discussion.   The tape recordings were scored with respect to the five dependent variables described above. Each of the experimenters scored 12 recordings collected by a different experimenter. To assess inter-experimenter reliability, all experimenters scored the recording of one randomly selected subject. There was perfect agreement among the five experimenters on the scoring of that subject's recording.

The five dependent measures were analyzed in a multivariate analysis of variance with average on the three previous exams ("A," "C," or "F") as the independent variable. There was a significant multivariate main effect of previous average, $F(10, 106) = 77.72, p < .001$. The means from this analysis are shown in Table 1.

Univariate analyses of variance were then conducted to assess differences between "A," "C," and "F" students on each of the dependent measures. Following each analysis, the performance differences between "A" and "C" students and between "C" and "F" students were assessed with a priori F-tests. A .001 significance level was adopted for each of the ten tests (two comparisons on each of five dependent variables) so that the experiment-wide probability of a Type I error was .01.

The scores of the three groups of students on the current exam significantly differed, $F(2, 57) = 87.83, p < .001$; "A" students ($M = 64.20$) scored significantly better than "C"

Table 1. Performance on the Current Exam as a Function of Average Score on the Three Previous Exams

| | Previous Exam Average | | | | | |
| | "A" | | "C" | | "F" | |
Current exam	M	SD	M	SD	M	SD
Performance Score	64.20	5.90	52.35	6.44	35.65	8.02
Answers read per question	3.66	.63	1.82	.51	1.48	.60
Number of anticipated answers	40.90	9.54	7.65	4.84	2.30	3.50
Critiques of incorrect answers per question	1.93	.25	.20	.19	.07	.12
Number of questions initially skipped	5.40	3.41	1.25	1.45	.40	.82

students ($M = 52.35$), who scored significantly better than "F" students ($M = 35.65$). Despite the unusual conditions under which subjects took the exam, each group's performance on this exam was very similar to that group's average performance on the three previous exams. In terms of individual students, there was a positive relationship between scores on the current exam and previous exam average ($r = .73$). This suggested that students were not unduly handicapped by the experimental procedure.

All students were required to read each question aloud, but the students significantly differed in the mean number of alternatives per question they read aloud, $F(2, 57) = 81.97, p < .001$. "A" students ($M = 3.66$) read significantly more alternatives than "C" ($M = 1.82$) or "F" ($M = 1.48$) students who did not significantly differ from each other. Consideration of all alternative answers would seem to be an important strategy for optimizing performance and only "A" students used this strategy with any consistency. Even when "A" students found the first or second alternative appealing, they tended to read the remaining answers. "C" and "F" students, on the other hand, tended to stop reading alternatives as soon as they found one that seemed suitable. In addition, these poorer students often started reading with the third or fourth alternative, a strategy rarely employed by "A" students. The best students almost always read the answers in the order in which they were presented.

The students significantly differed in the number of times they anticipated an answer to the question before reading the alternatives provided, $F(2, 57) = 207.18, p < .001$. "A" students ($M = 40.90$) anticipated an answer to significantly more questions than did "C" ($M = 7.65$) or "F" ($M = 2.30$) students. The difference between "C" and "F" students was not statistically significant, and it can be seen that both groups of poorer students rarely used the anticipation strategy on the 70-question exam. When "A" students used the anticipation strategy, they compared their anticipated answer with each of the alternatives provided, choosing the alternative that best matched their answer. This strategy provided "A" students with another means of evaluating the correctness of each alternative, a method which was presumably unavailable to poorer students.

Each question contained three incorrect alternatives, each of which was incorrect for one or more reasons. Students significantly differed in the frequency with which they eliminated incorrect alternatives by stating the reasons they were inappropriate answers to the question, $F(2, 57) = 575.03, p < .001$. Three critiques of incorrect alternatives could be stated per question; "A" students ($M = 1.93$) offered significantly more critiques than "C" ($M = .20$) or "F" ($M = .07$) students whose frequencies of critiquing alternatives did not significantly differ. The strategy of analyzing and dismissing incorrect alternatives provides a method for determining the correct answer by the process of elimination. The best students took advantage of this strategy whereas the poorer students did not.

Question skipping was the final strategy considered in the present study. Students significantly differed in the number of times they initially skipped a question, $F(2, 57) = 29.85, p < .001$, with "A" students ($M = 5.40$) skipping significantly more questions than "C" ($M = 1.25$) or "F" ($M = .40$) students. The latter two groups of students did not significantly differ. Most "A" students (18 of 20) initially skipped at least one question, but only 11 "C" students and 5 "F" students used this strategy. The effect of question skipping on total exam score was assessed by comparing the performance of those who did and did not skip questions. Within each group of students, the exam scores of those students who skipped questions did not significantly differ from the scores of students who did not skip questions. This result is in contrast to Rindler's (1980) finding that skipping questions on a verbal aptitude test benefited high ability students and reduced the performance of students with average or low ability.

The results of the present study indicated that "A" students used different test-taking strategies on an experimental multiple-choice exam than did "C" or "F" students. In general, the strategies of the best students were characterized by a more thorough consideration of the alternative answers for each question. There was also a concomittant increase in the number of verbalizations produced by these students. Because the relationship between level of performance in the course and test-taking behavior is correlational, one can only speculate about the cause of the observed strategy differences. Perhaps "A" students possessed superior reading skills which permitted them to read all the alternatives with relative ease. It is also possible that "A" students were better able to verbalize their thoughts than were "C" or "F" students and, consequently, that their strategies were more faithfully revealed. Nevertheless, the present results are suggestive of strategy differences between better and poorer students. Presumably similar strategy differences would occur on exams written by other instructors.

Since completing this investigation, I have described the results to introductory psychology students seeking to improve their performance on my multiple-choice exams. Some of these "C" and "F" students later commented that they used the strategies characteristic of "A" students, and they reported an improvement in their exam scores. Formal evaluation of the benefits of teaching poorer students to use these strategies is an interesting topic for future research.

References

Bath, J. A. Answer-changing behavior on objective examinations. *The Journal of Educational Research*, 1967, *61*, 105-107.

Best, J. B. Item difficulty and answer changing. *Teaching of Psychology*, 1979, *6*, 228-230.

Edwards, K. A., & Marshall, C. First impressions on tests: Some new findings. *Teaching of Psychology*, 1977, *4*, 193-195.

Johnston, J. J. Sticking with first responses on multiple choice exams: For better or for worse? *Teaching of Psychology*, 1975, *2*, 178-179.

Johnston, J. J. Exam-taking speed and grades. *Teaching of Psychology*, 1977, *4*, 148-149.

Johnston, J. J. Answer-changing behavior and grades. *Teaching of Psychology*, 1978, *5*, 44-45.

Mueller, D. J., & Wasser, V. Implications of changing answers on objective test items. *Journal of Educational Measurement*, 1977, *14*, 9-13.

Paul, C. A., & Rosenkoetter, J. S. The relationship between the time taken to complete an examination and the test score received. *Teaching of Psychology*, 1980, *7*, 108-109.

Rindler, S. E. The effects of skipping over more difficult items on time-limited tests: Implications for test validity. *Educational and Psychological Measurement*, 1980, *40*, 989-998.

Strategies in Answering Essay Tests

Gabriel Cirino-Gerena
University of Puerto Rico

In discussing the value of essay tests in education several strengths and weaknesses have been mentioned. The main limitations seem to be that the sample from the achievement domain being measured is very small and that the scoring of the tests is biased and unreliable. The principal strength seems to be that essay tests can tap higher mental processes such as creativity, critical thinking and evaluative skills. The usual recommendations of test experts is to use essay tests to supplement objective tests and only when higher mental processes are to be measured.

In spite of demonstrated weaknesses the essay test continues to be used as the preferred method of testing by many educators, especially those in the humanities. It has been suggested that essay tests are the only type of written test to be used in courses where there are no right or wrong answers and what counts is the ability of the student to come up with reasoned opinion based on data available to him or her. This goal presupposes a climate of mutual trust in which the student feels free to express opinions without worrying about being penalized for disagreeing with the professor. On the other hand, the subjectivity of the grading process of essay tests makes the possibility of being penalized, at least unconsciously, for disagreeing from his professor a real one.

Research on the social psychology of experiments provides evidence that subjects tend to fulfill the perceived expectations of the experiment (Rosenthal & Fode, 1963; Orne, 1962). The "demand characteristics" are present in a situation in which a person has power over another person (Orne, 1962). The classroom seems to be one of such situations. Are there demand characteristics in the classroom? I think there are. Some of my students have indicated that they tend to express opinions similar to their professors in the classroom while they disagree with them privately. When taking tests they write what the professor expects them to write. If this is a generalized practice then the main goal of essay tests is not being met.

Method. In order to obtain some information regarding the question, a study on the strategies used by students in answering essay tests was done. The sample consisted of students attending two General Psychology classrooms selected randomly from 18 of such classrooms. The cooperation of teacher and students was requested for the administration of a short questionnaire on strategies for taking essay tests. All 45 students agreed to respond. Two of the questionnaires were dropped from analysis because the students failed to respond to all but one or two questions.

The students answered the questionnaire anonymously but provided general data on sex, year of studies, number of essay tests taken in the last year and estimated grade point average.

Results. The frequency and percentages of students using each of the strategies is presented in Table 1. These results show that the most popular strategy in answering essay tests for this group of students was: "Express a similar opinion to that of the teacher." About four of every five students reported using this strategy and there was no sex difference. Other popular strategies have to do with the ability to write extensively and rephrase. The second, third and fourth most popular strategies were: Discuss extensively what I know and very little what I don't (77%); write extensively (67%); and rephrase arguments several times (63%). Only 28% of the students reported preparing an outline before answering,

Table 1. Incidence of Students of Each Sex Using Each Strategy While Taking Essay Tests

Rank	Strategy	Men		Women		Total	
		F	%	F	%	F	%
1.	Express a similar opinion to that of the teacher.	21	81	14	82	35	81
2.	Discuss extensively what I know and very little what I don't.	20	77	13	76	33	77
3.	Write extensively.	17	65	12	70	29	67
4.	Rephrase arguments several times.	16	62	11	65	27	63
5.	Budget my time for each question.	15	58	10	59	25	58
6.	Quote books and/or articles.	16	62	8	47	24	56
7.	Use big letters to fill up more space.	13	50	7	41	20	46
8.	Rephrase the question conveniently.	13	50	5	29	18	42
9.	Admit I do not know.	10	38	3	18	13	30
10.	Make up an answer.	11	42	2	12	13	30
11.	Prepare an outline before answering.	9	26	3	18	12	28
12.	Include irrelevant material in my answer.	10	38	6	11	11	26
13.	Copy from a friend, the book or the notebook.	7	27	0	0	7	16
14.	Write illegibly so the teacher will not understand.	0	0	1	6	1	2

30% admitted making up an answer and 16% admitted copying.

When students' answers were tabulated in terms of their reported academic record it was found that students reporting 3.0 or better GPA tend to use the following strategies more often: Quote books and/or articles; rephrase arguments several times; include irrelevant material in my answer; and rephrase the question conveniently. Students reporting academic GPA of less than 3.0 more often tend to admit that they do not know. This may indicate more use of bluffing among the most able students.

Men tend to use the following strategies more often than women: Rephrase the question conveniently; quote books and/or articles; include irrelevant material in my answer; admit I do not know; make up an answer; and copy from a friend, the book or the notebook. Thus men more often use strategies related to higher grade point average, but also are more inclined to admit they don't know, make up answers and copy from a friend.

Discussion. The results tend to show that expressing a similar opinion to that of the teacher is the most common strategy among students, and that it is done equally by men and women, good students and poorer students. The results cast doubt upon the generally accepted assumption that essay tests provide the opportunity for students to exercise creativity and critical thinking. It may point to the probability that there are demand characteristics in test-taking situations which result in students answering according to their perceptions of teachers expectations. Satisfaction of teachers with essay tests may be due, at least in part, to satisfaction of seeing their own ideas reflected in students papers. The study also provides evidence that copying and guessing are strategies used with essay tests.

Research is needed in this area to confirm these findings and to learn more about what specific behaviors of teachers provide the cues as to when to feel free to present own opinions in essay tests and when to express an opinion similar to that of the teacher.

Other popular strategies have to do with ability to write extensively, rephrase and discuss extensively what they know and very little what they do not know. Research is also needed in this area to determine how effective these strategies really are and how they affect the validity of the tests.

References

Orne, M. T. On the social psychology of the psychological experiment with particular reference to the demand characteristics and their implications. *American Psychologist*, 1962, *17*, 776-783.

Rosenthal, R., & Fode K. L. The effect of experimenter bias on the performance of the albino rat. *Behavioral Science*, 1963, *8*, 183-189.

d. Changing Answers on Multiple Choice Tests

Changing answers on multiple choice tests is the theme of the following group of articles. There have been at least 33 studies reported on this topic since 1928. Despite an extensive amount of research to the contrary, most students (from 68% to 100%) and the majority of faculty members (55%) thought that answer changes would lower test scores. The article by Ludy Benjamin (Texas A&M University), Timothy Cavel (Louisiana State University) and William Shallenberger (Texas A&M University) offers a thorough review and critique of the literature. The article can be helpful to student advisers by clarifying the sometimes conflicting findings. Additionally, the authors categorized relevant moderator variables, such as academic ability, gender, personality, item difficulty, and so forth. There are also instructive suggestions for future research.

James Johnston authored two articles on answer changing by using students from introductory and industrial psychology classes at the University of Wisconsin in Stevens Point. The results of both studies were consistent and demonstrated that students made more wrong to right changes than right to wrong and that answer changing was more helpful than harmful.

Nicholas Skinner surveyed students in an introductory psychology course at King's College. He asked them about their beliefs, including whether the first alternative chosen on an exam was probably correct. In addition, two observers independently examined answer sheets for a multiple choice exam. The observers determined the number and direction of changed answers. From the results, the author concluded that because of the belief that the first alternative chosen was probably correct most students were reluctant to change answers and thus did so only when they were highly confident in the change. The author concluded that such a rationale contributed to the higher rate of wrong to right than right to wrong changes. Furthermore, the author interpreted the findings as supporting the widespread belief against answer changing on multiple choice exams. Finally, the article reported that women changed their answers twice as often as men.

John Best from Indiana University investigated the incidence of answer changing behavior among students with high, medium, and low grade levels as a function of item difficulty and type of answer change, e.g., wrong to right. Results showed that students at different performance levels respond differently to the difficulty of the item when making a change. For example, students in the lower third ran a higher risk of making a right to wrong change, than a wrong to right change. Those and other findings indicate that advisers should give students more sophisticated advice than "don't change your first impression."

Anthony Edwards snd Carol Marshall found further evidence about the students' widespread beliefs about "staying with your first answer." Their research with students at Minot State College indicated that teachers were often the source of those false beliefs. For example, 43% of the students stated that their instructors advised them that their first impressions were most likely to be correct. Readers might ask themselves what their students' responses would be to a similar question.

Staying With Initial Answers on Objective Tests: Is it a Myth?

Ludy T. Benjamin, Jr., *Texas A&M University*
Timothy A. Cavell, *Louisiana State University*
and William R. Shallenberger, III, *Texas A&M University*

> The common advice to not change answers appears to be a mistake, but before that is certain, additional information is needed.

Since 1928, at least 33 studies have been published concerning a number of issues surrounding answer-changing behavior on objective tests. Although results in these studies have sometimes been at variance, the one consistent finding is that there is nothing inherently wrong with changing initial answers on objective tests. In fact, the evidence *uniformly* indicates that: (a) the majority of answer changes are from incorrect to correct and (b) most students who change their answers improve their test scores. None of the 33 studies contradicts either of those conclusions.

Most of the research in this area has been aimed at testing the accuracy of "first impressions" in test-taking. This bit of academic folk wisdom is typically stated as the belief that one should not change answers on objective tests because initial reactions to test questions are intuitively more accurate than subsequent responses.

Prevalence of the Belief and Potential Sources. That this belief is widespread among test-takers is supported by a number of studies. Surveys of students' attitudes toward the results of answer changing are fairly consistent in their outcomes revealing that most students (between 68% and 100%) do not expect changed answers to improve their score. Indeed, approximately three out of every four of these students felt answer changes would lower their score. The percentages of students reporting an expected improvement have ranged from 0% to 32% (Mathews, 1929; Foote & Belinky, 1972; Lynch & Smith, 1975; Mueller & Shwedel, 1975; Ballance, 1977; Smith, White & Coop, 1979).

Because a majority of test-takers believe that changing answers will not improve their scores, the obvious question to ask is where they acquired such a belief. One potential source would be manuals or articles on "how to take tests." Actually very few books on test-taking strategies have been identified as either perpetrators of the belief of "first impressions" or as proponents of answer changing. Interestingly, which side of the fence these strategists were on was often not clear. For example, Huff's (1961) position was both pro and con, depending on the article in which he was cited (Jacobs, 1972; Pascale, 1974; Davis, 1975; Lynch & Smith, 1975; Stoffer, Davis, & Brown, 1977). For the record, Huff's position is a qualified "yes" to answer changing, except in "a case that is very close to sheer guess" (p. 36). However, there have been some blatant examples cited of advice contrary to all the extant research. In defense of these strategies, though, it should be said that they rarely recommended complete abstinence from answer changing, rather they strongly qualified those occasions when it seemed beneficial. Millman, Bishop, and Ebel (1965) have written that a tendency to make judicious changes in one's answers is a characteristic of "test-wiseness." More recently, Mehrens and Lehmann (1978) have urged teachers to disabuse students of the misconception, but Crocker and Benson (1980) advise classroom teachers "specifically *not* to discourage response changing" (p. 239).

Because a half-dozen studies have shown the prevalance of the belief among college students, it is possible that it is reinforced by their instructors. No investigator to date has looked at faculty opinions. That oversight prompted our survey of faculty at Texas A&M University in the Colleges of Education, Liberal Arts, and Science using a brief questionnaire that inquired about belief in the outcome of answer changing on objective tests. Those faculty who indicated that they used objective tests were also asked about any instructions they gave to students about answer changing Like students, most faculty (55.2%) believe that changing the initial answer will lower scores. Only 15.5% of those responding said they thought answer changing would improve a student's score. Interestingly, the majority of the faculty in that group (77.7%) were members of the College of Education (see Table 1). Apparently they are more familiar with the many studies in this area, which is not surprising because much of this research has been published in the educational literature.

Do faculty members give instructions to their students about changing answers? Of those responding, about a third (32.7%) indicated that they did, and of that group, nearly two-thirds (63.1%) warned their students not to change their answer because the likely outcome would be a greater number of wrong answers. The remainder essentially cau-

Table 1. Faculty Responses to Question about the Outcome of Changing Initial Answers on Objective Tests

College	N	Improve the Test Score	Hurt the Test Score	No Change	Don't Know
Education	23	30.4%	52.2%	13.0%	4.3%
Liberal Arts	19	5.3%	52.6%	5.3%	36.8%
Science	16	6.2%	62.5%	12.5%	18.8%
All Faculty	58	15.5%	55.2%	10.3%	19.0%

tioned their students to be judicious in changing their answers as they reassessed their first responses. No instructor, even those who indicated their belief that answer changing would improve scores, advised students to change answers on that basis.

College faculty may contribute to the initiation and/or maintenance of the belief, but they are not the sole source as indicated by studies noting the prevalence of the belief in high-school students and even some non-student populations. Although no investigator has asked the question, it is likely that many test-takers acquire the admonition on answer changing from their peers.

The Attitude-Behavior Question. Given the discrepancy between existing data that belie the validity of the belief regarding changing initial answers and the evidence for its persistence, one may rightfully question the influence of a belief which does not seem to affect answer-changing behavior. At least four authors have dealt with this question, although each in a different manner. Mathews (1929) encouraged his students to make changes, for doing so was "more apt to raise than lower their final scores." The effect of this encouragement upon total changes and/or benefits from changing answers is indiscernible, however, due to an imposed penalty for guessing (which probably inhibited some answer-changing behavior) and the absence of a comparison group. After having first surveyed students' attitudes toward answer-changing results, Foote and Belinky (1972) provided feedback to the same individuals in the form of the percentages of items on two multiple-choice tests changed from wrong to right (W/R), right to wrong (R/W), and wrong to wrong (W/W). Despite the fact that for the two tests combined, the percentages (55% for W/R changes, 21% for R/W changes, and 23% for W/W changes) disagreed with students' expectations (only 32% expected to gain), answer-changing behavior on two subsequent tests was not noticeably altered, in terms of both the number of answers changed and results of those changes.

Likewise, Jacobs (1972) found no relationship between perceived outcomes from changing answers and net gains made. One study (Ballance, 1977) was designed expressly to look at the effect of students' expectations on their answer-changing behavior. Having grouped subjects according to their stated belief, Ballance concluded there was no "evidence to support the conjecture that beliefs asserted by a student have an effective relationship with the number of answer changes . . . [or] fluctuation in test score resulting from answer-changing" (p. 165).

Assuming that reported expectancies are a valid measure of actual expectancies, one might then argue that answer-changing behavior was poorly correlated with students' expectations. Implicit in this argument is the added question of the utility of debunking a "myth" which has no impact on test-taking behavior. However, in response it should be noted that on the average about 16% of all test-takers do not change any of their answers, and of those who do change answers, the average number of responses changed is around 3%. In addition, given the amount of selective perception that seems to exist among students with respect to their own answer-changing results, expectancies may still be exercising some inhibitory effects upon answer-changing behavior. Bath (1967) has pointed out that

students seldom remember those items that they changed and got correct. Would positive expectations concerning answer-changing results alter answer-changing behavior? In the one study which grouped students by their expectancies, Ballance (1977) found no differences among the groups in terms of their answer-changing behavior. However, considering the small number of subjects (N = 12), conclusions here must be rather tentative. Thus, it may be the case that changing one's belief about the consequences of one's behavior is a difficult task, but it does not necessarily follow that answer-changing behavior is independent of the beliefs surrounding the consequences of this behavior.

Returning to the notion of selective perception among students, one could view that as a much more plausible explanation for the maintenance of this widely reported belief of "first impressions" than that of misleading test-taking manuals or occasional misinformed teacher's instructions (Lynch & Smith, 1975; Stoffer, et al., 1977; Smith, et al., 1979). Moreover, there would have to be at least equally widespread ignorance of the data which refute this myth. In fact, this apparent ignorance has extended into the circle of those who could be expected to know better, that is, the researchers in this area. For example, Foote and Belinky (1972) in an article published after no less than ten other studies in this area, reported finding "no published research on this question" (p. 667).

Empirical Studies of Answer Changing. Given the persistence of this belief among faculty and students, it is hoped that the literature review provided here may serve to make faculty aware of the accumulated evidence on answer changing and cause them to evaluate their test-taking instructions. Such awareness may eventually alter student expectations on this question. However, the principal purpose of this review is to provide a groundwork for the future directions in research discussed at the close of this article. Although research on this topic has spanned more than 50 years, the collective knowledge gained from this research is disappointingly small. This state of affairs is due to problems of experimental design, narrowness of the questions researched, and duplication of previous studies, presumably due to ignorance of their existence. As an aid in this review, Table 2 provides a summary of test format, test content, types of subjects, and results obtained in 33 studies published between 1928 and 1983.

In this review we will analyze the research in terms of techniques for assessing answer changing, the extent of answer changing, the consequences of those changes, as well as the various subject and item variables that have been studied.

Measurement Strategies to Determine Answer Changes. Researchers have employed varied strategies in an attempt to measure accurately both the number and results of changed answers on objective tests. The vast majority, however, have simply relied upon their own ability to detect changes as indicated by observed erasures and crossouts. Several authors reported using this basic procedure (Mallinson & Miller, 1956; Bath, 1967; Johnston, 1975; Crocker & Benson, 1980). Some studies reported using interobserver agreement to check the degree of accuracy associated with

Table 2. Summary of Conditions and Results in Studies on Answer Changing

First Author (date)	Test Type[a]	Item[b] TF	Item[b] MC	Test Content	Type of Ss	Percent of changes Items	W-R	R-W	W-W	W-R/R-W[c]	Percent of[d] Changers	Gainers	Losers	Samers
Lehman (1928)		X		Educ.[e]	Col.[e]						78.0	51.0	36.0	13.0
Lowe (1929)	Ach	X		EdPsy.[e]	Col.[e]	2.9	66.4	33.5	N/A	1.98		48.8	16.0	
Mathews (1929)	AchT	X		EdPsy.	Col.	3.2	65.3	32.3	N/A	2.13				
Mathews (1929)	AchT		X	EdPsy.	Col.	2.6	52.4	21.1	26.5	2.49				
Lamson (1935)	AchT	X		Psy&Ed	Col.	2.2	65.6	34.4	N/A	1.91				
Hill (1937)	AchT	X		Educ.	Col.	2.5	58.9	41.1	N/A	1.43				
Berrien (1939)		X	X	Psy.	Col.						96.1	66.9	23.0	10.1
Jarrett (1948)		X		Psy.[e]	Col.[e]	2.8	71.3	28.7	N/A	2.49	89.7[f]			
Jarrett (1948)			X	Psy.[e]	Col.[e]	3.9	69.3	16.6	14.1	4.18	89.7[f]			
Reile (1952)	AchT		X	Psy.	Col.	6.2	48.9	23.0	28.1	2.13				
Mallinson (1956)	AchT		X	Sci, SS	Col.		48.0	26.7	25.1	1.80				
Archer (1962)	AchT		X	Educ.[e]	Grad.						86.2	68.1	24.6	7.2
Archer (1962)	AchT		X	Educ.[e]	Grad.						95.6	76.9	4.6	18.5
Clark (1962)	AchT		X	ChildDev	Col.		56.0	24.0	20.0	2.33	88.0	64.6	15.9	19.5
Bath (1967)	AchT		X	EdPsy.	Col.	4.3	59.8	20.1	20.1	2.97	93.5			
Copeland (1972)	AchT		X	Chem.	Col.	3.3	44.5	16.5	39.0	2.70	71.3			
Foote (1972)	AchT		X	Psy.	Col.	3.8	54.5	21.6	23.9	2.52				
Jacobs (1972)	AchT		X	Meth.	Grad.	32.7[g]	55.9	20.1	23.9	2.78				
Reiling (1972)	AchT		X	Econ.	Col.	9.0								
Pascale (1974)	AchT		X	Meas.	Col.	7.0								
Davis (1975)	AchT		X	Med.	Med.	5.5	58.0	21.0	21.0	2.76				
Davis (1975)	AchT		X	Med.	Med.	5.4	57.6	20.3	22.1	2.83				
Johnston (1975)	AchT		X	Psy.	Col.						74.5	69.6	30.3	2.9
Lynch (1975)	AchT	X	X	Educ.	Col.	2.5	56.5	26.9	16.7	2.10	83.0			
Mueller (1975)	AchT	X	X	Educ.	Grad.	3.7				5.30	80.0	66.5	17.0	18.0
Smith (1976)	AchT		X	GED	H.S.	4.0	46.5	19.2	34.0	2.43				
Ballance (1977)	AchT		X	Stat.	HlthCare						84.8	60.8	11.4	12.7
Edwards (1977)			X	Psy.	Col.	2.5	66.7	6.7	26.7	10.00				
Stoffer (1977)	AchT		X	Psy.	Col.	3.8	65.0	20.0	16.0	2.83	60.7	67.0	17.0	13.0
Stoffer (1977)	AchT		X	AcftRep	U.S.A.F.	3.1	64.5	17.0	18.5	3.79	60.3	72.0	14.0	14.0
Beck (1978)	AptT		X	Reading	3rd Grdrs	2.8	58.0	18.7	23.3	3.10				
Johnston (1978)			X	Psy.	Col.							75.5	10.0	
Best (1979)	AchT		X	Psy.	Col.	3.2	61.7	20.8	17.4	2.96		74.7	10.3	
Smith (1979)	AchT		X	EdPsy.	Col.	6.1	62.3	25.6	12.1	2.44	86.0			
Crocker (1980)	AchT		X	Math	7th Grdrs	4.0					57.0	47.0	2.4	
Sitton (1980)	AchT		X	Psy.	Col.		61.7	25.0	13.3	2.50				
Vidler (1980)	AptT		X	Crit.Thk.	Col.	3.8	61.5	38.5		1.60				
Range (1982)	AchT		X	Psy.	Col.	3.7	55.7	20.0	24.5	2.80				
Skinner (1983)	AchT		X	Psy.	Col.	4.0	51.5	26.3	22.3	2.00				

[a] Ach = Achievement; Apt = Aptitude; T = Timed
[b] TF = True-False items; MC = Multiple choice items
[c] Ratio of W-R changes to R-W changes
[d] Outcome of answer changing: "Gainers" are those with net increases; "Losers" are those with net losses; "Samers" are those answer changers whose net score does not change
[e] Not clearly specified in the study
[f] Figure combines data from true-false and multiple-choice tests
[g] Special testing instructions and procedures appear responsible for this value

the measurement of changes (Archer & Pippert, 1962; Foote & Belinky, 1972; Stoffer, et al., 1977; Beck, 1978; Smith, et al., 1979). Typically these studies reported high interobserver reliability (e.g., 99.5%), and several chose to include only those items for which there was 100% agreement among observers. Several studies (Foote & Belinky, 1972; Davis, 1975) sought to enhance accuracy of detection of changes by back-lighting answer sheets. In one study (Archer & Pippert, 1962) this approach also included checks by another independent judge. The high interobserver agreement provides support for a number of authors who have commented on the ease and unambiguousness of detecting answer changes (Hill, 1937; Jarrett, 1948; Archer & Pippert, 1962; Foote & Belinky, 1972).

In other studies some type of obtrusive measure was used to get at the "true" number and direction of answer changes. For some, students were given special instructions (e.g., "Do not erase," "Draw a line through your first judgment that I may know what it is.") As a result of these instructions, answer-changing behavior may have been inhibited. Thus Lehman (1928) reported a relatively low rate of changers (roughly six percentage points below the median reported figure of 84%), but Lamson (1935) reported the lowest rate of items changed (2.2%) among all studies. One study (Smith, et al., 1979) which required students to use a pen resulted in 6.1% of the items being changed, one of the highest percentages reported, excluding two highly deviant observations produced apparently by special answering formats. That this figure supports an argument that many erasures go undetected is plausible but certainly not evidence enough.

Special answer sheets were used in three studies. Typically these sheets included spaces for marking subsequent, as well as initial, answers. Edwards and Marshall (1977) also used tests with carbon backing (for detecting erasures) and imposed a penalty for answer changing. In their 1929 study, Lowe and Crawford required that students read over the entire test before marking any answers in the "second answer" space. Jacobs (1972) used a slide projector to present test items. Items were exposed for only 30 to 45 seconds, depending on their word count. After all slides had been viewed and attempted, mimeographed copies of the test were passed out with red pencils for making answer changes. Considering that the median reported percentages of all items which are changed is 3.3%, one would suspect each of these last two strategies to be a factor in their substantially larger percentages—10.2% and 32.7%, respectively.

In short, the use of obtrusive strategies for detecting answer changes cannot be justified in light of the evidence. Reports of high interobserver reliability in unobtrusive procedures, the possibility of altered change rates using obtrusive procedures, and the apparent ease of detecting answer changes all argue against the use of obtrusive measures.

Extent of Answer-Changing Behavior. Most people change at least one or more answers on exams. The data on percentage of changers are somewhat clouded by the fact that some studies have reported results per exam, but other studies averaged figures across exams. This problem notwithstanding, data from 15 studies indicate that the percentage of persons changing one or more answers ranged from 57% to 96% with an estimated median 84%. This *estimate* of the median of the combined studies is simply the median of the reported medians. For the combination of other research, the same procedure is used.

In terms of the proportion of items which were changed, the amount was consistently very small except, as indicated earlier, in those instances where an obtrusive experimental measurement strategy was employed. Excluding those two studies which reported such highly inflated percentages, the data from the 28 studies reporting this figure ranged from a low of 2.2% to a high of approximately 9.0%. The estimated median percentage of items changed was only 3.3%. These percentages are based on a large number of response observations ranging from a low of 1,800 to a high of 144,370 with the median number of responses being approximately 12,000. These percentages on the extent of answer-changing behavior are comparable to those reported in an earlier article by Mueller and Wasser (1977), even though the current review contains data from an additional eighteen studies. In short, the data on this question are very consistent in terms of the proportion of persons changing answers and the proportion of answers changed.

Consequences of Answer-Changing Behavior. That most individuals improved their scores and that most item response changes are from wrong to right (W/R) are two

observations found consistently throughout the literature on answer-changing behavior. For purposes of discussion of these data we will define "gainers" as individuals who improve their score through changes, "losers" as those whose score is lowered after making changes, and "samers" as those whose score is neither raised nor lowered as a consequence of changing answers. Data on the proportions of these outcome categories should only be compared with respect to the item formats used on exams. True-false items, unless ultimately left blank, involve only W/R and R/W changes, whereas multiple-choice items also allow for W/W changes. Moreover, the nature of the item formats may entail response tendencies which differ in their propensity to be changed in a particular direction (W/R, R/W, W/W). Thus, not only is it the case that one who changes an initially wrong answer on a true-false test marks a correct answer, and such is not necessarily true for multiple-choice tests, but it is also the case that multiple-choice and true-false items may involve recall tasks of different natures with correspondingly different results. This distinction is most critical when discussing answer change results by item responses since there is no W/W category for true-false item change results.

Two studies have reported response changes by individual subjects taking tests involving only true-false items, and one of those (Lowe & Crawford, 1929) listed only the percentage of students who made only W/R changes (49%) and only R/W changes (16%). Consequently, those individuals who made both changes (35% of all changes) but were also possible gainers, losers, or samers were not included in the data. In the other study, Lehman (1928) found 51% of all changers were gainers, 36% losers, and 13% samers. Two studies which used individuals as the unit of analysis involved tests with combined multiple-choice and true-false formats (Berrien, 1939; Mueller & Shwedel, 1975). The respective percentages from the two studies were as follows: 67% and 65% improved their score, 23% and 17% lost points, and 10% and 18% did neither.

A general discussion of the consequences of answer-changing behavior by students taking multiple-choice tests (see Table 3) is hindered by the fact that some studies, rather than report the proportion of *changers* who gained,

Table 3. Range and Estimated Median Values for Six Studies on Answer Changing Outcome in Multiple-Choice Tests

Measure	Students who Gained	Students who Lost	Students who Stayed the Same
Highest	76.9%	30.3%	18.5%
Lowest	47.0%	2.4%	2.9%
Estimated Median	67.5%	15.0%	14.0%

etc., chose to report the proportion of *total test-takers* who experienced the consequences of answer changes. Using this format, Johnston (1978) and Best (1979) reported virtually identical results with 75% of all subjects gaining, 10% losing, and 15% either staying the same or changing no answers.

The percentages of changers (based on six studies) who gained points on multiple-choice tests ranged from 47% to 77% with an estimated median of 67%. One can see that had Johnston (1978) and Best (1979) excluded those students who had made no changes, their figures would have been even higher, and thus some of the largest percentages reported. The percentages of losers ranged from 2.4% to 30% with an estimated median percentage of 15. The estimated median percentage of students who neither improved nor hurt their grade, but did change answers, was 14%, with a range of samers from 3% to 18%.

Recognizing the sparse data on true-false items, there nevertheless seems to be an increase in the proportion of individuals who gain changing item responses as the test formats change from true-false to multiple-choice. This fact is illustrated by the median ratios of numbers of gainers to losers for true-false (1.43 to 1), combination (3.9 to 1), and multiple-choice formats (5.3 to 1). Regardless of test format, all studies concluded that the majority of students improve their score by changing initial answers.

Answer changing results as reported by item responses are typically stated in terms of the percentages of total changes which were W/R, R/W, and W/W changes (see Table 4A). For true-false tests, W/R changes ranged from 59% to 71% with an estimated median of 66% from the five

Table 4. Range and Estimated Medians of Answer Changes by (A) Outcome and (B) Ratio of Gainers to Losers

Category	Highest	Lowest	Estimated Median
A. By Percent of Outcome of Change			
Multiple-Choice Studies (N = 20)			
Wrong to Right	69.3	44.5	57.8
Right to Wrong	26.7	6.7	20.2
Wrong to Wrong	39.0	12.1	22.8
True-False Studies (N = 5)			
Wrong to Right	71.3	58.9	65.6
Right to Wrong	41.1	28.7	33.5
B. By Ratio of Gainers to Losers			
Multiple-Choice Studies (N = 20)	10.00 to 1	1.80 to 1	2.77 to 1
True-False Studies (N = 5)	2.49 to 1	1.43 to 1	1.98 to 1

studies reporting. The one study (Lynch & Smith, 1975) that used both types of items in one format and which looked at these proportions found 57% of all item responses changes were in the W/R category. Twenty studies used tests having only multiple-choice items. Percentages ranged from 44% to 69% with an estimated median of 58% for W/R changes. For R/W changes, the true-false item studies had percentages ranging from 29% to 41% with an estimated median of 33%, for the one combined format, 27% of the changes were R/W, whereas multiple-choice formats produced R/W change percentages ranging from 7% to 26% with an estimated median of 20%. Of course, no data exist for W/W changes on true-false tests, but the one combination format produced 17% W/W changes. For multiple-choice item W/W changes, percentages ranged from 12% to 39% with an estimated median of 23%.

Figures on the ratios of W/R to R/W changes offer a good summary of item response change results from the different test formats. Studies using true-false items had ratios ranging from 1.43 to 1 to 2.49 to 1 with an estimated median of 1.98 to 1. Mueller and Shwedel (1975) used a combination format but did not report on the breakdown of percentages

for each change category. However, they did find a ratio of W/R to R/W changes of 5.3 to 1 compared to a ratio of 2.1 to 1 in a similar study reported by Lynch and Smith (1975). Combining the data from these two studies produces an estimated median ratio of 3.7 to 1. Multiple-choice item response changes produced W/R:R/W ratios (see Table 4B) ranging from 1.80 to 1 to 10 to 1 (the next highest being 4.18 to 1) with an estimated median of 2.77 to 1. Ignoring the figures from the combination formats (based on only two studies using unstated proportions of true-false to multiple-choice items), and focusing on the median ratios of true-false and multiple-choice item response change results, allows the following conclusions: Approximately every three changes on the true-false tests examined resulted in two correct and one incorrect answers whereas every four changes on multiple-choice tests have produced three correct and one incorrect answers. This second ratio does not include W/W answer changes because those changes do not hurt the students' performance.

Subject Variables. Many studies have attempted to differentiate between changers and non-changers and among gainers, losers, and samers based on some external criterion. Typical variables investigated have been academic ability, sex, and several personality variables.

Academic Ability. The variable most often used to indicate a student's ability has been the student's test scores: sometimes scores for the entire course and sometimes scores for the particular exam under study. Of course, there exists a confounding of any relationships proposed to exist between test scores and numbers and types (W/R, R/W) of revisions made due to the fact that the former is partly a product of the latter. Lehman (1928) was the first to note this relationship and others have followed suit (e.g., Mueller & Shwedel, 1975; Best, 1979) attempting either to circumvent or minimize the importance of this problem. Lehman reexamined tests using initial answers only and found only "two or three" students whose position changed with respect to the median. Mueller and Shwedel chose to look at the relationship between test scores and W/W changes in order to assess independently which students made the greatest gains in answer changing. They reported a significant negative correlation (−.22) between total scores and W/W changes. Thus higher-scoring students made fewer W/W changes. Best emphasized the unimportance of such confounding after observing the small proportion of items changed per test compared to the number of points necessary to alter one's grade. Best's observations, while they may be valid in the context of his study, are not necessarily generalizable to all studies of this sort.

The problems of using test scores as a subject/classification variable notwithstanding, several investigators have looked at the possible relationship between a student's test score and his or her answer-changing behavior. If one were to view extensive answer changing as a sign of test-taking uncertainty, then it is not surprising to find that most authors report an inverse relationship between test scores and the numbers of revisions made by students: Six studies reported a statistically significant negative relationship (Lynch & Smith, 1975; Mueller & Shwedel, 1975; Stoffer et al., 1977; Johnston, 1978; Best, 1979; Sitton, Adams & Anderson,

1980) but five others reported nonsignificant results in the same direction (Reile & Briggs, 1952; Reiling & Taylor, 1972; Pascale, 1974; Smith & Moore, 1976; Crocker & Benson, 1980). Only in one study is there a positive relationship (Beck, 1978) and it was nonsignificant, and two other studies showed no trend in either direction (Bath, 1967; Copeland, 1972). Although it is true that most subjects benefit from answer changing regardless of test score, and that most item response changes are from wrong to right, it is obvious that one cannot assume a positive linear relationship between test scores and the number of answer changes.

The statement that increased answer changing will improve one's score is tempered, not only by the data on test scores, but also by the conflicting data on net gains enjoyed versus the numbers of revisions made: Six studies have shown that profit from answer changing increased significantly with the number of revisions (Reiling & Taylor, 1972; Pascale, 1974; Mueller & Shwedel, 1975; Stoffer et al., 1977; Sitton et al., 1980; Range, Anderson & Wesley, 1982), three others found negative but nonsignificant trends (Lehman, 1928; Mathews, 1929; Archer & Pippert, 1962), and one study showed no relationship in either direction (Berrien, 1939). Obviously a point must be reached where answer changes are no longer beneficial to the test-taking student. Assuming revisions are not made randomly, an individual changing an exorbitant number of answers soon leaves behind the rationale for answer-changing behavior that produces the gains typically reported.

Given that approximately 70% of all subjects gain from changing answers, can it be assumed that those who enjoy greater profits actually have better test scores? The answer is basically "yes," for eleven studies a positive relationship was found between test score and net profit (Lehman, 1928; Reile & Briggs, 1952; Mallinson & Miller, 1956; Archer & Pippert, 1962; Copeland, 1972; Reiling & Taylor, 1972; Lynch & Smith, 1975; Mueller & Shwedel, 1975; Smith & Moore, 1976; Stoffer et al., 1977; Beck, 1978), with six of those showing significant results.

Other subject variables pertaining to achievement or ability have provided few clues in determining why some people change answers and, of those who change, why some profit and others do not. Achievement variables include course grade and grade point average (G.P.A.), whereas scores on Borgatta and Corsini's (1964) Quick Word Test (QWT), the Scholastic Aptitude Test (SAT), and the Airman Qualifying Exam (AQE) have been used as ability variables. Individuals who were rated low on these variables typically were found to change more answers (Mathews, 1929; Reiling & Taylor, 1972; Pascale, 1974; Stoffer, et al., 1977), however, in only the last of those studies was there found a significant relationship between ability (as measured by the SAT) and frequency of answer changing. In none of these studies was there any relationship between any of the achievement/ability variables and the degree of profit from answer changing.

Sex. Sex has also been investigated as a subject variable in predicting answer changing frequency and/or gains in a number of studies (Reile & Briggs, 1952; Mallinson & Miller, 1956; Bath, 1967; Copeland, 1972; Reiling & Taylor, 1972; Pascale, 1974; Mueller & Shwedel, 1975; Stoffer, et al., 1977; Beck, 1978; Sitton, et al., 1980; Skinner, 1983). Three

of these studies showed a slightly higher frequency of answer changing by females and one study (Skinner, 1983) reported the only statistically significant sex difference, finding that females changed twice as many answers as males. With regard to gains made from answer changing, Reile and Briggs (1952) reported that females profited less, but Bath (1967) found that females made larger gains than males. Both studies have problems. Reile and Briggs suggested that their findings might be confounded by some pre-existing performance differences which restricted the potential for gains by females, but an analysis of Bath's data on sex differences simply does not support his conclusion. In short, if sex differences do exist, they seem to be in the frequency of answer changing and not in the gains made from those changes.

Personality. Several writers have suggested that personality variables may contribute to the separation between changers and nonchangers and between gainers and losers. To date, only three investigators have reported research in this area. In an *a posteriori* analysis of subjects' scores on Rotter's I-E scale, Stoffer, et al. (1977) found no relationship between the I-E measure and the number of revisions a student made. Sitton, et al. (1980) and Range, et al. (1982) have correlated a host of personality variables with frequencies and outcomes of answer changing. They report that anxious students change more answers than non-anxious ones, and that nondepressed students are more successful in their answer changes. One variable that may be related to answer changing is impulsivity (Mueller & Shwedel, 1975), however it has not been investigated to date.

Item Variables. Researchers have only occasionally looked at the characteristics of test items in their efforts to detect some distinguishable pattern of answer-changing behavior. Item difficulty and item position are the variables that have received the most attention.

Item difficulty has been defined in varying ways by researchers. Most often, *p*-values (i.e. the proportion of students who answered an item correctly) were used, either derived from the sample data or from previously studied samples. Jacobs (1972) and Beck (1978) used previously obtained *p*-values to establish item groups based on level of difficulty. Lynch and Smith (1975) and Jackson (1978) apparently based their correlational analysis of item difficulty on *p*-values, also. Best (1979) formed his easy-difficult item grouping based on whether items fell above or below the median percentage correct for all test items. Berrien (1939) and Pascale (1974) chose to rate whole tests as either "difficult" or "easy," the former doing so intuitively and the latter doing so empirically based on the mean *p*-values of the two tests employed. As with test scores, measures of item difficulty derived from the sample data may be open to confounding if linked to measures such as net profit due to answer changing. Still it seems unlikely that item difficulty values would be substantially affected by response changes (Best, 1979).

Generally it can be said that difficult items are more likely to be changed than easier ones. Most of the studies indicate trends in that direction, however, only four (Lynch & Smith, 1975; Beck, 1978; Jackson, 1978; Vidler & Hansen, 1980) have reported results that reached statistical significance.

Of course for poorer students, that is, those who are ill-prepared for the test, many more items will be seen as difficult (Lynch & Smith, 1975). That observation can be used to explain the fact that those students typically change more of their answers.

Data on the relationship between item difficulty and profit are conflicting, and the reason for these conflicts are not at all apparent. Jacobs (1972) found most net gains involved changes of items which were either moderately or highly difficult. Similarly, Pascale (1974) found a significant positive correlation between a test's difficulty and the number of additional correct answers due to revisions. Beck (1978), however, reported that changes on easy items were significantly more likely to be correct than changes on hard items. Controlling for test performance, Best's (1979) data provide further evidence on the opposing side based on a comparison of W/R:R/W ratios for difficult (2.47) versus easy items (4.28).

It seems reasonable to conclude that item position might be an important variable. Most tests have a time limit, so review of the answers may not proceed beyond the earlier test items. In addition, seeing items later in the test may provide a context in which answers for earlier items might be reviewed and changed. Thus, on an intuitive basis, one could argue that items at the beginning of a test would be changed more frequently than items at the end. Only two studies have examined the effect of item position on answer-changing behavior and both found that fewer changes were made near the end of the test (Reile & Briggs, 1952: Jackson, 1978). Jackson also examined alternatives within an item subgroup using partial correlation. Results showed item position within a test subgroup of "some specific stimulus material" produced significant zero-order correlations with the number of answers changed. The trend was for earlier items to have more changes, an effect described by Jackson as due to novelty. No one has looked at the relationship between item position and net gains from changing.

In addition to level of difficulty and position, two other item variables have been researched. Reiling and Taylor (1972) attempted to relate items which involved "analytical reasoning" to answer-changing behavior but found no relationship to exist with either the amount of answer changing or the net gain enjoyed. Jackson (1978) did find some evidence (significant results for one of the three samples he tested) that items of low discriminating power tend to be changed more than answers to other items.

Although the research on the influence of item variables on answer-changing behavior is fairly sparse, Jackson's view that changed items are often misinterpreted items is given some credence by the results. Item difficulty, novelty, position, and discriminability would all seem to affect, to varying degrees, the propensity of an item being changed.

Conclusions and Future Directions. After more than a half-century of research on this topic, what do we know about answer changing? Based on the 33 studies reviewed in this article we know that: (a) only a small percentage of items are actually changed, (b) most of these changes are from wrong to right answers, (c) most test-takers are answer changers, and (d) most answer changers are point gainers. These findings would appear to refute the widespread belief about

the consequences of answer changing as well as questioning what effect, if any, that belief may have on actual behavior.

Having established that most test-takers change answers on objective tests in spite of their purported beliefs, what are their reasons for making those changes? Amazingly, no researcher to date has attempted seriously to answer that question. Obviously there are different reasons for changing an answer, for example, marking the wrong space on the answer sheet or simply misinterpreting the item (e.g., not seeing the negative in the stem of the item). In these cases it is most unlikely that the test-taker will believe the assertion about the correctness of initial answers, and thus will readily make those changes. Another reason for changing an answer is that the test-taker is unsure of the answer; indeed, it may have been a guess. In this situation, answer changing may be pursued with greater reluctance. In fact, it is possible that in this latter case, the myth may be no myth at all.

In short, the research to date has treated all answer changes as though they were the same. That procedure does not permit a real answer to the questions, indeed, it ignores the crucial question on this topic. Future research on answer changing must begin with a way to segregate answer changes with respect to the reasons for those changes and should focus on those answer change situations in which the answer is altered due to some cognitive evaluation. Indeed, studies of the decisional process itself could shed more light on answer changing. In the research to date we are limited to studying the items that were actually changed, and are unable to know how many other items were considered but left unchanged. Both of these issues, that is, the reasons for change and the consideration of items that were not changed, could be studied by an inquiry procedure immediately following the test. Such a procedure would be awkward under most testing conditions, which is to say that researchers may need to construct their own testing situations specific to the problem, rather than relying exclusively on extant samples and tests that are part of college courses.

A related variable to be considered in this research is the confidence the student has in a particular answer. What confidence level has to exist before a student would be willing to change an answer? Only Skinner (1983) has looked at that question. He reported that students felt a different answer should have a high probability (74.6%) of being correct before a change was made. Further, how is confidence level as a variable affecting answer changing related to the student's level of belief in the caveat about answer changing? These questions are the most basic in this area, yet they have been largely ignored in the extant research.

Almost all of the studies to date have used regular course exams to evaluate answer changing. These are achievement tests which are typically administered under a time limit, although they are not speed tests in the strictest interpretation of that label. Students may have time to answer all of the questions, but it is unlikely that they have the opportunity to review their answers thoroughly, thus adding to the potential for answer change. Although it was impossible to discern in all cases, we could not identify a single study in the 33 reviewed here which used a testing procedure that allowed test-takers as much time as they wanted to complete the test. Time constraints are always a critical variable in test taking, and in research assessing answer changing one ought to be concerned that students have the opportunity to change answers. It seems quite plausible to assume that rates and, perhaps, consequences of answer changing could be affected by timed versus power testing conditions.

Other test variables are also potentially important issues in this research. Do test-takers perform differently in terms of answer changing on aptitude versus achievement tests? To date only two studies (Beck, 1978; Vidler & Hansen, 1980) have used an aptitude test. Similarly, these studies have used tests that are largely norm-referenced and few that are domain-referenced. Answer changing may or may not differ between those types of tests. It is impossible to answer that question based on the research to date, but we believe it is a question worth pursuing. Researchers in this area need to state the purpose of the tests they are using. Although testing purpose is often implied, a more definitive statement would add to the understanding of this literature. Further, penalties for guessing should be studied as they affect the frequency of answer changing and the outcome of those changes.

Another area for future research concerns the apparent discrepancy between what students say about answer changing and what they actually do, an issue which we referred to earlier as the "attitude-behavior question." So much evidence in psychology has indicated a strong correspondence between belief and action that it calls for investigation of this discrepancy. Yet such an analysis cannot be answered unless we know why students change answers, and under what conditions. That information is mandatory if we are to understand the way in which the belief operates.

Further, we would encourage additional research focusing on the interrelationships of item variables (such as difficulty and nature of item distractors) and cognitive strategies of test takers. Research to date has emphasized academic ability, using mostly confounded measures, while ignoring some better measure of both cognitive ability and style. Among the subject variables, we believe that cognitive variables are likely to be far more meaningful than others studied thus far, such as sex or certain personality traits.

In conclusion, this review has noted a remarkable consistency of results across 33 separate investigations. That kind of consistency is rare in psychology and the authors are duly impressed with the harmony of those data. That consistency of results has caused a number of researchers in this area to argue that the statement about the accuracy of first impressions is a myth. That conclusion may be accurate, but we do not believe that it is justified on the evidence provided to date. Until researchers are able to segregate answer changing responses, thus separating those that are the result of "second impressions" from other kinds of changes, the conclusions of this research must be considered tentative.

The question of whether answers should be changed or not is an important one, not only for test-taking strategies, but for an understanding of the psychological processes involved in that behavior. Our hope is that future research will seek to systematically answer the questions raised in this review.

References

Archer, N. S., & Pippert, R. Don't change the answer! An expose of the perennial myth that the first choices are always the correct ones. *Clearing House,* 1962, *37,* 39-41.

Ballance, C. T. Students' expectations and their answer-changing behavior. *Psychological Reports,* 1977, *41,* 163-166.

Bath, J. A. Answer-changing behavior on objective examinations. *Journal of Educational Research,* 1967, *61,* 105-107.

Beck, M.D. The effect of item response changes on scores on an elementary reading achievement test. *Journal of Educational Research,* 1978, *71,* 153-156.

Berrien, F. K. Are first impressions best on objective tests? *School and Society,* 1939, *50,* 319-320.

Best, J. B. Item difficulty and answer changing. *Teaching of Psychology,* 1979, *6,* 228-230.

Borgatta, E. F., & Corsini, R. J. *Quick word test.* New York: Harcourt, Brace & World, 1964.

Clark, C. A. Should students change answers on objective tests? *Chicago Schools Journal,* 1962, *43,* 382-385.

Copeland, D. A. Should chemistry students change answers on multiple-choice tests? *Journal of Chemistry Education,* 1972, *49,* 258.

Crocker, L., & Benson J. Does answer-changing affect test quality? *Measurement and Evaluation in Guidance,* 1980, *12,* 233-239.

Davis, R. E. Changing examination answers: An educational myth? *Journal of Medical Education,* 1975, *50,* 685-687.

Edwards, K. A., & Marshall, C. First impressions on tests: Some new findings. *Teaching of Psychology,* 1977, *4,* 193-195.

Foote, R., & Belinky, C. It pays to switch? Consequences of changing answers on multiple-choice examinations. *Psychological Reports,* 1972, *31,* 667-673.

Hill, G. E. The effect of changed responses in true-false tests. *Journal of Educational Psychology,* 1937, *28,* 308-310.

Huff, D. *Score—the strategy of taking tests.* New York: Ballantine Books, 1961.

Jackson, P. F. Answer changing on objective tests. *Journal of Educational Research,* 1978, *71,* 313-315.

Jacobs, S. S. Answer changing on objective tests: Some implications for test validity. *Educational and Psychological Measurement,* 1972, *32,* 1039-1044.

Jarrett, R. F. The extra-change nature of changes in students' responses to objective test-items. *Journal of General Psychology,* 1948, *38,* 243-250.

Johnston, J. J. Sticking with first responses on multiple-choice exams: For better or worse? *Teaching of Psychology,* 1975, *2,* 178-179.

Johnston, J. J. Answer-changing behavior and grades. *Teaching of Psychology,* 1978, *5,* 44-45.

Lamson, E. E. What happens when the second judgment is recorded in a true-false test? *Journal of Educational Psychology,* 1935, *26,* 223-227.

Lehman, H. C. Does it pay to change initial decisions in a true-false test? *School and Society,* 1928, *28,* 456-458.

Lowe, M. L., & Crawford, C. C. First impression versus second thought in true-false tests. *Journal of Educational Psychology,* 1929, *20,* 192-195.

Lynch, D. O., & Smith, B. C. Item response changes: Effects on test scores. *Measurement and Evaluation in Guidance,* 1975, *7,* 220-224.

Mallinson, G. G., & Miller, D. J. The effect of second guessing on achievement scores of college tests. In *Yearbook of the National Council on Measurement in Education,* Volume 13, 1956, pp. 24-26.

Mathews, C. O. Erroneous first impressions on objective tests. *Journal of Educational Psychology,* 1929, *20,* 280-286.

Mehrens, W. A., & Lehmann, I. J. *Measurement and evaluation in education and psychology.* New York: Holt, Rinehart and Winston, 1978.

Millman, J., Bishop, C. H., & Ebel, R. An analysis of test-wiseness. *Educational and Psychological Measurement,* 1965, *25,* 706-726.

Mueller, D. J., & Shwedel, A. Some correlates of net gain resultant from answer changing on objective achievement test items. *Journal of Educational Measurement,* 1975, *12,* 251-254.

Mueller, D. J., & Wasser, V. Implications of changing answers on objective test items. *Journal of Educational Measurement*, 1977, *14*, 9-13.

Pascale, P. J. Changing initial answers on multiple-choice achievement tests. *Measurement and Evaluation in Guidance*, 1974, *6*, 236-238.

Range, L. M., Anderson, H. N., & Wesley, A. L. Personality correlates of multiple choice answer changing patterns. *Psychological Reports*, 1982, *51*, 523-527.

Reille, P. J., & Briggs, L. J. Should students change their initial answers on objective-type tests?: More evidence regarding an old problem. *Journal of Educational Psychology*, 1952, *43*, 110-115.

Reiling, E., & Taylor, R. A new approach to the problem of changing initial responses to multiple choice questions. *Journal of Educational Measurement*, 1972, *9*, 67-70.

Sitton, L. R., Adams, I. G., & Anderson, H. N. Personality correlates

of students' patterns of changing answers on multiple-choice tests. *Psychological Reports*, 1980, *47*, 655-660.

Skinner, N. F. Switching answers on multiple-choice questions: Shrewdness or shibboleth? *Teaching of Psychology*, 1983, *10*, 220-222.

Smith, A., & Moore, J. C. The effects of changing answers on scores of non-test-sophisticated examinees. *Measurement and Evaluation in Guidance*, 1976, *8*, 252-254.

Smith, M., White, K. P., & Coop, R. H. The effect of item type on the consequences of changing answers on multiple-choice tests. *Journal of Educational Measurement*, 1979, *16*, 203-208.

Stoffer, G. R., Davis, K. E., & Brown, J. B. The consequences of changing initial answers on objective tests: A stable effect and a stable misconception. *Journal of Educational Research*, 1977, *70*, 272-277.

Vidler, D., & Hansen, R. Answer changing on multiple-choice tests. *Journal of Experimental Education*, 1980, *49*, 18-20.

Sticking with First Responses on Multiple-Choice Exams: For Better or For Worse?

James J. Johnston
University of Wisconsin

There is a bit of folk wisdom often heard in student circles which goes something like "don't change your answers on a multiple choice test—your first impulse is usually right." This piece of advice was tested by recording observable changes from a right answer to a wrong one, and vice-versa, in two sections of introductory psychology (31 and 35 students) and three sections of industrial psychology (20, 30, and 21 students), taught by the author over a two semester period. Each of these students took several multiple choice quizzes comprising a total of about 150 questions. Since individual changes are not independent (i.e., a particular student may have a strong tendency to make wrong-to-right or right-to-wrong changes), the appropriate unit for comparison was the student. Ignoring students who made some, but equal numbers of wrong-to-right and right-to-wrong answers (3 students), and those who made no changes of either kind (32 students) left an N of 102. Of these students, 71 showed more wrong-to-right changes, and 31 showed more right-to-wrong

changes. Comparison with an even (51 to 51) split, gives a chi-square of 15.686; with 1 degree of freedom, p< .005. This suggests that better advice than that given above might be, "if in doubt, go ahead and reconsider."

One methodological point should be mentioned. It was not possible to detect the existence of all changes. The quizzes were hand, rather than computer, scored, so students who used ink or felt pens simply crossed out answers and marked other alternatives to change answers. Many of those who used pencils did this too, or made an erasure which was easily detectable. It is possible, though, that some students who used pencils erased so thoroughly that no change was detectable. There is, however, no reason for any such changes which might have occurred to show a systematic difference from the result for detectable changes. To require the use of a pen could affect the results by making some subjects aware that changes could be observed, or at least that something was unusual.

Answer-Changing Behavior and Grades

James J. Johnston
University of Wisconsin

Both Bath (1967) and Johnston (1975) have found that changing answers on multiple choice examinations is more likely to be helpful than harmful. Bath (1967) also investigated the relationship between answer-changing and grades; however, he used no tests for statistical significance and the unit used for analysis was the individual response-change. I feel that a more appropriate unit would be the

student, since response-changes are not independent (i.e., a single student might account for a relatively large number of changes of a particular kind—either wrong-to-right or right-to-wrong).

The present study was therefore conducted to investigate whether there were any statistically significant differences in answer-changing patterns among students at different performance levels, using the individual student as the unit of analysis.

Procedure. The subjects were 94 students enrolled in an Introductory Psychology class taught by the author. Each student took five multiple-choice quizzes comprising a total of 148 questions. For each student, the number of right-to-wrong, wrong-to-right, and wrong-to-wrong changes (as indicated by erasure or crossing out) was recorded. Chi-square was used to test for the following: (a) Whether students tended to help, rather than hurt, themselves by changing answers, as previously found by Bath (1967) and by Johnston (1975), (b) whether students at different performance levels tend to show different amounts of answer-changing, and if so, whether the patterns are also different for (c) wrong-to-right and (d) right-to-wrong answer-changing specifically.

For (b), (c), and (d), the students were categorized as nearly as possible into high, middle, and low thirds on both performance (percentage of correct answers on the 148 questions) and on number of (the appropriate kind of) answers changed.

Results. Of the 94 Ss, 71 were "helped" (more wrong-to-right than right-to-wrong changes) and 9 were "hurt" (more right-to-wrong than wrong-to-right changes) by answer-changing. Comparing this to an even split (40 helped—40 hurt) gives a chi-square of 48.04 ($p<.001$) thus supporting the earlier conclusion of Bath (1967) and of Johnston (1975) that answer-changing is more often helpful than harmful.

A test of the hypothesis of independence between grades and overall answer-changing (3X3 table) gives a chi-square of 30.7 ($p<.001$), leading to rejection of the hypothesis. The tendency is for those who get low grades to do the most answer-changing and for those who get high grades to do the least answer-changing.

When wrong-to-right changes and grades are tested for independence, independence is rejected (chi-square = 12.7, $p<.02$) with a tendency for grades and changes to be inversely related. When right-to-wrong changes and grades are tested for independence, independence is rejected (chi-square = 20.9, $p<.001$) again with a tendency for grades and changes to be inversely related.

Conclusions. More students raise their grade than lower it by changing answers. Students who get low grades are likely to be high in answer-changing, and those who get high grades are likely to make relatively few changes, whether total, wrong-to-right, or right-to-wrong answers are consid-total, wrong-to-right, or right-to-wrong answers are considered. This tendency is stronger for right-to-wrong than for wrong-to-right answers. (It would be surprising if this were not so, since the grades were affected by the kinds of changes made.)

Bath (1967) found that the best students had the greatest, and average students the least, tendency to change responses. The discrepancy between his results and the present findings should be tested further. It may be caused by the fact that he used the response-change, rather than the subject, as the unit of analysis; there may have been a few Ss in his high-grade category who made a large number of changes, thus making a large contribution to the total for that category.

References

Bath, J. A. Answer-changing behavior on objective examinations. *Journal of Educational Research*, 1967, *61*, 105-107.
Johnston, J. J. Sticking with first responses on multiple-choice exams: For better or for worse? *Teaching of Psychology*, 1975, *2*, 178-179.

Switching Answers on Multiple-Choice Questions: Shrewdness or Shibboleth?

Nicholas F. Skinner
King's College

Results of this study suggest that answers should not be changed unless probability of better performance is high.

The widespread assumption that one's first-chosen response to an objective-test question is usually correct and should not be changed (e.g., Bath, 1967; Johnston, 1975; Reiling & Taylor, 1972; Sitton, Adams & Anderson, 1980; Stoffer, Davis & Brown, 1977) has been called into question frequently during the past half-century by repeated demonstrations that more than half of all such changes are successful (e.g., Bath, 1967; Best, 1979; Johnston, 1975; Johnston, 1978; Lehman, 1928; Pascale, 1974; Reile & Briggs, 1952). This unanimity notwithstanding, two contradictions contaminate the literature.

First, although students switch answers despite their *own* beliefs that such a strategy is unproductive (Ballance, 1977),

paradoxically, they do not heed the *instructor's* suggestion that answer-changing will produce better grades (Foote & Belinky, 1972). Second, although females consistently alter more responses than do males, it is not clear whether their success rate is generally higher (Bath, 1967; Sitton *et al.*, 1980) or lower (Pascale, 1974; Reile & Briggs, 1952; Reiling & Taylor, 1972; Stoffer *et al.*, 1977). The investigation reported here was thus intended to (a) explain students' apparent disregard for advice that switching answers is beneficial, and (b) examine more closely sex differences in answer-changing.

Method. Forty-six females and twenty-two males from an introductory psychology course served as subjects; all but four were first-year students. Prior evaluation indicated no significant differences between females and males on measures of IQ and GPA.

During the first week of classes, subjects completed a 24-item "Student Information Survey" which included the following questions: (a) Have you heard of the advice that you shouldn't change your first-chosen answer on a multiple-choice question because it is usually correct?; and (b) What probability do you think a different alternative should have of being correct before you will change an answer? Next, at approximately the mid-point of the course, subjects completed a 70 min., four alternative, 100 question multiple-choice examination by indicating each chosen alternative in pencil directly on the test paper.

By scrutinizing the erasures and cross-outs made by each subject, two observers independently recorded the number and direction of all changed answers, i.e., Positive (wrong to right), Negative (right to wrong) and Neutral (wrong to wrong). Inter-inspector agreement was 98.8%.

Results and Discussion. In evaluating the results summarized in Table 1, it should be remembered that in previous

Table 1. Number and Patterns of Changed Multiple-Choice Answers by Sex

Change	Males ($n = 22$)		Females ($n = 46$)		Total ($n = 68$)	
	No.	%	No.	%	No.	%
Positive (W–R)	28	53.8	113	50.9	141	51.5
Negative (R–W)	13	25.0	59	26.6	72	26.3
Neutral (W–W)	11	21.2	50	22.5	61	22.3

investigations the incidence of answer changing was low, ranging from three to seven percent (Ballance, 1977, and Pascale, 1974, respectively). Thus, although the present *proportion* of answer changes from wrong to right was, as in other studies, relatively high (51.5%: Table 1), it is more important to note that the actual *number* of answer changes was again small, only 4.03%. The significance of this low rate of switching answers can be understood best in conjunction with the responses to the relevant items on the "Student Information Survey," which showed that virtually all subjects (67 of 68) knew of the common wisdom advising against answer-changing (Question a), and felt that before a change was made it should have a high probability ($M = 74.6\%$) of being correct (Question b).

Taken together, these results suggest that, precisely because of a belief that the alternatives they had chosen initially were probably correct, most subjects were reluctant to change answers (hence the low rate), and consequently did so only when they were highly confident in the change, with the result that more than half the changes were correct. In short, the folk-admonition against answer-changing was supported rather than disconfirmed, perhaps explaining why students do not heed suggestions to be less cautious about changing answers on multiple-choice questions (e.g., Foote & Belinky, 1972).

Sex differences in answer-changing were also analyzed. As in the majority of earlier studies, on a proportional basis females made significantly more changes than did male subjects ($t = 2.32, p < .05$); indeed, their rate of 4.83% was

more than double the male rate of 2.36%. Potential explanations can range from "the generally low expectancies [for success] of girls and women" (Frieze, 1978, p. 242) to the aphorism about a woman's prerogative to change her mind. However, it is more useful to consider the *implications* of the present findings, particularly within the context of the distinction between "power" and "speed" tests, namely, that correct solution on a power test is primarily a function of intrinsic item difficulty, whereas a speed test puts a premium on the ability to solve problems within an allotted time. (It is interesting that Foote and Belinky (1972) reported a higher rate of answer-changing by students required to complete 55 items in 50 min. than for the group given 50 min. for only 35 questions.)

Clearly, deliberating about answer-changing leaves less time available for other activities, such as answering multiple-choice questions not yet attempted, or doing other types of questions (e.g., essays). Thus, regardless of whether or not there is a functional relationship between the number of answer changes and time taken to consider and implement such changes, *on a speed test* the tendency for females to make more than twice as many answer changes as males may well be counterproductive, particularly in light of two further findings: first, the success rate for answer changes for women was not better than that for men (indeed, males made 54% successful changes, females 50%); and, second, female subjects achieved a mean grade of 65.9% on the examination, compared to 70% for the males. Further research is ongoing to determine whether the sex differences discovered in the present study are a function of item difficulty (Best, 1979) or a relatively greater vulnerability in females to evaluation by multiple-choice tests *per se*.

References

Ballance, C. T. Students' expectations and their answer-changing behavior. *Psychological Reports*, 1977, *41*, 163-166.

Bath, J. A. Answer-changing behavior on objective examinations. *Journal of Educational Research*, 1967, *61*, 105-107.

Best, J. B. Item difficulty and answer changing. *Teaching of Psychology*, 1979, *6*, 228-230.

Foote, R., & Belinky, C. It pays to switch? Consequences of changing answers on multiple-choice examinations. *Psychological Reports*, 1972, *31*, 667-673.

Frieze, I. H. Achievement and non-achievement in women. In I. H. Frieze, J. E. Parsons, P. B. Johnson, D. N. Ruble, & G. L. Zellman, *Women and sex roles*. New York: Norton, 1978. Pp. 234-254.

Johnston, J. J. Sticking with first responses on multiple-choice exams: For better or for worse? *Teaching of Psychology*, 1975, *2*, 178-179.

Johnston, J. J. Answer-changing behavior and grades. *Teaching of Psychology*, 1978, *5*, 44-45.

Lehman, H. C. Does it pay to change initial decisions in a true-false test? *School and Society*, 1928, *28*, 456-458.

Pascale, P. J. Changing initial answers on multiple-choice achievement tests. *Measurement and Evaluation in Guidance*, 1974, *6*, 236-238.

Reile, P. J., & Briggs, L. J. Should students change their initial answers on objective-type tests?: More evidence regarding an old problem. *Journal of Educational Psychology*, 1952, *43*, 110-115.

Reiling, E., & Taylor, R. A new approach to the problem of changing initial responses to multiple choice questions. *Education Measurement*, 1972, *9*, 67-70.

Sitton, L. R., Adams, I. G., & Anderson, H. N. Personality correlates of students' patterns of changing answers on multiple-choice tests. *Psychological Reports*, 1980, *47*, 655-660.

Stoffer, G. R., Davis, K. E., & Brown, J. R. The consequences of changing initial answers on objective tests: A stable effect and a stable misconception. *Journal of Educational Research*, 1977, 70, 272-276.

Notes

1. This study was funded by an award from the King's College Research Grants Committee to the author.

2. A preliminary version of the paper was presented at the Fifth National Institute on Teaching of Psychology to Undergraduates, Clearwater, FL, January 1983.

Item Difficulty and Answer Changing

John B. Best
Indiana University

The author replicates some earlier results and extends the analysis to show interactions with student performance and item difficulty.

Several recent examinations of answer changing behavior (Bath, 1967; Johnston, 1975, 1978) on multiple choice tests have cast some doubt on the wisdom of the old adage—"Stay with your first answer." These researchers have discovered that changing answers on a multiple choice test is more likely to be helpful than harmful. Also, Johnston (1978) found that students who get high grades were likely to be relatively low in frequency of answer changing and students who get low grades are likely to make more changes. However, these investigations have made no attempt to consider the difficulty of the item in determining whether or not answer changing is likely to be beneficial. Yet, it is commonly known that multiple choice test items vary in difficulty both within and across tests. The present investigation was undertaken to provide further substantiation for the effects discovered by Bath (1967) and Johnston (1975, 1978) and to determine what, if any, effects the difficulty of the item has on answer changing.

Procedure. Students in an introductory psychology class (N = 261) taught by the author were divided into upper, middle and lower thirds based on their performance on four 50-item multiple choice tests. The number of right-to-wrong, wrong-to-right, and wrong-to-wrong answer changes (as indicated by erasure, or crossing out) was recorded for each student. Each of these three kinds of answer changes was categorized as being made on an "easy" or "difficult" item. Easy items were those in which the percentage of the class getting that item correct was greater than the median percentage correct for all items on that test. Difficult items were those in which the percentage of the class getting that item correct was less than the median percentage correct for all items on that test. Chi-square tests were used to determine (a) whether the previous findings of Bath and Johnston could be replicated and (b) if students could be differentiated by the amount and kind of answer changing on easy vs. difficult items.

Results. More wrong-to-right changes than right-to-wrong changes were made by 195 of the Ss, who were thus "helped" by changing answers, and 27 Ss "hurt" themselves by making more right-to-wrong changes than wrong-to-right changes. When this finding is compared to an even split (111 helped, 111 hurt), a chi-square of 125.6 ($p < .001$) is obtained, thus replicating earlier findings by Bath (1967) and Johnston (1975, 1978): Answer changing is more likely to be helpful than harmful. A test of independence between test performance and overall answer changing yielded a chi-square of 17.1 ($p < .001$) thus rejecting the hypothesis of independence. The tendency is for students who get good grades to do the least amount of answer changing; with the middle and lower thirds doing approximately equal amounts of answer changing. Table 1 shows the overall answer changing pattern. It is important to keep in mind that the

Table 1.
Frequency and Kind of Answer Changes for Three Performance Levels

Third	Right-to-Wrong Easy	Right-to-Wrong Difficult	Wrong-to-Right Easy	Wrong-to-Right Difficult	Wrong-to-Wrong Easy	Wrong-to-Wrong Difficult
Top	13	78	98	231	9	48
Middle	34	95	137	226	22	81
Lower	50	78	176	163	27	104
Total	97	251	411	620	58	233

overall amount of answer changing was quite low. 261 students generated a total of 1670 answer changes across the four tests. The mean fequency of answer changing was therefore only about 1.6 items per student per test.

When wrong-to-right changes and grades are tested for independence, independence is not rejected (chi-square = 1.78). Overall, students with good grades made no more wrong-to-right changes than did students with lower grades. However, when a test of the independence of grades and wrong-to-right answer changes on easy and difficult items was carried out (3 x 2 table), independence was rejected (chi-square = 35.24, $p < .001$). The tendency is for good and average students to make more wrong-to-right changes on the *difficult* items, whereas students in the lower third make more wrong-to-right changes on the *easy* items.

When right-to-wrong changes and grades were tested for independence, independence is rejected (chi-square = 8.09, $p < .01$). As might be expected, the tendency is for students with high grades to make fewer right-to-wrong changes than students at other performance levels. When a test of independence of grades and right-to-wrong answer changes on easy and difficult items was carried out, independence was rejected (chi-square = 15.67, $p < .001$). For easy items, there is an inverse relationship between grades and frequency of right-to-wrong changes. For difficult items, average students made the most right-to-wrong errors, but students in the upper and lower thirds made an equal number of such changes.

Conclusion and Discussion. Students are more likely to help rather than hurt themselves by changing answers on a multiple choice test. Johnston's (1978) finding that the best students had a tendency to do the least amount of answer changing was also replicated. The difficulty of the question has a strong impact on wrong-to-right answer changing by students of different performance levels. Students in the top and middle thirds made more wrong-to-right changes on *difficult* items; the opposite was true of students in the lower third of the class. Regarding right-to-wrong changes, students in the middle and upper thirds of the class were more likely to make such changes on difficult rather than on easy items. This was not true of students in the lower third of the class—they were almost as likely to make right-to-wrong changes on *easy* items as they were on difficult items.

The point here is that students at different performance levels apparently respond differently to the difficulty of the item when making a change. Since (obviously) a person's overall grade could be affected by the number and kind of changes made it is important to discuss possible confounding between performance level and such changes. Clearly, if the amount of answer changing is high the possibility of confounded results increases. That is, if subjects, by and large, are capable of making wrong-to-right changes and do so often enough, there is the possibility that some students in the upper 1/3 of the class appear there *because of* a rather shrewd or novel answer changing strategy. However, there are strong indications that this is not so. The typical student changes approximately 1.6 answers per test. Even if all of these were wrong-to-right changes (itself unlikely), over the course of a semester such a student would raise his/her score by about 6 points. Given that the range from one third of the class to the next is approximately 25 to 30 points, it seems extremely unlikely that a student could alter his/her performance level simply by changing answers. Although the effect of changing answers from wrong-to-right certainly helps a student's test score, the effect is just not strong enough to bring about genuine confounding with performance level.

A second type of confounding could result from changes made on difficult items. Since wrong-to-right changes result in an item's becoming easier, it could be that an item's status (easy or difficult) is confounded with the number of wrong-to-right changes made on it. From Table 1 it can be seen that there were 620 wrong-to-right changes. Since some 200 items were administered to the class, the typical item received 3.1 wrong-to-right changes. However, given that the mean percentage of the class passing a difficult item was about 65% and the mean percentage passing an easy item was about 85%, it seems that any given item would have to receive 9 to 10 times the mean number of wrong-to-right changes before its status could be altered from a difficult to an easy item. The possibility of this occurring for very many of the 200 items appears quite remote. Hence it seems that there is no genuine confounding of wrong-to-right changes and an item's status.

This analysis seems to indicate then, that for students in the lower third of the class, the traditional conception of answer changing seems to fit pretty well. That is, answer changing can be seen as a pretty chancy business in which one runs a relatively high risk of "booting" an already correctly answered easy question. But for other students, particularly those in the top third of the class, the traditional picture does not seem to be accurate. Such students are much more likely to help themselves by answer changing. Thus, these findings suggest that it may now be appropriate to supply students with a more sophisticated answer changing strategy than "stay with your first answer."

References

Bath, J. A. Answer changing behavior on objective examinations. *Journal of Educational Research,* 1967, *61,* 105-107.

Johnston, J. J. Sticking with first responses on multiple-choice exams: For better or for worse? *Teaching of Psychology,* 1975, *2,* 178-179.

Johnston, J. J. Answer-changing behavior and grades. *Teaching of Psychology,* 1978, *5,* 44-45.

First Impressions on Tests: Some New Findings

K. Anthony Edwards
and Carol Marshall
Minot State College

First impressions on objective tests
are not necessarily best, but the
preferred strategy is to be careful.

Interest in student's responses on objective tests has been renewed by at least three studies (Davis, 1975; Johnston, 1975; Reiling & Taylor, 1972). Evidence from these and earlier reports (Lowe & Crawford, 1929; Mathews, 1929; Reile & Briggs, 1952) has indicated that students will score higher on multiple-choice and true-false tests by changing answers when changes are considered appropriate by the student. All studies agreed that students tend to change answers from wrong to right more often than from right to wrong. One study (Davis, 1975) showed that test scores are higher when students changed their answers. Thus, the commonsense notion that "first impressions are best" has apparently been quashed.

Several questions arise after reviewing these studies, however. The implications from them, for example, are that students will get a lower test score if there is no opportunity to change test answers. One wonders also if the so-called commonsense notion is a widespread belief or if it is "commonsense" to only a few. Furthermore, it seems that there should be some difference with respect to the time the exam is taken; i.e., will students change answers from wrong to right more often when the material is unfamiliar, as on a pre-test? Answers to these questions were sought in the present study.

Methods

Subjects Thirty-six students enrolled in a self-paced psychology of adjustment course at Minot State College participated in the study.

Apparatus. Two sets of answer sheets especially designed for this study were used. One set allowed students to select a multiple-choice answer from the first row of letters for each item. If a change was desired, the student was able to cross out the answer on the first row and place the changed answer on the row just below. There were five rows of letters for each question. Thus, students had four opportunities per item to change answers, although no student changed more than three times for any one question. With this procedure, we were able to detect changes from wrong to right, right to wrong, wrong to wrong, and right to right. Right to right changes were defined as any answer in which the student began with the correct answer and, after changing to an incorrect answer, later changed back to the correct answer. Only the first and last answers were counted in this study.

On the pre-course test, each answer sheet was backed by a sheet of carbon paper so that we could determine whether any erasures had been made during the examination. Most test items provided four alternatives; but, in some instances, as few as three or as many as seven were available. On the final exam, one group of students was issued an answer sheet that had only one row of letters per item on which answers could be placed. These students were told that any changes on their answer sheet would be counted incorrect. The students in the other group were issued the same answer sheet used on the pre-course test. All students used a ball-point pen. Because no erasures were detected to have been made on the pre-test, the carbons were not used on the final exam.

Procedures. All students received a 140-item multiple-choice test before and after the course. The test items were randomly ordered after use in a previous study (Edwards, 1976). As soon as the students completed all required course work, they were allowed to take the final exam in the self-paced course. A table of random numbers was used to assign students to one of two groups by student numbers. Students assigned to the Change group (N=17) received the type of answer sheets used in the pre-course test which allowed changes if they so elected. Those in the No-change group (N=19) received the answer sheets with only one row of letters on which they could place their answers.

Data were analyzed for the pre-course test and the final exam. Pre-course test scores for the Change and No-change groups were compared, using a t-test for means of independent samples (Ferguson, 1976) to determine whether there were initial differences between the groups prior to the use of different answer forms. Final exam scores were similarly compared to determine whether there were any differences between the two groups when one group was allowed to make changes and the other was not. The pre-course test scores were examined before and after changes were made, using a t-test for correlated samples (Ferguson, 1976). The Change and No-change group pre-course test scores were examined separately to determine whether the changes in the answers made any difference. The final exam scores were examined, using a t-test for correlated samples (Ferguson, 1976) for the Change group before and after answers were changed to determine whether the changes made a difference. Another comparison was made to determine whether the changes on the pre-course test differed from those made on the final exam (i.e., whether students in the Change group gained or lost more on the final exam compared with the pre-course test). The sign test (Siegel, 1956) was used to determine whether the number of students who gained by changing answers was greater. This test was used on the pre-course test for both groups and on the final exam for the Change group.

Results

Of major interest in this study was the percent changes made from wrong to right, right to wrong, wrong to wrong, and right to right. The percent changes made by students are shown for the pre-course test and the final exam in Figure 1.

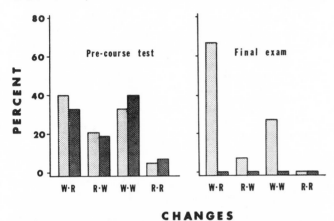

CHANGES

Figure 1. Percent of changes which were from wrong to right (W-R), right to wrong (R-W), wrong to wrong (W-W), and right to right (R-R) on the pre-course test and final exam. Darker stippled bars indicate the No-change group changes (N=108, pre-course; N=0, final exam). Lighter stippled bars indicate the Change group changes (N = 98, pre-course; N=60, final exam).

On the pre-course test, 206 changes were made by the 36 students in the two groups combined. Of these changes, 76 (37%) were from wrong to wrong, 75 (36%) were from wrong to right, 42 (20%) were from right to wrong, and 13 (6%) were from right to right. Sixteen of the 17 students in the Change group made changes and all 19 of the students in the No-change group did so. On the final examination, sixty changes were made by the 17 students in the Change group: 40 (67%) were from wrong to right, 16 (27%) were from wrong to wrong, 4 (7%) were from right to wrong, and none were from right to right.

Also of interest was whether the two groups differed on test scores after the students changed the answers. Comparison of the Change and No-Change groups on pre-course test scores showed no statistical differences between the groups ($t=1.0986$, $df=34$, $p>.05$). Comparison of the two groups on the final exam scores also yielded no statistical differences ($t=0.0614$, $df=34$, $p>.05$).

Comparison of the group scores before and after changes on the pre-course test showed significant improvement for the Change group ($t=2.2011$, $df=16$, $p<.05$), but no significant shift was shown for the No-change group ($t=1.3050$, $df=18$, $p>.05$). Comparison of the final exam

scores for the Change group before and after changes showed significantly higher scores after changes ($t=4.8542$, $df=16$, $p<.001$).

The number of gains and losses on the pre-course test was compared with the number of gains and losses on the final exam. Comparison yielded no significant difference between the two tests for the Change group ($t=0.6008$, $df=16$, $p>.05$). The number of students who showed positive changes from the pre-course test to the final exam were compared with the number of students who showed negative changes. Four students in the Change group showed negative changes on the pre-course test but no negative changes on the final exam. Three students who gained by making changes on the pre-course test made no changes on the final exam. One student who had made as many changes from right to wrong as from wrong to right on the pre-course test (5 each) gained by changing more answers from wrong to right (6) than from right to wrong (2) on the final exam.

Finally, it was questioned whether more students made more changes from right to wrong than from wrong to right. In the Change group, 11 students made more changes from wrong to right on the pre-course test while 4 students made more right to wrong changes than wrong to right ($\chi^2=3.2667$, $df=1$, $p>.05$). In the No-change group on the pre-course test, eight students made more changes from wrong to right than from right to wrong while seven students made more changes from right to wrong than wrong to right ($\chi^2=0.0667$, $df=1$, $p>.05$). On the final exam, the sign test was applied to the gains and losses made by the Change group students when making changes. The number of students who gained by changing answers (12) was significantly greater than the number of students who lost by changing answers (0) ($\chi^2=12.0000$, $df=1$, $p<.0001$).

Discussion

Results from this study agree with those of other studies. Changing test answers tends to produce more right than wrong answers by more students. More test answers were changed from wrong to right than from right to wrong and more students changed answers from wrong to right than from right to wrong. Why the Change group showed a significant change on the pre-course test and the No-change group did not, we do not know. It is possible that unfamiliar material may be less likely to product significant change from wrong to right answers, but this needs further study.

Clearly, students' scores from the Change group did not differ from those of the No-change group on either the pre-course test or the final exam. All students in the pre-course test were allowed to make changes on answers, but students in the No-change group were not allowed to make changes on the final exam. Although the students definitely improved their test scores on the final exam by making the changes, it apparently did not benefit them at all in terms of final exam scores when compared with their controls. This seems to indicate that students who are allowed to make changes are simply "sloppier" in answering questions the first time through the test than students whose first answer is the only opportunity.

Preconceptions. Although the myth of "first impressions" has been with us for a long time (Lowe & Crawford, 1929;

Mathews, 1929), it has never been clear just how prevalent it really is. Davis (1975) attempted to examine this question informally and found that the myth was probably quite widespread.

In the present study, after the experiment was completed, we also looked into this question. A survey was conducted in another class to determine students' preconceptions concerning changing answers on multiple-choice test items. The purpose of this survey of students' beliefs about changing test answers was to determine whether students had been previously advised on how to respond to questions on objective tests. It was also desired to determine how this advice, if given, affected their current modes of responding on tests.

Seventy students enrolled in a psychology of adjustment course were surveyed. The course was similar to the one used in the study described above; however, it was taught in a different term. On the survey, students were asked if they had received suggestions from a teacher on changing objective test answers. It was found that 43% of the students surveyed had been told by a previous instructor that their first impressions were most likely to be correct.

Question 2 asked the students to describe the advice received if any had been given. Out of 30 who received advice, 22 (73%) stated that the advice had been to stick with the first impression because it was the best. Six out of 30 (20%) stated that the advice was more on the order of a restatement of the question. For question 3, 19% reported that they do not change answers.

Question 4 asked students to describe why they changed answers on objective tests, regardless of whether they were advised to do so or not. Several students indicated that items later in the test provided a clue. Many others simply stated that they "changed their mind" without providing the reason for doing so. One student stated that the answer was changed if too many of the same letter appeared consecutively. Several students who answered "yes" stated that they did so reluctantly knowing that the first impression was probably correct anyway.

Question 5 asked students to state why they did not change answers if they had so indicated. Of the 13 who reported they did not do so, 11 stated it was because the first impression is the best. One stated simply that he or she was following the instructor's advice.

Implications. The present research suggests that students have been misinformed on how to perform a simple task by educators in a presumed "informed" society. In spite of studies reaching back as far as 1929, the myth goes on.

It seems that students who are allowed to make changes on multiple-choice test answers are simply "sloppier" at answering questions than those who are penalized for making changes. It should not be inferred, however, that punitive measures such as penalties for changing answers should be used. Teachers should certainly avoid the blanket statement that "first impressions are best" as others have previously stated; teachers should also avoid suggesting to students that they should make changes. Rather, the student should be told to be more careful when answering questions. Most of all, teachers should base their test-taking suggestions on empirical data rather than on folk myth or "commonsense."

References

Davis, R. E. Changing examination answers: An educational myth? *Journal of Medical Education*, 1975, *50*, 685-687.

Edwards, K. A. *An analysis of oral and written quizzes as teaching techniques.* Unpublished doctoral dissertation, Utah State University, 1976.

Ferguson, G. A. *Statistical analysis in psychology and education* (4th Ed.). New York: McGraw-Hill, 1976.

Johnston, J. J. Sticking with first responses on multiple-choice exams: For better or for worse? *Teaching of Psychology*, 1975, *2*, 178-179.

Lowe, M. L., & Crawford, C. C. First impression versus second thought in true-false tests. *Journal of Educational Psychology*, 1929, *20*, 192-195.

Mathews, C. O. Erroneous first impressions on objective tests. *Journal of Educational Psychology*, 1929, *20*, 280-286.

Reile, P. J., & Briggs, L. J. Should students change their initial answers on objective-type tests? More evidence regarding an old problem. *Journal of Educational Psychology*, 1952, *43*, 110-115.

Reiling, E., & Taylor, R. A new approach to the problem of changing initial responses to multiple choice questions. *Journal of Educational Measurement*, 1972, *9*, 67-70.

Siegel, S. *Nonparametric statistics for the behavioral sciences.* New York: McGraw-Hill, 1956.

Notes

1. A portion of this study was presented by the junior author at the meeting of the North Dakota Psychological Association, Fargo, North Dakota, October 1975.

3. INVESTIGATING GRADUATE EDUCATION IN PSYCHOLOGY

Each year, many psychology majors confront faculty members with questions about pursuing graduate study in psychology. Although the contents of this group of articles cannot hope to answer all of those questions, the articles will provide perspectives and information that should help faculty feel more confident in advising their students about this important area of their development. The articles that we selected consist of surveys of *Graduate Study in Psychology* that assess the role of selection factors among different program specialities and degree levels. We also found articles that provided indicators of success on the GRE, in graduate school, and in professional practice. The uneven distribution of students in clinical and experimental areas of psychology constitute the contents of two articles.

Students' questions about professional school in psychology can be particularly difficult to answer for those of us trained in the more traditional areas of psychology. Two articles provide background information about professional schools as well as expectations that those schools have for prospective students.

We also selected articles that provide advisers with information about the problems of licensure for those completing psychology related programs, a course for instructing students about graduate school and professional issues, the implications of the decline in graduate school enrollment on the undergraduate curriculum, and suggestions than can help faculty write more effective letters of recommendation.

a. Admission Variables

Randolph A. Smith from Ouachita Baptist University surveyed 539 graduate programs listed in *Graduate Study in Psychology 1983-1984* to provide information for advising psychology majors. He tabulated both the programs' preferences for courses in applicants' undergraduate background and ratings of five nonobjective criteria in relation to the programs' training speciality (e.g., clinical/counseling) and type of degree (master's only or doctoral). The type of training was significantly related to preferred courses and ratings of nonobjective criteria, whereas type of degree was relatively unimportant. The author discussed the data for each of the four program types, because each requires a different advising strategy.

James Couch and James Benedict from James Madison University surveyed the data in *Graduate Study in Psychology 1982-1983*. They analyzed the GRE, GPA, MAT scores, and the average number and per cent of students accepted into different types and levels of graduate programs in psychology. One finding was that admission to doctoral programs was consistently more competitive than to master's programs. Those who advise students planning to pursue graduate education may want to examine closely the detailed results of this survey. The authors also compare the results with previous studies.

Ronald Nowaczyk and Jerry Frey employed a path analysis to examine the relationship between SAT and GRE-P (psychology) scores of Clemson University students. The authors also examined the mediating influence of intervening academic factors. Using the path solution for the Direct/Indirect model, the authors discovered that SAT had both the greatest direct and indirect influence. On the basis of their findings, the authors questioned using the GRE-P as solely a measure of achievement. The results of this study may help advisers to predict their students' performance on the GRE-P. Delay in taking the GRE-P until students have completed as many psychology classes as possible would not seem to be supported by this study's findings.

Glenn Littlepage, David Bragg, and James Rust went beyond the scope of the first three articles to investigate the relationship between various admission criteria, graduate school achievement, and professional success in psychology. Participants in the study were Middle Tennessee State students receiving master's degrees in psychology or guidance and counseling. Results revealed that admissions measures were related to academic performance and that professional performance was a multidimensional concept. Implications exist for both undergraduate advisers and graduate program administrators.

James Korn and Marie Lewandowski from Sanit Louis University reported the results of a survey of psychology graduate students from four schools and of 33 APA-approved clinical programs. The authors sought to increase readers' awareness of the competitiveness for gaining admission to graduate school and of the varieties of alternatives to clinical and counseling psychology. The authors concluded that an existing clinical bias has a negative effect on undergraduates and on the profession. They emphasized that faculty should make students aware of alternative programs and employment options in the non-clinical area.

Dennis Wright and Donald Kausler's article reinforces portions of the previous one by describing their experience at the University of Missouri. They reported a relatively low number of applications for the experimental psychology program and lower GRE scores among those who did apply. Experimental psychology is one of psychology's non-clinical areas that we could encourage talented students to explore.

Advising Beginning Psychology Majors for Graduate School

Randolph A. Smith
Ouachita Baptist University

The 539 American graduate programs listed in Graduate Study in Psychology 1983–1984 *were surveyed in order to provide more information for advising psychology majors, particularly beginning majors. Undergraduate course preferences and ratings of five nonobjective criteria were tabulated in relation to the program's training specialty and type of degree offered. Programs were classified as offering one of four types of training—clinical/counseling, experimental, both clinical/counseling and experimental, or educational. The type of training was significantly related to preferred courses and ratings of nonobjective criteria, whereas type of degree was relatively unimportant. Results indicated a high preference for a course in statistics, a high rating for letters of recommendation, and a low rating for extracurricular activity. The data are discussed for each of the four program types, because each requires different advising.*

Advising students who are interested in going to graduate school is an important function of the psychology adviser. Students need information covering a broad range of graduate schools and related topics. Fortunately, there are many resources to help students select schools for the application process. Most notably, the American Psychological Association (APA) publication *Graduate Study in Psychology* (GSP) provides information about each graduate program's selection criteria so that students may make informed choices of prospective graduate schools.

Several studies have added to the APA information. Admission odds for clinical and counseling programs have been summarized (Korn, 1984; Korn & Lewandowski, 1981; Nyman, 1973). The 1978–1979 GSP contained a summary of 1974–1979 admission requirements. Two articles have contained summary data (from GSP editions) of students who were admitted to graduate programs. Stoup and Benjamin (1982) reported 1973, 1976, and 1979 data; Couch and Benedict (1983) provided 1980–1981 data.

Unfortunately, most of this information is directed toward upperclass students who are trying to select schools that are likely to accept them. Underclass students who are interested in graduate school are generally ignored. The APA has sought to meet this need with the publication *Preparing for Graduate Study in Psychology: NOT for Seniors Only!* (Fretz & Stang, 1980). This booklet provides information about how best to prepare oneself for graduate study. *Preparing for Graduate Study* alerts beginning students to the importance of research experience, getting to know professors, professional organizations, and so forth, but it does not provide enough information for the underclass student.

Students often ask "What courses should I take?" Many advisers probably rely on their own experience to answer this question, perhaps ignoring the fact that their experience may not match what the student wants or needs. Fretz and Stang (1980) point out that "beyond basic courses in introductory psychology, experimental psychology, and statistics, graduate programs fail to agree on which courses should be taken in psychology" (p. 19). Their statement is supported by the results of an earlier survey (Holder, Leavitt, & McKenna, 1958) of 149 graduate department chairpersons who selected vital undergraduate courses. Statistics was selected by 96% and Experimental by 95% of the chairpersons. The remainder of the top 10 courses and their listed percentages were Tests and Measures (59%), Social (57%), Learning (54%), Abnormal (53%), History of Psychology (52%), Physiological (52%), Personality (47%), and Schools and Systems (46%). These data are clearly outdated, both by time and by the increase in departments offering graduate training.

Certain programs list specific courses in *GSP*, but students probably do not use *GSP* until it is too late to take courses listed by a particular program. The need for specific information concerning the student's area of interest is probably more important than a list of necessary courses for graduate school in general. For these reasons, the courses and nonobjective criteria listed in the 1983–1984 *Graduate Study in Psychology* were analyzed with respect to both the type of degree and program specialty area offered by the graduate schools. This information should be valuable in advising underclass psychology majors for graduate school.

METHOD

The data in this report came from the Admission Requirements section of graduate program entries in the 1983–1984 volume of GSP (1982) and included only schools in the United States. Within that section, graduate programs may specify any undergraduate courses that they require or recommend. In addition, five nonobjective criteria (previous research activity, work experience, extracurricular activity, clinically related public service, letters of recommendation) are ranked low, medium, or high in importance for admission.

As the data for each program were recorded, the type of degree offered (master's only or doctorate) and type of training offered (clinical/counseling only, experimental only, both clinical/counseling and experimental, or educational) were noted. Doctoral programs offered PhD, PsyD, and/or EdD degrees and most also granted master's degrees. In order to avoid numerous subcategories, the definition of experimental programs included any training that did not fit either the clinical/counseling or educational categories, such as developmental, social, and industrial.

RESULTS

Of the 539 graduate programs surveyed, 343 (63.6%) listed at least one course in the Admission Requirements section of GSP 1983–1984. Courses were listed as required, recommended, or optional. Two guidelines were used to avoid listing too many courses in the survey. First, Introductory Psychology was not counted because its inclusion would have been superfluous. Second, only courses mentioned by at least 5% of the 343 programs listing courses were included. These criteria resulted in the 12 courses listed in Table 1, which also shows the rankings of the five nonobjective criteria for all programs surveyed. These data may be compared to the 1973, 1976, and 1979 data of Stoup and Benjamin (1982). Table 1 is an overall listing, which ignores both program type and degree.

Chi-square analyses (2×4) were used to compare each of the 12 courses in Table 1 across the four program specialties based on whether or not a course was listed. Significant differences among program types were found for 6 of the 12 courses, ($df = 3$, $N = 343$, $p < .001$ for all comparisons); Statistics: $\chi^2 = 29.31$; Experimental: $\chi^2 = 49.00$; Abnormal: $\chi^2 = 43.85$; Personality $\chi^2 = 31.76$; Developmental: $\chi^2 = 31.56$; Testing $\chi^2 = 27.21$. The type of program is an important variable in the listing of courses. These differences are summarized in Table 2. Only one course (Statistics) was ranked in the same position by the four program types. When the nonobjective criteria were compared across the four program types based on ratings of high, medium, or low importance with 3×4 chi-square analyses, three of the five criteria showed significant differences, Research: $\chi^2(6, N = 508) = 113.07$, $p < .001$; Work: $\chi^2(6, N = 509) = 56.60$, $p < .001$; Clinically Related Public Service: $\chi^2(6, N = 481) = 93.57$, $p < .001$. Differences were related to type of graduate training (see Table 2). Thus, both courses and nonobjective criteria vary significantly with type of program. Therefore, program specialty should be taken into account when advising undergraduates concerning courses and the importance of nonobjective criteria for graduate school.

Chi-square analyses (2×2) were used to compare courses between the master's and doctoral programs based on whether or not a course was listed for each of the four program specialties (e.g., a comparison of listing/nonlisting for Statistics in Experimental programs between master's and doctoral programs). In the large majority (42/48 or 87.5%) of these analyses, the course listings did not differ for master's and doctoral programs. In addition, 2×3 chi-square analyses were performed to compare the frequencies of high, medium, and low ratings for the five nonobjective cri-

Table 1. Course Preferences and Ratings of Nonobjective Criteria by American Graduate Programs (Overall)

Course	Course Preferences Percentages of Programs Listing Course[a]			
	Required	Recommended	Option	Total
Statistics	74.6	13.7	2.3	90.6
Experimental	60.9	11.7	4.4	77.0
Abnormal	14.9	2.6	12.2	29.7
Personality	9.6	5.2	13.4	28.2
Learning	9.9	6.4	9.6	25.9
Developmental	9.0	2.3	9.3	20.6
Testing	12.8	1.7	4.1	18.6
Physiological	4.1	3.5	7.6	15.2
Social	2.0	3.5	7.6	13.1
History and Systems	4.1	3.8	2.9	10.8
Child Development	3.8	1.2	2.9	7.9
Perception	0.9	1.5	5.2	7.6

Criterion	Ratings of Nonobjective Criteria Numbers of Programs Rating Criterion[b]			
	Low	Medium	High	Mean[c]
Previous research activity	70	182	256	2.37
Work experience	77	291	141	2.13
Extracurricular activity	299	138	13	1.36
Clinically related public service	88	249	144	2.12
Letters of recommendation	18	150	356	2.65

[a]A total of 343 programs listed at least one course.
[b]A total of 530 programs rated at least one criterion.
[c]Mean based on Low = 1, Medium = 2, High = 3.

Table 2. Percentages of Course Listings and Mean Ratings of Nonobjective Criteria by Different Program Types

Course Listing Percentages				
	Type of Program			
Course	C/C	EXP	BOTH	ED
Statistics	81.9	90.6	96.9	70.6
Experimental	60.7	75.5	88.7	41.2
Abnormal	62.3	13.2	22.6	38.2
Personality	54.1	15.1	21.6	41.2
Developmental	36.1	11.3	13.9	47.0
Testing	31.2	3.8	14.9	41.2

Mean Ratings of Nonobjective Criteria				
Criterion	C/C	EXP	BOTH	ED
Previous research activity	1.87	2.70	2.57	2.07
Work experience	2.34	1.93	1.98	2.41
Extracurricular activity	1.44	1.28	1.31	1.48
Clinically related public service	2.46	1.60	2.10	2.14
Letters of recommendation	2.61	2.71	2.64	2.64

Note. C/C = Clinical/Counseling programs (61 listed courses; 112 rated criteria); EXP = Experimental programs (53 listed courses; 95 rated criteria); BOTH = Clinical/Counseling and Experimental programs (195 listed courses; 231 rated criteria); ED = Educational programs (34 listed courses; 92 rated criteria).

teria (within each program specialty). Again, the vast majority (16/20 or 80%) of comparisons showed that the criteria were unaffected by the type of degree. It appears, then, that the type of degree offered should have little effect on how we advise students. Hence, the following descriptions will largely ignore the type of degree offered. The data are presented for the four program specialty areas because specialty accounted for the major differences.

Clinical/Counseling Programs

There were 112 programs classified as offering only Clinical/Counseling (C/C) training (20.8% of the total 539). Of those, 67 (59.8%) offered only master's degrees, and 45 (40.2%) were doctoral programs. Of the 112 programs, 61 (54.5%) listed at least one course advised for entrance. Table 2 shows the six courses previously mentioned and their frequencies of listing.

All differences between the data of Tables 1 and 2 mentioned hereafter have been verified as significant by chi-square tests. However, because the data of the two tables are not independent, only descriptions of the results will be reported. Abnormal, Personality, Developmental, and Testing were listed more often by C/C programs than in the overall listing, whereas Statistics and Experimental were listed less often. In addition, both Statistics and Learning were listed more often by doctoral than by master's programs.

All 112 C/C programs rated at least one of the nonobjective criteria (means in Table 2). In comparison with the overall ratings, C/C programs placed greater emphasis on work and clinical experience and less on research. However, the difference in research was due to a difference be-

tween types of degrees offered, as the mean ratings for research were 1.63 by master's and 2.18 by doctoral programs.

Experimental Programs

Of the 539 programs, 96 (17.8%) had only Experimental training. Of those, 31 (32.3%) offered only master's degrees and 65 (67.7%) offered doctoral degrees. Courses were listed by 53 (55.2%) of the programs. Experimental programs listed Abnormal, Personality, and Testing less often than overall. The pattern of Statistics and Experimental ranking far ahead of the other courses (as in Table 1) was duplicated.

Of the 96 Experimental programs, 95 (99.0%) rated at least one nonobjective criterion (see Table 2). Compared to the overall ratings, Experimental programs showed a reversal of the differences in the C/C area, as Experimental programs placed greater emphasis on research and less on work and clinic experience.

Both Clinical/Counseling and Experimental Programs

The largest number of the 539 graduate programs (237, or 44%) offered both Clinical/Counseling and Experimental training. Of those, 92 (38.8%) offered only master's degrees and 145 (61.2%) offered doctoral training. Selection criteria are probably different for C/C and Experimental areas within this category, but GSP information is only presented departmentally. Therefore, data are presented as they appeared in GSP.

Courses were listed by 195 of the 237 Both programs (82.3%). Compared to the overall listing, both C/C and Experimental listed Statistics and Experimental more often and Developmental less often (see Table 2). As in the overall and Experimental listings, Statistics and Experimental ranked far ahead of other courses. Within this category, master's programs listed Abnormal, Learning, Personality, and Testing approximately twice as often as doctoral programs did.

Of the 237 Both programs, 231 (97.5%) rated at least one nonobjective criterion (see Table 2). These programs valued research more and work experience less than in the overall ratings. Also, doctoral programs rated both research and letters of recommendation more highly than did master's programs.

Educational Programs

The majority of these programs offered either traditional educational psychology training or work in counseling (counselor education or counseling psychology). Because admission to APA-approved C/C programs is difficult (Korn, 1984), Educational programs might be appropriate for the student whose credentials are not strong enough for acceptance by a traditional Counseling program. Couch and Benedict (1983) reported acceptance rates of 16% for Counseling programs and 45% for Educational programs and that doctoral students accepted by Counseling programs outperformed those of Educational programs on the Graduate Record Examination (1148 to 1119), Miller

Analogies Test (64 to 52), and psychology grade-point average (3.55 to 3.36).

Of the 539 programs, 94 (17.4%) were classified as Educational. Doctoral degrees were offered by 66 (70.2%) and 28 offered only master's degrees (29.8%). Only 34 of the 94 (36.2%) listed courses for admission. Compared to the overall listing, Educational programs listed Statistics and Experimental less often, whereas Testing and Developmental were mentioned more often. Statistics stands far ahead of the other courses.

Of the 94 Educational programs, 92 (97.9%) rated at least one nonobjective criterion (see Table 2). Compared to the overall ratings, Educational programs rated research as less important and work as more important. Again, research was rated more highly by doctoral programs.

Comparison of Programs

From Table 2, it is apparent that Experimental and Both programs are similar in their course listings and criteria ratings and that the C/C and Educational programs are also similar. Because the different program types have independent data, chi-square tests are appropriate.

Analyses comparing the listing of courses showed that Experimental programs listed Experimental, $\chi^2(1, N = 248) = 5.18, p < .03$, and Testing, $\chi^2(1, N = 248) = 5.63, p < .02$, less often than did Both programs. C/C programs listed Abnormal, $\chi^2(1, N = 95) = 5.11, p < .03$, and History and Systems, $\chi^2(1, N = 95) = 4.26, p < .04$, more often than did Educational programs. No other course-listing differences were found between the Experimental–Both or the C/C–Educational pairings of programs.

The only criterion difference between program pairs concerned clinically related public service, as Both programs valued it more highly than did Experimental programs, $\chi^2(2, N = 291) = 44.65, p < .001$. Also, the C/C programs rated clinical experience more highly than Educational programs did, $\chi^2(2, N = 190) = 12.23, p < .01$.

DISCUSSION

These data should be interpreted with care because they are summary data and provide only general guidelines. Also, the four types of training programs showed a high degree of variability in reporting course preferences. Several conclusions, however, are supported by these data. The two most important findings concern the variables of program specialty and the type of degree offered. First, the potential graduate specialty of the student should be taken into account when giving academic advice. Table 2 demonstrates the differences between the four program specialties. With these data, students could carefully choose courses throughout their academic careers. Second, the type of degree offered by the graduate program is only a minor issue. In most cases, the course listings and ratings of nonobjective criteria within specialty areas did not differ between master's and doctoral programs. However, doctoral programs consistently rated previous research activity more highly than did master's programs.

Other general trends are difficult to isolate because of the variability among specialties. Clearly, Statistics is considered very important by a large majority of the graduate programs. Experimental is fairly important, but is listed differently by the various types of programs. The safest conclusion concerning specific courses beyond Statistics is that there is no consistent trend. Conclusions about the nonobjective criteria are somewhat clearer. Letters of recommendation are considered most important within all specialty areas and extracurricular activity is the least important. The other criteria must be evaluated by program specialty.

One noteworthy finding was that the Experimental programs and programs offering both Clinical/Counseling and Experimental training had similar response patterns, as did the Clinical/Counseling and Educational programs. This situation presents a quandary for underclass students who are interested in clinical or counseling training. Should they follow the Clinical/Counseling or the Both pattern? According to GSP 1983–1984, there were 116 APA-approved (or provisionally approved) clinical programs with full information listed; all but eight departments also offered experimental training. Of the eight exceptions, five were professional schools and one was a seminary. There were 28 APA-approved (or provisionally approved) counseling programs listed with 11 of those departments offering experimental training. However, 9 of the 17 exceptions were in the Educational classification. It appears that Both programs are more likely to have APA approval than either C/C or Educational programs. Thus, if students seek admission to an APA-approved program, the Both pattern is probably the wiser approach. Further, from the ratings of clinically related public service (Table 2), it does not appear that the Both data have been dramatically skewed toward the experimental side of the programs. Although the Both rating (2.10) is lower than the C/C rating (2.46), the Both value is much higher than the Experimental rating (1.60) and is essentially equal to the Educational rating (2.14).

CONCLUSION

In sum, this paper is intended to provide guidance for advisers of underclass students who are interested in preparing for graduate study in psychology. Perhaps the most important consideration is the type of graduate training that the student desires. Once that decision has been made, the present data and other resources can be used to help the student plan an appropriate undergraduate program and prepare for further study. Finally, information from the present study might also be useful in curriculum development. For example, if a department's goal is to prepare some of its students for graduate study, these data should be helpful in planning appropriate course offerings and determining requirements for a major in psychology.

REFERENCES

American Psychological Association. (1977). Graduate study in psychology 1978–1979. Washington, DC: Author.
American Psychological Association. (1981). Graduate study in psychology 1982–1983. Washington, DC: Author.

American Psychological Association. (1982). *Graduate study in psychology 1983-1984*. Washington, DC: Author.

Couch, J. V., & Benedict, J. O. (1983). Graduate school admission variables: An analysis of 1980-81 students. *Teaching of Psychology, 10*, 3-6.

Fretz, B. R., & Stang, D. J. (1980). *Preparing for graduate study in psychology: NOT for seniors only!* Washington, DC: American Psychological Association.

Holder, W. B., Leavitt, G. S., & McKenna, F. S. (1958). Undergraduate training for psychologists. *American Psychologist, 13*, 585-588.

Korn, J. H. (1984). New odds on acceptance into PhD programs in psychology. *American Psychologist, 39*, 179-180.

Korn, J. H., & Lewandowski, M. E. (1981). The clinical bias in the career plans of undergraduates and its impact on students and the profession. *Teaching of Psychology, 8*, 149-152.

Nyman, L. (1973). Some odds on getting into PhD programs in clinical and counseling psychology. *American Psychologist, 28*, 934-935.

Stoup, C. M., & Benjamin, L. T., Jr. (1982). Graduate study in psychology, 1970-79. *American Psychologist, 37*, 1186-1202.

Graduate School Admission Variables: An Analysis of 1980-81 Students

James V. Couch and
James O. Benedict
James Madison University

Requirements are highest for doctoral programs, but GRE scores have decreased and GPA scores have increased since 1975.

For a number of years we have been using the APA publication *Graduate Study in Psychology* in our advising work with students who are applying for admission to graduate school. The information contained in the individual departmental listings is very helpful to students once they have identified an area of specialization and a set of schools to which they may apply. Over the years, however, we have found that many questions about graduate school admission cannot be answered by consulting this resource. Examples of questions asked by students are "What are my chances of getting into a program in clinical or experimental psychology?" "What are the average GRE, GPA, or MAT, scores for programs in the area of industrial or school psychology?" An analysis of all the program statistics reported in the *Graduate Study in Psychology* would be required in order to answer these questions. The results of such an analysis are reported in this paper.

In addition to answering some of the student-generated questions, this type of analysis allows comparisons to be made with previously published results on graduate school admission. Specifically Nyman (1973) and more recently, Korn and Lewandowski (1981) have published results on admission parameters in clinical and counseling psychology programs. Furthermore, APA, in the 1978-79 edition of *Graduate Study in Psychology*, summarized admission requirements for 1974 through 1979. Finally, the 1979-80 summary report of the Survey of Graduate Departments of Psychology (Stapp, Note 3) reported data on enrollments in various doctoral program areas.

Given the scarcity of current information about admission statistics both across degree type and program area it was decided to analyze all of the program information provided in the 1982-83 edition of *Graduate Study in Psychology*. Results in this analysis could prove very useful in graduate school advisement activities with students, and could provide more information for comparing the admission statistics of different types of graduate programs in psychology.

Method. The data for the analysis came from the individual program listings in the 1982-83 edition of *Graduate Study in Psychology* and more specifically from the "Student Statistics 1980-81" section of each program listing. Thus, the results reported in this paper represent characteristics of the students admitted to graduate programs in 1980-81. All information was transferred to computer coding forms and then punched into computer cards.

The data recorded included the average scores of the students accepted for the Verbal component of the Graduate Record Examination (GRE-V); the Quantitative component (GRE-Q); the Total (Verbal + Quantitative) scores (GRE-T); the score for the Advanced component (GRE-Adv); the total grade point average (GPA); psychology courses only (GPA-P); the last 60 semester hours only (GPA-60); and the Miller Analogies Test score (MAT). In addition, the number of applications received and the number of students accepted were recorded for each program. This latter information was used to compute the program's percent acceptance by dividing the number of students accepted by the number of students who applied. Only those programs which reported either the GRE-T score or both the GRE-V and GRE-Q scores were included in the analysis. In addition to the above information pertaining to students, each program was coded by its degree level (masters, specialist, or doctoral) and its program area. The total analysis included 260 masters programs, 12 specialist programs, and 430 doctoral programs for a total of 702 programs.

Results. Table 1 shows the means for each of the various admission variables across the five graduate degrees. Not all programs reported scores for all of the admission variables. The number in parenthesis under each graduate degree indicates the number of programs that reported either GRE-T or both GRE-V and GRE-Q average. As can be seen in the table, the greatest GRE-T, GRE-Adv, GPA-P and GPA-60 scores were for students admitted to PhD programs. The highest MAT and GPA scores were for students admitted to EdD programs. The PsyD programs reported the lowest average percentage of students accepted; the Specialist, EdD, and Masters programs reported the largest acceptance percentages. It should be noted that the percent acceptance data do not account for multiple applications by students.

Table 2 illustrates the means for the admission variables across the 11 Master's degree program areas. The number in parentheses after each program indicates the number of programs reporting either GRE-T or both GRE-V and GRE-Q averages. The range of GRE-T averages for Master's programs was from a high of 1113 for personality programs to a low of 1012 for student personnel service programs. Mean GRE-Adv scores ranged from a high of 655 for social psychology programs to a low of 475 for student personnel service programs. Total GPA scores ranged from a high of 3.40 for social psychology programs to a low of 3.10 for personality programs. The average number of students accepted ranged from a low of 3 for social psychology programs to a high of 23 for counseling programs. Percent acceptance rates range from a high of 55% for personality programs to a low of 25% for social psychology programs.

Comparing the four largest program areas at the masters level (e.g. experimental, clinical, counseling, and school) the highest mean GRE-T score was for experimental psychology programs, the highest mean GRE-Adv score was for students enrolled in clinical psychology programs. The largest average *number* of students accepted was for counseling programs, but the highest acceptance *percentage* is for students who applied to school psychology programs.

Table 3 presents the mean scores for students admitted to

Table 1. Mean Scores of Students Separated by Graduate Degree: 1980-81

Score	Masters (260)[a]	Specialist (12)	Doctoral[b] (430)	PhD (413)	PsyD (10)	EdD (7)
GRE-V	540	524	604	604	608	616
GRE-Q	531	513	598	599	567	544
GRE-T	1071	1059	1197	1201	1174	1076
GRE-Adv	561	572	614	616	593	590
MAT	58	59	**72**	68	—	71
GPA	3.28	3.33	3.45	3.45	3.38	3.52
GPA-P	3.43	3.50	3.62	3.62	3.53	—
GPA-60	3.41	3.50	3.55	3.56	3.41	3.26
Number Accepted	14	19	8	8	16	10
Percent Accepted	42	52	17	17	13	44

[a]Number of schools reporting GRE-T or both GRE-V and GRE-Q.
[b]All doctoral programs combined.

Table 2. Comparison of Admission Variables Across Program Areas: Masters Degree

Program Area	Evaluation Measure								Average Number Accepted	Percent Accepted
	GRE-V	GRE-Q	GRE-T	GRE-Adv.	MAT	GPA	GPA-P	GPA-60		
Clinical (53)[a]	552	536	1085	568	61	3.33	3.49	3.47	14	32
Community (10)	501	507	1025	549	41	3.25	3.36	3.52	8	47
Counseling (40)	533	512	1046	560	57	3.16	3.35	3.25	23	44
Developmental (13)	507	503	1032	548	57	3.31	3.30	3.53	8	50
Educational (8)	548	544	1094	557	54	3.20	3.80	3.31	6	49
Experimental (58)	549	546	1098	563	57	3.31	3.40	3.42	10	43
I/O (16)	539	544	1080	581	59	3.23	3.53	3.47	11	40
Personality (2)	562	551	1113	521	—	3.10	3.28	3.52	4	55
School (36)	523	525	1054	534	60	3.36	3.45	3.42	10	50
Social (3)	587	523	1103	655	—	3.40	3.60	3.50	3	25
Student Personnel (7)	518	493	1012	475	—	3.26	—	3.45	9	42

[a]Number of schools reporting either GRE-T or both GRE-V and GRE-Q.
Where no entries appear, data not reported.

specialist degree programs. As can be seen there are a limited number of these programs that reported student statistics in the *Graduate Study* edition used for this analysis.

Table 4 presents the mean scores for students admitted to the 14 doctoral degree program areas. The range of GRE-T scores for doctoral degrees was from a high of 1287 for cognitive psychology programs to a low of 958 for student personnel programs. Mean GRE-Adv scores ranged from a high of 643 for personality programs to a low of 470 for community psychology programs. Mean MAT scores ranged from a high of 75 for personality programs to a low of 52 for educational psychology programs. Mean GPA ranged from 3.62 for personality programs to 3.28 for physiological psychology programs. The average number of students accepted ranged from 16 in both student personnel and school psychology programs to 3 in both quantitative and community psychology programs. The average percentage accepted ranged from 45% in educational psychology to 6% in clinical psychology.

Comparing the five largest program areas at the doctoral level (e.g. clinical, experimental, developmental, social, and counseling) indicates that the highest mean GRE-T, GRE-Adv, and MAT scores are reported for students admitted to clinical psychology training programs, but developmental psychology program students have a mean MAT score equal to clinical psychology students.

Table 5 presents a comparison of mean scores for students admitted to master's and doctoral programs in 1975-76, 1976-77, and 1980-81. The data for the 1975-77 students was reported in the 1978-79 edition of the *Graduate Study in Psychology* (1977).

Considering masters level training, Table 5 indicates a decline in GRE-V, GRE-Q, GRE-T, GRE-Adv, and MAT scores for the 1980-81 students as compared to the earlier years. However, for the GPA scores there has been an increase in average scores for the students admitted to graduate programs in 1980-81 as compared to students admitted in 1975-76 and 1976-77, except for GPA-60 which is essentially the same for the 1980-81 and the 1975-76 time periods.

A similar pattern emerges for the doctoral degree programs. That is, GRE-V, GRE-Q, and GRE-T scores have declined since 1975-76 with GRE-Adv scores being equal for the 1980-81 students and the 1975-76 students. MAT scores and the GPA scores show little change over the three comparison periods.

In interpreting the percentage acceptance data presented in Table 4, a complication arises because students submit multiple applications to graduate programs. Korn and Lewandowski (1981) tried to account for multiple applications by asking a sample of graduate students in clinical and counseling doctoral programs to indicate the number of schools to which they sent applications. They reported that clinical students applied to an average of 13 schools and counseling students applied to an average of 6.7 schools. Then they used this information to compute a candidate acceptance ratio (previously used by Nyman, 1973) by

Table 3. Comparison of Admission Variables Across Program Areas: Specialist Degree

Program Area	Evaluation Measure								Average Number Accepted	Percent Accepted
	GRE-V	GRE-Q	GRE-T	GRE-Adv.	MAT	GPA	GPA-P	GPA-60		
Counseling (4)[a]	523	498	1052	—	63	3.43	3.50	3.50	33	61
Educational (1)	540	510	1028	—	—	3.10	—	—	—	—
School (7)	522	520	1067	572	57	3.31	—	—	11	46

[a]Number of schools reporting either GRE-T or both GRE-V and GRE-Q
Where entries are missing, no data reported.

Table 4. Comparison of Admission Variables Across Program Areas: Doctoral Degree

Program Area	Evaluation Measure								Average Number Accepted	Percent Accepted
	GRE-V	GRE-Q	GRE-T	GRE-Adv.	MAT	GPA	GPA-P	GPA-60		
Clinical (102)[a]	631	613	1243	632	72	3.50	3.68	3.61	12	6
Cognitive (12)	638	649	1287	624	73	3.55	3.63	3.60	4	20
Community (4)	504	503	1021	470	—	3.49	3.66	3.56	3	7
Counseling (42)	559	560	1148	599	64	3.45	3.55	3.50	10	16
Developmental (42)	601	596	1192	622	72	3.52	3.68	3.53	5	18
Educational (17)	569	559	1119	592	52	3.48	3.36	3.47	13	45
Experimental (79)	591	590	1181	609	66	3.38	3.61	3.60	6	22
I/O (14)	622	646	1261	633	64	3.38	3.64	3.41	6	10
Personality (7)	657	579	1273	643	75	3.62	3.76	3.78	4	16
Physiological (25)	590	615	1205	616	72	3.28	3.56	3.44	4	18
Quantitative (10)	557	632	1188	603	60	3.51	3.86	3.62	3	40
School (26)	578	549	1114	568	63	3.40	3.66	3.46	16	32
Social (41)	595	609	1208	590	71	3.45	3.53	3.53	5	16
Student Personnel (3)	552	534	958	—	—	3.50	—	—	16	23

[a]Number of schools reporting either GRE-T or both GRE-V and GRE-Q
Where entries are missing, no data reported.

Table 5. Mean Scores on Admission Variables For Master's and Doctoral Programs

Evaluation Measure	1975-76[a]	1976-77[a]	1980-81
Master's programs			
GRE-V (234)[b]	574	568	540
GRE-Q (234)	567	562	531
GRE-V + Q (260)	1132	1123	1071
GRE-Adv (130)	567	567	561
MAT (41)	62	59	58
GPA (188)	3.25	3.20	3.28
GPA-P (118)	3.39	3.38	3.43
GPA-60	3.43	3.29	3.41
Doctoral programs			
GRE-V (392)	633	618	604
GRE-Q (392)	638	612	598
GRE-V & Q (430)	1263	1252	1198
GRE-Adv (247)	616	607	615
MAT (90)	70	70	69
GPA (314)	3.44	3.47	3.45
GPA-P (133)	3.71	3.59	3.62
GPA-60 (145)	3.54	3.52	3.55

[a]Data from *Graduate Study in Psychology: 1978-1979.*
[b]Number of programs reporting data.

Table 6. Candidate Acceptance Ratios 1980-81 Students

Program Area	Mean Applications/ Department	Mean Acceptances/ Department	Mean Applications/ Student[a]	Candidate Acceptance Ratio
Clinical	261.64	11.51	13.0	1.75
Counseling	80.87	10.41	6.7	1.16

[a]From Korn and Lewandowski (1981)

dividing the mean number of applications per department by the mean number of applications per student. This result is then divided by the mean number of students accepted by each department. They report a candidate acceptance ratio of 1.9 and 1.6 for clinical and counseling programs respectively, meaning that 1.9 applications were received by clinical programs for every student admitted and 1.6 applications were received by counseling programs for every student admitted.

Table 6 presents the results necessary to calculate the candidate acceptance ratios for the 1980-81 students entering doctoral level programs in clinical and counseling psychology. The mean number of applications per student was taken from Korn and Lewandowski (1981)—this information is not found in the *Graduate Study in Psychology*. Table 6 shows that for the present data there were 1.75 applications for each student admitted to a clinical psychology program with 1.16 applications for each student admitted to a counseling program.

Discussion. There are several conclusions which can be drawn from the current analysis. First, for most program areas, the mean scores on the admission variables are higher for students admitted to doctoral programs than for students admitted to either masters or specialist programs. The mean

qualifications of a student admitted to a masters program in year 1980-81 were a GRE-T of 1071, GRE-Adv of 561, a GPA of 3.28, GPA-P of 3.43 and a GPA-60 of 3.41. For a doctoral program (combining PhD, PsyD, and EdD programs), the mean qualifications were a GRE-T of 1197, GRE-Adv of 614, a GPA of 3.45, GPA-P of 3.62, and a GPA-60 of 3.55.

Second, the number of students admitted was much larger for masters programs (mean = 14) than for doctoral programs (mean = 8). Also the percentage of students accepted in masters programs was higher (*M* = 42%) than in doctoral programs (*M* = 17%). Third, since 1975-76 there has been a drop in GRE scores for masters students along with an increase in average GPA scores. A similar decline in GRE scores is evident for doctoral programs. It is not clear as to the reason for the decrease in GRE scores. It may be an artifact of the data because there were several schools in the *Graduate Study in Psychology* edition which did not include either GRE-T or both GRE-V and GRE-Q scores and thus were not included in this analysis. But given the large number of schools that were included (N = 702), it is more likely that the decline in GREs is a real characteristic of the 1980-81 student statistics. Either graduate schools are admitting more students and thus becoming less selective or fewer applications are being received by the graduate schools thus forcing them to become less selective. Previous issues of *Graduate Study* do not present summary statistics that could be used to evaluate which hypothesis is correct.

The present data do show that the candidate acceptance ratios were more favorable, from the student's perspective, given the present data, than were Korn and Lewandowski's data. One might conclude from these analyses that it was somewhat easier to obtain admission to graduate school during the year 1980-81 than during the immediately preceeding years.

One final outcome of the present analysis was the generation of a computer listing[1] that rank ordered graduate programs by degree type and program area using the GRE-T variable. The purpose of this listing was to allow a student to quickly identify those graduate schools that have accepted students who have average GRE-T scores similar to their own. We find so many students spending a great deal of time and money making application to schools to which they have little chance of being accepted. This behavior is a function of at least two different antecedants. First, students have not looked closely enough at the student statistic section of the *Graduate Study* guide, or if they had they have ignored the information found there. Second, students do not know which schools in the country accept students that have qualifications similar to their own. The computer listing compiled from the 1982-83 *Graduate Study in Psychology* has the potential of eliminating both of these antecedants.

References

American Psychological Association. *Graduate study in psychology, 1978-1979.* Washington, DC: Author, 1977.

American Psychological Association. *Graduate study in psychology, 1982-1983.* Washington, DC: Author, 1981.

Korn, J. E., & Lewandowski, M. E. The clinical bias in the career plans of undergraduates and its impact on students and the profession. *Teaching of Psychology*, 1981, *8*, 149-152.

Nyman, L. Some odds on getting in PhD programs in clinical and counseling psychology. *American Psychologist*, 1973, *28*, 934-935.

Notes

1. A copy of the computer listing has been submitted to the *Journal Supplement Abstract Service*. A limited number of copies of the listing are available from the authors.
2. Charles Stoup and Ludy Benjamin, Jr. presented a paper at the 1981 APA meetings that provided an analysis of *Graduate Study* *in Psychology* from 1971 to 1980.
3. Stapp, J. Summary report of 1979-80 survey of graduate departments of psychology. American Psychological Association, 1980.

Factors Related to Performance on the GRE Advanced Psychology Test

Ronald H. Nowaczyk
and Jerry D. Frey
Clemson University

Academic factors, such as GPA, do contribute to GRE-P performance, but SAT scores contribute more, so is GRE-P a measure of achievement?

The advanced Psychology test of the Graduate Record Examination (GRE-P) is a standardized test often used in considering an applicant for admission into a graduate program in psychology. Published research using this test (Ewen, 1969; Mehrabian, 1969; Stricker & Huber, 1967) has been directed at identifying its ability to predict success in graduate school. However, little emphasis has been placed on determining the factors that contribute significantly to performance on the GRE-P itself.

Although past studies were concerned with the predictive validity of the tests, statistics on academic factors that might influence GRE-P performance were also included. The Mehrabian (1969) study included overall undergraduate grade-point average (GPA-U). The Stricker & Huber (1967) and Ewen (1969) studies also included grade-point average for psychology courses (GPA-P), and the Ewen study also added the number of psychology courses completed at the time of testing. The relationship between the GRE-P and GPA-U was nonsignificant in all three studies, $r = .18$ in the Mehrabian study, $r = .23$ in the Stricker and Huber study, and $r = -.03$ in the Ewen study. The relationship between GRE-P and GPA-P was no better, $r = .13$ in the Stricker and Huber study and $r = .01$ in the Ewen study. Furthermore, Ewen reported a nonsignificant relationship between the GRE-P and the number of psychology courses completed, $r = .30$. The lack of significant findings in these studies may be the result of a restricted range problem (Dawes, 1975) in that the subjects in these studies were graduate school applicants (Mehrabian, 1969) or graduate students (Ewen, 1969; Stricker & Huber, 1967). Furthermore, the fact that the students came from different undergraduate institutions makes it somewhat difficult to make meaningful comparisons among students in terms of GPA-U and GPA-P (Ewen, 1969).

The fact that no relationship could be found between the GRE-P and these academic factors is intriguing inasmuch as the GRE-P is designed to assess undergraduate achievement in psychology. Even if the relationship between GPA-U and GRE-P is low, one might expect a somewhat stronger relationship between GRE-P and factors directly related to the subject material such as GPA-P and the number of psychology courses completed. The present study investigated the relationship between the GRE-P and previously studied factors, GPA-U, GPA-P, and the number of semester hours completed in psychology (HRS-P). In addition, the student's overall SAT score was considered. These past studies have found a significant relationship between GRE-P and overall GRE score and because few of the students in our sample had taken the GRE, we decided to include their overall SAT score in our analysis. In addition, we were interested in determining how predictive SAT performance might be for the GRE-P test.

As noted, previous studies have used only graduate students or applicants to graduate school. The present study overcomes the problem of a restricted range by including many students who were not planning on applying to graduate school. Furthermore, all students in the sample attended the same university, allowing for greater comparability on academic factors than was possible in previous studies that used students from different institutions.

Two models were proposed to explain performance on the GRE-P. The academic factors were assumed to directly influence GRE-P performance in both models. In one model (Indirect Model), SAT is assumed to influence GRE-P performance only indirectly, through the academic factors. This is supported by the finding (DuBois, 1972) that SAT and GPA-U are related. In the other model (Direct/Indirect Model), SAT is assumed to influence performance on the GRE-P not only indirectly through the academic factors, but also directly.

These two models can be tested as causal models. An introduction to causal modeling and a review of recent work in the area are presented by Bentler (1980). Although causal models must be evaluated by a variety of criteria, including meaningfulness, they can be tested statistically for adequacy of representation through path analysis. Path analysis is superior to ordinary regression analysis because it allows the investigator to move beyond the estimation of direct effects, the basic output of regression, when the factors can be ordered temporally as is the case in this study. Whereas regression analysis would allow one to determine only the extent to which SAT scores predict GRE-P scores, path analysis enables one to determine the extent to which the influence of SAT on GRE-P is mediated by the intervening academic factors.

Method. For three successive years, psychology majors with junior status at Clemson University were strongly encouraged to take the GRE-P test as a way of determining their own strengths and weaknesses in psychology. Psychology majors in their senior year were also permitted to take the test the first year it was offered. Across the three years of testing, 75 percent of the listed majors with junior status took the test (44 were female and 17 were male, which is comparable to our departmental women-to-men student ratio). Because the department was interested in evaluating its program, the test was administered at departmental expense.

Each year the test was scheduled for an afternoon in the latter half of the Spring semester. Students were notified of the date and were encouraged to register for the test. They were told that the cost of the test would be handled by the psychology department and that our primary interest was in assessing the adequacy of our program. Students were informed that taking the test could benefit them as well. However, permanent recording of their scores by ETS was left to their discretion. Following completion of the test we asked each student for permission to check his or her academic records for factors we felt would be predictive of performance on the test.

Results and Discussion. The data revealed that the mean GRE-P score of our sample was comparable to the national norm.[1] Summary statistics for the GRE-P and the academic factors are included in Table 1. A measure of skewness

Table 1. Summary Statistics for GRE-P, SAT, and Academic Factors

Variable	Mean	SD	Minimum	Maximum	Skewness
GRE-P	455.24	62.49	310.	640.	.51
SAT[a]	990.41	150.05	650.	1350.	.19
GPA-U[b]	2.97	.57	1.52	3.90	−.20
GPA-P	2.99	.71	1.00	4.00	−.44
HRS-P[c]	20.21	8.37	3.00	45.00	.57

[a]Combined Verbal and Quantitative Scores.
[b]GPA based on 4-point grading scale.
[c]A semester course is equivalent to three course hours.

based on the third moment about the mean is included for each variable. Based on this measure and the minimum and maximum values reported, it appears that each variable is normally distributed. The data for GPA-U and GPA-P indicate that our subjects were performing "B" work on the average. The mean number of courses completed in psychology was approximately seven. This figure does not include psychology courses that subjects were enrolled in at the time of testing. For the sake of completeness, the correlation matrix for all variables is shown in Table 2.

Table 2. Correlation Matrix for GRE-P, SAT, and Academic Factors

Variable	SAT	GPA-U	GPA-P	HRS-P
GRE-P	.65	.49	.44	.30
SAT		.39	.41	.15
GPA-U			.86	.07
GPA-P				.10

Note. With N = 61, r > .25 to be significant at p < .05.

The data on all variables were standardized ($M = 0$, $SD = 1$). Separate multiple regression analyses using the General Linear Model program from the SAS computer package (1979) were conducted based on the two models described earlier. The Direct/Indirect model accounts for a highly respectable 54 percent of the variance in GRE-P, compared to 32 percent for the Indirect model. The path solution for the Direct/Indirect model is presented in Figure 1. It is clear that the Indirect model must be rejected as inadequate because

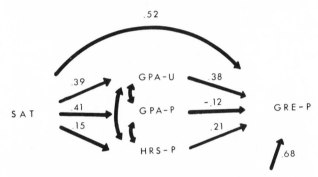

Figure 1. Representation of Direct/Indirect Model.

this model assumes that the magnitude of the direct linkage between SAT and GRE-P is zero, which clearly is not the case.

The Direct/Indirect model is more appropriate, given that the direct influence of SAT on GRE-P is greater than that of GPA-U and HRS-P. Only GPA-P does not have a significant ($p < .05$) influence on GRE-P. This lack of a significant contribution can be attributed to the fact that the GPA-P was equally weighted for all students regardless of the number of course hours it was based on, 3 to 45 hours, and the fact that GPA-U and GPA-P are highly related. The only academic factor not influenced by SAT was HRS-P, which was not unexpected.

SAT not only has the greatest direct effect on GRE-P, it also has an indirect effect on GRE-P, primarily through GPA-U. Whereas the direct effect is given as the simple path coefficient, indirect effects are given by multiplying the path coefficients associated with the academic variables. Therefore, SAT influences GRE-P directly (.52) and also indirectly, through GPA-U (.15). Similarity between SAT and GRE-P in test format and test-taking strategies may be an important source for this direct influence.

Based on these findings, it appears that the Direct/Indirect Model better explains performance on the GRE-P. The relatively small contribution of academic factors found in this study was consistent with previous studies using only graduate students or applicants (Ewen, 1969; Mehrabian, 1969; Stricker & Huber, 1967). This small contribution is surprising, given that the GRE-P is presumably an achievement test based on knowledge accumulated during the undergraduate years. The present study does find that academic factors do contribute significantly, but the fact that SAT directly contributes more to performance on the GRE-P, 27 percent of the total variability, leads one to question the validity of the GRE-P as solely a measure of achievement. It occurred to us that the lower contribution of academic factors to GRE-P performance might be the result of our subjects having completed too few courses in psychology. However, the average student in our sample had completed five upper-level content courses in psychology in addition to Introductory Psychology and a Statistics and Methods course. Virtually all of our students were enrolled in and were near completing one or more additional upper-level psychology courses at the time of testing.

The present study overcame the problem of a restricted sample that was present in previous studies using graduate students or applicants. And, as a result, significant relationships between the GRE-P and the academic factors of GPA-U and HRS-P were found. However, the weakness of these relationships is disturbing, especially when one considers the strength of the relationship between SAT and GRE-P reported in this study (or between overall GRE and GRE-P reported in previous studies). Further research on the influence of undergraduate performance, especially in psychology courses, on the GRE-P is needed. The research to date has not revealed academic factors to be the strongest influence on perfomance on the GRE-P.

References

Bentler, P. M. Multivariate analysis with latent variables: Causal modeling. *Annual Review of Psychology*, 1980, *31*, 419-456.

Dawes, R. M. Graduate admission variables and future success. *Science*, 1975, *187*, 721-723.

DuBois, P. H. Review of the Scholastic Aptitude Test. In O. K. Buros (Ed.), *The seventh mental measurements yearbook*. Highland Park, NJ: Gryphon Press, 1972.

Ewen, R. B. The GRE psychology test as an unobtrusive measure of motivation. *Journal of Applied Psychology*, 1969, *53*, 383-387.

Mehrabian, A. Undergraduate ability factors in relationship to graduate performance. *Educational & Psychological Measurement*, 1969, *29*, 409-419.

SAS User's Guide. Raleigh, NC: SAS Institute, Inc., 1979.

Stricker, G., & Huber, J. T. The graduate record examination and undergraduate grades as predictors of success in graduate school. *Journal of Educational Research*, 1967, *60*, 466-468.

Notes

1. Educational Testing Service reported a mean score of 476 for juniors who took the test between October 1973 and September 1976.
2. We would like to thank DeWayne Moore for his comments and suggestions on an earlier draft of this manuscript.

Relations Between Admission Criteria, Academic Performance, and Professional Performance

Glenn E. Littlepage, David M. Bragg
and James O. Rust
Middle Tennessee State University

Although predictor relationships to on-the-job performance are modest, some leads are found for further work.

Currently, there is intense competition for admission to most graduate programs in psychology (APA, 1976; Kiesler, 1977). In an attempt to select the best candidates, schools have generally found it necessary to screen students on the basis of their past academic performance, achievement test scores, and a variety of other types of information. Although most schools utilize essentially the same types of admission criteria (APA, 1976), the validity evidence indicating the relationship between admission criteria and graduate school performance is not strong and consistent. Furthermore, it has not been clearly demonstrated that the persons selected make the best professional psychologists. Therefore the present study was designed to examine the relationship between various admission criteria, graduate school achievement, and professional success in psychology.

Prediction of Graduate School Performance. Among the information used to screen potential graduate students,

Graduate Record Examination (GRE) verbal, quantitative, and advanced scores, Miller Analogies Test (MAT), undergraduate grade point average (GPA), and letters of recommendation are most common (APA, 1976). These variables have indeed been found to be related to success in many graduate psychology programs (i.e. Psychological Corporation, 1970; Lannholm, Marco, & Schrader, 1968; Lannholm, 1972). However, it is also clear that the predictive utility of the various types of information is highly variable between programs. For example, a summary of MAT scores shows their relation to graduate grades in psychology ranged from .43 in one study to −.23 in another, both satistically reliable (Psychological Corporation, 1970). A similar pattern of results has been found for GRE scores. In a review published by Educational Testing Service (ETS), Lannholm, et al. (1968) show that GRE verbal, quantitative, and advanced scores ranged from moderately positive correlations with psychology graduate school performance (.35, .45, & .35

respectively) to moderately negative correlations (−.28, −.24, and −.35 respectively). Even undergraduate GPA is sometimes unrelated to graduate school performance (Hackman, Wiggins, & Bass, 1970). Thus, the relationship between predictors and psychology graduate school performance is much weaker and much less consistent than selection procedures would seem to indicate. One possible reason is that persons admitted to graduate psychology programs are generally quite homogeneous with respect to the selection measures, severely restricting the range of the measures.

Relation Between Graduate School Performance and Professional Success.
A review of the available literature shows a relatively small number of studies concerning the relationship between academic success and vocational success, and only two studies relating directly to psychology. Lunnenborg (1974) studied recent BA graduates in psychology and found that GPA was not related to employment status (i.e., whether the student was employed on a full time basis, part time, attending school, or unemployed). A study by Hackman, Wiggins, and Bass (1970) examined the relation between both admission-type measures and measures of graduate school success to professional success among former PhD students in psychology at a major university. They found that, of five quantitative measures of graduate school performance, only grades in one of four core courses were predictive of professional success. Overall first year graduate GPA was not related. However, faculty ratings and self-reports were related to post-graduation success. Thus, there is evidence that some aspects of graduate school performance, particularly subjective judgments, are related to professional success.

Relation Between Admission-Type Criteria and Professional Success.
Two studies have correlated admission-type information and professional success; the Hackman, et al. (1970) study mentioned above, and a classic study by Kelly and Fiske (1951). The Kelly and Fiske study examined the professional performance of PhD clinical psychology students in training situations. In that study, more than one hundred potential predictors were used involving intellectual tests, interest tests, personality tests, clinically derived measures, and subjective judgments. Although the specific correlations varied from criterion to criterion, objective tests generally correlated moderately with professional performance. In the 26 years since this classic study, little attention has been directed to determining antecedents of professional success in psychology.

The Hackman, et al. study, (1970) examined the relation of 13 admission-type criteria to professional success. Only two significant positive relations and three significantly negative relations were found. Quality of undergraduate school (r = .43) and the advanced psychology section of the GRE (r = .32) were related to success. Undergraduate GPA in physical science courses, biology courses and number of hours of foreign language courses were negatively related to professional performance.

Two limitations of the Hackman et al. study should be noted. First, as in most studies involving admission criteria, the range of scores on admission criteria was severely limited. Second, the criteria of professional success was rather narrow. It reflected faculty judgments of the former students' jobs six years after admission. This was primarily a measure of the job status, and probably does not reflect an accurate assessment of the quality of performance on the job. The Kelly and Fiske (1951) study, using a variety of professional success criteria, was conducted during a supervised internship, had a somewhat limited range of scores on admission criteria, and is nearly thirty years old.

Because of the lack of research available and the limitations of the previous research, the present study examined the relationships between admission-type criteria, graduate school performance, and professional success among masters level psychology graduate students. The study attempted to correct common limitations of other studies in this area by employing a variety of professional success criteria, and by using as subjects, students from a less selective program, thus allowing a wider range of scores on admission-type variables. Since professional success in psychology has been studied at the bachelors and doctorate level only, a study of masters level psychologists would assess the generality of previous findings to a different level of training.

Method

Subjects. Subjects were graduates from masters programs in the psychology department of a regional state university of about 10,000 students. They had received either a MA degree in Psychology or a ME degree in Guidance and Counseling from the Psychology Department. The degrees were granted between August 1973 and December 1974. Between 6 and 24 months following graduation, questionnaires were sent to 171 potential subjects; 15 were returned for incorrect addresses, so 156 questionnaires presumably reached their subjects. After a reminder letter, 103 questionnaires were returned, 60% of those sent and 66% of those presumably reaching the subjects.

Procedure. Information from the subject questionnaire included a description of their job title, duties, and salary, along with permission to contact their employers and to examine their university and departmental records. The questionnaire also included questions concerning subjects' opinion of their jobs and of their graduate courses; these data were not included in the present study, but are described elsewhere (Bragg, 1976).

Measures of admission-type information were obtained from records. These included graduate GPA, whether the student's undergraduate major was psychology, MAT scores, English Cooperative Test Scores (Educational Testing Service, 1970), and Verbal and Quantitative scores on the GRE. Because they were not required for admission, GRE scores were available for only 24 of the subjects.

Measures of graduate school performance consisted of undergraduate GPA and percentile scores on a comprehensive examination required for the master's degree. An additional measure of graduate school performance was obtained by having each subject rated for "overall academic performance as a graduate student" on a 10 point Likert-type scale (ranging from 1 = poor to 10 = excellent). For most subjects, the student was rated by the thesis advisor, but for 20 subjects this was not possible. They were rated by other faculty members who knew the subject, and were assigned the mean of these ratings.

Responses from the subjects' questionnaires provided information concerning salary, duties and job title. Salary was used as one dependent measure of professional success. Another measure of professional success involved the subjective rating of the quality of the job. Because of the specialized nature of the jobs, established scales of job status such as Roe's (1956) could not be used. Instead, two psychology professors looked at the job title, description of duties and salary and rated each job on a ten point Likert-type scale of "success for Master's level graduates in psychology." A high correlation was found between ratings, $r(99) = .79$, $p < .01$, indicating close agreement between raters. The average of their ratings was a measure of professional success. In order to further assess reliability, three other faculty members independently rated the jobs. The mean correlations between their ratings and the previously attained mean rating was .72. Both salary and this subjective job rating seem to reflect the level of the position obtained by the subject.

A questionnaire was sent to employers of 82 subjects who had given permission to contact their employers. After a follow-up letter, 67 were returned for an 82% return rate. This short questionnaire asked the supervisor to rate his employee on two, five-point Likert-type scales. Scores were labeled as poor, coded 1, to excellent, coded 5. Supervisors responded to the following items: 1. "How would you rate this person's performance in his present job?" 2. "How would you rate this person's potential for advancement?" Thus we had two measures of job performance. A third, overall measure of the supervisor's opinion of the subject was obtained by summing the ratings to these two questions. These three measures reflect performance on the job.

Of the several measures of the subject's professional performance obtained, some seem to reflect the status or quality of employment, whereas others seem to indicate the competence and professionalism with which the subject accomplishes the job. Since both are thought to be important aspects of professional job performance, one final composite index of job performance was created to reflect equally these two components. This composite rating was obtained by summing the subjective job rating which indicated the level of the job, and the sum of the supervisor's ratings which measured how well the subject was performing his job duties. Thus, a subject receiving a high score would have a high quality job and would be performing at a high level.

Results

Prediction of Graduate School Success. Table 1 shows the correlations between screening measures used to select applicants for graduate school and various measures of graduate school performance. Significant correlations were found between both the MAT, and undergraduate psychology major and all three measures of graduate school success. All other admissions measures were related to at least one success measure. GRE verbal, while showing a significant correlation to only the comprehensive exam scores, had correlations above .32 for the other two measures, but perhaps because of the small number of persons

Table 1
Correlations of Preadmission Variables With Graduate School Performance

Predictor	Graduate GPA	Comprehensive Exam %ile	Professors' Rating of Grad School Performance
Miller Analogies Test	.277* (73)	.512** (78)	.313** (71)
GRE Verbal	.358 (23)	.495* (24)	.323 (23)
GRE Quantitative	.456* (23)	.319 (24)	.092 (23)
English Cooperative	.056 (96)	.275** (102)	.010 (94)
Undergraduate GPA	.019 (79)	.216* (85)	−.038 (78)
Undergraduate Psych Major	.235* (97)	.201* (103)	.243* (95)

The N for each correlation is given in parentheses.
*$p < .05$
**$p < .01$

with these scores, they were not significantly related to the other success measures.

Predictors of Professional Success. Ninety-two respondents were working full time at various jobs. Five were currently working toward advanced degrees, five were seeking employment, and one had other means of support.

The major purpose of this study was to determine what correlations exist between screening measures, graduate school performance and various criteria of professional success. Correlations between the various independent variables and the six criterion measures of professional success are listed in Table 2.

MAT scores, undergraduate psychology major, and professors' rating of graduate school performance were all predictive of the composite measure of professional success. In addition, GRE verbal showed a correlation to overall success higher than any of the other predictors; however, because of the limited number of GRE scores, this correlation did not reach conventional levels of significance. In sum, the composite rating of professional success was moderately related to some of the admissions criteria, and one measure of graduate school performance (See Table 2).

Since professional success depends both upon the nature of the position and the performance level in the position, these two aspects will be considered separately. Correlations between job level measures and job performance measures were all small and non-significant, indicating that these are two relatively independent factors in professional success. Salary did not correlate with either present performance, $r(67) = -.02$, ns, or potential, $r(67) = .03$, ns. Similarly, the subjective job rating was unrelated to present performance, $r(67) = .09$, ns, and potential $r(67) = .12$, ns.

Two measures of level of the job were available: salary and the faculty rating of the job quality. Salary was not significantly related to any of the independent variables, but faculty job rating was related to undergraduate psychology

Table 2
Correlations Between Predictors and Professional Success

Predictor	Job Level		Performance			
	Faculty Subjective Job Rating	Salary	Employer Questionnaire Ratings			Composite Job Success
			Performance	Potential	Sum	
Miller Analogies Test	.107 (78)	.109 (76)	.328* (49)	.329* (49)	.353** (49)	.282* (49)
English Cooperative	−.027 (102)	.181 (100)	−.039 (66)	.191 (66)	.093 (66)	.172 (66)
GRE Verbal	.114 (24)	.186 (24)	.165 (17)	.389 (17)	.301 (17)	.336 (17)
GRE Quantitative	−.023 (24)	−.067 (24)	.028 (17)	.190 (17)	.118 (17)	.163 (17)
Undergraduate GPA	−.118 (85)	−.106 (84)	.231 (55)	.285* (55)	.288* (55)	.047 (55)
Undergraduate Psych Major	.332** (103)	−.028 (101)	−.012 (67)	.007 (67)	−.002 (67)	.297* (67)
Graduate GPA	.173 (97)	.120 (95)	.181 (64)	.224 (64)	.225 (64)	.187 (64)
Comprehensive Exam %ile	.234* (103)	.018 (101)	.043 (67)	.336* (67)	.218 (67)	.145 (67)
Professors' Rating of Academic Ability	.273** (95)	.149 (93)	.069 (64)	.144 (64)	.120 (64)	.301* (64)

The N for each correlation is given in parentheses.
* .05 level
** .01 level

major, comprehensive exam percentile, and professors' rating of graduate school performance (See Table 2).

Performance Level was measured by two questions answered by the supervisors. These revealed the supervisor's rating of the subject's present level of job performance ($M=4.21$, $SD=.70$) and potential for advancement ($M=4.19$, $SD=.78$). Because of the limited range of the supervisor's scales, correlations with level of job performance measures might be somewhat constricted. Current job performance was related to only MAT, but potential was related to MAT scores, undergraduate GPA, and comprehensive exam percentile rank. GRE verbal showed a higher correlation with advancement potential than any of the other predictors, but because of the small number of GRE scores, was not statistically reliable. The sum of these two performance ratings was significantly related to MAT scores and undergraduate GPA. A moderate but nonsignificant relationship with GRE verbal was observed. Thus, there is evidence that admission criteria are moderately related to the quality of on-the-job performance (See Table 2).

Discussion

Results indicate that the various admission measures were related to performance in graduate school. Although most of the admission criteria were not related to all measures of graduate school success (graduate GPA, comprehensive exam percentiles, and professors' ratings), each admission variable was related to at least one of these graduate school success measures. Although the various predictors relate to different aspects of graduate school performance, all are positively associated with some aspect of success in graduate school. Thus, at least for this pro-

gram, the admission criteria have a measure of validity. However, the inconsistent findings of previous research suggest that these positive relationships do not generalize to all programs.

It appears that for masters level psychology graduates, professional performance is a multidimensional concept which reflects both the level of the job and the level of performance on the job. These two dimensions were not correlated and show a different pattern of relationships with admission and graduate school success measures. It appears that attempts to assess professional success should use multidimensional measurement criteria.

Job level was assessed by salary and a subjective rating. Salary was unrelated to any of the admission or graduate school success measures. The job level rating was related to three predictors, (a) majoring in psychology as an undergraduate, (b) comprehensive exam percentiles, and (c) professors' rating of graduate school performance. These three predictors seem to reflect the amount of the students' knowledge of psychology. Thus, it appears that the level of the job attained is related to knowledge of the field of study. The positive correlation between job level and faculty ratings of the students' graduate school performance might indicate that professors' opinions, through letters of recommendation and informal contacts, influence the students' job prospects. These faculty ratings of students gain some validity since they relate to two other measures of knowledge of the subject matter. Thus it appears that professors' impressions are consistent with other measures of knowledge and are related to the level of the job the subject attains. Hackman, et al. (1970) had also found that faculty ratings of students were related to their job levels.

It should be noted that neither undergraduate nor graduate grades are related to the quality of job attained. This result is consistent with findings for undergraduate psychology majors (Lunnenborg, 1974), PhD psychologists (Hackman, et al. 1970), and for graduates of other fields (i.e. Hoyt, 1965, Muchinsky & Hoyt, 1973). As others have noted, grades tend to be poor predictors probably because of restricted range and uneven grading standards. Hackman et al. (1970) also found that GRE-quantitative scores were related to their rating of job success. Their criterion corresponds most closely to the job level rating in this study, but in the present study, none of the standardized test scores were related to job level.

Once on the job, potential for advancement was related to various admissions criteria as well as to comprehensive examination percentile. Thus, it seems that the admissions criteria have some validity as predictors of the quality of professional performance. Professionals who were judged by their employers to exhibit high potential for advancement tended to score high on several admissions measures.

The level of validity exhibited by the prediction instruments, although encouraging, may not hold for all specialty areas and for all levels of training. There are no other studies among psychologists which relate admissions criteria to post-graduation measures of on-the-job performance. Results from industrial settings fail to show a consistent pattern between admission-type criteria and level of job performance (ETS, 1970). Therefore, research assessing the generality of these finding to other programs, various specialties, and various levels of training is needed.

This study found several variables significantly related to professional success among masters level psychologists. However, correlations with both admission criteria and graduate school performance were relatively small. Although multiple predictors could be expected to increase the predictive utility of these measures to some degree, it seems that they would still account for a relatively small portion of the variance in professional success. Thus, how can prediction be improved? One possible route for future research is to shift from the current conceptual model underlying graduate selection. This model has been described as a unidimensional talent model (Willingham, Note 1). Willingham has suggested a selection model based on more specific criteria. That is, a prototype of the kinds of professionals hoped for by the department could be developed along with specific indicators of professional success appropriate to that model. Then, intermediate criteria of graduate school performance, and finally predictor variables could be identified. Such an approach clearly requires much work, (e.g. Kelly & Fiske, 1951) but psychologists have designed sophisticated selection procedures for other professions, such as maintenance mechanics, communica-

tions consultants, and middle management (e.g., Bray & Campbell, 1968; Bray & Grant, 1966; Champion, 1972). Surely the selection and training of psychologists deserves at least as much thought.

References

American Psychological Association. *Graduate study in psychology, 1977-78.* Washington, DC: Author, 1976.

Bragg, D. M. *Job success and its correlation to various academic measures for master's recipients.* Unpublished master's thesis, Middle Tennessee State University, 1976.

Bray, D. W., & Campbell, R. J. Selection of salesmen by means of an assessment center. *Journal of Applied Psychology*, 1968, *52,* 36-41.

Bray, D. W., & Grant, D. L. The assessment center in the measurement of potential for business management. *Psychological Monographs*, 1966, *80,* (17, Whole No. 625).

Champion, J. E. Work sampling for personnel selection. *Journal of Applied Psychology*, 1972, *56,* 40-44.

Educational Testing Service. Cooperative English Examination (1970 Revision). New York: Author, 1970.

Hackman, J. R., Wiggins, N., & Bass, A. R. Prediction of long-term success in doctoral work in psychology. *Educational and Psychological Measurement*, 1970, *30,* 365-374.

Hoyt, D. P. The relationship between college grades and adult achievement: A review of the literature. *ACT Research Reports* (No. 7). Iowa City: American College Testing Program, 1965.

Kelly, E. L., & Fiske, D. W. *The prediction of performance in clinical psychology.* Ann Arbor, MI: University of Michigan Press, 1951.

Kiesler, C. A. The training of psychiatrists and psychologists. *American Psychologist*, 1977, *32,* 107-108.

Lannholm, G. V. *Summaries of GRE validity studies 1966-1970.* Graduate Record Examinations Special Report 72-1. Princeton, NJ: Educational Testing Service, 1972.

Lannholm, G. V., Marco, G. L., & Schrader, W. B. *Cooperative studies of predicting graduate school success.* Graduate Record Examinations Special Report 68-3. Princeton, NJ: Educational Testing Service, 1968.

Lunnenborg, P. W. Can college graduates in psychology find employment in their field? *Vocational Guidance Quarterly*, 1974, *23,* 159-166.

Muchinsky, P. M., & Hoyt, D. P. Academic grades as a predictor of occupational success among engineering graduates. *Measurement and Evaluation in Guidance*, 1973, *6,* 93-103.

Psychological Corporation. *Miller Analogies Test Manual* (1970 Revision). New York: Author, 1970.

Roe, A. *The Psychology of occupations.* New York: Wiley, 1956.

Notes

1. Willingham, W. W. Predicting success in graduate education. In Educational Testing Service. *Papers presented at the Graduate Record Examinations Board research seminar at the 12th annual meeting of the Council of Graduate Schools.* Princeton, NJ: Author, 1973.

2. The authors are grateful to Dr. Willard Kerr and Dr. Robert Aden for their assistance and cooperation in obtaining graduate school admission and performance measures.

3. This paper is based on the second author's masters thesis (Bragg, 1976) from Middle Tennessee State University.

The Clinical Bias in the Career Plans of Undergraduates and Its Impact on Students and the Profession

James H. Korn and
Marie E. Lewandowski
Saint Louis University

From a survey study, it is concluded
that career advisement of undergraduates
needs to be expanded and improved.

Every year in the spring, psychology teachers all over the country encounter students like this one: He enters your office looking sad, not his usual enthusiastic self ("good verbal skills, works well in a group"). You hope he wants to discuss his excellent term paper ("writes well, creative approach to research, good data analysis skills"). However, as you feared, he says, "I was rejected by all six schools: Minnesota, Missouri, Iowa. . . .Even my back-up school turned me down. Now what do I do?"

This student wanted to be a clinical psychologist. He was a good student, but apparently not good enough. His GRE scores were in the 500 range and he had only a few B and C grades on his transcript. The ability and motivation were there and you tried to emphasize that in your letter of recommendation. This student and others like him might have become good psychologists. Now he'll go into retail sales or hospital administration or some other field where he can use his human service skills. He will survive and both of you will get over your disappointment, but we think this student exemplifies a problem that must be addressed. It is a problem for students and for the profession. The purpose of this paper is to investigate the extent and source of this problem and to argue that the solution is largely the responsibility of psychology teachers.

The data which brought this problem to our attention were the imbalance in undergraduate applications to psychology graduate programs. Clinical applications outnumber others by a factor of about five. Furthermore, it is much less likely that a student will be admitted to clinical or counseling programs than to other psychology graduate programs. We have labeled this situation as a "clinical bias" to reflect our hypothesis that students underestimate career opportunities in nonclinical areas of psychology. Furthermore, we suggest this bias exists because of the popular image of psychologist as clinician, an image which has not been corrected by undergraduate education.

Why is it an important problem? First, because it produces unreasonable psychological pain for our students: self actualization is blocked, they are frustrated and angry, identity is threatened, there is a feeling of failure, the future is uncertain, considerable time is seen as wasted. This pain may be prevented or reduced. In our discussion we will suggest how prevention might be done both in and out of the classroom.

There is also a problem for the profession. We may be losing large numbers of persons who have the potential for making a contribution to the promotion of human welfare. We are familiar with the argument that the profession of psychology is overcrowded and the only jobs available may be for clinicians and eventually even those will be hard to find. At the same time we see a wide range of human needs that are not being adequately served and could best be served by persons with graduate training in areas other than clinical psychology. Poverty, desegregation, aging and pollution demand the knowledge and skills of developmental, social, educational and other applied psychologists. An APA publication discusses these career opportunities in some detail (Woods, 1976). Teachers of psychology should convey these opportunities to their students.

The clinical bias in applications to graduate programs was documented by Nyman (1973). After statistically controlling for the fact that students make multiple applications to graduate programs, Nyman computed candidate/acceptance ratios of 4.6 for clinical and 2.4 for counseling programs. "Another way of looking at these figures underlines the observation that clinical psychology turns away from its doors close to 80% of the candidate population, and counseling psychology rejects close to 60%. . . ." (Nyman, 1973, p. 934). The ratio for clinical psychology was higher than the 2.7 computed for medical school candidates.

The present study provides more recent information on applications and admissions into graduate programs in both clinical and non-clinical psychology as reported in *Graduate Study in Psychology 1979-1980*. In addition, a survey was conducted to determine the average number of psychology programs to which students apply and to explore certain variables related to the application process which may give a possible explanation for the disproportionate number of applicants to clinical and counseling programs. The study attempts to increase the awareness of the realities of graduate admissions and the range of opportunities for graduate study in psychology beyond the clinical/counseling options.

Method. Seventy first-year graduate students in psychology at Saint Louis University, Vanderbilt University, Washington University, and University of Missouri at Columbia voluntarily completed a two-page anonymous questionnaire.

The questionnaire asked students to give their current area of specialization, the areas of psychology in which they made graduate school applications during the previous year, and the number of acceptances received in each area. They also were asked which of fourteen sources were responsible for their interest in a career in psychology. Distribution of the questionnaires was made through the department chairperson at each of the four universities. Completed surveys were returned to that office and forwarded to us for data processing.

A random sample of 33 graduate psychology departments in which there was an APA-approved clinical program was taken from *Graduate Study in Psychology* for 1979-80 to obtain information on number of applications and acceptances in clinical, counseling and other areas of graduate study in each department.

Results. The areas of specialization for the 70 students who completed the survey were clinical (33), counseling (7), personality/social (10), school (4), physiological (3), perception (3), evaluative-applied (3), developmental (2), cognitive/learning (2), general experimental (2), and teaching (1).

The means, ranges and ratios of applications and acceptances for the current study and for Nyman (1973) are presented in Table 1. Nyman's department data came from a survey of APA-approved clinical programs, whereas in the current study we used the APA *Graduate Study* book. Although the number of applications reported for 1979 is lower than that for 1973, the number of acceptances changed less, resulting in lower application/acceptance ratios. Nyman did not report data for non-clinical/counseling programs. It is clear that in 1979 the number of applications, acceptances and the ratio is much lower for these other programs.

Table 1 also presents information on number of applications per student.[1] The current study surveyed students at four universities. Nyman surveyed one. Candidate/acceptance ratios were computed by dividing mean applications/department by mean applications/student, then dividing the result by mean acceptances/department. The ratios computed in our study are less than half the size obtained by Nyman, although the ratio for clinical is still the largest.

When asked to indicate what their most preferred choice was as a senior undergraduate for graduate work, 80% of the clinical/counseling students reported it was their current area of psychology, 12.5% listed graduate work in another area of psychology (clinical, educational, developmental, and general/experimental), and 7.5% listed other. Of the 30 non-clinical students, 57% listed their current area as first choice, 37% indicated graduate work in another area of psychology and 6% listed graduate work in an area other than psychology (e.g. sociology) or other.

The number of students indicating specific sources as responsible for their interest in a psychology career is presented in Table 2. Clinical and counseling students were more influenced by work experience and practicing psy-

Table 2. Number of Students Indicating Specific Sources as Responsible for Interest in Psychology Career[1]

Source	Clinical and Counseling (N=40)	Other (N=30)
Psychology teacher in high school	6	5
Psychology teacher in college	12	16
Psychology teacher or advisor outside of course	8	9
Course material or content	15	12
Guidance counselor	1	0
Practicing psychologist	15	3
Work or volunteer experience	21	10
Information from the APA	2	2
Reading	7	4
TV or movies	1	0
Parent	2	2
Other relative	3	2
Friend	6	5
Other source	2	1

[1]Each student could indicate more than one source.

Table 1. Means, Ranges and Ratios of Applications and Acceptances
For the Current Study and for Nyman (1973)

Variable	Nyman (1973)		Korn & Lewandowski (1979)		
	Clinical	Counseling	Clinical	Counseling	Other
Applications/Dept.[1]					
N	42	9	29	15	33
Mean	456	204	256	151	24
Range	175-1349	50-360	119-600	67-300	3-274
Acceptances/Dept.					
Mean	13.3	11.6	10.6	14.5	9.2
Range	6-33	6-24	4-34	4-2	
Applications/ Acceptances	34.3	17.6	24.2	10.4	2.6
Applications/Student[2]					
N	40	—	33	7	30
Mean	7.4	—	13.0	6.7	5.0
Range	1-19	—	2-30	1-20	1-15
Candidate Acceptance Ratio	4.6	2.4	1.9	1.6	0.5

[1]Nyman's data for Departments were obtained by a survey of APA approved clinical and counseling training programs. The Korn & Lewandowski data are from *Graduate Study in Psychology 1979-80*.
[2]Nyman's data for students are from a survey of graduate students and senior undergraduates at one university. Korn & Lewandowski surveyed first-year graduate students at four universities.

chologists than were students in other areas. Many students in both groups indicated teachers and advisors as significant sources of influence.

Discussion.   There is a problem, although it is less severe than Nyman's 1973 data indicated. Our candidate/acceptance ratio for clinical psychology suggests that at least half the students who apply to clinical programs do not get into any program. That means there are hundreds of rejected students, most of whom are lost to the profession. This may be a conservative estimate since it is based on the average number of applications of a sample of students who were successful in gaining admission to graduate study. Students who do not make it may apply to fewer schools. If so, our estimate of applications per student is too high and our candidate/acceptance ratios are too low.

Compared to 1973, a much larger proportion of students applying to graduate school in psychology are being accepted. This appears to be primarily a function of a decrease in the number of applications. Although the growth in the popularity of psychology as a major has leveled off, it has not declined. Perhaps undergraduate majors have gotten the message that if you are admitted to graduate school in psychology, you won't get a job after you get a PhD. They also have heard that although there are lots of jobs for clinical psychologists, it's very hard to get into clinical graduate programs. This negative view of the future could account for the decline in applications from a total pool which has not been shrinking. The prediction for the 1980s, of course, is that the pool *will* shrink. What will happen to our ratios then?

Clinical psychology remains the most popular field for graduate school applicants and the most difficult one in which to be accepted. At one major university, 42% of all psychology majors hoped to enter a career in clinical or counseling psychology (Malin & Timmreck, 1979). We wonder how much these students know about what clinicians do and how students might otherwise achieve their career goals. Perhaps this is an expression of the popular image of the psychologist as psychotherapist. What PhD psychologist, clinical or experimental, has disclosed her/his occupation at a party and not been told, "I bet you want to psychoanalyze me." The nature and impact of this cultural image needs further investigation.

Many of the clinical and counseling students in our survey might have been quite knowledgeable about the field of their choice. They said that the common sources of their interest in psychology as a career were practicing psychologists and work experience. A selection bias may be operating here, however. These are students who made it into graduate programs, based in part on their experience and recommendations. We also would like to know why they sought specific work experiences and contacts. Perhaps they were seeking confirmation of an interest in clinical work that developed earlier.

In nonclinical areas it appears that if students with reasonable credentials apply to enough programs, they are certain to be accepted. This is a bad news, good news situation. The bad news is that as a profession we have not figured out how to help graduate students achieve both educational and employment goals, especially in the areas of experimental psychology. A capable student who is excited by the study of perception should be able to pursue that interest in spite of the fact of limited academic employment possibilities, *but* with some preparation for employment in non-academic settings.

The good news for undergraduates who pursue the nonclinical route is that employment opportunities are excellent in many areas such as industrial psychology. program evaluation and school psychology. Students who want to help people can do so. Although they cannot do one-on-one psychotherapy without a clinical degree, they can have an impact on many more people in a large organization than by seeing one patient an hour. If money is the motive, the various consulting fields are quite lucrative.

Other frequently listed sources of interest in psychology as a career both for clinical students and others were teachers and other people. To what extent are these people aware of the opportunities that exist outside of clinical psychology? If their awareness is so low, their good advice will contribute to the clinical bias. Recent publications from the APA Central Office present a realistic and more optimistic picture of the non-clinical job market and should be useful to undergraduate advisors (Fretz & Stang, 1980; Woods, 1976, 1979). Few of the students in our sample were directly influenced by material from APA.

The burden of solving the clinical bias problem is on undergraduate teachers of psychology. They must be made aware of the opportunities in the nonclinical applied psychology fields. Given this awareness, they must present the opportunities to undergraduates in their classes and in their role as advisors. Undergraduates can be encouraged to accept field placements in settings which will expand their awareness of career opportunities. Guest speakers can be brought to the classroom to provide information and examples of career alternatives.

Having provided information about the positive and negative aspects of career opportunities in psychology, the undergraduate teacher should encourage good students to prepare for graduate study. Our definition of "good student" goes beyond grades and GRE scores. Equally important criteria are motivation for graduate work, human relations skills, communication ability, and successful experience in working with people. These characteristics are not measured by the GRE. Excessive reliance on the GRE may result in the "loss" to the profession of many highly competent persons. This is the kind of student mentioned in the introduction to this paper. As teachers we have great confidence in the ability of these students to succeed in graduate school. High GRE "cut off" scores prevent them from even being considered.

Our data indicate that good students who want to make a contribution to the promotion of human welfare can be admitted to graduate study. Although the likelihood of acceptance to nonclinical programs is greater, the process of preparation for graduate study is just as difficult. Fretz and Stang (1980) have provided students and their advisors with an excellent discussion of this process. They emphasize that it is important for a student to begin the process early in one's college career. We wish to emphasize how important it is for faculty to help students become aware of the range of opportunities open to them in psychology. This awareness, coupled with information gained through reading and experience, may reduce the possibility of rejection for students and the loss of human resources to the profession of psychology.

Summary. We have argued that applications to graduate programs indicate a clinical bias which has a negative impact on undergraduates and on the profession of psychology. Although the proportion of applicants being accepted into graduate programs is greater now than in 1973, clinical psychology continues to account for the greatest number of applicants and rejections. Students must be made aware of training programs and employment opportunities in nonclinical fields.

References

American Psychological Association. *Graduate study in psychology, 1979-1980.* Washington, DC: American Psychological Association, 1978.

Fretz, B. R., & Stang, D. J. *Preparing for graduate study in psychology: Not for seniors only!* Washington, DC: American Psychological Association, 1980.

Malin, J. T., & Timmreck, C. Student goals and the undergraduate curriculum. *Teaching of Psychology,* 1979, *6,* 136-139.

Nyman, L. Some odds on getting into PhD programs in clinical and counseling psychology. *American Psychologist,* 1973, *28,* 934-935.

Woods, P. J. *Career opportunities for psychologists: Expanding and emerging areas.* Washington, DC: American Psychological Association, 1976.

Woods, P. J. *The psychology major: Training and employment strategies.* Washington, DC American Psychological Association, 1979.

Notes

1. As a reliability check, first-year graduate students at Saint Louis University in 1980 were asked to indicate the number of programs to which they applied. The mean number of applications for eight clinical students was 12.5; for five non-clinical students the mean was 3.8.

Commentary: Advising Students About Graduate Work

Dennis C. Wright and Donald H. Kausler
University of Missouri

Recently we have observed two interesting phenomena that we believe to be related. First, the number of applicants for admission to our graduate program in experimental psychology was incredibly low this year. What makes this year so remarkable is that it follows several years in which we expected the decline in number of applicants to "bottom out." We also had expected that the declining quality of applicants would have bottomed-out. It didn't. When we consider transcripts, recommendations, GREs, MATs, and GPAs, we discover that many of this year's applicants we rated "Do accept with stipend" would have not made it to our "second alternate" list ten years ago. After a brief period of stubbornly maintaining standards, we've changed.

We think this startling result is not unique to our department. We think so because we've lost some of those "accept" applicants to better offers from other departments competing with us for potential students in what seems to be an impoverished talent pool. In short, there appears to be fierce competition for even marginal (e.g., combined Quant Verbal GRE of 800) students.

Could all this be because undergraduates have been steered away from graduate school in experimental? Have horror stories about "the job market" played a role?

The undergraduates in our classes seem no less bright and no less eager to do research than in the past. Have we stopped telling undergraduates "you're good and you should pursue a career as a teacher/scientist"?

Second, the number of recent PhD applicants to our department for an open faculty position in experimental this year was incredibly low. Although some of those applicants possessed outstanding qualifications, most did not. The faculty position will remain open. Our "better than ever" offers to the best applicants got bettered elsewhere.

You doubtless now see why we believe that these phenomena may be related. When the quantity and quality of new graduate students is lowered, the quantity and quality of new PhDs must drop within a predictable time span. We can guess why this has happened.

In the early '70s we responded to what looked to be a declining job market in academe by reducing the number of entrants to that market. Many schools instituted voluntary "birth control" measures by reducing the number of students admitted to their experimental psychology programs. This voluntary reduction led to relatively tough standards for admission. Undergraduates got the word and also began to hear about the imminent death of academe. Applications dropped (and eventually, so did standards). The "birth control" has now become involuntary. The problem is real for all of us.

If our hypothesis is correct, we should be telling good undergraduate students that in many experimental psychology graduate programs the demand for good students currently far exceeds supply. Let them know that there are some who believe that graduate school in experimental psychology still can be a delightful, thrilling experience and the entrée to a rewarding career. Tell them that good people can get jobs in academe and that research funds do exist. Above all, tell the very best that they represent the future for graduate and undergraduate education in psychology, and the continuation of psychology as a science.

James Scheirer wrote this article while working for the American Psychological Association. He discussed the professional school movement, the difference between PsyD and P hD degrees, and the implications of accrediting programs. Readers and their students will find the author's description of the Boulder Model and the practitioner-oriented programs instructive. One can also learn about the characteristics of professional school programs. The details about quality indicators and accreditation are particularly important. In the final analysis, students can use this article to help in deciding which type of program is for them.

David Cole, now retired from Occidental College, surveyed professional schools to determine their perceptions about the priorities used in selecting graduate students, particularly those factors that relate to undergraduate training. The results will encourage students enrolled in a program that emphasizes traditional courses in psychology and field training.

Professional Schools: Information for Students and Advisors

C. James Scheirer
American Psychological Association

These graduate programs emphasize the public practice of psychology, often offer a different degree, and they give less emphasis to research.

Many undergraduate students aspire to careers in the delivery of professional psychological services. There is little systematic information available, however, on educational alternatives leading to such careers. In particular many academic advisors have little familiarity with the "professional school" programs specifically oriented to training psychological practitioners. The purpose of this paper is to fill that gap with a discussion of professional schools and the professional school movement. Here professional school refers to a program, department, or school whose avowed mission is to train students to deliver psychological services. The term "professional" used in this manner refers to the service delivery aspect of the program, and is not meant to imply that other schools are non-professional.

Most psychologists involved in training and advising undergraduates were themselves trained in so-called Boulder-model, or scientist-practitioner model, programs (Raimy, 1950) that stress training in research skills. This is necessarily the case because professional schools, also called Vail-model programs (Korman, 1976), are relatively new and because graduates of professional schools tend to go into service delivery areas of psychology and not into academe. Therefore, it seems particularly critical to make accurate, up-to-date information on professional schools available so that students can make educational choices on an informed basis. It is hoped that this article can be a resource both for students considering application to doctoral programs in professional psychology, and to faculty advising these students.

I will discuss the professional school movement as an alternative to more traditional models of training; the difference between the PsyD and PhD degree; and the implications of accreditation, both regional and specialized, for quality of programs. This paper is intended as a discussion of doctoral training in professional psychology; nondoctoral programs are not discussed because there is little systematic knowledge about these programs. For this reason the Education and Training Board (E&T) of the American Psychological Association (APA), through its Committee on Graduate Education, is currently collecting data in this area. It should also be noted that it is the policy of APA that the doctoral degree is the minimum standard for the independent, unsupervised direct delivery of professional services. This policy is consistent with most state licensing laws.

The Boulder and Vail Models of Professional Education. The traditional model for the training of professional psychologists is referred to as the scientist/practitioner model, or the Boulder Model, after the Conference on the Training of Clinical Psychologists held in Boulder, Colorado in 1949 (Raimy, 1950). That conference systematized the training of psychologists. Taking into account the nascent state of the science, the Boulder Conference proposed that all clinical psychologists be trained as both scientists *and* practitioners. The conference provided a major step in the definition of psychology as a profession, and the model proposed was widely adopted as the training model for professional psychologists.

A program in the science/practitioner model trains professionals to function both as scientists (i.e., to do basic research) *and* as practitioners (i.e., to deliver psychological services). Training thus includes both rigorous scientific training as well as professional training. Normally, early in their graduate career, a student begins to work with a professor, the mentor, in an apprenticeship role for the purpose of learning how to do research. This apprentice relationship for scientific training generally continues through the student's graduate career. Concurrently, the student takes professionally oriented courses and engages in research training. The science/practitioner model is consistent with the theoretical position that psychology is a scientific discipline and, as such, has a major responsibility to develop new knowledge. The Boulder Model assumes that their scientific training will incline students toward research activities, while their professional training will orient this research toward more applied areas.

For many years, the science/practitioner model, as defined by the Boulder Conference, was the major model of training of doctoral-level professional psychologists. This model was reaffirmed as the appropriate training model at a conference in Chicago in 1965 (Hoch, Ross, & Winder, 1966). But, in spite of the formal acceptance of the Boulder Model of training, criticisms of the model increased over the post-war years. The Chicago Conference had proved divisive even though eventually the scientist-practitioner model had been supported. Criticism of the scientist/practitioner model centered around several issues. Briefly these issues were:

(1) Boulder Model programs produced too few practitioners to meet mental health needs. For example, in the early sixties less than 20 PhD clinical psychologists were being produced in the entire state of California each year (Peterson, 1982).

(2) It was argued that the scientist/practitioner programs did not train either scientists or practitioners well, nor did it capitalize on student interests and strengths. There was simply not enough time to train students competently in both the scientific and the applied aspects of psychology.

(3) Students from Boulder Model programs were not providing research to advance the field. The modal number of publications among such PhDs was zero (Levy, 1962).

(4) The practitioner part of the scientist/practitioner model was being short-changed. The academics who trained professionals were scientists first, and had little desire to produce practitioners.

These arguments formed the logical basis for the development of programs whose primary purpose was to train psychologists specifically for professional practice. (For a more detailed discussion of the history of the professional school movement see Peterson [1982], from which this outline is drawn, or Fox [1982].).

The first of the practitioner-oriented programs was established in the Department of Psychology at Adelphi University in 1951; this program later became Adelphi's Institute of Advanced Psychological Studies. In 1968 the Department of

Table 1. Professional Schools Known to APA, and Selected Information

School[1]	Accred. Status[2]	NCSPP Mem.[3]	Degree Offered
Adelphi University, Institute of Advanced Psychological Studies	APA	Yes, A	PhD
Antioch/New England Graduate School	Reg.	Yes, C	PsyD
Baylor University	APA	No	PsyD
California Graduate Institute	No	Yes, C	PhD
California Institute of Integral Studies (Formerly California Institute of Asian Studies)	Reg.	No	PhD
California School of Professional Psychology, Berkeley	Reg.	Yes, A	PhD
California School of Professional Psychology, Fresno	Reg.	Yes, A	PhD
California School of Professional Psychology, Los Angeles	APA	Yes, A	PhD
California School of Professional Psychology, San Diego	APA	Yes, A	PhD
Caribbean Center for Advanced Studies (San Juan)	Reg.	Yes, A	PhD
Chicago School of Professional Psychology	Reg.	Yes, B	PsyD
Central Michigan University	Reg.	No	PsyD
University of Denver, School of Professional Psychology	APA	Yes, A	PsyD
Fielding Institute	Reg.	Yes, A	PhD
Florida Institute of Technology, School of Professional Psychology	Reg.	Yes, A	PhD & PsyD
Forest Institute of Professional Psychology	Reg.	Yes, A	PsyD
Fuller Theological Seminary	APA	Yes, A	PhD
Hahneman Medical College and Hospital	APA	No	PsyD
Hawaii School of Professional Psychology	No	Yes, C	PsyD
Humanistic Psychology Institute	Reg.	No	PhD
Illinois School of Professional Psychology	Reg.	Yes, A	PsyD
Indiana State University	Reg.	Yes, C	PhD
Massachusetts School of Professional Psychology	Reg.	Yes, B	PsyD
New York University	Reg.	No	PsyD
Northwestern University Medical School	APA	No	PhD
Nova University School of Professional Psychology	Reg.	Yes, C	PhD & PsyD
Oregon Graduate School of Professional Psychology	Cand.	Yes, C	PsyD
Pace University	Reg.	No	PsyD
Psychological Studies Institute	No	Yes, C	PhD
Rosemead Graduate School of Professional Psychology	APA	Yes, A	PhD & PsyD
Rutgers University, School of Applied and Professional Psychology	APA	Yes, A	PsyD
United States International University	Reg.	No	PhD
Virginia Consortium for Professional Psychology	Reg.	Yes, A	PsyD
Wisconsin School of Professional Psychology	Cand.	Yes, C	PsyD
Wright Institute, Berkeley	Reg.	No	PhD
Wright State University, School of Professional Psychology	APA	Yes, A	PsyD
Yeshiva University, School of Professional Psychology	Reg.	Yes, A	PsyD

[1]Addresses for schools can be obtained by writing to Educational Affairs Office, American Psychological Association, 1200 17th Street, NW, Washington, DC 20036, or see Graduate Study in Psychology.
[2]APA = APA accreditation; Reg. = regional accreditation; Cand. = candidate for regional accreditation
[3]Membership in National Council of Schools of Professional Psychology; A = full; B = associate; C = affiliate

Psychology at the University of Illinois became the first professional program to offer the PsyD degree. In 1973, programs oriented specifically to the training of professional psychologists were "approved" at a conference in Vail, Colorado. At that conference it was stated that, "...psychological science has sufficiently nurtured to justify creation of explicitly professional programs" (Korman, 1976). According to the most recent list available to APA, presented in Table 1, there are now 37 professional school programs in psychology in the United States and Puerto Rico which are either regionally accredited or are members of the National Council of Schools of Professional Psychology (see below). A major source of the growth of professional schools has been the number of qualified, but unsuccessful, applicants to clinical programs in more traditional graduate schools of psychology. It has been estimated by the Council of Directors of Clinical Training in Psychology that there are about six applications for each admission, corrected for multiple applications, to graduate school in clinical psychology. The corresponding number for medical school is 2.5 (Note 1).

Practitioner-model schools exist in many settings. One is in a medical school; one is based in a consortium of three graduate schools and a medical school; one is in a theological seminary; whereas most are based in universities, either in Departments of Psychology or as separate Schools of Professional Psychology. Over the past decade a number of free-standing professional schools, with no formal affiliation with other organizations, have developed. All, however, have as their primary purpose the training of professional psychologists. A discussion of the implications of organizational context can be found in Peterson (Note 2).

Characteristics of Professional School Programs. As is true with graduate training programs in general, there are substantial differences among individual professional programs. Thus, any student interested in investigating the possibility of admission to a specific program should write to that school for a catalog and associated documents. In addition, several professional school models and the theory behind them are discussed in Caddy, Rimm, Watson, & Johnson (1982). This book also provides several background chapters on the development of professional schools. Another excellent resource focusing on current issues in professional psychology is McNamara and Barclay (1982). Fulcher (Note 3) and Stapp (Note 4) present summaries and overviews of doctoral production in health-science areas. Finally, students should be aware that most states require professional psychologists to be licensed. Therefore, students should know that their selection of a graduate program might affect their eligibility for licensing.

In spite of the unique character of individual professional programs, there appear to be some commonalities. It must be remembered, however, that these commonalities are generalizations representing the synthesis of the author—they do not apply universally—but they are compatible with earlier trends discussed by Cole (1979). Professional schools tend to enroll larger classes than traditional programs. Traditional programs tend to limit the size of classes for two reasons. First, they are training students in many areas of psychology and prefer to maintain a balance among numbers of students in each area. And second, they practice an apprentice model

of research training which requires a very low faculty-student ratio. Professional programs, on the other hand, limit their training to one, or at most a few, areas of psychology. And, research in professional schools is often taught in a more didactic manner than in traditional programs, although several professional schools require research dissertations.

Course sequences in professional schools tend to be structured throughout the curriculum. This is consistent with the idea that there is a specific body of knowledge that needs to be transmitted. Because of the structured nature of the course work, students entering together tend to graduate together, usually in four years. In contrast, the average time to graduate from a "typical" scientific/practitioner program is about 5½ years. By no means is all of the education in a professional school program didactic, however. As is the case with traditional training programs, students tend to be involved in practical work (practica) early and consistently throughout their education.

Finally, students in professional schools often tend to be older and tend to have had practical working experience in areas related to applied psychology, compared to those in Boulder Model programs. There are also more people who enter with Master degrees. It is the practice of some practitioner programs to seek out students with advanced degrees, and all of them value practical experience highly (Shannon, 1982).

Entrance requirements vary widely among all graduate schools. In general, however, professional schools weigh non-traditional criteria more heavily than traditional programs. A few do not require GRE scores (Shannon, 1982). Many stress prior clinical experience (Cole, 1979), and most require an interview, a practice that is increasing among traditional programs as well.

Quality Indicators. The above description of practitioner-oriented programs does not address a major concern of the student and the advisor, however: the concern for quality. One cannot measure quality directly, one can only examine indicators of quality. The ability to grant degrees, even doctoral degrees, does *not* necessarily indicate quality. The authority to grant degrees rests solely with the states, and states differ drastically in the oversight they exercise to ensure quality. In all states professional psychologists must be licensed, and the acquisition of a doctoral degree is, by itself, generally not sufficient to sit for the licensing exam. Rather, educational backgrounds are screened by licensing boards on a case-by-case basis prior to establishing eligibility to take the licensing exam. *Any student planning to seek licensure after completion of training should contact the state licensing board in the state they intend to practice prior to enrolling in any graduate program.*

A better indicator of program quality is accreditation status. There are two types of accreditation, regional and specialized. Regional accreditation is administered by six accrediting organizations chartered by the U.S. Department of Education and the Council of Post Secondary Accreditation (COPA). Regional accreditation "certifies" that educational *institutions* meet some minimum criteria of acceptability. Regional accrediting bodies examine such things as libraries, financial resources and administration; thus regional accreditation guarantees a minimum level of institutional educational quality. Regional accreditation is not required by an institution to operate, but most institutions seek regional accreditation. At present, 32 professional schools are in institutions which are fully accredited regionally (Table 1), and several others are candidates for accreditation, a status which normally leads to regional accreditation in a short time. Regional accreditation applies to an institution as a whole.

Specialized accreditation, such as APA accreditation, accredits specific programs within institutions. Thus accreditation by the American Psychological Association applies only to the doctoral specialty accredited. APA accredits only doctoral programs in clinical, counseling, school, and combined professional-scientific psychology in regionally accredited institutions. In the APA accreditation process, each program receives a site visit by a team of three psychologists who recommend an action to the Accreditation Committee. The committee reviews the report of the site visit team and other self-study documents from the program before making a decision to accredit. APA accreditation signifies that the program (not the department or institution) is in sufficient compliance with the criteria set forth by APA. If one has graduated from an APA-accredited program, one may automatically sit for licensure in most jurisdictions, provided one has met appropriate "experience" requirements. Thus APA accreditation guarantees that a specific program is maintaining a level of quality acceptable to APA. There are presently 11 APA accredited professional schools in clinical psychology (see Table 1).

Accreditation by APA is optional. Thus there is no guarantee that an institution which does not have APA accreditation does not have equivalent educational standards, but APA accreditation is much sought after. There are at present 181 APA accredited professional programs in both Boulder and Vail model programs. Graduation from an APA accredited program is required for some jobs and for many APA accredited internship placements. The Veterans Administration has recently announced that only graduates of APA approved programs will be eligible for employment in VA facilities. APA accreditation has become the accepted standard in accreditable specialty areas of psychology.

Finally, quality is also a major concern of the professional schools themselves who have formed an association, the National Council of Schools of Professional Psychology (NCSPP). One of the goals of NCSPP is "to provide standards for the education and training of professional psychologists." Table 1 indicates the membership status in NCSPP of currently operating professional schools.

PhD—PsyD. The Vail Conference which "legitimatized" the professional school concept, also recommended that ". . . where primary emphasis in training and function is upon direct delivery of professional services . . . the Doctor of Psychology degree is appropriate" (Korman, 1976). The Doctor of Psychology degree (PsyD) was offered by the Department of Psychology at Illinois when they began their professional program. The rationale was, and is, that the PhD should be reserved for research training, and that the PsyD, like the EdD, MD, DDS, and JD, be reserved for those trained in a profession. This distinction is most easily seen at Rutgers University, where a student graduating from the School of

Professional Psychology receives a PsyD, and a student graduating from the Department of Psychology receives a PhD. Both programs offer training in clinical psychology, and each is accredited by APA.

The PsyD has come to be equated with professional training, and indeed that is its philosophical base. But fewer than half of the professional schools award the PsyD degree; the rest award PhDs. There are several reasons for this disparity. The California School of Professional Psychology felt that their new (at that time) training model of a freestanding professional school was sufficiently innovative that they did not want the additional burden of a new degree (Peterson, 1982); other schools felt that their professional training was as "scholarly" as those in traditional programs, and so retained the PhD; and it would be naive to fail to recognize that some schools offer a PhD simply because of its acceptability and status. In any case, PsyD and professional schools are not synonymous. (For a further discussion of this issue see Fox [1980].)

Does it matter whether a program offers a PsyD or a PhD? Apparently not, according to the criterion of degree acceptability (Peterson, Eaton, Levine & Snepp, 1982). Respondents to Peterson's survey actually reported believing that the degree placed them at an advantage in the jobs they were seeking. Not surprisingly, however, these jobs were mainly in service delivery areas and not in universities.

Selecting a Graduate Training Program.   What are some of the criteria that a student should use to decide between a professional school program in psychology and a traditional program? The most obvious one is the orientation of the student. Is the student interested specifically in the *practice* of psychology? This is a critical decision because one's options can be limited at this stage. Although graduates of professional schools do not seem to be at a disadvantage in clinical settings, and may even be at an advantage, this is certainly not true in research/academic settings. All professional schools expose students to research, most teach "evaluation research" courses, and a few require research dissertations. Professional schools, however, aim to develop consumers of research, not research scholars. Because traditional academic departments value research productivity, it is unlikely that a student with a degree from a professional school would be considered for faculty appointment in a traditional academic department unless the student had demonstrated research competence in another context. On the other hand, PhD graduates from programs designed on the Boulder model do obtain positions in professional practice.

A second major factor in the selection of a training model is the academic background of the student. Increasingly, scientifically based clinical training programs are emphasizing preparation in the natural sciences and mathematics. If a student has not completed such courses, her/his chances of admission are diminished. On the other hand, many professional schools look upon "hands-on" experience with favor. Such activities as "hot-line" attendant, counselor, etc. show a commitment to the helping professions. They also provide for the opportunity for students to see if they would like a vocation in applied psychology.

Care must be taken, however, not to over interpret the

training which is valued by professionally oriented and scientifically oriented departments. No department will be excited by an applicant who has taken *only* non-science courses, even if they have field experience. And *everyone* will be interested in a student with good grades, a solid mix of science and other courses, and some hands-on experience. All programs wish to maximize the probability of academic success among their students. The differences among selection criteria are in emphasis, not absolute.

The choice between training in a professional school and in a more traditional department of psychology is an important one. There are, however, major differences between specific programs, even of the same model. A rough guide to specific programs can be found in *Graduate Study in Psychology*[5] published yearly by APA (APA, 1982). This book can help in a preliminary screening of programs, but specific and detailed information should be gathered from a wide variety of training programs. The whole process of preparation for, application to, and selection of a graduate program is described in detail in *Preparing For Graduate Study in Psychology: Not For Seniors Only* (Fretz & Stang, 1980).

Conclusion. Psychology can prove an exciting career. In exchange for a commitment of time, a minimum of four years plus an internship year, and at least a year of supervised practice; and temporary financial deprivation, one can expect a relatively secure and rewarding future. Graduates of psychology programs report an overwhelming satisfaction with their career choice. Starting salaries are moderate, the median salary for a clinical psychologist engaged in direct human services (in 1982) was $23,000, but career prospects are bright; the corresponding median salary with 10 years experience is $40,000 with 25% of the people reporting salaries over $55,000 (Note 6). In addition, unemployment rates among doctoral level psychologists has remained under 2% for several years. Complete data on the current status of psychological employment can be found in the August, 1981 issue of *American Psychologist* which is devoted solely to human resources issues.

It should be clear from the above discussion that professional schools provide a viable path to a career in professional psychology. Although many professional schools are still in the developmental stage, it is clear that the professional school movement will have an increasing impact on the profession of psychology. It is hoped that students now contemplating a career in the profession of psychology can enter the educational path with a clear view of the alternatives available.

References

American Psychological Association. *Graduate study in psychology 1983-1984.* Washington, DC: Author, 1982.

Caddy, G. R., Rimm, D. C., Watson, N., & Johnson, J. H. (Eds.). *Educating professional psychologists.* New Brunswick, NJ: Rutgers Professional Psychology Review, Vol. 1, 1982.

Cole, D. L. Undergraduate preparation for admission to professional schools of psychology. *Teaching of Psychology,* 1979, 6, 179-180.

Fox, R. E. The need for a reorientation of clinical psychology. *American Psychologist,* 1982, 37, in press.

Fox, R. E. On reasoning from predicates: The PhD is not a professional degree. *Professional Psychology,* 1980, 11, 887-891.

Fretz, B. R., & Stang, D. J. *Preparing for graduate study in psychology: Not for seniors only.* Washington, DC: American Psychological Association, 1980.

Hoch, E. L., Ross, A. O., & Winder, C. L. (Eds.). *Professional preparation of clinical psychologists: Proceedings of the conference on the professional preparation of clinical psychologists meeting at the Center for Continuing Education, Chicago, IL, Aug. 27-Sept. 1, 1965.* Washington, DC: American Psychological Association, 1966.

Korman, M. (Ed.). *Levels and patterns of professional training in psychology: conference proceedings: Vail, CO, July, 1973.* Washington, DC: American Psychological Association, 1976.

Levy, L. H. The skew in clinical psychology. *American Psychologist,* 1962, 17, 244-249.

McNamara, J. R., & Barclay, A. G. *Critical issues, developments, and trends in professional psychology.* New York: Praeger, 1982.

Peterson, D. R. Origins and developments of the Doctor of Psychology concept. In G. R. Caddy, D. C. Rimm, N. Watson, & J. H. Johnson, (Eds.), *Educating Professional Psychologists.* New Brunswick, NJ: Rutgers Professional Psychology Review, Vol 1, 1982.

Peterson, D. R., Eaton, M. M., Levine, A. R., & Snepp, F. P. Career experiences of Doctors of Psychology. *Professional Psychology,* 1982, 13, 268-277.

Raimy, V. (Ed.). *Training in clinical psychology* (by the staff of the Conference on Graduate Education and Training held at Boulder, CO, Aug. 1949). New York: Prentice Hall, 1950.

Shannon, D. T. Entrance requirements and assessment of performance of PsyD students. In G. R. Caddy, D. C. Rimm, N. Watson & J. H. Johnson (Eds.), *Educating professional psychologists.* New Brunswick, NJ: Rutgers Professional Psychology Review, Vol. 1, 1982.

Notes

1. Grey, J. Discussion of undergraduate advisement at the Council of Undergraduate Psychology Departments meeting. Meetings of the Eastern Psychological Association, Baltimore, MD, April 1982.
2. Peterson, D. R. Organizational dilemmas in the education of professional psychologists. Paper prepared for the Conference on Quality in Professional Psychology, San Diego, CA, February, 1981.
3. Fulcher, R. The production and employment of PsyD recipients. Paper presented at the meeting of the American Psychological Association, Los Angeles, CA, July, 1980.
4. Stapp, J. *Summary report of 1979-80 survey of graduate departments of psychology* (Technical Report). Washington, DC, American Psychological Association, July, 1980.
5. The title of this annual guide will be changed to Graduate Study in Psychology and Related Fields.
6. Stapp, J., & Fulcher, R. *Report of the 1982 APA Salary Survey* (Technical Report). Washington, DC, American Psychological Association, August, 1982.
7. This article represents the viewpoint of the author and does not necessarily represent the viewpoint of the American Psychological Association.
8. I would like to express my sincere appreciation to Dr. Richard Kilberg and Anne Rogers of APA for their careful reading and constructive comments on an earlier draft of this paper. I would also like to thank Professors Donald Paterson, Eugene Shapiro, Gordon Derner, and Ronald Fox for their careful reading and helpful comments. Unfortunately, even with all of this expert advice, I must still remain responsible for errors of fact and interpretation.

Undergraduate Preparation for Admission to Professional Schools of Psychology

David L. Coyle
Occidental College

The past decade has seen a marked growth in the number of graduate schools of professional psychology. A professional school is one which has as its primary aim the training of psychologists to be practitioners (for the most part as clinicians) in contrast to the aim of preparing people primarily for academic and/or research positions. Even though a professional school may adhere to the "Boulder model" of the scientist-practitioner, the emphasis is quite clearly on the practitioner. Some professional schools are part of established universities, whereas others are "free standing" in the sense that their existence is independent of a larger institution.

The increasing number of such professional schools and the success they enjoy in attracting students suggests that this area of training is going to take on more significance in the coming years. If this is true, it is appropriate to determine the impact that these programs are likely to have on undergraduate education in psychology. So the American Psychological Association's Committee on Undergraduate Education undertook to survey these schools in order to determine perceptions of the priorities used in selecting graduate students, particularly as these relate to the applicant's undergraduate training.

At the time of the initiation of the study, 14 professional schools were known by APA Central Office, and five others were in the planning stage. These numbers are already out of date, but the list provided a pool of potential respondents for the present survey. A letter was sent to the administrative officer at each of these schools explaining the interest of the Committee. Answers were requested to each of the following questions:

1. What qualifications do you look for in an applicant to your program?
2. Are the expectations for applicants to your campus different from what you would expect to find in a traditional graduate school, and if so, how?
3. If the applicant pool is currently over-represented with older persons, will these expectations change if, over time, the applicant pool becomes younger?
4. Will you be apt to favor students with particular experiential backgrounds?
5. Are there field training experiences or other special opportunities which an undergraduate department would be wise to provide for its students to enhance their likelihood of being accepted into your program?
6. Are there experiences which a student could gain on his/her own, apart from the curriculum, which would be valuable?

Results. Eleven of the 14 established schools responded, as well as three of the five in the planning stages. One of the latter was too far away from initiation of its program to provide useful data.[2]

What follows is a summary of the information provided by the respondents. Because the questions were broad and overlapping, the information has been synthesized, and will not be presented on a question by question basis. The reader is reminded that these replies indicate what the respondents say they expect. We did not check on actual practice.

It seems quite clear that these schools are expecting applicants to bring traditional and substantial backgrounds in undergraduate psychology. Two respondents specified that an undergraduate major in psychology was not necessary, but they asked for considerable background in its subject matter. Content or methods areas which were specified as expected of applicants by at least half of the respondents included: Abnormal, Developmental, Experimental, Learning, Personality, Physiological, and Statistics. None recommended clinical courses *per se*, although as will be seen below, field experiences were considered very important by most. Two respondents specified tests and measurements, but in general the content and methods expectations were very similar to what would be expected for someone entering a traditional program. Three respondents specified the advanced psychology section of the GRE, and four specified "academic excellence." In various ways, nearly all respondents made it clear that they expected academically gifted students.

Only one respondent failed to comment on the value of field experience. Three indicated that it would be useful but not critical. For the others, it occupied a much higher priority. Four stated that they expected supervised field experience, something on the order of a "clerkship." Four others indicated they preferred supervised experience, but would accept it unsupervised if other qualifications were high.

Only the more recently established professional schools noted that their typical student was many years older than the average college graduate at the time of the AB degree. Some schools reported that when their program began they had served an older student pool, but that age levels had dropped later. Three schools reported a modal applicant age of 23—an age strongly suggesting that the large majority of their acceptances were now going to students just completing the AB.

The declining age of applicants takes on added significance when it is noted that seven of the respondents stressed the importance of "psychological maturity" in their applicants and others appeared to be talking of this in less direct terms. In addition, "stability of personality" was stressed by six of the respondents and alluded to by others. These variables are very difficult to evaluate from a transcript. Two of the respondents mentioned the importance of

Discussion. Although these data suggest that professional schools ask for much the same prerequisites as are traditional, the emphasis on carefully monitored field train-letters of reference and four noted the importance of the personal interview. Two administrators mentioned a desire to find women applicants, and three mentioned minorities. ing experiences is new. It is in this area that the rise of professional schools may influence undergraduate curricula. Although field training experiences are not rare in undergraduate work, it is less clear that these are typically supervised with the same care that an undergraduate receives in laboratory work. Reallocation of faculty time to provide such supervision may become increasingly necessary as professional schools take a heavier proportion of those students who enter graduate work.

The concern with psychological characteristics such as "maturity" and "stability" may lead to an increasing use of the personal interview as a selection procedure, a path currently followed much more by medical schools than by graduate departments of psychology. If this happens, the question of the validity of impressions gained through interviews will be a haunting one. At present we use instruments of minimal demonstrable validity in screening applicants. The interview could easily join that list. It is hoped that if the interview does indeed become a common selection procedure we will use research to seek to validate its use.

Notes

1. Adapted from a paper presented at the American Psychological Association meetings in Toronto, 1978.
2. The 13 professional schools providing useable data for this survey were: Adelphi University, California School of Professional Psychology (separate replies from campuses in Fresno, Los Angeles, San Diego and San Francisco), University of Denver, Fuller Theological Seminary, Massachusetts School of Professional Psychology, New York School of Professional Psychology, Ohio School of Professional Psychology, Pacific Graduate School of Psychology, Rutgers University, Wright Institute, Berkeley.

c.   Additional Issues

Douglas Henderson offered his experience as a member of an undergraduate psychology department at the University of Wisconsin at Stevens Point and of a state psychology examining board. He pointed out the problems that licensing boards can have when trying to evaluate the credentials from individuals who have obtained degrees from programs identified with departments other than psychology. Students should not take such a caveat lightly.

Michael Gottlieb designed a course for sophomore and junior psychology majors or prospective majors at Southern Methodist University. The purpose of the course was to communicate basic knowledge about psychology as a profession. Readers will find the author's course outline and list of readings of considerable assistance in developing a course of their own.

Patricia Lunneborg from the University of Washington conducted a survey of the 511 department chairs listed in *Graduate Study in Psychology 1981-1982.* She asked them several questions about enrollment reductions and curricular adjustments for graduate and undergraduate students. After summarizing and discussing her findings, the author used her respondents' own words to describe four paths for undergraduate programs. She recommended that readers determine which approach is most compatible with the many variables that departments must consider.

Philip Zimbardo drew from his experience at Stanford University and provided suggestions for students who ask faculty to write letters of recommendation. The article contained several guidelines. In addition, the author provided a copy of the memo that he developed and distributed to students. As a first step in developing your own guidelines or as a reference for reviewing existing ones, this article should please you.

On Advising Undergraduates About Graduate School in Professional Psychology

Douglas B. Henderson
University of Wisconsin

As a member of an undergraduate department of psychology for six years, and a member of a state psychology examining board for five years, I have frequent exposure to both the academic and professional aspects of psychology. In my academic role as one of three licensed clinicians in a 14-member department, I often advise students who wish to continue their education at the graduate level. In my professional role as an examining board member, I frequently encounter applicants for licensure as a psychologist whose graduate academic background is not "in psychology" as it is defined in our Wisconsin licensing law, in the licensing laws of other states, and at the national level.

Psychology, as we teach our introductory students, is a young and evolving field of study, both as a science and as a profession. However, recent cooperation between representatives of both major elements of our field has led to a widely accepted definition of a "doctoral degree in psychology." The definition, based on work by Wellner (1978), has now been accepted in similar form by the American Association of State Psychology Boards and the National Register of Health Service Providers in Psychology. Nearly one-half of the State Psychology Examining Boards have used, or intend to use, this definition as the basis for revisions in their statutes. A slight modification of this definition in draft form is also being used by the American Psychological Association Task Force on Education and Credentialing in its pilot study for a nationwide system of designating doctoral programs in psychology (APA, 1981). The definition has ten specific criteria and details of these may be obtained from the APA or state licensing boards. Most important of these ten criteria are the requirements that, to be a graduate program "in psychology," the program must be identified by title as a psychology program, and must have, as its purpose, the training of students in psychology. There are also specific course content and administrative requirements.

Given these recent developments, the important role played by teachers of undergraduate psychology occurs as we advise our students about their choice of potential graduate programs. Students are confronted by a variety of professional programs available in departments identified by titles such as Counseling and Guidance, Counselor Education, Child and Family studies, Human Services, Human Development, and so forth. These programs look attractive to students interested in further education in psychology. Many of these programs are in graduate schools of high reputation and many have a number of individuals who are classically trained and well known psychologists on their faculties. However, the vast majority of such programs do not produce graduates who meet the requirements for licensure as a psychologist, because the program is not "in psychology." As undergraduate advisors, we have a clear obligation to inform our students of the current status of professional licensing both at the national level and within our own states, so that they can choose a graduate program which will prepare them to be a licensable psychologist if that is their desire.

All too often, members of state licensing boards are confronted by doctoral level applicants who, while claiming to have always wanted to be a psychologist, clearly do not meet the requirements for licensure. A few of these applicants have, for example, an undergraduate major in English, a masters degree in religion, and a doctoral degree in child and family studies. Their understanding of what a psychologist is and even of basic psychology sometimes seems questionable. However, a distressingly large number of such applicants have at least a bachelor's degree in psychology and, it would seem, should have known better. Some states have "equivalency provisions" which offer some hope of licensure to these non-traditionally trained individuals, but in many states these students can not become a licensed psychologist. Perhaps some of these individuals are students who tried but couldn't get accepted into a proper psychology training program. Perhaps, however, some well-timed advice about how to become a psychologist from an undergraduate faculty member could have saved considerable difficulty both for the individual student and for the licensing board the student later angrily confronts.

Two final issues must be briefly raised. Although this message is directed primarily at undergraduate faculty members, it would seem that psychologists who are members of graduate programs both in and out of psychology departments also have a role to play. These psychologists should see to it that applicants to their programs know whether or not graduates can reasonably expect to qualify for licensure as a psychologist.

Also, the issue of academic freedom often enters into the licensing/certification controversy. Certainly, academic departments can offer whatever courses they desire, with whatever content and whatever titles they desire. Students can take whichever of those courses from whatever department they wish. No outside group should dictate what is taught on a university campus. However, if an individual student wishes to become a licensed psychologist (or to join any profession for that matter) the path to follow to that goal should be both clear and available. The clarity of the path is in part the responsibility of undergraduate advisors. The availability of the path is the responsibility of both the student, though his or her quality of work, and the graduate program, through the professional identification and course content it offers.

References

American Psychological Association. *Draft designation handbook and procedures manual* (July 1981 Revision). Washington, DC: Author, 1981.

Wellner, A. *Education and credentialling in psychology*. Washington DC: American Psychological Association, 1978.

Introduction to the Fields of Psychology:
A Course Proposal

Michael C. Gottlieb
Southern Methodist University

Describing a course designed to
assist in the better preparation of
undergraduates for graduate school.

In recent years undergraduate students have become increasingly interested in pursuing psychology as a career. Until the recent economic decline, most graduate programs were capable of accepting a reasonable number of promising students. Unfortunately the number of applicants substantially increased at the same time that these programs were forced to reduce their admissions because of reduced funding. The well-known result was a virtual flood of applicants desperately trying to obtain admission with the hope of eventual professional employment.

Such a condition places undergraduate teaching institutions in a rather difficult position. If one has the avowed purpose of training students to compete and succeed at the graduate level, such an endeavor becomes rather ludicrous if the students cannot gain admission to the school of their choice. Undergraduate institutions then seem faced with modifying their offerings and purposes to reflect more accurately the current conditions.

To complicate the matter even further, it has been our experience that students often choose psychology on a rather capricious basis. Former students, who did gain graduate admission, often return telling of how well prepared they were academically, but how poorly informed they were about psychology as a profession, and about its relationship to their personal goals. Furthermore, the knowledge they do have has usually been obtained in random fashion, and is often incomplete. Such ignorance is even more pervasive among undergraduates who try to piece together information on the fields of psychology, often compiling a fascinating pastiche of fact and fiction.

In response to this situation, our department proposed a new course called Introduction to the Fields of Psychology. The course is designed for the Sophomore-Junior student who is (or is planning to be) a major in psychology. Its purpose is to impart basic knowledge about psychology as a profession. Hopefully students will gain a more realistic perception of the field, specifically in terms of its rewards, limitations, requirements, and potentialities. Such a course should lead to more enlightened career choices (be they for or against psychology) and to more appropriate choices for graduate training. The purpose of this article is to acquaint other psychologists with the course so that they may consider developing a similar one.

Course Outline

I. **Fields of Study** (3-4 weeks). This first and primary section should focus upon the areas or fields in which Psychologists work, what they do, and the subject matter they study. A second (optional) purpose would be to investigate the methods of study each area employs such as the experimental method, clinical observation, testing, etc.
   A. Learning Motivation and Emotion, Sensation and Perception, and Physiological
   B. Developmental, Child, Social
   C. Clinical, Counseling, School, Rehabilitation
   D. Industrial, Organizational

II. **Work Settings** (3 weeks). The section examines where psychologists find employment, and the functions performed in these settings. That is, who employs psychologists, and in what capacities.
   A. Research
   B. Teaching
   C. Professional services—public and private
   D. Business and Industry
   E. Government
   F. Administration
   G. Consultation

III. **Graduate Training** (2-3 weeks). Attention should be directed to the process of applying to graduate school, the admissions process, training requirements, and the ways in which research and training are funded.
   A. Application—requirements and procedures
   B. Admissions—policies and criteria
   C. Training requirements—years, credit hours, dissertation, language, and internship
   D. Funding—representative agencies and restrictions e.g., NIMH, VA, etc.

IV. **Levels of Training** (1 week). Professional psychologists function at three levels based upon their academic degrees. Discussion should center upon differences in skill, function, capacity, responsibility, and advancement.
   A. BA
   B. MA
   C. PhD

V. **Licensure and Certification** (1 week). A brief section on national and state regulation of psychologists including: academic requirements, examinations, experience, definition and limitations of practice. Other current topics may be relevant here, such as ABEPP or the *National Register of Health Service Providers*.

VI. **Professional Organizations and Publications** (1 week). Psychologists are literally flooded with information from a myriad of sources. The section is designed to acquaint the student with the literature and organizations available to psychologists. Some effort should be made to distinguish between professional organizations and interest groups, and scholarly journals and magazines.

VII. **Professional Ethics and Issues** (2 weeks). The section should cover basic principles of conduct related to the various areas of professional functioning, accompanied by relevant contemporary issues. Flexibility should be maintained here in an effort to accommodate issues of interest to both instructor and student e.g., deception research, social involvement, the MA—PhD membership controversy, and criteria for graduate training.

VIII. **Future Trends** (1 week). The purpose of this section is, as time permits, to impart some idea of those questions to be faced in the future such as: The future of applied psychology, biofeedback, ongoing professional education, behavioral technology etc.

Readings

Because of the unavailability of an appropriate text book, and the continuously changing nature of the material, no required text is recommended. If the instructor does choose to use one however, Guilford's *The Fields of Psychology* would be appropriate for Part I. For subsequent sections, the instructor will be required to determine which materials he feels will be most relevant, valuable, and interesting. Below, the reader will find a brief list of suggested readings to aid in course preparation.

Please note that any such list is arbitrary and reflects the bias of the author. The purpose of the list is simply to offer guidelines and stimulation for the reader in considering preparation of his own material.

I. Fields of Psychology

Guilford, J. P. *Fields of psychology* (3rd ed.). Princeton, N. J.: Van Nostrand, 1966, (selected chapters).

Task Force on the Practice of Psychology in Industry. Effective practice of psychology in industry. *American Psychologist,* 1971, *26,* 974-991.

Supplemental: *Publication manual of the American Psychological Association* (2nd ed.). Washington, D.C.: 1974.

II. Work Settings

Cates, J., Mensh, I., & Witkin, H. Psychologists in medical schools. *American Psychologist,* 1972, *27,* 434-440.

Norton, F. Two-year college instruction: Opportunities for psychology. *American Psychologist,* 1972, *27,* 445-450.

Speisman, J. Distribution of psychologists in universities and colleges. *American Psychologist,* 1972, *27,* 431-433.

Sundberg, N., Taplin, J., & Tyler, L. *Clinical psychology: Expanding horizons* (2nd ed.). New York: Appleton, Century, Crofts, 1973, 3-29.

III. Graduate Training

American Psychological Association. APA approved doctoral programs in clinical, counseling, and school psychology. *American Psychologist,* 1974, *29,* 844-846.

American Psychological Association. APA approved internships for doctoral training in clinical and counseling psychology. *American Psychologist,* 1974, *29, 841-843.*

Astin, H., & El-Khawaw, E. Current enrollment characteristics of graduate students in psychology. *American Psychologist,* 1972, *27,* 457-461.

Davis-Silka, L., & Scott, W. Applying to graduate school in psychology: A perspective and guide. JSAS *Catalog of Selected Documents in Psychology,* 1975, 4, 33 (MS.No. 597).

Supplemental: *Graduate Study in Psychology for 1975-1976.* Washington, D.C.: American Psychological Association, 1974.

IV. Levels of Training

Jones, A. Masters' level training. *Conference on the Professional Preparation of Clinical Psychologists: Preconference materials,* Washington, D.C.: American Psychological Association, 1965.

Korman, M. National conference on levels and patterns of professional training in psychology: The major themes. *American Psychologist,* 1974, *29,* 441-449.

V. Licensure and Certification

American Psychological Association. Some characteristics of psychology laws. 1972 (mimeographed).

Directory of Diplomates. Rochester, N. Y.: American Board of Professional Psychology, Inc., 1974, 2-3.

Texas State Legislature. *Vernon's Annual Civil Statutes.* Psychologists certification and licensing act, Article 4512 C, 61st Legislature, regular session, 1969.

Supplemental: Texas State Board of Examiners of Psychologists. *Roster.* Austin, Texas, 1975.

VI. Professional Ethics and Issues

American Psychological Association. Ethical standards of psychologists. *American Psychologist,* 1963, *18,* 56-60.

American Psychological Association, Division of Psychotherapy. Recommended standards for psychotherapy education in psychology (mimeographed).

Blau, T. Exposure to competence: A simple standard for graduate training in professional psychology. *Professional Psychology,* 1973, *4,* 133-136.

Caplan, N., & Nelson, S. On being useful: The nature and consequences of psychological research on social problems. *American Psychologist,* 1973, *28,* 199-211.

Robinson, D. Therapies: A clear and present danger. *American Psychologist,* 1973, *28,* 129-133.

VII. Professional Organization and Publications

Sundberg, N., op. cit., 502-519. Professional organizations and ethics.

Sundberg, N., op. cit., 543-545. Major journals and series relevant to clinical psychology.
Supplemental: A list of journals in the behavioral sciences from the campus library may be compiled and annotated.

VIII. Future Trends

Albee, G. The uncertain future of clinical psychology. *American Psychologist*, 1970, *25*, 1071-1080.

Dubin, S. Obsolescence or lifelong education: A choice for the professional. *American Psychologist*, 1972, *27*, 486-498.

Krauskopf, C., McAleer, C., Thoresen, R., & Wender, D. The future of applied psychology: Are we building a buggy whip factory? *American Psychologist*, 1972, *27*, 134-139.

Methods

Our department chose to offer the course for two semester hours credit. This decision was based primarily upon the fact that it would fit easily into our undergraduate program for psychology majors. Some would suggest that such a course not be offered for academic credit, but instead relegated to non-credit colloquia or seminars. Each department will have to come to terms with this issue in its own way. Obviously it was our feeling that the course should carry academic credit and that it was of sufficient value to be considered as part of our curriculum.

Although the course offers only two hours of credit, students are expected to meet three times weekly. The third meeting is exclusively devoted to hearing speakers primarily from the local community. The speakers are utilized extensively to give students an opportunity to meet these persons, learn about what they do, how they were trained, and how they came to occupy their current position. A primary focus for the author in this regard is to give students some appreciation for the great variety of training, background, experience, and interest of psychologists. Related area professionals, such as a psychiatrist, social worker, and marriage and family counselor, are also invited.

Grading is a difficult problem at best. Our decision was to offer the course on a pass-fail basis even though psychology majors in our department are required to take all courses in their major for credit. This decision was frankly a compromise with those who felt that the course should not be offered for credit. As with all such decisions, there is no perfect solution; however, the pass-fail system does seem well suited to such a course. It will obviously reduce to a minimum any atmosphere of competition between students, and will also permit them greater latitude in pursuing their respective interests.

Course evaluation is another area over which many will differ. Three options in various combinations seem viable. First, periodic examinations would be useful in determining if students are learning the material covered in the lecture portion. Such examinations would probably not be exceedingly rigorous, but would establish basic competency in the area. Second, term papers may be of value depending upon how the course is structured. Certainly library research on representative issues would be appropriate. A third option, again depending upon structure, is the term project. Such projects are often less academically oriented, but do offer a needed flexibility for meeting individual student needs. When the author taught the course last year on a pilot basis, a contract system was employed in which students made individual agreements with me employing various combinations of the three options listed above.

A note should be made regarding instructor requirements. One's area of specialization does not seem critical to the success of the course, although applied psychologists may find the assignment more related to their work. The critical variables however seem to be a basic commitment on the part of the instructor to psychology as a profession, and an ability to excite students using his own enthusiasm as a vehicle.

Finally, a course such as this will be immeasurably enhanced by student feedback at the end of the semester. Since the basic purpose focuses upon students' interests and goals, time should be devoted to obtaining input for future planning. Although such a procedure is advisable at the beginning of the course, it seems a necessity at the end. Students should have an opportunity to respond not only to procedures and methods, but to content as well, so that the course may be periodically revised. In this way the course will retain viability long after many issues of the day have been resolved.

Notes

1. The author would like to thank Drs. Richard Hunt and William Tedford for their support and critical reading of this paper.

How Are Changes in Graduate Admissions Affecting the Teaching of Undergraduate Psychology?

Patricia W. Lunneborg
University of Washington

This report of a survey indicates modest declines in graduate enrollment, but also very little planning for reduced support.

Certainly 1981 was earmarked as the year when psychology would have to face up to a government whose spending priorities placed defense far ahead of social service and social science (Cole, 1981). Or was it? What impacts were proposed budget cuts in training and research support actually having on psychology graduate programs? Assuming that such effects inevitably would trickle down to the undergraduate level, what accommodations were departments making in their baccalaureate programs? These two questions were the focus of the present study.

The device chosen to assess these questions was a brief survey for departmental chairs which began by describing it as "an attempt to collect and disseminate some data on the reductions in federal and state support for graduate training in psychology." The items were designed both to measure the extent of changes in graduate admissions and to gather information on adjustments departments were making at the undergraduate level. Ironically, a week after the surveys were mailed, the July *APA Special Monitor* carried an article about a similar survey done in April by the Central Office and Council of Graduate Departments of Psychology (VandenBos & Roesler, 1981).

Method. The chairpersons of all 511 U. S. master's and doctoral level programs in *Graduate Study in Psychology 1981-1982* (1980) were mailed a one-page survey with a return envelope on July 1, 1981. As of August 7th, 274 had been received of which 260 (51%) were usable and provided the data for this report. This compares favorably with the VandenBos and Roesler reponse rate of 48%. Schools had to be rejected primarily for omitting complete identification necessary to classify them as master's or doctoral level based on *Graduate Study* descriptions.

The survey inquired first as to how many graduate students had been admitted fall 1980 and fall 1981 in clinical and in "all other" areas. There followed five open-ended questions concerning (1) most important reason for cutting back admissions, (2) extent of contemplated reductions in 1982, (3) how departmental requirements of applicants might change over the next few years, (4) what adjustments were being made to make undergraduates more competitive for graduate school, and (5) what other adjustments in the undergraduate program might be made given changes in graduate enrollments. In instances where respondents gave more than one response to these items, the first listed was used.

In addition to frequency and percentage tallies, chi-square tests were performed where appropriate between master's and doctoral level results. Analyses for questions (4) and (5) above were performed only for departments that had undergraduates.

Results. Forty-two percent (109) of respondents were master's level and 58% (151) doctoral level programs. Programs having undergraduates as well, 206 schools in all, were 45% master's and 55% doctoral. Most of the programs without psychology undergraduates were in school, counseling, and educational psychology; only six were professional schools of psychology.

The percentages of clinical and other students admitted fall 80 and 81 were highly similar. Table 1 presents these data in terms of gains and losses in eleven categories for master's and doctoral programs separately. Programs were omitted from the table if they listed zero admits for both 1980 and 1981, indicating they didn't have programs of that particular type.

Examining the totals in the middle of Table 1, at master's and doctoral level the number of departments which admitted more students in 1981 than 1980 was about the same. More doctoral programs, however, were losing students than master's programs in both clinical and other programs in 1981. Both gains and losses were most frequent in the 1-5 students category.

Sums, means, and standard deviations for the four groups represented in Table 1 appear in Table 2. Actual mean differences between 1980 and 1981 are slight and when

Table 1. Differences between Fall 80 and 81 in Graduate Student Admits

Number of Students	Master's level		Doctoral level	
	Clinical $n = 54$	Other $n = 99$	Clinical $n = 88$	Other $n = 142$
Gains (% of responding programs)				
>20	0	0	0	0
16-20	0	1	1	0
11-15	0	0	0	0
6-10	6	2	3	3
1-5	24	25	24	27
Total % gained	30	28	28	30
Total % no change	31	43	30	28
Total % lost	39	28	42	42
Losses (% of responding programs)				
1-5	30	20	39	30
6-10	6	5	1	8
11-15	4	2	2	3
16-20	0	0	0	1
>20	0	1	0	0

Table 2. Enrollments in Graduate Programs 1980 and 1981

	1980	1981	81 - 80[a]
Ph.D. clinical (n = 88)			
Total new admits	1247	1227	−20
Mean	14.17	13.94	−.23
SD	13.76	15.32	4.55
Ph.D. other (n = 142)			
Total new admits	2675	2562	−113
Mean	18.84	18.04	−.80
SD	18.23	17.83	4.48
Master's clinical (n = 54)			
Total new admits	866	845	−21
Mean	16.04	15.65	−.39
SD	18.03	18.25	4.09
Master's other (n = 99)			
Total new admits	2111	2058	−53
Mean	21.32	20.79	−.54
SD	27.28	26.05	6.02

[a]Based on difference scores calculated for each department.

losses are added together by department by program, 207 fewer students were admitted in 1981 than in 1980. PhD clinical programs overall reduced their admissions by 20 students, a decrease of 1.6%. The other decreases were 4% for PhD other programs, 2.4% for master's clinical programs, and 2.5% for master's other programs.

Given the number of departments in which admittances were unchanged or increased, it is not surprising that 63% said "no cuts" or left blank the item that inquired as to the most important reason for cutting graduate admissions. Of the 37% who did give a reason, 15% said lack of funding, 10% lack of (qualified) applicants, 8% lack of faculty or desire to maintain a good student/faculty ratio, and 4% were "other" responses including job market, economic anxieties. These percentages were essentially the same when the 206 departments with undergraduate programs were separately examined.

The second open-ended question was preceded by a simple request to indicate if reductions in admissions were contemplated next year. "No" was the response of 84%, "maybe" given by 5%, and "yes" by 11%. Of the 30 respondents who said "yes", the extent of reduction was less than 10% for one school, 10-20% for 15 schools, and more than 20% for 7 schools. Two said they would cut programs, not students, and 5 gave incalculable responses such as "several students."

Did departments foresee that what they required of graduate applicants would change over the next few years? Seventy-three percent said "no," 3% said "maybe," and 23% said "yes." As to how requirements would change (72% gave no response), the chief reaction by 14% was that requirements in terms of academic record, experience, etc., would be more stringent. Five percent said students would have to support themselves more, 3% said students must have more applied interests, 2% said they would be taking more part-time students, and 1% said they would have less stringent requirements. (There were 3% in the "other" category.) Again, these percentages were the same for departments with undergraduate students examined separately.

What adjustments were they making in the undergraduate program to make students more competitive for graduate appointments? Of the 206 departments with undergraduate programs, 52% said none or they didn't know. The chief adjustment given by 14% was to strengthen core requirements, increase breadth, require more science, math, statistics, laboratories. Eight percent said they would require more research of students, and 8% said they would require more applied, practical experience. To 5% the answer was to strengthen the honors program, small seminars, graduate school preparation. Three percent said advising would be improved including GRE preparation and there were 9% in the "other" category.

What other adjustments in the undergraduate program might be made given changes in graduate admissions? Again, just for the 206 undergraduate departments, 71% said none or don't know. The most popular response was to make the program more applied (13%). Requiring more research or quantitative science was given by only 3%, greater breadth by 2%, and improved advising by 4%. Six percent fell in the "other" category and only 1% cited negative effects on teaching for lack of graduate TA's.

There was a highly significant chi-square value for a test of whether level of program (master's, doctoral) was related to reasons given for making cuts. PhD programs less often reported they had made no cuts and 31% gave funding or lack of faculty as reasons vs. only 12% for these combined reasons among master's programs. Chi-square tests for program level vs. the response categories of the last three open-ended questions were not significant.

Discussion. VandenBos and Roesler (1981) found overall a 10% decrease from the 1980 level among doctoral programs. In the present study decreases were never more than 4% and the overall picture was one of relative stability for both clinical and other programs, at both master's and doctoral levels. There are at least two explanations for the discrepancy between APA's April survey results and these findings. (a) *Item differences and timing.* In April, programs were "estimating" fall 81 admissions vs. July when they gave the numbers of students actually admitted. Projected estimates appear to have been conservative relative to behavior three months later. (b) *Sample differences.* VandenBos and Roesler noted enormous differences in enrollment declines among different types of programs. The percent decrease ranged among research programs from 2% for Educational to 22% for cognitive, and among applied programs from 1% for counseling to 76% for community. Inasmuch as here all programs other than clinical were subsumed under an "other" label, the difference between the composition of our doctoral sample with VandenBos and Roesler's sample probably accounts for most of the discrepancy.

The evidence for denial or wishful thinking or apathetic indecisiveness in psychology departments facing adverse political/economic realities is very strong. First, less than a half of departments had reduced the numbers of graduate students they admitted from 1980 to 1981. Second, the reductions proved minuscule. Third, a full 84% said no reductions in admissions were contemplated for 1982.

Looking at the 37% who gave reasons for cutting back graduate admissions, only 15% cited lack of funding as the chief reason and less than 4% said economic anxieties and the job market were factors. Looking at the 28% who said they might change admissions requirements for graduate students over the next few years, only 5% said students would have to support themselves more and 2% said they would probably accept more part-time students (so that students could also be employed).

Many departments appear to have adopted a wait-and-see attitude rather than thinking about and planning for the problems that lack of funding would necessarily entail. Instead of a reason for cutting, they wrote, "We're holding constant." "Holding steady." "No current plans to alter our admissions." "Remaining the same." Certainly there was little evidence of the "depression era mentality" feared by some and considered "contrary to the Administration's theory of what should be happening" (VandenBos & Roesler).

On the other hand, lack of long-range planning in relation to graduate education may mean that departments will have to adjust very quickly to future economic realities. When they do, they will have little practice at planning for the reverse of expansion—fewer grants, fewer applicants, unreplaced faculty positions, etc. Optimal decisions seem unlikely when procrastination can suddenly no longer be afforded and individuals and institutions must face up to the fact that the money simply isn't there.

The adjustments suggested at the undergraduate level, with very few exceptions, were to add new elements or strengthen old elements to programs. These reactions indicated there were four primary paths being considered. First, there was the level at which the program could be geared. Departments can either strengthen it as graduate school preparation or as a terminal BA program. Second, within these two levels, departments can emphasize either breadth and core of psychological knowledge or applied/technical skills. These four paths combining different levels and emphases are best described using the words of respondents:

BA Level, Breadth/Core Psychology Emphasis
Emphasize breadth of education and general skills.
Train in broader ways; emphasize general undergraduate preparation.
An increase in computer science courses would give our majors an additional competitive edge regardless of whether or not they plan to enter graduate school.
Broader training; development of better communication skills.
An even greater increase on standards and overall development.
BA Level, Applied/Technical Emphasis
60-80% of undergraduate majors are targeted for nursing, business, etc. We are contemplating courses to serve these students and hence, to develop a clientele of serious but nongraduate school bound students.

Increase offerings in applied psychology to lead to some marketable skills at bachelor's level.
Emphasis on interdisciplinary programs, e.g., business and psychology.
We have had to make available for undergraduates more practicums—to get jobs.
Making undergraduate major more applied. Almost none of our UGs go on to a graduate program.
Graduate Preparation Level, Breadth/Core Psychology Emphasis
Strengthening core areas, providing students opportunities to add professional items such as papers and presentations to the vita.
Stricter, broader core requirements with more emphasis on quantitative skills.
Grad type education will occur at UG level.
Continue our strong (2-year) undergraduate honors program involving students in research.
Better advising to emphasize need for advanced experimental courses and independent research.
Graduate Preparation Level, Applied/Technical Emphasis
Addition of courses in organizational psychology and computer interfacing.
We require a "Careers in Psych" course utilizing the texts by Woods and Fretz and Stang.
Major revisions in undergraduate program with several applied areas, e.g., industrial/organizational, human services, etc.
Better preparation for seeking applied graduate training.
Provide some applied courses and practica.

The question remains, how can these new course offerings and program options be added in an era of diminishing resources? Which courses on the books will be sacrificed? Who will develop and teach these new courses? Could any program go in all four directions, or is more than one direction beyond the budgetary limitations of most departments? How will departments decide which way to go?

It is hoped that delineating four possible future emphases provides a focus for faculty discussions as to which solution is most compatible with teaching and research interests, material resources, undergraduate student characteristics, graduate admissions rates, and the host of other variables departments must consider as they seek to maintain quality undergraduate education in psychology in the 1980's.

References

Cole, D. L. Teaching tomorrow's psychology students: Who pays the piper? *American Psychologist*, 1981, *36*, 506-513.
VandenBos, G. R., & Roesler, M. 1981 graduate admissions in psychology—A survey. Memorandum to Michael S. Pallak. Washington, DC: American Psychological Association, June 1, 1981.

Reducing the Agony of Writing Letters of Recommendation

Philip G. Zimbardo
Stanford University

One of the more important tasks that a faculty member is called upon by students to undertake is to write letters of recommendation for them—for jobs, for admission to other schools, for awards, etc. It is also one of the most onerous of teaching functions when the number of such students begins to proliferate and your knowledge of most of them is not as adequate as you would like it to be. I am always distressed when I indicate to a student that I have not had enough personal contact over a sufficient period of time to be able to write a strong letter, and he or she replies, "but no one else here knows me any better than you do!" Our large lecture sections, overworked faculty, student shyness, the diversity of courses, the necessity of after-school jobs, commuting, and the like all conspire to reduce the level and quality of personalized interaction between faculty and students as in many academic settings. In addition, a surprising number of students are unaware of their need to secure a series of recommendations until it is too late, as well as being uninformed about the non grade-related dimensions of such recommendations that are important.

To help remedy this annual problem, I suggest the following:

1. Make a formal statement about the nature and the process of obtaining recommendations; to be presented at the end of the introductory psychology course, in written statements to all new majors and even incorporated into a freshman orientation guide, if your school has one.
2. Inform students of the "transient" nature of graduate TAs, visiting faculty and untenured assistant professors; thus the need to have them file a letter with the department as soon after the "favorable" contact period as possible.
3. Where the student has worked closely with a graduate TA, the TA should prepare the letter, discuss it with the TA's faculty advisor; the final letter being sent under both signatures.
4. Provide students with an outline guide to help them in making the recommender's task easier and more effective. The guide I have used is given below, and has been received enthusiastically by my undergraduates. It encourages them to think through some of the information they need for their autobiographical statement; they can use it (with modifications) for each of their other recommenders; they become aware if the basis of contact with a faculty member is too slight to permit him/her to write a solid letter; it discourages some students because of the effort it entails; it is a sample of the student's writing and thinking; and it is remarkable how much new information you learn even about students with whom you are well acquainted.

On the basis of my positive experience using this memo on letters of recommendation, I strongly recommend its use to my colleagues.

Memo on Letters of Recommendation
To: Stanford Undergraduates
From: Philip Zimbardo

In order for me to write the best possible (strongest) letter in support of your application, you should provide me with the kind of information I've outlined below. It will help me to personalize and individuate my recommendation of you and make it easier for me at times when I have a considerable number of such letters to write. Please feel free to speak well of yourself—if you do not think you are good and deserving of whatever position you are applying for, how can anyone else? Thanks and good luck!

A. Please supply me with a copy of your transcript and your letter of purpose, autobiography or similar statement (as requested by the school or job). If you want constructive criticism on that statement, indicate that you do and when you need it returned to you. Include a stamped, self-addressed envelope for that and/or for a copy of my letter of recommendation for your files. Indicate if you wish the letter of recommendation sent to the University's Academic Information Center or to various schools. If the latter, include addressed, stamped envelopes for each school. Also, indicate if you maintain an *open* or *closed* recommendation file by signing the attached "waiver" or "right to inspect" form—I will not give you a copy of my letter if your file is closed.

B. On a separate form, please provide the following information in an outline format:

1. Name and current address.
2. Current date.
3. Deadline for each letter of recommendation.
4. Indicate application for: type of school (list specific ones if you know them); type of job; general file.
5. The basis of *our* contact: Formal courses (title, grade, other aspects of your special performance); honors research; teaching proctorship; independent reading/research; informal contacts; other.
6. Academic Achievement: Tell me about your grades (GPA), major, strengths and weaknesses, how your academic background has prepared you for what you are being recommended for. Include anything "extra" or unique about your academic background. If you have any Board scores, let me know them.
7. Non-Academic background; Jobs, hobbies, sports, community work, political or social involvements, overseas campus, travel, etc.
8. Pre-College background: Anything of note in your family or earlier life history?
9. What would you like to be doing with your life ten years from now (in an ideal, just world)?
10. List your five major personal/social traits.
11. List your five major academic/work traits.
12. What about your emotional stability, maturity?
13. And of course, what about your character?
14. If you get what you are applying for, what are the chances you will "stick it out" or will drop out?
15. Suppose you don't get in anywhere you are applying to—what then? P.S. I'd like to know the outcome of your applications.

4. PROMOTING GRADUATE STUDENT DEVELOPMENT

The focus of the following collection of articles contrasts with those in the preceding group by examining and evaluating concerns of graduate versus undergraduate students. The first selection of articles describes the following topics: the development of self-confidence and competence, the characteristics of superstar students, and the factors that favor the admission into doctoral programs of students from master's-only programs.

The acquisition of teaching skills during graduate school constitutes the theme of articles in the second group. Authors relate their experiences including a conceptual framework for training college teachers, a two-day workshop for graduate teaching assistants, a co-operative program that provides graduate students with full time teaching experience in community colleges, and faculty recruiters' insights about the transition from graduate student to faculty member.

The student's development of scholarly skills lies at the core of graduate education. Learning by collaborative efforts with one's peers is the topic of one article. A second article describes strategies for preventing or dealing with problems associated with doing a dissertation. Dissertation and thesis supervisors can especially appreciate the contents of that article. The last three articles are intimately related to one another; they describe advantages and disadvantages to students of the pressure to publish scholarly work.

a.   Personal Development

Paul Delfin and Michael Roberts were graduate teaching assistants when they participated in this study. The purpose was to assess the process of change in students' perceptions of themselves. This repeated measures design assessed two classes of graduate students four times during their first year of school. Findings revealed increases in self-confidence and decreases in incompetence in relation to specific behavioral objectives following training. The authors candidly acknowledged the limitations of the study when drawing conclusions. Nevertheless, faculty responsible for training practitioners will find many valuable insights and suggestions.

Larry Bloom and Paul Bell from Colorado State University provided a novel description of graduate students' qualities that faculty value. The authors asked about 40 colleagues from across the country to identify the behaviors that distinguished superstars from other students. Bloom and Bell pointed out that these five factors did not include qualities often used in selecting students for graduate school. One could speculate that maybe they should. Nevertheless, the study provides useful suggestions to current and prospective graduate students about those behaviors that elicit favorable reactions from faculty.

Baron Perlman and Patricia Dehart investigated the differences between students who applied and/or gained admission to doctoral programs with those who did not apply. Participants were students completing a terminal master's in clinical at the University of Wisconsin at Oshkosh. The results of the study provided a profile of personal characteristics associated with successful admission to doctoral programs even though 71% of the sample had been denied admission before master's training.

Self-Perceived Confidence and Competence as a Function of Training in the Beginning Graduate Student in Clinical Psychology

Paul E. Delfin, *Reading Hospital and Medical Center*
and Michael C. Roberts, *University of Alabama*

This repeated measures study pioneers into the realm of students' self assessment of graduate training experience effectiveness.

Current training in clinical psychology has been influenced heavily by the scientist-practitioner model, within which the clinician is both service-provider and service-evaluator. The model dictates multimodal training in clinical skills, research skills, and an overall attitude of scientific inquiry (APA Committee on Training in Clinical Psychology, 1950). Despite some debate on the relative weight which ought to be assigned to research or practice, there has been considerable agreement that this model can facilitate the training of innovative, adaptive professonal psychologists who are critical observers of their own and others' work (e.g., Lloyd & Newbrough, 1966). It seems, however, that most graduate students are "critically observed" only in terms of overt measurable behavior (classroom, clinical and expository), presumably in hopes that they will introject the faculty's standards and eventually become independent self-evaluators. Rarely are the students' self-perceptions and "internal" standards observed and taken into account, even though they influence not only interactions with clients and faculty, but also the very professional behaviors which students choose to acquire or exhibit.

There are some measures of students' attitudes in the form of the evaluations of the course and the instructor. Such evaluations reflect how a course is perceived and probably interact with what the student will learn as well as provide feedback to aid in improving the instruction. Other factors which may aid in enhancing acquisition of desirable attitudes and behavior also need to be investigated.

The current study represents a first attempt at assessing the process of change within students' perceptions of themselves and their abilities relative to the intense performance demands of graduate training. We posed problems in the realms of both measurement and politics. As no previous measures were available, we decided to develop our own questionnaire to assess student attitudes. Thus, the device is admittedly unproven for reliability and validity. A major difficulty lies in the often tenuous relationship between self-report and actual behavior. However, since the study's purpose was to assess the students' self-perceptions, self-reports are inevitable.

The political considerations of such a study revolved around our presentation of the research questions to faculty and students. We were, in effect, proposing to evaluate part of the training program in terms of the extent to which some desired objectives (positive student self-perceptions) were being reached. In addition, the fact that the study was presented as desirable could have been read as an implicit challenge to the program's underlying assumption that the development of the student's critical self-observation was in fact being facilitated. Suchman (1967) has pointed out that with staff "ego involved" in the training program, there is likely to be some resistance to the implied questioning of assumptions having "time honored validity." The students, already feeling the pressure of evaluation, might also have resisted an intrusive exploration of their self-perceptions.

Our solutions to these problems were to (a) use a measure which had face validity, but which had unproven predictive or criterion validity, and (b) involve the faculty in the design of the study by asking them to define the behavioral objectives of the first-year sequence in clinical psychology, which we agreed to use as the focus of the study. Our intention was to gain greater faculty and student cooperation by using an obviously crude (and therefore nonthreatening) measure, within boundaries set by the faculty who might otherwise be concerned about the breadth of our "evaluation" of their teaching. Our fears were unrealized as the faculty accepted the project. Some students asked about the use of the data and grumbled about time taken to complete the questionnaire.

Method. The subject population consisted of all students in their first-year of graduate training at an APA approved clinical program based on the scientist-practitioner model. Two groups of first-year students were surveyed as data were collected for two consecutive years (total number enrolled each year was 12). Only eight students in each group completed all questionnaires and were included in the study (approximately 67% cooperation). Three of the clinical psychology faculty were responsible for the course sequence in assessment and interviewing skills over the two years of the study. Graduate teaching assistants (the authors) distributed and collected the questionnaires.

The course instructors described 26 behavior objectives for the two semester course consisting of situations in which the instructors wanted expertise developed. A questionnaire was then devised by the authors consisting of a list of the 26 situations. These were combined into 10 general categories (see Table 1). The following skills objectives were the topics of inquiry at each of the four periods during the year when measurement was made: (periods 1-2) administering, scoring, and interpreting the Stanford-Binet, writing test reports, consulting with teachers, principals, and parents, interviewing adults and children, and behavioral assessment; (periods 2-3) experience with WISC-R, WPPSI, and WAIS; (periods 3-4) mental status examinations and behavioral programming. However the latter two categories were not covered, although they had been scheduled. Of course, many of the activities continued throughout the school year (e.g., report writing and interviewing).

The questionnaire asked the students to rate their self-perceived levels of confidence and incompetence on the 26 items. Confidence was defined as "feeling able to handle the situation and comfortable with their level of functioning within the role." Incompetence was defined simply as "self-perceived lack of skills." Nine-point, Likert-type scales were used for the attributes of confidence and incompetence ranging from "none" to "total." "Incompetence" was used as a rating rather than "competence" to discourage students from giving scores identical to their "confidence" ratings. For anonymity, students' names were not associated with the forms; only the last three digits of the student's Social Security number were used for later matching of questionnaires over time.

The measures were taken four times (periods) over the course of an academic year: at the beginning and middle of each of the two semesters in the student's first year. Because the last quarter of the second semester was devoted to special topics and issues not tapped by the questionnaire (e.g., ethics), we elected not to administer the questionnaire at the end of that semester. A multiple-baseline design is apparent in that the measures were taken on all behaviors including ones for which training had not yet been given. Thus, the design may be viewed as involving the presentation of successive units of training as the independent variable with the measured effects on the students' self-ratings. A functional relationship may be demonstrated if the changes in the self-perceptions correspond to the changes in training. In summary, the design involved four repeated measures of confidence and incompetence over two semesters for two consecutive years on a different group of first-year students each year.

Results. Only the data from the students completing all four ratings were retained for analysis here. Concerning the "unretained" data, four students in each year had each omitted one questionnaire out of the four given. Examination of those forms which the unretained students did complete revealed no major differences with the results reported here. The results of the surveys retained for the second group of students are reported in Table 1. Some of the categories listed are the average rating for several items relating to the central objective (e.g., work with the Stanford-Binet test included separate ratings of administration, scoring, and interpretation). Each entry in the table represents the average rating for the students on the questionnaire items or more general categories. Higher numbers indicate a higher rating for the attributes—confidence and incompetence. As can be seen in the table, in general, the students' self-perception of confidence increased over the first year in graduate school but ratings of incompetence decreased over time. This general conclusion of positive changes is true for both years surveyed.[1]

In order to provide statistical confidence in the observed trends in the self-perceptions, the ratings for the second year of the study were analyzed by repeated measures Analyses of Variance (ANOVA). A Duncan's multiple range test was computed where a significant effect was found on the ANOVA as depicted in Table 1. All ANOVA's had degrees of freedom of 3, 21; all significant F ratios were greater than 4.4; all p values less than the .05 level. Where Duncan's test subscripts are not depicted, no significant effects were obtained.

Following the multiple-baseline type of design, the observation may be made of significant change in self-perceptions over time with some particular time periods more important for change on certain activities than other time periods. These particular findings become even clearer when compared with the clinical and classroom activities during each semester. Students achieved the largest boost in self-confidence and decrease in incompetence for that measurement following instruction in and practical work with the rated situations. For example, the students worked with the Stanford-Binet intelligence test and report writing between the first and second measurement. They worked with the WISC-R, WPPSI, and WAIS between the second and third measurements. Accordingly, students showed statistically significant changes in their ratings at those times.

Table 1. Mean Ratings of Confidence and Incompetence for Course Objectives by First-Year Graduate Students

Objective	Confidence Self-Perceptions Periods of Measurement				Incompetence Self-Perceptions Periods of Measurement			
	First	Second	Third	Fourth	First	Second	Third	Fourth
Stanford-Binet (3)	4.0	7.3_a	7.3_a	7.5_a	6.4	2.8_a	2.6_a	2.3_a
Report writing (1)	3.9	6.9_a	7.1_a	7.1_a	6.5	3.0_a	3.0_a	2.8_a
Consultation (5)	4.4	6.2_a	6.3_a	6.8_a	6.2	4.1_a	3.5_a	3.4_a
Interview (5)	5.1	6.8_a	6.4_a	7.0_a	4.7_a	3.7_{ab}	3.4_b	3.0_b
Behavioral assessment (1)	4.1_a	6.4	6.0_a	7.5	6.3	3.4_a	3.1_a	2.8_a
WISC-R (3)	4.4_a	4.9_a	7.4_b	7.7_b	6.1_a	5.5_a	2.5_b	2.3_b
WPPSI (3)	3.9_a	4.3_a	7.4_b	7.7_b	6.7_a	6.3_a	2.5_b	2.3_b
WAIS (3)	4.0_a	4.0_a	7.0_b	7.7_b	6.6_a	6.6_a	3.0_b	2.3_b
Mental status exam (1)	3.6_a	5.8_a	5.4_a	7.0	7.0	3.8_a	3.5_a	3.1_a
Behavioral programming (1)	4.9_a	5.4_a	5.4_a	6.8_a	5.4_a	4.8_a	4.1_a	3.4_a

Notes: Numbers in parentheses refer to the number of items contributing to category. Means in a row which do not share a common subscript differ significantly at the .05 level by Duncan's multiple range test.

Discussion. Self-perceived confidence and competence (or lack of incompetence) in relation to specific behavioral objectives were shown to be a function of training for those objectives in first-year graduate students in clinical psychology. In eight of the ten categories, confidence increased and perceived incompetence decreased after the point in the year when the behaviors within each category had been trained and tested in the classroom. The exceptions to general positive changes were the mental status report and behavioral program design. We later found that although these items had been listed initially as course objectives, they were not taught during the year. Thus, we inadvertently included control items on our measure!

Recognition of student self-perceptions as important concomitants to training goals should enhance training and may facilitate student acceptance of critical components by communicating a concern for the effects on the student of the training process. For example, professionalism and acceptance of the training model may be increased by attention to the feelings of the students, as suggested by Rogers (1967). Other significant factors might include self-perceptions of anxiety, of professional role identity, of ability to help clients, of personality traits, or of professional behavior.

The students who agreed to return the questionnaires consistently (and who might therefore be characterized as more compliant) may have been simply responding to the demand characteristics of the situation by reporting more positive self-evaluation as the year went on. However, the findings on mental status exam and behavioral programming are discrepant with this idea. Apparently, the students were able to discriminate areas in which their self-perceptions were not congruent with the situational demands.[2] The specific findings of this project are predictable to some extent from a "common-sense" position. One would expect changes to be made in self-perceptions after receiving training for particular skills. However, there has been no previous attempt at verification. More important, this project exemplifies the attitude educators must take in assessing the effects of the educational process on the student, especially in our graduate training.

The questionnaires did not tap the students' actual abilities for the situational categories. Because of guaranteed anonymity, it was not possible to correlate the self-ratings with instructors' ratings of the student for each activity listed in the course objectives. It can be argued that these self-reports have little utility in evaluation, since there is no demonstrable correlation with actual behavior. However, a continued awareness of these and other factors (such as anxiety levels) may be important for monitoring and understanding the processes of change in students. This report has attempted to document some of the attitudinal changes which result from training and which are often noted only informally by students and faculty. The way in which students perceive the acquisition of skills and knowledge likely influences their behavior. Students' attitudes about themselves and perceptions of their own abilities can affect the learning process. Most important, these self-perceptions help the student define his or her future professional role as a psychologist.

References

APA Committee on Training in Clinical Psychology (E. L. Kelly, Chairman). Standards for practicum training in clinical psychology: Tentative recommendations. *American Psychologist,* 1950, *5,* 594-609.

Lloyd, D. N., & Newbrough, J. R. Previous conferences on graduate education in psychology: A summary and review. In E. L. Hoch, A. O. Ross, & C. L. Winder (Eds.), *Professional preparation of clinical psychologists.* Washington, D.C.: APA, 1966.

Rogers, L. R. Graduate education in psychology: A passionate statement. *The Clinical Psychologist,* 1967, *20,* 55-62.

Suchman, E. A. *Evaluative research.* New York: Russell Sage Foundation, 1967.

Notes

1. The results from the earlier group were analyzed in a 26-variable repeated measures ANOVA with significant effects probed by the method of individual comparisons. These data are too cumbersome to present here, but the observed trends were virtually identical to those presented in Table 1. Unfortunately, we were unable to reanalyze the first group's data in a way comparable with those from the second year because the original questionnaires were lost. Copies of the questionnaire and more complete information on the analyses are available from the authors.

2. The same questionnaire was given informally at various times to second-year students in the program. Their responses indicated a stable high sense of confidence, but, surprisingly, increasing levels of incompetence as their chronological distance from the first year course work increased. This lends further support to the statement that students were not merely responding to demand characteristics.

3. Data reported in this study were collected by the authors while graduate students at Purdue University. Thanks are extended to Francis Gilbert, James P. Curran, Donald R. Ottinger, and James D. Linden for their assistance.

4. The order of authorship of this paper is arbitrary as the authors made equal contributions to the project.

Making it in Graduate School: Some Reflections About the Superstars

Larry J. Bicom and Paul A. Bell
Colorado State University

For some students, graduate education in psychology is a traumatic experience fraught with an overabundant dosage of uncertainty, anxiety, and paranoia. Many of them harbor resentments about faculty and program requirements, spend a significant amount of time bemoaning the noxiousness of their education, and in general come to devalue academia. Others find graduate school much less punitive and anxiety-provoking; they seem, much of the time, to even enjoy their graduate education. Within this latter group are a smaller sample of students which, for the sake of this paper, we have labeled the "superstars." These are the few who proceed through the program with a minimum amount of difficulty and a maximum amount of quality performance. They are respected by the faculty, they receive the best financial assistance, they receive accolades, and as a group, they end up with the best employment. Who are these students and, more important, what makes them superstars?

During our own graduate education, we can recall, some faculty made a concerted effort to delineate to their students the contrasting behaviors of superlative and "average" graduate students. In one case, an advisor made it a policy to spend one lecture at the beginning of each year for imploring students to become "superstars." Distinctions between "superstardom" and "satisfying degree requirements," however, must be more difficult for novice students to comprehend than for faculty more familiar with the merits of graduate education. Indeed, it was not until we became faculty for a few years ourselves that we gained peak experience insight into the virtues of having superstar students around.

Stimulated by Maslowian logic and a curious preoccupation with "class," we then took it upon ourselves to study the superstars by talking with those individuals, i.e., faculty, who are instrumental in anointing students with superstar status. Employing a superstar characteristic ourselves, we even collected data on the topic, although in the most informal manner of asking approximately 40 colleagues (all with earned doctorates from established psychology programs across the country) to define the behaviors that distinguish superstars from others. The standard first request was: "Think of the best student you ever worked with or ever knew and tell me what he/she was like, what behaviors he/she emitted to deserve your praises." Those faculty who elected themselves were encouraged to think of an alternative selection. (If they nominated themselves again, they were dropped from the sample.) This first request was usually followed by: "What are some behavioral predictors of graduate superstardom?" Responses to these questions were amazingly consistent. Those qualities which were endorsed overwhelmingly included the following:

Visibility.
The most often mentioned behavioral characteristic was visibility. Superstars were observed to be physically present in the department, during and often after working hours.

Hard Working.
The next most often mentioned quality was they they were hard working. It is important to point out that the superstars were perceived as hard working because faculty actually saw them working hard. Other students may have worked harder, but because they were working hard at home or in the library they were not perceived to be as hard working as the superstars.

Reflection of program values.
A consistently mentioned quality was the faculty's perception of their professional values. These values were concordant with program values of research and scholarly excellence. *All* of the superstars were engaged in ongoing research projects in addition to their MA and PhD theses. Non-superstars did research because it was a degree requirement. Superstars viewed research as an integral part of the discipline and as a desirable and worthwhile activity for any professional psychologist. They were curious enough

about a problem to want to see data on it. In addition, superstars readily recognized the value of having contact with broad areas of psychology, even though their own program might be highly specialized.

Professor Attachment.
From the time they entered graduate school almost all superstars attached themselves to one or two faculty members with whom they continued to work during the course of their training.

The W Factor.
The final characteristic was that superstars had the ability to make faculty feel worthwhile and rewarded. Typical faculty responses here were "early on, they were easy to teach," "they picked up things quickly," "they could receive and use feedback well," "they were not constant complainers," "they were able to grow into colleague status without taking advantage." In essence, the superstars listened, learned, grew, and produced, which in turn made the faculty member feel worthwhile and rewarded for his/her investment and chosen occupation.

It is curious that the above list does not contain the factors of high intelligence, excellent grades in courses taken, ratings of practicum supervisors, interpersonal skills, verbal facility, or writing ability—qualities often used in formal student evaluations. Perhaps these qualities are assumed to be inherent in the qualified few who enter graduate school or perhaps they are subsumed under the basic qualities mentioned above.

The present survey can be criticized on a number of grounds. The "data" are very informal. It would have been useful to gain information from the superstars themselves. There is a noted lack of female impressions of superstars; only three faculty members in this survey were female. All of the impressions were gained from psychologists who came from research-oriented Ph.D. programs, none came from "professional" or nonresearch programs.

Nevertheless, this paper may have important implications for entering graduate students and their faculty. Because faculty are educators seeking to turn out competent psychologists, why not educate students on how to become superstars? Rather than just one or two faculty in a program giving an initial lecture on superstardom, all faculty could actively encourage students in this direction. Superstar training could begin at an initial meeting for all new graduate students. During this meeting, in addition to conveying to students the standard information discussed at such meetings, faculty could convey to students as specifically as possible those behaviors that correlate with, i.e., predict, superstardom. This process might reduce casualties and it could be extremely beneficial to those students who might roam aimlessly wondering what they need to do to make it in graduate school. At its worst, it might make graduate education a more enjoyable experience for students and faculty alike. Although there are undoubtedly more characteristics of the superstars, the present survey suggests that students can increase their chances of success in graduate school by becoming visible, letting faculty see that they are working very hard, conveying an attitude which reflects program values, attaching themselves to a professor, and making faculty, who have dedicated a large part of their lives to graduate education, feel worthwhile and rewarded—in effect validated. Especially to students, it may all sound very autocratic and asymmetrical in the balance of power. The reality here is that it is indeed this way. The reality is also that the superstars not only learn the game but play it extremely well, much to their benefit.

The Master's-Level Clinician: Application and Admission to Doctoral Programs

Baron Perlman
University of Wisconsin—Oshkosh

Patricia Dehart
Winnebago Mental Health Institute

The effect of having a master's degree on doctoral program application and acceptance/nonacceptance remains unclear. All former master's-level clinicians (N = 89) in an MS psychology program for an 11-year period were sampled; 65 individuals responded. Of those who applied to doctoral programs (n = 28), 86% gained admission. Results indicated significant differences between this accept group (n = 24) and a noapply group (n = 37). The noapply group had significantly lower GRE Quantitative scores, took significantly more time to complete the master's degree, were significantly older, chose the master's degree because at the time of master's application they did not want a doctorate, and had a higher percentage of women. Four primary implications of the data are discussed.

The value of a terminal master's degree to those seeking doctoral program admission remains uncertain. On the one hand, some doctoral programs seem reluctant to accept such individuals (Albee, 1971; Annis, Tucker, & Baker, 1978; Howell & Murdock, 1972; Saccuzzo & Schulte, 1978). On the other hand, some research and writing support the value of a terminal master's degree for doctoral program admission (Mealiea, 1973; Ward & Ziegler, 1973). It is difficult to gain admission to many PhD and PsyD programs, and a master's degree may be the only choice for some qualified individuals (or the degree of choice for others). One *can* earn a master's degree and apply to doctoral programs with hopes of admission (Annis, Tucker, & Baker, 1978; Mealiea, 1973; Perlman, in press; Tucker & Annis, 1981).

Korn (1984) recently estimated that the odds on gaining doctoral program acceptance seem to be improving (although he did not look at master's-level individuals per se) while LeUnes, Bourgeois, Bond, and Oppenheimer (1982) argue for in-depth follow-up of master's programs. The present research addresses both issues. It is an 11-year follow-up on doctoral program applications for all students in a MS Psychology Program–Clinical Emphasis. The study focuses not only on those who apply and are accepted or denied admission to doctoral programs, but also on those who have never made application. This latter group has been ignored in the literature.

The purpose of this research is to determine if differences exist between students trained in a terminal master's program with a clinical emphasis who applied and/or gained admission to doctoral programs and those who did not apply. Learning more about these master's clinical persons may be of assistance to faculty members who teach in terminal master's-level clinical programs in planning and assessment; that is, program goals and curricula could differ depending on whether students go on for doctoral study, work in the field, or both. These data may also benefit both undergraduate and graduate students (and faculty members advising them) in educational and career planning and decision-making.

METHOD

Subjects

Students who had completed all coursework (but not necessarily the thesis) for the master's degree in psychology with a clinical emphasis at the University of Wisconsin–Oshkosh from 1971 to 1982, inclusive, were sampled (N = 89).

The Program

The MS Psychology–Clinical Emphasis program has an 18–21 credit "core" with courses in experimental design, statistics, learning, experimental psychology, theoretical issues, and thesis. Clinical courses include individual intelligence testing, projective tests, objective tests, psychopathology, psychotherapy, community mental health, four semesters of community agency practicum, and two semesters of psychodiagnostic practicum. The program requires 45 semester credits in total.

Instrument

Data were collected by means of a questionnaire that took 10 minutes to complete. Respondents' age and sex were obtained. Undergraduate data included major, grade point average, and degree earned. Data on master's clinical training included: (a) amount of time between receipt of bachelor's degree and beginning of master's training; (b) amount of volunteer experience prior to master's training—measured on a 5-point scale coded from none to more than 1 year; (c) amount of paid human service/mental health work experience—measured on a 1- to 4-point scale coded from none to 1 year or more full-time; (d) when master's training was begun; (e) when coursework was completed; (f) when thesis was completed; (g) age when coursework was completed; and (h) grade point average. Five items with a 1- to 5-point Likert-type scaling (*strongly agree* to *strongly disagree*) asked about reasons behind the decision to attend a clinical master's program (feeling doctoral program admission would be impossible, doctoral training taking too long, doctoral education seeming too expensive, not wanting a doctorate at the time master's clinical program application was made, and doctoral program admission being denied).

Post-master's program data were gathered for all persons sampled. Those accepted into doctoral programs were asked to supply information in response to questions applicable at the time of first doctoral program admission. Questions included (a) amount (years and months) of full-time and part-time salaried mental health work; (b) post-master's scholarly experience (number of paper presentations, symposium participations, manuscripts published); (c) number of workshops, conventions, and training sessions attended; (d) amount, if any, of research activity; and (e) Graduate Record Examination scores (Verbal, Quantitative, Analytic, and Advanced).

Those respondents who had not made doctoral program application answered additional items, including a question with a 6-point Likert-type scale (*very unlikely* to *very likely*) on the likelihood that doctoral program application would be made in the future. They were also asked six questions, scaled on a 5-point Likert-type scale (*agree* to *disagree*), about their reasons for not making doctoral program application (unable to relocate, financial, belief admission would be denied, thesis incomplete, family considerations, present employment too good).

Respondents who had been accepted into doctoral programs answered questions about (a) the year first acceptance into a doctoral program occurred; (b) number of years in a row all doctoral program applications were denied; (c) total number of applications made and number of acceptances; and (d) whether the respondent had attended a doctoral program and, if so, the university and program emphasis. Those who attended doctoral training programs responded to items asking about (a) degree level of their class, that is, all master's-level, majority master's-level, majority bachelor's-level; (b) credit received for master's training (all, part, none); (c) number of credits of pre-master's work required in the doctoral program; and (d) whether the person had graduated, was still in, or had dropped out of the doctoral program.

Those persons who had applied and never gained admission to a doctoral program answered questions about the number of years doctoral program application had been made and the total number of applications submitted.

Procedure

A cover letter, questionnaire, and self-addressed, postage-paid, return envelope were sent to each of the 89 former students, with a 2-week follow-up.

RESULTS

Thirteen questionnaires were returned "addressee unknown," decreasing the usable sample to 76. Completed questionnaires were received from 65 former students (41 males and 24 females, average age = 27.7 years), a response rate of 85.5% (73% of all clinical graduates in 11 years). Thirty-seven (57%) respondents indicated that they had not applied to doctoral programs since completing their master's training (noapply). Twenty-four (37%) respondents indicated that they had gained admission into one or more doctoral programs following completion of their master's training (accept). Four (6%) respondents indicated that they had applied to, but had not been accepted by, any doctoral program since finishing their master's training (noaccept). Thus, 86% of all master's individuals who had applied to doctoral programs gained admission. The noaccept group was dropped from further study due to its small size.

To determine if the noapply and accept groups differed significantly, chi-square analyses or separate t tests were performed. For the latter, an F statistic for homogeneity of variance at the .05 level of probability was computed for each item analyzed. When homogeneity of variance was assumed, t values with pooled variance estimates were used. In those instances where homogeneity of variance could not be assumed, t values with separate variance estimates were used. All t tests were nondirectional, using .01 as the level of significance.

Those who were accepted to doctoral programs (19 males, 5 females) may be characterized, compared with their noapply peers (19 males, 18 females) as: wanting a doctorate even when gaining admission to a master's program; being younger, $t(59) = 2.86$, $p < .001$, M = 27.7 years versus 31 years; having a higher GRE Quantitative score, $t(49) = 3.97$, $p < .001$, M = 616 versus M = 521; and taking less time to complete the master's degree, $t(43) = 3.42$, $p < .001$, M = 26 months versus 35 months, including thesis. A chi-square analysis revealed significant differences for number of males and females in the two groups, $\chi^2(1, N = 61) = 4.79$, $p < .05$. An inspection of individual cells reveals the noapply group is 49% female, the accept group 21% female. The noapply group is not firmly established at the master's-level with 15 individuals stating they were still planning to seek doctoral training, 12 not planning to do so, and 10 undecided.

Pre-Master's Training Data

A bachelor's degree with a psychology major was predominant for both groups (accept group = 88%, noapply group = 97%) (χ^2, n.s.). For the noapply group the BS degree was held by 68%, whereas only 37% of the accept group had this degree (63% had a BA degree). A chi-square analysis on type of bachelor's degree was significant, χ^2 (1, N = 61) = 5.33, $p < .025$. There is a relationship between type of degree and whether one makes doctoral program application after master's training with a greater percentage of those who do apply for doctoral study possessing a BA degree. The undergraduate GPA (computed on a 4-point scale) for the accept group was 3.16; for the noapply group, it was 3.32 (t test, n.s.). The noapply and accept groups averaged 11.84 and 18.83 months, respectively, between conclusion of bachelor's and beginning of master's training (t test, n.s.). Finally, 62% of the noapply and 75% of the accept groups had volunteer experience in mental health, and 54% of the noapply group and 50% of the accept group had salaried work experience in mental health (chi-square values on these latter two findings were not significant).

Master's and Post-Master's Training Data

The accept and noapply groups had the following mean GRE scores: (a) Verbal GRE equaled 568 and 538, (b) Analytic equaled 613 and 581, (c) Advanced equaled 610 and 551, respectively. The accept group had a mean master's-level graduate GPA of 3.65 and were 25.5 years old at the completion of master's-level training; the noapply group had a graduate GPA of 3.54 and were 27 years old when they received their degree. The t-test analyses on these variables yielded nonsignificant results.

The accept and noapply groups were compared for scholarly experience, research activity, and attendance at workshops, conventions, and training sessions after master's training. Chi-square analyses on the first two variables and a t test on the latter yielded nonsignificant results. Six members (of 37) in the noapply group and 5 members (of 24) in the accept group reported research activity. Scholarly experience (paper presentations, symposium participation, publishing of manuscripts) was limited for individuals in both groups. Only 8 persons in the noapply group and 7 persons in the accept group reported engaging in any scholarly work. Finally, on the average, those in the noapply group attended 6 workshops, 1.5 conventions, and 4 training sessions. Those in the accept group reported attending an av-

erage of 3 workshops, 1 convention, and 4 training sessions after master's work and before first doctoral program acceptance.

Doctoral Application Data

Of the 61 individuals studied, 32 applied to doctoral programs prior to master's-level clinical training. Of these 32, 26 (81%) were denied admission. It is interesting to note that 18 individuals in the accept group had applied to doctoral programs (before master's training) and 17 had been denied admission. In other words, 17 persons denied admission to doctoral programs before terminal master's clinical study gained doctoral program admission after master's training.

Table 1 provides data on reasons for attending a terminal master's program and not pursuing a doctorate in psychology directly after undergraduate training. Each statement was scaled from 1 = *strongly disagree* to 5 = *strongly agree*. The Disagree category represents Responses 1 and 2, the Agree category combines Responses 4 and 5. The t-test analyses comparing those in the accept and noapply groups on the uncollapsed 1- to 5-point scaled items yielded one significant result, "I decided to attend a clinical master's program rather than directly pursuing a doctorate because I did not want a doctorate at that time," t (59) = 4.49, $p < .001$. Those in the noapply group had a higher mean (2.76) response to this item than persons in the accept group (1.42).

Members of the noapply group were asked to indicate their reasons for not seeking a doctoral degree in psychology since they completed master's training. Items were scaled 1 to 5 with Responses 4 and 5 in the Agree category. The percentage of respondents who agreed with each reason were: (a) present employment satisfactory (70%), (b) family considerations (51%), (c) expense of a doctoral education (38%), (d) unable to relocate (32%), (e) thesis incomplete (8%), and (f) belief admission would be denied (4%).

Analyses of accept group data revealed that the group's mean age at time of first doctoral program acceptance was 27.7 years and the mean amount of time between completion of coursework for the master's degree and first doctoral program acceptance was 22.5 months. Fifty-eight percent indicated the thesis was complete when first accepted into a doctoral program. Respondents in the accept group were

Table 1. Percentage of Respondents Giving Various Reasons for not Directly Pursuing a Doctorate in Psychology after Undergraduate Training

Reasons	NOAPPLY				ACCEPT			
	Disagree	Undecided	Agree	N	Disagree	Undecided	Agree	N
Length of a doctoral program	68	8	24	37	87	0	13	24
Expense of a doctoral education	73	5	22	37	79	8	13	24
Not interested in a doctorate	57	0	43	37	92	0	8	24
Belief that admission would be denied	62	5	33	37	29	4	67	24
Application to doctoral program made and admission denied	36	0	64	14	6	0	94	18

also asked to indicate when (after master's training) they achieved their first doctoral program acceptance. Results revealed that 11 individuals (46%) gained acceptance into at least one doctoral program during their first year of application, seven individuals (29%) were admitted during the second year of application, with five respondents (21%) successful during their third or fourth year of application. One individual (4%) was not able to gain admission into any doctoral program until the seventh year of application.

Members of the accept group were also asked to indicate the total number of doctoral applications made, the emphasis of the programs to which they applied, and the number of programs that accepted them. Twenty-three individuals applied to Clinical programs; 11 gained admission (48%), but only 12% of their applications were accepted. Some applicants applied to over 25 Clinical programs! Thirteen persons applied to Counseling programs with six gaining admission (46%), 12 applied to PsyD programs with five gaining admission (42%), and all eight who applied to "Other" (School Psychology, Industrial/Organizational) programs gained acceptance. The acceptance rate of applications submitted was 24% for Counseling programs, 53% for PsyD programs and 92% for "Other" programs. Nine persons applied to both PsyD and PhD Clinical programs. No one was accepted to both, 5 individuals were accepted to PsyD programs, 3 were accepted to PhD Clinical programs, and 1 person was denied both Clinical and PsyD admission, but was accepted in an "Other" doctoral program.

Doctoral Program Attendance Data

Of the 24 members of the accept group, 21 (88%) attended doctoral programs in psychology. Of these, 5 persons attended PhD Clinical programs, 4 PsyD programs, 4 Counseling programs, and 8 attended "Other" programs in psychology. Calculation of amount of master's work accepted revealed 13 respondents (62%) who reported that all master's work was accepted. No student accepted into a doctoral program had all master's work denied. Mean number of courses repeated by these master's-trained individuals once in doctoral training was 2.4

The high success rate of the accept group may be due in part to their selection of programs. Respondents who attended doctoral training were asked to provide their best estimate on the percentage of their doctoral class with a master's degree; 10 stated that their entire doctoral class had master's degrees, 7 stated that a majority admitted were at the master's level, and 4 claimed that the majority admitted were at the bachelor's level.

DISCUSSION

The terminal master's degree with a clinical emphasis is not a dead-end precluding doctoral work. Eighty-six percent (24 out of 28) of the respondents who applied to doctoral programs gained admission and of these 24, 17 had been denied admission before master's training. Almost half of those accepted gained admission to PhD clinical programs, and training in PsyD programs was also possible. Admission to School Psychology and Industrial/Organizational doctoral training was almost certain. What is not

known is whether the acceptance rate is good because of improved credentials due to master's training, better advising, a more reasonable choice of programs, being older, having more work experience, or other factors. The finding that a greater percentage of those in the accept group compared to the noapply group have a BA degree, not a BS, cannot be explained by the authors.

The accept group, as a whole, seems to have chosen the master's degree as a second choice or as a "stepping-stone" to the doctorate. Two groups emerge in the research. For the accept group, primarily male, a career path includes doctoral work. For the second group, equally men and women, the master's degree becomes the end point of formal academic training in psychology (a chosen alternative for some, for others a result of family, good employment, realization that doctoral program acceptance is remote, and other considerations). Thus, advisers, students, and faculty members have some insight into who will and who will probably not go on for doctoral work. Those who will probably do so report (in retrospect) that they wanted a doctorate when earning a BA/BS degree, are younger, more likely to be male, have a higher GRE Quantitative score and, once in a terminal master's program, finish sooner. This study encompasses a 1971–1982 time period; it will be interesting to see if similar research in the future reports a higher percentage of women attending doctoral programs after master's training.

The data lend support to the argument of the possible "solidity" of the terminal master's-level clinician. Based on the one program sample reported here, there are few differences between those who go on for doctoral work and those who do not apply, many of whom work in the field at the master's level. The differences in applying for doctoral work and eventually earning this degree seem to be those of motivation and nonwork considerations, not of overall ability as measured by GPA, most GRE scores, and so on. This research provides limited evidence that one may be in error to think of the person with terminal master's-level training in the clinical area as a "PhD dropout" with the negative connotations this phrase may carry with it.

Although applicants are probably wise to choose doctoral programs that accept those with master's degrees, antimaster's bias may still be encountered. One respondent accepted into a Developmental/Clinical doctoral program commented that the admissions committee at that university "does not prefer" to admit master's-trained individuals, and added that she was "the first one" to be admitted. Another individual who had gained acceptance into a PhD program in Industrial/Organizational psychology commented, ". . . having a master's kept me from being admitted. I had to beg." Persistence and appropriate assertiveness may be needed for master's-trained individuals seeking doctoral program admission.

Generalization of these findings should be made cautiously because of the single program studied, its characteristics, the sample's characteristics (GRE scores, years of work experience, age, etc.), and individuals' perseverance in making doctoral applications. It is also not known what quality of counsel these students received about doctoral program applications and the reasons students selected programs for application. The high response rate, number of comments on questionnaires, and the fact that all but two of the respondents requested a copy of the results seem to suggest that this is an issue that elicits both interest and strong emotion. The research reported here should be useful for students in psychology, advisers, and faculty members.

REFERENCES

Albee, G. W. (1971). Master's level education in psychology. In *Master's level education in psychology: Report of a conference held November, 1970*. Washington, DC: American Psychological Association, 1–11.

Annis, L. V., Tucker, G. H., & Baker, D. A. (1978). What happens to PhD program applicants who have master's degrees? *American Psychologist, 33*, 703–705.

Howell, R. J., & Murdock, M. I. (1972). The questionable value of a master's degree for a PhD-pursuing student. *American Psychologist, 27*, 647–651.

Korn, J. H. (1984). New odds on acceptance into PhD programs in psychology. *American Psychologist, 39*, 179–180.

LeUnes, A., Bourgeois, A., Bond, T., & Oppenheimer, K. (1982). The master's program in psychology: A 10-year follow-up study. *American Psychologist, 37*, 1060–1062.

Mealiea, W. L., Jr. (1973). The unquestionable value of a master's degree for a PhD-pursuing student. *American Psychologist, 28*, 938–939.

Perlman, B. (in press). The master's degree in psychology. In G. F. Sumprer & S. Walfish (Eds.), *Clinical, counseling and community psychology: A student guide to graduate training and professional practice*. New York: Irvington.

Saccuzzo, D. P., & Schulte, R. H. (1978). The value of a terminal master's degree for PhD-pursuing students in psychology. *American Psychologist, 33*, 862–864.

Tucker, G. H., & Annis, L. V. (1981). The ideal function of the terminal master's degree program for a PhD-pursuing student. *Professional Psychology, 12*, 336–340.

Ward, B., & Ziegler, D. J. (1973). On Howell and Murdock. *American Psychologist, 28*, 91.

NOTES

1. The authors would like to thank E. Alan Hartman, Lee McCann, and Robert Lane for assistance with earlier drafts of this paper.

b. Teaching Skills

Angus Strachan, Veronica Welch, Chris Barker, Bruce Compas, and Mary Ferguson described a conceptual framework for training college-level psychology instructors while they were at UCLA. Their model, which can also serve as the foundation for other programs, consists of five basic processes for training particular teaching skills. The authors elaborated on the processes that consist of a) informing, b) modeling, c) experiencing, d) discussing, and e) feedback. Even experienced teachers are likely to discover some challenging suggestions in this article.

Graduate teaching assistants and fellows at West Virginia University have found a structured two-day workshop waiting for them before the start of the fall term. Kennon Lattal provided a thorough description of the workshop that focused on information about questions, policies, and problems that affect teaching of all courses. The author noted that he will provide more detailed information on request.

J. Grosslight described a cooperative program that developed between Florida State University and several community colleges to provide graduate students with substantial teaching competency. The article delineated the program's characteristics, advantages, and disadvantages. The program may be particularly noteworthy for PhD candidates interested in obtaining academic positions.

First-time seekers of academic positions will also appreciate the insights and views of these seasoned recruiters of college teachers from Barat College. Paul Hettich, Sandra Lema-Stern, and Joseph Rizzo collaborated in producing this article. Topical ideas consist of an examination of the differences between graduate and undergraduate education, the role of teaching experience, preparation for the employment interview, and an evaluation of teachers' values and goals. Interested readers may find that the authors' experience can facilitate the transition from graduate student to faculty member.

A Framework for Training College-Level Teachers of Psychology: Five Basic Processes

Angus Strachan, Veronica Ortega Welch,
Chris Barker, Bruce Compas, and
Mary Lund Ferguson
University of California

This paper presents a conceptual framework for training college-level instructors of psychology in teaching skills. The UCLA Department of Psychology has developed two teacher training courses: a practicum in discussion group leadership skills for undergraduates and a training course for graduate teaching assistants. From the experience of planning, implementing, and refining these programs, five basic processes have emerged as essential to consider when designing such courses: (a) informing, (b) modeling, (c) experiencing, (d) discussing, and (e) feedback. This framework can help identify the best methods for training particular teaching skills. They can be used as "building blocks" in the design of other programs.

Informing. Informing is the direct delivery of information about teaching by verbal presentations and written or audiovisual material. As used here, the direct delivery of information has the particular disadvantage that the student teacher receives the information passively and gets no actual practice in teaching concepts. Therefore, we use informing in combination with other active training processes which require the student teachers to observe and try various teaching practices. When applied in this manner, we have found the process of informing to be useful in three ways: (a) providing a rationale and cognitive structure for the other training processes, (b) concisely transmitting psychological principles of learning and memory, and (c) describing alternative teaching roles such as those of discussion leader or project consultant.

The advantage of informing is that information can provide a structure for organizing and anticipating experience, and can be delivered and absorbed quickly. Thus, it can be very useful to present psychological principles relevant to lecture organization, such as the use of active processing and a variety of encoding methods in improving memory. Overall, our programs downplay training by the delivery of information. Thus, although we find that providing facts about lecture organization helps the student teachers structure their lecture material, providing facts about lecture delivery is less helpful for improving lecture performance than the more active processes discussed below.

Modeling. Modeling is an inevitable process in the training of teachers, whether intended or not. Rather than leave the modeling process to the whims of incidental learning, we use modeling as a major training technique to help student teachers acquire intricate response patterns, eliminate behavioral deficits, and reduce fears and inhibitions. We analyze the models to which students have been exposed in the past and use peers and the teacher trainer as new models.

The most salient role model is the trainer. In our programs, the teacher trainer intentionally models by demonstrating the various techniques he or she wishes the students to learn. The trainer can model an organized versus a disorganized lecture, or the use of "ice-breaking" discussion techniques. These demonstrations are especially useful when repeated after discussion. It is particularly important to model several questioning and active listening techniques, such as open-ended questions, summary reflections, and pauses. Finally, a trainer can disclose covert thought processes and problem-solving strategies and thus provide a model of a human "coper" rather than a fully-fledged "master."

Experiencing. The experiential portion of our programs can be divided into two parts: simulated teaching and actual teaching. The simulated teaching consists of role plays and "micro-teaching" in which students practice teaching techniques with their peers and receive videotape and verbal feedback (Ivey, 1971). The simulations vary to the extent to which the roles are spontaneous or scripted ("be yourself" or "be authoritarian"); the extent to which the skills are specific (questioning strategies or facilitating group process); and the manner in which feedback is given (verbal or video).

The advantage of role-playing is that it is probably the most effective way of changing attitudes and ideas about teaching by allowing students to try new styles of teaching in a non-threatening atmosphere. Role-plays can also teach particular skills effectively by reinforcing and shaping desired behavior, particularly when preceded by modeling and followed by feedback. Finally, it can be used to desensitize students to anxiety-provoking situations, either by practicing prior to facing the actual situation, or by "reliving" a difficult situation and finding a different outcome.

Discussing. Weekly group discussion opportunities for student teachers are also a central part of our programs. The structure and format of the group discussions varies week to week from a focus on a selected theoretical issue to an open-ended discussion of problems which are most pressing to the student teachers. In either case, an essential part of the experience is to allow students to share the common elements in their work as beginning teachers. In addition, the discussion process generates a supportive and cohesive atmosphere among the participants. Although group discussions are included in educational programs for a wide variety of reasons (e.g., increased rate of learning and improved retention), group discussions are particularly valuable in that they provide the participants with an opportunity to share perspectives on material which has been presented didactically, and to generate problem-solving strategies for problems encountered in their practicum experiences. Finally, the group discussions can provide an opportunity for the participants to learn about group dynamics. Students can more clearly observe and discuss communication patterns and phases of group development when they have been participants in a group process themselves. In addition, the student teachers are more able to appreciate the relation between the leader's behavior and the group's performance when they have consciously participated in both roles.

Feedback. As part of our program, the use of feedback on teaching performance greatly enhances training by the other four processes. The purpose of this section is twofold: (a) to present a graded hierarchy of techniques for providing feedback, and (b) to show how the program teaches giving and getting verbal feedback.

A major problem with beginning teachers is their reluctance to be observed. They are afraid of criticism or personal judgment. This is not surprising since teaching involves putting oneself on view. The additional embarrassment of receiving feedback overwhelms some beginning teachers. The question seems to be how to provide useful feedback in a minimally threatening way. Some techniques are more threatening than others. Being videotaped while one is teaching a class is a powerful learning experience, but it is unsettling. Feedback from faculty can be threatening and may not always be informed. It is our experience that feedback from peer teachers is effective if the peers are trained in observation techniques and in ways of giving feedback.

We have found that feedback is most effective when a graded hierarchy of techniques is used to desensitize the beginning teacher to receiving feedback. We shall present this graded hierarchy starting with the least threatening technique and moving to more powerful techniques.

1. *Observation of a Faculty Member Teaching.* Student teachers visit a faculty member's class, observe, take notes, and share their observations with the group. Washington, in her book "Expert Teacher Action Program" (1971), provides an excellent list of 25 variables to observe. A shortened list may be useful in a brief training course. Observation can be of broad variables such as course organization, student participation or student-teacher rapport. These can be reduced to smaller skill-segments for particular teaching situations. Observing a lecture, one might focus on blackboard technique, movement on the stage, or the organization of the lecture material. In learning to observe these behaviors, student teachers become sensitive to them in themselves.

2. *Audiotape of Student Teacher's Class.* The student can listen to the tape for self-analysis. This is not very threatening. Even so, until they grow accustomed to their own style and voice they may be somewhat scared and embarassed by early tapes.

3. *Microteaching with Trainee Peers.* The student teacher gives a brief lesson (3-5 minutes) to the rest of the group of peers who act as students. The lesson is videotaped and replayed to generate feedback from the others. The video can be used to "anchor" the feedback with concrete examples. An additional advantage of this method is that they get exposed to a variety of teaching styles.

4. *Observation of a Peer Teaching a Real Class.* Student teachers join a peer's class and observe with minimal disturbance. We advise observers to meet briefly with the teacher before and immediately after the class with more detailed feedback being given later.

5. *Videotape of Student Teaching a Real Class.* The teacher should announce that the purpose of the observation is to monitor the teacher, not the class. The peer group can observe the videotape and provide feedback directly. Alternatively, the tape can be stopped at any time and the experience of the teacher explored (Kagan, 1976).

We have discovered the following to be useful guides to giving verbal feedback whether in a micro-teaching or a live teaching situation: (a) Before the class meets, ask the teacher for the objectives and any specific behaviors which should be observed. (b) After the class, give the teacher an opportunity for self-evaluation. It is surprising how much people are aware of strengths and weaknesses of their own teaching. (c) When giving feedback, first give positive feedback focusing on specific behaviors. (d) Then give constructive feedback, again focusing on specific behaviors. These can be pointed out on the video, and alternative behaviors suggested. Observers should be sensitive to the effects of feedback on the teacher. Feedback presented in a caring, objective manner is easier to accept. Telling one's own reactions instead of judging performance is more useful and less threatening to the teacher, e.g., "I could not follow your blackboard diagram," rather than "your blackboard diagram was not clear." (e) Finally, non-defensiveness on the part of the teacher can make the process of feedback much smoother. The teacher can try to be open in hearing the feedback. It is sometimes hard to remember, but the feedback refers only to a specific display of a special skill, and not to one's value as a person.

Basic courses in psychology have become a crucial part of college education. Thus, teachers of psychology are challenged to present psychological materials in stimulating ways to large numbers of college students with diverse interests and backgrounds. The conceptual framework for training which we have presented here can be used to introduce training programs for teachers of psychology which should improve the quality of undergraduate education in psychology.

References

Ivey, A. E. *Microcounseling: Innovations in interview training.* Springfield, IL: Charles C Thomas, 1971.

Kagan, H. *Interpersonal process recall.* Lansing: Michigan State University, 1976.

Washington, E. *Expert teacher action program.* Belmont, CA: Fearon, 1971.

Notes

1. The last three authors participated equally and are cited in random order.
2. Portions of this paper were first presented as papers at the 1978 meeting of the Western Psychological Association.
3. We wish to thank Morris Holland for his inspiration and support.

A Workshop for New Graduate Student Teachers of Undergraduate Psychology Courses

Kennon A. Lattal
West Virginia University

Many new graduate students, only a few months past being undergraduates themselves, are placed in positions of teaching responsibility in larger psychology departments. Frequently they are without teaching experience and have little information on basic classroom procedures, administrative requirements, and performance expectancies by faculty. While many of these deficits can be ameliorated only by actual classroom experience in teaching, the transition from student to teacher can be eased by supplying information on the academic community's resources and requirements and by providing experiences in handling general types of problems likely to be encountered in teaching. Because student teachers in our department are assigned to individual courses of faculty members who provide supervision of instructional techniques, content-related information, and specific procedures for their courses, we focus on providing information on questions, policies, and problems that more generally affect teaching of all courses and all undergraduate students in the department.

The format is a two-day (11 hour) workshop conducted before the start of classes in the fall term. During the preceding summer, a letter is sent to all new graduate teaching assistants and teaching fellows, announcing the time and schedule of the workshop and that the workshop is required of them. Fourteen students participated in the first workshop.

During the first two-hour session, responsibilities and rules concerning undergraduate teaching are presented by administrative personnel of the department. Next, all curriculum requirements of the university, college and department for obtaining the Bachelor's degree are discussed. This is followed by a consideration of the administrative mechanics of teaching, e.g., reporting of grades; which forms to use for changing a grade or dropping a course; which secretary or office to refer students for specific types of problems; and procedures for obtaining undergraduate student evaluations of teacher performance.

The next two three-hour sessions are devoted to departmental and university resources for teaching. The departmental component includes a tour of the psychology building with brief stops in the various laboratories, in classrooms available for teaching, in the department testing center, and, most important, in the departmental offices where the secretarial staff is introduced. This is followed by a two-hour training session in the use of instructional equipment available in the department; specifically, they are given experience in operating various film projectors, video equipment, and tape recorders. Next, representatives from the library, academic advising center, student counseling center, and reading and writing laboratories each provide a 15-30 minute talk on the services they offer. In this section, we are concerned primarily with student teachers

knowing where to send their students when specific academic and/or personal problems appear.

The workshop concludes with a three-hour session in which example problem situations which have arisen in various faculty members' teaching experiences are presented for discussion. Students are divided into groups of five or six and participate in role playing and problem solving of each of fifteen situations. A faculty member serves as discussion leader for each group. The problems cover such areas as interpersonal relations with students, professional and ethical behavior of teachers, use of students as research subjects, cheating, confidentiality of student data, and a category labelled "being reasonable and fair with students." Some examples of the problems and the type of problem they exemplify are as follows:

1. At the beginning of the semester you indicate that the course grading will be 90% of total points=A; 80%=B, etc. You go on to illustrate this by showing that of the 400 possible points in the course, a student must earn 340 to receive an *A*. On the last day of class you catch your mistake and realize that 340 points is 85% and not 90%. Some of your students have been working for an A, expecting to have to earn only 340 points and not 360 (.90 x 400). What should you do? (Being reasonable and fair with students).

2. Following a class discussion on IQ testing, in which you acknowledge your skill as a psychometrist, a student asks you if you would give him/her an IQ test. Should you? (Professional Behavior.)

3. You meet one of your students from Psych 1 at a social gathering in the local pub. You would like to continue seeing him/her and you contemplate inviting him/her over to your house the following weekend to see your incredible movie on "Token Economies with Amphibians." Should you or should you not pursue this relationship with your student? (Interpersonal relations with students.)

4. Mr. Jackson calls you and wants to know how his son Dave is doing in your Psych 1 course. (Should you give him the information?) As you check your records, you discover that he has dropped the course. Further checking with Mrs. Watson, the Undergraduate Secretary, indicates that young Dave dropped out of the university three weeks ago. What do you do now? (Confidentiality of student data.)

Reaction to the workshop, assessed by a written evaluation conducted at the end of the last session, was very favorable. On a scale of 1=poor and 10=excellent the average rating (N=14) of the overall value of the workshop was 8.69 (range=8-10). The graduate students noted that much of the mystery of departmental and college administrative operations had been removed. They felt that they had substantial resources available to assist in teaching and advising undergraduate students. The problem solving session was singled out as the most enjoyable component of the workshop. A follow-up evaluation held three months after the workshop indicated that most students had encountered situations where the administrative information was valuable and that the example problems covered were indeed representative. The students generally reported that, as a result of the workshop, they were better prepared to deal with teaching-related problems.

A detailed outline of the workshop, including a list of the situations used in the problem solving sessions, may be obtained from me on request.

Note
Dr. William J. Fremouw's assistance in constructing the example problem situations and in serving as discussion leader for the groups is gratefully acknowledged.

The Teaching Apprentice: A Community College-University Program

J. H. Grosslight
Florida State University

With the cooperation of several community colleges (Note 1), a program has evolved in the Department of Psychology at Florida State University for preparing graduate students with substantial teaching competency. Concern about the teaching competency of new PhD's interested in academic positions prompted the program's inception seven years ago. Professional literature was replete with moans and groans concerning the lack of teaching skills characteristic of PhDs graduated from primarily research-oriented departments (Note 2). Most attempts to train teachers of psychology were limited by and to the practicum experience. Even in those departments allowing graduate students to participate in introductory courses, graduate students were primarily involved in research and academic requirements, and were teachers only secondarily, and then for only a small portion of their work week. Consequently, they experienced a small and truncated sample of college teaching duties and responsibilities. Teaching a course, or even two, as a graduate student is quantitatively and, I suspect, qualitatively different from teaching as a full-time faculty member. From this viewpoint, it was deemed necessary to devise a program to provide our graduate students with a more realistic and appropriate teaching experience.

Currently, this program allows our graduate students to function as full-time faculty members in *non-local* community colleges. Selected graduate students, with a minimum of a master's degree, are assigned for a full semester. During that time, they assume the role and duties of regular college faculty in order to experience a total immersion in teaching and collateral activities.

The teaching assignments consist of three classes, occasionally four, with the constraint that no more than two preparations are needed. Further, the community colleges attempt to provide classes representing different student populations. Although these teaching apprentices generally teach a population of day-time, young, community college students, they also experience distinctly different groups for one or more classes: adult-evening-working population; culturally disadvantaged and/or minority population; early-college-placement high school population; and we hope they are exposed to the growing senior, retired, continuing-education population.

While on apprenticeship, they are paid as faculty members by the community college. Their initial teaching endeavor is supervised by one or more senior faculty members at the community college. In fact, the relationship of the apprentice and the community college faculty is usually reciprocal: the student is supervised and often also participates in the supervisor's and other faculty members' classes.

In addition, members of our faculty visit the apprentice and his/her classes. During this visit, informal, mini teaching seminars are conducted for discussions of teaching style, methods, and problems. This informal interaction is advantageous for the apprentice, the community college faculty, and our faculty.

In preparing the graduate students for their assignment, a departmental "teaching seminar" is conducted at the University. The seminar focus is on preparation for teaching rather than on extensive formal content. Students are made aware of the history, goals, and philosophies of the community colleges, of methods of performance evaluation of both teachers and learners, and of procurements of audio-visual materials. Discussions of various teaching procedures—i.e., lecture, discussion, tutorials, and contingency-managed modes of instruction, etc.—are an important aspect of the seminar. Video-taped lectures by the students are viewed and discussed by the whole group (Note 3). Student statements of objectives for an introductory course, as well as complete outlines, are shared and discussed.

Finally, during this summer period, the apprentices are interviewed by appropriate representatives of at least two colleges. To a considerable extent, these are real interviews that "don't count," inasmuch as no long-term consequence is involved. These interviews, however, do relate to the community colleges' eventual selection of their apprentices.

The advantages and disadvantages of the apprentice program, from the University Department's point of view, require comment. First, an obvious advantage is better prepared and more experienced teachers for later consumption in the academic marketplace. This advantage has been measured more by observation than by empirical data: Teaching performance continues to defy purely empirical evaluation.

However, two outcomes are apparent. First, the improved quality of preparation and presentation in subsequent graduate courses, seminars, colloquia, and paper presentations is apparent to all our faculty. So dramatic has been this result that any initial resistance has been replaced with strong support.

The second relates directly to our own instructional program. For many years we did not allow graduate students to teach our undergraduate courses, the assumption being that undergraduates should have the best instruction possible. Now, selected apprentices are assigned introductory classes upon their return to campus. These Teaching Associates are paid a significantly higher stipend than other assistantships within the Department. The evaluations of these Teaching Associates by our undergraduate students has been overwhelmingly positive; so positive, in fact, that undergraduates are now requesting particular Teaching Associates.

Potential problems and difficulties also need to be recognized. To begin with, the program breaks the continuity of the graduate student's course of study. Initially viewed as a stumbling block, experience has indicated that the increased communication skills and the increased overview of general psychology acquired by the apprentices far outweigh the short break in research experimentation.

Second, the possibility that the community college will perceive the apprentices as "cheap" labor, as part-time employees, rather than as trainees in a full-time task is curtailed through continued review of each student's duties and experiences. When this happens, as it has on occasion, the arrangement is either quickly repaired or entirely discontinued.

Finally, some apprentices become so enthusiastic about their teaching experience that they are tempted to seek immediate employment rather than to return to finish their degrees. Several students have considered this option, but none has carried it out. Further, some apprentices, upon return to the university, find it difficult to once again assume the usual graduate student role.

The benefits of the program for the community colleges, from our perspective at Florida State University, is important. Ignoring any cost or savings in salaries, the community colleges receive highly trained, subject-area specialists. These colleges each year have new faculty with different interests and skills, without the restraint of long-term commitment. In fact, as different instructional needs arise semester to semester at the community colleges, an apprentice with particular subject-area expertise can be invited. The flexibility afforded by this arrangement, in terms of faculty and schedule, allows the community college to be exceptionally responsive to its instructional needs.

Further, the Department of Psychology at Florida State University offers its instructional and demonstrational resources as a support system to the community college. This Department has lent (and even built) equipment to establish small teaching laboratories and demonstrations. Members of our department have given lectures on specialized topics and participated in the community college programs. In essence, each psychology course or program at the community colleges can acquire an extensive back-up through the University Department.

In conclusion, the interaction between the community colleges and the University has kept the University aware of the larger teaching mission of the community colleges and the problems they face. It has helped the University faculty to be involved more effectively in the overall State System of education. It has demonstrated to our graduate students the importance and value of teaching as part of the commitment to an academic career. And, it has provided earnest and well-trained new faculty to satisfy the changing needs and interests of community college students, affording the colleges the opportunity to expand temporarily their psychology faculty without making long-range commitments.

Notes

1. Lake City Community College, Seminole Community College in Sanford, Valencia Community College in Orlando, Broward (North) Community College in Ft. Lauderdale, and Valdosta State College of Georgia.
2. Several institutions proposed and instituted a special degree, the Doctor of Arts, aimed at achieving teaching competence. To date, the Doctorate of Arts has not been adopted widely and has not had a substantial effect on training procedures or on the philosophy of PhD-granting institutions.
3. The video-tape assignment involves a short lecture on the topic in psychology which the student knows *best*. The rationale arises from the observation that new teachers have the most difficulty teaching their own specialty areas. Since good teaching in an introductory class is often as dependent upon what is left unsaid as what is said, the "familiar" topic assignment forces the new teacher to learn how to leave things unsaid and not dilute core materials.

Dear Graduate Student (and Future Professor):

Paul Hettich, Sandra Lema-Stern,
and Joseph V. Rizzo
Barat College

Being a timely sharing of the issues and
insights that may ease the transition
from graduate student to faculty member.

When you began your graduate studies you may have thought about the possibility of teaching in a small, two-year or four-year college. Now that you are entering the job market, this possibility likely looms even larger in your thoughts as the limited number of positions in college and university teaching becomes forcefully evident to you. Despite the fact that there are over 1700 four year colleges (excluding universities), and nearly 1300 two year colleges, the teaching market nevertheless remains very tight. Darley and Zanna (1979) have discussed some of the issues involved in the process of job searching and negotiating at larger colleges and universities, and we would like to share some thoughts regarding your impending job hunt at smaller schools.

In the past five years we have interviewed three times at regional conventions and advertised in the *APA Monitor*. These recruitment efforts resulted in about fifty personal interviews and over three hundred resumes for our review. In addition, we typically receive fifty to sixty unsolicited resumes even during years when we are not seeking faculty. In this process, we have developed some insights that we think generalize well beyond our own institution and which may be of help to you. These ideas relate to enculturation in graduate school milieu, pre-employment teaching experience, interviewing skills, and a teacher's values and goals.

Examine Your Graduate School Subculture. Graduate schools clearly develop their own subcultural values and biases. In order to survive in a graduate program, you have probably developed an acute awareness of the subculture's social and organizational hierarchy and its power structure. In addition to being reasonably bright, you have probably become more or less compulsive, constructively (and sometimes frighteningly) paranoid, and cooperative with your instructors and advisors on most essential matters. You have likely modeled many of your instructor's attitudes and behaviors. As a result of course specialization, you may value and know only the narrow content of your advisor's specialty area and your dissertation. Also, you may believe that research is more demanding and more important than teaching, that the best teaching occurs in graduate programs, and that the best undergraduates inevitably enter graduate programs. You may believe that people with degrees in education or psychiatry frequently don't know research methods and that they have little firm knowledge of human behavior. You have probably come to believe that psychologists clearly have the most sophisticated training in research skills and, therefore, something of a monopoly on understanding behavior. Finally, you may be in a graduate program characterized by hostility and distrustful interpersonal communication (though, hopefully, your experiences have been more positive). The communication patterns that you have developed in graduate school may not be appropriate in future job settings.

Check your assumptions. When you begin teaching in an undergraduate institution you will make some discoveries. You will learn, for example, that not only is undergraduate teaching demanding, but also it is more difficult than graduate level instruction. Instead of wallowing in one's own more or less narrow research interests as graduate instructors often do (while assuming that competent students will learn whatever they need to learn on their own), you will have to learn to teach. You will have to learn to communicate clearly and concisely with students whose primary interests are often not in psychology but in art or history or education.

You will also learn that mastery of content in your discipline is not the only component of an education, nor even necessarily the most important one. You may discover that students learn more from your attitudes, your intellectual values, and your self-presentation than they do from your lectures.

You will discover that compulsive thoroughness is not always a virtue as you hear student minds click shut while you brilliantly expose flaws in each of the two or three dozen studies that you are reviewing on a single, often obscure, issue. Instead, you will recognize the necessity of making decisions regarding the value of certain ideas and studies without having the luxury of qualifying every statement. Consequently, you will be exposing yourself to potential criticism from students or colleagues for missing a study, failing to have read a review, or misunderstanding an issue.

In addition, you will learn that some people with education or psychiatry degrees are smarter than you, that you can best relate to peers on a collegial rather than an adversary level, that other disciplines have a lot to say about human behavior even though they do not express it in probability levels, and most important, that good teaching is damn hard.

In short, you will have to learn that the culture you modeled in graduate school may be vastly different from the one you join when you sign your first contract. In fact, after a few years, you may even enjoy discarding some of the cultural trappings of the graduate school. For an incisive elaboration of these and related issues see Mahoney's (1976) chapter "Rites of Passage: Selected Absurdities in Graduate Training."

Prepare to Teach. Over the years we have interviewed many bright and articulate psychologists with impressive vitas, a string of publications, and recommendations from eminent psychologists. Nevertheless, we often place their resumes behind those who appear to have accumulated successful teaching experience. Other things being equal (and they rarely are), we prefer a candidate who may have only one or two graduate courses in a particular area, but who has also had one or two semesters of teaching experience in that area. We believe that it is easier to learn content than it is to learn to teach effectively, and in a small liberal arts college, we cannot afford to have students serve as guinea pigs for inexperienced instructors. Remember, in two-year and four-year colleges, especially smaller liberal arts schools, teaching and not research is the primary *raison d'etre*. You would be well-advised to try to teach as many different courses as often as you can, perhaps in extension programs or even at local community colleges (Ewens, 1976).

Teaching alone, however, has limited value without feedback or an opportunity to examine the teaching-learning process. Enroll in a course or seminar on college teaching if your program offers one. If it does not, discuss the possibility of establishing one with interested faculty and classmates. There are a variety of models for developing college teaching skills that could form the basis for interesting student-faculty dialogues (e.g., Ericksen, 1973; Finger, 1969; Strachan, *et al.*, 1980). It is ironic to note that department chairs regard teaching ability as the second most important characteristic of the "balanced" college professor, but believe that only one-sixth of a student's graduate training in psychology should be devoted to the development of teaching skills (Williams & Richman, 1971).

You may also find it is useful to subscribe to the quarterly *Teaching of Psychology,* to attend the workshops and conferences on teaching (such as that offered annually by the University of Illinois Department of Psychology), and to determine whether your university offers faculty development programs, a faculty resource center, or a center for teaching. Such centers typically subscribe to periodicals (e.g., *Change, Journal of Higher Education),* purchase books on teaching (e.g., Hoover, 1980; McKeachie, 1978; Milton, 1978), and sponsor workshops. They are staffed by faculty interested in discussing teaching. One of the writers, for example, attended a self-improvement program at the Center for the Teaching Professions at Northwestern University. This experience, combined with teaching experiences, gave her a decided edge over many other highly qualified candidates.

If none of these services is available, you could develop feedback groups in which you and a few colleagues attend each other's classes two to four times a semester to observe specific pre-determined teaching behaviors and provide mutual feedback.

In summary, since teaching is the most important activity at the two- and four-year college, we hire persons who have a mature interest and some successful experiences in teaching. By the way, if your teaching experiences are successful, don't hesitate to bring summaries of course evaluations or letters from supervising teachers.

Construct an Interview "Roadmap." Despite the importance of a job interview, we are repeatedly surprised to encounter so many applicants with so little skill in self-presentation during the interview. An extensive literature on job interviewing has developed in recent years (e.g., Platt *et al.*, 1978), and many workshops are available to sharpen interviewing skills. Use them. However, don't "market" yourself as a product that ceases to exist once you've signed the contract. Our most qualified applicants are also good interviewers of us and have sufficient insight to know whether they will be able to fit comfortably into our setting.

Before interviewing, prepare a "roadmap" for yourself so that you inquire about such issues as: (a) course load and number of preparations; (b) departmental philosophy and biases; (c) support for development of teaching skills or research; (d) availability of departmental assistants and copy services; (e) films, supplies, and budgets; (f) procedures and criteria for promotion and tenure; (g) rank and tenure status of other departmental members; (h) institutional financial stability, identity, and atmosphere; (i) salary, salary increments, merit pay, fringe benefits, publication bonuses and convention funds; and (j) the quality of the library and its services. These questions, plus others that may be personally important to you, are vital if you are to make an informed decision about an institution in which you are going to work and grow.

Examine Your Values and Goals. Finally, you need also to ask yourself a series of important questions about your own values and career goals. First, are you willing to become a generalist? For example, in many small colleges, courses are taught only once a year. It is not uncommon for an instructor to teach four to six different courses a year. You must be flexible enough to develop interests in many different areas and willing to do tremendous amounts of work for each preparation. You need not feel that you've betrayed your primary research interest when you develop new research interests, including those of students. In a few years, you'll become less of a specialist and more of a generalist. Some of us *enjoy* being generalists.

Second, are you genuinely committed to working with students? You'll need to be willing to schedule generous office hours and to work intensively with academically weak students outside of classes. You should view students first as persons whose lives extend beyond some narrow area of psychology, and secondly as members of your class. You must be sufficiently stable, patient, and socially adaptable to teach and work with a large variety of students: those who are extremely bright and mature; and those who are immature and who need guidance. In addition to teaching, advising—both course and career oriented—is a very important and time-consuming activity. According to the Williams and Richman survey, student advising is the third most important characteristic of the "balanced" college professor.

Third, are you willing to contribute to the life of the college community? Committee work, often more time consuming than teaching, is expected of faculty in most colleges. Similarly, you'll be asked to participate in panel discussions, student-faculty sports, recruitment, and similar events.

Fourth, can you interact effectively with other faculty? You may have to work with that curmudgeon of an Ancient History Teacher (or is that an ancient History teacher?). You may soon find yourself involved in the volatile politics of a small college campus where it is not uncommon to find a strong adversary on your promotion committee. You'll have to practice (not just preach) the social psychology of groups, power, organizational structures, and decision-making while remaining honest to yourself and relatively unscarred.

If you are able to answer these questions and face these issues honestly, you are well on your way to making what may be the most important career decision of your life. Do not force or fake these answers, however, especially if you are desperate for a position. The people interviewing you already have struggled seriously with these issues; they know the answers which they are looking for, and they'll be able to gauge your responses with surprising accuracy.

References

Darley, M. M., & Zanna, M. P. On getting your first job in academic psychology. *Catalog of Selected Documents in Psychology*, 1979, 9, 45-46.
Ericksen, S. C. The apprentice teacher. Center for Research on Learning and Teaching. Ann Arbor, MI: University of Michigan, #51, March, 1973, pp 1-6.
Ewens, B. Preparing for teaching: Suggestions for graduate stud-
ents of sociology. In *On Teaching Undergraduate Sociology.* Washington, DC: American Sociological Association, 1976, pp 1-5.
Finger, F. W. Preparation for a career in college teaching. *American Psychologist*, 1969, 24, 1044-1049.
Hoover, K. H. *College teaching today: A handbook for post-secondary instruction.* Boston, MA: Allyn and Bacon, 1980.
Mahoney, M. J. *Scientist as subject.* Cambridge, MA: Ballinger Publishing Co., 1976.
McKeachie, W. *Teaching Tips: A guidebook for the beginning college teacher.* Lexington, MA: Heath, 1978.
Milton, O. (Ed.). *On college teaching.* San Francisco, CA: Jossey-Bass, 1978.
Platt, J. S., Goeres, E. R., & Deschler, D. D. Questions to ask when interviewing for a university or college faculty position. *Contemporary Education*, 1978, 50, 5-8.
Strachan, A., Welch, V. O., Barker, C., Compas, B., & Ferguson, M. L. A framework for training college-level teachers of psychology: Five basic processes. *Teaching of Psychology*, 1980, 7, 180-183.
Williams, J. E., & Richman, C. L. The graduate preparation of the college professor of psychology: A survey. *American Psychologist*, 1971, 26, 1000-1009.

Notes

1. This article is based on a paper of the same title presented at the meeting of the American Psychological Association, September 1980, Montreal.

c. Scholarly Skills

David Glenwick and Aden Burka drew from their graduate student experiences to discuss the advantages and difficulties of peer research collaboration barriers interfering with extensive collaboration, and means for overcoming such barriers. Advantages of collaborative graduate student research activity include mutual learning, cooperative and emotional support, greater breadth and depth of investigation, and professional socialization. Although the authors pointed to evidence indicating some faculty reluctance to graduate student collaboration, we hope that the contents of the article will foster graduate student scholarly development.

Judith Blanton conducted nine structured interviews with graduate faculty members from five different institutions. The article attempted to clarify problems that arise developmentally in supervising dissertations and ways in which faculty can aid in preventing or dealing with those problems. The author concluded by pointing out that although the supervisor's own research competence is a necessary condition, it is not a sufficient condition for assuring a developmental experience for the student. One lesson to learn from this article is that the goal of research training is not limited to the acquisition of specific skills, but it also includes developing an excitement about and interest in scholarly activity.

In the following three articles, two authors challenge us to evaluate the reasons for and consequences of doing research. Dennis Fox's article can prompt us to reflect on whether our scholarly pursuits have made us lose sight of the goal of research. As a returning graduate student at Michigan State University, he was struck by a perceived increase in the emphasis on the product of scholarship, publication, and a decrease in time devoted to education.

Martin Heesacker commented on each of Fox's assertions about the negative consequences of publishing research as a student. In particular, the author drew from his experience of supervising graduate and undergraduate student research at the University of Southern Illinois. He observed that research activity facilitates students' reading, discussion, listening, and thinking. Finally, Heesacker concluded that the gains from research would not have been possible from classroom experience.

In his rejoinder, Dennis Fox acknowledged that the pressure to publish can result in important advances in knowledge. However, he also argued that conducting research for the sole purpose of publishing the findings is a corruption of the ideals of education. Finally, Fox pleaded with readers to recognize publication pressure's escalating costs to psychology, society, students, and ourselves. A re-examination of one's goals for and priorities in doing research may be an important outcome associated with reading this article.

Research Collaboration Between Graduate Students: Facilitating the Rites of Passage

David Glenwick
Kent State University
and Aden A. Burka
University of Maryland

Rites of passage—ceremonies whereby a society confers adult status upon its younger members—are a common phenomenon, ranging from the wilderness experiences of African tribes to such religious rituals as confirmation and bar mitzvah in our own society. Graduate school in psychology, too, may be viewed as containing a series of hurdles which collectively comprise rites of passage no less anxiety-arousing than the illustrations cited above. Chief among these tests of adulthood are such research demands as the master's thesis and the dissertation. Our major contention here is that collaborative efforts between graduate students can ease the traumatic aspects of research requirements, as well as achieve positive educational ends. Drawing upon our own experiences as collaborators in a graduate school project, we will discuss advantages and difficulties of such collaboration, barriers currently standing in the way of extensive joint research, and means of overcoming such barriers.

Mutual Learning.   Graduate student collaboration promotes the goal of students learning from each other, as they share theoretical, methodological, and factual input. In this manner, the differing strengths of the individuals collaborating may be capitalized upon, while weaknesses are remediated.

Although the direct transmission of knowledge represents the most obvious type of reciprocal learning, a second form is the learning of professional habits (e.g., compulsiveness in organizing and saving data) through observation at an eyeball to eyeball level. Interpersonal style can be observed and is particularly crucial in applied research, where one must learn to deal effectively with varied segments of the lay community. The particular "roles" that collaborators take during the course of a project would appear to reflect the various interpersonal strengths (e.g., directness, graciousness) they bring to the venture. It is hoped that these differing strengths can be appreciated and assimilated by both collaborators. Such experience in acquiring professional and interpersonal habits may be more difficult to obtain from faculty, because the time spent with them is briefer and more focused.

Mutual learning is also enhanced by the collaborators trying out conceptualizations, offering interpretations, and raising questions with each other that they might be unwilling to disclose to faculty for fear of appearing ignorant and inadequate. Ideally, in opening up all facets of the research process to such "blue skying," a dialectic process occurs in which the collaborators' separate viewpoints synthesize into a new, more encompassing perspective.

Interpersonal Relationships and Roles.   Collaborative efforts can transform the interpersonal set from one of competitiveness ("me vs. you") to one of mutuality ("we're in this together"). This change of set increases the exchanging, as opposed to the hoarding, of knowledge as if it were professional gold. Additionally, it provides a ready source of emotional support for each partner during the ups and downs and unforeseen complications present in any research endeavor. Thus there can be a sharing of affect, with less internalization of emotion. Such an emotional safety valve can lessen the sense of pressure and isolaton which psychology graduate students all too frequently feel.

Scope of Research Projects.   With the greater total person-hours of work provided by two or more persons, a problem can be investigated in greater breadth and depth. This is especially helpful in applied and field studies, where the more variables one can study, the better the chance of understanding the relationships among the several factors entering into a given set of results. Expressing similar thoughts to our own, Rotter (1973, p. 320) has noted that "clinical research, [which] often requires more than one experimenter to avoid bias, do ratings, and carry out manipulations [involving] long expenditures of time and effort, . . . can best be done by having several people working cooperatively" and that such research "might very well involve several students working on theses and dissertations at the same time."

Commitment to, and Interest in the Research.   Because graduate student collaborative efforts are usually master's theses or dissertations, the projects typically have high priority for all involved, resulting in an intensive and fairly equal investment of time and energy. Furthermore, as the scope of the project becomes more ambitious, there is normally a proportionate rise in interest without necessarily a great increase in the amount of work required of each individual. These conditions may serve to prevent the occurrence of differential commitment, a problem identified in a recent survey of doctoral level psychologists (Hallauer & Glenwick, Note 1) as the principal drawback of research collaboration in general.

Professional Socialization.

Collaboration is the way most psychological researchers function, with the respondents to the Hallauer and Glenwick survey (Note 1) reporting that 67% of their publications had a joint author. Consequently graduate student collaboration provides a chance to learn professional skills which will be valuable in conducting post-doctoral research. Issues of pertinence here include establishing a division of labor, setting contracts, and agreeing upon order of authorship. Additionally, students, being less experienced and (sometimes) more immature than faculty, may benefit from the opportunity to become more adept at handling personality and stylistic divergences and differences of opinion between partners. Thus lapses or differences in judgment which might arise in the course of graduate student collaboration, although possibly unpleasant and counterproductive in the short run, can avert errors in one's later professional work.

Why, then, does graduate student collaboration appear to occur relatively seldom? Faculty attitudes may account in large part for this state of affairs. Thus, in the Hallauer and Glenwick survey (Note 1) 89% of respondents felt that psychology students should be encouraged to engage in collaborative research with faculty members, but only 72% believed that collaboration between students should be fostered. It seems to us that graduate student collaboration is rarely promoted and, in fact, is often actively discouraged. This may stem from faculty members' fears of inability to allocate responsibility and attribute credit to individual students for components of the overall project.

Although such fears are understandable, there are methods of avoiding the coordination and evaluation problems presented by student collaboration. Each individual's tasks (e.g., division of labor, assignment of primary responsibility for analysis of particular variables and relationships) and credits (e.g., decisions regarding coauthorship of publications) should be well-defined at the earliest possible stages of the project, subject to subsequent modification by mutual agreement of students and faculty advisor. The negotiation of contracts, varying in formality, can aid in clarifying responsibilities.

Concerning formal evaluation by faculty of student collaborators' activities, Rotter (1973, p. 320) has suggested that among the factors that should be taken into consideration are "the time and effort . . . expended, the amount . . . learned and contributed to the group effort, and . . . skill and adequacy in analyzing . . . data and reporting . . . results." With goodwill on the part of all participants, such a task should not prove unduly burdensome to faculty. An added incentive may be the possibility that the advantages outlined above might produce a reduction in faculty supervision time, as the students adopt the role of colleague/advisor with one another.

One may wonder how generalizable our collaborative experience, and attitudes concerning that experience, might be. Reflecting upon this, we are struck by the resemblance that collaborative research bears to a marital relationship. Like marriage, collaboration is not for everyone; also, one may be a satisfied (and satisfying) collaborator with some partners but not with others. Successful collaboration depends upon the interaction of the abilities and styles of the particular individuals involved, with issues of similarity and complementariness being as pertinent here as in the attractiveness literature of social psychology. Some may find their Individuality, creativity, power needs, etc. cramped by the compromises that collaboration inevitably demands. Certain personality types (e.g., extremely passive or unassertive persons) would probably gain more from having total responsibility for a project than from "collaborating" in an effort in which they supplied only minority or token input.

Thus there are caveats to be remembered when considering whether to enter into collaboration with a fellow graduate student. Nevertheless, while subject to the strains of any close relationship, the collaborative experience can, we believe, foster increased self-awareness and interpersonal sensitivity as a psychologist and person, as well as competency as a researcher.

Reference

Rotter, J. B. The future of clinical psychology. *Journal of Consulting and Clinical Psychology,* 1973, *40,* 313-321.

Notes

1. Hallauer, D., & Glenwick, D. S. A survey of psychologists' behaviors and attitudes toward collaborative research. In F. Vance (Chair), *Contemporary issues in collaboration in psychological research.* Symposium presented at American Psychological Association annual convention, San Francisco, August, 1977.
2. A version of this paper was presented at the American Psychological Association's annual convention, San Francisco, August, 1977. An extended version is available from the first author.

Midwifing the Dissertation

Judith S. Blanton
California School of Professional Psychology

> Good teaching may not ensure good research supervision. So you may profit from this account of problems and their solutions.

The dissertation is a critical element in doctoral training. It can be one of the most satisfying and educational parts of a program, yet, too often the process is painful and tedious for both faculty and students. A substantial number of those who do complete their dissertations do not undertake further research. This seems to be particularly common in programs that train practitioners (Goldenberg, 1973, p. 73).

There are a number of books and manuals to assist students in technical aspects of writing (Allen, 1973; Steinberg, 1977; Weedman, 1975). There have also been studies examining students' experiences (Katz & Hartnett, 1976), emotional problems (Lowenberg, 1969), development (Patch, 1978; Clark, 1980), and relationship with the supervisor (Markle, 1977). Yet, very little attention has been given to improving the chair's ability to direct the thesis. A notable exception is the work of Seeman (1977), who suggested that research learning would "take place most fully when (a) the learning climate is designed to foster conditions of creativity, (b) research learning is seen as a task related to the development of personal effectiveness and personal goals and (c) explicit provisions are made to foster growth toward autonomy and professional maturity." He believes that effective teaching stimulates students to become more aware of their own curiosity and to respect the questions they are asking themselves. According to Seeman, learning in the early stages of inquiry is fostered by an open structure in which ambiguity is accepted and "form and method are not prematurely emphasized." The creation of this climate is the responsibility of the faculty member. Unfortunately, many faculty, even those who are good classroom teachers, are not prepared to supervise dissertations effectively. The manuscript is produced by the student but skilled midwifery by the faculty member can make the process much easier.

In an attempt to clarify the problems which arise in the supervision of dissertations and the ways in which faculty can aid in preventing or dealing with these problems, nine graduate faculty from five different institutions were interviewed about their experiences.

Three of those interviewed were currently teaching in large universities. Although two were currently teaching in state colleges that had no doctoral programs in psychology, both had substantial experience supervising doctoral students in earlier positions in the university and still regularly served on doctoral committees as outside members. Four were currently employed in three different free standing graduate schools of psychology although all but one had several years of experience within state universities.

The aim was not to test hypotheses but to gather case study material of practical import and to generate questions for further study. Faculty members were selected because of their interest in the dissertation process and their experience. As a group, these faculty had directed 138 dissertations and served on another 157 committees. Five had taught dissertation seminars. Each faculty member was interviewed for approximately 90 minutes using a structured interview schedule.

Probably everyone who has directed at least one dissertation would have additional suggestions to add to those of this group, e.g. starting with a larger N than needed in order to avoid disaster from drop-outs. A worthy project for any graduate institution would be to share these individual insights. Junior faculty, in particular, might find this a valuable process because, unfortunately for them and their students, such learning too often comes from painful experience.

Interview Results. Dissertation supervision can be a very stimulating and enjoyable task for faculty. The reasons they give for liking the process can be clustered into three primary categories: (a) Intellectual/creative reasons (enjoyment of the co-creative process, the stimulation of finding creative solutions to problems, an empathetic sense of adventure). When the faculty member is not currently doing research, it seems to be a way to keep involved in such activities indirectly; (b) Developmental reasons (seeing the student develop personally and as a researcher/scholar); (c) Feelings of making a contribution to the student, society and/or the field.

Supervision can also be an unpleasant task for faculty members. Among the things faculty disliked were: (a) Interpersonal conflicts (manipulative behavior, hostility, resistance, hassles); (b) Having to work with poor students (students who lacked basic conceptual, writing, and/or research skills); (c) Time constraints (Faculty feel pressed for time and sometimes feel they do not have time to provide the type of supervision they would like to provide.)

Although most of the written rhetoric about dissertations focuses on its scientific contribution, in practice the dissertation serves an educational and a developmental function. Rather than an opportunity for a student to demonstrate what he or she already knows, in most cases, the project seems to prove an opportunity for students to learn. Conceptual skills, writing skills and research skills are often honed during the dissertation process. Certainly, the dissertation also provides an opportunity for personal development. This is an intriguing and little studied area of investigation, but one which merits attention (Clark, 1980). Many students seem to mature as persons as well as scholars during this phase of their graduate education. Their abilities to set priorities, organize time, and manage conflict often improve. Rather than just having to please a single instructor, they must learn to juggle the expectations of an entire committee and, at an even higher level, to take responsibility for and evaluate their own work.

Phases of the Dissertation Process. Chronologically, the dissertation process can be separated into five stages: planning, beginning, data gathering, writing, and finishing. The next section will briefly summarize some of the major kinds of problems which arise in each phase, and strategies faculty might employ in dealing with such problems.

Planning. All faculty interviewed considered the planning phase to be the most critical. Many of the problems which appear later could have been prevented with more careful attention to planning. During this phase the student and the committee must work out their style of working together. Clarification of rights, obligations, and expectations early on can save much confusion and conflict later. Faculty in professional schools or alternative schools with less of an established tradition regarding faculty-student roles or agreement about the "proper" form(s) of research may need to give more attention to these issues than those from schools with a more established tradition.

Data from interviews suggested that some of the traditions of the dissertation are not being taken for granted as they were even ten years ago. Students and faculty are questioning the value of the dissertation, the necessity that the dissertation be a piece of research, questioning what constitutes research, and even questioning the value of research altogether (Skadegaard & Robe, 1975). In some cases, the dissertation is seen merely as a hurdle, an annoyance to be gotten out of the way as soon as possible. Rather, they expressed concern that such views were sometimes found among their students and fellow faculty. Clinical students, in particular, seem vocal in questioning the value of a research dissertation for their future careers. Those interviewed complained that some other faculty do not take the dissertation process "seriously" enough, and did not role model the researcher. This seems to be an issue when those who identify primarily as practitioners, not researchers, are responsible for supervising research dissertations.

Strategies which faculty have found useful in dealing with difficulties in the planning phase include: (a) making sure the topic is interesting to the student but not so emotionally close that perspective is lost; (b) providing a choice of methodologies which reflect the resources of the student, and providing some means of outside consultation if the methodology is outside of the chair's range of expertise; (c) having the student write down key terms, define them, and complete a one-page summary of their dissertation plan; (d) having students find and critique a role model research study in the style or area they are exploring.

As well as identifying planning goals and style of working with each other, the chair and student must select and develop a procedure of working with other committee members. Faculty interviewed brought up several specific questions which must be addressed at this stage, such as: (a) the availability and time commitments of the chair and other members; (b) means of reaching and recording agreements with the committee and student; (c) methods of communication and conflict resolution between committee members; (d) specific expertise responsibilities of each member; (e)

the distinction between suggestions and requirements in feedback to the student.

Other major tasks in the planning phase include selecting a topic and moving from a topic to a specific question. Faculty must assist students to avoid the pitfalls of: (a) diffusion; (b) triviality; (c) grandiosity; (d) a topic which is too personally charged; (e) a topic which does not sustain the interest of the student; (f) moving ahead to data collection before basic issues are clarified.

Good supervision at this stage seems to require skills similar to those described by Carkhoff and Berenson (1967) in their research on effective psychotherapy: accurate empathy and concreteness.

The Socratic method of question asking appears to be a major supervision technique in the planning phase. Other useful techniques include summarizing, rephrasing, clarifying, and pointing out implications of a student's statement.

Beginning. Problems in the middle three phases (beginning, data gathering, and writing) tend to be more technical. When working with a student who is well prepared, these stages are relatively less demanding for faculty as the student must take on the major burden and the faculty member serves as a resource and provides supervision. When a student is not prepared, however, this phase can be very frustrating for faculty. In such cases, faculty must take on a major instructional role. They may actually do some of the work themselves, or help the student deal with the painful fact that the process will take much longer than they had planned. Among the problems that the faculty must assist the student to deal with during the beginning phase are: (a) determining what should be reviewed in the literature review; (b) moving from a cataloging of literature to a thoughtful analytic critique; (c) moving from a topic to a question and/or specific hypotheses; (d) determining specific methods and measurement tools; (e) determining, finding and obtaining the cooperation of subjects; (f) determining the plan for data analysis. (In many cases, students pressure to postpone the data analysis plan until later, but data suggest that handling it early seems to avoid many problems later.)

Particular strategies for avoiding problems common to this phase included: (a) selecting measures that are appropriate by reviewing a wide range, taking into account that names of tests and subscales can be misleading. Outside measurement consultations can be useful at this time; (b) setting up realistic expectations and timelines for each phase, taking into account emergencies, "acts of God," predictable hitches (finding subjects from a narrow subject pool, human subjects delay for an ethically complicated proposal, etc.); (c) initial criticism should focus on the general concepts and ideas, in the manner of mutual problem-solving. Later phases of the dissertation process are more appropriate for detailed, specific, criticisms. Combine criticism with support, in the spirit of teaching and improvement of the work.

Data Gathering. "Acts of God" cause problems in this phase: subjects drop out, data are lost or contaminated, a child gets the measles, a parent dies, etc. Faculty can not eliminate such problems but they assist by warning students that they might occur, setting up strategies to reduce the likelihood of data being lost or destroyed and allowing leeway in the timetable to cope with problems that do arise.

In some cases, such as lack of cooperation by subjects, the problem can itself become data and be discussed analytically in the dissertation.

Writing. Problems in the writing phase included: (a) lack of technical writing skill; (b) inability to organize the material conceptually—sometimes caused by having too much data, sometimes by lack of an organizing principle; (c) inability to see meaningful patterns—sometimes caused by lack of conceptual skill, sometimes by lack of confidence that what is seen is important; (d) lack of loyalty to the data. This generally occurs when a student is over-invested in a particular viewpoint whether or not the data support it. Assertions are made that are not supported by the data.

Some faculty play a major role in editing both the ideas and the writing. Others merely refer students to an editor or insist on more drafts. Further discussion of the ethical questions about how much editorial assistance is appropriate seems needed. Standards seem to vary a great deal among institutions and among faculty within institutions.

Finishing. The final stage again seems to require more faculty attention. This phase appears to be the most emotionally stressful for students. Issues which were not dealt with in the earlier stages may surface here and cause conflict between student and faculty or among committee members. Such conflicts generally arise around issues of what is "acceptable," what is "quality" work, and how much revision is necessary to have the manuscript approved. These issues may have become even more salient when another rewrite can mean that the student will have to pay hundreds or even thousands of dollars in tuition, or when a potential internship or job is jeopardized by not completing the doctorate on schedule. Problems in this last phase included: (a) losing energy for the task—fatigue and depression; (b) integration of the parts into a coherent whole; (c) dealing with the myriad details necessary for a finished piece of work— proofing, getting references checked, organizing and checking tables, etc.; (d) lack of clarity about expectations for an approved dissertation; (e) last minute time pressures to complete; (f) anxieties about the dissertation defense.

Faculty interviewed offered several practical suggestions to assist in this final phase of the dissertation process: (a) warning the student early about the number of technical details that have to be completed at the last phase. Be sure sufficient time is allocated for this activity. The student can prepare for this by setting up mock tables, keeping meticulous notes on references, etc. Check on the possibilities of using a word processor as a way to speed up the revision process; (b) not allowing the student to have each chapter typed in final form until the entire piece has been written and reviewed to check for internal organization and flow. Some faculty require that the student take a two week break at this phase to be able to come back and take a fresh look at the whole; (c) in preparing for the final oral defense of the dissertation, the chair might want to spend at least one session describing the process and preparing for it by asking the kind of questions that will be asked. Some faculty have the student make a short professional presentation of the overall findings to start the sessions.

Working With Problem Students. An important subsection of the interviews dealt with the issue of working with problem students. Among the strategies suggested by those interviewed were the following: (a) If a student is excessively dependent, set specific tasks to be done before the next meeting. Have him or her take on responsibilities for calling meetings of the committee, setting up an agenda, etc. Avoid the pressure to make the decision *for* the student. Avoid *doing* the work for the student but rather teach *how* to do it. For example, make careful corrections on a few pages and then give it back to the student to review in the same manner; (b) If a student is manipulative, make it clear at the beginning what constitutes a legitimate and an illegitimate demand, make sure communication is direct and clear among committee members; (c) If a student is reluctant to ask for needed assistance, make sure he or she realizes that the chair is accessible, set up a series of regular meetings, insist that the student get a sign off at each stage before proceeding to the next stage; (d) If the student is below par academically or intellectually, be sure faculty are willing to take on the extra commitment that working with such students requires. Help the student set a realistic timeline given his or her skills. Help them pick a research topic and method within their scope. In general, this type of student should not be encouraged to pursue a theoretical or qualitative dissertation which requires a high level of analytic ability and fluent writing. A very specific research question using well defined methods might be more feasible.

A wide variety of skills are required of faculty in order to direct the dissertation effectively. Although the supervisor's research competence is necessary, it is not sufficient to assure a developmental experience for the student. The goal in research training is not merely to produce a single acceptable piece of research, nor to train students in specific methods, but to excite student's creativity and their interest in the research process. Thoughtful and skilled midwifery by the faculty member may yield, not only a dissertation, but a sense of joy in the doing of research.

References

Allen, G. A graduate students guide to theses and dissertations. San Francisco, CA: Josey-Bass, 1973.

Carkhoff, R. R., & Berenson, B. G. *Beyond counseling and therapy.* New York: Holt, Rinehart and Winston, 1967.

Clark, A. The influence of adult developmental processes upon the educational experiences of doctoral students (Doctoral dissertation, The Humanistic Psychology Institute), 1980.

Goldenberg, H. *Contemporary clinical psychology.* Monterey, CA: Brooks/Cole, 1973.

Katz, J., & Hartnett, R. (Eds.). *Scholars in the making: The development of graduate and professional students.* Cambridge, MA: Ballinger, 1976.

Lowenberg, P. Emotional problems of graduate education. *Journal of Higher Education,* 1969, *40,* 610-623.

Markle, G. Student and supervisor interactions: A model of the thesis completion process. (Doctoral dissertation, University of Toronto, 1977). *Dissertation Abstracts International,* 1977, *38,* 3214A-3215A.

Patch, G. An investigation of the dissertation process as a training in will power: Will power's relation to spiritual development, and their mutual implications in the educational process. (Doctoral dissertation, University of Massachusetts, 1977). *Dissertation Abstracts International,* 1978, *38,* 5363A-5364A. (University Microfilms No. 77-30, 568,198).

Seeman, J. On supervising student research. *American Psychologist,* 1977, *28,* 900-906.

Skadegaard, R., & Grabelsk, R. The dilemma of the emerging psychologist, *Professional Psychology,* 1975, *6,* 201-203.

Steinberg, R. *Writing the psychology paper.* Woodbury, NY: Arron's Educational Series, 1977.

Weedman, C. *A guide for the preparation and evaluation of the dissertation or thesis.* San Diego, CA: Omega, 1975.

The Pressure to Publish: A Graduate Student's Personal Plea

Dennis Fox
Michigan State University

"Of course," added Bill McGuire, "those of you without tenure yet can ignore what I'm going to say." Laughter.

McGuire, speaking at the 1982 Murray Lectures at Michigan State University (Note 1), went on to offer several now-familiar suggestions for improving the quality of research done by personality and social psychologists, a theme highlighted at the conference by Salvatore Maddi and others and written about at least for the past decade (McGuire, 1973). The laughter of the audience did not seem to be a rejection of the suggestions; rather, it seemed to be an (uneasy?) acknowledgement of the inconsistencies often found between theory and reality.

The American Psychological Association's *Publication Manual* (1974) points out that "some problems that arise in manuscripts may be attributed to the publish-or-perish spirit in which they are written" (p. 22). This pressure to publish—and to publish as often as possible—directly interferes with the kind of research advocated by Maddi, McGuire, and the others: research that is multi-dimensional, longitudinal, collaborative, and relevant to life in the real world. Indeed, the *Publication Manual* points out how "we become content with rapid, mediocre investigations where longer and more careful work is possible" (1974, p. 22).

Publish-or-perish as a guideline for untenured faculty has now become something of a mania even for graduate students. How else, we are told by our professors, will you find a job? It's a jungle out there, and a list of publications to flesh out the curriculum vitae is supposed to be our first line of defense. It doesn't much matter *what* we publish, or whether we actually write anything original or useful or thoughtful; what matters is how long a list of publications we can present to the Search Committee of whatever institution we hope to work at.

The lip-service given to calls for a reappraisal of where the field is headed is sometimes impressive. "Sure I agree with what he says," said one graduate student in reference to McGuire's lecture, "but he's right—you won't get published that way." Another student tells of a professor's comment that whether or not research results are *valid* is less important than whether or not they are *publishable.*

Upon returning to the university to complete my doctorate after a decade outside the halls of academia, I was quite unprepared for today's frantic push to publish. In the early 1970s, in retrospect, there seemed to be a quite reasonable understanding that graduate school was a place to become educated. Publication was certainly not discouraged, but it was not stressed to the point of exhaustion either. We were expected to do a thesis and a dissertation, but intensive additional research and publication was for the most part something to be done after graduate school.

In 1982, education seems to have given way to career training. There's nothing exactly *wrong* with career training—don't get me wrong, I would like a job when I get my doctorate—but making career training the *priority* over education seems to me to be a misguided trend. Putting pressure on graduate students to perform unending experiments *for the sole purpose of getting published* is a corruption of the ideals of what an education is supposed to be. When are we supposed to read, to discuss, to listen, to think? How can we learn to relate one field of study to another when we are pushed to produce, to specialize, to become prematurely socialized into the role of worried (untenured) faculty? Well-meaning advice by concerned professors to "read only the first sentence of every paragraph in books you 'have' to get through" is not helpful.

The pressure to produce can be resisted to some extent by a stubborn refusal to worry about the future, though such a posture is difficult to maintain; I am, after all, writing this article. The danger, though, is that some students will drop out entirely, discouraged by the senselessness of it all. Social psychology attracts many undergraduates who see in the field a way to approach the problems of real people in modern society. Many of the best of these students become understandably disillusioned once they reach graduate school and discover that relevance may stand in the way of career.

Some undergraduates discover this while still in college. A junior in a class I'm teaching told me about a professor who is trying to get her to publish *now.* The student, with some justification, does not feel the need at this point in her life to worry about publication; she is still trying to sort out her place in psychology, trying to decide if social psychology will allow her the flexibility and relevance she wants. The response of the professor, though, was to point out the necessity of publishing in order to get *into* graduate school!

The time has long since come for Search Committees and Tenure Committees to seriously question the value of "publishing" as a motivating force in academic life. Certainly at least those students primarily interested in their own education would be better served by a faculty that stressed thought rather than output. I would also argue that psychology as a field and society as a whole would likewise be better served by a psychology oriented toward thoughtful relevance rather than rushed publication. Societal trends toward conservatism and economic pressures toward job competitiveness should not be allowed to stand in the way of a well-rounded education in psychology that is meaningful to the student's life in the real world.

Note

1. McGuire, W. J. *Explorations in the spontaneous self-concept: Going beyond self-esteem and the reactive self.* Paper presented at The Michigan State University Henry A. Murray Lectures in Personality, East Lansing, MI, April 1982.

References

American Psychological Association. *Publication manual of the American Psychological Association* (2nd ed.). Washington, DC: Author, 1974.

McGuire, W. J. The yin and yang of progress in social psychology: Seven koan. *Journal of Personality and Social Psychology,* 1973, *26,* 446-456.

From One Without Tenure: A Response to Fox

Martin Heesacker
Southern Illinois University

Fox (1983), in a recent issue of *Teaching of Psychology,* took the position that pressure to publish research while in graduate or even undergraduate school results in the following negative consequences: (a) publishability is valued over research validity; (b) educational ideals are corrupted; (c) time "to read, to discuss, to listen, to think" is taken away (p. 177); (d) the ability to "learn to relate one field of study to another" is removed (p. 177); (e) "some students will drop out entirely, discouraged by the senselessness of it all" (p. 177); (f) "many of the best students become understandably disillusioned once they reach graduate school and discover that relevance may stand in the way of career" (p. 177). An alternative viewpoint to Fox's will be presented.

First, submitting research for journal publication represents the scientific community assessing the validity and importance of the psychologist's work. Publishing and validity go hand in hand. Invalid work is not likely to be published in research journals. Journal reviews of unacceptable work document how the research has failed and how it might be improved.

Second, educational levels are *exemplified* by publishing psychological research, not corrupted by it. In general, the educational ideals involve creating knowledge, disseminating knowledge, and using knowledge to benefit humanity. Encouragement to do research of publishable quality can cause research to be done, which results in knowledge being created. The publication of research disseminates knowledge. The dissemination of knowledge is required for its application.

Third, my own experience with over 20 graduates and undergraduates on research teams (whose purpose was to produce publishable research and whose efforts resulted in several published articles) was that doing this research *facilitated* reading, discussion, listening and thinking. As a result of this research experience, students have been able to add a dimension to their education that no classroom experience could provide. Most impressive is how much students' thinking was sharpened over the course of a research team's work. For myself, the *academic* work with which I am most pleased is associated with research projects I have done. Doing publishable research made me a better student. It should also be noted that the Four-Year College and University 1983 Teaching Award for Division 2

went to Ernest D. Kemble, a professor who coauthored 27 articles with undergraduates and had 37 students go on to graduate and professional schools (Bond, 1983).

Fourth, for me and for many others, the most thoughtful relating of one field to another was accomplished while doing research. I am currently involved in research on the interface of social and counseling psychology, research that has come about because of awareness, through doing research, of new and important developments in attitude change theory that can help explain counseling processes and help improve counseling interventions.

Fifth, research accepted for publication is research judged by the community of scientists to be the most valid and important. If such work appears senseless to a person, a competent vocational psychologist might suggest pursuit of a different occupational environment, one which makes more sense to that person.

Sixth, the best students I know have not become disillusioned. They have become challenged to do *better* research, teaching and therapy than they have seen. These aspirations are the seeds of progress in psychology. Additionally, doing relevant research is more valued by journal editors and reviewers than doing irrelevant research and as a consequence is more likely to be published. Therefore, relevance should *enhance* a research career, not stand in the way of it.

Seventh, Fox (1983) implied that research that is more arduous to conduct is more psychologically relevant than that which is easier to conduct. In reality, the dimensions of relevance and ease of execution are orthogonal. As students of adult development methodology know, longitudinal designs confound age and time of measurement effects (Kausler, 1982, p. 89), resulting in the inability to tell if getting older, per se, caused any observed differences. Yet, these designs are certainly difficult to conduct. On the other hand, as Mook (1983) has convincingly pointed out, easily conducted lab studies, such as Higgins and Marlatt's (1973) research on drinking and tension reduction, have resulted in important modifications in theory and, thus, improved relevance. Of course, regardless of the ease of execution, researchers who do not take the time to do careful work will not produce good research. Their research is less likely to be published than research of those who do careful work.

Finally, Fox implied that publishing should not be considered by tenure and search committees. Publishing is one of several very good ways to gauge a faculty member's pursuit of the educational ideals. Knowing that a faculty member's work is regularly being accepted by his or her scientific colleagues for dissemination is one indication that the work is important and well done. Of course, no single measure is perfect. An appropriate indication of a faculty member's *overall* research contribution would be acceptance as an APA Fellow or receipt of a Distinguished Contributor award. Tenure and search committees are charged to assess quality as well as quantity of the research and allowances are made for important research which takes time to conduct. Good research is not a hindrance to thought and relevance, but rather is both thoughtful and relevant. Bad research is not what journals are in business to publish.

References

Bond, T. 1983 teaching award winners. *Teaching of Psychology,* 1983, *10,* 131-132.

Fox, D. The pressure to publish: A graduate student's personal plea. *Teaching of Psychology,* 1983, *10,* 177-178.

Higgins, R. L., & Marlatt, G. A. Effects of anxiety arousal on the consumption of alcohol by alcoholics and social drinkers. *Journal of Consulting and Clinical Psychology,* 1973, *41,* 426-433.

Kausler, D. H. *Experimental psychology and human aging.* New York: Wiley, 1982.

Mook, D. G. In defense of external invalidity. *American Psychologist,* 1983, *38,* 379-387.

Alternative Perspectives on the Pressure to Publish

Dennis R. Fox
Michigan State University

In an earlier article, I called on "Search Committees and Tenure Committees to seriously question the value of 'publishing' as a motivating force in academic life" (Fox, 1983, p. 178). In his response, Heesacker (1984) described what he took to be the many benefits of that pressure to publish. Readers of the two articles might be excused for wondering if we are talking about the same academic world. Is this just another argument about whether the glass is half empty or half full?

Rather than simply repeat the points I have already made, which Heesacker has clearly listed and disagreed with, I would like to suggest here that those on both sides of the publish-or-perish debate may have more separating them than their level of optimism or pessimism. It may be instead that those who criticize psychology's status quo (on this and other issues) and those who defend it have significantly different conceptions of what psychology and psychology education are (and should be) about. Discussion of these important issues requires more than advising those who are dissatisfied with things as they are that "a competent vocational psychologist might suggest pursuit of a different occupational environment" (Heesacker, 1984, p. 239).

In informal discussions with other graduate students and professors at Michigan State and at other institutions, I have heard occasional defenses of the publish-or-perish system that parallel those of Heesacker: Publication represents the scientific community at work and stimulates thought; research that strikes some people as trivial might be fascinating to the people doing it; and so on. I have even heard a tenured professor insist that there really is no pressure to publish beyond that which is self-motivated, and that the purpose of virtually all research is the accumulation of knowledge rather than the attainment of tenure; this last claim is so far from the experience of most others I have spoken to that, like Heesacker's claims, it illustrates the

ability of different people within a single system to maintain entirely different perspectives.

I certainly don't mean to imply that all research is worthless, or that Heesacker's views have no merit. I think, however, that his perspective is probably a minority one, and I continue to believe that "putting pressure on graduate students to perform unending experiments *for the sole purpose of getting published* is a corruption of the ideals of what an education is supposed to be" (Fox, 1983, p. 177).

The pressure to publish is not an isolated problem that affects only graduate students looking for jobs and assistant professors seeking tenure. The pressure, for example, is partly responsible for the proliferation of journals and conferences primarily designed to provide an outlet for career-motivated research, and for the consequent "self-limiting" specialization that Bevan (1982) called "the most serious question facing organized psychology today" (p. 1311). (Sanford, 1982, similarly complained that psychology has become "fragmented, overspecialized, method centered, and dull" p. 902.) Many senior faculty members privately criticize current trends; many assistant professors just as privately acknowledge that much of their own research is done *only* for career reasons and that they have no choice but to try to publish everything they do, *even when they decide the research has little merit;* many also acknowledge that they give their undergraduate students minimal attention because, as one untenured professor put it, "They won't decide to keep me or get rid of me on the basis of my courses" (see Boice, 1984, p. 6, for a listing of several studies illustrating the lack of academic rewards for teaching quality).

That the issue of publication pressure extends beyond the halls of any one institution is reflected in the letter sent to me by the editor of *Teaching of Psychology* to inform me that my original article was accepted for publication. The editor repeated the reviewer's comment that "if you are brave enough to write it, we certainly should be willing to distribute it—these things need to be said" (R. S. Daniel, personal communication, January 28, 1983). The tendency to attribute "bravery" to one who criticizes the status quo can be taken, perhaps, as another sign of problems in a field where "these things" need to be said more often.

Outside psychology the situation apparently is much the same. A philosophy professor told me he retired partly because the joy of teaching lessened in the mid-seventies when, he said, "even philosophy students" started overspecializing in response to job pressures. Hyde (1983), a poet and translator looking at science in the context of a "gift community," argued that:

> It is precisely when people work with no goal other than that of attracting a better job or getting tenure or higher rank, that one finds specious and trivial research, not contributions to knowledge. When there is a marked competition for jobs and money, when such supposedly secondary goals become primary, more and more scientists will be pulled into the race to hurry "original" work into print, no matter how extraneous to the wider goals of the community. (In the literary community, at least in the last few decades, the need to secure a job has certainly accounted for a fair amount of the useless material that's been published, both as literature and as criticism.) (p. 83)

Montagu (1981), an anthropologist, criticized our education system on related grounds:

> Too much of our learning is done without thought, and such learning is labor lost. . . .What passes for education is largely instruction. . . .As one proceeds from Bachelor's degrees to Master's and Doctor's degrees, one dies both intellectually and spiritually by degrees. (p. 140)

Michael Birt, chairperson of the Australian Vice-Chancellors' Committee and Vice-Chancellor of the University of New South Wales, recently noted that Australian universities "cannot afford to support research by every professor, nor are all professors capable of creative research" (Maslen, 1984, p. 31), and he called upon universities to redefine promotion standards. His conclusion, that he didn't know whether professors "would be better off doing something other than research, but I know that the system would be" (p. 32), may be equally applicable to the United States.

The disparity between what might be good for psychologists' careers and what might be good for psychology as a field and society as a whole is a crucial one. This issue is only one of many ideological, theoretical, and methodological controversies that have surfaced in recent years (e.g., Caplan & Nelson, 1973; Ginsburg, 1979; Manicas & Secord, 1983; Peters & Ceci, 1982; Sampson, 1981; Sarason, 1981).

It is interesting that an MSU "Psychology and Controversy Discussion Group" that met for several months to examine a number of these topics lost its momentum, perhaps predictably, as publication and other time pressures built up (Fox, in press).

Clearly, as Heesacker (1984) noted, the pressure to publish can result in important advances in knowledge. Yet to argue that such a beneficial result happens routinely, and that the established institutions of the field work just fine the way they are, is to ignore the reality faced by hordes of harried students and professors who see a different truth but who assume that nothing can be done about it. It is time we examined our assumption of impotence in the face of "things as they are," before the costs to psychology, to society, to our students, and to ourselves escalate even further.

References

Bevan, W. A sermon of sorts in three plus parts. *American Psychologist*, 1982, *37*, 1303-1322.

Boice, R. The relevance of faculty development for teachers of psychology. *Teaching of Psychology*, 1984, *11*, 3-8.

Caplan, N., & Nelson, S. On being useful: The nature and consequences of psychological research on social problems. *American Psychologist*, 1973, *28*, 199-211.

Fox, D. R. The pressure to publish: A graduate student's personal plea. *Teaching of Psychology*, 1983, *10*, 177-178.

Fox, D. R. Psychology and controversy: Points for discussion. *Society for the Advancement of Social Psychology Newsletter*, (in press).

Ginsburg, G. P. (Ed.). *Emerging strategies in social psychological research*. Chichester, England: Wiley, 1979.

Heesacker, M. From one without tenure: A response to Fox. *Teaching of Psychology*, 1984, *11*, 238-239.

Hyde, L. *The gift: Imagination and the erotic life of property*. New York: Vintage Books, 1983.

Manicas, P. T., & Secord, P. F. Implications for psychology of the new philosophy of science. *American Psychologist*, 1983, *38*, 399-413.

Maslen, G. Expectation that all professors do research called "unrealistic" by Australian official. *Chronicle of Higher Education*, April 18, 1984, 31-32.

Montagu, A. *Growing young*. New York: McGraw Hill, 1981.

Peters, D. P., & Ceci, S. J. Peer-review practices of psychological journals: The fate of published articles, submitted again. *The Behavioral and Brain Sciences*, 1982, *5*, 187-255.

Sampson, E. E. Cognitive psychology as ideology. *American Psychologist*, 1981, *36*, 730-743.

Sanford, N. Social psychology: Its place in personology. *American Psychologist*, 1982, *37*, 896-903.

Sarason, S. B. *Psychology misdirected*. New York: Free Press, 1981.

Section II
Career Development

An examination of the publication dates of this section's articles reveals that over 70% of them appeared in the 1980s. This growth in writing about students' career needs follows many years of informal discussion and action. The following topics reflect our colleagues' broad scope of interest in students' career development.

The organization of topics assumes that career development is a process that can be fostered in a variety of ways; it also assumes that students can gain most from information about occupational alternatives and opportunities when they know about themselves (i.e., their interests, values, and abilities) and how congruent their personal characteristics are with the work demands of different occupations. Skill development further prepares students for post graduate pursuits. An assessment of the success of occupational pursuits and student satisfaction with those pursuits provides a concluding view of the process.

1. STIMULATING CAREER EXPLORATION AND DEVELOPMENT

This first group of articles describes a model program, courses, and a colloquium series that faculty developed. The articles share a common theme of promoting career exploration and development by stimulating student self exploration and by providing information about occupational alternatives.

Thomas McGovern's description of the evolution of a career development program for undergraduate psychology majors stands as a comprehensive and thorough approach for others to model. The program, designed at Virginia Commonwealth University, consisted of a variety of workshops, a career fair, and a career booklet. The use of student feedback at each stage in the development of the program constitutes a distinctive feature.

The design and evaluation of a Career Development course for upper level psychology majors at Creighton University is the subject of two studies that Mark Ware reported. Course objectives consisted of increasing students' knowledge about themselves, the world of work, and career implementation skills. The second article described the contents of the course that was an elective for three semester hours credit. A more detailed description is available from the author. The studies pre- and posttested students on several dimensions and compared their performance with a group of psychology majors (and in the first study, non-psychology majors) who were not taking the course. The studies found that students taking the course showed significant increases in career decisiveness, self knowledge, job knowledge, skills knowledge, cognitive and behavioral vocational information seeking, and career maturity. The results of those investigations provide encouraging evidence for the effectiveness of the course in achieving its objectives.

A more economical one semester hour course for second semester sophomore and junior psychology majors was the focus of Kennon Lattal's article. This course, taught at West Virginia University, included a review of various areas of psychology, of employment opportunities for bachelor level psychology majors, and of pertinent information about graduate school, as well as workshops on employment interview procedures. Readers may find the author's suggestions for course format very helpful in developing their own.

Venus Bluestein described an elective Fields of Psychology course at the University of Cincinnati. The course evolved as one way for the department to provide career counseling for its several hundred majors. One of the course's primary goals was to engage students in self study, including their reasons for attending college and majoring in psychology. The author described the satisfactions with and obstacles to teaching such a course.

The final article in this group described a novel colloquium series that Mark Ware and Janet Matthews designed at Creighton University; the series sought to promote career exploration and research among undergraduate psychology majors. The authors' instructive guidelines and caveats for developing a series can assist others in avoiding many pitfalls. Students' evaluation of this ongoing series and anecdotal evidence indicated that it had surpassed its objectives.

Development of a Career Planning Program For Undergraduate Psychology Majors

Thomas V. McGovern
Virginia Commonwealth University

The purpose of this paper is to describe the evolution of a career development program for undergraduate psychology majors at Virginia Commonwealth University. V.C.U. is an urban university in which the majority of students are somewhat older, more experienced, and realistically invested in career preparation. The Department of Psychology is one of the largest in the College of Arts and Sciences with twenty-seven full time faculty and 350-400 undergraduate majors. The undergraduate curriculum includes the traditional requirements for an arts and sciences degree, and a minimum of thirty hours in psychology. When the career program was formally begun in 1976, much of the curriculum "groundwork" and positive attitude of the faculty had already been accomplished. There were opportunities for a major to participate in one year of field work or in a one year behavior technology program as part of the psychology electives. Support from the Dean's office was also explicit and enthusiastic about career orientation.

Phase I: Initial Needs Assessment. In Fall, 1976, a needs assessment instrument was prepared. It consisted of a list of career exploration and information workshops which we had the resources to deliver. The list was distributed in all of the upper level psychology courses and the majors were asked to rank order the workshops based on their specific needs.

Seven workshops were offered during the academic year, 1976-1977. In the fall and spring, we offered a two-hour exploration session entitled "Careers in Psychology." The attendance (N = 50) included sophomores, juniors, and seniors, and was the best for our series. A twelve-hour "Art of Helping" training program was also successful. The remaining four workshops which emphasized very specific informational needs were less well attended. These included: "Applying to Graduate School," "Job Search Skills," "Preparing a Resume," and "Job Interview Techniques."

In reviewing the first year's efforts, several important issues emerged for subsequent planning. By listening carefully to students' comments during the "Careers in Psychology" session, I became aware of their aspirations to be psychotherapists, and their stereotypic images of business as an unfit place to use their interests in psychology. In addition to some unrealistic ideas about work, most had no understanding of how to translate their academic coursework into marketable skills. Workshops which focused on a single, informational topic could best be combined into a "career fair" format with extensive use of handout materials. One of the most significant accomplishments of the first year's activities was the preparation of a career library in the department with catalogues, books, and free hand-out materials.

Phase II: Second Needs Assessment. During the fall semester 1977, two studies were completed to assess the expectations, goals, and interests of the psychology majors. The students in my course on Occupational Information and Career Development interviewed senior majors (N = 58). In a separate study, an undergraduate who worked with me on an independent research basis interviewed a representative sample (N = 40) of freshman and sophomore majors. Concerning post-graduation plans, 63% of the freshmen and sophomores surveyed planned to attend graduate/professional school, 5% planned to work, and 32% had no plans at all. In contrast, 59% of the seniors planned to work; 51% planned to attend graduate school in one, two, or three years after they had worked and were financially able to continue. While 89% of the seniors felt that their course work might help them find a job, only 15% felt that their courses had given them any actual "training" for a job. However, 55% felt that their volunteer work gave them the necessary experience, insight, and personal contacts to find meaningful employment. In the freshman-sophomore group, the primary reason for choosing to major in psychology was "to learn more about myself and to help other people." However, 25% of this group had absolutely no idea where a person with a bachelor's degree in psychology could work.

To meet the needs of the graduating seniors, the students in the occupational information class designed a career fair which was held in the fall 1977. Starting with the hand-out material which had been developed the previous year, the students came up with an impressive set of resources. They designed hand-outs on salary expectations, a "roadmap" for the state and federal civil service hiring process, and specific job settings and positions within the city civil service system. Attendance (N = 75) was very good and the evaluation forms showed an enthusiastic response by the people who came and talked with their "peer consultants."

The three major conclusions which could be drawn from the assessment completed during this phase were: (1) Most psychology students (across all class levels) had a fairly clear understanding of why they chose the major. The two orientations were social and investigative—helping other people and understanding the causes of human behavior; (2) Psychology students chose their courses for intrinsic appeal, faculty preferences, or randomly. Almost all of the students surveyed saw little or no relationship between their courses and marketable skills; and (3) Job title jargon and specific employment settings for a bachelor's degree in psychology were virtually unknown. Based on these conclusions, the career development program shifted gears and a major emphasis was placed on educational programming at the freshman and sophomore class level.

Phase III: Curriculum Evaluation. Because of the lack of awareness of students about the translation of academic course material into marketable employment skills, we did a major evaluation of our curriculum in the fall semester 1977. Every faculty member was interviewed in order to identify for every course what a student learned *how to do* during that course. The skills and courses were then clustered into the two main areas of human relations and scientific research. The first part of this matching of skills with academic courses has been completed. The next step is to extend the course/skill relationship to actual job titles and settings so that the student will be able to see a step-by-step sequence from course selection, to clustering, to entry into the workplace.

A booklet, "Career Development Planning with a B.A./B.S. in Psychology," was prepared for distribution to all psychology majors during the fall semester 1978. The booklet serves as a handbook for both the undergraduate major and the faculty advisor. It includes a description of our workshops and information resources, an overview of career development planning, the course/skills/job titles matching, opportunities for work experience within our curriculum, and graduate school options.

Phase IV: Future Directions. At this stage, I have identified four goals for the future: (1) Continue to offer and evaluate the information materials and career fair format to meet the needs of graduating seniors; (2) With the "Career Development Planning" booklet as a primary resource, introduce every new psychology student to the concepts of course planning, skills identification, and job settings/titles; (3) Develop a set of "skills resumes" which will more accurately present the psychology student's marketable credentials to an employer. More traditional resume formats only perpetuate employers' stereotypes of the qualifications of a B.S. in psychology; and (4) Establish some "external validity" for the course/skill/job title relationship through interviews with possible employers. Such placement contacts will serve both a public relations-consciousness raising function as well as a test of our actual marketability.

In sum, we have begun to develop some good methods and have found specific, positive answers for the question posed by one of our skeptical students, "Is there any life after graduation with a bachelor's degree in Psychology?"

Evaluating a Career Development Course: A Two Year Study

Mark E. Ware
Creighton University

Compared with control groups, students in this course showed gains in a number of criteria related to their career readiness.

The attention that some psychologists have given to the career concerns of undergraduate psychology majors (Caffrey, Berger, Cole, Marx, & Senn, 1977) is part of a more general trend in higher education (Bachhuber, 1977; Figler, 1975; Kirts & Fisher, 1973). The last few years have seen a growth in the number of career development courses and most have been directed toward students in the first two years of college (Haney & Howland, 1978).

Over 1000 colleges and universities offer courses in career development. However, there are relatively few reports that evaluate the effectiveness of those courses, and some of the reports have methodological deficiencies. The failure to include a no treatment control group is a common limitation (Evans & Rector, 1978; Heppner & Krause, 1979; Touchton, Wertheimer, Cornfeld, & Harrison, 1977). In general, those studies reported on career development courses for freshmen and sophomores who were undecided about the choice of a major and/or the preference for an occupation. Collectively, they reported finding increases in career decision making, in knowledge of self awareness and of the world of work, and in cognitive complexity.

Babcock and Kaufman (1976) employed a control group and evaluated a career development course for junior and senior female students in a College of Human Ecology. The investigators used the Career Development Inventory (Super, Bohm, Forrest, Jordaan, Lindeman, & Thompson, 1972) and found significantly greater increases in self-knowledge, and in planning to become informed about career alternatives for students enrolled in the course versus those in the control group.

Ware and Beischel's research (1979) is the only one found in the literature that investigated the effectiveness of a career development course for junior and senior psychology majors. Their findings indicated significant differences in cognitive skill and decisiveness for students enrolled in the course versus a control group of psychology majors who were not taking the course. Ware and Beischel also reported that a second study was in progress and indicated that several dependent variable measures would be used to assess the course's effectiveness. The present investigation is that second study.

The primary purpose of this study was to evaluate further the effectiveness of a career development course for upper level psychology majors. Moreover, the study identified the pre-course similarities and differences among psychology majors who were taking the course and psychology majors and non psychology majors who were not taking the course. Finally, the study evaluated the content of the course by examining students' reactions to each of the course's components.

Method. The Psychology Department at Creighton University offered the course, Career Development in Psychology, during the 1979 and 1980 spring semesters. The instructors for the course were Beischel in 1979 and Ware in 1980. The change in instructors resulted from the first instructor's decision to make a career change. The course consisted of three components corresponding to the three objectives of the course, including increasing knowledge about one's self, educational/occupational opportunities, and the occupational implementation skills of resumé writing and interviewing. Ware and Beischel (1979) provide a more detailed description of the course components.

A total of 148 junior and senior college students participated in the study. The 31 psychology majors who enrolled in the course constituted the experimental (E) group. A total of 59 psychology majors who were not in the course made up the control major (CM) group. A total of 29 non psychology majors who were not in the course made up the control, non major (CNM) group. There was a slightly greater percent of males than females in each of the groups. Students in the CNM group had academic majors in the humanities (31%), business administration (21%), social sciences (17%), natural sciences (14%), and other (17%). Inclusion of the CNM group permitted an evaluation of the similarities and differences between students majoring in psychology and those in other disciplines. Thus, the primary variable in this study was the treatment variable consisting of E, CM, and CNM groups.

The second variable that this study examined was a confounded one. The confounding existed between the student who comprised the samples used in 1979 and 1980 and the instructors who taught the course on those two occasions. Thus, the second variable is called the students/instructors variable. In the case of a significant difference in pre/post-course scores involving this variable, no firm conclusion can be drawn about which of the two factors is more important. In the case of a significant difference in pre-course scores involving this variable, one can draw a conclusion about sample selection differences between the two years.

The materials used in this study consisted of several forms. They included those with atheoretical and theoretical origins.

The first one informed students that in choosing and implementing an occupational choice, individuals have different degrees of information available to them. The form instructed each student to rate his/her degree of knowledge about him/herself, job opportunities, and resumé writing and interview skills. The rating scale was a six point Likert scale that varied from low (1) to high (6). Thus, the first form evaluated the course's effectiveness in realizing its objectives.

The second form was the Vocational Checklist (Aiken & Johnston, 1973). The copy of the Checklist that the author acquired consisted of 50 sentence stem items that asked the students to indicate the approximate number of times they emitted a specific information seeking response during the preceding three weeks. Students responded by using a seven point scale that varied from never (0) to very frequently (6). The Checklist provided two scores, including a cognitive or thought response and a behavioral or action response. The second form evaluated the course's effectiveness in instigating covert and overt information seeking activity.

The third form was the Decision Making Task: Occupation Scale (DMT-O) of the Assessment of Career Decision Making (Harren, 1966; Harren, Note 1). Harren developed the Assessment of Career Decision Making in the context of Tiedman's theory (Note 2). The theory contends that as people resolve career decision making tasks they gradually increase control over their own behavior and environment. Resolution of career decision making tasks results in progress through several stages. The DMT-O contains 40 items and uses an agree-disagree format. Subtest scores indicate which of four stages a student is in regarding a career decision. The stages include exploration, crystallization, choice and clarification. An overall score provides a measure of how advanced a student is along a decision making continuum.

The Career Maturity Inventory-Attitude Scale (CMI-AS) constituted the fourth form (Crites, 1973). Crites (1974)

described career maturity in the context of a developmental theory of career counseling. Career maturity is viewed as progressing from orientation and readiness for career choice to decision making and reality-testing. The CMI-AS consists of 50 true-false items. The resultant score provides a measure of career maturity in which higher scores indicate higher levels of maturity.

Administration of the forms described above occurred during the first (pre) and last (post) two weeks of the semester. Students in the course completed the forms as part of the course requirements, but students in the control groups were volunteers. At each administration, students needed about 35 minutes to complete all forms. Students' failure to complete all items on one or more forms and/or to complete the post-course test resulted in a 20% loss of subjects.

Items included on the student's evaluation of the course are listed in the Results section. They are grouped according to the course objectives. Students responded to each item by circling a letter indicating whether they strongly agreed (SA), agreed (A), undecided (U), disagreed (D), or strongly disagreed (SD) with the statement.

A 3 x 2 analysis of variance was used to evaluate the results. The unequal number of subjects in the cells of the factorial design required the use of harmonic-mean analysis. In the first set of analyses, students' pre/post-course difference scores were the data. These analyses evaluated whether significant differences in pre/post-course variations existed between the groups. In the second set of analyses, students' pre-course scores were the data. These analyses provided one way to identify the similarities and differences between psychology and non psychology majors as well as between those who elected to take or not to take the course.

Results. Table 1 contains the mean pre/post-course difference scores for the experimental and control groups. Analy-

Table 1. Means and Standard Deviations for Treatment Groups

Groups	Knowledge			Voc. Info. Seeking		Decision Making	Career Maturity
	Self	Job	Skills	Cognitive	Behavioral		
Pre/Post-Course Difference Scores							
Experimental							
Mean	.45	1.52	2.52	13.90	30.35	1.94	2.45
SD	.89	1.15	1.91	16.38	36.83	3.12	4.03
Control, Major							
Mean	− .03	.12	.22	− .64	5.24	.44	.00
SD	.76	1.10	1.00	18.81	17.69	3.00	3.55
Control, Non Major							
Mean	.17	.14	.31	2.21	1.14	1.13	.79
SD	.66	1.27	.97	18.60	25.68	3.23	3.94
Pre-Course Scores							
Experimental							
Mean	4.77	3.45	2.42	53.97	40.58	25.32	36.03
SD	.92	.89	1.36	20.16	27.15	2.21	5.37
Control, Major							
Mean	4.95	3.69	3.33	54.37	35.20	27.05	38.54
SD	1.02	1.28	1.33	24.84	20.85	3.07	5.04
Control, Non Major							
Mean	4.76	4.03	3.52	51.79	44.52	26.59	39.45
SD	.69	1.32	1.40	19.23	25.04	3.03	3.98

sis of the self knowledge ratings revealed a significant difference for the treatment variable, $F(2,113) = 3.31$, $p < .05$. Results of protected t-analyses (Welkowitz, Ewen, & Cohen, 1976) revealed that students in the E group reported significantly greater increases in self knowledge than those in the CM group, $t(113) = 2.78$, $p < .01$.

Analysis of the job knowledge ratings revealed a significant difference for the treatment variable, $F(2,113) = 24.59$, $p < .01$. Protected t-analyses revealed that students in the E group reported significantly greater increases in job knowledge than students in the CM, $t(113) = 5.98$, $p < .01$, and CNM groups, $t(113) = 5.06$, $p < .01$. Moreover, analysis of job knowledge ratings revealed a significant treatment by students/instructors interaction, $F(2,113) = 11.10$, $p < .01$. Table 2 contains the mean pre/post differences scores for the interaction. Inspection of Table 2 reveals that the students' ratings in the CM group for 1980/Ware largely accounted for the interaction. Only the ratings by those students reflected a decrease in career knowledge.

Table 2. Mean and Standard Deviation for Job Knowledge Scores

Groups	1979/Beischel	1980/Ware
Pre/Post-Course Difference Scores		
Experimental		
Mean	.88	2.29
SD	.86	.99
Control, Major		
Mean	.46	−.55
SD	1.02	.94
Control, Non Major		
Mean	.00	.22
SD	1.67	1.00
Pre-Course Scores		
Experimental		
Mean	3.88	2.93
SD	.60	.92
Control, Major		
Mean	3.36	4.35
SD	1.20	1.18
Control, Non Major		
Mean	3.64	4.28
SD	1.12	1.41

Analysis of the skills knowledge ratings revealed a significant difference for the treatment variable, $F(2,113) = 34.88$, $p < .01$. Protected t-analyses revealed that students in the E group reported significantly greater increases in skills knowledge than students in the CM, $t(113) = 7.97$, $p < .01$, and the CNM groups, $t(113) = 6.56$, $p < .01$.

Analysis of the cognitive vocational information seeking revealed a significant difference for the treatment variable, $F(2,113) = 6.17$, $p < .01$. Protected t-analyses revealed that students in the E group exhibited significantly greater increases in cognitive information seeking than students in either the CM, $t(113) = 3.57$, $p < .01$, or in the CNM groups, $t = 2.47$, $p < .05$.

Analysis of behavioral vocational information seeking revealed a significant difference for the treatment variable, $F(2,113) = 12.53$, $p < .01$. Protected t-analyses revealed that students in the E group exhibited significanty greater increases in behavioral information seeking than students in

either the CM, $t(113) = 4.37$, $p < .01$, or the CNM groups, $t(113) = 4.37$, $p < .01$.

Analysis of the decision making scores revealed no significant differences.

Analysis of the career maturity scores revealed a significant difference for the treatment variable, $F(2,113) = 4.41$, $p < .05$. Protected t-analyses revealed that students in the E group exhibited significantly greater increases in career maturity than students in the CM group, $t(113) = 2.95$, $p < .01$.

Table 1 also contains the mean pre-course scores for the experimental and control groups. Analysis of the self knowledge ratings revealed no significant differences between groups.

Analysis of the job knowledge ratings revealed a significant treatment by students/instructors interaction, $F(2,113) = 7.16$, $p < .01$. Table 2 also contains the mean pre-course scores for the interaction. Inspection of Table 2 and results of protected t-analyses revealed that the 1979/Beischel students in the E group provided significantly higher ratings of job knowledge than those in the CM group, $t(113) = 2.08$, $p < .05$. However, the 1980/Ware students in the E group provided significantly lower ratings of job knowledge than students in the CM, $t(113) = 5.67$, $p < .01$ and the CNM groups, $t(113) = 4.60$, $p < .01$.

Analysis of the skills knowledge ratings revealed significant differences in scores for the treatment variable, $F(2,113) = 6.67$, $p < .01$. Protected t-analyses revealed that students in the E group reported significantly less skill knowledge than students in either the CM, $t(113) = 3.02$, $p < .01$, or the CNM groups, $t(113) = 3.13$, $p < .01$.

Analysis of pre-course cognitive and behavioral vocational information seeking responses revealed no significant differences.

Analysis of students' decision making scores revealed a significant difference for the treatment variable, $F(2,113) = 3.33$, $p < .05$. Protected t-analyses revealed that students in the E group exhibited significantly lower decision making scores than students in the CM group, $t(113) = 2.72$, $p < .01$.

Analysis of pre-course career maturity scores revealed a significant difference for the treatment variable, $F(2,113) = 4.89$, $p < .01$. Protected t-analyses revealed that students in the E group exhibited significantly lower career maturity scores than students in either the CM, $t(113) = 2.31$, $p < .05$, or in the CNM groups, $t(113) = 2.13$, $p < .05$.

Listed below are items from the students' course evaluation, including the percent of students who agreed or strongly agreed with each item. Inspection reveals that students discriminated among the several course components and that more than three out of four responded favorably to all class activities.

Self Knowledge
1. The self-exploration exercises in the beginning of the course helped me to know myself better. (81)

Job Knowledge
2. It was very important for me to have the different areas or jobs in psychology differentiated. (90)
3. Realizing job opportunity and salary level in areas of psychology was very important to me. (90)
4. The video-tapes and professionals who came to class helped me very much in my own decision making. (84)
5. The lectures on graduate school application and acceptance were very important for me. (77)

6. The lectures on resumé writing and letter of application were very important to me. (100)
7. The resumé and letter of application writing exercises were very important to me. (97)
8. The lectures on the interviewing process were very important to me. (97)
9. The opportunity to practice interviewing in class was very important to me. (84)

Recommendation
10. I think this course should be taken by every psychology major. (87)

Discussion. The E group's superior increases in ratings of knowledge about self, job opportunities, and skills were consistent with the course's objectives. Moreover, the findings of significant increases in self knowledge for students taking a career course are consistent with those that Babcock and Kaufman (1976) reported.

The results of cognitive and behavioral vocational information seeking responses indicated that the course contributed to instigating both thoughts and actions directed toward acquiring career-related information. Babcock and Kaufman (1976) also reported finding significant increases in becoming more informed about careers. However, the findings of the present study indicated that information seeking activity is not limited to merely thinking about getting information.

At least two explanations account for the failure to find significantly greater increases in decision making scores for the E group. The findings may indicate that the course was ineffective or that the total score index was insensitive for those students. The author undertook an *ex post facto* examination of the DMT-O subtest scores. Inspection of the pre/post-course modal response category (stage of decision making) for the groups revealed that students in the E group began the course at stage 2, crystallization, and ended the course at stage 3, choice. Students in both control groups began and ended the course at stage 3. These findings suggest that the total score on the DMT-O was insensitive and that subtest scores were more sensitive to detecting changes brought about by the course. Indirect support for this conclusion is found in research by Evans and Rector (1978) who found significant increases in DMT-O scores among freshmen and sophomores who took a career course. Inspection of the mean DMT-O scores revealed lower values than those found in this investigation using juniors and seniors. Thus, the total DMT-O score appears less sensitive with older college students.

Finally, the course appeared effective in increasing the students' career maturity scores. These results confirmed an *ex post facto* finding that Ware and Beischel (1979) reported.

One conclusion from this study is that the theoretical orientations of Harren (Note 2) and Crites and his colleagues (Super, Crites, Hummel, Moser, Overstreet, & Warnath, 1957) can provide useful contexts for planning and evaluating courses in career development. A conclusion about the effectiveness of the course is tempered by the limitations associated with the use of a quasi-experimental design.

The students' pre-course performances revealed that there was no instance in which students in the CM and CNM groups differed significantly from each other. Thus, psychology majors who didn't take the course were similar in career-related behaviors to a broad range of other college undergraduates.

The significant differences in ratings of skill knowledge, decision making, and career maturity between those who took the course and those who did not can be interpreted in at least two ways. Students who took the course may be more willing to acknowledge their needs, that is, they were less defensive. The results may also indicate that those who took the course recognized and acted on their perceived need for the course. Future research should address these and alternative explanations.

The pre-course data are also valuable for identifying the characteristics of students who are the most likely to profit by taking the course. The results suggest that students who think they have deficient knowledge about skills, who are at a crystallization stage of decision making, and/or who have lower career maturity scores are more likely to benefit from the course. These findings argue against the students' favorable response to the item on the course evaluation that asked about requiring this course for all psychology majors. Moreover findings reported by Hanes, Adams, Lloyd, and Woodman (1978) offer several promising leads for identifying additional variables for predicting who can benefit the most by taking a career course.

Overall, the students responded favorably to the course, and that finding is consistent with results that Ware and Beischel (1979) reported. Students in the present study responded most favorably to the skills component of the course. Examination of students' ratings of skill knowledge revealed that they entered the course thinking that they were deficient in that area. Thus, the course appeared to be particularly effective in addressing this perceived need of students.

The course described in this paper provides one alternative for communicating more effectively with students about post graduate alternatives. For those interested in resources that describe a myriad of educational and occupational alternatives available to students with an undergraduate major in psychology, the author recommends the following: Cates (1973), Davis (1979), Lunneborg (1974; 1978), Malnig and Morrow (1975), Titley (1978), and Ware and Meyers (1981).

Another recommendation is the development of a more comprehensive program of career development. One element in such a program is a career development course similar to the one described in this investigation. Another is the type of professional training that Caffrey et al. (1977), Korn and Nodine (1975), and Nish (1979) emphasized. A third component consists of field experiences that many have described and recommended as an important part in the career development of undergraduates (Davis, 1979; Korn & Nodine, 1975; Lunneborg, 1974; Matthews, 1979. Ware and Matthews (1980) described a fourth and novel approach to foster career development. They designed a colloquium series to stimulate career exploration and research among undergraduate students. Finally, McGovern (1979) described a career planning program for undergraduate psychology majors that recommends a developmental orientation and the multifaceted qualities that are required to meet the variety of students' educational and occupational needs.

The comprehensive program recommended in this article does not require substantial revision or sacrificing of a traditional curricular approach to teaching undergraduate psychology. However, it does require faculty commitment to the challenge posed by the frequently asked question, "What can I do with a major in psychology?"

References

Aiken, J., & Johnston. Promoting career information seeking behavior in college students. *Journal of Vocational Behavior*, 1973, *3*, 81-87.

Babcock, R., & Kaufman, M. Effectiveness of a career course. *Vocational Guidance Quarterly*, 1976, *24*, 261-266.

Bachhuber, T. Career development in higher education: Process, program, or problem? *Journal of Employment Counseling*, 1977, *14*, 31-38.

Caffrey, B., Berger, L., Cole, S., Marx, D., & Senn, D. Integrating professional programs in a traditional undergraduate psychology program. *Teaching of Psychology*, 1977, *4*, 7-13.

Cates, J. Baccalaureates in psychology: 1969 and 1970. *American Psychologist*, 1973, *28*, 262-264.

Crites, J. *The career maturity inventory*. Monterey, CA: CTB/McGraw-Hill, 1973.

Crites, J. Career counseling: A review of major approaches. *The Counseling Psychologist*, 1974, *4*, 3-23.

Davis, J. Where did they all go? A job survey of BA graduates. In P. Woods (Ed.), *The psychology major: Training and employment strategies*. Washington: American Psychological Association, 1979.

Evans, J., & Rector, A. Evaluation of a college course in career decision making. *Journal of College Student Personnel*, 1978, *19*, 163-168.

Figler, H. *PATH: A career workbook for liberal arts students*. Cranston, RI: The Carroll Press, 1975.

Hanes, P., Adams, J., Lloyd, R., & Woodman, R. Career planning: Who's ready for it? *Journal of College Placement*, 1978, *79*, 47-50.

Haney, T., & Howland, P. Career course for credit: Necessity or luxury? *Journal of College Placement*, 1978, *39*, 75-77.

Harren, V. The vocational decision-making process among college males. *Journal of Counseling Psychology*, 1966, *13*, 271-277.

Heppner, P., & Krause, J. A career seminar course. *Journal of College Student Personnel*, 1979, *20*, 300-305.

Kirts, D., & Fisher, R. TRIPOD: A systems approach to career planning. *Journal of College Placement*, 1973, *33*, 42-49.

Korn, J., & Nodine, B. Facts and questions concerning career training of the psychology major. *Teaching of Psychology*, 1975, *2*, 117-119.

Lunneborg, P. Can college graduates in psychology find employment in this field? *Vocational Guidance Quarterly*, 1974, *23*, 159-166.

Lunneborg, P. *Why study psychology?* Monterey, CA: Brooks/Cole, 1978.

Malnig, L., & Morrow, S. *What can I do with a major in...?* Jersey City, NJ: Saint Peter's College Press, 1975.

Matthews, J. Undergraduate field placement: Survey and issues. *Teaching of Psychology*, 1979, *6*, 148-151.

McGovern, T. The development of a career planning program for undergraduate psychology majors. *Teaching of Psychology*, 1979, *6*, 183-184.

Nish, W. W. A psychology technician training program. *Teaching of Psychology*, 1979, *6*, 206-209.

Super, D., Bohm, M., Forrest, D., Jordaan, J., Lindeman, R., & Thompson, A. *Career development inventory*. New York: Teachers College Columbia University, 1972.

Super, D., Crites, J., Hummel, R., Moser, H., Overstreet, P., & Warnath, C. *Vocational development: A framework for research*. New York: Teachers College Bureau of Publications, 1957.

Titley, R. Whatever happened to the class of '67? *American Psychologist*, *1978, 33*, 1094-1098.

Touchton, J., Wertheimer, L., Cornfeld, J., & Harrison, K. Career planning and decision-making: A developmental approach to the classroom. *The Counseling Psychologist*, 1977, *6*, 42-47.

Ware, M., & Beischel, M. Career development: Evaluating a new frontier for teaching and research. *Teaching of Psychology*, 1979, *6*, 210-213.

Ware, M., & Matthews, J. Stimulating career exploration and research among undergraduates: A colloquium series. *Teaching of Psychology*, 1980, *7*, 36-38.

Ware, M., & Meyers, A. Career versitility of the psychology major: A survey of graduates. *Teaching of Psychology*, 1981, *8*, 12-15.

Welkowitz, J., Ewen, R., & Cohen, J. *Introductory statistics for the behavioral sciences* (2nd Ed.). New York: Academic Press, 1976.

Notes

1. Harren, V. A. Assessment of career decision making (ACDM). Unpublished paper, 1976 (Available from Vincent A. Harren, Department of Psychology, Southern Illinois University, Carbondale, IL 62901).

2. Harren, V. A. An overview of Tiedeman's theory of career decision making and summary of related research. Unpublished paper, 1976 (Available from Vincent A. Harren, Department of Psychology, Southern Illinois University, Carbondale, IL 62901).

Career Development: Evaluating a New Frontier For Teaching and Research

Mark E. Ware and
Mark L. Beischel
Creighton University

A case is made for treating the subject in terms of an intellectual experience, and a favorable student evaluation of the course is shown.

Although in former years many curricula emphasized preparing students for graduate school, increasing numbers of programs now are attending to the needs of the majority of psychology majors who are not going to graduate school. Korn and Nodine (1975) described the central feature of undergraduate professional training as emphasizing off-campus experience. Caffrey, Berger, Cole, Marx and Senn (1977) presented a program consisting of four professional areas for the training of undergraduates. Lunneborg (1974) reported on the effectiveness of a program which was similar to those two. A survey of psychology graduates of a bachelor's program with a vocational emphasis revealed that 25% were employed in jobs directly related to the major, whereas only 16% attributed difficulty in getting a job related to the major. Although such programs might provide encouragement, the career development approach described in this paper offers promise for psychology students whether they plan immediate employment or additional education. In part, career development is understood as a process in which persons develop realistic goals and strategies for professional and personal life-style futures.

A program of career development recognizes the range of students' problems. Some students have not decided and others seem incapable of deciding on a training specialization. For them the problem may involve inadequate knowledge about themselves and/or deficient career decision making skills. Other students have made a decision but are deficient in knowledge about opportunities and/or effective implementation behaviors. Super and Hall (1978) summarized the considerable literature on career development in educational settings. However, the bulk of the research was at the pre-college level. Moreover, courses in career development at the college level have tended to be limited to freshmen and sophomores (Haney & Howland, 1978). Harkness (1976) provided an excellent account of several approaches to workshops, seminars, and courses in career development. The research literature contains relatively little about programs for upper classmen. One exception was a description of a career awareness mini-seminar for advanced psychology majors (Hackney & Williams, 1975). Another by Patterson (Note 1) described the contents of a course in career development for psychology undergraduates. Neither study reported systematic evaluation.

The purpose of the present study is to describe and evaluate the contents of a course in career development for advanced psychology majors. The objectives of the course included increasing students' knowledge about themselves, educational/career opportunities, and career implementation skills. Moreover, the study evaluated the effectiveness of the course in developing cognitive skills, altering one's identity and increasing decisiveness about career plans.

Method. The students enrolled in the course constituted the experimental group and included 12 junior and senior psychology majors. A total of 13 junior and senior psychology majors who were not enrolled in the course made up the control group. Students enrolled in the course served in the investigation as a part of the course requirements. All other participants were volunteers.

The materials consisted of a course evaluation and two questionnaires. The course evaluation consisted of items designed to elicit students' responses to issues related to each of the course objectives. Students indicated their reactions by responding on a five point Likert scale which varied from strongly disagree to strongly agree. Table 1 contains the items on the course evaluation. They are grouped according to the course objectives. The first questionnaire consisted of one of the competency scales (WSTD) from Crites' Career Maturity Inventory (1973). The WSTD scale measures skill at solving problems of a career-related nature. The second questionnaire was the Identity Scale (Holland, Gottfredson & Nafziger, 1975). High scores on the scale reflect a clear and stable self-picture of personality, interest, and talent. Students also rated their degree of decisiveness about the choice of a career. All materials were administered to both groups at the beginning and end of the semester.

The Psychology Department offered the Career Development course for 3 semester hours credit during the spring semester. Enrollment was limited to junior and senior psychology majors. The class met three times a week for 14 weeks. The instructor assigned readings from the texts (Dunphy, Austin, & McEneaney, 1978; Super & Super, 1976) and several other miscellaneous sources throughout the semester.

The course consisted of three components corresponding to the three objectives, including increasing knowledge of one's self, educational/career opportunities, and the career implementation skills of resumé writing and interview skills. During the first part of the course students were

Table 1
Student Evaluations of Course Components

Item	Median Response Category	Percent ≥ Agree
Self-Knowledge		
1. The self-exploration exercises were very effective in helping me to know myself better.	Agree	85
2. The group discussions that followed the self-exploration exercises were very helpful.	Agree	60
3. The career aptitude test and its interpretation was a very good way to enable me to know my abilities more accurately.	Agree	92
4. The group discussions that followed the aptitude test results was very important to me.	Agree	62
Job Knowledge		
5. The part of the course in which different job descriptions were clarified was very good.	Strongly Agree	87
6. Realizing educational/career opportunity and salary level in areas of psychology was very important to me.	Strongly Agree	87
Skill Development		
7. The lectures on resume writing were very helpful to me.	Strongly Agree	87
8. The resume writing exercise was very good for me.	Strongly Agree	87
9. The lectures on the interviewing process were very helpful to me.	Strongly Agree	92
Overall		
10. This course is among the best I have ever taken.	Agree	62

encouraged and directed to acquire a greater awareness of their interests and abilities. The instructor administered the Self-Directed Search (Holland, 1972) and the General Aptitude Test Battery. He also provided an interpretation of the results. The students evaluated those data in small group discussions. Students were informed about the services of the university counseling center and encouraged to use them for acquiring additional information about themselves.

The second portion of the course emphasized the world of work. Students investigated career opportunities requiring degrees in psychology from the bachelor to doctoral levels. Psychologists representing several doctoral specializations visited the class and described their experiences in graduate training and the employment setting. Students examined other areas of training and work closely affiliated with the practice of psychology, including paraprofessional activity, social work, special education, etc.

Students studied procedures for applying to graduate school and evaluated their likelihood of gaining admittance. Although the course concentrated on graduate school in psychology, the instructor generalized the principles to those situations confronting students seeking admission to medical, dental, or law school.

The final component of the course included instruction and practice in resumé writing and interviewing. The university's placement office director provided assistance in describing the content and organization of a resumé. Furthermore, he encouraged students to make use of the facilities in his office to obtain employment. Several periods were devoted to videotaping simulated interviews. The tapes were replayed and the instructor and students identified strengths and weaknesses in each interview.

Results. Table 1 contains items relating to the objectives of the course. It also reports the median response category for, and the percent of students who agreed or strongly agreed with, each item.

Inspection of items 1 and 3 in Table 1 reveals that a very high percentage of students responded affirmatively to items about the value of activities designed to increase knowledge about themselves. Students gave less positive reactions to group discussions following each of those activities, as indicated by responses to items 2 and 4. Students' responses to the clarification of job descriptions, educational/career opportunities, and salary levels were at the highest level. The median response category was strongly agree on both items 5 and 6.

Items 7 and 8 addressed the value of the lectures on resume writing and the interview process. The median response category was strongly agree on both. Ninety-two per cent of the students responded favorably to the exercise of writing and revising a resume. The last item on the evaluation assessed the students' overall reactions to the course. The results indicate that 62% of the students regarded the course as among the best they had ever taken.

Table 2 contains the pre- and post-test results for experimental and control groups on measures of cognitive

Table 2
Summary Data for Groups

Groups	Cognitive Skill		Identity		Decisiveness	
	Pre	Post	Pre	Post	Pre	Post
Experimental						
Mean	13.9	13.9	12.7	13.7	4.6	5.3
SD	1.4	2.0	2.4	1.6	.7	.7
Control						
Mean	11.4	12.2	11.7	12.9	4.3	4.3
SD	2.2	1.1	2.5	1.6	1.1	1.4

skill, identity, and decisiveness about a career. A 2 x 2 analysis of variance with repeated measures on the second factor was used on each measure. The results revealed that significant differences existed between experimental and control groups in cognitive skill, $F(1,21) = 13.80$, $p < .01$. Inspection of Table 2 reveals that students who enrolled in the course originally had and maintained a higher level of cognitive skill than those who did not take the course.

Analysis of the identity data revealed a significant increase in identity scores from the beginning to the end of the semester, $F(1,23) = 8.34$, $p < .01$. Inspection of the means of both groups indicates similar increases from the beginning to the end of the semester.

Finally, analysis of decisiveness ratings indicated a significant increase in scores from pre- to post-testing, $F(1,21) = 4.39$, $p < .05$, and a significant interaction between groups and trials, $F(1,21) = 8.38$, $p<.01$. Inspection of Table 2 indicates that the experimental group experienced an increase in decisiveness but the control group remained unchanged.

Discussion. The results of the students' evaluation of the course were generally very favorable. Students indicated that the activities designed for self understanding and awareness were effective. However, there was less agreement about the importance and helpfulness of group discussion associated with those activities. Two explanations are offered. On the one hand, the products of group discussion may not have been perceived as effective as simply obtaining the data. On the other hand, some students may have reacted defensively at the public disclosure of data inconsistent with the social image they desired. Observations of students' nonverbal behavior in class and conversations between students and the instructor outside the class supported the latter explanation.

The second part of the class focused on job descriptions and educational/career opportunities. The strong favorable reaction to this part of the course was not surprising. Given the widespread attitude that a person cannot get a job with a bachelor's degree in psychology, this part of the course seemed to alleviate much anxiety for some students and provide considerable encouragement about opportunities. Moreover, other students reported satisfaction at discovering viable alternatives to doctoral programs in psychology, such as social work, school psychology, college student personnel, etc. If this part of the course were characterized as promoting career awareness and discrimination, our students were pleasantly surprised by their insights.

The last part of the class, emphasizing resumé writing and interviewing skills, was also responded to very favorably. In part, the satisfaction might be understood as a general response associated with the acquisition of a skill or competence. But in addition, students expressed confidence in undertaking the processes of applying for a job or to post graduate school. In sum, the objectives of the course were fully realized as evidenced by the satisfaction expressed by students taking the course.

The effectiveness of the course was also evaluated by assessing relevant career-related behaviors. The results of the measures of problem solving skills indicated that the students enrolled in the course were superior to those who did not take it. Students who were more sophisticated in making career-related decisions seemed more disposed to take the course. Although at a cognitive level they may have had less of a need for the course, they were better equipped to evaluate their need for more information and for making a decision about post graduate plans.

The results of the identity measure were inconclusive. The groups did not differ from one another, and both increased significantly in their views of themselves. Whether the change represented a general developmental influence or a similar impact by differential forces can't be answered by this study.

In the experimental group, the change in decisiveness about a career was an anticipated consequence. The course did not attempt to force students to make a career decision. However, it was expected that decisiveness would increase with greater information about one's self,

educational/career opportunities, and career implementation skills. The change in decisiveness can be explained in the context of Crites' theory (1974). As measured by the Career Maturity Inventory-Attitude Scale, vocational maturity includes an assessment of the students' involvement in the choice process, independence in decision-making, preference for vocational choice factors, orientation toward work, and conceptions of the vocational choice process. Individuals who are more vocationally mature have been found to be more decisive about their careers. The more vocationally mature students are also understood to be more realistic and to have integrated existing data into career directed decisions. Students in the class completed the Attitude Scale and their scores increased from 37.8 to 41.7 from the beginning to the end of the course, $t(11) = 3.91$, $p<.01$. The absence of career maturity measures on the control group limits the interpretation. Moreover, one weakness of the quasi-experimental design used in this study is the possible influence of a selection-maturation interaction. A conclusion about the effectiveness of the course in producing increased certainty about one's career plans should be regarded as tentative.

Some might question the propriety of offering academic credit for a career development course. The justification for the course was viewed in the same context as other psychology courses. Specifically, it requires a disciplined study of certain related facets of behavior in which the objectives are understanding, prediction and control. Finally, the conventional academic standards of student contact hours, scholarly pursuit of the subject matter and a critical evaluation of performance were applied with comparable rigor in the career development course.

A second study on the effectiveness of the Career Development course is in progress. The subsequent study includes an additional control group consisting of non-majors. The study will examine changes in career maturity, stage of decision making, and cognitive and behavioral career information seeking responses. The objectives include evaluating the effectiveness of the course and identifying the similarities and differences between psychology majors and non majors with regard to career-related behavior. Similarities between the two would support the extension of a course such as this to majors in other disciplines.

A convincing case is emerging for viewing the career development of college students as a worthwhile endeavor for teachers of psychology, as well as a viable area of investigation. Major theoretical perspectives include self concept and development (Super, Stariskevsky, Matlin, & Jordaan, 1963), social learning theory (Krumboltz, Mitchell, & Jones, 1976), and stages of development (Harren, Note 2). The efforts of other investigators will be eagerly awaited.

References

Caffrey, B., Berger, L., Cole, S., Marx, D., & Senn, D. Integrating professional programs in a traditional undergraduate psychology program. *Teaching of Psychology,* 1977, *4,* 7-13.

Crites, J. O. *The career maturity inventory.* Monterey, CA: CTB/McGraw-Hill, 1973.

Crites, J. O. The career maturity inventory. In D. E. Super (Ed.), *Measuring vocational maturity for counseling and evaluation.* Washington, DC: American Personnel and Guidance Association, 1974.

Dunphy, R., Austin, S., & McEneaney, T. *Career development for the college student* (4th ed). Cranston, RI: Carroll Press, 1978.

Hackney, L., & Williams, C. Career awareness miniseminar. *The Vocational Guidance Quarterly,* 1975, *24,* 365-366.

Haney, T., & Howland, P. Career course for credit: Necessity or luxury? *Journal of College Placement,* 1978, *39,* 75-79.

Harkness, C. A. *Career counseling.* Springfield, IL: Charles C Thomas, 1976.

Holland, J. *Professional manual for the self directed search.* Palo Alto, CA: Consulting Psychologist Press, 1972.

Holland, J. D., Gottfredson, G. D., & Nafziger, D. H. Testing the validity of some theoretical signs of vocational decision-making ability. *Journal of Counseling Psychology,* 1975, *22,* 411-422.

Krumboltz, J. D., Mitchell, A. M., & Jones, G. B. A social learning theory of career selection. *The Counseling Psychologist,* 1976, *6,* 71-81.

Korn, J. H., & Nodine, B. Facts and questions concerning career training of the psychology major. *Teaching of Psychology,* 1975, *2,* 117-119.

Lunneborg, P. Can college graduates in psychology find employment in their field? *The Vocational Guidance Quarterly,* 1974, *23,* 159-166.

Super, D. E., & Hall, D. T. Career development: Exploration and planning. *Annual Review of Psychology,* 1978, *29,* 333-372.

Super, D. E., Stariskevsky, R., Matlin, N., & Jordaan, J. P. *Career development: Self-concept theory.* New York: College Entrance' Examination Board, 1963.

Super, D., & Super, C. *Opportunities in psychology careers today.* Louisville, KY: Vocational Guidance Manuals, Inc., 1976.

Notes

1. Patterson, B. Didactic group training in career development for psychology undergraduates. In E. Krimsky-Montague (Chair), *A career-decision making course for psychology undergraduates.* Symposium presented at the meeting of the American Psychological Association, Toronto, Canada, 1978.

2. Harren, V. A. An overview of Tiedeman's theory of career decision making and summary of related research. Unpublished paper, 1976 (Available from Vincent A. Harren, Department of Psychology, Southern Illinois University, Carbondale, IL 62901).

3. The first author was primarily responsible for the design, statistical analysis, and write up of the investigation. The second author was primarily responsible for teaching the course. The second author now holds a position with the Department of Correctional Services, State of Nebraska. The first author is now responsible for teaching the course.

"Psychology as a Profession"; A Brief Course Providing Career Information for Psychology Majors

Kenneth A. Lattal
West Virginia University

Baccalaureate graduates in psychology often have little systematic information about career options in psychology or how to begin planning their career while still an undergraduate student. To ameliorate this problem, McGovern (1979) developed workshops and booklets, but Ware and Matthews (1980) implemented a colloquium series focusing in part on career development. Alternatively, we provide career information in a one-hour credit elective service course entitled "Psychology as a Profession."

Course Design. The course has been offered in its present form for two years. Enrollment (about 40 students) is limited to second-semester sophomore and junior psychology majors. Grading is pass-fail; attendance at eleven or more of the thirteen weekly one-hour meetings is the only requirement for a grade of pass. No texts are required, but relevant APA publications are ordered for optional purchase through local bookstores.

Career development through relevant educational and work experiences is presented first. Included is a review of the various areas of psychology and required levels of academic training and skills needed for employment in each. Students receive ideas for courses and experiences available in the department (e.g., directed research projects; off-campus, semester-long training programs in mental health facilities around the state; volunteer projects; the department's honors program) that might help in shaping different psychology-related careers. Vocational counseling is offered through the student counseling center to students unsure of their vocational objectives.

Employment opportunities in psychology at the Bachelor's degree level is the next topic. Considered are such things as employment data on recent departmental graduates, the advantages and disadvantages of not going to graduate school immediately, use of the university placement service, and places to look for positions in the state. Representatives from mental health facilities in the area visit the class to discuss their facilities' needs for and uses of Bachelor's level employees.

We then focus on professional issues likely to affect our graduates. In addition to APA's code of ethics, we cover such topics as the purpose and organization of APA, licensing and certification issues, training models for clinical psychology (Boulder and Vail) and different types of graduate training in Psychology (e.g., MA vs. PhD vs. PsyD).

A survey of graduates of our department between 1971 and 1977, conducted by Dr. Ralph R. Turner, indicated that 46 percent of those graduates continued their education beyond the Bachelor's degree. We therefore devote several sessions to graduate study. This begins with a rather detailed description of how to apply to graduate school. Obtaining information on programs and schools, guidelines for selection of schools (e.g., ways of assessing the quality of different schools), matching a student's interests with graduate programs, taking required tests, and suggestions on completing application forms, are covered. Here we also discuss the relative importance of grades, recommendation letters, required test scores, employment and volunteer experiences, admission interviews. Psychologists from the department visit the class to describe graduate training in their areas of specialization. Since about 60 percent of our graduates who continue beyond the Bachelor's degree do so in areas other than psychology, such areas as social work, vocational rehabilitation, counseling and guidance, medicine, law, education, and child development are discussed by guest-speaker professionals.

The course concludes with a workshop on interviewing skills conducted by the University Placement Service. A didactic session on how to interview is followed by a videotaping of each student during a mock interview with an employer and a review of the tape with the student by a number of the placement service staff.

Evaluation and Discussion. Of 31 students completing the course evaluation at the end of the Spring 1979 semester, over 80 percent rated the statements, "This course provided valuable information about employment opportunities"; "This course provided valuable information about post-graduate educational opportunities for psychology majors"; and "The information I obtained in this course was information which I have not previously known about" as 1 or 2 on a scale from 1-5 where 1 signified strongly agree and 5 signified strongly disagree.

By a wide margin, students expressed a preference for the present class format over either written material or optional colloquia-type meetings (cf. McGovern, 1979; Ware & Matthews, 1980). To the statement, "The present course should be dropped and the relevant information made available to psychology majors through a written booklet," 85 percent of the students gave a rating of 4 or 5 on the 5-point scale. Sixty-six percent rated as 4 or 5 an item suggesting the course be dropped in favor of optional evening meetings. In addition to student preferences, there are other advantages that recommend the course format for disseminating career information. The opportunity for discussion and in-depth questions and answers, characteristic of courses, are precluded with written material. Face-to-face contact with students over an entire semester optimizes both the opportunity for questions and answers and for a systematic, cohesive development of the careers topic. A regularly scheduled class meeting time where there are explicit consequences for non-attendance insures continuity from topic to topic for students. Since attendance is near perfect, anxiety on the part of the instructor about a "good showing" of students for guest speakers also is minimized. Workshops, on the other hand, must be offered during the academic year at mutually convenient times, usually in the evenings or on weekends, to avoid conflict with classes. Unfortunately, during these times concurrently available activities often preclude regular workshop attendance, resulting in disjointed topic coverage for sporadic attenders.

Several issues related to course organization were considered in arriving at the present format. Specific course requirements, such as developing a resume (although students at this level have very little to enter on a resume), a statement of career objectives, or research into different professional areas or issues, and use of a more evaluative grading system for such activities could be made easily without appreciably changing the course format or objectives. However, the pass-fail grading and lack of substantive course requirements were implemented to create a relaxed atmosphere where providing help to students, and not evaluation of them, was central. Because majors are limited in the number of hours of psychology courses they can take, it was important to provide maximum information and minimum interference with the credit hours students should acquire in more substantive psychology courses (cf. Ware & Beischel, 1979). The one hour credit course permits coverage of a great deal of information at minimal cost both in terms of credit hours and faculty time. Some difficulty with overlap and redundant information has occurred when guest speakers were not precisely informed about what topics to discuss. Another problem has been to provide the information to students at a time when it can be optimally useful. Unlike Ware and Beischel (1979), we have not found the material to be very useful to seniors. For example, even first-semester seniors have already availed themselves of most departmental opportunities and, by the time discussion of graduate school comes around, deadlines are near or past for the coming academic year. Offering the course in the spring semester seems best, for it gives second semester juniors time to plan for the following year when they will begin applying for jobs and graduate programs.

References

McGovern, T. V. Development of a career planning program for undergraduate psychology majors. *Teaching of Psychology,* 1979, *6,* 183-184.

Ware, M. E., & Beischel, M. L. Career development: Evaluating a new frontier for teaching and research. *Teaching of Psychology,* 1979, *6,* 210-213.

Ware, M. E., & Matthews, J. R. Stimulating career exploration and research among undergraduates: A colloquium series. *Teaching of Psychology,* 1980, *7,* 36-38.

Variations on the Fields of Psychology Course

Venus Bluestein
University of Cincinnati

The Fields of Psychology course offered at the University of Cincinnati is similar in purpose and content to that proposed by Gottlieb (1975), but differs in some respects which, perhaps, makes it unique.

In less developed cultures, career choices are limited, role models are readily visible, and one's work often is more a function of birthright than of desire. The more complex the society, the more options there are and the more difficult it is for individuals to obtain information about the world of work. My experience has been that, all too frequently, career choices are more the result of chance occurrences than careful study. Ideally, career counseling should begin at an early age and continue throughout one's life. Although the Federal Government advocates the concept of career education from kindergarten through grade twelve, few such formal programs exist.

At the college level, students frequently select a major for the wrong reasons. Psychology is particularly attractive in this respect. Further, it is not uncommon for majors to assume that the BA will prepare them for careers as psychologists. As is true of other campuses, UC makes career counseling available. However, these facilities cannot reach all students who are in need of the service. Consequently, our department decided to explore ways in which we could provide career counseling for our own 600 majors, and the Fields of Psychology course was conceived.

As envisioned, the course would serve several functions: (1) present psychology as a potential career; (2) serve as a vehicle for imparting information about requirements, optional learning experiences, the faculty, and the department; (3) afford an opportunity to become acquainted with faculty members; (4) teach some basic skills which apparently were not being obtained elsewhere.

During the first meeting, our chairman describes the composition of the department and faculty and how the department operates. One session is held in the library while the psychology-education reference librarian describes facilities and discusses relevant psychological references, guides, services, periodicals, etc. One meeting is devoted to the improvement of study skills. Most weeks, time is set aside for one or more faculty member to meet with the group. Each tells something about his/her courses, research, and other professional interests, and informs students of opportunities to serve as teaching or research assistants or for independent study.

One of the primary goals of the course, however, is to engage students in self study. They are urged to think about their motivation for attending college and their reasons for selecting psychology as a major. What are their career goals? Is psychology the most appropriate route to those goals? What sort of learning experiences should they plan for themselves while they are undergraduates in order to maximize the likelihood of accomplishing their goals? Students are given a number of exercises, such as those suggested in Bolles (1972), which help them to define their interests, skills, values, life goals, aspirations, and the type of work they might enjoy. Students who are undecided about careers are encouraged to refer themselves to the Counseling Center for vocational testing.

Fields is not an easy course to teach. The content is vague; its approach and goals are unique as courses go. The topics do not lend themselves to stimulating group discussions and students sometimes fail to appreciate the value of the experience until later. Evaluations from the more perceptive students have been favorable and their personal reports and anecdotes indicate that the course does accomplish its goals for most of the participants.

We had hoped to make the course a requirement for all psychology majors, but soon discovered that we lacked the faculty resources to accommodate some 200 students annually. The content and goals do not lend themselves to large lectures and it's not the sort of course one is likely to undertake if not committed to the concept of career education. Currently, Fields is an elective, but we are hopeful of discovering a means of reaching more students in the future.

References

Bolles, R. N. *What color is your parachute?* Berkeley: Ten Speed Press, 1972.

Gottlieb, M. C. Introduction to the fields of psychology: A course proposal. *Teaching of Psychology*, 1975, *2*, 159-161.

Stimulating Career Exploration and Research Among Undergraduates: A Colloquium Series

Mark E. Ware and
Janet R. Matthews
Creighton University

The most frequent question asked of advisors in psychology was answered in this department by an ongoing undergraduate colloquium program.

Recently, considerably greater attention has been given to the needs of undergraduates regarding preparation for post graduate years, particularly when that entails immediate entrance into the job market (Caffrey, Berger, Spurgeon, Marx, & Senn, 1977; Korn & Nodine, 1975; Turner, 1974; Mink, Note 1). Although the process of career development is familiar to professionals in counseling and student personnel (Holland, 1959; Super, 1953), it is a relatively new phenomenon to more academically-oriented psychologists. Ware & Beischel (1979) may be the first to report on the content and effectiveness of a career development course for psychology majors. However, most teachers of undergraduate psychology are acutely sensitive to the challenge posed by the question, "What can I do with a major in psychology?"

Another challenge faced by many teachers of undergraduate psychology is to stimulate student research. Forsyth (1977) and Yoder (1979) reported on the importance of students' involvement in an actual investigation when learning about research methodology. Another relevant variable is the kind of researcher, role model projected by the teacher. Being an effective model may not seem possible in the face of heavy institutional demands for teaching and service unless novel strategies are developed to reduce one's teaching load (Ware, Gardner, & Murphy, 1978; Morris, Note 2). Despite teaching load reductions, the stimulation of observing and opportunity for presenting research are often lacking. One may ask, "How can I contribute to a scholarly atmosphere in my department?"

The two questions raised above were the background against which a colloquium series was initiated and evaluated at our institution. The purposes of this investigation were: (a) to assess students' reactions regarding the effectiveness of the series, (b) to identify and evaluate events associated with planning and implementing an undergraduate colloquium series.

Guidelines. In the planning stage, we discussed and identified several issues influencing the implementation of the series. The first task consisted of specifying objectives for the series. The following objectives reflected the needs and values of our circumstances: (a) to illustrate the variety of activities engaged in by psychologists; (b) to provide a public forum for psychology faculty and students to present their scholarly work; (c) to stimulate additional scholarly activity among faculty and students.

We agreed that one of the greatest dangers associated with our enthusiasm for the series was an unrealistic expectation about faculty and student interest. Stated more positively, we sought to schedule enough speakers to stimulate but not satiate the anticipated audience. Thus, we scheduled three speakers during the fall and three speakers during the spring semesters.

Because of the limited size of our department and of the diversity of the discipline, speakers were sought from within the department and from the community at large. Student presentations were not scheduled until the second year of the series. That delay was designed to allow students time to develop research projects with faculty.

Anticipated by-products of the series included students' cognitive development and improved faculty-student interpersonal relations. We decided that an informal social gathering following each presentation would facilitate faculty-student interaction. We distinguished the cognitive and social aspects of the series by serving refreshments in the departmental office. Members of the psychology club assumed responsibility for setting up facilities and hosting the social gathering.

Alternatives for publicizing the series received special attention. Initial plans recommended use of mimeographed handouts. Subsequently, we decided to have brochures prepared professionally. The objective was to communicate an air of importance and respectability to the series.

Scheduling the series presented some problems. We selected a time which was convenient to all faculty members. However, no one time was convenient to all psychology majors. Videotape recordings of each presentation provided interested students an opportunity for viewing at a later date.

Implementation. Once the guidelines were established, the task consisted of locating speakers. Obtaining faculty participation posed no difficulties. Moreover, we were pleasantly surprised by the reaction of psychologists in the community. They readily donated time and were highly cooperative in orienting their presentations to the sophistication level of undergraduate students. Although we were not usually acquainted with persons outside the university, serendipity and a willingness to contact strangers resulted in two years of a series with which we were very satisfied. Topics in the first year covered career development, the role of the paraprofessional, animal research on learned helplessness, industrial-organizational psychology, history of a psychology department, and the training of a psychologist outside of a traditional psychology department. In the second year, topics were school psychology, counseling psychology, social work, human services, and pediatric psychology. Students' presentations included the impact of the wording of test questions on performance, a model for career decision making, and a study of the content of adolescent diaries.

Preparation of the brochure in the first year produced the greatest obstacle. We experienced repeated delays from the personnel responsible for designing the layout for the brochure. Consequently the finished product was received only after the first presentation. The long term consequences of the delay were insignificant, and the quality of the brochure more than offset the short term disappointment.

Evaluation. Several alternatives for evaluating the series were discussed. We finally decided that an evaluation form should be administered following each presentation and that the form should include both rating and open-ended items. The rating scale consisted of 5 steps which varied from "poor" (1) to "excellent" (5) with intermediate steps of "fair," "good," and "very good."

A total of 232 students attended 12 presentations during the two year period. About 90% of the students were psychology majors. The remainder represented a variety of disciplines. Overall, 78% of the students completed an evaluation form. One third to one half of those attending the presentations also attended the social gatherings afterward. Attendance by the psychology faculty was consistent at about 85%.

Item 1 of the evaluation form asked about the series' effectiveness in stimulating career exploration. The median response for all presentations was "good." Item 2 questioned the presentation's effectiveness for stimulating additional investigation into that area. The item provided a gauge of the series' effectiveness in stimulating research in a broader sense. The median response was "good." Item 3 asked about the value of the presentation for acquiring new information. The item was designed to assess the effectiveness of the series for cognitive development. The median response for all presentations was "very good." Finally, item 4 assessed students' reaction to the format of the presentation. The median response was "very good."

A modified version of the evaluation form was used for the students' presentations. Item 1 inquired about the effectiveness of the presentations for illustrating the variety of research engaged in by students. The median response was "very good." A median response of "very good" was also given to an item about the series providing a forum for student research. Item 3 questioned the effectiveness of the presentations for stimulating students to engage in research. The median response was "very good." The last item asked about the acquisition of new information, and the median response was "good."

Responses to the open ended questions and unobtrusive observations provided additional information. The most frequently expressed criticisms on the open-ended questions involved the use of a classroom for the series. Students reported that they felt the classroom inhibited give-and-take discussion. One of the most frequent positive comments was related to the acquisition of new information. Many of those comments related the new information to career planning. An unobtrusive observation noted the difference in students' behavior at the presentations versus the social period following the program. Most of the students who attended the social gathering engaged in extended conversation with the speaker and faculty members. Portions of conversations which were overheard included requests for additional information or clarification about some topic covered during the formal presentation.

A comparison of students' responses to speakers from outside versus within the university revealed a more favorable evaluation for the former. The magnitude of the difference was slight, about one half of a scalar unit, but consistent for the items about career exploration, investigation, and information. There was no difference between types of speaker for item 4 on the effectiveness of the format.

Discussion. The results of the formal student evaluation provided support for the effectiveness of the series in increasing student awareness regarding career alternatives. Moreover, the observation of student interaction with speakers during the social segment of the series revealed genuine interest in the career aspects of the presentation. Anecdotal evidence highlighted those findings. One student noted the contribution of the series to his decision to switch from pre-medicine to psychology. Another student reported a change to psychology as a major after observing faculty-student interaction in the series. Thus, the series seemed to contribute either directly or indirectly to increased student awareness about career-related alternatives. However, the effectiveness of the series must also be viewed in the context of other factors including a student advising program, a course in career development, and periodic meetings on career development issues.

Favorable student responses to the effectiveness of presentations for stimulating research support a conclusion

that the series contributed to a scholarly atmosphere in the department. Moreover the series provided an immediate public forum for students to present their scholarly work and an opportunity for them to serve as models for their peers. Informal comments from students indicated interest in participating in the series next year. One student made plans to work with a faculty member in the fall to be ready for the student presentations in the spring. Anecdotal evidence also revealed that the series contributed to the efforts of three undergraduates who authored or co-authored papers at a regional psychology convention. A steady growth in research activity is directly related to the series. Although other contributing factors exist, the series maintains a pivotal position.

Student responses to the item about the acquisition of new information were consistent with anticipated outcomes. The series is viewed as serving a complementary role to the standard curriculum. Assessing social interactions was more difficult. Although student attendance at the social gatherings was less than hoped for, the quality of the interactions was amicable. Faculty-student and student-student relationships emerged which would not have developed in the absence of the series.

Several explanations exist to explain the more favorable reactions toward the speakers from outside the university. Included among them are such variables as novelty, competence, and status. Whatever the sources of influence, we intend to continue taking advantage of the impact. Departmental speakers contributed substantially to the series. But, all agree that outside speakers provided a vitality, making them a valuable component of the series.

Students' responses to the format supported the authors' view that planning decisions contributed to an effective program. After two years' experience, we think the decision to limit the number of speakers to a total of six for the academic year was a good one. The rationale was derived from a theatrical tradition. Namely, it is better to leave the audience wanting more than to provide them with too much. As yet, we have no solution to the limitations posed by holding the series in a classroom setting. For those undertaking a colloquium series, we recommend moderate optimism about student attendance at the presentations and social gatherings. In retrospect, we realize that no single activity sponsored by the department can hope to attract as many students as originally expected. Consequently, we have concentrated on maximizing the gain for students who do attend the series. The third year of the program will include a psychologist with national prominence to celebrate the centennial year of psychology's founding. It will also include an academic psychologist from another university within the state to initiate an interinstitutional exchange of scholars.

In sum, we think the investigation demonstrated the series' effectiveness in realizing its objectives. Moreover, we are discovering that the series is expanding beyond our original expectations.

References

Caffrey, B., Berger, L., Spurgeon, C., Marx, D., & Senn, D. Integrating professional programs in a traditional undergraduate psychology program. *Teaching of Psychology,* 1977, *4,* 7-13.

Forsyth, G. A. A task-first individual differences approach to designing a statistics and methodology course. *Teaching of Psychology,* 1977, *4,* 76-78.

Holland, J. L. A theory of vocational choice. *Journal of Counseling Psychology,* 1959, *6,* 35-45.

Korn, J. H., & Nodine, B. F. Facts and questions concerning career training of the psychology major. *Teaching of Psychology,* 1975, *2,* 117-119.

Super, D. E. A theory of vocational development. *American Psychologist,* 1953, *8,* 185-190.

Turner, R. H. What happens to the liberal arts BA in psychology who doesn't go to graduate school? *Teaching Psychology Newsletter,* 1974, (Feb.), 3-4.

Ware, M. E., & Beischel, M. L. Career development: Evaluating a new frontier for teaching and research. *Teaching of Psychology.* 1979, *6,* 210-213.

Ware, M. E., Gardner, L. E., & Murphy, D. P. Team teaching introductory psychology as pedagogy and for faculty development. *Teaching of Psychology,* 1978, *5,* 127-130.

Yoder, J. Teaching students to do research. *Teaching of Psychology,* 1979, *6,* 85-88.

Notes

1. Mink, W. Majors and Careers for BA Degree Holders. In G. R. Francois (Chair), *Some Problems and Proposed Solutions of Psychology Departments in Private Liberal Arts Colleges.* Symposium presented at the meeting of the Midwestern Psychological Association, Chicago, 1976.

2. Morris, C. J. Psychology Departments in Private Liberal Arts Schools: Some Problems and Proposed Solutions. In G. R. Francois (Chair), *Some Problems and Proposed Solutions of Psychology Departments in Private Liberal Arts Colleges.* Symposium presented at the meeting of the Midwestern Psychological Association, Chicago, 1976.

2.   IDENTIFYING OCCUPATIONAL OPPORTUNITIES FOR PSYCHOLOGY MAJORS

We have heard a frequent refrain from students, their parents, and even our colleagues from around the country : "You can't get a job with a psychology major!" The following articles are representative of a larger body of literature that rejects such claims. The evidence indicates that psychology attracts students with diverse interests and backgrounds. The evidence also reveals that those students find employment in a wide variety of occupations and that they pursue education in many professions and disciplines.

Mark Ware and Ann Meyer investigated the occupational and educational pursuits of Creighton University's psychology graduates. They adopted John Holland's theoretical model. The results contradicted the conventional wisdom that asserts that students with psychology majors can't get a job and that those who do are primarily in human services settings. All respondents reported being employed or in graduate or professional school. The majority of those employed were in Holland's enterprising and social categories. A striking gender difference was that the majority of males selected enterprising occupations and the majority of females chose social occupations. Among those surveyed, 59% pursued post graduate education. Readers will find the graduates' evaluation of the psychology program quite instructive in providing information about curricular evaluation and for advising students about elective courses.

The post graduate occupational and educational pursuits of psychology graduates from Western Illinois University constituted the focus of the study that Paula Wise, Gene Smith, and Frank Fulkerson reported. The types of occupations that students pursued most frequently were similar to the previous study, however the gender differences were not as pronounced. They also examined students' reactions to eight features of their undergraduate education and their likelihood of majoring in psychology if they had it to do over again. Ratings of the program were generally favorable, but about one-third of the students indicated that they would not major in psychology if they had it to do over again. The findings of this and the previous study provide a candid picture of how psychology majors view their educational experience.

Finally, Carol Erdwins and James Olivetti provided a bibliography of articles published in the 1970's that described human-service employment settings for students completing an undergraduate major in psychology.

Career Versatility of the Psychology Major: A Survey of Graduates

Mark E. Ware and
Ann E. Meyer
Creighton University

Analysis of graduates by training level, sex, and Holland's occupational types shows a wide choice of jobs after graduation.

Among the prevailing views expressed about students who major in psychology is that their employment opportunities are limited or non existent without graduate level training. In addition, many assume that students who major in psychology are likely to pursue occupations in the area of human services. Although one would not be surprised at the expression of those views by individuals outside of psychology, it is disheartening to discover that psychology majors themselves are uninformed or misinformed about the occupational merit of their training (Quereshi, Brennan, Kuchan, & Sackett, 1974).

In recent years, several investigators have recognized and addressed the occupational needs of undergraduate psychology majors. Some have described programs with professional training components and/or fieldwork for psychology majors who were not going to graduate school (Caffrey, Berger, Cole, Marx, & Senn, 1977; Korn & Nodine, 1975; Lunneborg, 1974). McGovern (1979) described a program and Ware and Beischel (1979) described and evaluated a course on career development for psychology majors regardless of their post graduate plans. These latter two programs include components on the career opportunities for psychology majors.

Reports exist on the post graduate career activities of psychology majors (Cates, 1973; Davis, 1979; Lunneborg, 1974; Titley, 1978). Only Lunneborg (1974) presented results in a career development framework, specifically that by Roe (1956). Holland provides a more contemporary theory of careers (1973) and assessment and classification booklets (Holland, 1974) that promote systematic career exploration by students.

The primary purpose of the present study was to investigate the post graduate career activity of psychology majors within the framework of Holland's theory. Furthermore, it sought to address the views that little opportunity exists for psychology majors who do not go to graduate school, and that human service occupations are the most likely choice of psychology majors whether or not they go to graduate school. Secondary purposes included the identification of graduates' reactions to the undergraduate program.

Method.   A total of 339 students acquired bachelor's degrees with a major in psychology from Creighton Unversity between May 1973 and August 1978. Preparation of a mailing list used the Creighton University Alumni Directory 1979 (1978). Reasons for eliminating graduates included the failure of the directory to list them and the return of envelopes that were undeliverable. Thus, the sample that was surveyed consisted of 275 graduates.

Mailing of a 12 item questionnaire commenced on October 15, 1979. A cover letter described the purposes of the survey and indicated that the results were confidential. One month later a follow up letter was sent. The letter thanked those who returned the questionnaire and asked the others to complete and return theirs as soon as possible. The graduates returned a total of 152 questionnaires (55%) within two months after the first mailing (105 males and 47 females). Returns by the sexes were consistent with the sample that was surveyed. Moreover, the percentage of questionnaires that graduates of each year returned was approximately equal. Thus, there was no evidence of selective levels of return for the sexes or by graduates of different years.

The questionnaire provided data on several dimensions: additional education (type and amount), employment status (type and number, as well as full or part time), income (starting and current), courses you wish you had taken, and satisfaction with major. The last two items used a seven step Likert-type scale, which varied from very unsatisfied (1) to very satisfied (7).

The authors divided the returns into groups that varied in the amount of additional education. Group 1 included graduates who had taken no graduate level coursework or who were not working for an advanced degree. Group 2 included graduates who had acquired a masters degree or who were actively pursuing that degree. Group 3 included graduates who had acquired a doctoral level degree or who were working for that degree. The authors independently subdivided the current occupations of graduates in Groups 1 and 2 into one of Holland's six occupational types: realistic,

investigative, artistic, social, enterprising, and conventional (Holland, 1973). The subdivision of graduates in Group 3 was on the basis of the field of doctoral training each was pursuing. The authors agreed in their assignment of graduates to occupational types in more than 95% of the cases.

Results.   Table 1 contains the percent and number of male and female graduates who comprised Groups 1, 2, and 3. Inspection reveals that, in general, more than half of the

Table 1. Percent of Graduates in the Educational Groups

| Sex | Groups | | | |
	1. AB	2. MA	3. PhD	Total
Males	36 (38)	20 (21)	44 (46)	69 (105)
Females	51 (24)	32 (15)	17 (8)	31 (47)
Total	41 (62)	24 (36)	36 (54)	100 (152)

Values in parentheses are the actual number of graduates.

graduates sought additional formal education. Moreover, a chi-square test revealed that a significant difference existed in the number of males and females making up the three groups ($\chi^2(2) = 10.21, p < .01$). Inspection reveals that males constituted a disproportionate percentage of doctoral level students and that females constituted a disproportionate percentage of those who did not pursue additional formal education.

Table 2 contains the percent and number of male and female graduates making up the occupational types for Groups 1, 2, and 3. A chi-square test revealed significant

Table 2. Percent of Graduates by Educational Group and Occupational Type

Group	Occupational type	Males	Females
1. Bachelors	Social	13 (5)	58 (14)
	Enterprising	55 (21)	17 (4)
	Other	32 (12)	25 (6)
2. Masters	Social	62 (13)	73 (11)
	Other	38 (8)	27 (4)
3. Doctors	Investigative	67 (31)	38 (3)
	Other	33 (15)	63 (5)

Values in parentheses are the actual number of graduates

differences in the number of Group 1 male and female graduates in the Holland occupational types ($\chi^2(2) = 15.36, p < .01$). Inspection reveals that the majority of males and females selected occupations described as enterprising and as social, respectively. A partial list of occupations reported by graduates in group 1 is shown below.

Males (Social type): counselor, program manager, parent training research coordinator, surgical orderly, admissions counselor, quality assurance, bartender, fast foods manager, recreation aide.

Males (Enterprising type): sales, personnel department, store manager, small business owner, loan officer, marketing representative, legal technician (FBI), warehouse manager, transportation director, congressional aide.

Males (Other types): landscaping foreman (R), receiving clerk (R), waiter (R), filling station attendant (R), computer programmer (I), phlebotomist (I), filmmaker (A), interior decorator (A), budget director (C), accountant (C).

Females (Social type): case evaluator/social worker, residential youth counselor, recreation assistant, probation officer, rehabilitation advisor, resident advisor, executive director (YMCA), occupational therapist, quality inspector (Hallmark), nurse.

Females (Enterprising type): store manager, manager, insurance underwriting supervisor, sales service coordinator.

Females (Other types): paint line foreman (R), laboratory assistant (I), public relations (A), secretary.
(Letters in parentheses for other types indicate the Holland type)

Inspection of Table 2 also reveals the percent and number of Group 2 male and female graduates in the Holland occupational types. The authors collapsed the occupational types to two to produce large enough expected values for analysis. A chi-square test revealed no significant differences in the number of males and females in the occupational types ($\chi^2(1) = .13, p > .05$).

Finally, Table 2 contains the percent and number of Group 3 male and female graduates in the Holland occupational types. The authors collapsed the occupation types to two to produce large enough expected values for analysis. A chi-square test revealed no significant differences in the number of males and females in the occupational types ($\chi^2(1) = 1.52, p > .05$) An examination of the number of graduates pursuing different types of doctoral training revealed that dentistry was most common with 41%, followed by medicine and law with 19% each. Among those pursuing doctoral training, 13% selected psychology and 8% selected other programs.

Table 3 contains the median starting and current annual salary for Group 1 and 2 male and female graduates.

Table 3. Median Salaries for Graduates

Group	Salary	Males	Females
1. Bachelors	starting	$11,000	$9,000
	current	>14,000	13,000
2. Masters	starting	11,000	13,000
	current	>14,000	13,000

Inspection reveals that the median salary for males exceeded that of females in three out of four comparisons. However, the results of median tests revealed no significant differences in the salary for the sexes.

Table 4 contains the number and percent of courses that graduates identified as those they wished they had taken.

Table 4. Percent of Courses Identified as
Those That Graduates, Subdivided by
Educational Groups, Wished They Had Taken

Courses	Groups		
	1. AB	2. MA	3. PhD
Psychology	54 (35)	80 (40)	70 (39)
Business	32 (21)	10 (5)	11 (39)
Science	6 (4)	6 (3)	18 (10)
Other	8 (5)	4 (2)	2 (1)
Total	100 (65)	100 (50)	101 (56)

Values in parentheses are the actual number of graduates.

Psychology courses made up the majority of courses reported by graduates. In general, no pattern of courses emerged except for Business courses among Group 1 graduates. Graduates reported the following courses in order of frequency: Business (in general), Management, and Accounting.

A 2 x 2 analysis of variance of graduates' responses to the question about satisfaction with major revealed a significant difference in satisfaction for the three groups ($F(2,146) = 5.50, p < .01$). The mean satisfaction scores were 4.77, 5.55. and 5.43 for Groups 1, 2, and 3 respectively. Protected t-tests (Welkowitz, Ewen, & Cohen, 1976) revealed that Groups 2 and 3 were significantly different from Group 1 but were not significantly different from each other. There was no significant difference in satisfaction between the sexes or for the Groups x Sex interaction.

Discussion. Results of the present study are consistent with findings that somewhat greater than half of psychology majors plan to and pursue additional education after receiving the undergraduate degree (Cates, 1973; Davis, 1979). By themselves, the results do not indicate whether students who select psychology are more inclined to pursue additional education or if there are experiences associated with majoring in psychology that encourage students to remain in school. Some combination of the two may provide a more complete explanation.

The significantly greater number of males pursuing post graduate education is not consistent with one study (Davis, 1979) that reported only slightly fewer males obtaining advanced degrees. If the findings of the present study are generalizable, then one must be discouraged at the effectiveness of efforts to provide encouragement and opportunities for females to pursue professional development. The results suggest that social forces of a more widespread character are at work that discourage females from developing career expectations like those of males.

The previously mentioned sex difference expresses itself differently in the types of occupations that Group 1 males and females pursued. The tendency for males with a bachelor's degree to select enterprising occupations is consistent with findings reported by Titley (1978). Moreover, the trend for females to pursue social occupations is consistent with Lunneborg's report (1978) about females' enthusiastic endorsement of social activities. Sex role-related behaviors manifest themselves in occupations that these bachelor's level graduates selected.

The considerable variety of occupations that bachelor-level psychology majors select is not a finding unique to this study. Lunneborg (1974) listed several occupational titles that were directly related to the psychology major. Moreover, Davis (1979) and Titley (1978) reported lists that had considerable occupational diversity. Thus, the evidence challenges those who contend that a student with a psychology major cannot find employment.

The failure to find a significant difference in the number of doctoral level males and females associated with the investigative type may be an encouraging sign. If the results reflect a nonsexist basis in selecting an occupation, then females may be assuming an autonomous stance in career development. However, the optimism is mixed with a healthy skepticism. Among graduates pursuing doctoral training, males constituted 85% and females 14% versus a 2:1 ratio in the total sample. Thus, although doctoral level females may achieve independence in career selection, they are not representative of females in general.

The variety of doctoral level programs that the psychology graduates in this study pursued is consistent with results of previous investigations (Cates, 1973; Quereshi, 1977). Although the percentage of graduates pursuing one versus another program differs from study to study, the range of programs is similar. Psychology graduates broadly distribute themselves across the professional ranks.

The overall finding of educational and/or occupational variability associated with Groups 1, 2, and 3 should help lay to rest the views identified in the introduction of this paper. The evidence does not support the views that bachelor-level psychology graduates cannot find a job and that the available occupations for psychology graduates are in only the human service areas. However, the results are consistent with Lunneborg's perspective (1979) about the career versatility and adaptability of the major in psychology.

The results of this study demonstrate the use of Holland's model for assessing the post graduate alternatives for psychology majors. The authors recognize the limitations of the sampling in the present study and encourage other investigators to explore this issue using the same or a different career development model.

The lack of a significant difference in the salary levels of males and females is similar to trends reported by Cates (1973). However, these discrepancies will be a source of irritation to all who argue for equal pay for equal work. The discrepancy at the bachelor's level can be understood in part by examining the types of occupations that the graduates chose. The service-type work associated with social occupations does not pay as well as the enterprising occupations regardless of sex. To those for whom the size of the salary is a highly valued component of employment, we recommend that they critically examine income generated by the social type of occupations.

In response to the question about courses that they wished they had taken, Group 1 graduates expressed the greatest need for coursework in the area of business. These findings echo the recommendations of Davis (1979) and Lunneborg (1974). Advising students in the judicious selection of electives can be one of the most beneficial services that faculty members provide. Additionally, Korn & Nodine (1975) recommended the inclusion of off campus experiences for the psychology major. The combination of a psychology major, appropriate electives, and real-life experience can make the graduate a more attractive job applicant.

The significantly lesser degree of satisfaction with the major by Group 1 graduates can be understood by referring to a finding by Quereshi (1977). He reported that graduates exhibited a greater concern about occupational matters than they did when they were students. The occupational concern can be severe when competing for employment without occupational knowledge and career skills. The latter findings may also reflect a weakness of many undergraduate psychology programs. Specifically, how do faculty prepare their students for the actual work world? Alternative answers are emerging and include programs (McGovern, 1979) and courses (Ware & Beischel, 1979) in career development. These alternatives do not require substantial curricular revision nor do they employ a trade school attitude. Career development does not train students for an occupation, but rather it teaches a process of assessing one's self, exploring occupational alternatives, and developing career implementation skills. A program in career development does not sacrifice the traditional program of undergraduate psychology, but it can provide students with advantages that many academic psychologists have neglected.

References

Caffrey, B., Berger, L., Cole, S., Marx, D., & Senn, D. Integrating professional programs in a traditional undergraduate psychology program. *Teaching of Psychology*, 1977, *4*, 7-13.

Cates, J. Baccalaureates in psychology: 1969 and 1970. *American Psychologist*, 1973, *28*, 262-264.

Creighton University Alumni Directory 1979. White Plains, NY: Bernard C. Harris Publishing Co., 1978.

Davis, J. Where did they all go? A job survey of BA graduates. In P. Woods (Ed.), *The psychology major: Training and employment strategies*. Washington: American Psychological Association, 1979.

Holland, J. *Making vocational choices: A theory of careers*. Englewood Cliffs, NJ: Prentice-Hall, 1973.

Holland, J. *The self directed search*. Palo Alto, CA: Consulting Psychologists Press, 1974.

Korn, J., & Nodine, B. Facts and questions concerning career training of the psychology major. *Teaching of Psychology*, 1975, *2*, 117-119.

Lunneborg, P. Can college graduates in psychology find employment in their field? *Vocational Guidance Quarterly*, 1974, *23*, 159-166.

Lunneborg, P. Service vs. technical interest—biggest sex difference of all? *Vocational Guidance Quarterly*, 1979, *28*, 146-153.

Lunneborg, P. *Why study psychology?* Monterey, CA: Brooks/Cole, 1978.

McGovern, T. The development of a career planning program for undergraduate psychology majors. *Teaching of Psychology*, 1979, *6*, 183-184.

Quereshi, M. Evaluation of an undergraduate psychology curriculum. *The Journal of Experimental Education*, 1977, *45*, 42-50.

Quereshi, M., Brennan, P., Kuchan, A., & Sackett, P. Some characteristics of undergraduate majors in psychology. *The Journal of Experimental Education*, 1974, *42*, 65-70.

Roe, A. *The psychology of occupations*. New York: Wiley, 1956.

Titley, R. Whatever happened to the class of '67? *American Psychologist*, 1978, *33*, 1094-1098.

Ware, M., & Beischel, M. Career development: Evaluating a new frontier for teaching and research. *Teaching of Psychology*, 1979, *6*, 210-213.

Welkowitz, J., Ewen, R., & Cohen, J. *Introductory statistics for the behavioral sciences* (2nd Ed.). New York: Academic Press, 1976.

Occupations of Psychology Majors Receiving Undergraduate Degrees from Western Illinois University

Paula Sachs Wise, Gene F. Smith,
and Frank E. Fulkerson
Western Illinois University

This paper reports the findings of a questionnaire survey sent to all bachelor graduates with a major in psychology prior to fall semester, 1979 and who had an address registered in the Alumni Office. The department was established in 1960 and the first psychology majors were graduated in 1964. Therefore the surveys reflect 15 years of alumni.

One hundred and eighty-three of the 600 mailed surveys were completed and returned yielding a return rate of about 30.5%. Although the return rate is fairly low, there is at least a partial explanation. Many of the surveys mailed out were returned as undeliverable. Unfortunately, no tabulation of these "dead letters" was maintained. However, if only the alumni actually receiving the survey had been considered, the response rate would be much higher, perhaps even approaching 50%.

The survey was designed to obtain several types of information. Alumni were asked to complete a section of general information—name, year and quarter of graduation, current address, and sex. They were also asked about additional education and employment history since graduation, which courses or aspects of training had proved the most valuable since graduation, what improvements they would suggest for the undergraduate curriculum, when and why they decided to major in psychology, and "If you were starting at WIU in 1980 would you still want to major in Psychology/Why or Why not?" In addition, alumni were asked to rate certain aspects of their training in psychology at WIU (e.g. quality of faculty, variety and difficulty of coursework, and academic advising).

Results. Answers from completed surveys were tabulated and analyzed. Table 1 depicts the current occupations of

Table 1. Current Occupations of Psychology Majors Graduating from SIU (in percent)

Occupational Group	Male (n = 113)	Female (n = 70)	Total (n = 183)
Social Services	31.0	30.0	30.6
Education	15.1	24.3	18.6
Management	14.2	15.7	14.8
Sales	14.2	2.9	9.8
Graduate School	10.6	11.4	10.9
Professional Trades	10.6	2.9	7.7
Clerical	0.9	11.4	4.9
Miscellaneous	3.5	0.0	2.2
Unemployed	0.0	1.4	.5

those alumni responding to the survey. More than half of the female respondents (54.3%) were employed in social service and education occupations. Thirty-one percent of the males were employed in social service occupations, and approximately equal numbers (14-15%) were employed in education, management and sales-related occupations.

The general categories in Table 1 were determined after examining the data and looking through some of the studies previously reported. The "social services" category includes, but is not limited to, respondents working as counselors, therapists, social workers, psychometrists, and pastors; "education" includes teachers, professors, school psychologists; "management" includes nearly all business-related personnel not considered to be in sales or clerical positions; "sales" includes stockbrokers and insurance agents as well as those directly involved in selling; "professional trades" include mail carriers, police officers, construction workers, and so on; and, "miscellaneous" includes those whose occupations "defied" classification as well as those individuals labeling themselves "self-employed."

The question of whether the alumni were working in jobs related to their studies in psychology requires a more subjective judgment than does a listing of occupations. It might be said that only working as a psychologist relates to the study of psychology. On the other hand it might be argued that there are few if any occupations unrelated to psychology. Looking at the list of occupations in Table 1, it would appear that the first five categories—social services, education, management, sales, and graduate school—would seem to relate at least indirectly to some aspects of undergraduate training in psychology. Without more elaborate data about the particular occupations, a more specific answer cannot be given to the question.

The question of how many former students completed graduate degree work was easily answered. Of the 183 total respondents, 62 had received Master's degrees (a category which included MA, MS, MSW and MBA degrees). Five of the alumni had received PhD degrees, and two received JD degrees. With 20 former students still in graduate school, the total number of advanced degree aspirants, candidates, or recipients is 89 out of 183 or near 50 percent. In addition, 40 alumni reported at least some graduate coursework.

Alumni were also asked to rate eight separate aspects of their education in the Psychology Department at WIU. These eight aspects were quality of professors, difficulty of coursework, academic advising, preparation for graduate school, helpfulness of faculty toward students, opportunities for students to engage in research, and quality of textbooks. At least 50% of the respondents rated each of the items as excellent, very good, or average. Ratings were highest for quality of professors (73.4% of respondents assigned ratings of excellent or very good); quality of textbooks (60.4% assigned ratings of excellent or very good); and helpfulness of faculty toward students (59.4% assigned ratings of excellent or very good).

Finally, students were asked, "If you were starting at WIU in 1980 would you still want to major in psychology?" Students' responses were as follows: 42.4% answered with an unqualified yes; 8.2% gave a qualified yes; 10.4% were undecided; 7.1% gave a qualified no; 30.6% gave an unqualified no. The reason given most frequently for why they would not want to major in psychology revolved around lack of appropriate employment opportunities and/or low salaries in related jobs.

Discussion.   One of the concerns most often raised, especially by parents of undergraduate psychology majors, is "Can you find a job with a bachelor's degree in psychology?" It should prove comforting to the parents of present psychology majors, to the majors themselves, and to faculty in departments of psychology that of the 183 respondents only one was unemployed. A second question or concern which is frequently heard is, "What type of job can you obtain with a bachelor's degree in psychology?" This question is more difficult to answer because the range of jobs reported by respondents is so broad.

Although the present study represented the most thorough and systematic survey of alumni for the Psychology Department at WIU, there were a few questionnaire-related difficulties which became apparent during the data analysis phase of the study. The condensation of 183 current occupations into a few meaningful occupational categories was one such difficulty. It was obvious that "professor" or "school psychologist" should be considered education-related careers, that "secretary" was "clerical," and that "salesman" came under the rubric of "sales." What about the person who wrote "librarian" or "counselor" without specifying the locale? Is a nursing home administrator employed in a social service or a management setting? These and similar questions were resolved on a case-by-case basis by the authors but the decisions were admittedly somewhat arbitrary.

The possibility of sample bias is also a concern in a survey such as this one. Can the results of the present survey be generalized to all of the alumni of WIU's Psychology Department? Do the respondents reflect the total alumni group, or are the alumni who respond more likely to be those who feel as though they have succeeded?

The authors do believe that the present study is valuable in providing information about the employment and educational histories of psychology alumni. Responses to this survey as well as to a previous survey have aided us in advising current and potential psychology majors and have indirectly led to two new course offerings. One course, Field Experiences, was developed in response to respondents' perceived desire for more first hand experience in mental health-related settings. A second course, Training and Employment Strategies in Psychology, was developed to make psychology majors aware of existing job opportunities and their educational prerequisites. Finally, the information that 182 of 183 former psychology majors sought and obtained gainful employment is a noteworthy finding in and of itself.

Psychology Related Employment Settings for Graduates of Submaster's Programs in Psychology: A Bibliography

Carol Erdwins and L. James Olivetti
George Mason University

Over the past several decades an ever increasing number of undergraduates have elected psychology as their major field of study. For the 1973-74 academic year alone over 52,000 baccalaureates in psychology were awarded, and it is predicted that this number will increase substantially during the next few years (NCES, 1976; Cates, 1973). What happens to all of these students after graduation? According to most recent studies approximately fifty per cent choose to begin graduate work either in psychology or a related field such as medicine, social work, or education (Cates, 1973; Daniel, 1974). Unfortunately until very recently very little notice has been taken of the other fifty per cent (Fields, 1976). Perhaps it was just assumed that they went out into the world and lived happily ever after. In fact there may have been some basis for this feeling since the job market of the sixties seemed able to absorb all of our college educated. This picture has changed rather dramatically within the last several years, however; and it now appears that many liberal arts students including psychology majors are having difficulty finding employment after graduation.

Students are showing increased concern with their employment opportunities, and those of us engaged in teaching psychology may find ourselves devoting more time to giving advice and counsel on the realities of the current job market. Some of us may also be contemplating changes in our undergraduate programs or the initiation of special course sequences which might increase the employability of our graduates. In fact, descriptions of several innovative undergraduate programs have already appeared in the literature (Korn, 1974; Pinkus and Korn, 1973; McPheeters, 1972), and the Vail conference also made several recommendations with regard to these submaster's training programs (Korman, 1976).

Before launching full-scale into either student advising or program alteration it might be helpful to get as full a picture as possible of the positions in which psychology majors are already employed, particularly those human-service or psychology-related positions that most students view as highly desirable. Many probably chose psychology as a major in order to obtain such jobs in the first place. The following bibliography lists recent articles that have described human-service settings or positions in which persons having only undergraduate course work in psychology have been employed. The reader will see that the possibilities, although not large, are certainly varied, ranging from abortion counselors to psychometric technicians.

References

Cates, J. Baccalaureates in psychology: 1969 and 1970. *American Psychologist*, 1973, *28*, 262-264.

Daniel, R. S. Surveys of psychology baccalaureate graduates. *Teaching Psychology Newsletter*, February 1974, 8-10.

Earned degrees conferred (U.S. National Center for Educational Statistics 76-106). Washington, D.C.: U.S. Government Printing Office, 1976.

Fields, C. M. 5-10 pct. of students major in psychology, but after graduation, what do they do? *Chronicle of Higher Education*, 1976, 8, 9.

Korman, Recommendations of the conference. In *Levels and patterns of professional training in psychology; Conference proceedings, Vail, Colorado, 1973*. Washington, DC: American Psychological Association, 1976.

Korn, J. H. Training and employment of BA psychologists: Report of a symposium. *Teaching Psychology Newsletter*, 1974, 10-12.

McPheeters, H. L. The middle-level mental health worker, II. His training. *Hospital and Community Psychiatry*, 1972, *23*, 334-335.

Pinkus, R. B., & Korn, J. H. The preprofessional option: An alternative to graduate work in psychology. *American Psychologist*, 1973, *28*, 710-718.

Bibliography

Aiken, J., Brownell, A., & Iscoe, I. The training and utilization of paraprofessionals in a college psychological service center. *Journal of College Student Personnel*, 1974, *15*, 480-486.

Baker, E. The mental health associate: One year later. *Community Mental Health Journal*, 1973, 9, 203-214.

Bartels, B. D., & Tyler, J. D. Paraprofessionals in the community mental health center. *Professional Psychology*, 1974, *5*, 442-452.

Bleeker, D. A survey of occupational opportunities for BA psychology majors. *Psi Chi Newsletter*, 1972, *2*(1), 6-7.

Bouhoutsos, J. The nontraditionally trained mental health worker: Fad or future. *Professional Psychology*, 1970, *1*, 455-459.

Brinson, L. C., & Alston, P. P. Graduate and undergraduate training: A comparison of the impact on counselor performance and job satisfaction. *Journal of Applied Rehabilitation Counseling*, 1973, *4*, 110-117.

Brown, W. F. Effectiveness of paraprofessionals: The evidence. *Personnel and Guidance Journal*, 1974, *53*, 257-263.

Calder, B., Tyrrell, M., & Franklyn, G. The case for counsellor technicians and counsellor assistants. *Canadian Counsellor*, 1973, *7*, 133-138.

Daniel, R. S. Surveys of psychology baccalaureate graduates. *Teaching Psychology Newsletter*, February 1974, 8-10.

Dauber, B. Profile of an abortion counselor. *Family Planning Perspectives*, 1974, *6*, 185-187.

Felton, G. S., Wallach, H. F., & Gallo, C. L. New roles for new-professional mental health workers: Training the patient advocate, the integrator, and the therapist. *Community Mental Health Journal*, 1974, *10*, 52-65.

Fretz, B. R. Finding careers with a bachelor's degree in psychology. *Psi Chi Newsletter*, 1976, *2*(2), 5-13.

Gentry, W. D. Symposium: The emerging profession of psychological technician. *Professional Psychology*, 1974, *5*, 206-226.

McPheeters, H. L., King, J. B., & Teare, R. J. The middle level mental health worker, his role. *Hospital and Community Psychiatry*, 1972, *23*, 329-334.

Nadolsky, J. M. Guidelines for the classification and utilization of vocational evaluation personnel. *Rehabilitation Literature*, 1974, *35*, 162-173.

Rosenbloom, A., & Randall, T. The role of the low vision assistant in the care of visually impaired persons. *New Outlook for the Blind*, 1975, *69*, 20-24.

Rudow, E. H. Paraprofessionals in a drug education program. *Personnel and Guidance Journal*, 1974, *53*, 294-297.

Talbott, J. A., & Ross, A. M. The paraprofessional teaches the professional. *American Journal of Psychiatry*, 1973, *130*, 805-808.

True, J. E. Education and work performance of associate degree mental health workers as related to group therapy. *International Journal of Group Psychotherapy*, 1974, *24*, 383-392.

Turner, R. H. What happens to the liberal arts BA in psychology who doesn't go to graduate school? *Teaching Psychology Newsletter*, February 1974, 3-4.

Vidaver, R. A new framework for baccalaureate careers in the human services. *American Journal of Psychiatry*, 1973, *130*, 474-478.

3. DEVELOPING OCCUPATIONALLY RELATED SKILLS

The authors of this collection of articles share the common perspective of recognizing the value to students of identifying and fostering the acquisition of skills. However, the authors approach that theme in somewhat different ways.

Thomas McGovern and Susan Ellett asked the psychology faculty at Virginia Commonwealth University to identify the skills that students could acquire from psychology courses. Readers may want to try this exercise in their own departments; the findings could be as enlightening to your faculty as they were to the VCU faculty. In a subsequent stage of the project, the authors matched those skills to job titles. They were able to list 49 discrete occupations requiring a bachelor's degree in psychology as the entry level training. This approach of identifying the match between personal characteristics and occupational demands is consistent with John Holland's career model.

Students at Illinois Valley Community College took a required course, Human Relations in the World of Work. In his article, William Marzano elaborated on the component of the course that taught job-entry skills. The skills consisted of completing application forms, constructing resumes, obtaining references, and developing appropriate dress and grooming behaviors for interviews. Graduates provided feedback indicating that they valued the course's content.

Paul Korn's approach to skill development consisted of designing a course to compliment the fieldwork and traditional academic courses. He introduced students at Suffolk University to the theory of helping behavior, to supervised practice in a classroom setting, and to a forum for integrating theory, practice, and personal concerns about being a helping person. The results of an evaluation revealed that students acquired accurate empathy skills, thereby indicating that the course was effective in achieving its objectives. The article provides readers with a summary of the course content and activities.

Readers in urban or rural settings may discover some helpful information from Frank Prerost and Michael Reich's work at Western Illinois University and Lewis University, respectively. They conducted a survey of employers of undergraduate psychology majors to determine their preference for students' educational experiences and the importance they attached to the personal interview, letters of recommendation, field experience, and the school's reputation. Although there were similarities in the rating that urban and rural employers gave to specific courses, there were also differences. For example, Motivation and Gerontology courses were at the opposite ends of the list for the two types of agency. The authors pointed out that faculty should be aware of employers' needs and preferences if they wish to help their bachelor level students be competitive for the limited number of entry level positions in human services settings.

Bridging the Gap: Psychology Classroom to the Marketplace

Thomas V. McGovern and Susan E. Ellett
Virginia Commonwealth University

A recent longitudinal study by Titley (1978) provides more reason for optimism than is commonly held by the undergraduate psychology student. The author followed up students with a bachelor's degree in psychology from Colorado State University one, five, and ten years after their graduation. Titley looked at the jobs held by these graduates and categorized them by three fields (psychology, education and human services, business-professional-trades) and by three levels (1 = high school education required/on-the job training; 2 = college preferred or moderate to extensive, related work experience; 3 = college degree required, degree in special field and extensive experience often preferred). The graduates showed a clear upward mobility by the defined levels. None of the subjects were in level one jobs ten years after graduation; 53% of the most recent graduates were. The results for the employment fields were also informative. Titley observed that much shifting seemed to occur within but not across fields. "Those who begin careers in one of the general fields tend to stay there" (p.

1097). Business-professional-trades field jobs employed the highest percentage of graduates in their first year.

Although this study gives psychology graduates some reason for optimism about their opportunities over time, the delay of gratification for five or ten years seems a mixed message, at best. Such high percentage of recent graduates in level one jobs needs more attention, since the experiences of Colorado State graduates are probably not unique. This article will elaborate on the authors' attempts to provide a systematic method for psychology majors to enter the labor market in a field and at a level more consistent with their education. Our career development program is based on two theoretical systems in vocational psychology research: John Holland's (1973, 1976) typology of persons and environments and Donald Super's (1969) self-concept/career development theory.

Super's theory describes the process by which students try to express in occupations their ideas of the kind of individuals they are and hope to be. Most of our students are drawn to psychology for its scientific or human relations content. They interact with faculty role models who reflect these two orientations. Unfortunately, the students' attempts to implement their self-concepts in actual job positions cause much floundering. Many experience difficulty in translating the experiences of their psychology training into potential occupational experiences and work settings. For the business or engineering student, subject material covered in classes is directly related to post-graduation job tasks. For the psychology major, this relationship is not always so clear. This is where Holland's theory is especially useful.

Holland identified that people choose educational and work environments which match their own personality types. In Holland's model, there are six discrete types by which a person/environment can be categorized: *R*ealistic, *I*nvestigative, *A*rtistic, *S*ocial, *E*nterprising, and *C*onventional. Our psychology department includes graduate faculty who teach in experimental, clinical, and counseling programs as well as the majority of our undergraduate offerings. Our environment can thus be defined as a combination of the I, S, and A themes since the occupational code for experimental psychologist is ISA and for a counseling/clinical psychologist it is SIA. An undergraduate student should therefore experience congruence if his/her individual personality pattern matches that of the ISA or SIA combinations. Using this typology, undergraduates can make decisions about other environments in the same way that they chose a psychology curriculum. Occupations and work settings can be examined for their investigative or social primary characteristics.

Students need to understand one more variable, however, in their decision making equation. It has been our experience that the translation of one's educational experiences into specific, behaviorally concrete skills is crucial to make the transition from academia to work. For the psychology major, some bridge is needed to translate what is learned in experimental, developmental, or social psychology courses into possible job requirements. The identification of what the student learns *how to do* in every course or part time work activity provides the necessary bridge.

In sum, we have tried to (1) define the environment of the psychology major by its investigative and social characteristics; (2) identify marketable skills learned in every course; (3) identify the match between specific skills and job title/job settings for a baccalaureate in psychology and (4) expose the psychology major through innovative techniques to the methods and outcomes of career planning.

Every faculty member in our department was interviewed to identify a set of skills which could be learned from each department offered course. This served as a consciousness raising experience for the faculty who had never themselves "translated" their course's inputs and outputs into marketable skills. The skills clustered around two areas, "human relations," which reflects Holland's S theme, and "research and writing," which reflects a combination of the I and A themes. Seven skills clustered under human relations (e.g., how to follow standard procedures to administer and score specific tests; how to do a formal interview as either the interviewer *or* interviewee) and nine skills (e.g., how to collect and code research data; how to make and record behavioral observations) clustered for research and writing.

Most of the skills were derived from the traditional "bread and butter" courses in the department's offerings (child, social, experimental, personality, adjustment, industrial). Some of the skills were primarily a function of individual faculty interests (advertising, occupational information, linguistics). Two special programs, Behavior Technology and Field Work (see Thomas, 1975), also served to enhance those skills originally modeled and learned in traditional classroom settings.

The major work of occupational information research was undertaken next. Using the *Dictionary of Occupational Titles* and individual job description published by the Federal Government, Commonwealth of Virginia, City of Richmond, independent community service agencies, and private business and industry, we matched these skills to job titles. Forty-nine discrete occupations requiring a bachelor's degree in psychology as the entry level training were identified. (Note: All of these titles would be considered level three jobs in Titley's classification!) This information was then written up in a career planning booklet (Ellett & McGovern, 1978) in which we described Holland's theory and the concept of skills as the bridge to the work world, as well as the actual matches between courses taken/skills learned/possible work settings/concrete job titles. During the summer of 1979, the second author also contacted 29 employers in the private sector. The two clusters of human relations skills and research and writing skills struck a responsive chord among the employers. Job titles such as management trainee, personnel trainee, public relations and community representative, and sales representative were most commonly identified as positions in which the psychology major could find openings. However, the consistent message delivered by the private employers was that the undergraduate needs to be taught to do his/her "homework" about what an area, company, job position require. Many of these requirements can be met through courses and part-time experience, and then addressed in the cover letter, resumé, and job interview. Once again, the "translation" concept from academic content to job related skills seemed most helpful.

We prepared a series of "skills resumés" which model for the undergraduate student an effective entry approach. The traditional chronological approach on a resumé which covers education, work experience, and extracurricular activities is seen repeatedly by employers. Unfortunately, most employers use only their stereotype of "junior shrink" when reviewing a candidate with a B.S./B.A. in Psychology. The skills resumé (Crystal & Bolles, 1974) emphasizes the student's qualifications in behavioral terms first, then lists the history and sources where those qualifications were developed. It is very important, we found, for the student to research the potential employer first, and then to match that environment's tasks with his/her concrete skills. Finally, we developed four new psychology courses tailored for four different age groups and the correlate problems of that developmental period. They are entitled: "Basic career exploration and educational planning," "Advanced career planning and job search," "Mid-life career planning and decision making," "Retirement planning and decision making." Each semester course is for two credits and combines didactic, experiential, and testing components. With course credit and more structured times, we hope to provide a strong incentive for students of all ages to do some career development work and to move easily from school to work and back again, when necessary.

At this point, our programs have received high ratings on the consumer satisfaction evaluations administered after individual and group sessions. However, a formal, annual follow-up procedure is planned to assess the components of the program which were most effective, and those which need modification. The "success stories" which have begun to filter back to us increase our belief that departmental career programs is an idea whose time has certainly come.

References

Crystal, J., & Bolles, R. *Where do I go from here with my life?* New York: Seabury Press, 1974.

Ellett, S., & McGovern, T. *PSY 2001: A career odyssey for persons with a bachelor's degree in psychology.* Unpublished manuscript, Virginia Commonwealth University, 1978.

Holland, J. *Making vocational choices: A theory of careers.* Englewood Cliffs, N. J.: Prentice-Hall, 1973.

Holland, J., & Gottfredson, G. Using a typology of persons and environments to explain careers: Some extensions and clarifications. *The Counseling Psychologist,* 1976, *6*, 20-29.

Super, D. Vocational development theory: Persons, positions and processes. *The Counseling Psychologist,* 1969, *1*, 2-9.

Thomas, E. An alternative approach to undergraduate training in psychology. *Teaching of Psychology,* 1975, *2*, 80-81.

Titley, R. Whatever happened to the Class of '67? *American Psychologist,* 1978, *33*, 1094-1098.

Individualizing Job-Entry Skills

William A. Marzano
Illinois Valley Community College

The increase in the number of psychology course offerings in the past decade has been well documented by Lux and Daniel (1978). Within 2-year colleges, an increase of 50% in the number of applied psychology offerings was specifically identified. Because 2-year colleges increasingly service occupational students in addition to their traditional transfer-oriented students, this trend in course development is readily understood.

Students enrolled in 2-year occupational curricula at Illinois Valley Community College, for example, are required to take an applied psychology course titled Human Relations in the World of Work. This offering has been specifically designed for occupational students, and it acquaints them with industrial and organizational psychology and a variety of conditions in the work-a-day world, such as motivation, stress, and communication.

An entire unit of the course is devoted to the job application process. In addition to acquiring the necessary skills and knowledge from their occupational curricula, these students also need to develop job-entry skills to compete successfully in their specific job markets. The unique learning experiences of this unit are designed to increase their chances for success in securing entry-level employment.

The students are given an overall perspective of the job application process, including the filling out of sample application forms, the construction of resumes, and the securing of references. Also, practical tips on appropriate dress and grooming for interviews are presented.

Hoover (1979) has identified the intructional techniques of role-playing and simulation as powerful methods for individualizing and internalizing teaching objectives. These techniques are employed to individualize the job-entry skills development of students in the following way. First, the students prepare an interview form specifically designed for a typical job in their chosen field. This form includes both standard questions and specific questions tailored to their occupational curricula.

Standard interview questions are procured from a list of questions developed by the professional job-placement agency of Allen and Associates (1983). Examples of such standard questions would be items such as: "Why do you want to work for this company?"; "What skills and qualifications can you offer us in this position?"; "Why did you choose this particular career or field of employment?" Specific interview questions vary, depending on the occupational field. These questions are developed in consultation with college instructors in the particular occupational programs who are familiar with entry-level positions and qualifications. The following are examples of such specific questions. A student in automotive technology may propose a question like "What diagnostic procedure would you employ if a vehicle failed to start repeatedly?" A student in the mid-management program may propose a question like "What is your personal management philosophy and leadership style?" Finally, a student in the robotics curriculum may propose a question like "What safety devices can be employed to protect workers who must work in close proximity to robots?" The preparation of this interview form thus allows each student to anticipate both general and specific interview questions individualized to their occupational goals.

These interview forms are then used in a simulated interview experience. Students engage in a role-playing activity where one serves as the interviewer and the other as the interviewee. The interviewer asks the interviewee all the questions from the previously prepared, individualized interview form. After the simulation, the interviewer completes the role-play by evaluating the performance of the interviewee by filling out a standard form. Specific areas of performance on this evaluation form, such as eye contact, manners, enthusiasm, and verbal expression, were developed in reference to a list of critical interview behaviors identified by a professional job-placement agency. The purpose of this evaluation is to provide feedback and constructive criticism.

The simulated interview is also videotaped for later viewing by both the instructor and the interviewee. This viewing presents another opportunity for evaluation and the identification of strengths and weaknesses in the interview performance.

Having prepared an individualized interview form, participated in the simulation, and secured feedback on their performance, these students improve the skills needed to market themselves in the increasingly competitive employment situation. As they usually participate in this experience shortly before they engage in real job applications, they are more prepared and confident. Feedback from former graduates usually indicates their perceived value of the experience. In fact, a number of students report that their real interviews were relatively easy as compared to the arduous and thorough simulation experience.

REFERENCES

Allen and Associates. (1983). *The total job campaign manual.* Schaumburg, IL: Author.

Hoover, K. H. (1979). *College teaching today.* Newton, MA: Allyn and Bacon.

Lux, D. F., & Daniel, R. S. (1978). Which courses are most frequently listed by psychology departments? *Teaching of Psychology, 5,* 13–16.

An Undergraduate Helping Skills Course: Skill Development and Career Education

Paul R. Korn
Suffolk University

Students in this course learned to help each other and become more self-disclosing as they developed skills for career goals.

During the past decade, there has been a continual increase in the training of undergraduates to provide mental health services (Cowen, Gardner, & Zax, 1967; Guerney, 1969) as well as an increase in the inclusion of field experiences as legitimate courses for credit in undergraduate curricula (Caffrey, Berger, Cole, Marx & Senn, 1977; Harrison, Fink, Lilliston, Aponte & Korn, 1978; Korman, 1974; Kulik, 1973; Shemberg & Keeley, 1976; Shiverick, 1977). These trends dovetail to produce two effects. The first is more relevance in the training of undergraduate psychology majors, which will increase the marketability of those not continuing for advanced degrees (Korn & Nodine, 1975; Pinkus & Korn, 1973). The second effect is the growing number of trained paraprofessionals used to meet the help-giving needs of the community (Baker, 1972; Cowen, Gardner, & Zax, 1967; Riessman, 1967).

The use of undergraduates as paraprofessionals during their college careers affects colleges and universities, the helping professions, and the community at large. Conceptions of undergraduate education are changing. Students are being trained to provide peer counseling services on college campuses as well (Aiken, Brownell & Iscoe, 1974; Leventhal, Berman, McCarthy & Wasserman, 1976). Whether choosing helping professions or not, college graduates who have some training in helping skills or some experience in a helping setting are moving into many different careers, professions, and social settings.

The Helping Skills Course described here was piloted in response to the trends described. The course was designed to complement the fieldwork experience and the traditional classroom experience of undergraduates interested in the helping professions. Traditional courses provide students with necessary cognitive frameworks and intellectual skills. Supervised fieldwork and practica offer relevant professional exposure, on-the-job training, and contacts with potential employers. The Helping Skills Course was conceived to add a third and necessary element in light of the growing reliance on paraprofessionals. The course provided an introduction to a widely applicable theory of helping, supervised practice in a classroom setting, and a forum to integrate theory, practice, and personal concerns about being a helper.

Course Structure. The Helping Skills Course was conducted during a twelve-week semester at a small urban commuter university. Classes were held weekly, each lasting two and one-half hours. The students were 13 advanced undergraduates, all working in helping settings, either as part-time employees (nursing home, welfare department), as practicum students from the university's psychology and sociology departments, or as volunteers at the university peer counseling center. Although some of the students had received training and some supervision, none had any formal training in helping skills. The instructor was a clinical psychologist who is a faculty member and who is also a clinician at the university counseling center.

The design of the course was based on three components: (a) providing conceptual understanding of a helping model and the helping process; (b) providing opportunities for increasing self-awareness and relationship-awareness; and (c) offering guided helping skills practice and feedback. Table 1 presents a simplified course syllabus specifying the integration of these three components.

The conceptual component was built around the Carkuff (1969) model of systematic skills training. Egan's text, *The Skilled Helper* (1975a) and his *Training Manual* (1975b) were used. Weekly reading assignments, weekly reading reports,

Table 1. Summary of Course Content and Activities

Activities and Focus[a]	Assignment for Next Class[ab]
Session 1	
1. Orientation to Course/Grading Contract	1. Chapter 1: Helper and Helpee (C)
2. Introduction to One Another	2. Chapter 2: The Helping Model (C)
3. Wood Blocks Activity: Diagnosing Personal Helping Styles (A)	3. Personal Journal and Reading Reaction (CAP)[c]
4. Written Helping Survey: Examples of "Real" Clients (AP)	
Session 2	
1. Videotape Play (A)	1. Chapter 3: Skills of Attending (C)
2. Discussion of Chapters 1 and 2 (C)	2. Handout: "Why It Is Sometimes Hard To Be A Counselor" (C)
3. Lecturette/Activity on Observation and Feedback (CP)	3. Preparation for Role-Playing (A)
4. Triad Practice (Helper, Helpee, Observer) (P)	4. Personal Journal and Reading Reaction (CAP)[c]
Session 3	
1. Discussion of Chapter 3 (C)	1. Chapter 4: Skills of Stage I: Primary Accurate Empathy, Respect, Genuineness, Concreteness (C)
2. Practice Discrimination/Communication (A)	
3. Triad Practice of Attending With Video Option (P)	2. Helping Skills Inventory (AP)
Session 4	
1. Lecturette on Paraphrasing	1. Reread Chapter 4
2. Practice in Pairs (P)	2. Speaking Concretely (AP)
3. Triads/Video Option (P)	3. Values as a Helper (A)
4. Discussion of Feedback From Triads and From Helping Skills Inventory (CA)	
Session 5	
1. Concreteness/Vagueness Practice (A)	1. Reread Chapter 4(C)
2. Role-Playing/Discussion Helping Interactions (CP)	2. The Language of Emotions (A)
3. Triads/Video Option (P)	
Session 6	
1. Lecturette on Emotions (C)	1. Chapter 5: Skills of Stage II Advanced Accurate Empathy, Self-Disclosure, Confrontation, Mutuality, Immediacy (C)
2. Expressing and Recognizing Emotion (A)	
3. Triads/Video Option (P)	2. Written Dialogue Between You the Helpee, and You the Helper (A)
Session 7	
1. Learning to Use Stage I Skills in a Group/Group Task (AP)	1. Reread Chapter 5(C)
2. Listening to and Discussing Tape of Carl Rogers (C)	2. Identifying Common Mistakes When Using Accurate Sympathy (A)
Session 8	
1. Identifying Personal Life Themes and Practicing Extracting Themes From Others Statements (AP)	1. Reread Chapter 5(C)
2. Discussion of Common Mistakes Using Accurate Empathy/Role-Play (CAP)	2. Learning to Differentiate Primary From Advanced Accurate Empathy (A)
3. Triads/Video Option (P)	
Session 9	
1. Lecturette: Stage II as Making Demands on the Helpee (C)	1. Chapter 6: Skills of III: Action Planning, Problem-Solving, Force-Field Analysis (C)
2. Demander/Resister Pairs (A)	
3. Triads/Video Option (P)	
Session 10	
1. Lecturette/Discussion of Action Planning (C)	1. Reread Chapter 6 (C)
2. Group Feedback - Incomplete Sentence Blanks (A)	2. Written Dialogue Using Stage II Skills (A)
3. Triad Practice Based On Life Themes (P)	
Session 11	
1. Lecturette/Discussion of Force-Field Analysis (C)	1. Final Preparation of Contracted Assignments
2. Brainstorming Practice (A)	
3. Triad Practice (P)	
Session 12	
1. Collect and discuss journal summaries, papers, video reports (C)	
2. Retake Helping Survey (See Session 1) and Compare Changes (A)	
3. Course Feedback and Goodbyes	

[a]Activities and assignments are annotated with (C) Conceptual, (A) Awareness, and (P) Practice to indicate the balancing of these three elements throughout the course.
[b]Chapter assignments are made from Gerard Egan's *The Skilled Helper*.
[c]Personal journals and reading reactions are handed in *every week* two days before class.

and classroom lecture/discussions focused on clarifying the nature of the helping relationship and the helping model.

At least half of most class sessions and frequent homework assignments were devoted to awareness activities. Sharing these activities helped build a closer, more trusting group. Experiential learning about self and others is consistent with Egan's (1975) ideas of training-as-treatment. A number of sources exist for awareness activities that are relevant to teaching helping skills (e.g., Pfeiffer & Jones, 1975; Stevens, 1971; Egan, 1975b). The following are two brief examples of awareness activities used during the course.

During the first class session, students were asked to close their eyes and participate in a guided fantasy. The instructor suggested: "Imagine yourself in a recent situation where you were helpful. Try to attend to the details of the interaction. What was said? How did you feel? What did you do?" After the fantasy, students formed pairs. Following discussion of the fantasy, each pair was given some wooden building blocks and a blindfold. Taking turns, each student was blindfolded and, after thinking of a structure, was helped by his or her partner to build something with the blocks. When everyone was finished, students spent some time alone and then in group discussion thinking about and sharing what they noticed about their styles of giving and receiving help.

Later in the course, while focusing on advanced helping skills, students were asked to form pairs, with one person asking for an unnamed "something" in as many ways as he/she could, while the other person refused and resisted giving that "something." After taking turns asking and refusing, the group members spent some time thinking about their styles of asking and refusing. A group discussion followed about situations in a helping setting when the helpee refuses help or advice.

In another effort to raise students' awareness of self-as-helper, homework assignments from Egan's training manual supplemented classroom activities. In addition, personal journals were handed in every week, including responses to class sessions and descriptions of helping interactions which occurred during the week. Students were asked to attend to all helping interactions, both formal, as might be related to their practicum assignment, and informal, with friends, family, or roommates. The journal entries also provided the instructor with constant information about students' progress and reactions.

The third component of the course, guided skills practice and feedback, focused on six skills: (a) primary level accurate empathy skills; (b) observation and attending skills; (c) feedback skills; (d) advanced accurate empathy skills; (e) confrontation skills; and (f) problem-solving skills. At least one class session was devoted to each of these skills. The class included lecture, awareness activity, demonstration, skills practice, and feedback. Because of the limits of time and the beginning level of the students, the bulk of classroom sessions was spent learning and practicing the first three skills.

About one-third of each class session was spent practicing the current skill in groups of three. Students rotated through the roles of helper, helpee, and observer. During each class session, one group worked with the instructor and a videotape system. Every student practiced and received feedback every week; and each student received videotape and instructor feedback regularly.

Students were evaluated and graded with a contract system. Grades were based upon how much work the student performed. The minimum contract included class attendance, weekly reading reports, weekly journal entries, and a journal summary at the end of the semester. Students could contract for higher grades by choosing to write one or two papers on approved topics and by providing a 15-minute videotape of themselves in a helping interaction. These tapes were self-evaluated and also were evaluated by the instructor in the presence of the student.

Course Evaluation. A pre-post test was used to evaluate acquisition of accurate empathy skills. A paper and pencil form drawn from The Helping Relationship Inventory (Pfeiffer & Jones, 1973, pp. 53-70) was administered to students in the Helping Skills Course and to a control group of students in an experiential group dynamics course. The test presented statements by eight people of different backgrounds talking about a variety of issues (e.g., loneliness, suicide, jealousy, falling in love). Students were instructed to write one or two sentences which would be a helpful response to the person making the statement. The same form of the test was used for the pre-measure and the post-measure to control for variability in the problem statements.

Carkuff's (1969) revised five-point empathy scale was used by two independent judges to rate levels of empathy. Interjudge reliability for total empathy scores of each student was $r = .81$. Ratings were averaged for each student and divided by the number of statements to provide scores comparable with other research on empathy (Payne, Weiss & Kapp, 1972; Payne & Woudenberg, 1978; Ritter, 1978).

For the students in the Helping Skills Course, scores on the Carkuff (1969) five-point scale were pre $M = 1.29$, $SD = .325$; post $M = 2.36$, $SD = .476$. The average gain was $+1.07$, $t(20) = 5.94$, $p < .001$. The correlation of pre-post scores was $r = .327$.

On initial scores of empathy, there was no difference between students in the Helping Skills Course and control group students. Also, there were no significant changes over time for the control group students (pre $M = 1.22$, $SD = .172$, post $M = 1.15$, $SD = .125$). This finding is consistent with previous studies (Payne & Woudenberg, 1978).

At the end of the semester, students in the Helping Skills Course rated self-perceived changes using a post-course questionnaire on objectives. The questionnaire consisted of eleven seven-point scales, on which the students indicated their skill/understanding level before the course and at the end of the course. Table 2 presents group means of "before" and "after" ratings, differences, and t statistics.

Allowing for problems interpreting self-report data, students reported changes which were statistically significant in regard to: (a) understanding Egan's model and concepts: (b) ability to use various helping skills; (c) awareness of self-as-helper; and (d) confidence in the helping situation. The greatest changes in understanding and skill were reported for objectives relating to primary-level accurate empathy. This result is consistent with the fact that most of the course time was spent discussing and practicing the basic skill of primary-level accurate empathy.

Non-quantifiable information was gathered from journal summaries, written course evaluations, self-evaluations of videotapes, and instructor evaluations of videotapes. Students reported a great amount of excitement and satisfaction with the course. They wrote that they had learned definite skills and had acquired a more realistic idea about the rewards and difficulties of being a helper.

Self-evaluations revealed that the students were able to evaluate their own helping skill level objectively, noting both positive and negative attributes. Students emphasized the importance of classroom practice in small groups. They valued receiving feedback in these groups and also the opportunity every week to be in the helpee role, being helped with their own problems. The students indicated clearly that they

Table 2. Means, Differences, and t-Tests Comparing "Before" and "After" Ratings on Objectives

Objective	"Before"	"After"	Difference	t value*
Understand Egan's helping model	1.18	5.09	3.91	12.22
Understanding concept of primary-level accurate empathy	1.82	6.09	4.27	10.17
Skill in using primary-level accurate empathy	2.09	5.73	3.64	10.06
Understanding concept of advanced accurate empathy	1.36	5.45	4.09	10.44
Skill in using advanced accurate empathy	1.27	4.55	3.36	10.88
Skill in communicating respect/genuineness	3.18	5.91	2.73	7.13
Skill in speaking concretely	2.18	4.73	2.55	7.50
Skill attending to own and others' feelings	2.45	5.64	3.18	8.37
Skill communicating about own/others' feelings	2.36	5.36	3.00	7.50
Awareness of own strengths and weaknesses as helper	1.91	5.64	3.73	8.70
Confidence being a helper	1.91	4.82	2.91	8.50

*All t values are significant, $p < .001$, $df = 10$.

would benefit from a continuation of the course in order to develop and practice their helping skills.

Discussion and Implications. The pilot semester of Helping Skills Course for Undergraduates has been described and evaluated. Helping skills were taught as part of an academic program to complement traditional courses, fieldwork practica, and the growing demand by undergraduates for relevant training. In striking a balance between theory, self-awareness activities, and skills practice, the course was meaningful, and class sessions were active, involving, and exciting for students and instructor alike.

Within the limitations of a quasi-experimental design, the results of a comparison between students from the Helping Skills Course and students from a control group indicate that on a paper-and-pencil measure, Helping Skills students learned to respond to problem statements with accurate empathy. In addition students' self-assessments indicate an increase in understanding of helping skills concepts and an increase in skills level. Although these results must be interpreted tentatively, they provide support for the conclusion that undergraduate students in a one-semester course learn basic helping skills as well as an orientation to the helping process.

The nature of this Helping Skills Course increased the personal development of the students as they grew closer, became more self-disclosing, and received meaningful help from one another. The responsibilities and problems of being a helper were experienced in a context wherein they could be discussed. Students interested in the helping professions were able to get a "hands on" sense of helping in the relatively safe atmosphere of a classroom. This experience added to the actual helping experiences in the field, which usually have less opportunities for risk-taking and immediate feedback. Undergraduates who did not enter the helping professions took from the course certain basic skills which can be put to use in any career or social setting.

Although similar courses are regularly included in graduate programs for helping professions (Anthony, Slowkowski & Bendix, 1976; Ritter, 1978), the results and reactions to this pilot course suggest that undergraduates also can learn from supervised classroom training in helping skills. Including such a course in undergraduate curricula would require that instructors modify graduate courses and/or be trained to teach such a subject to undergraduates. The politics of a changed conception of undergraduate education may give rise to problems similar to those met when efforts were first made to include fieldwork as part of the undergraduate curricula.

Further experimentation and evaluation of undergraduate skill development courses is necessary to create meaningful and relevant training programs and to validate the effects of such programs.

References

Anthony, W., Slowkowski, P., & Bendix, L. Developing the specific skills and knowledge of the rehabilitation counselor. *Rehabilitation Counseling Bulletin,* 1976, *19,* 456-462.

Aiken, J., Brownell, A., & Iscoe, I. The training and utilization of paraprofessionals in a college psychological center. *Journal of College Student Personnel,* 1974, *15,* 480-486.

Baker, E. J. The mental health associate: A new approach in mental health. *Community Mental Health Journal,* 1972, *8,* 281-291.

Caffrey, B., Berger, L., Cole, S., Marx, D., & Senn, D. Integrating professional programs in a traditional undergraduate psychology program. *Teaching of Psychology,* 1977, *4,* 7-13.

Carkuff, R. *Helping and human relations,* (Vols. 1 & 2). New York: Holt, Rinehart, & Winston, 1969.

Cowen, E., Gardner, E., & Zax, M. *Emergent approaches to mental health problems.* New York: Appleton-Century-Crofts, 1967.

Egan, G. *The skilled helper: A model for systematic helping and interpersonal relations.* Monterey, CA: Brooks/Cole, 1975a.

Egan, G. *Exercises in helping skills: A training manual to accompany "The Skilled Helper."* Monterey, CA: Brooks/Cole, 1975b.

Guerney, B. *Psychotherapeutic agents: New roles for nonprofessionals, parents, and teachers.* New York: Holt, Rinehart, & Winston, 1969.

Hess, A., Harrison, A., Fink, R., Lilliston, L., Aponte, J., & Korn, J. Critical issues in undergraduate training in various community settings. *Teaching of Psychology,* 1978, *5,* 81-86.

Korman, M. National conference on levels and patterns of professional training in psychology. *American Psychologist,* 1974, *29,* 441-449.

Korn, J., & Nodine, B. Facts and questions concerning career training of the psychology major. *Teaching of Psychology,* 1975, *2,* 117-119.

Kulik, J. *Undergraduate education in psychology.* Washington, DC: American Psychological Association, 1973.

Leventhal, A., Berman, A., McCarthy, B., & Wasserman, G. Peer counseling on the university campus. *Journal of College Student Personnel,* 1976, *17,* 504-509.

Payne, P., Weiss, S., & Kapp, R. Didactic, experiential, and modeling factors in the learning of empathy. *Journal of Counseling Psychology,* 1972, *19,* 425-429.

Payne, P., & Woudenberg, R. Helping others and helping yourself: An evaluation of two training modules in a college course. *Teaching of Psychology*, 1978, *5*, 131-134.

Pfeiffer, J., & Jones, J. *The 1973 annual handbook for group facilitators*. La Jolla, CA: University Associates Publishers, 1973.

Pfeiffer, J., & Jones, J. *A handbook of structured experiences for human relations training*, (Vols. 1-4). La Jolla, CA: University Associates Publishers, 1975.

Pinkus, R., & Korn, J. The preprofessional option: An alternative to graduate work in psychology. *American Psychologist*, 1973, *28*, 710-718.

Riessman, F. Strategies and suggestions for training nonprofessionals. *Community Mental Health Journal*, 1967, *3*, 103-110.

Ritter, K. A case for skills training. *Teaching of Psychology*, 1978, *5*, 148-149.

Shemberg, K., & Keeley, S. Training undergraduates as subprofessional community mental health workers. *Teaching of Psychology*, 1976, *3*, 118-121.

Shiverick, D. A full-time clinical practicum for undergraduates. *Teaching of Psychology*, 1977, *4*, 188-190.

Stevens, J. *Awareness: Exploring, experimenting, and experiencing*. Moab, UT: Real People Press, 1971.

Notes

1. This article is based upon a paper presented at the meeting of the American Psychological Association, New York City, September 1979.

Factors Affecting Evaluation of Undergraduate Job Applicants: Urban vs Rural Human Service Delivery Systems

Frank J. Prerost
Western Illinois University
and Michael J. Reich
Lewis University

The locale of an agency does make a difference in the preferred academic preparation of AB job applicants.

During the last decade special regard has been shown about the career matters of undergraduate psychology majors (Caffrey, Berger, Cole, Marx & Senn, 1977.) This concern has stimulated an expansion in the range and diversity of coursework available to the psychology major (Barton & Duerfeldt, 1980). Modifications in traditional degree programs have afforded students course options focusing on field experience (Matthews, 1979), career development (Ware, 1981), and applications of psychological principles (Mann, 1982). In fact, some universities have designed alternative major tracks of study, one in preparation for graduate school and another for entering the job market in applied psychology (Nazzaro, 1976).

Korn and Nodine (1975) stated that the majority of psychology majors enter the job market with a bachelor's degree as sole preparation for career work. The career plans envisaged by psychology students focus on the human services because students develop a bias toward clinical areas (Korn & Lewandowski, 1981). Yet, undergraduate students often are unaware of the occupational opportunities open to them in the human service field (Quereshi, Brennan, Kuchan & Sackett, 1974). Korn and Lewandowski (1981) cited inadequate career advising for the human services and inadequate curricular preparation as deficiencies in many psychology programs. Prerost (1981) found that a high proportion of students with field experience coursework were successful in attaining human service employment.

Boltuck, Peterson and Murphy (1980) have indicated that academic advisors typically recommend that undergraduates pursue coursework centering on traditional scientific content. The extent to which a broad background in psychology as a science is advantageous in obtaining entry level positions in the human services has remained unanswered. With the increased number of course options available to undergraduate majors in psychology, a number of pertinent questions pertaining to the value of specific courses for career preparation should be addressed. The purpose of the present study was to survey employers of psychology majors to ascertain what they prefer in the educational history of new employees. Information related to the value placed on specific topic areas by employers in the human service field can assist both in the advising of psychology majors and in modifying curricula. White and Lindquist (1982) reported such feedback from human service agencies assisted in the validation and development of a master's-level psychology training program at one institution.

In order to acquire data on the factors affecting hiring practices in the human services, agencies that service either urban or rural districts were surveyed. It was expected that the agencies would show a preference for coursework reflecting the applied areas of psychology, and that preference be demonstrated at both rural and urban locations. This study also focused on the attitudes of psychology majors in choosing coursework which they perceive as beneficial in the acquisition of employment at human service agencies.

Method. A questionnaire was mailed to 140 human service officers serving either urban or rural populations. The Chicago metropolitan area served as the urban locale for sampling 70 human service facilities. The remaining agencies, representing the rural half of the sample, were housed in agricultural communities with a maximum population of 30,000. The agencies in the sample provide a wide range of psychological and related services including diagnostics, individual and group psychotherapy, drug and alcohol rehabilitation, and inpatient care.

In addition to the sample of human service agencies, data were collected from 120 psychology majors attending either a small liberal arts college or a medium sized university in the Midwest. The student population ranged in age from 20 to 26. Only junior and senior year majors were sampled, because employment issues would be of greater relevance to them.

One hundred eleven agencies responded with completed questionnaires (52 urban, 59 rural) giving a 79% return rate. The questionnaire was typically completed by the agency director or person in charge of hiring at the facility. The respondents typically held a PhD or terminal degree in social work. Although the rural agencies reported a higher percentage of professional staff holding bachelor and master degrees than did urban facilities, there was no significant difference in the academic degree held by the individuals completing the questionnaires. Thus, the hiring decisions were typically assumed by doctoral level professionals at the surveyed locations. The questionnaire listed 32 undergraduate psychology courses with brief catalogue descriptions. The list was an exhaustive compilation from a review of midwestern university catalogues. The respondents were required to rate each course on a five-point scale as follows: (1) Not at all useful; (2) Somewhat useful; (3) Moderately useful; (4) Definitely useful; (5) Extremely useful (indicating importance in preparing students for entry level employment at the agency).

In addition to the courses, the agency respondents were asked to assign the relative importance of the following factors in hiring of entry level personnel: personal interview, letters of reference, volunteer/practicum experiences, undergraduate coursework, workshops/seminars, and reputation of the student's college or university. These factors were judged using the five-point scale described above. The same instruments were given to the sample of students who were directed to indicate the expected importance of each in helping them secure employment in the applied areas of psychology.

Results.   Review of the ratings completed by personnel from the urban and rural respondents yielded some dissimilarities in the perceived importance of undergraduate courses. Mean ratings of courses by the rural group of agencies demonstrated an interest in the applicants who have completed coursework in the clinical and gerontological subject areas, as shown in Table 1. The courses viewed as least beneficial by the rural agencies were largely methodological and experimental.

The urban agencies showed a pattern somewhat different. The most preferred for new employees were mainly preclinical, basic courses. Three of the lowest ratings were the same courses identified in the rural list, whereas the other three were mainly biologically oriented. Notice that two courses (Motivation and Gerontology) were at opposite ends in the two agency lists. Nevertheless, the correlation between the

urban and rural mean ratings for the courses was .62 (p<.01).

Concerning the factors affecting an applicant's evaluation during the hiring process, both urban and rural agencies rated the personal interview of highest importance and

Table 1. Mean Ratings of Psychology Courses by Urban and Rural Agencies

Rural Agencies		Urban Agencies	
Course	Mean Rating	Course	Mean Rating
Most Useful Courses			
Gerontology/Aging	4.41	Social	4.28
Abnormal	4.37	Developmental	4.14
Adjustment	4.19	Personality	4.01
Tests & Measurement	4.06	Field Practicum	3.96
Field Practicum	3.91	Abnormal	3.85
Psychotherapy	3.83	Motivation	3.73
Least Useful Courses			
Statistics	1.55	Gerontology/Aging	1.79
Research Design	1.52	Psychobiology	1.41
Cognitive	1.31	Research Design	1.38
Learning	1.28	Statistics	1.31
Industrial	1.12	Industrial	1.19
Motivation	1.08	Perception	1.10

Note. Ratings based on a five-point scale with (5) equal to extremely useful.

usefulness (urban $M = 4.78$; rural $M = 4.63$). Rural agencies viewed the applicant's coursework as being more important for hiring decisions than did the urban group (rural $M = 4.29$; urban $M = 3.16$). Letters of reference from professors were considered of minor usefulness in the hiring process (urban $M = 1.98$; rural $M = 2.24$). Practicum experiences were rated as useful (urban $M = 3.75$; rural $M = 3.86$), but workshops (urban $M = 2.83$; rural $M = 2.48$), and the academic institution's reputation (urban $M = 2.89$; rural $M = 3.21$) were judged of moderate significance.

Student ratings of psychology courses showed a perceived importance of courses reflecting clinical and applied topics. The courses garnering highest ratings were: abnormal $(M = 4.75)$, child psychopathology $(M = 4.63)$, adjustment $(M = 4.51)$, community mental health $(M = 4.33)$, and counseling/psychotherapy techniques $(M = 4.39)$. The courses with the lowest evaluations were: aging/gerontology $(M = 1.84)$, psychobiology $(M = 1.66)$, cognitive $(M = 1.47)$, statistics $(M = 1.23)$, and research design $(M = 1.15)$. Students perceived letters of recommendation to be highly important in the hiring process $(M = 4.46)$. Of the remaining factors such as school reputation and workshop experience students judged them to be of minor importance.

Discussion.   Rural agencies appear to desire students prepared in specific skill areas related to the practice of psychology. Understanding psychopathology, its assessment and treatment, appears to be the knowledge needed by students when applying at rural offices. The high ratings given to the psychology of aging by rural facilities may indicate that the elderly are served extensively by these agencies. The rural agency may expect the entry level employee to assume direct service activities with minimal on-the-job training. A shortage of personnel may be present in rural agencies to provide training and supervision. A new employee at a rural facility may be expected to assume a broad range of duties making practical knowledge and experience critical to employment.

The urban centers evaluated the basic psychology core courses as preferred in the education of new employees. Background in social, developmental, and personality were rated as useful course experiences. This finding may illustrate the urban agency's desire to do the training of individuals who possess fundamental psychological knowledge for specific direct service functions. The question arises if urban facilities are more oriented toward training and supervision of new personnel than are the rural offices.

Because both rural and urban agencies placed minor emphasis on statistics and research design courses, minimal understanding of the usefulness of such topics for mental health workers may be present. Students rated the same topic areas as being of minor importance in securing jobs at human service agencies and may reflect their dislike of these topics.

Considering the limited number of entry level positions in the human services that students are competing for each year, it seems important for academic institutions to be aware of the needs and preferences of agencies which employ undergraduates. Students, depending upon the geographic location of their potential job market, might benefit from courses useful in securing employment. Letters of reference from academic instructors are not highly prized as evaluation instruments by human service employers, therefore students might be best served by attending to the development of practical skills, and selecting courses for specific topic coverage. The results of this study need to be weighed with the potential long range benefits of successfully completing courses in statistics and experimental design.

References

Barton, E. J., & Duerfeldt, P. H. Undergraduate psychology practica pragmatism. *Teaching of Psychology*, 1980, *7*, 146-149.

Boltuck, M. A., Peterson, T. L. & Murphy, R. J. Preparing undergraduate psychology majors for employment in the human service delivery system. *Teaching of Psychology*, 1980, *7*, 75-78.

Caffrey, B., Berger, L., Cole, S., Marx, D., & Senn, D. Integrating professional programs in a traditional undergraduate psychology program. *Teaching of Psychology*, 1977, *4*, 7-13.

Korn, J. H. & Nodine, B. F. Facts and questions concerning career training of the psychology major. *Teaching of Psychology*, 1975, *2*, 117-119.

Korn, J. H. & Lewandowski, M. E. The clinical bias in the career plans of undergraduates and its impact on students and the profession. *Teaching of Psychology*, 1981, *8*, 149-152.

Mann, R. D. The curriculum and context of psychology. *Teaching of Psychology*, 1982, *9*, 9-14.

Matthews, J. R. Undergraduate field placement: Survey and issues. *Teaching of Psychology*, 1979, *6*, 148-151.

Nazzaro, J. Identity crisis in psychology. *Change*, 1976, *8*, 44-45.

Prerost, F. J. Post-graduation educational and occupational choices of psychology undergraduate practicum participants: Issues for the psychology profession. *Teaching of Psychology*, 1981, *8*, 221-223.

Quereshi, M. J., Brennan, P. J., Kuchan, A. M. & Sackett, P. R. Some characteristics of undergraduate majors in psychology. *Journal of Experimental Education*, 1974, *42*, 65-79.

Ware, M. E. Evaluating a career development course: A two year study. *Teaching of Psychology*, 1981, *8*, 67-71.

White, G. D., & Lindquist, C. U. Survey of mental health agencies in curriculum development of a master's-level psychology training program. *Teaching of Psychology*, 1982, *9*, 212-215.

4. ASSESSING JOB SATISFACTION AMONG PSYCHOLOGY MAJORS

The two articles constituting this group provide a fitting conclusion to the topic of career development. Not only must students recognize the importance of the career decision making process (how they decide) and product (what they decide), but they should also know how to obtain a position.

Patricia Lunneborg and Vicki Wilson examined the role of job satisfaction components by asking psychology graduates from the University of Washington the following questions: "How long does it take to find a good job?" — "What's the best way to search for it?" — "Is employment in some fields more satisfying than others?" Their answers to these and other questions can provide future graduates and those who advise psychology majors with suggestions for undertaking the job search and for selecting elective courses.

One lesson from the final article in this section is that it is not enough to expect that the psychology major's career versatility guarantees occupational satisfaction. Patricia Lunneborg drew that conclusion from the results of an investigation that examined the satisfactions and dissatisfactions that graduates from the University of Washington reported. The author's forewarnings to psychology majors provide challenging reading material for all.

Job Satisfaction Correlates for College Graduates in Psychology

Patricia W. Lunneborg
Vicki M. Wilson
University of Washington

This survey emphasizes the value of job preparation while still in college, and gives some important tips in finding jobs.

Ware & Meyer (1981) felt that many psychology departments neglect to prepare undergraduates for the actual work world. Programs and courses in career development were suggested as one way to meet the occupational needs of students. Among the aims of such courses is imparting knowledge about how previous generations of psychology majors fared in the job market. Certainly a major point that would be stressed is the considerable variety of work into which psychology graduates go (Davis, 1979; Titley, 1979; Ware & Meyer, 1981; Woods, 1979).

The primary purpose of the present study was to identify important components of job satisfaction in psychology baccalaureates. How long does it take to find a good job? What's the best way to search for it? Is employment in some fields more satisfying than others? Both the correlates of job satisfaction and the compilation of advice for future graduates provide useful material for career development classes, departmental advisors, and placement office personnel.

Method. Between August 1977 and December 1979, 908 people received bachelor's degrees from the University of Washington's Department of Psychology. The present report is based on the responses of these graduates to a brief postcard survey mailed in May 1980 (and followed up in August 1980). A total of 720 surveys proved deliverable and 425 of these were completed (a 59% return rate).

Of the 425 respondents, the 304 who had received BA degrees provided the data for analysis here. The 121 BS recipients were not included because their curriculum is pure psychology graduate school preparation and, indeed, there was a significant difference between the two groups in current enrollment in post-baccalaureate studies (25% BA's vs. 47% BS's). Returns from more recent BA's were higher (54% of the class of 1977, 58% of 1978, and 65% of 1979), however, the proportions of the sexes in this sample are the same as in the total group of graduating BA's, 70% women, 30% men.

The postcard survey provided 12 variables for analysis in addition to job titles, employers, and comments. In addition to the criterion, (a) job satisfaction (rated not at all, somewhat, or very), there was (b) sex status, (c) current primary activity, (d) interest area of employment, and whether employment was (e) full-time or not, (f) psychology-related or not, and (g) career choice or not. Solicited as well were (h) how long the graduate had searched for a job, and (i) the job search method that succeeded. Graduates were given five reasons for majoring in psychology and asked to indicate (j) their primary reason, followed by (k) an item measuring degree satisfaction, "How well did BA/S meet this goal? Not at all? Somewhat? Very?" The five reasons for the major were interest, psychology graduate school preparation, non-psychology graduate or professional school preparation, personal growth, and job preparation. The last variable was (l) type of further degree being sought.

Variable e, interest areas of present employment, was coded by the authors using Roe's (1956) classification system. As all 12 variables were categorical data, including the eight Roe occupational groups, chi-square analyses were used throughout.

Results. Only 8% said they were "not at all" satisfied with their jobs; 37% were somewhat satisfied and 55% were very satisfied with their jobs. Looking at the respondents who gave job satisfaction ratings, chi-square analyses revealed no difference between the sexes in job satisfaction. There was also no difference between those who said their *primary* activity was currently school, or work, or both school and work. Five percent were unemployed, 15% primarily in school, and 70% primarily employed (but 10% were "primarily" both employed and in school). Likewise, excluding those who did not rate job satisfaction, full-time work (held by 84% of the sample) was no more satisfying than part-time work.

There were highly statistically significant associations between job satisfaction and whether or not the job held was psychology-related and in the respondent's career choice area. Greater satisfaction resulted from jobs related to psychology and in one's projected career, as might be expected. Of particular interest was a chi-square value significant at the .05 level (26.38 with 14 df) between interest area of job and job satisfaction. Greater satisfaction was associated with working in the Business Contact and General Cultural fields, lesser satisfaction with Organizational and Technical jobs. The percentages of BA's in these eight areas are given in Table 1.

Job satisfaction was also significantly related at the .02 level to *length* of job search and at the .05 level to the *method* used successfully in the job search. The longer the search, the greater was job satisfaction. The methods associated with greater satisfaction were "self-initiated, self-created" and "worked/volunteered there previously." The search methods associated with lesser job satisfaction were "want ads" and "employment agency or service." Table 1 contains the details of these results.

The five reasons for majoring in psychology (see Table 1) were not related to job satisfaction. However, the extent to which one's goal in selecting the major had been met *was* related at the .01 level to job satisfaction. The more satisfied graduates were with their degrees (for whatever reason) the

Table 1. Job Satisfaction Variables for Psychology Baccalaureates (N = 304)[a]

Variable	Percent
Interest Area of Present Employment (N = 237)	
Service	29
Business Contact	11
Organization	27
Technical	10
Outdoor	1
Science	6
General Cultural	13
Arts & Entertainment	3
Length of Search for Current Job (N = 234)	
One month or less	60
Greater than 1 month to 6 months	28
Seven to twelve months	7
Over twelve months	4
Job Search Method That Succeeded (N = 241)	
Friends, relatives, contacts, referrals	24
Direct contact with employer	15
Previously employed or volunteered there	15
Want ads, newspapers, posted notices	14
Employment agency or service	8
Self-initiated, self-created	7
College placement center	7
Other	10
Primary Reason for Majoring in Psychology (N = 289)	
Interest	50
Personal growth	19
Job preparation	17
Psychology graduate school preparation	8
Professional school preparation	6

[a]214 women, 90 men

more satisfied they were with their jobs. Nine percent were "not at all" satisfied with their degrees, 56% were somewhat satisfied, and 35% were very satisfied with their BA degrees.

The comments of these graduates made seven points that bear repeating in any career class or advising sessions. The seven points were:

1. As an undergraduate you need to supplement psychology with another field if you expect to find work appropriate for someone with a college degree.

2. You need relevant work experience *before* you graduate—part-time job, volunteer work, internships—to get a good job when you graduate.

3. People in college who have career goals related to the psychology major are very satisfied later in their work.

4. You shouldn't graduate unless you have a career goal and are prepared to pursue it. Otherwise you are likely to be underemployed and continue to be undecided about your career direction for years.

5. Don't leap at your first job offer. Unless you hold out for an appropriate job, *perhaps for as long as a year,* you are likely to be very unhappy in a job where you won't apply psychology at all.

6. Counseling and social service are currently poor areas of employment—work at very low levels for very low pay.

7. For a career that pays well you should plan to do graduate work. Master's degrees in business administration, public affairs, education, social work, religion, and communications were recommended.

In regard to Number 7, the last point, 30% of this sample was pursuing or had pursued further education. Nineteen of these 91 individuals were in professional programs (14 in law, dentistry, medicine) or doctoral programs (5 getting psychology PhDs); 26 were doing additional work at the bachelor's level; and a total of 46 were getting master's degrees in social work (4), business and public administration (10), education (15), counseling (7), and "other"—health education, communications, physical therapy, divinity, librarianship, history (10). Not one BA was pursuing a master's degree in psychology.

Discussion. The extent to which career goals are *not* paramount in the choice of the psychology major is seen in the 69% who selected it primarily out of interest or for personal growth. This lack of career orientation poses a problem for faculty and advisors concerned about helping students link their undergraduate education to future employment.

Perhaps one manifestation of this lack of concern is the 60% who said they had found their jobs in one month or less—surprising at a time of rising unemployment. The positive relationship, however, between job satisfaction and length of search suggests that an unfortunate amount of jumping at the first opportunity occurred, which turned out to be an unhappy "choice." Graduates should expect a search between 7 months and a year for a satisfying job.

What was the best way to search for a job? While leads through friends, relatives and contacts, and directly contacting prospective employers were the two most frequently used methods, those that led to greater job satisfaction were "being previously employed" or "having volunteered" there and creating the job oneself. As an "employee communications consultant" said, "I turned a part-time boring job I had as a student into a full-time challenging job with lots of responsibility."

The next thing for psychology baccalaureates to consider is that greater satisfaction was found among those who were in their career choice area and those whose jobs were related to psychology. This latter relationship was strictly in the eye of the jobholder. Respondents gave as "psychology-related" such jobs as marketing consultant, systems analyst, flight attendant, insurance agent, claims representative, real estate salesperson, and account executive, in addition to, as one might expect, social worker, teacher, nurse, counselor, and personnel assistant.

Regarding the association of greater job satisfaction with work in Business Contact and General Cultural and lesser satisfaction with Organizational and Technical employment, it should also be mentioned that there was a significant sex difference in areas of present employment. Women were more employed in Service, Organization, and General Cultural jobs and men more employed in Business Contact and Technical jobs. Our impression from the raw data is that many women in Organization were in very low-level clerical jobs and the men in Technical were similarly working at a low level—driving trucks, fishing, remodeling houses. This low-level factor may be behind the significant relationship between job satisfaction and interest area of job. In contrast, men in sales and women in teaching were more satisfied.

The diversity of jobs into which psychology baccalaureates go, whether they consider them related to psychology or not, was once again confirmed. Further, the diversity of graduate education for which this bachelor's program prepared them was equally obvious. This is a further fact about which psychology majors need to be informed. It parallels Ware & Meyer's (1981) finding that among BAs pursuing doctoral level programs, only 13% were in psychology. Their students, too, had used the psychology major as preparation for dentistry, law, medicine, and many other graduate degrees.

Perhaps the content of the University of Washington's BA curriculum is worth mentioning. Required courses are at a minimum: introductory, scientific methodology, statistics, and one laboratory. The remainder of each student's program (50 quarter credits) is guided by individual career goals. BA students are urged to take supplementary courses in another major, basic skills courses (English, mathematics, speech), job-related skills courses such as computer programming, and fieldwork.

References

Davis, J. Where did they all go? A job survey of BA graduates. In P. Woods (Ed.), *The psychology major: Training and employment strategies.* Washington, DC: American Psychological Association, 1979.

Roe, A. The psychology of occupations. New York: John Wiley, 1956.

Titley, R. Whatever happened to the class of '67? Psychology baccalaureate holders one, five, and ten years after graduation. In P. Woods (Ed.), *The psychology major: Training and employment strategies.* Washington, DC: American Psychological Association, 1979.

Ware, M., & Meyer, A. Career versatility of the psychology major: A survey of graduates. *Teaching of Psychology,* 1981, *8,* 12-15.

Woods, P. Employment following two different undergraduate programs in psychology. In P. Woods (Ed.), *The psychology major: Training and employment strategies.* Washington, DC: American Psychological Association, 1979.

Job Satisfactions in Different Occupational Areas Among Psychology Baccalaureates

Patricia W. Lunneborg
University of Washington

The present study addresses the issue of job satisfaction among psychology majors employed in different occupational areas. The career versatility of the major is well-documented by Ware and Meyer (1981) and Woods (1979). But the question remains, are our majors equally satisfied in the wide variety of occupations that they enter?

Malin and Timmreck (1979) noted an overwhelming desire among University of Houston undergraduates for careers in psychology or closely related fields. Forty-two percent wanted careers in clinical and counseling. Korn and Lewandowski (1981) labeled this phenomenon "the clinical bias in the career plans" of majors and argued for making students more aware of employment opportunities in nonclinical fields, as have Titley and Titley (1982). If our graduates are less satisfied using their psychological skills and knowledge as office managers and loan officers, how advisable is it to say, "Look at all the jobs you can do with your BA in psychology?" Surely we must point out the types of satisfactions and dissatisfactions previous psychology majors say are associated with employment in different fields.

METHOD

The participants in this study were 178 psychology baccalaureates of the University of Washington who graduated between March, 1978 and March, 1979. A total of 354 psychology majors graduated over these 5 quarters, of whom 304 had addresses to which the survey was deliverable (59% return rate). The postcard surveys were mailed in November, 1983 and follow-ups occurred in December, 1983 and February, 1984.

The sample consisted of 65% females and 35% males, and of 69% BA recipients and 31% BS recipients. These proportions do not differ significantly from the population as a whole. Thirty-two percent had supplemented psychology with another major as undergraduates, while 55% had pursued further education and 80% (N = 142) were currently employed. Their jobs were coded by the author using Roe's (1956) vocational interest framework, which embraces eight groups. The percentages of the 142 employed respondents in each of Roe's groups are: service 24%, business contact 7%, organization 30%, technical 11%, outdoor 0%, science 12%, general cultural 14%, and arts and entertainment 1%. General cultural jobs include teaching, law, librarianship, and academic psychology posts.

The data were gathered through a postcard survey, which asked for occupational and educational information, and had graduates rate their satisfaction with the psychology BA/BS in six aspects. Following these ratings appeared one of four different career items, including the one which is the focus of this report. It asked "How true of your job are these facts?", followed by eight job satisfactions. Ratings were of the form: 0 = not, 1 = some, 2 = medium, and 3 = very ("satisfied" in the case of the six psychology degree aspects, and "true" in the case of the eight job satisfactions). Data were analyzed using chi-square and analysis of variance. All differences reported here were significant at the .05 level.

RESULTS

The means (with standard deviations in parentheses) for the job satisfactions in descending order are: satisfied with job 2.29 (.78), job fits long-range goals 2.10 (1.06), satisfactory career progress 2.10 (1.02), good prospects for advancing 1.99 (1.07), skills fully utilized 1.81 (.97), well-paid 1.80 (.98), have policy responsibility 1.73 (1.10), and set own hours 1.42 (1.22).

Analyses of variance were preformed for each job satisfaction in relation to eight vocational and educational variables: BA or BS psychology degree, whether coursework in supplementary area was taken, whether further education was pursued, type of further degree, area of post-baccalaureate study, whether current job is psychology-related, whether current job is in career choice area, and occupational interest area of current employment.

One of the eight job satisfaction measures was unrelated to any background feature, the one with the poorest rating, "set own hours." Similarly, two background variables were totally unrelated to any job satisfaction—whether supplementary work had been taken along with the psychology major and type of further degree pursued.

Two other background variables were significantly related to only one job satisfaction: (a) Area of post-baccalaureate study was solely related to being well-paid. (People who had subsequently studied engineering, business administration, and medicine were most satisfied, while people who had studied humanities, social sciences, or education were least satisfied with their earnings.) (b) BS graduates were more satisfied with their jobs overall than BA graduates. But the three background variables of job related to psychology, job in one's career choice area, and further education pursued, all enhanced satisfaction on five or six of the job satisfaction measures.

The variable of greatest interest here, however, is the impact of working in different interest areas upon job satisfaction. Job interest area did not relate significantly to either "set own hours" or "have policy responsibility," but it did to the other six satisfaction measures in the following ways. Skills were more fully utilized in jobs in the service and general cultural areas, and *underutilized* in organizational jobs. "Satisfactory career progress" was occurring more in technical, scientific, and general cultural jobs, and occurring least in organizational jobs. Prospects for advancement were brighter for graduates working in business contact, technical, scientific, and general cultural jobs, and least promising for workers in service and organizational jobs. And again, with respect to both "job fits long-range goals" and "satisfied with job," the technical, scientific, and general cultural areas were most satisfying, while organization was least satisfying. Only with respect to "well-paid" did an area of interest other than organization rate poorest: service jobs, and to some extent general cultural jobs, were less satisfying in this regard, compared to business contact and technical jobs.

DISCUSSION

It is important in reading the following to remember that 41% of these 1978-79 graduates chose not to participate. This imparts an inevitable degree of uncertainty to any conclusion.

These results are consistent with those based on a sample which overlapped to some extent with the present one (Lunneborg & Wilson, 1982). There we found that general job satisfaction was associated with business contact and general cultural jobs and not associated with organizational and technical jobs. The underlying details of these earlier results are now clearer and will be elaborated with actual job titles observed in this sample.

1. Psychological skills and knowledge were best utilized in social service jobs (mental health therapist, special education teacher) and general cultural jobs (high school teacher, attorney). However, skills utilization was apparently the only satisfaction that service jobs provided.

2. For high pay, business contact jobs (insurance agent, stockbroker) and technical jobs (computer programmer, human factors engineer) were the best. Service and general cultural jobs especially disappointed these respondents.

3. For the other kinds of satisfactions one can expect for those 5 years out of college, three areas stood out. In addition to technical and general cultural jobs, scientific jobs were satisfying (nurse, dentist, physician).

4. For overall job *dissatisfaction*, organizational jobs had no peer. There was little redeeming said by the 43 people who found themselves as bookkeepers, owners of small businesses, executive secretaries, administrative assistants, and department supervisors.

Curiously, the areas of study most often selected by these dissatisfied people in organization, if they had it to do over again, were business administration and computer science. Thus, although organization may not have been their ideal career choice, they now wish they had had more appropriate business training rather than wish they had entered teaching, a medical field, or counseling.

These results pose a dilemma for undergraduate advisers of psychology majors. On the one hand, the bulk of jobs in American society for recent college graudates is in Roe's organizational area. On the other hand, the satisfactions reported from these jobs by psychology graduates do not compare favorably with the satisfactions to be found in the technical, scientific, and general cultural areas. Even business contact sales jobs pay more, and low-paying service jobs at least use the skills and knowledge gained from the major.

What good, then, is the psychology major for the many people who must take organizational jobs because that's what's available? Are the degree's only virtues those of the liberal arts tradition and personal growth? Will these satisfactions be sufficient to outweigh disillusionment with psychology as career preparation for the business world?

Surely we must forewarn our majors that (a) organization *is* where the jobs are, (b) they may not be very happy in those jobs, and (c) additional degrees in business administration or computer science will probably be necessary for success. To say you can do "anything" with a BA in psychology is as irresponsible as saying there is "nothing" you can do with it. Our students need all the empirical data we can give them on the fates of those who majored before them, the bad news along with the good.

REFERENCES

Korn, J. H., & Lewandowski, M. E. (1981). The clinical bias in the career plans of undergraduates and its impact on students and the profession. *Teaching of Psychology, 8,* 149–152.

Lunneborg, P. W., & Wilson, V. M. (1982). Job satisfaction correlates for college graduates in psychology. *Teaching of Psychology, 9,* 199–201.

Malin, J. T., & Timmreck, C. (1979). Student goals and the undergraduate curriculum. *Teaching of Psychology, 6,* 136–139.

Roe, A. (1956). *The psychology of occupations.* New York: John Wiley.

Titley, R. W., & Titley, B. S. (1982). Academic advising: The neglected dimension in designs for undergraduate education. *Teaching of Psychology, 9,* 45–49.

Ware, M. E., & Meyer, A. E. (1981). Career versatility of the psychology major: A survey of graduates. *Teaching of Psychology, 8,* 12–15.

Woods, P. J. (Ed.). (1979). *The psychology major: Training and employment strategies.* Washington, DC: American Psychological Association.

Section III
Field Placement

Researchers have identified a growing trend in psychology departments to provide field placement experiences for majors. In fact by 1981, more than two-thirds of the psychology departments offered a placement course. They are known by a variety of names including externship, internship, and practicum. We have used the term "field placement" since this term has not been applied to couses that focus specifically on graduate, full-time, or vocational training as the other terms have.

We have organized more than 30 articles into four groups: exploring administrative issues, describing undergraduate placements, describing graduate placements, and evaluating programs. This section can serve as an invaluable resource for both novice and experienced placement supervisors who are searching for implementation techniques, tips for new placement settings, and/or research ideas.

A reader may wonder why we included a field placement section with sections on advising and career development. A brief review of this section's contents will reveal field placement experiences promote academic and career development. For example, field placements afford students an opportunity to acquire experience and to apply their knowledge of psychology to "real-life" situations. Students can begin to integrate the discipline and practice of psychology. Moreover, students can investigate specialized areas of psychology and the world of work. Field experiences provide them with the opportunity to make more informed decisions about career alternatives, including graduate school. Additionally, students can use the experience to identify and evaluate their personal strengths and weaknesses. Finally they acquire work experience and personal contacts. It is not uncommon for placement personnel to offer students full-time jobs upon graduation. Thus, we decided that the intimate relationship between advising, career development, and field placement activities supported inclusion of the latter topic in this book.

1. EXPLORING ADMINISTRATIVE ISSUES

Since the field placement course differs greatly from traditional academic courses, the supervisor often faces many complex and often ambiguous issues. Some of the issues center around peers' resistance to awarding academic credit. However, peer acceptance, if not support, of the course seems the trend more recently. The central issues of concern to most authors in this group of articles were: supervision, selection, training, requirements for credit, placement goals, and agency-university interface. Readers will find themselves considerably enlightened from the thorough discussion of those issues from a variety of perspectives.

Leon VandeCreek and Mitchell Fleischer from Indiana University of Pennsylvania surveyed a stratified sample of 291 psychology departments to describe the role of the field placement course in the undergraduate psychology curriculum. Their study compared the demographics of schools with and without placement programs. The issues they investigated included: course supervision, teaching load reduction, insurance coverage, selection procedures, and course credit requirements. Concluding that programs vary significantly on many of these variables, the authors stated that field placement courses need to be more formalized if they are to attain a more stable position in the academic structure. Their recommendations consisted of the development of formal course outlines, site descriptions, and others. This article provides important insights for "curriculum architects" who want to strengthen their undergraduate offerings with a field placement course. Experienced supervisors can benefit from the comparison of their departments' programs with those described in this article.

Janet Matthews conducted a survey of small liberal arts colleges shortly after she became director of the field placement course at Creighton University. Variability describes the results of her findings. Departments varied considerably in the amount of academic credit they awarded, the educational requirements for on-site supervisors, the length of time the course had existed, the size of student enrollment, and the prerequisites for students taking the course. However, one common finding was the failure of individuals and institutions to carry malpractice insurance. The author emphatically stated that field placement supervisors needed to be informed about the pertinence for carrying malpractice insurance. We encourage readers to evaluate seriously this caveat.

Leon Vande Creek from Indiana University of Pennsylvania and Glenn Thompson from Allegheny College summarized their concerns about the proper management of field placement programs. They offered guidelines to promote the inclusion of psychology content and to justify the awarding of academic credit. The authors also elaborated on the supervisor's responsibilities and the role of malpractice insurance. We can only reiterate our previous comment about the serious attention readers should give to the issue of malpractice insurance.

Edward Barton and Pryse Duerfeldt offered some practical advice and strategies that they developed as field placement supervisors at Northern Michigan University. They identified goals that the field experience typically accomplishes and listed typical problems encountered in supervising placements; such as, unethical student behavior. The authors also described strategies to avoid pitfalls when establishing placements, such as: clarification of client-instructor roles, maintenance of agency rapport, and formal evaluation of student performance. The formal evaluation consisted of a skills' checklist, skills' mastery quizzes, and a record requiring the instructor's signature. This article will appeal to supervisors attempting to improve the quality of their placements and of their students' evaluation.

Donald Wolfgang from Virginia Wesleyan College focused on the problems of supervising placement courses. Maintaining that proper supervision is a chore for which many instructors are unprepared, and in fact underestimate, the author elaborated on six principal supervisory functions. The functions were: creating an attitude among students that the placement is a worthwhile experience, monitoring both the student and the agency, grading the student, helping the student relate the field experience to class work, and counseling the student to reflect on the experience and apply the learnings. This article is particularly noteworthy for new placement directors. It emphasizes the importance of instructor commitment, thorough planning, monitoring, and follow-up to the operation of a field placement course.

Dana Anderson and Debra Stein drew from their experience at Pennsylvania State University in Erie. Their article focused on identifying and meeting the goals of placement students, agencies, and instructors. For example, psychology majors must see the practicum as an important aid to career decision-making or as an opportunity to develop marketable skills. Agencies must increase their service with minimum expense to their personnel. Psychology departments must justify rewarding academic credit for the course. How the program is administered determines the success in meeting these goals. To address these issues, the authors recommended a contract-based procedure for interfacing with the placement agency. Department administrators who have responsibility for assuring the professional and efficient conduct of the course will find the pointers offered here beneficial.

Peter Keller described a method for identifying specific goals and evaluating student progress that he used in conducting field placement courses at Mansfield State College. He drew from eight years of experience with a semester long full-time placement course completed by more than 400 students. His program required students to identify five specific goals that they expected to accomplish during the placement, to maintain weekly progress notes, and to meet with faculty for a goal progress review. His goal-oriented approach has applicability to many placement programs, both large and small, and should be studied by supervisors who want a technique for maintaining controls and avoiding conflicts in evaluating programs and students.

James Dalton from Bloomsburg University of Pennsylvania, focused on ethical issues that he discussed in the seminar component of a placement course. Since ethical issues arise in mental health settings, the course should include discussions about their impact on patients' lives. For example, clients' right to confidentiality and freedom may clash with agencies' responsibilities to parents or the courts. To develop students' ability to deal with those issues, the author suggested discussion of means versus ends, and ethics versus politics. He also provided the address for a placement coordinators' newsletter. Readers concerned about ethics will find Dalton's article a handy resource for a reading list.

The Role of Practicum in the Undergraduate Psychology Curriculum

Leon VandeCreek and
Mitchell Fleischer
Indiana University of Pennsylvania

Although practicum is frequently available to majors, variety in nature and quality is striking, and it seems to lack a mission.

Recommendations on the undergraduate curriculum in psychology have come from several sources in the past 30 years. One of the first reports on the role of psychology as it emerged as an academic discipline was the Harvard Commission Report. Completed in 1947, it was entitled, "The place of psychology in an ideal university" (Gregg, 1970). The report recommended that because scientific methodology was the core of the discipline, psychology courses would be of most benefit if students were taught to approach the subject matter in a questioning or scientific manner. Laboratory courses were the heart of the Commission's recommended curriculum. Career or professional training was not to occur at the undergraduate level, and psychology majors were not to be identified as "psychologists."

In subsequent years three national surveys of undergraduate curricula in psychology have been reported (Kulik, 1973; McKeachie & Milholland, 1961; Wolfle, Buxton, Cofer, Gustad, MacLeod, & McKeachie, 1952). Each report offered searching reviews of undergraduate education and a variety of suggestions for improvement. The first, known as the Wolfle Report, reiterated the recommendations of the Harvard Commission Report that all courses should include scientific methodology. A separate course on experimental methodology would be redundant. Specifically *excluded* were courses aimed at improving student adjustment or imparting technical skills other than methodological ones.

In 1961, the Michigan Report (McKeachie & Milholland, 1961) again recommended that scientific methodology should be the core of the curriculum. However, it acknowledged that a variety of curricular designs was available, including special courses in methodology and independent study projects.

By the time of the most recent report (Kulik, 1973) several trends in course offerings were apparent. During the twenty-year period since the Wolfle Report, courses following a natural science, laboratory model (learning, motivation, physiological) and independent study courses had shown the greatest percentage of increase. Applied courses such as educational psychology, vocational psychology, and personal adjustment courses had shown the greatest decline. However, this decline in applied courses was offset by an increase in experiential components in traditional courses and by separate courses called field work or practicum. Approximately 44% of the respondents to Kulik's survey in 1969 indicated that they offered courses which included at least one hour per week of field experience. Although the Kulik Report noted that a few departments had developed an entire course for field experience, no frequency data were available about this. Kulik suggested that field experiences could play an important role in the psychology curriculum. The enthusiasm of both students and participating faculty seemed encouraging, although the Report concluded that the relationship between conventional classrooms and field sites required clearer articulation.

In subsequent years, this innovation in field experience coursework appears to have grown rapidly, and many participating faculty have described their programs (Barton & Duerfeldt, 1980; Hess, Harrison, Shantz, Fink, Zepelin, Lilliston, Aponte and Korn, 1978; Prerost, 1981; VandeCreek & Thompson, 1977). Problems with site and student selection, evaluations of students, agency supervision, amount of academic credit, and financial and time constraints on the departments have been popular issues. Other authors have described specific types of settings in which students have been placed (Caffrey, Berger, Cole, Marx & Senn, 1977; Hess et al., 1978; Prerost, 1981).

These practicum courses can be clearly distinguished from vocational training and graduate professional training. In vocational training the goal is to produce a set of marketable skills for a specific job. In contrast, practicum courses have typically been described as part of the psychology major or minor and as enhancing the goals of a liberal education. Although there may be career advantages inherent in taking a practicum course, this has not been the primary intent (however, see Pinkus and Korn, 1973, for an obvious exception). Undergraduate practica often have incorporated some amount of training in professional skills such as interviewing, but the extent of such training is minimal compared to graduate professional education.

The number of reports about practicum programs suggests that such courses have been adopted by many departments. Yet, little is known about this innovation. Consequently, the authors conducted a national survey to provide some initial data which could guide departments in the management of their curricula as well as elicit debate within the discipline.

There were few guidelines available to follow in constructing the survey. Consequently, articles which described specific practicum programs were reviewed and questions were devised to elicit data about the ingredients of these courses. Other questions were included based on our experiences in managing the department's program. A copy of the complete survey is available from the authors.

Method

Selection of the Sample. A sample of 499 schools was selected from a comprehensive list of all U.S. colleges and universities offering the bachelor's degree. This sample was stratified by the size of the college/university (tiny = 1-999 students, small = 1000-4999, medium = 5000-9999, large = 10,000 +) and by the region of the country in which it was located (East = New England and Mid-Atlantic states, South = south of the Mason-Dixon line and west to and including Texas, Midwest = all else east of the Rocky Mountains, and West = west of the rockies). Thus, there were 16 cells in the sample, each with approximately 31 schools.

Survey Instrument. The four-page survey consisted of 37 multiple choice and open-ended items. It was sent to the psychology department chair at each school in the sample with a cover letter requesting that it be passed along to the department's practicum coordinator or director, if there was such a person (otherwise the chair was to complete it). The person completing the form had the option of simply checking a space that indicated they had no practicum program and returning the survey. An identical survey was mailed to non-respondents three weeks after the initial mailing.

In addition to the survey instrument, additional data about each department were obtained from the APA's *Graduate Study in Psychology* (APA, 1981) and about the school's locale from the 1970 Census (U.S. Bureau of the Census, 1972).

Respondents. Of the 499 surveys mailed, 291 were returned and completed by a member of a Psychology Department. An additional 29 surveys were returned with the indication that the school had no psychology majors. The total return rate was not consistent across cells, with western schools somewhat less likely to respond, and southern and mid-western schools more likely to do so.

A sample of 48 nonrespondents was telephoned in an attempt to estimate the representativeness of the respondents. Twenty-three percent of these nonrespondents had no psychology department, as opposed to only 9% of respondents. Fifty-seven percent of the nonrespondents claimed to have an undergraduate practicum program, as compared to 65% of respondents. Given the relatively high return rate of the surveys (an estimated 68% of schools with psychology majors) and the apparent similarity of nonrespondents to respondents, as determined by the follow-up, it seems likely that survey respondents are fairly representative of the entire sample. Nevertheless, the reader should be cautioned that the respondents may differ in subtle ways from non-respondents.

Data Analysis. The majority of items used a multiple-choice format which did not involve rater decisions. Open-ended items from the survey were content analyzed by having two raters develop rating schemes and then scoring responses independently. Satisfactory levels (greater than 80% agreement) of inter-rater reliability were achieved for all items.

Analysis of the data was divided into two parts. The first received that amount of credit. Eight percent reported that the "quality" of the learning experience was a major factor in determining the number of credits received. Thus, if a student could be expected to learn more at a site, more credit would be allowed. Usually other factors were combined with this in the final determination of credits. Finally, 16% said that some unspecified combination of factors was involved, or that a negotiation process between student and faculty determined credit. All schools said that students were required to work a certain number of hours per week on-site for each credit hour earned. The mean number of hours per week was 3.1 per semester hour of credit.

In addition to working at the site for a certain number of hours, many schools required their students to participate in classroom activities. Fifty-nine percent reported that they had a formal class meeting for their students. Of these, 62% held weekly meetings, 17% held monthly meetings, and 21% held meeting with some other frequency. Thus, a formal academic experience was an important component of a large number of programs.

Grading. For many students one of the most important elements of any course is the determination of their grade. Traditional grades (A, B, C, etc.) were used by most (74%) of the departments, and the rest used Pass-Fail grades only. Respondents were asked to choose from a list of seven grading mechanisms. The most commonly used mechanisms were agency supervisor ratings (83% selected this) and ratings of a student's daily journal (64%). The next most frequently used were self-evaluations (34%), on-site observations by faculty supervisors (34%), seminar participation (30%), and a research paper (30%). Almost all departments (95%) reported that they used more than one of these grading mechanisms.

A closer look at these data revealed some interesting differences among departments. Of particular interest was the distinction between a research paper and seminar participation on the one hand, as more "traditional" grading mechanisms, and journals, observations and supervisor ratings as being less so. Schools with doctoral programs were significantly less likely to use journals (a less traditional mechanism) in determining grades (X^2 (2) = 8.11, $p<.05$). Only 18% of PhD departments used journals, but 44% of MA departments and 37% of BA departments did so. Similarly, PhD departments were significantly less likely to use on-site faculty observations (another less traditional mechanism) in determining grades (X^2 (2) = 6.67, $p<.05$). Forty-six percent of PhD departments used on-site observations, 63% of MA departments and 71% of BA departments did so.

Site Issues. Respondents were asked to select among 8 site-selection criteria. Two criteria were selected by the majority of respondents: student demand/interest (91%) and agency reputation (85%). Also of some importance were the criteria of distance from campus (43%), faculty supervisor interest (34%), and academic degree of site supervisor (32%). The criteria of professional field of site supervisor (19%), licensure of site supervisor (13%), and number of staff at agency (5%) were clearly of less relevance.

Although less than half of the departments reported using distance from campus in selecting sites, most sites were close to campus. Forty percent of the departments said that was a comparison of schools that had a practicum program with those that did not. The second was an effort to comprehensively describe the programs that were reported. Throughout the analysis, comparisons were made between subgroupings based on the highest degree offered by the department (BA, MA, PhD) and rural vs. urban/suburban location based on the U.S. Census Standard Metropolitan Statistical Area (U.S. Bureau of the Census, 1972).

Results

Who Has a Program? Sixty-five percent (188 of 291) of the respondents claimed to have a practicum program. Because of the structure of the survey it was possible to obtain only a small amount of information about departments that did not have a program. However, enough information was available to permit several interesting comparisons. Departments offering the PhD were significantly less likely to have a practicum program in their undergraduate curriculum than were departments offering only bachelor or masters degrees (Table 1, X^2 (2) = 9.04, $p<.02$). In addition, departments at smaller schools were found to be more likely to offer a all of their sites were local (within 20 miles of campus). Over all respondents, a mean of 85% of sites were local. On the average, 11% of sites were between 20 and 50 miles away, and only 4% were more than 50 miles from campus. More than half of the departments (51%) had no sites more than 20 miles from campus, and 77% had no sites more than 50 miles away.

Another set of questions asked about the types of

Table 1. Incidence of Practicum by Highest Departmental Degree and Geographic Region

	No	Yes	Total
Highest Degree Offered*			
BA	45	101	146
MA	18	45	63
PhD	40	42	82
Total	103	188	291
Geographic Region**			
East	21	52	73
Midwest	28	54	82
South	42	47	89
West	12	35	47
Total	103	188	291

* X^2 (2) = 9.04, $p<.02$.
** X^2 (3) = 8.87, $p<.04$.

practicum (F(1, 285) = 5.33, $p<.05$). The mean number of students at schools offering practicum was 6735, whereas schools without a practicum had a mean of 8990 students. However, no differences were found based on the size of the psychology department itself, as determined by number of faculty teaching undergraduates or by the number of undergraduate majors. Another interesting observation was that schools in the South were less likely to offer practicum (Table 1, X^2 (3) = 8.87, $p<.04$). Finally, there were no differences found between schools located in rural settings and those in urban/suburban settings.

Age and Size of Programs. Practicum programs seem to be a relatively recent phenomenon. Respondents were asked in what year their program had begun. From 168 responses, the range was from 1953 to 1981 (the year of the survey). However, more than 80% indicated a start in 1970 or later, and 38% indicated that their programs had started since 1975.

The size of the programs varied greatly. All respondents with a program indicated they provided placements during the academic year. The number of students enrolled during placements that each program used. Not surprisingly there was a strong emphasis on mental health settings. Eighty-nine percent indicated they used residential treatment settings, and 77% said they used outpatient mental health settings such as community mental health centers. Other types of settings that received heavy use were medical/health settings (66%), schools (60%), and community action and advocacy agencies (60%). Settings receiving relatively low usage included industrial/organizational (I/O) settings (42%), outpatient correctional settings (34%), and what might be termed "self-contained" settings such as the Washington Center for Learning Alternatives or the Deveraux Foundation that provide a variety of field placement experiences under their direction (16%). The relatively low use of I/O placements is surprising considering the current emphasis by many students on business oriented careers. A final point of interest here is the question of variety. The mean number of types of placements chosen was 4.8, with a range from 1 to 9 (out of a possible 10 including "other").

Problems with Practicum Programs. The final question on the survey asked "What are the major problems you face with practicum?'' A total of 216 separate statements were reported from 156 respondents to this question. These statements were content analyzed and divided into 20 response categories. The problem most frequently cited (by 15% of the respondents) was that the program was too time consuming or that there were too many students to supervise. Ten percent cited problems with agency supervisors such as lack of time spent with students or incompetence. Nine percent stated they lacked enough agencies in their local area, and 6% stated that lack of teaching credit was a problem. Another 6% cited the general ''low quality'' of the experience their students received at agencies.

The 20 categories were then pooled along conceptual lines. Thus defined, 21% cited a variety of agency problems (including supervision, exploitation of students, etc.); 15% cited student problems (including lack of student interest and transportation problems); 9% cited location problems (not enough sites in the area); 23% cited administrative problems within their college/university, and 13% cited lack of support or interest among their colleagues. Only 10% of the respondents stated outright that they had no problems with their practicum program.

Discussion

It is clear that what was once regarded as an innovation by a few departments in the 1960s has now become a very widely available course. The 1969 Kulik survey (Kulik, 1973) did not even ask about the availability of courses devoted entirely to field experience. However, by 1981, two thirds of departments offered such a course. In addition, many departments offer it for variable credit with a few students received that amount of credit. Eight percent reported that the ''quality'' of the learning experience was a major factor in determining the number of credits received. Thus, if a student could be expected to learn more at a site, more credit would be allowed. Usually other factors were combined with this in the final determination of credits. Finally, 16% said that some unspecified combination of factors was involved, or that a negotiation process between student and faculty determined credit. All schools said that students were required to work a certain number of hours per week on-site for each credit hour earned. The mean number of hours per week was 3.1 per semester hour of credit.

In addition to working at the site for a certain number of hours, many schools required their students to participate in classroom activities. Fifty-nine percent reported that they had a formal class meeting for their students. Of these, 62% held weekly meetings, 17% held monthly meetings, and 21% held meeting with some other frequency. Thus, a formal academic experience was an important component of a large number of programs.

Grading. For many students one of the most important elements of any course is the determination of their grade. Traditional grades (A, B, C, etc.) were used by most (74%) of the departments, and the rest used Pass-Fail grades only. Respondents were asked to choose from a list of seven grading mechanisms. The most commonly used mechanisms were agency supervisor ratings (83% selected this) and ratings of a student's daily journal (64%). The next most frequently used were self-evaluations (34%), on-site observa-

tions by faculty supervisors (34%), seminar participation (30%), and a research paper (30%). Almost all departments (95%) reported that they used more than one of these grading mechanisms.

A closer look at these data revealed some interesting differences among departments. Of particular interest was the distinction between a research paper and seminar participation on the one hand, as more ''traditional'' grading mechanisms, and journals, observations and supervisor ratings as being less so. Schools with doctoral programs were significantly less likely to use journals (a less traditional mechanism) in determining grades ($X^2(2) = 8.11$, $p < .05$). Only 18% of PhD departments used journals, but 44% of MA departments and 37% of BA departments did so. Similarly, PhD departments were significantly less likely to use on-site faculty observations (another less traditional mechanism) in determining grades ($X^2(2) = 6.67$, $p < .05$). Forty-six percent of PhD departments used on-site observations, 63% of MA departments and 71% of BA departments did so.

Site Issues. Respondents were asked to select among 8 site-selection criteria. Two criteria were selected by the majority of respondents: student demand/interest (91%) and agency reputation (85%). Also of some importance were the criteria of distance from campus (43%), faculty supervisor interest (34%), and academic degree of site supervisor (32%). The criteria of professional field of site supervisor (19%), licensure of site supervisor (13%), and number of staff at agency (5%) were clearly of less relevance.

Although less than half of the departments reported using distance from campus in selecting sites, most sites were close to campus. Forty percent of the departments said that all of their sites were local (within 20 miles of campus). Over all respondents, a mean of 85% of sites were local. On the average, 11% of sites were between 20 and 50 miles away, and only 4% were more than 50 miles from campus. More than half of the departments (51%) had no sites more than 20 miles from campus, and 77% had no sites more than 50 miles away.

Another set of questions asked about the types of placements that each program used. Not surprisingly there was a strong emphasis on mental health settings. Eighty-nine percent indicated they used residential treatment settings, and 77% said they used outpatient mental health settings such as community mental health centers. Other types of settings that received heavy use were medical/health settings (66%), schools (60%), and community action and advocacy agencies (60%). Settings receiving relatively low usage included industrial/organizational (I/O) settings (42%), outpatient correctional settings (34%), and what might be termed ''self-contained'' settings such as the Washington Center for Learning Alternatives or the Deveraux Foundation that provide a variety of field placement experiences under their direction (16%). The relatively low use of I/O placements is surprising considering the current emphasis by many students on business oriented careers. A final point of interest here is the question of variety. The mean number of types of placements chosen was 4.8, with a range from 1 to 9 (out of a possible 10 including ''other'').

Problems with Practicum Programs. The final question on the survey asked ''What are the major problems you face with practicum?" A total of 216 separate statements were reported from 156 respondents to this question. These statements were content analyzed and divided into 20 response categories. The problem most frequently cited (by 15% of the respondents) was that the program was too time consuming or that there were too many students to supervise. Ten percent cited problems with agency supervisors such as lack of time spent with students or incompetence. Nine percent stated they lacked enough agencies in their local area, and 6% stated that lack of teaching credit was a problem. Another 6% cited the general "low quality" of the experience their students received at agencies.

The 20 categories were then pooled along conceptual lines. Thus defined, 21% cited a variety of agency problems (including supervision, exploitation of students, etc.); 15% cited student problems (including lack of student interest and transportation problems); 9% cited location problems (not enough sites in the area); 23% cited administrative problems within their college/university, and 13% cited lack of support or interest among their colleagues. Only 10% of the respondents stated outright that they had no problems with their practicum program.

Discussion

It is clear that what was once regarded as an innovation by a few departments in the 1960s has now become a very widely available course. The 1969 Kulik survey (Kulik, 1973) did not even ask about the availability of courses devoted entirely to field experience. However, by 1981, two thirds of departments offered such a course. In addition, many departments offer it for variable credit with a few students permitted to earn as much as 20% of their undergraduate credit in practicum. It is likely that no other undergraduate psychology course has grown this rapidly. Its growth is all the more remarkable in light of the conclusion of the Wolfle Report (Wolfle, et al., 1956) that such coursework was to be specifically excluded.

Other comparisons with the data of the Kulik Report further attest to the high visibility of practicum. Kulik reported the percentages of departments which offered a set of thirty different courses in 1969. When those data are compared with the frequency (65%) with which practicum is *now* found, only five courses received a higher ranking by Kulik: General, Social, Abnormal, Tests and Measurements, and Independent Study. Courses in Experimental Methodology receive about an equivalent ranking.

The frequency with which practicum is available does not imply popularity with all faculty members, nor does it indicate that courses have become fully accepted into the curriculum. In fact, in nearly half of the cases, critical decisions about practicum are made by only one person, and in more than one-third of the departments, the entire operation is managed by a single individual. Forty percent of schools with practicum offer no teaching credit for faculty supervision, and more than half receive no travel reimbursement for on-site visits. Many respondents also cited a lack of support or interest among their faculty colleagues as a problem. These factors indicate that the practicum course has not yet become entrenched into many departments and, in those departments, is not yet regarded as a full-fledged part of the curriculum. One

wonders how many of these programs would be discontinued if the current faculty manager left the department. Pinkus (1979) has described the demise of one career oriented program due to lack of faculty interest.

The availability of practicum and the way the program is managed varied according to the degree-granting capability of the departments. Departments offering doctorates were less likely to provide practicum for their undergraduates. Perhaps such departments have faculty who are more interested in doing research, or their jobs require a higher output of publications than do faculty of purely undergraduate departments. Such "doctoral departments" might be less likely to initiate a practicum because supervision of practicum is less likely to lead to successful grants or publications. It also may be viewed as less prestigious and less likely to earn a promotion.

Respondents to the survey gave high endorsement to two purposes for practicum programs. "Career development" was given the highest rating. The second purpose, "to observe in action material taught in other courses," is more of a liberal education goal. That both purposes should receive high ratings suggests that many respondents viewed practicum as being able to fulfill both functions. Some critics of practicum (Enteman, 1979; French, 1979; Goldwin, 1976) have described the career development function of practicum as a serious threat to liberal education. They view these two functions as antagonistic, and fear that the popularity of practicum-type courses reflects the shift of undergraduate education toward vocational training. The survey data offer no clues to how departments integrate these two purposes, but some guidance for this question can be found in educational philosophy.

Most classroom learning follows a pattern that Coleman (1976) has called information assimilation. It includes four steps: (a) transmitting information in lecture or written form, (b) organizing this information into general principles, (c) learning how to apply the general principles in new situations, and (d) applying the principles. The weakness of many courses is that learning often stops at the second step without opportunity for application. The failure to provide opportunity for application also reduces the excitement of the material for the student, and instructors frequently must resort to external motivators such as grades. Candland (1980) made a similar point when he stated that a good education should produce persons "who both think and act" (p. 195), and that this combination of thinking and acting provides the best of education. The action component of learning can be built into some courses through laboratories. Many psychology courses also incorporate a research project to provide an "action" component in learning how to do research.

But courses which emphasize content over research methodology may have no application phase available. For example, where is the application in courses such as Child Psychology, Abnormal Psychology, or Industrial-Organizational Psychology? While field trips, role playing, and classroom simulations may provide some opportunity for application, these classroom strategies pale in comparison with the learning that could occur if the students were actually placed in a real "laboratory" such as a head start program or a personnel office. Practicum can be the vehicle for such applications.

If practicum is to provide the third and fourth steps in the information assimilation pattern of learning, then it must be closely tied to the general principles supplied by the other courses. One of the responsibilities of the faculty supervisor should be to insure that students complete these last two steps in the learning pattern. This will require firm direction from the supervisor since the student may quickly become involved in the exciting activities of the site without regard to application of general principles.

Practicum courses can contribute to a liberal education through the application of a second model of learning as well. This model may be called experiential learning (Coleman, 1976). Both thinking and application are required in this model, too, but the steps proceed in an opposite order from the first model. The steps include (a) carrying out an action in a particular situation, (b) understanding the effects of this action, (c) comprehending the general principle under which this particular action and situation falls, and (d) applying the general principle in new situations. In this model students do not necessarily begin with applying principles from other courses although this might be possible. Rather, this model permits students to first experience the activities of the setting and then to generate general principles. Whereas students are usually more enthused by this pattern of learning because of the heavy action component, the risk is that they will not proceed to steps three and four to understand the general principles involved. The faculty supervisor's job in this case should be to assist the students in comprehending the new principles resulting from their experiences.

Vocational training can be distinguished from experiential learning as defined here. Vocational training primarily emphasizes the first two steps of the experiential learning model. That is, the learning and application of general principles is not necessary, or at best is secondary to the acquisition of specific skills. Thus, a practicum course can easily disintegrate into vocational training if the student is not guided into formulating general principles from experiences. At the same time it is obvious that students who complete a practicum under either model will have learned some skills which will provide career advantages. The same could be claimed for the student who obtained a research assistant job because of good research skills acquired in research methodology courses.

It is important to see that though students may be enthused by practicum in either model, it is essential for the faculty supervisor to assure that students progress through all four steps. If the information assimilation model is used, then general principles learned in other courses must be identified and then observed or applied in the practicum setting. If the experiential model of learning is chosen then general principles must be developed from the experiences themselves. The supervisor's task in either case is a difficult one, and if it is to be done well, the supervisor will need adequate resources such as time, teaching credit, and personal access to the student. Kramer and Harshman (1979) have recently described one university-wide approach to manage some of the supervisory problems.

Conclusion

Undergraduate practicum is now riding a wave of popularity. It is probably one of the most widely accepted innovations in undergraduate education in psychology. Yet, there is cause for concern. Practicum has developed without any guiding principles from the discipline of psychology. In spite of the rate at which practicum credit may be accruing on students' transcripts, practicum as a course is not well integrated into many departments.

If practicum is to survive and attain a more stable position in undergraduate curricula, then it must assume a more formal academic structure. The steps to such stability might include developing more checks and balances such as policy committees in the college/university and department; requiring formal course outlines or practicum site descriptions which spell out course purposes for review by faculty and students; involving more department faculty in such aspects of the program as student selection, placement, site selection, and general course requirements; and obtaining some of the typical academic accoutrements such as teaching credit, reasonable faculty-student ratios, and travel reimbursement. Without these elements of academic respectability, practicum may face serious cutbacks in competition for shrinking budgets.

The overriding conclusion to be drawn from the data that have been presented here is that, although practicum is frequently available, it is different things to different departments. The variety is more striking than the similarities, and there are few consistently found mechanisms of quality control. It has grown rapidly without any overriding sense of mission. What is needed is discussion about its purposes, its operation, and its evaluation.

References

American Psychological Association. *Graduate study in psychology*. Washington, DC: Author, 1981.

Barton, E. J., & Duerfeldt, P. H. Undergraduate psychology practica pragmatism. *Teaching of Psychology*, 1980, *7*, 146-149.

Caffrey, B., Berger, L., Cole, S., Marx, D., & Senn, D. Integrating professional programs in a traditional undergraduate psychology program. *Teaching of Psychology*, 1977, *4*, 7-13.

Candland, D. K. Speaking words and doing deeds. *American Psychologist*, 1980, *35*, 191-198.

Coleman, J. S. Differences between experiential and classroom learning. In M. T. Keeton and Associates, *Experiential learning: Rationale, characteristics, and assessment*. San Francisco: Jossey-Bass, 1976.

Enteman, W. F. When does liberal education become vocational training? *Liberal Education*, 1979, *65*, 167-171.

French, D. Closet vocationalists among proponents of the liberal arts. *Liberal Education*, 1979, *65*, 470-477.

Goldwin, R. The future of liberal education. *Educational Record*, Spring 1976, 111-116.

Gregg, A. The place of psychology in an ideal university. *American Psychologist*, 1970, *25*, 391-410.

Hess, A. K., Harrison, A. O., Shantz, D. W., Fink, R. S., Zepelin, H., Lilliston, L., Aponte, J. F., & Korn, J. H. Critical issues in undergraduate training in various community settings. *Teaching of Psychology*, 1978, *5*, 81-86.

Kramer, T. J., & Harshman, E. A model for faculty supervision of interns. In P. J. Woods (Ed.), *The psychology major*. Washington, DC: American Psychological Association, 1979.

Kulik, J. A. *Undergraduate education in psychology*. Washington, DC: American Psychological Association, 1973.

McKeachie, W. J., & Milholland, J. E. *Undergraduate curricula in psychology*. Chicago: Scott, Foresman, 1961.

Pinkus, R. L. Career training and the definition of liberal arts education: Philosophy, politics, and money. In P. J. Woods (Ed.), *The psychology major*. Washington, DC: American Psychological Association, 1979.

Pinkus, R. B., & Korn, J. H.   The professional option: An alternative to graduate work in psychology. *American Psychologist,* 1973, *28,* 710-718.

Prerost, F. J.   The feasibility of undergraduate field experience in child psychology: Program factors and suggestions. *Teaching of Psychology,* 1981, *8,* 19-22.

U.S. Bureau of Census.   *Census of population: 1970; Characteristics of the population, Part A, number of inhabitants.* Washington, DC: U.S. Government Printing Office, 1972.

VandeCreek, L., & Thompson, G.   Management of undergraduate psychology internships. *Teaching of Psychology,* 1977, *4,* 177-180.

Wolfle, D., Buxton, C. E., Cofer, C. N., Gustad, J. W., MacLeod, R. B., & McKeachie, W. J.   *Improving undergraduate instruction in psychology.* New York: Macmillan, 1952.

Notes

1. The contribution of the two authors was equal; author order was determined by coin flip.

Undergraduate Field Placement: Survey and Issues

Janet R. Matthews
Creighton University

A summary of responses from 29 Liberal Arts College psychology departments shows some trends in the offering of experiential learning.

This survey stemmed mainly from the author's curiosity about undergraduate field placement programs. Having recently been appointed as director of such a program, the author began reading about these programs. One result of this reading was that many additional questions were raised. What types of field placement program exist within undergraduate psychology departments? What is the typical enrollment in such a program? How often does the campus supervisor visit the placement site? What types of credentials do site supervisors need to have? What about malpractice coverage for such programs?

Since the undergraduate student on field placement is frequently viewed as being a "paraprofessional," perhaps some definition of this term is also needed. According to O'Leary and Wilson (1975), a paraprofessional is someone who works as an assistant to a person with a professional degree, license, or certificate. Thus, it is an umbrella term which does fit the field placement student's role, regardless of the type of setting in which the student is placed.

A somewhat different approach to identifying the potential role of the undergraduate field placement student is taken by Christensen, Miller, and Munoz (1978). The distinction which they make between "partners" and "paraprofessionals" has direct bearing on the training which is, or in some cases is not, provided for the undergraduates we are placing in field sites. They suggest that the title "paraprofessional" carries responsibility and that such a person needs to have prior training for specific functions. They suggest that the term "partners" is more appropriate for most undergraduates on field placement. This term is used to indicate individuals who will participate in treatment programs as assistants, data gatherers, or companions.

Regardless of the confusion about the label for, and functions of, the undergraduate psychology student on a field placement, the experience appears to have justification. The student on placement has the opportunity to observe in action the theories taught in many of our classes. Such an experience can make class material more mean-

ingful. The field placement course also serves a career development function. What may sound like a fascinating career when described in a textbook may not be right for a given individual. Having a small sample of the demands of certain jobs while an undergraduate seems preferable to the investment of many years in graduate school in terms of choosing a potential career.

Sample.   In order to tie together the demands of directing an undergraduate field placement program and the reasons for having one at all, some compilation of information on these programs appeared warranted. Since it would not have been feasible to write all undergraduate psychology departments to ask about the presence of a field placement program, some small listing of such schools was needed. Small liberal arts colleges appeared to be an appropriate source of information; and thus, the 43 programs included in the Cole and Van Krevelen (1977) study of small liberal arts colleges were used. A letter explaining the purpose of the present investigation as well as a one page questionnaire was sent to each of these psychology departments. According to Cole and Van Krevelen, the schools within this group have a median full-time psychology faculty of 4.2 with the range being from 2 to 10. Of the 43 psychology departments contacted, 29 responded to this survey. The student body of these responding institutions ranged from 600 to 2275 with a median of 1260. Geographically, the schools ranged from coast to coast and included 19 different states. Many of the respondents provided considerable detail about their programs in addition to that requested on the questionnaire. Although the departments described in this survey are not meant to be a representative sample of undergraduate psychology departments, they do provide data upon which to build in terms of considering the scope and problems of undergraduate field placement programs.

Survey Data.   As can be seen in Table 1, the majority of the programs responding to this survey do have field placement programs. While graduate students in field placements may be paid for their work, from the data reported here it appears that this is not the typical arrangement for the undergraduate student. Perhaps as a method of assuring some degree of academic achievement for the educational credit given, most of these programs require some work in addition to that which is done at the placement site. This additional work included required readings, a formal written paper, seminars, a final examination, and keeping a journal of the activities in the applied setting.

Table 1
Answers to General Questions About
Field Placement Programs

Questions	Yes	Occasionally	No
Program Available?	22		7
Are Students Paid?	2	5	15
Malpractice Insurance Available?			22
Additional Work Required?	18	1	3

Yet another way of approaching the academic training in conjunction with a field placement course was provided in additional comments from one responding institution. The field placement at that school is seen as one course with a normal term load being four courses. Taken concurrently with the field placement is a "practicum seminar." This seminar meets for three hours each week as part of the student's regular course load.

Since academic credit is being given for the field placement experience, an area of interest is the amount of credit allowed. In some programs, the credit is variable. The specific number of credit hours given may be related to the number of hours/week spent at the placement site and/or the amount of additional academic work agreed upon by the student. In other programs, credit for field placement is treated like other academic courses with a standard number of hours being specified. Data from this survey indicate that half of the schools offer the rather standard three semester hours credit for their field placement course. The range was from one semester hour to 16 quarter hours. The school reporting the possibility of 16 quarter hours credit raises another issue relative to the undergraduate field placement course. Is it better to treat this experience as equivalent to other courses and conduct it in a similar manner to those courses or to treat it more like the internship experience of the graduate student in one of the applied fields of psychology? Shiverick (1977) has reported on what he describes as a successful full-time clinical practicum for undergraduate students. Such a program, however, was not typical of those responding to this survey.

Perhaps the most distressing data from Table 1 involves malpractice insurance. Vande Creek and Thompson (1977) have previously suggested that malpractice-type problems associated with student field placement experiences may not be covered by standard university insurance programs. Despite this information, none of the 22 programs responding affirmatively in this survey carried such special insurance. One respondent did add that university did not have malpractice insurance yet. Such a remark could be taken to indicate that they are considering it. Cole (1977) reported that the placement agencies used for his undergraduate

practicum in clinical psychology accepted legal responsibility for the work done by the students. This article does not state, however, whether Cole, as the students' university supervisor, or his university are covered in the event of malpractice problems.

Typically the undergraduate field placement program is directed by only one faculty member rather than several being involved in the program. This may be because of faculty size or perhaps it is limited to those whose degrees are in applied areas of psychology. In a few cases, the faculty member in charge of the program was the one whose area of specialization was most closely related to the type of placement being used rather than approaching the field placement as a course taught by a particular faculty member. Such an approach to field placement appears to treat the experience more like an independent study project than an ongoing class.

An issue which might be raised about field placement for academic credit is whether or not such a course should receive a letter grade. Some programs have moved to the position of using a pass/fail system for experiential courses including field placements. The majority (68%) of those responding to this survey, however, chose to use the more traditional letter grading system. The data available from this survey do not provide information on the basis for such grades. It is possible that the sources vary depending upon the types of additional work required as well as the willingness of the site supervisors to participate in the grading process.

This issue of grading leads to questions about the types of supervision these students are receiving at their respective field placements. One item on this survey dealt with requirements for the educational level of the supervisory staff at the field placement site. Of the 22 programs having field placement courses, 9 had no specific educational requirements for the field supervisors. An additional 4 programs required that the supervisor be "competent" in the particular field but did not specify any educational level relative to such competence. In several of these 13 programs which did not specify an educational level for field placement supervision on site, they added that although they would prefer someone with at least a master's degree, such people were just not always available. A question might be raised as to whether we are lowering academic standards in order to obtain field placement experience for our students. This statement is not meant to be critical of those making such a comment, as the author is well aware, from personal experience, of the dilemma involved. The comment is intended, however, to lead to some personal questioning of our motivations in choosing field placement sites. When community programs which have the potential to provide a good learning experience are directed by people with minimal formal education, a decision must be made regarding the acceptability of the placement. Some universities are located such that limited choice of available field placement sites is a definite problem. Seven of the 22 field placement programs stated that they required a minimum of a master's degree from their site supervisor and the final 2 programs required a terminal degree (MSW, Ph.D., or MD.)

Not all of the supervision is done by someone at the field site. Since the work is done for course credit at a university, there is also someone on the academic faculty who is involved. This faculty member or members will typically make site visits to the various facilities at which students are placed. Considerable variability was reported, however, in the frequency of such visits. One or two visits per student during the term was the most frequently reported level of activity (45%). In 23% of the programs in this survey, it was reported that the frequency of site visits varied, but no specific numbers were provided. Reasons for this variation included the distance to the site and the type of facility used. An additional 18% of the programs reported 2-3 site visits per student. The remaining programs reported site visits of 2-10 per student, 4-5 per student, and weekly visits. One important factor for the university course supervisor to remember, regardless of the number of site visits which are made, is to clearly establish where the jurisdictions of the university and site supervisors, respectively, end. Harrison (1978) reported on the difficulties which can arise for the student if the university supervisor tells the student to do one thing and the site supervisor says that the student is to do just the opposite.

Enrollment in this type of course was found to vary considerably. The range was from 1 to over 20 with the median class having 5 or less students. Although data are not available on the typical course enrollment at the institutions included in this survey, it seems quite possible that many of the other courses offered have larger enrollments. There are several potential reasons for the low enrollment in field placement courses. It is possible that limited placements are available and only a few students could be accommodated during any given semester. Alternatively, faculty and/or student interest may not be strongly supportive of such a course. Cole and Van Krevelen (1977) reported in their survey of liberal arts colleges that none of the schools contacted considered field work to be indispensable to a major in psychology. It is also possible that university faculty find it unwieldy to supervise more than ten students during any given term and thus limit the enrollment in such courses. Regardless of the reason for the limited enrollment in these classes, it seems to be an issue worth considering. If universities demand specified numbers of student contacts per faculty member, the psychology faculty member who supervises such a program may be in a somewhat untenable position.

The length of time these programs have been in existence varied as greatly as did the enrollment. There was one respondent who stated that although that department did not currently offer a field placement program, such a program was in the planning stage and was expected to begin within the next two years. From those programs already in existence, the duration was from 1 to 20 years with a median of 4 years. Thus, the idea of field placement in the undergraduate psychology department appears to be a relatively new phenomenon. The recency of the development of these programs may be contributing to the small enrollment as well. While novelty in a course may be attractive to some students, others may feel more comfortable following a well-established sequence of course offerings.

A final area covered in the survey was the prerequisites for this course. From the information in this survey, there appears to be no standard prerequisite for undergraduate field placement enrollment. Only one of the programs said that they had no prerequisites. Some programs used junior or senior standing as a prerequisite and others limited enrollment to junior and senior psychology majors. Several programs reported screening procedures through which "inappropriate" people were identified. This screening might be conducted by a single individual, such as the course director or department chairperson, or by a departmental committee. Approval by the staff of the potential placement was also mentioned as an acceptance requirement. Terms such as "responsible" and "mature" were used to describe those students who were considered appropriate for field placement. Three programs mentioned the importance of a student having preprofessional plans prior to acceptance for field placement. One program specified that in order to be admitted to the field placement course, a student must have at least a 3.0 GPA in the major. Perhaps the most stringent criteria of those responding to this survey was senior standing and completion of the psychology major. To complete the psychology major in that program the student must pass written and oral comprehensive exams and complete an undergraduate thesis. With such requirements it is not surprising that only 1-3 students per term are enrolled in this field placement course.

Conclusions. From the material presented in this article, different readers may be able to find material which is of importance to them and their programs. It was gratifying to see the amount of additional information which was provided by many of those who responded to this survey. From this limited sample, there is an indication that undergraduate field placement programs do exist in many regions of the country. These programs appear to vary more than we would hope other courses of like title do. Although there are individual differences in what is covered in introductory psychology, for example, there is a tendency to see them as comparable. If a student transfers from one school to another, many of the courses taken at the first school are seen as comparable to ones at the second school and easily accepted. But what about student field placements? Is there some basis for working on comparability of these experiences? It seems that a forum is needed for increased communication among faculty who direct such programs. On the graduate level, for example, directors of clinical training meet and communicate with each other. This author is unaware of any such system of communication among the directors of undergraduate field placement programs.

Another issue which is illustrated in this survey, but certainly not resolved, is malpractice coverage for undergraduate field placement programs. If these programs are to continue to exist and be made into strong educational experiences, perhaps it is time for their directors to stop ignoring the issue of insurance coverage. The naive faculty member could agree to direct such a course without even realizing the potential financial problems resulting from a malpractice suit. Some universities may have insurance which covers such courses, but that did not appear to be the typical situation.

It is hoped that this survey will stimulate others to write about unique aspects of, and problems with, their own field placement programs. Such a sharing of information seems of particular importance for this type of course because of its relative recency within academic psychology on the undergraduate level. It is a course which was not an option for most faculty when they were undergraduate students. They are thus more removed from it than from many of their other classes. Directors of these programs could profit from the successes and problems of their colleagues to compensate for their own lack of personal experience.

References

Christensen, A., Miller, W. R., & Munoz, R. F. Paraprofessionals, partners, peers, paraphernalia, and print: Expanding mental health service delivery. *Professional Psychology,* 1978, *9,* 249-270.

Cole, D., & Van Krevelen, A. Psychology departments in small liberal arts colleges: Results of a survey. *Teaching of Psychology,* 1977, *4,* 163-168.

Cole, S. Practicum in clinical psychology. *Teaching of Psychology,* 1977, *4,* 9-10.

Harrison, A. O. Intervention in battered child families. *Teaching of Psychology,* 1978, 5, 81-82.

O'Leary, K. D., & Wilson, G. T. *Behavior therapy: Application and outcome.* Englewood Cliffs, NJ: Prentice-Hall, 1975.

Shiverick, D. D. A full-time clinical practicum for undergraduates. *Teaching of Psychology,* 1977, *4,* 188-190.

Vande Creek, L., & Thompson, G. Management of undergraduate psychology internships. *Teaching of Psychology,* 1977, *4,* 177-180.

Management of Undergraduate Psychology Internships

Leon Vande Creek
Indiana University of Pennsylvania
and Glenn Thompson
Allegheny College

Pitfalls and rewards for teachers operating or planning internship programs are assessed by these two experienced intern supervisors.

Many psychology departments today include in their curricula one or more courses which involve work in an off-campus agency. These courses have increased in number and variety for many reasons, chief among them probably being the heavy student demand for relevance in education. In addition, there have been repeated documentations of the manpower shortage in the mental health field (Albee, 1959, 1968); reports of successful internship programs, beginning with Holzberg and his colleagues (Holzberg, 1963; Holzberg, Whiting & Lowry, 1964; Umbarger, 1962); and evidence that college students could be effective therapeutic agents (Gruver, 1971).

Although only a few such undergraduate internship programs have been described in the professional literature, discussions with psychology departments, many other departments, and with mental health agencies have quickly uncovered the fact that a multitude of such programs exist today. For example, at Indiana University of Pennsylvania, a small to moderate sized university, there are now about 17 departments which offer, or are hoping to offer, some kind of internship experience. During the past four years the psychology department has placed students in at least 15 different settings. Allegheny College, a small independent liberal arts college, presently offers 34 internship settings representing 12 different departments. The psychology department alone offers seven different intern placement settings. Most of this internship emphasis has developed during

the past two years, and current expectations are that fieldwork will continue to expand. Such rapid development places a strain on quality control efforts.

This article summarizes several serious concerns of the authors about guaranteeing proper management of undergraduate psychology intern programs, especially if they are to continue to warrant academic credit for the work.

Academic and Professional Considerations. Within the psychology department, undergraduate internships run the risk of being viewed as providing easy grades, technical job training, or "credit for living," rather than a course in which psychology content is emphasized and for which academic credit should be offered. Consequently, it is important for a department to clearly define the ingredients of an internship program. The following guidelines are suggested: (1) An internship must emphasize supervised learning in an activity not otherwise available within the department. (2) The setting should have a professional person assigned to supervise the intern. (3) The internship should be planned in advance of the intern's arrival with both agency and academic supervisors agreeing on the content of the program for the intern. (4) The goal must be an increase in the intern's knowledge and/or skills regarding a specific area of the profession, not the carrying out of "busywork" or enhancing the staff of an agency.

These guidelines are intended to assure that the intern's

academic program will be enhanced. The authors can think of many interesting experiences that would provide a valuable learning experience for students (getting married, traveling across the country, etc.), but for which academic credit should *not* be allotted. Similarly, participating in volunteer work that is available to anyone should not qualify for credit unless it is very clear that it fits adequately into an academic plan for the student. Experience in living does not warrant academic credit.

If the intern is to be actively involved in agency activities, then an ethical issue is immediately raised. At what point is a student to be seen as a psychologist? The APA ethical standards (1963) state that the student of psychology who assumes the role of psychologist shall be considered a psychologist. The code emphasizes the importance of maintaining the highest standards of service and competence and discouraging the practice of psychology by unqualified persons. On the other hand, the psychologist as teacher is enjoined to recognize his primary obligation to help others acquire knowledge and skill. It is clear, then, that the supervisor must insure that the intern understands and follows the code of ethics.

A second issue is whether an intern can provide an effective service to the agency and to the clients of that agency or whether service should even be a goal of an internship program. There is considerable research support demonstrating the effectiveness of student therapists. It would not be possible to review these data in this paper, but as far back as 1966 Poser found that untrained college women produced more positive change in hospitalized chronic schizophrenics than did professionals. Other studies with varied samples present similar support. Gruver (1971) presented a good review of the situation. Student therapists have been shown to be particularly effective with adolescents and children, and with the proper incentive and personality characteristics and training, they can be of potential service to the needs of the mental health field. In spite of this, if academic credit is involved, the major reason for internships should not be service, but training of the student. Service can only be seen as a possible by-product.

Credit and Grades. Because undergraduate internships are often regarded by faculty as being unworthy of much, if any, credit, a vicious cycle may develop. If intern programs are not deemed academic, then inadequate resources and staff time will be allotted to the operation of the intern program. Such programs run the risk of becoming casual, hit-or-miss, not worthy of formal academic recognition. Eventually students recognize the lackluster attitude of faculty and begin to cut corners in their intern activities, leading their setting supervisors to deny them all but the most routine tasks because they appear to be unreliable.

If internships are to receive academic recognition there must be more involved than just a work experience. A variety of instruments exist to assure academic rigor and to mesh the internship with previous and future coursework. The most commonly used methods are the writing of daily or weekly logs, research or evaluation papers, written tests, assigned readings related to the experience, faculty supervisor visits, and the presenting of seminars by interns. Settings can also be encouraged to add their own "academic" requirements to enhance their particular work.

If students receive extensive credit for an internship (e.g., 12-15 hours) a dilemma often arises about how to give grades. It is unlikely that many interns will warrant 12 hours of an "A" or "B" grade. Rather, varying degrees of competence or learning will have occurred in different facets of the experience. One avenue is to offer only 3-hour sections and enroll each intern from one to four times depending on the total credit of the experience. A 12-hour intern can then receive four different grades to reflect varying levels of competence in different aspects of the work.

Selection Procedures. Should every student who is interested and highly motivated be accepted for an internship? Or, if selection procedures are used, what criteria should be enforced?

One commonly used criterion is prerequisite coursework. There are two ways to approach this criterion. One is to argue that a student should complete extensive coursework *before* becoming an intern because only then can one be adequately prepared to absorb relevant information from the experience. The internship becomes a chance to put into practice theoretical knowledge and to gather advanced knowledge and experience not available in the classroom. Because seniors are the only students likely to have completed extensive prerequisites, they would make up the majority of interns. A second perspective is to view the internship as a time and place for the student to integrate basic knowledge and skills. This intern is then expected to return to campus for further coursework and thereby enrich these courses both for himself and the other students.

The most difficult part of intern selection has to do with personality variables. It would seem that the type of person who would function best as an intern is one who is emotionally stable and secure, self-confident, tactful, open and responsive to new situations, and has at least adequate communication skills. Additional factors are important depending on specific settings. For example, if interns are placed in correctional settings, the person may have to be able to work effectively in an atmosphere with hostile and sexual overtones.

It is obviously difficult to select interns with these qualities, especially when most applicants have only minimal knowledge of or experience in the potential settings. Yet, it is certainly possible to screen out gross negatives. A suggested procedure consists of four steps: (1) Interested students receive information about all available settings and activities through written descriptions and meetings with current interns. (2) Student completes application which includes a description of previous relevant coursework, grades, and a self statement regarding internship preferences and motives for choices of settings. (3) Applicants who meet minimal criteria are interviewed by two clinical staff persons. These interviewers then meet to make tentative intern assignments. (4) Selected interns then interview the potential agency supervisor. The intern may reject the setting at this point and ask for reassignment and/or the agency supervisor may reject the intern. This process takes several weeks and occurs midway during the semester prior to the assignment. A great deal of staff and student time is consumed in this process, but we are convinced that it pays off handsomely in performance.

Faculty Supervisor. From the psychology department point of view, the success or failure of the internship program rests with the faculty supervisor. This person must be highly motivated and willing to keep close contact with agency personnel, students, and other faculty. Some early internship programs placed the burden of generating new settings and selecting interns on the students themselves. It was argued that any student who could convince an agency that he or she ought to be accepted, would be the sort of student who would succeed. The result was that internship programs were dominated by highly motivated self-starters who had little bargaining power with the agency over appropriate activities, little sense of who might or might not be a good supervisor, and little back up from their major department. Such programs have mixed results at best. In fact, we have found, even with attempts at close supervision by faculty, that intern settings continually change and falter, and need to be renegotiated.

It is a faculty supervisor's task to coordinate and carry out the advertising of intern settings and the selection process, to investigate new settings, and to maintain faculty support for the program. This supervisor also must keep up-to-date on intern progress through logs and/or personal contacts, make on-site visits to obtain agency supervisor evaluations of interns, assure that they are all receiving an academic experience, and finally evaluate each intern's overall learning.

The teaching load of the faculty supervisor is also a crucial variable in running a manageable program. If large numbers of students are managed by one person there is increased risk of poor supervision and watered-down academic rigor. One possible guideline for determining the maximum number of students to be supervised can be patterned after the experience of student teacher supervision in Education, where a half-time teaching load might consist of working with 10-12 student teachers, each of whom earns 12 hours of credit. This generates up to 144 semester hours of credit for this faculty member's half-time teaching load.

Using this model as a rough guideline, an intern supervisor could supervise 10-12 full-time interns or about 45 interns at 3 hours credit each for a half-time teaching load. Obviously, it is not practical for any one supervisor to manage 45 interns, so a second rule of thumb should be to limit the total number of different interns to about 15, regardless of credit generated, for which any faculty supervisor is responsible. Slightly more may be manageable if several interns are working at the same setting and carrying out similar tasks. It is felt that every setting should be visited by the faculty supervisor at least once each semester. If the student is working full-time in an internship, then two or three personal visits with the student are necessary, plus regular logs and telephone calls. Internships clearly entail far more work per student by the faculty supervisor than is required in standard courses and it is important that the supervisor and department recognize this.

Another question, and one to be most carefully considered by the academician, is whether or not the internship provides an effective educational experience. The answer seems to be affirmative on this point. There are obvious benefits in terms of professional training, experience, and introduction into a professional field. Numerous studies have shown personal growth occurring in students after such experiences. For example, Umberger *et al.* (1962) reported that students thought they learned more about psychology in their internship experience than in their formal courses. They reported a gain in insight into their relationship with other people. Interviews with students in our present programs bear out this contention. The major thrust of the intern program's value is that it has the triple outcome of fostering better personal development, enriching school and college curricula, and developing potential interest and involvement in the mental health field.

As a result of the positive outcome of internships, the internship programs in the two departments of the authors have been gradually enlarged. Now interns are placed in public schools, community mental health centers, state hospitals, vocational rehabilitation workshops, drug and alcohol counseling centers, crisis intervention centers, various facilities for the aging, and state government offices.

Paid Internships. Until very recently the majority of interns have not usually received payment for their intern work. Two developments are changing this situation. First, state government internships have become available to psychology majors in several states, and these internships include payment. In addition, specific state agencies and county agencies periodically provide funding. Secondly, increased federal pressure to increase field experiences within the rubric of work-study money for college students has recently produced the option of work-study money for intern work.

An obvious danger exists that with such incentives a dramatic increase in number of interns will occur without a corresponding control on the quality of experience. Abuse of intern programs can only add fuel to the arguments that credit may be earned for doing almost anything in today's academic world.

Liability and Malpractice Insurance Problems. The insurance question is of increasing concern to professionals, but the vast majority of undergraduate intern programs with which the authors are familiar have limited insurance coverage or assume that a college or university blanket insurance policy covers all intern activities. Recent discussions with several insurance vendors who sell blanket policies to academic programs have elicited serious reservations about their company's intent to cover malpractice-type problems. In fact, one vendor stated that they were currently busy writing several disclaimer clauses to clearly *exclude* malpractice coverage in future policies to schools. Examples may help to clarify the potential malpractice problem:

1. An intern in a mental hospital is recognized as "staff" by a client. The intern fails to report to a supervisor that the client has told him that she has swallowed a handfull of broken glass. The intern thought the client was hallucinating, but the client or guardian later sue the intern, the hospital, and the academic supervisor for not responding appropriately to the crisis. While the hospital will have a policy to cover its staff, this policy may not cover persons not on the payroll.

2. An intern is working with a child client and while playing outside, the child darts into the street and is struck by a car. The parents sue the intern and the supervisor. Even if the supervisor *is* covered by the academic policy the student will likely have to pay for his own defense or sue the supervisor or school to cover legal costs.

Many academic personnel do not understand the nature of the malpractice risks involved in internships. The standard insurance coverage which colleges and universities hold is usually designed to handle academic problems which might arise between students and staff. Internship programs involve persons outside of the academic setting (agency personnel and clients of the agency) who have no relationship to the school except through the intern. The potential for legal suit here is not between intern and supervisor but between an agency client and the intern, with the agency and academic supervisors and school also likely included in the legal action.

To add further confusion to this matter is the fact that the opinions which one may solicit from academic administrators or even the state attorney general's office regarding insurance coverage or likelihood of legal suit are *only opinions*. A court or insurance company is not bound by such opinions, and there are few guidelines available from previous court cases to help predict the outcome of a potential malpractice suit in intern programs. It would seem advisable, then, for faculty supervisors to question the insurance company which covers their institution regarding liability and malpractice coverage. In conversations with insurance companies it is important to describe clearly the nature of off-campus intern work and the possible kinds of malpractice problems which might arise.

In the long run, the viability of undergraduate practica will depend upon the maintenance of quality rather than quantity. While practica are currently popular with students and some teachers, we must not be deluded into offering academic credit for just any interesting experience without foresight into the possible danger of weakened academic quality.

References

American Psychological Association. Ethical standards of psychologists. *American Psychologist*, 1963, *18*, 56-60.

Albee, G. W. *Mental health manpower trends.* New York: Basic Books, 1959.

Albee, G. W. Conceptual models and manpower requirements in psychology. *American Psychologist*, 1968, *23*, 317-320.

Gruver, G. G. College students as therapeutic agents. *Psychological Bulletin*, 1971, *76*, 111-127.

Holzberg, J. D. The Companion Program: Implementing the manpower recommendations of the joint commission on mental illness and health. *American Psychologist*, 1963, *18*, 224-226.

Holzberg, J. D., Whiting, H. S., & Lowry, D. G. Chronic patients and a college companion program. *Mental Hospital*, 1964, *15*, 152-158.

Poser, E. G. The effect of therapist's training on group therapeutic outcome. *Journal of Consulting Psychology*, 1966, *30*, 283-289.

Umbarger, D. C., Palsimer, J. S., Morrison, A. P., & Breggin, P. R. *College students in a mental hospital.* New York: Grune & Stratton, 1962.

Undergraduate Psychology Practica Pragmatism

Edward J. Barton and
Pryse H. Duerfeldt
Northern Michigan University

Some practical advice is presented from two psychologists who have supervised practica and solved some of the problems.

As the 1980's begin more and more practica in psychology are being offered in undergraduate programs. Although many explanations of this trend can be posited, such as increased student demand for relevance in education and evidence that college students can be effective therapeutic agents (Van de Creek & Thompson, 1977), two factors are probably salient. First an undergraduate psychology degree without applied training makes it extremely difficult for an individual to find employment in a market flooded with unemployed MA and PhD psychologists. Second, in this highly competitive endeavor of applying to graduate programs in psychology, an individual without applied training is at a disadvantage. Although a multitude of undergraduate practica exist today, very little professional journal space has been devoted to pragmatic issues in establishing such programs. In a perusal of the literature we found only 15 pages devoted to this topic (Shiverick, 1977; Van de Creek & Thompson, 1977; Yates, 1980). This paucity appears quite disproportionate given the potential impact of the practicum on the student as well as the University and the community. Therefore, the purpose of the present paper was to: (a) identify the goals, (b) discuss inherent problems, (c) provide strategies for avoiding potential pitfalls, and (d) conclude with a cost benefit analysis of the undergraduate psychology practicum.

Goals. The goals of undergraduate psychology practica, of course, differ depending upon the perspective taken (i.e., the client's, the agency's, the practicum student's, or the practicum instructor's viewpoint). For the client the goal of the practicum is to overcome or modify some personal problem in a rather nonthreatening, friendly sort of manner. For the agency, the goals are: (a) to help resolve a client's problems, (b) to help reduce the workload of the agency agents,[1] (c) to avoid creating new problems for the client, the agency, or the agency agent, and (d) to develop a meaningful and, we hope, rewarding learning experience for the student. For the practicum student the goals are: (a) to get a feel for the "real world" through in vivo assessment and treatment, (b) to improve his/her vita, (c) to determine if this is the sort of career he/she really wants to pursue, (d) to be successful, and (e) to become cognizant of personal limitations. Finally, for the practicum instructor, the goals are: (a) to provide the practicum student with an experience that will be meaningful and that will allow for demonstration of competency on a number of behavioral objectives, (b) to provide enough supervision so that the student's work will be successful and thereby increase the probability that the student will continue to pursue this endeavor, (c) to avoid any legal, ethical, or political repercussions, and (d) to continue to develop and expand rapport with community agencies. Thus, potentially the undergraduate psychology practicum can meet the needs of all the parties involved in its execution.

Problems.   Like any other arena in which there are a divergent variety of goals, it is very difficult to realize all of them. When goals are not met or are in conflict, problems develop. What are some of the pitfalls of the undergraduate practicum? The first problem, which is most obvious but also common to all professional and paraprofessional change agents, is a failure to help the client. While it is true that the successful modification of the client's behavior is not always expected even with professional service providers, the "sweet smell of success" brings a smile to everyone's face and makes it more likely that the other goals will be met. Unfortunately, in some instances the client gets worse. This has been referred to as the deterioration effect (Bergin & Lambert, 1978).

A second problem is that some of the practices of the practicum student may be unethical or even illegal. For example, the student may fail to ensure the confidentiality of the client's records as dictated by the *Standards for Providers of Psychological Services* (APA, 1977; Section 2.3.5). The student also may fail to follow the intent of recent court decisions (e.g., Wyatt v. Stickney, 1972) concerning the question of coercion and the right of the client to refuse treatment, all of which suggests that the simplest, least intrusive, and most positive approaches be used before less benign ones (refer to Budd & Baer, 1976, and Heads, 1978, for critical reviews).

A third problem is that the practicum student may create or be incapable of dealing with political problems.[2] Our experiences with community psychology suggest that providing adequate solutions to political problems is often one of the most difficult tasks for the student. For example, the practicum student unknowingly may insult the agency agent's expertise or actually may increase the agency's workload. A fourth problem is how does the practicum instructor go about establishing a practicum site and overcoming initial agency resistance? For example, some agencies may fear being under the scrutiny of a PhD psychologist or may have memories of a prior student-placement fiasco. A fifth problem is in what manner, by whom, and how much supervision should be provided? Thus, the undergraduate

practicum has the potential of developing problems for the client, the practicum student, the agency agents, and the practicum instructor far beyond those expected in more traditional advanced undergraduate courses.

Strategies for Avoiding Pitfalls.   Clearly the instructor must structure the undergraduate practicum so as to avoid propagating problems. In this section strategies that we have developed and instituted at Northern Michigan University (NMU) to circumvent potential problems will be discussed.

Upon deciding to develop a practicum, the first task for the instructor is to establish placement locations. At the larger institutions practicum sites are often available on campus (e.g., medical centers and exceptional child centers). At smaller institutions these opportunities usually are absent and at the larger universities these facilities sometimes are unsatisfactory for a practicum placement. Thus, the instructor typically has to establish a cordial liaison with local agencies. This step involves having individual meetings with representatives from each potential placement location (which take a considerable amount of time). In addition, some agencies may be hesitant to become involved in this type of semester-long commitment. Beyond the obvious need for finesse and good interview skills, a clear statement of the student behavioral objectives is extremely helpful in this process.

It is our belief that in most cases, catastrophic practicum experiences are a result of a lack of student objectives and inadequate supervision. We have found that even the most initially hesitant agency agents can be enticed to cooperate through a clear statement of what the student will be doing and how his/her behavior will be monitored. This tactic can be further supplemented by providing the agency with information about potential benefits for the agency (e.g., a reduced workload for agency staff). Once the practicum has been conducted for a semester, it is much easier to establish additional placement sites because its credibility will be communicated by the agency to other agencies. The instructor can facilitate this process by providing the agency agents at potential practicum sites with a copy of all the reports of the practicum cases for the previous semester.

Another important consideration in the establishment of the practicum placement site is its location. Even though some practicum students do have cars, driving makes the management of the practicum much more difficult and costly. For example, during the Winter 1979 semester the first author had a practicum student placed in an agency which was located 6.5 miles from school. To supervise this student at the agency 13 times cost the instructor 6.5 hours extra driving,[3] $25.35 in travel costs,[4] numerous phone calls, and coordination problems. Given our current fuel shortage and in the spirit of President Carter's May 1979 directive about energy conservation, agencies which are located within walking distance of the campus are preferred.

Once a practicum placement has been made there are a number of other things that the instructor can do in an attempt to maintain good rapport with the agency. First and foremost, it is imperative that clear delineation be made of the roles and responsibilities of the agency and the instructor in supervising the practicum student. Anecdotal comments by colleagues and our own subjective observations suggest that initially it is best to have the instructor assume the major role. Once the instructor is comfortable that the agency agent possesses or has developed the appropriate monitoring behaviors, then the supervisory authority can be transferred to the agent. If the agency is unwilling to go along with this approach, then the placement probably should not occur. On the other hand, if the instructor is willing to allow the agency to have the major responsibility from the start, then the agents must be provided with plenty of feedback and positive reinforcement for their supervision in order to assure quality control. Second, it also is important that the instructor communicate to the agency agents that all problems related to or created by the practicum student, no matter how small, should be brought to the instructor's attention immediately. By utilizing this system and acting on these problems immediately it is less likely that political, ethical, or legal problems will develop or that the agency will build up animosities toward the practicum. Third, the instructor can demonstrate an honest interest in the practicum by visiting the agency weekly to monitor the student. Although the instructor should be careful not to interrupt the agency's ongoing activities, positive interactions with the agents are desirable (e.g., praising an aide for how much progress she has made with a child's speech). A final suggestion for maintaining rapport with the agency is to provide the agent with a copy of the case reports which have been written by the student and evaluate the practicum experiences that were conducted in their agency. In addition, it is good public relations to provide the agency with a final instructor's report which includes an anthology of all the cases that were dealt with during the school year.

Probably the most difficult part of conducting a practicum is the determination of what and how much work to expect of the students and how to supervise and provide guidance for them. At some universities where graduate students provide the supervision, undergraduate practicum students are required to be present at the agency as much as two hours daily but are not required to attend class. At other institutions the practicum students may be required to attend regular class sessions but working in the agencies may occur as little as 1 hour per week. In general, 4 to 10 hours of attendance (i.e., at the classroom and/or agency) are required of practicum students. Although we at NMU do not have the assistance of graduate students, we are currently requiring the undergraduates: (a) to work one hour per day in the agency, 5 days per week on a minimum of one and maximum of two cases, (b) to attend class 3 days per week, and (c) to meet individually with the instructor a minimum of three times per semester. In order to structure the student's activities at the beginning of the semester, each is provided via the syllabus with dates for the class assignments (e.g., tentative treatment plan) and the setting assignments (e.g., parent meeting) as well as a calendar describing the topic of each class meeting (e.g., case staffings). Some of the types of treatment cases with which the students have been involved include: on-task behavior, nonverbal interaction, verbal interaction, thumbsucking, drooling (Barton & Madsen, 1980), vomiting, tongue thrust control, echolalia, color discrimination, repetitive dysfunctional behaviors such as rocking, head swaying, and arm flapping, truancy, elective mutism, physical aggression, and assertiveness training.

Even with course prerequisites, students sometimes enter the practicum with serious deficiencies in their behavioral repertoire. Therefore, to increase the probability that the students will be successful in the practicum, they are required to demonstrate mastery of some prerequisite skills that should have been incorporated into their repertoire during previous psychology courses. The prerequisite skills are based partially upon a checklist used in a graduate practicum at Utah State University (Ascione, Note 6). Their mastery of these skills is demonstrated by passing quizzes over each of the areas listed below. However, prior to taking the quiz the students are provided with a list of readings to review, develop, or solidify their knowledge in each of these areas:

A. OBSERVING and RECORDING BEHAVIOR. The student will be able to:

1. define behavioral and environmental events operationally
2. describe and use each of the following recording methods:
   (a) narrative, (b) event, (c) duration, (d) interval
3. describe the conditions under which each recording system is appropriate
4. devise a data sheet appropriate for use with each recording method
5. collect data
6. operate a cassette audio recording device and stopwatch
7. represent the data in graphic form and summarize in written form
8. select and use the correct formula for computing observer agreement for each recording method
9. follow "rules for observers" when observing in classrooms or homes

B. METHODOLOGICAL ISSUES in behavioral observation. The student will be able to discuss how:

1. different methods of computing observer agreement are influenced by the frequency of the behavior and the observer behavior
2. observational systems may be subject to "instrument decay"
3. to determine the best method for insuring high observer reliability
4. to reduce observer bias and observer reactivity
5. to assess convergent validity of behavioral definitions
6. various factors influence behavioral observations

C. ETHICS. The student will be familiar with the ethical guidelines and will be able to discuss current issues concerning the ethics of assessment and treatment

D. ACCOUNTABILITY through the use of single-subject designs. The student will be able to

1. define subject, task, and environmental confounding variables
2. describe the advantages and disadvantages of reversal, multiple-baseline, multi-element, and changing-criterion designs
3. select the appropriate design for a given behavior change program
4. portray graphically data gathered using each design

After they pass this hurdle, the students devote the remainder of the semester to developing their skills in the areas of in vivo assessment and treatment.

The student will have a comprehensive working knowledge of how to set up, implement, and evaluate behavioral management programs. Specifically, the student will be able to: (a) determine and operationally define target behaviors; (b) set up a workable observation sheet; (c) observe behavior reliably; (d) set up a workable and ethical treatment program; (e) set up and conduct a parent meeting; (f) act in a professionally appropriate manner; (g) identify and deal with potential political problems; (h) carry out a treatment program under the instructor's supervision; (i) assess and/or facilitate generalization of treatment gains across time, settings, individuals, groups, and responses; (j) conduct a minimum of two case staffings; (k) terminate the case appropriately; (l) write up a short case report; and (m) write up a longer technical report.

Competency in these areas is demonstrated at the agency and on homework assignments. Each student is provided with a record sheet which lists all the behavioral objectives. When a student satisfactorily completes an objective[5] the instructor dates and signs the record sheet.

One of the obvious goals of the practicum for the student is to be successful. There are a number of methods for increasing the probability that this goal will be realized. First, if after the narrative recording has been completed the student chooses more than one behavior for more than one client that he/she would like to work on, then the instructor can make the final selection as to who works with whom on what. By analyzing the capabilities and limitations of each student as well as the complexity of the problem and the supporting environment, the instructor can greatly enhance the likelihood that the case will be successful. In addition, through the use of class discussions, role playing, and case staffings, the student can gain valuable suggestions for his/her cases. The instructor can supplement this further by conducting a few individual conferences with the student.

Cost-Benefit Analysis. Although there are obvious payoffs for the student, the client, the agency agents, and the instructor, the benefit analysis has been limited to the student. The most evident outcome for the student is the expansion of his/her behavioral repertoire. The practicum produces a large increment in ability to use assessment and treatment techniques—a much greater enhancement than typically occurs at the undergraduate level. In addition, the practicum gives the undergraduate student an opportunity to investigate novel treatment techniques that may merit presentation at a professional convention or publication in a scientific journal (e.g., Barton & Madsen, 1980), These professional experiences, when listed on a vita, greatly augment the student's probability of getting accepted into graduate school (APA, 1979).

Another source of information which is pertinent to the benefit analysis is an end-of-the-semester questionnaire which has been given during the last three semesters at NMU. As can be seen from the first four items on Table 1, the students found the practicum very beneficial. The next three items disclose that the students perceived the class meetings and daily class sessions as very necessary. Furthermore, they reported the parent meetings were a valuable experience.

Although the potential benefits are great, so are the costs. Items 8 and 9 in Table 1 show that the students reported that the practicum required a lot of work but that this activity was necessary to meet the course objectives. The students also indicated in additional written comments that the course should be given more academic credit by NMU. In spite of the costs to the students, their overwhelming responses to Item 10 suggest that the benefits far exceed the costs.

Table 1. Mean Ratings on Evaluative Items for Three Semesters

Items[a]	Winter 1978	Fall 1978	Winter 1979	Total Mean
Regarding General Value:				
1. This class was rewarding and beneficial	4.86	4.71	4.86	4.81
2. Overall course evaluation	4.71	4.50	4.86	4.69
3. Course evaluation (content only)	4.71	4.67	4.71	4.70
4. Knowledge gained as compared to other NMU courses	4.71	4.83	4.71	4.75
Regarding Specific Experiences:				
5. I enjoyed the daily therapy sessions	4.29	4.60	4.43	4.44
6. I enjoyed the class meetings	4.29	4.29	4.71	4.43
7. The parent meeting was beneficial	4.29	4.14	4.43	4.29
Regarding Effort Cost:				
8. This class required a lot of work	4.71	4.29	4.14	4.38
9. That much work was necessary to meet the course objectives	4.71	4.80	4.86	4.79
10. I would recommend this class to a friend	5.00	4.57	4.86	4.81

[a]Scores ranged from 1 (strongly disagree/unsatisfactory) to 5 (strongly agree/excellent).

The price of conducting the practicum is also great for the instructor. Although enrollment in the course has been relatively low (7 to 8 students per semester), overall the instructor has expended approximately 17.7 hours per week conducting the practicum. This figure only includes direct supervision of the students in the classroom, in the agency, and in individual conferences. It does not include class preparation, homework correction, or community liaison work. Without a doubt, the undergraduate practicum imposes a serious burden on instructors who do not have graduate students to help supervise. Even more disheartening is the realization that larger enrollments will place an even greater time commitment on the instructor.

Conclusion. In summary, it is possible to conduct an undergraduate practicum that satisfies the needs of the student, the client, the agency, and the university. The benefits which can be accrued from the practicum are great—possibly greater than the costs. It is clear, however, that a lack of careful supervision and planning will turn the practicum into a disaster. Therefore, if the demands of supervision can be met, the undergraduate practicum can be a panacea. On the other hand, if the rigors of supervision cannot be met satisfactorily, then the practicum has no place in an undergraduate curriculum.

References

American Psychological Association. *Standards for providers of psychological services.* Washington, DC: Author, 1977.
American Psychological Association. *Graduate study in psychology for 1980-1981* (13th edition). Washington, DC: Author, 1979.
Barton, E. J., & Madsen, J. J. The use of awareness and omission

training to control excessive drooling in a severely retarded youth. *Child Behavior Therapy*, 1980, *2*, 55-63.

Bergin, A. E., & Lambert, M. J. The evaluation of therapeutic outcomes. In S. L. Garfield & Allen E. Bergin (Eds.). *Handbook of psychotherapy and behavior change: An empirical analysis* (2nd ed.). New York: Wiley, 1978.

Budd, K., & Baer, D. M. Behavior modification and the law: Implications of recent judicial decisions. *The Journal of Psychiatry and Law: A Special Reprint*, 1976 (Summer), 171-244.

Heads, T. Ethical and legal considerations in behavior therapy. In D. Marholin (Ed.). *Child behavior therapy*. New York: Gardner Press, 1978.

Shiverick, D. D. A full time clinical practicum for undergraduates. *Teaching of Psychology*, 1977, *4*, 188-190.

Van de Creek, L. V., & Thompson, G. Management of undergraduate psychology internships. *Teaching of Psychology*, 1977, *4*, 177-180.

Wyatt v. Stickney. 344 F. Supp. 373 (M.D. Ala. 1972, North. Div.).

Yates, B. T. Benefits and costs of community-academia interaction in a paraprofessional training course. *Teaching of Psychology*, 1980, *7*, 8-14.

Notes

1. The term "agency agent," as used in the present article, refers to all individuals who work for and represent the agency (e.g., directors, community mental health therapists, teachers, aides, etc.).

2. The term "political problem," as used in the paper, refers to problems between the practicum student and the agency agents, client, client's guardian, or significant others which hinder the therapeutic process.

3. There were a number of occasions when the first author had planned to supervise but could not because of the time required to drive that far.

4. This figure was based on the 1977-78 State of Michigan mileage reimbursement figure (i.e., 15¢ per mile).

5. For most of the competency areas satisfactory completion of an objective by a student is a somewhat subjective decision by the instructor. However, evaluation of competence on Objective 3 (i.e., observer reliability) is made by a second practicum student who observes the same behavior once per week.

6. Ascione, F. R. Personal communication, September 1977

7. This paper is based partially on an invited address given by the authors at the Fifth Annual Convention of the Association for Behavior Analysis, Dearborn, MI, June 1979.

8. We are indebted to Frank R. Ascione, J. Grayson Osborne, Roger L. Peterson, and Joel D. West for their helpful suggestions.

The Psychology Teacher and Undergraduate Field Experience Courses: The Problem of Supervision

Donald G. Wolfgang
Virginia Wesleyan College

Many undergraduate departments, believing that experiential learning is a worthwhile complement to the more traditional classroom courses, have instituted field experience courses in which students receive academic credit for working at an agency which provides human services or does psychological research. This joint venture involving student, school, and agency offers a unique educational experience and an opportunity to see classroom material come to life. The observations which follow may be of help to teachers initiating such a program.

As more students are being given the opportunity to enroll in field experience courses an increasing number of teachers are being called upon to administer them. These responsibilities include placement, supervision, and evaluation/grading of the students' efforts.

Three years of experience with faculty responsibilities in an undergraduate field experience program has taught me that the most difficult, most time-consuming, and most important aspect of faculty involvement in such a program is that of supervision. The necessity and difficulty of adequate supervision is probably not fully appreciated by many academic deans, department heads, or tenure and promotion committees. Therefore, teachers involved in supervising students as part of their teaching load may find the efforts vastly undervalued. However, students in such programs who are adequately supervised will recognize and appreciate the efforts involved. Supervision is a chore for which many teachers are unprepared, and many of the teachers themselves may underestimate the importance of the responsibility. There should be an agency representative who provides on-the-job supervision, but with one involved it is seductively tempting to leave *all* the supervising responsibilities to the agency. The results of this tactic, however, can be deleterious for all parties involved.

A conscientious job of student placement in the field experience program makes proper supervision an easier task. Care must be taken to place the student in a position suitable to his/her interests, abilities, educational preparation, and career goals and then to establish appropriate, relevant learning objectives. It is necessary to consider the needs and objectives of the agency as well as those of the student. Once need assessment and learning objectives have been decided upon collectively by the student, the agency, and the teacher, it would seem most prudent to prepare a written agreement to be signed by all three parties. Having this contract available will make supervision more systematic, providing a framework for evaluating, monitoring, and giving feedback.

As a means of emphasizing the importance of adequate supervision the principal supervisory functions and purposes should be noted. First, and perhaps most important, the teacher, by taking the time to supervise, and the school, by providing faculty time, convey to both the student and the agency an attitude which indicates that the internship is a worthwhile experience which merits faculty involvement. Unlike a *laissez faire* attitude, such a demonstration of caring is likely to promote a favorable attitude in both the student and the agency representative so that both are more likely to perform their duties optimally.

A second function of supervision is that of providing ongoing evaluation and monitoring of both the student and the agency, and providing appropriate feedback to both

182

parties. This role of supervision will be facilitated if placement of the student has considered the unique needs of both, and if the responsibilities of each have been clearly and specifically defined by contract before the actual internship experience begins. The teacher can use the contract to ensure that both parties' needs are being met and that the agreed activities are taking place in proper sequence. This includes making sure that the responsibilities of the supervising agency representative are being carried out.

Related to this aspect of supervision is the function of assuring that neither the student nor the agency are exploiting either each other or the school. There are some agencies which, rather than providing proper experiences, will attempt to use students as if they were clerical help. On the other hand, there are some students who may see such a non-academic course as a chance to earn credits for doing nothing. Proper supervision can minimize or prevent such exploitation and make the students' participation more rewarding.

The third function of supervision is an extension of the second. Adequate supervision greatly facilitates evaluation of the student so that the grade given at the end of the course will be more valid. The more contacts and the closer the student has been followed throughout the school term, the more confidence the teacher can have in the formal assessment of the student's performance.

A fourth function of faculty supervision is to help the student relate the field experience to class work and to be a resource person providing guidance and reading resources. A closely related function is to give encouragement and to be available when problems arise, helping the student resolve the problem and/or letting the student ventilate. Often students' constructive observations, complaints, or suggestions about the agency have more credibility when they have the backing of the faculty member. The teacher must be sensitive to such situations and handle them tactfully. Some or all of the agency staff may view students and sometimes faculty as outsiders who are intruders to be viewed with suspicion and hostility.

A sixth function of ongoing supervision is one that also requires sensitivity. An important role of supervising is counseling. This includes getting feedback from the student about his/her experience, but more specifically it means allowing the student to reflect on that experience. Counsel-ing can add a great deal to the meaningfulness of a field experience course and can provide a better understanding of psychology, the agency and the people it serves, the student's career objectives, and the student himself. A properly administered internship program is more than an educational activity—it is a personal growth experience.

Adequately carrying out all of these functions is obviously a task requiring both commitment and ample time from the faculty member—the main limiting factor. I would like to propose the following supervisory scheme as one which makes most efficient use of faculty time, yet still meets the required needs.

Early in the school term more time may be required than later on. During this time, the learning objectives previously agreed upon may be judged to be either inadequate or too ambitious. The student may experience considerable anxiety and self-doubt. During this initial phase it seems especially crucial for the teacher to be available for student conferences. Once a reasonable amount of stability is established, weekly scheduled meetings with the student and bi-weekly scheduled contacts with the agency appear to be a workable routine.

I prefer the idea of a co-requisite seminar course consisting of weekly meetings in which all the students receive instruction and discuss experiences. This seminar enables the students to share in each others' learning and to support one another. Some time should be allotted for meeting individually with each student, preferably on an informal basis. Often these individual conferences can be facilitated by the use of daily or weekly logs of the internship experience recorded by each student.

I believe that the teacher's contacts with the agency representative are best made by phone. There may, of course, be times during which a personal visit by the teacher to the agency would be preferable. For example, there may be a problem to be resolved, or the student may have some situation he/she wants the teacher to observe. In addition, approximately once every six weeks it is advantageous to arrange a meeting at the agency with all three parties.

Being a good supervisor of field experience work is not unlike being a good psychology teacher in other courses. It requires good planning, good implementation (monitoring and observation), and good follow-up. And, as in any other course, being available for spontaneous conferences with one's students is especially desirable.

Organization and Administration of the Psychology Practicum: Meeting Student, Agency, and Program Goals

Dana D. Anderson and Debra K. Stein
Pennsylvania State University

The psychology practicum course offers students a valuable opportunity to translate classroom theory into practical skills. However, at many colleges and universities the course is not well-designed and the placements are not properly supervised. At the Pennsylvania State University, The Behrend College, the practicum course has developed into a highly organized and essential part of the psychology curriculum. This has occurred, we believe, because the format of the course allows it to meet three types of goals: (a) those of the individual student choosing the practicum; (b)

183

those of the community agency sponsoring the practicum; and (c) those of the psychology department offering the practicum as an educational experience.

Goals. Although practica are designed to be highly individualized learning experiences some common student goals are apparent. First, psychology majors see the practicum as a chance to apply their knowledge of psychological theory to practical problems—to understand the complementary relationship between work in the classroom and the field. Awarding academic credit for the practicum experience is an important means of making this relationship salient to students.

Second, in choosing practicum sites students are able to sample their area of specialization and test the appropriateness of their career decisions. If a student finds a practicum in a particular speciality area unsuitable this is done before a long-term educational or employment commitment has been made.

A third student goal is the identification of strengths and weaknesses through field work. Under the close faculty and staff supervision offered in a practicum, weaknesses are more apt to be detected, analyzed, understood and remediated, and strengths may be reinforced and supported with accelerated study.

A fourth and very important goal for most students enrolling in practica is the accumulation of work experience and the personal contacts necessary for post-baccalaureate employment or graduate training. In some cases students who have performed well have been offered full time employment with their sponsoring agency—a fringe benefit rarely overlooked by students.

Practica serve agency goals such as the maintenance of good community relations and the identification of potential employees. However, the major agency goal is to increase service with minimum expense to agency clientele. Although quite appropriate to the agency's mission, this goal may conflict with those of the student and psychology program. Agencies on occasion inadvertently overwork students or assign them to necessary but non-educational tasks. A formal contract drawn up between the student, agency, and the psychology program's supervising faculty member clarifies each parties' responsibilities and serves to minimize conflicts.

A major goal for departmental faculty is to meet student needs in a manner that justifies awardng academic credit for practical experience. In our program this is accomplished by assigning advanced readings relevant to the practicum. Also, students are required to keep daily journals relating these readings to their field experiences. The journals serve as the basis for term papers summarizing and evaluating the practicum experience. Care is taken that faculty evaluations of the journals and term papers meet the same rigorous standards as traditional courses and weigh heavily in the grading process.

The close supervision offered by a practicum provides a unique opportunity for faculty to contribute to their students' growth as persons and professionals, a primary goal of all undergraduate programs. Weekly sessions are scheduled to monitor student progress and to review journals, facilitating the discussion of ideas and problems arising in the field. This informal one-on-one interaction also enables the establishment of a more personal relationship than that found in other college courses.

Practica can also strengthen student moral and involvement in the department. For example, at Behrend, the student-run psychology club provides a forum for practicum agency staff to come and speak, and this generates discussions of theoretical issues and career options. This community contact increases the department's visibility in the community and helps to serve the college's recruitment goals.

Organizing and Administering the Practicum Program. Behrend's practicum program is able to fulfill these diverse sets of goals through the establishment of academic and placement contracts that must be signed by the student, the agency staff member supervising the student's practicum, and the supervising faculty member. The academic contract specifies the number of credit hours assigned the practicum, the frequency of faculty supervision sessions, the assigned readings, required written work, and criteria for grading. It is important that the academic contract stipulate that the final course grade is determined by the faculty supervisor on the basis of both the quality of the academic work and the quality of job performance as reflected by agency feedback. Three credit hours per term, roughly ten field hours per week, seems the minimum for an educationally worthwhile practicum.

The placement contract clearly defines the student's duties to the agency and the agency's responsibilities to the student. This contract also specifies the days and hours to be worked per week, the location(s) where the work is to be performed, the tasks assigned the student, the frequency of staff supervision sessions, the criteria used to evaluate student performance, and the form of the final written evaluation. It is important that the placement contract note that this final evaluation will weigh heavily in determining the student's final grade.

Implicit in the program's administration is the recognition that the faculty sponsor and the agency accept certain responsibilities to each other. It is assumed that the faculty member will retain signed copies of both contracts, that the faculty and staff supervisors will regularly review the student's performance, and that the faculty member will be available to intervene on behalf of the student or agency if conflicts arise. The faculty member's control over the assignment of a final grade to the student and provision of additional students to the agency in the future insure faculty ability to intervene effectively.

This contract-based procedure makes it relatively easy for Behrend's practicum program to meet the diverse agency, department, and student goals outlined above. Evalution of the student's academic and field performance is straightforward, and the student's evaluation of the agency as a practicum site is useful in placing future students in appropriate settings. Feedback from participating agencies and students has been quite positive. A total of 20 placement sites are now available to our students, and a majority of upper-level psychology students enroll in one or more practica.

Although the administration of a practicum program requires considerable faculty time, we find that practica have added greatly to the development of our students and psychology program. College administrators should be made aware that the implementation of worthwhile practica represent a legitimate part of a faculty member's course load. They require the components of preparation, instruction, and evaluation essential for the presentation of all college courses.

Identifying Goals for Undergraduate Internships

Peter A. Keller
Mansfield State College

Practical issues related to the planning and management of undergraduate psychology internships have been adequately discussed in several recent articles (Schiverick, 1977; Vande Creek & Thompson, 1977). The purpose of the present article is to describe a method which can be utilized to identify specific individualized goals for undergraduate psychology interns.

Students in the Department of Psychology at Mansfield State College have been involved in undergraduate internships for eight years. Qualified majors in the Department have the option of completing an internship, a research apprenticeship, or a supervised independent study project to satisfy requirements for graduation. More than half currently choose the internship option, and, to date, over 400 students have participated in semester-long, full-time placements under the program.

While seeking opportunities which can provide rigorous supervision, the Department has always been relatively flexible in selecting various agencies which meet the interests of individual students. For example, placements have included mental health and children's service agencies, prisons, schools, and industrial personnel offices. The result is that students have had very diverse experiences, some much more clearly structured than others.

The members of the Department have not been displeased with the diversity and flexibility of the program, but there has been a strong belief that the faculty should have an effective method of monitoring each student's plans and activities during the internship. Consequently, a goal-oriented internship program was designed.

The plan has been in effect for two years and approximately 35 students have utilized the process. The reaction from students, placement supervisors, and faculty have been uniformly positive. The goal-oriented program provides an efficient and effective means of informing faculty of the goals and activities of each student intern. Faculty can consequently determine the level of their involvement which is necessary to ensure adequate supervision and a productive internship for each student. A description of the goal-setting process follows.

Identifying Goals. During the planning process which precedes a student's actual placement, only general expectations and internship activities are delineated. These are described in correspondence between the Department and placement facilities. Specific goals are purposely not included at this point because we believe that each student should have an informed participation in a process of identifying goals. Consequently, the task of planning specific goals is designed to occur during the initial stage of the internship.

Within 10 days from the start of the internship, each student is expected to work with his or her supervisor to define a minimum of five specific goals which can reasonably be accomplished during the remainder of the internship. The goals are submitted on an appropriate form to the Department faculty for review and approval. Faculty may offer comments and suggestions or require the student to make changes if the goals are unsuitable.

With advisement from the internship supervisor and the faculty advisor, the student may make modifications in goals or add new goals during the semester. Such changes are formally reported to the Department via a mid-semester report and a final report at the end of the semester. There is latitude for the faculty to have as much or as little involvement in the process as seems necessary for the success of each internship.

Evaluating Goal Achievement. Once the goals have been established, the student is required to maintain weekly progress notes in relation to each goal. The progress notes are recorded on forms designed specifically for this purpose and contain the following information for each goal: (1) the plan for attaining the goal; (2) the results from implementing the plan; (3) the student's comments or observation regarding the plan and goal.

The progress notes are designed to fulfill several purposes. First, the notes are helpful in giving the student a perspective on the progress toward each goal. Second, the notes can be of help in focusing constructive supervision from the internship supervisor. Third, the notes are helpful in providing the faculty advisor with specific information about the student's activities and progress when visits are made to the internship facility. Also, if some aspect of the internship is problematic, the faculty advisor can ask to review the progress notes as often as necessary.

In addition to the weekly progress notes, each student is required to submit both mid-semester and final reports which take progress toward the goals into account. The identified goals and the student's actual accomplishments as described in the progress notes and final reports provide a clear picture of what has been achieved during an internship.

Discussion. The goal identification process has several important advantages over the more traditional forms of internship planning and supervision. First, it is adaptable to diverse types of internship settings. Second, the student becomes an integral part of the internship planning process. Third, the goal identification process and weekly progress notes provide the Department with more specific information about the activities of each intern.

Most important, the process provides a basis for evaluating infernships. For departments wishing a concrete form of evaluation, the method of goal attainment scaling (Kiresuk & Sherman, 1968) could easily be applied to measure internship outcome. Goal attainment scaling is a precise method for measuring achievement of operational goals. Although it has been used primarily to evaluate mental health treatment programs, its application here would be straightforward.

References

Kiresuk, T. J., & Sherman, R. E. Goal Attainment Scaling: A General Method of Evaluating Comprehensive Community Mental Health Programs. *Community Mental Health Journal,* 1968, *4,* 443-453.

Shiverick, D. D. A full-time clinical practicum for undergraduates. *Teaching of Psychology,* 1977, *4,* 188-190.

Vande Creek, L. & Thompson, G. Management of undergraduate psychology internships. *Teaching of Psychology,* 1974, 4, 177-180.

Discussing Ethical Issues in Practicum Courses

James H. Dalton
Bloomsburg University of Pennsylvania

The resurgence of academic interest in values and ethical issues is having many effects on undergraduate education. This resurgence is occuring even in disciplines like psychology that have traditionally sought to be "value-free." A field work, internship or practicum course, by virtue of its emphasis on practical decisions and interventions, is perhaps more directly concerned with values and ethical issues than any other course in the undergraduate psychology curriculum. Incorporating systematic consideration of ethical issues and dilemmas into these courses, however, is not a simple task. Many coordinators of such courses simply rely on their own experience and practical intelligence to identify ethical issues. Two problems arise from exclusive reliance on this method.

First, students' learning is limited by the supervisor's awareness of ethical dilemmas and assumptions; issues not recognized by the superior often are not recognized or mentioned by students. Second, students receive an inductive and narrow body of knowledge about specific ethical issues, rather than a general set of skills that can be used to identify and deal with ethical aspects of practical problems. Although overviews of supervision issues in undergraduate practica have recently appeared in this journal (Fernald, Tedeschi, Siegfried, Gilmore, Grimsley & Chipley, 1982; VandeCreek & Fleischer, 1984), a more detailed discussion of ethical concerns is appropriate. In this brief paper, I will review some concepts and methods for considering value issues more systematically in a practicum course.

An ethical issue arises in a practicum setting when the goals or activities of the organization or individual conflict with the rights of clients or employees, or with the expectations of society regarding the organization's purposes. For instance, in juvenile probation settings, the clients have rights to confidentiality, access to staff when needed, and advocacy for their interests against unfair treatment by parents, educators, or other adults. In addition, society (in the form of parents, educators, police, the press, and others) has strong expectations regarding agency performance. These are to control and punish criminal activity and to "rehabilitate" clients and prevent future criminal acts. Because these expectations often contradict each other, and conflict with some concepts of clients' rights, virtually everything a probation officer does has ethical overtones. A second example concerns residents in a total institution, who certainly have rights to adequate food, shelter, privacy, and daily activities. But what if their behavior can become more active and adaptive if these rights are satisfied contingent on the performance of certain socially-approved target behaviors? This can be considered a conflict of rights to basic necessities versus the right to treatment.

Means versus Ends. To identify ethical aspects of practical situations, students must distinguish between means and ends, and analyze both. Means involve the intermediate steps taken to reach a desired goal. Ends include not only the attainment of that goal, but the other, perhaps undesirable, consequences of action. In American society and psychology, both of which emphasize outcomes and "results," it is often easy to overlook the means of an action. However, desirable outcomes (e.g., the welfare of a client, a just policy or decision) are often difficult to define or achieve in practice, whereas means are readily observable. Kennan (cited in Ewing, 1977) asserts that his colleagues in diplomacy held high-minded goals, yet it was the *methods* of working toward those goals that molded the quality of their lives. The analysis of means or methods is essential in a practicum placement. For instance, behavioral treatments (including positive reinforcement) are manipulative and even coercive when used without explicit client consent—a condition often found in token economies and programs for the institutionalized. A student in such a setting needs to discover the difficulties in obtaining consent from a possibly reluctant client, assess the effectiveness of behavioral techniques for that client in that setting, and experience the conflict of means and ends in planning treatment.

Ends also deserve close examination. Students need to learn and use a simple version of a rational cost-benefit framework for examining goals and planning actions. But they also need to ask, "Whose costs? Whose benefits?" and

"How are individual rights and welfare involved here?" They need to grapple with the difficulties of fitting values and intangible factors into this framework, just as they learned in earlier psychology courses about the difficulty of measuring abstract psychological concepts.

Means and ends can be analyzed at an organizational as well as at an individual level of analysis. Students in psychology tend to focus on individual motives and actions rather than the mandates, policies, and actions of institutions. They often do not recognize that the latter have ethical dimension. Discussion of *de facto* and *de jure* discrimination, or of institutional racism and sexism, often challenges and widens these students' perspectives. The overwhelming concern of the mental health system with treatment rather than prevention (Albee, 1982) is another area in which institutional mandates structure the assumptions, interests and activities of employees, students and clients.

Ethics and Organized Politics.   Ethical conflicts occur within a social context. In a practicum setting, professional staff often share a set of assumptions and values. They may, for instance, define a problem with ethical overtones as a benign matter of professional expertise rather than an ethical conflict of values. ("We cannot expect our clients to design their own treatment, so explicit consent is not necessary"). A student-novice, who does not share the professionals' experience and assumptions, may recognize more clearly an ethical issue, but be reluctant to discuss it. The interpersonal consequences of taking an ethical stance can be strong: Issues begin to be defined in dichotomous right/wrong terms, advocates easily become moralistic zealots, compromises can be seen as sellouts, coercive solutions become more likely, and declarations often supplant discussion. Weick (1984) cogently discusses these forces, which can affect both students and professionals. Discussing whether this risk is appropriate to a specific situation is a useful group-supervision tactic. It encourages critical thinking and interpersonal sensitivity.

Facilitating Discussion of Ethical Issues.   In practicum supervision meetings on campus, several approaches exist for discussing ethical issues. All of them are probably enhanced by requiring an ethics, moral problems, or social issues course as a prerequisite. Readings coupled with a reaction paper or similar assignment effectively deepen student knowledge and class discussion. Films or structured exercises can be used to build student awareness of their values, or to discuss specific ethical situations. Finally, a section of the students' summary papers or journals could concern observed or potential ethical dilemmas and discussion of alternative solutions.

A variety of readings exist. The APA statement of ethical principles (American Psychological Association, 1981) is six pages long and easily reproduced. This statement is primarily addressed to professionals with graduate degrees, but several sections are relevant to students. Fernald, et al (1982) discuss specific applications of the APA code to undergraduate practica.

Textbooks for helping skills, behavior modification, community psychology, and abnormal psychology courses also are useful resources. These are beginning to include an ethical perspective either as a chapter, or integrated in traditional content chapters. Issues to look for include the influence of values on a helping relationship, informed consent, confidentiality, sexism, racism, ageism, and rights of institutionalized persons. Altrocchi (1980), in an abnormal psychology text, includes a chapter that presents sixteen principles of community intervention for the mental health system. A handout summarizing these may be helpful in initiating class discussion of local concerns. Allen's (1977) text on psychotherapy includes an insightful discussion of helpers' self-sustaining beliefs that affect their relationship with clients (pp. 228-233). Steiner's (1976) conception of the Rescue game is also insightful. Sociopolitical issues, such as blaming the victim, community control of helping services, and ethical dilemmas in prevention, are better covered in community psychology texts such as Rappaport (1977) or Heller, Price, Reinhart, Riger and Wandersman (1984). Books discussing a single ethical or social issue in detail (e.g., Terry, 1970; Chesler, 1972; Ewing, 1977), provide valuable background material.

Directly related to supervisory session activities are the individual and group exercises in Okun (1982) and Corey, Corey and Callanan (1984). A film that facilitates discussion of sexual harassment is "Work Place Hustle" (Clark Communications, 903 Howard Street, San Francisco, CA 94108). Finally, a newsletter for coordinators of undergraduate psychology practica, the *Community Connection,* covers issues, resources, and teaching materials. You can be added to the newsletter list by writing one of the editors at the address given in Note 1.

References

Albee, G. W.   Preventing psychopathology and promoting human potential. *American Psychologist,* 1982, *37,* 1043-1050.

Allen, G. J.   *Understanding psychotherapy.* Champaign, IL: Research Press, 1977.

Altrocchi, J.   *Abnormal behavior.* New York: Harcourt, Brace, Jovanovich, 1980.

American Psychological Association. Ethical principles of psychologists. *American Psychologist,* 1981, *36,* 633-638.

Chesler, P.   *Women and madness.* Garden City, NY: Doubleday, 1972.

Corey, G., Corey, M. S., & Callanan, P.   *Issues and ethics in the helping professions* (2nd ed.). Monterey, CA: Brooks-Cole, 1984.

Ewing, D.   *Freedom inside the organization.* New York: McGraw-Hill, 1977.

Fernald, C., Tedeschi, R., Siegfried, W., Gilmore, O., Grimsley, D., & Chipley, B.   Designing and managing an undergraduate practicum course in psychology. *Teaching of Psychology,* 1982, *9,* 155-160.

Heller, K., Price, R., Reinhart, S., Riger, S., & Wandersman, A.   *Psychology and community change* (2nd ed.). Homewood, IL: Dorsey Press, 1984.

Okun, B.   *Effective helping.* Monterey, CA: Brooks/Cole, 1982.

Rappaport, J.   *Community psychology.* New York: Holt, Rinehart, Winston, 1977.

Steiner, L.   Rescue. In H. Wyckoff (ed.), *Love, therapy and politics.* New York: Grove Press, 1976.

Terry R.   *For whites only.* Grand Rapids, MI: Eerdmans, 1970.

VandeCreek, L., & Fleisher, M.   The role of practicum in the undergraduate psychology curriculum. *Teaching of Psychology,* 1984, *11,* 9-14.

Weick, K.   Small wins redefining the scale of social problems. *American Psychologist,* 1984, *39,* 40-48.

Notes

1. A previous draft of this paper appeared in the *Community Connection*, a newsletter for instructors of undergraduate practicum and classroom-based courses in applied and community psychology. The *Community Connection* may be obtained free of charge from the author, or from Maurice Elias, Department of Psychology, Tilleh Hall, Livingston Campus, Rutgers University, New Brunswick, NJ 08903.

2. The author wishes to thank Maurice Elias, Anne Wilson and Susan McCammon for their helpful comments on previous drafts of this paper. Chuck Laudermilch provided *For Whites Only* for review. A number of practicum students have also contributed indirectly to this paper by their honest reactions to readings and exercises. Sandra Long provided expert secretarial assistance.

2.   DESCRIBING UNDERGRADUATE PLACEMENTS

This selection of articles includes descriptions of more than 20 placement programs and 30 settings. It also contains detailed examples of specific activities that students have performed in those settings. Authors demonstrated considerable creativity in using novel placements. An examination of the index also reveals diversity of placements.

The programs differ greatly in scope and purpose. Some included a placement experience as part of an academic course, and a few were full-time placements that were part of a technical training program. Generally, the placements consisted of 10 and 15 students working 3 to 9 hours per week for a semester. The first group of articles focuses on programs that offered placements with varied settings and/or clientele. The next group reviewed programs that limited participants to a particular type of setting. Five of the seven articles consisted of settings with children. The last group of articles describes placements that prepared students for specific jobs.

a.   Diversified Settings and/or Clientele

In an article condensed from a symposium presented at the APA convention, several authors described field experiences in a variety of settings. In addition, they commented on the critical issues common to most placements. Algea Harrison identified the goals of a battered child program at Oakland University where students spent 4 hours per week for two semesters with a family who had experienced abuse problems. David Shantz, also from Oakland University implemented a foster-grandparents program for retarded adolescents. Robert Fink enumerated students' learning experiences as suicide "therapists" in the Oakland program. Allen Hess from Auburn University identified some training issues that he faced when he provided a dozen students with service experience in prisons. Harold Zeplin also from Oakland University described a 40 to 50 hour field work program in applied gerontology. Finally, Joseph Aponte, Lawrence Lilliston (both from the University of Louisville), and James Korn (from St. Louis University) elaborated the critical issues in training undergraduates to perform in the field. This article's lesson is that students can be meaningfully involved in a wide diversity of activities. We hope that faculty at all institutions are inspired by this selection's novel placement sites.

This next selection is a summary of a symposium presented at a meeting of the Southeastern Psychological Association. The article focused on a broadly based field placement course that has been in operation for more than 10 years at the University of North Carolina at Charlotte. Several faculty members participated in the program by supervising eight students each. C. D. Fernald and Richard Tedeschi's discussion of general planning and placement issues will be informative to those who want some concrete suggestions for getting a placement course underway. William Siegfried and David Gilmore, two industrial psychologists, identified special problems created by industrial placements. Their detailed discussion will be informative for even seasoned placement supervisors, who may want to expand their programs to include business settings. Douglas Grimsley, a department chairperson, discussed the unique academic issues that arise with placement courses and the solutions used to resolve them. The article also provided a unique view of placements from the perspective of an agency director, Beth Chipley of the Center for Human Development in Charlotte. Together, these authors gave us a particularly well organized and in-depth examination of a successful program.

Robert Sherman described a course taught at the University of California at Santa Barbara. The course ran for an academic year and placed 15 seniors for 6 hours of work per week in a variety of mental health settings. The thrust of Sherman's article was on developing a synergistic relationship between the university and placement settings. He used individualized readings and analytical weekly progress reports to strengthen the academic component. This article provides strong support for the academic value of the placement experience.

Critical Issues in Undergraduate Training In Various Community Settings

Allen K. Hess, *Auburn University,*
Algea O. Harrison, David W. Shantz,
Robert S. Fink, Harold Zepelin,
Lawrence Lilliston, *Oakland University*
Joseph F. Aponte, *University of Louisville*
James H. Korn, *St. Louis University*

Teachers planning undergraduate field experience programs will find here some problems, as well as some merits, requiring consideration.

Several trends have developed in recent years changing the nature and delivery of solutions to social problems, and the mandate of universities in training students. New manpower needs have arisen and led to the training and use of personnel called paraprofessionals. Simultaneously, student demands for "relevance" caused educators to re-examine curricula, and the mission of higher education. Convergence of these trends forms the focus of this symposium which deals with training undergraduates in delivering service and applying didactic coursework in community settings.

Intervention in Battered Child Families

The battered child program is a two semester course with practical experience open to junior and senior psychology majors, and is limited to ten students who spent at least six months with a family in order to adequately serve as a change agent. The students spent at least four hours a week with a family and attended a two hour seminar each week. Group discussions of the problems of each student served as a source of: (a) possible suggestions for actions (e.g., "Why don't you contact this agency"), (b) realistic perspective (e.g., "My family is not the only one that's mixed up"), and (c) appraisal of personal reactions (e.g., "I got so mad at that mother. How could she say such a dumb thing"). The student journal records of interactions with their family allowed for (a) the teaching of objective observation of human behavior, (b) the showing of how theories of psychology are useful to understanding human behavior, and (c) material for group discussions.

In the first class session after meeting their family the students had to identify the target member of the family with whom he or she was working (i.e., mother, child, father, etc.) and the short-term and long-term goals of the relationship. The essence of the relationship was to be a trusting friend of the target person. Goals were specific. For example, one student wanted to expose his target person to the cultural institution in which the youngster had expressed an interest, and another student wanted to help her target person prepare for the high school equivalency examination.

Problems Encountered. Although they had been exposed intellectually to the issue of battered children, it still was not enough to counteract the effects of personal exposure to insensitive and punitive acts of one human to another. I think the fact that they were sensitive was commendable, but it was difficult to instruct them in how to control their reactions in order not to alienate the family.

Different orientations by predominately middle-class students and the lower-class families caused turmoil. One of my major tasks was to keep the students from resorting to stereotypic thinking about welfare people (e.g., poor people, lazy people) in their reactions.

Conflict in authority arose between the agency personnel and myself. For example, one of my students was forbidden further contact by her client's husband who threatened the student. I forbade the student to make further contacts with the client. However, the agency kept pressuring her to continue seeing the client.

Maintaining Focus on Goals. Problems included (a) establishing realistic goals for what the students wanted to accomplish with the target person. Difficulties may have arisen because I required them to establish goals so early in the relationship. Also, students were overly optimistic about how they can change human behavior. Realistic feedback from their peers and myself corrected this problem. (b) The nature of the families: these multiproblem families first viewed the student as another social worker there to service their needs (i.e., rides to the doctor, provide food stamp applications, etc.). The agency, too, had trouble in understanding the students' role as distinct from a social worker's despite prior agreements and explanations. (c) Dependency needs of the other family members distracted the students.

Termination of Relationship. A month before the end of the course the student was to bring up termination in casual conversation with the target person, talk about mutually enjoyable experiences, and about what the person would be doing in the future without the student. The student prepared a summary of interactions with the target person for the agency, recommended further actions, and, when possible, introduced the target person to their new aide. Some of the students have not completely severed connections with their target person although they do not see them on a regular basis. —Algea Othello Harrison

Undergraduate Students and Foster-Grandparents in a Group Home for Severely Retarded Adolescents.

Two years ago our department was approached by a state agency responsible for finding community placement for institutionalized retarded children and adolescents. They specifically wanted our assistance in designing, staffing, and supervising a small residential treatment setting for institutionalized children who had severe behavioral and self-help problems, precluding community placement.

The Home was under the day-to-day direction of a live-in-houseparent — a recent graduate of our Master's program in clinical psychology — and his wife. The staff consisted of a number of Oakland undergraduate psychology majors who were employed on a 10-hours per week basis, and five foster grandparents. These grandparents were provided by another agency at no cost to our program. I was employed, on an eight hour a week basis, to work with the houseparent in the development of both individual and group programs that would help prepare our residents for successful *permanent* placement in the community.

In those first few hectic weeks after the home opened we all became profoundly impressed with the extent to which our boys' behavior was influenced by their external environment. As good behavior modifiers, we were prepared for the impact our rewards and punishments would have in their subsequent behavior. What we were not prepared for was the considerable effect that *antecedent* or eliciting stimuli had on their behavior! We suddenly began to appreciate the fact that serving meals table-style elicited significantly less jumping-up-and-running-around-the-dining-room behavior than did serving meals cafeteria style; or that washing the Van, and playing with balloons *elicited* more good behavior and less bad behavior than did coloring, drawing, or "artsy-craftsy" activities. Unfortunately, we also began to appreciate the fact that our theoretical and conceptual backgrounds did not provide much in the way of answers to the crucial question "What kinds of activities, procedures, and ways of relating to these kids will tend to elicit good rather than bad behavior?" To answer this question we were going to have to rely heavily on the child-care staff — the people with the most intimate knowledge of the residents. Accordingly, we adopted procedures whereby the houseparents and I would develop instructions and suggestions for the staff; they would implement them, and then report back and participate in the discussion of modifications and changes that appeared necessary in the light of their experiences. By working with the child care staff in this fashion it became obvious to them that they were an important and valued part of the operation, and their level of effort and enthusiasm was high!

One problem involved relationship with people in the State agency funding the project. They had no direct responsibility for the program and care of the residents, but were obviously concerned about the quality of care and that we did not abuse the residents. This concern led to such conflicts as to whether or not we could build and use a time-out-from-reinforcement room. The Agency was obviously afraid of newspaper headlines about our kids being placed in solitary confinement. We eventually got the room, but we were never able to get permission to put a hook on the outside of the time-out door! These problems were fully discussed at our staff meetings and we were able to make certain points to our staff with an impact that could never be achieved in a classroom; for example, the tremendous effect that consistency of outcome had on the residents' behavior. All the boys learned within two days not to try to get into the screened-in porch, because the door was locked, and their attempts were always unsuccessful. Since the time-out door was not locked, however, boys were periodically successful in leaving without being detected for a time, so this behavior was never successfully extinguished. To take another example, our problems with the Agency over time-out and other procedures spotlighted with considerable intensity the question as to whose interests a service facility should serve, and the complexities involved in trying to work out a compromise which strikes an appropriate balance between the interest of the clients, the staff, and the people funding the service. Here again, our students had an opportunity to learn things they would not have learned in a classroom, or in a field-placement which did not allow them access to the inner-workings of the operation. —David W. Shantz

Students as Suicide/Crisis Therapists: What Do They Learn?

The advent of practicum activities as an extension of many courses in psychology derives from the pragmatic philosophy and pedagogy of Dewey. Essentially this is the perspective that theory is learned by experiment, participation in the activities of the community, and the analysis of these experiences. Thus it is assumed that concepts and an enlarged personal sensibility are gained, as well as the mechanical competency for the particular task. The outcome is a more thoughtful, discriminating, and informed person.

Our weekly supervision had three foci: (a) problem solving aid from group members (e.g., do you know of the free pregnancy examination clinic?), (b) the student's ego involvement in the counseling situation, as well as the pattern of the interpersonal process and, (c) the relationship of theories of crisis and intervention to particular cases.

Every student did not have each of the seven learning experiences that will be enumerated. The extent and quality of their intellectual and self development varied greatly. I cannot make definitive "how much" statements. My purpose is more preliminary.

(1) Initially, the students' concepts of help were predominantly to share experiences with someone ("rapping"), give advice or instructions as to a course of action, provide material assistance, encourage emotional ventilation, and sympathetic comfort. The students assimilated new images, including facilitation of the client's decision making process rather than making the choice for him; listening, with the helper listening more than the individual receiving help; providing feedback that prompts the client to short out, acknowledge, and understand his feelings and problems; and through an active, relative directive mode of interaction, facilitating the client's recognition of his responsibility in determining the outcome of the therapeutic contact and course of action. In short, these new images all involved a definition of help that stressed action and change in a context where the student has significant limits of responsi-

bility, no real power leverage, and tends to be ineffectual by simply extending sympathy and support.

Many students found these new images jarring with their older ones. At first they felt withholding and limited. The conflict inherent in this learning process is probably an inevitable experience in being a therapist. Indeed, Ernest Jones' biography of Freud provides a gorgeous illustration. Freud, after maintaining the analytic detachment during the therapy hour, sometimes followed his patient into the coatroom and advised him on practical matters.

Besides this reconceptualization of help, many students attained a sharper definition of therapy. Commonly therapy was placed in a more modest light, with a dimming of its popular phosphorescence as a magical psychic scalpel.

(2) A second learning involved the enrichment of concepts of psychological crisis. Many students achieved understanding of how crises may develop and be manifested in unspectacular everyday behavior and situations, and that the individual's response to his situation is an integral aspect of any crisis. They learned this with a vividness that a strictly academic format simply could not capture.

(3) Self understanding: Through the analysis in supervision of their therapy work, some students gained a "feelingness" identification of certain of their personality tendencies as they are expressed in action. For example, several students discovered that they could not empathize with bleakly suicidal clients.

(4) Some developed a greater ability to maintain some perspective in their own crises. (5) Students understood how helping forms are shaped, partly but crucially, by nontherapeutic forces.

(6) The students learned that helping forms are shaped through direct interaction with community organizations and through the attitudes, values, and ideologies of the social institutions on which they are based. (7) Students gained a vocational direction from their experience.

How would I evaluate their educational experience in a formal fashion? Such research would be difficult, and suffers the pitfalls of research in psychotherapy and teacher effectiveness. If the educational goal is to facilitate the growth of individuals who are thoughtful, discriminating, and informed then a longitudinal research approach seems to be essential. —Robert S. Fink

On Putting Students in Prison: Some Issues in Training

I have brought about a dozen students into prisons in both research and service capacities. The students and I were familiar with each other from courses. Thus personal styles of the students and myself were at least minimally compatible. I was particularly careful to choose people who understood clinical concepts and were not in academic difficulty, and even more important, were socially skilled.

The student undertook a set of readings before or concurrently which focused on clinical, research, and organizational approaches to criminal justice. This served several purposes: (a) Didactic information learned in classroom was linked up to student experiences, (b) reading materials served to lend a structure or discipline and a tangible manifest task to the group, (c) the course structure served as a commitment by the students to the project for a specific

time frame, and (d) the notion was established to use the literature to help solve problems encountered in the prison.

I used an initial trip to the prison (a) to explore students' expectancies and fears of the prison (one male and one female expressed fear of residents raping women); (b) to review prison protocol (specifically, what constitutes contraband, and how to deal with requests such as delivering a letter for a prisoner to someone outside), and (c) to formalize the entry of the students and program with the responsible administrator so they could begin to relate to each other. Usually on the return trip the students were exhilarated and the degree to which they had integrated the research or service program, reading assignments, and their experience, was apparent. I was able then to assess any areas needing review. Often issues of values arose, including concerns about the ethics of delivering a program in a system so hollow in terms of human services. One fellow with Third World allegiances began crying on the trip home. He exclaimed that he would do all he could to destroy the prison, how the administrators were monsters and that his activities would be direct and would interfere with the project. Mutually we agreed that the experience was overwhelming to him and that his honest functioning in the research project would be too compromised for him to continue. More constructively, the students discussed plans of action, what goals they could reasonably aim for, how to achieve them, in which ways personnel we met would be helpful.

Using females in prison is a controversial topic. The issue of security was easily handled by telling all the students that their activities were centered in a specific area, that they should be in direct contact with each other, and that the females must be escorted into other areas by a male. No problems occurred. Females were qualitatively more effective than males. Attendance was high, language more modulated, personal appearance and grooming more attended to, and morale quite high when females were present. I might add, this occurred among male students as well as male residents. Body language, sexual societal attitudes, heterosexual relations become central topics in supervision as well as topics for residents' discussion.

One mention about race before ending this section: Race problems in prison are critical. Residents self segregate, and conflict is constant. I was unable to recruit involved black students. The students told of the continuing racial issues generated and asked for a black student participant.

I can report that all students went on to graduate school, employment in corrections, or both. For example, one fellow worked as Director of Education in Detroit's City Jail, winning the job over 30 other applicants partly as a result of his experience in the course. There is an unexplored, difficult, boundlessly rich field for program development using students in prisons to help change both. —Allen K. Hess.

Training in Applied Gerontology: The Combination of Theory and Practice

Gerontological psychology is a broad field that includes age-related cognitive change and personality change, problems of morale in old age, age-related psychopathology, and the effects of institutionalization on the aged in nursing homes.

It has research and applied aspects that enable students to explore vocational possibilities and help them to crystallize their occupational identities, including fields such as medicine, social work, clinical psychology, and political science.

The foregoing reasons stimulated my development of a series of courses on aging. The series was initiated with a traditional type of lecture course in which half of a semester was devoted to the psychology of aging. This course attracted as many as 150 students per semester. Student surveys showed that many favored a semester-long course on aging, and a significant number also expressed an interest in obtaining field experience in work with the elderly. As a result, the course offerings were expanded to include a course based on field work.

"Work With the Elderly" required the students to do from 40 to 50 hours of field work during the semester, either in an institution such as a nursing home, or with a community agency. Readings and lectures on physiological, social, and psychological aspects of aging were integrated with the field work. One class session a week was devoted to lectures, and one class session a week to reports and discussion of field experience. These discussions focussed on: (a) the characteristics of the clients, illustrating the aging process and the position of the aged in American society, (b) an evaluation of the work being done by the agencies, and (c) the role of the student in working with clients.

The appeal that field work has for the student probably comes from the satisfaction of making direct contributions to the well-being of elderly people who are in difficult circumstances. Critical to this experience, though, is the organization of the field work. The agencies selected for field placements have allowed for initiative by the students, so that the students are not just doing chores or carrying out rigid instructions. Where possible, especially in nursing homes, the students have been assigned in teams of two or more, so that they can give each other support and exchange information. In addition, classroom discussion of field experiences allows the students to learn from each other and the instructor. A provision for the guiding role of faculty seems essential because agencies serving the elderly (especially nursing homes) often lack the necessary expertise for the supervision of students.

The students contribute to the agencies. This seems especially true of nursing homes, which are seriously understaffed and often give little attention to the psychosocial needs of residents. In several instances, nursing homes have been spurred to carry on programs initiated by students. At least four students have taken jobs in nursing homes or other agencies. The field work program has led faculty into advocacy for the aged, for example, in the form of testimony before a state legislative committee on the needs of patients in nursing homes, and stimulated "action research" by faculty. Increasingly, agencies see the university as a resource. The university is in a position to provide not only training for students, but also, through the work of its students and faculty, to help upgrade the services for the elderly in the surrounding community.

But can a psychology department, by itself, develop in-depth training in special psychological skills, and also maintain responsibility for a program with a great variety of field placements? The concepts of community psychology may suggest that a psychology department is capable of "going it alone." But it may be dangerous to overlook the particular contributions that sociologists, social workers, and members of other disciplines can make to training students for work with the elderly. —Harold Zepelin

Discussion: Critical Dimensions in Undergraduate Training[1]

The first critical dimension, the *value base,* reflects the provision of services to the community, and secondly, the provision of training experiences to students through which they can acquire useful skills. A critical issue is who determines the ideology and value base? Is it the university? Is it the total community? Or is it the setting with which one has a training relationship?

Regarding *program goals and objectives,* a number of critical questions arise. What kind of student does the program turn out? Is the student eventually going to apply his/her undergraduate training in a service setting or go into graduate training? Flexible training allows the student to go to either setting.

The *units of study* in the above described programs predominantly focus on individuals but also encompass the study and work with families, particularly in the Battered Children Program. A critical issue is the focus of each of the community activities. How well do the experiences complement or supplement each other? One could, for example, have an undergraduate course in group processes that potentially would have relevance to all of the different community activities that have been described. Or one could teach group process skills within the framework of community activities, such as the prison program and crisis intervention program.

Another critical dimension is the *knowledge and research base* of the training program. Is there actually a bridging of research, theory, and actual field practice? This issue is critical to all training programs — undergraduate and graduate — and it is usually difficult to accomplish.

The fifth dimension deals with the skills that students acquire in the program and fluctuates according to the community activity. It is critical to specify the nature and extent of the skills. What specific services are the graduates capable and not capable of doing?

In looking at the total psychology training program, another critical issue is the *specification of core courses and their sequencing.* Who determines what these core courses are? Is it the university or is it the service program where the student is placed? Situations potentially exist where the service setting can actually have a great deal of impact in determining the type of content in the courses and the type of field experience.

The *format dimension* involves several key issues. One issue is how the various courses interlock with each other. How much duplication is there in the acquisition of skills? What are the differences and similarities among the various types of courses and practicum experiences? Descriptions have been provided of a variety of field placements where students are performing different kinds of tasks. How does that student pull all these together in the end?

Supervision varies depending upon the type of setting the student is placed in and the relationship between the university and the community setting. How does one go about *selecting these students?* What specific criteria or experiences are critical in the selection of students? What is the role of the community setting in the selection of students? What are the *specific roles of the student and faculty?* What are the specific roles of the people at the service agencies? It is a very complex set of questions because it really depends upon the type of setting. Is the faculty member an outside consultant, a part of the staff setting, and/or a supervisor? All of these questions and their answers have different implications for entrance, continuity, and termination of activities in community settings. And what are the student roles in relationship to the different levels of agency personnel?

How do you go about determining the needs of the community setting? Oftentimes when students are placed in settings, there is little awareness of these needs. They should be clearly identified and community setting expectations articulated in detail.

A critical issue that has not been addressed in the presentations is the *nature of the role models* for the students. The faculty is *not* a role model because of its status and university affiliation. This is particularly critical if the students are going to be terminating at the baccalaureate level. Does the role model come from the service setting? Who, if anybody, does the student identify with?

Related to role model identity is the critical issue of the existence of personnel classifications at local, state, and federal levels that would allow students to get jobs. If no match exists between the skills that these students acquire in the training program and the job specifications, it will then be difficult for them to find employment. New job classifications may have to be created. How much mobility is there for the student who completes the program, not only in terms of career ladders, but also in terms of career lattice. Can the individual move vertically up the career ladder, and move horizontally to other types of jobs within a system?

Finally, there needs to be both short-term and long-term *evaluation.* What happens to the students who complete the program and also what happens to the particular settings where the students are placed? These questions need to be answered.   —Joseph F. Aponte

Discussion: Critical Issues in Undergraduate Training

Importance of field experience. I am convinced that programs such as those presented here facilitate a kind of learning that is an essential part of a student's education. First, field education provides a vehicle for career decision making. As Dr. Fink's students demonstrated, these decisions can be either positive or negative, that is, a student may confirm his or her interest in a career area or find that it really isn't the right place to be. Second, values can be clarified and developed in ways that cannot happen in a classroom. For example, students may learn directly about human cruelty (see Harrison above) or the value of human life (see Fink above). Conflicts among economic, political, and moral values become more real.

This view of the importance of field experience appar-

ently is not widely accepted in academic psychology. The APA report on undergraduate education (Kulik, 1973) showed only 15.6% of four-year colleges listing field experiences as a "curriculum innovation." These experiences ranged from class visits to a local zoo to apprenticeships in behavior modification. I suspect many examples can be found of sending students out to see what they can see with no analysis of experience. One of the conclusions of the APA report was that techniques for coordinating field experience with classroom learning are still to be discovered. The programs reported here are at least partially responsive to this problem.

Is field experience important enough that it should be a more established feature of undergraduate psychology curricula, at least as important as a course in statistics? It should have that degree of importance only under certain conditions. First and most important, there must be *analysis of the experience.* The college or university is uniquely suited to the analytic function. If we do not provide that, the student could just as well do volunteer work and save the tuition money. Field work must also be *significant.* That is, students should behave as professionals and not serve in maintenance or clerical roles. Finally, we should do everything possible to make the experience a successful, *rewarding* one for the student. The student will learn more, and his or her success is likely to lead to a good recommendation for later employment.

Selection. Should any student be allowed in these programs? Hess chose students who were compatible with the instructor and who were socially skilled. Fink lists "personal characteristics" of students. Were these factors necessary in selection? Not much data can be found to help with this issue. I think most students can handle just about any placement given reasonable levels of interest, skill, and confidence. Still some screening should take place to protect both students and clients in the placement settings. Regular contact with agency supervisors should then be maintained to monitor student performance.

Placement of students in jobs. For what are they being trained? It is possible to give an extensive list of job titles suited to psychology majors (and most other liberal arts majors for that matter). What we need more are methods and systems for assessing markets for these jobs. Since that is not likely to happen we may have to create job markets, in effect to advertise. One way to do this is to acquire contacts in our communities. Helping students find jobs may often have as much to do with who you know as with the student's background.

Why should we do this? Because training implies a job. We have an obligation to students when we accept them into programs labeled as training or career preparation. In addition to our own efforts to open doors for our students, we should provide them with job-finding skills such as where to find information, assertiveness training, and interviewing strategies. An excellent source in this area is Richard Bolles' *What Color is Your Parachute?* (1972).

Another part of this issue is program flexibility. Many programs, especially those labeled "paraprofessional," are very limited in scope. They provide highly specific skills for specific jobs. We should strive for a degree of breadth in skills and experience. A student should combine two or more of these programs and achieve quite a versatile background.

Evaluation of effectiveness. It is difficult to find programs that provide useful data. Most programs do have goals, teaching of some kind of skill, that could be assessed. There should be more attempts to discover whether those skills are learned and used in other situations.

There is a danger here. If these programs are effective, these people with baccalaureate degrees pose a real threat to those higher in the educational hierarchy. People with higher academic degrees hold the power in many placement settings and we must be aware of a potential threat to their academic egos. This danger appears small in comparison to the need for competent people in the helping professions, whether or not they call themselves psychologists. Programs like those described here are powerful vehicles for learning, and we should take full advantage of their potential. — James H. Korn

References

Bolles, R. N. *What color is your parachute? A practical manual for job-hunters and career-changes.* Berkeley, CA: Ten Speed Press, 1972.

Kulik, J. A. *Undergraduate education in psychology.* Washington, DC: American Psychological Association, 1973.

Notes

1. These dimensions have been previously developed and utilized by Drs. Bernard Bloom, Ira Iscoe, Robert Reiff, and Charles Speilberger.
2. This paper is a condensed account of a symposium presented at the 83rd Annual Convention of the American Psychological Association in Chicago, 1975.

Designing and Managing an Undergraduate Practicum Course in Psychology

C. D. Fernald, Richard G. Tedeschi,
William D. Siegfried, David C. Gilmore,
Douglas L. Grimsley
University of North Carolina at Charlotte
and Beth Chipley
Center for Human Development, Charlotte

This is a comprehensive report of procedures, problems and values in a broadly based program from a department with 10 years' experience.

The faculty-supervised, off-campus learning experience, known by a variety of names including internship, clinical, and practicum, is not a new teaching methodology. It has been a familiar part of Bachelor's level programs in education, engineering, and nursing for decades. It is also a well-established component of graduate-level psychology programs. But the inclusion of practicum as part of undergraduate coursework in psychology is relatively recent in most institutions. For example, in 1969 undergraduate practicum was one of the least frequently offered psychology courses, but by 1975, forty-five percent of four year colleges taught undergraduate practicum (Lux & Daniel, 1978). A more recent report (Mink, 1979) indicated over 70% of colleges and universities surveyed provided undergraduate internships in psychology.

Traditionally, most undergraduate coursework has been theory-oriented rather than skill-oriented, and has been a preparation for graduate training or part of a general liberal arts curriculum rather than a preparation for a post-BA job in psychology. With the increase in the use of para-professionals in agencies such as community mental health centers, there are new opportunities for the BA psychology graduate. A survey of Fryrear (1979) of sunbelt cities showed that 38% of community social agencies employed people with BA degrees. Most of these agencies required experience prior to

entry into the job. Psychology practica provide just that type of experience.

In spite of the fact that there is apparently great interest in and need for undergraduate practica in psychology, there has been little systematic examination of the practicum in the literature. Barton and Duerfeldt (1980) found that only 15 pages in the literature had been devoted to practicum. Other articles have described specialized practica (e.g., child psychology, Prerost, 1981; behavioral training, Barton & Duerfeldt, 1980; Allen, 1978) or have focused on particular aspects of the course (e.g., supervision, Kramer & Harshman, 1979; placement sites, Hess, Harrison, Fink, Lilliston, Aponte & Korn, 1978; goal identification, Keller, 1979). Most articles, however, have not provided a comprehensive description of such courses nor have they dealt with the specific issues of ethics, industrial placements, administrative and legal aspects, and concerns of placement agencies. The purpose of this paper is to describe our experiences with the undergraduate practicum course that has been in operation for over ten years at the University of North Carolina at Charlotte. First, we discuss general issues concerning planning and implementing an undergraduate practicum. Next, our industrial psychologists address the special problems that arise when students are placed in business and industrial settings. Third, the unique administrative issues that arise with practicum are discussed by our departmental chairman. Last, the perspective of an agency that provides a placement site for students is described by their volunteer coordinator.

Planning and Implementing the
Undergraduate Practicum Course

Benefits of Undergraduate Practica. Since we have introduced undergraduate practica into our program, we have recognized the benefits of this course both for the student who intends to proceed to graduate school as well as for the student who is looking forward to a job with a BA degree. First, students may learn how theory can be applied in solving real-world problems when the instructor emphasizes this connection in supervisory sessions. A second benefit of practicum is that it allows acquisition of skills and knowledge from agency professionals that may be difficult for a single instructor to provide in a classroom. A third function of practicum is that it provides career opportunities and information to students that is difficult to obtain in any other way. It allows students to try out career options and see what people in various jobs actually do. Students develop personal contacts and the experience which can be so important in landing jobs in the competitive human services area after graduation. Finally, students demonstrate their abilities on the job, so that supervisors can accurately judge their potential as professionals. This is helpful for students when they seek recommendations for jobs or graduate school.

Student Selection. We have found that in order to have adequate time to arrange placements, it is necessary to select students by at least the midpoint of the preceding semester. We limit the number of students to six to eight per faculty supervisor to ensure close, high-quality supervision. Selections are made on the basis of grades, previous courses, faculty references and class standing, and are limited to junior and senior psychology majors. A delicate situation that arises from time to time concerns the student whose academic qualifications are satisfactory, but whose interpersonal style or skills are inappropriate or even harmful for work in a human service agency, and might jeopardize the success of the practicum program. This is a dilemma because the University's primary commitment is to the student's learning, and these students are the ones that need to learn the most. We have found that it is best to alert agency personnel to the potential problems with these students, but to leave the final decision of acceptance up to the agency. Often an appropriate placement can be found for these students and some turn out to be surprisingly successful.

Arranging Placement Sites. We are fortunate to have approximately 30 excellent agencies and organizations nearby that are pleased to accept psychology practicum students. Many of these sites have been developed through personal contacts that faculty members have with staff psychologists. In addition, large agencies have volunteer services coordinators who are useful in establishing placements, although it is important early in the deliberations for the faculty member to communicate directly with the staff member who will be the student's immediate supervisor.

It is important to make clear to the agency from the outset the role of the agency supervisor. The agency has the primary responsibility to ensure good client services, but they must also be willing to make a commitment to help the student. Agencies must understand that the practicum is primarily an academic experience and that any benefit the agency derives from the students' work is of secondary importance. It must also be understood that the student should be engaged in specific activities that will allow attainment of certain skills or knowledge. Active participation of the student is usually preferable to mere observation.

Course Requirements. Many problems that arise in the practicum course can be prevented by specifying all the details of the course in writing before the start of the semester. We use a standardized form for each student to complete to indicate learning goals, activities in the agency, schedule at agency, supervision requirements, and academic requirements, which usually includes class presentations, maintaining a journal, and writing a paper. The student, faculty member and agency supervisor each sign the form and keep a copy.

Normally the faculty supervisor spends one hour per week in class with the practicum students to ensure that students will develop a minimal level of clinical competence. It also provides an opportunity for students to exchange information and experiences among themselves. They are usually reassured and excited to find that others are encountering similar frustrations and insights. Class topics include ethical issues, basic helping skills such as active listening, behavioral principles such as observing and reinforcement, crisis intervention such as handling suicide threats, and treatment planning. Role playing and videotaping are useful ways of practicing these skills and providing students with feedback.

Most academic courses use various evaluation techniques to encourage students to perform high quality work, and this is the case with practicum courses as well. Although examinations may be given in practicum courses, other possibilities present themselves because of the small class size or individualized supervision. Evaluation can be based upon logs or journals, oral and written reports, class discussion and individual supervision sessions. Assessments of agency work can also be made through observation, work samples such as tape recordings or copies of written work done by the student, and reports of agency supervisors.

Assigning grades to students is more difficult in practicum than in other courses. Course objectives are not as easily defined and are less objectively measured than in conventional courses. Goals and activities will vary with individual students and different placement sites, making comparisons across students more difficult. Also, some of the information that the faculty member uses to evaluate student performance comes from third parties (i.e., agency supervisors) and it is difficult to gauge the validity of these judgments. Because of these problems with grading, we have moved to assigning practicum grades on a pass/no credit basis. One problem with this change is that students complain that the work load is too great to justify merely a "pass" grade.

The success of the student practicum experience probably depends more on the quality of supervision, especially agency supervision, than any other single variable. The purposes of supervision are to monitor progress and to anticipate and prevent problems, to provide feedback to the student about his or her strengths and weaknesses, and to delineate and help the student process what he or she is learning and how it relates to the theory and data of psychology. We require that the faculty and agency supervisors each spend approximately one-half hour weekly with the student in supervision. Furthermore, the faculty member is expected to talk with the agency supervisor at least once monthly by phone and visit the agency at least once each semester. While these activities are time consuming, they ensure that the student is learning and they prevent the development of serious problems by maintaining communications among all parties concerned.

Inasmuch as the Ethical Standards of Psychologists (APA, 1979) are designed to apply to students of psychology functioning in the role of psychologists, these standards should guide students in their practicum experience. The relevance of the various principles for an individual student will vary according to the duties performed at an agency, but certain principles have especially important messages for most undergraduates enrolled in practica. For example, the principle of *responsibility* requires students to maintain high standards of quality in their work and to accept the consequences of their decisions. The guidelines on *competence* are especially meaningful for students because there are obvious questions about the limits to their abilities. Some students are uncertain about testing their abilities, whereas others are anxious to exceed the limits of their competence in their enthusiasm for working and learning. The practicum course should include a component that encourages students to accurately assess their competence, and to formulate an approach to agency staff and clients that promotes an appropriate perception of the students' roles and capabilities. Furthermore, supervisors must be willing to address the personal styles or problems of students that affect performance at the agency, because this has implications for others as well as for the student. The principle of *confidentiality* becomes especially important for students when class discussions of agency work are designed into the course, and when the student wishes to talk with others outside the course about the interesting experiences. *Professional relationships* are often difficult for practicum students who are new to an agency, unaware of hierarchies of authority, and who may represent a threat to some established staff members. Agencies must understand that the practicum experience is designed primarily to educate the student, but the student must be aware that any contacts with agency clients must be handled with a concern for the *welfare of the consumer* remaining uppermost in importance, while the student's learning goals are viewed as secondary.

With the proper attention paid to these general issues and to those ethical principles which apply to specific student activities, students should be equipped to make ethical decisions in the course of their work. This in itself is an extremely important learning experience in the process of professionalization that takes place in a good practicum course.

C. D. Fernald and Richard G. Tedeschi

The Psychology Intern in Industry

In the past two years, many more students have entered the industrial/organizational concentration in our psychology program. This change has also increased the interest in industrial practicum experiences and it has been especially difficult to develop sites to meet the demand. There are several specific problems that must be solved before the industrial/organizational psychology student can enjoy the access to practical experiences that the more clinically oriented student has had.

The Development of Internship Sites. Private sector, profit-making organizations have no history of "volunteerism," and are often confused by the possibility of receiving "free labor." In dealing with private sector companies it has been necessary to address quickly issues related to pay, insurance, social security, etc., because often the first question asked is, "How much do I have to pay them?"

It is often to the advantage of the sponsoring organization to place a student on the payroll. Many managers feel that this ensures the student's commitment and motivation. It also has the effect of making a student an employee, thus binding him or her to company rules and regulations. However, in addition to some unresolved legal issues regarding compensation, there is the risk of turning the practicum into a part-time job rather than a learning experience. The net result is that many companies are reluctant to supervise a student without pay, while the university is reluctant to allow the student to be compensated.

Based on the competitive nature of private enterprise, organizations are reluctant to share company secrets with students who in turn will share them with faculty supervisors. This is a particular problem in cases where a student enters the internship while simultaneously holding a job in another (perhaps competing) organization. It must be made very clear from the beginning exactly what information will and will not be made available to the faculty supervisor.

Many organizations are surprised that industrial psychology skills reside in the psychology department rather than in business administration departments. Many personnel and training people will often contact that business school first, giving little thought to psychology. It is necessary to establish an image in the community so that people are aware of the diverse nature of psychology and come to see psychologists as having skills other than clinical.

Special Problems of Industrial Placements. Much of the training in psychology concerning ethical issues involves therapist-client relationships which are different from the typical situations that students face when studying organizational processes. For example, one student intern was asked by the personnel director of an organization to determine if operating managers might need to be trained to conduct better employment interviews, and the personnel director suggested that the student pose as an applicant to see what the typical interview involved. This type of deception may be necessary to get an accurate picture of the organizational process, but it obviously puts the student in a very awkward situation. In another situation, the personnel director suggested that a practicum student attend a union organizing meeting so that he might better understand the employee/union position on a number of issues. We don't think that the students were being used as spies, but it presents a number of ethical problems. Also, the practicum student in an organization is often supervised by a person with little or no psychological training, and that supervisor may have a different set of ethical considerations than would a person with psychological training.

One problem, more specific to industrial settings, is that many companies have dress codes. We have found that students often need to be told that business dress is required. Although a rather "scruffy" looking student may be a welcome extra hand working in a mental health setting, such appearances would definitely be out of place in the "3-piece" world of private business.

Whereas it may not be unique to industrial placements, sexual harassment has created some problems. Two of the twelve female practica students placed in the past two years have complained about sexual advances by their male supervisors. In both cases the offenses were fairly minor, such as asking to go out for a drink or excessive physical contact. The biggest problem, however, was a reluctance to discuss the problem until it reached the point that the entire practicum experience was affected. In one case the faculty supervisors were not aware of the problem until the agency supervisor called to report that the student had not come to work for a two or three week period. Confrontation with the student was not easy, and it took quite a while before the true nature of the problem was mentioned.

Some organizations see the practicum as the opportunity for free organizational consulting. In some instances organizations assume that our students are organizational consultants who can solve a wide variety of complex organizational problems in a single semester. In these cases we must remind the organization that these are undergraduate students who have some, but limited, expertise and that they are attempting to learn in their practicum. If the student realizes that he/she cannot solve all of the organization's problems, the student turns to their faculty advisor for "what should I do" answers. In this case the student becomes a "broker" and the faculty advisors become organizational consultants. We expect a reasonable amount of that type of activity in return for a good learning situation for our students, but we must draw the line somewhere.

Much of what psychology departments teach in undergraduate curricula involves considerable theory, but personnel managers, training directors, and other organizational supervisors tend to be concerned with practical problems. In the clinical type practica many of the agency supervisors have had training in psychology and may be more tolerant of our students who have been taught to deal with theoretical issues. In industrial situations, a theory-laden student who cannot move to a practical level quickly may be viewed as inappropriate for such work. Allegedly, practica are intended to provide the practical experience necessary to transfer theory into everyday use. However, we have an unconfirmed suspicion that practicum students in industrial organizations may be expected to make that transition more quickly than in the "helping relationship" practica. Part of this problem may be the background of the agency supervisors (often little psychological training) and part of the problem may be the pragmatic approach to problem solving prevalent in many organizations.

Recommendations.   Because of some of the problems we have described above, we have found that the most feasible industrial/organizational practica sites are not found in private industry, but rather in the public sector. Local mental health facilities, university personnel offices, local city government, are all performing functions found in private industry, such as personnel and training. These organizations have a history of using volunteers, are not as concerned with profit (only cost) and are eager to support the university. Legal issues are minimized, profits are not threatened, and competition is non-existent. Although the setting is different, and perhaps the prestige is lacking, we have found these organizations to be extremely valuable practicum sites. Although students sometimes are reluctant to give up the hope of working for a "name" company, their actual practicum experience is usually far superior.

William D. Siegfried and David C. Gilmore

Psychology Department Administration and the Practicum Program

The administration of a practicum program requires attention to a number of details prior to the time the program is initiated. It is essential that there are competent faculty and students who desire such an approach and that the rationale and goals are clearly stated.

There are a number of different approaches to administering the practicum program in a department. It might be established and run by individual faculty members (with little departmental endorsement or involvement), by department chairpersons or their designee, or by a university coordinator or director.

Credit Hours.   It is difficult to decide how to assign credit to practicum courses so that it is comparable to that in regular courses. We assign variable amounts of credit, from one to four semester-hours per semester, depending upon the student's work plan. As a rule of thumb, the student must work at least two hours weekly at the agency for each one hour of credit. This is similar to how credits for laboratory courses are assigned. We limit the total number of credit hours the student may take (8 semester hours) and even further limit the number that can satisfy major requirements (3 semester hours) to prevent students from taking too much practicum.

Serious concern would also have to be raised about the issue of transferability of practicum courses. If most of the students in an institution later transfer to complete their degree, it is essential that the articulation with the upper division institution be established.

Faculty Compensation.   One of the most significant issues in establishing practicum courses involves faculty compensation. How will a faculty member's workload be determined when practicum supervision is involved? In some departments, practicum supervision doesn't count as part of the teaching load and must be done on an overload basis; there is no compensation or reduction in workload. We allow faculty to count as part of their teaching load (one course equivalency) practicum supervision of about 8 students. We also permit faculty to supervise one or two students at a time on an overload basis and "bank the credit" until such time that they have accumulated enough credit to receive a course reduction. Because faculty who teach practicum carry considerably fewer students than they would in a regular course, practicum is a relatively "expensive" course. However, we feel that the potential gains are important enough to justify the additional costs.

A very significant aspect of faculty compensation involves the potential for considerable expense in the supervision of students in the field. Budgets in a department offering practicum supervision should be supplemented or arranged to provide for travel, and related parking expenses, and often meals, if the supervision is to be done properly.

Legal Issues.   There are a number of potential legal issues that arise concerning practicum. Questions such as university and faculty liability for student misconduct, violations of minimum wage laws and liability for accidental injuries during practicum activities are just a few. We have not been able to locate any definitive, comprehensive source that addresses these questions, although one booklet discusses many issues concerning paid "cooperative education assignments" (Hunt, 1980). It is our impression that the university and faculty are not liable unless they have performed their duties in a negligent manner. Thus competent, diligent, conscientious instruction and supervision of students should relieve the faculty members and the university from fault for accidents or misconduct over which they had no control.

Apparently minimum wage and other fair labor standards do not apply to practicum students as long as the training is for the student's benefit, it is understood in advance that the student will not receive pay, the student knows he is not necessarily entitled to a job at the end of the practicum, and the employer derives no immediate advantage from the activities (Hunt, 1980). "The Department of Labor is concerned with situations where the employer would be using the student on a regular and somewhat permanent basis to perform a basic and required function that would normally require a paid employee working on a part-time or fulltime schedule" (Hunt, 1980, p. 8). All employee issues, such as employee selection procedures, unemployment compensation and social security benefits are concerns with paid internships, but apparently these do not arise with unpaid internships. In any case, because there are complex legal issues involved, the university attorney should be consulted when they arise.

Douglas L. Grimsley

The Perspective of the Human Service Agency

The University of North Carolina at Charlotte is fortunate to have good working relationships with a large number of human service agencies. The following section describes the practices at the Center for Human Development, but they are typical of most of the larger agencies we work with.

Purposes.   There are two mandates of many human service agencies that call for student involvement: (a) Casefinding. Unless people know the agency and what it does, it can't help them. Students/volunteers involved in the programs become public relations people. They talk about their experiences with their classmates, roommates, and parents and in doing so will "spread the word" about the services and programs. (b) Human Resources Development. The Center for Human Development has an obligation to see that there is a continuous pool of professionals available to provide developmental disability service. That obligation includes intro-ducing students to this career field and hopefully providing interested students with the experience and information needed to complement their academic studies as well as encourage them to join us in providing services to the developmentally disabled populations in the future.

Other reasons agencies like to have students around include the fact that it's just plain fun to have the fresh ideas and the "shot in the arm" of somebody thinking that the staff's jobs are special and wanting to follow in their footsteps. An extra pair of hands is attractive, too; staff can accomplish a great deal with the assistance of a well-trained student. Some suggestions students make are so good that they become standard agency practices. One further advantage is that supervising students is good training for staff who haven't had the opportunity of supervising previously. It gives staff new skills.

Agency Procedures.   At the Center for Human Development, there are two primary staff members involved with each practicum student: the Volunteer Services Coordinator and the staff person who will supervise the student. The Volunteer Services Coordinator has the following responsibilities:

1. Assist staff in writing a volunteer job description for the student.
2. Recruit an appropriate student.
3. Conduct an initial screening and agency tour with the student.
4. Provide training in Volunteer Utilization for staff planning to supervise the student.
5. Monitor the relationship between the student and the agency throughout the semester.
6. Conduct an exit interview with the student at the close of the practicum experience.
7. See that the student's folder contains the required documents: application, job description, time card, student evaluation, staff evaluation, and any correspondence or notes concerning that student. This folder will be kept by the Volunteer Services Coordinator in the event that the student wishes to use the Center as a reference for a job or graduate school.

These are the responsibilities of the staff supervising the practicum student:

1. Participate in writing the job description.
2. Interview the student after the initial screening to assure that there is a match between the needs of the student and the needs of the staff person, and to clarify expectations.
3. Train the student to do the jobs outlined in the job description.
4. Integrate student into the agency.
5. Provide regular, meaningful supervision sessions throughout the semester.
6. Document time spent supervising and teaching student.
7. Evaluate student's performance at the end of the semester, for both the university and the agency.

What Do Agencies Need From Instructors?   What agencies need from instructors, in a word, is involvement. Having an active, involved instructor on the other side of the student gives us some leverage in simple things such as attendance and completing the semester's commitment.

The instructor can help a student process what is seen and experienced at the agency. Many times a student will share problems, anxieties and questions with the "third party" instructor before saying anything to their supervisor at the agency. The instructor can then alert the agency and problems can be smoothed out before they blow out of proportion.

Credibility is given to the students by the involvement of the instructor, and the staff responds well to phone calls or site visits by the instructor. Also, the relationships developed between the instructor and staff can provide an on-going placement slot for future students.

Finally, the evaluation of the program by instructors is most important to the agency. This is done informally throughout the semester and more formally at the end of the experience. The Volunteer Services Coordinator can make adjustments in the volunteer program to match the needs and recommendations of particular instructors and the different student referral sources.

Beth Chipley

Conclusion

Frequently students report that they have learned more in Practicum than in any other course, because they learn more by doing than by just reading and talking. Whether this is true is difficult to determine, but the practicum course should not just provide practical job training. It should also enable the student to integrate the theory and data of the classroom with "real world" experience. It should provide good services for clients and organizations as well as for students. Students should acquire new skills and insights that are important for their intellectual and personal development. Successful practicum experiences do not occur without careful planning and monitoring: careful selection of students and their placements; thorough planning of course goals and activities; close, frequent supervision by faculty and the agency; maintenance of high expectations and standards of student performance; adequate administrative support for the faculty; and close cooperation between the university and the agencies. Careful attention to these issues can help make practicum one of the best courses an undergraduate takes.

References

Allen, J. L. A January interim behavior modification seminar/ practicum. *Teaching of Psychology*, 1978, 5, 156-157.

American Psychological Association. *Ethical standards of psychologists*. Washington, DC: Author, 1979.

Barton, E. J., & Duerfeldt, P. H. Undergraduate psychology practica pragmatism. *Teaching of Psychology*, 1980, 7, 146-149.

Fryrear, J. L. Community agency employment opportunities and requirements. In P. J. Woods (Ed.), *The psychology major*. Washington, DC: American Psychological Association, 1979.

Hess, A. K., Harrison, A. O., Fink, R. S., Lilliston, L., Aponte, J. F., & Korn, J. H. Critical issues in undergraduate training in various community settings. *Teaching of Psychology*, 1978, 5, 81-86.

Hunt, D. C. *Legal considerations in cooperative education administration*. Detroit: Cooperative Education Program, University of Detroit, 1980.

Keller, P. A. Identifying goals for undergraduate internships. *Teaching of Psychology*, 1979, 6, 240-241.

Kramer, T. J., & Harshman, E. A. Model for faculty supervision of interns. In P. J. Woods (Ed.), *The psychology major*. Washington, DC: American Psychological Association, 1979.

Lux, D. F., & Daniel, R. S. Which courses are most frequently listed by psychology departments? *Teaching of Psychology*, 1978, 5, 13-16.

Mink, W. The Undergraduate major: Preparation for career or graduate school. In P. J. Woods (Ed.), *The psychology major*. Washington, DC: American Psychological Association, 1979.

Prerost, F. J. The feasibility of undergraduate field experiences in child psychology: Program factors and suggestions. *Teaching of Psychology*, 1981, 8, 19-22.

Notes

1. This paper is a summary of a symposium presented at the annual convention of the Southeastern Psychological Association in Atlanta, 1981.

Psychology Fieldwork: A Catalyst for Advancing Knowledge and Academic Skills

A. Robert Sherman
University of California, Santa Barbara

With certain features, a fieldwork course can promote a synergistic relationship between academic and experiential components.

It is the "experiential" component of psychology fieldwork courses that is often responsible for attracting the enthusiastic interest of students and offending the scholarly values of educators. Such courses are viewed by some as social diversions which afford academic credit with little intellectual effort or benefit. Others view them as honorably motivated but differ in their expectations as to whether academic goals will be appreciably served by fieldwork observation and participation. As advocated by Vande Creek and Thompson (1977), "The goal must be an increase in the intern's knowledge and/or skills . . . , not the carrying out of 'busywork' or enhancing the staff of an agency" (p. 177). It is the contention of this paper that a psychology fieldwork course can promote a synergistic relationship between academic and experiential components to advance the student's knowledge and academic skills of inquiry, analysis, and communication, in a manner which is satisfactory to students and educators alike.

Conceptual Framework. Within this conceptual perspective, the fieldwork experience is seen as a catalyst in augmenting the intellectual challenges and academic benefits associated with other course activities. With certain features, such a course can advance the student beyond the gains normally derived from separate, uncoordinated participation in academic and experiential functions.

Something certainly will be learned from standard coursework and from volunteer fieldwork experienced independently, but there may be certain limitations. For example, how many students would still be able to pass the final exam in their abnormal psychology course if the exam were presented to them a year later? And to what extent would the retained knowledge coincide with their actual needs if they subsequently found themselves confronted with the real-life challenges of working in a clinical facility? Conversely, how much benefit would the student volunteer derive from spending several hours per week at a clinical facility with little academic preparation, minimal supervision, and hours that vary with other educational, job, and social demands that are given priority over the student's volunteer commitment?

It is here hypothesized that the learning afforded by these two kinds of experiences, standard coursework and volunteer fieldwork, can be enhanced considerably through their integration into a psychology fieldwork course which includes certain additional features designed to facilitate the synergistic process. These features include individualized reading, analytical writing, and multidimensional evaluation, as represented in a fieldwork course introduced in 1970 at the University of California, Santa Barbara, with continued refinement from year to year.

The Course. The course was designed to provide superior psychology students with an opportunity to broaden their undergraduate training through academic coursework supplemented by supervised field experience in settings providing psychological services. The course begins each Fall Quarter and runs through the academic year, accommodating about fifteen senior psychology majors who are selected from a long list of applicants on the basis of overall academic performance and past performance in psychology. At the outset, students are given a course syllabus, an overview of the course, a description of the fieldwork facilities, and a summary of the basic course objectives. The objectives include helping the student to:

(1) Develop a broader and deeper knowledge of the theories and methods of psychological intervention employed in real-life settings.
(2) Become familiar with the specialized literature on psychopathology and its treatment related to the type of facility and population of the assigned fieldwork setting.
(3) Become partly desensitized to the stresses and challenges of establishing a personal identity in a "helper" role at a psychological-service facility, as well as to the frustration of discovering that well-intended personal efforts are not always successful or appreciated.
(4) Gain a more realistic perspective on the strengths and weaknesses of existing psychological facilities, their staffs, and the methods they employ.
(5) Learn about the structure and functions of other psychological facilities through visits, presentations by professional staff, and discussions by students working at other facilities.

(6) Improve and refine academic skills of inquiry, analysis, and communication.
(7) Conduct small-scale research projects with an individual or group if such an activity is within the student's interest, and is feasible at the assigned facility.

In accordance with their preferences, three or four students are assigned to each of four available facilities for the year. These facilities vary in their client populations (e.g., psychotic adults; emotionally-disturbed adolescents; mentally-retarded children; etc.), structures (e.g., residential; day treatment; outpatient; etc.), and intervention approaches (e.g., behavioral; psychodynamic; group or individually-administered; etc.). Students spend approximately six hours per week at the psychological setting, at least one hour of which consists of a group supervision session conducted by a qualified staff member of the facility. Students also attend weekly class meetings with the course instructor, during which time fieldwork experiences are shared and discussed, readings are reviewed, special guest speakers are occasionally invited, and various psychological issues are considered.

Weekly progress reports, which are submitted to the instructor two days prior to each class session so that they can be evaluated and returned in class, are an important academic feature of the course. The progress report consists of two sections. The Fieldwork Experience section begins with a summary of the salient features of the student's fieldwork for the preceding week, and this is followed by the student's evaluative thoughts about the fieldwork experience. The Reading Critique section begins with a listing and summary of the individualized readings completed during the preceding week, and this is followed by a critical analysis and evaluation of the reading material and its relationship to the student's fieldwork. The progress reports are designed to encourage students to think critically and creatively about their readings and fieldwork; the reports also enable the instructor to stay in close touch with the experiences of each student, as well as to identify issues that are likely to be of interest for general class discussion.

Grades in the course are based primarily upon students' weekly progress reports, individual meetings with the instructor, quarterly evaluations of fieldwork performance provided by students' supervisors, and participation in class sessions.

Special Features. There are three special features of the course which appear to serve an important function in facilitating the synergistic relationship between the academic and experiential components:

Individualized Reading. The challenges of the fieldwork motivate the student to search for relevant literature resources to fill personal gaps in knowledge and to facilitate effective fieldwork participation, which often includes the formulation and execution of a small-scale research project. It is expected that the student who is prompted to review the current literature on, for example, paranoid schizophrenia as a result of encountering patients with that diagnosis will learn and retain more about the nature and insufficiency of our knowledge than will the student whose exposure is limited to either reading alone or encountering alone.

Analytical Writing. Preparation of a weekly progress report requires the student to think actively and creatively about the readings and fieldwork, and to gain useful experience in analytical writing. It is expected that the student who is compelled to formulate his or her thoughts and impressions in writing will achieve a greater depth of understanding than the student whose involvement in readings or fieldwork is more passive and transitory.

Multidimensional Evaluation. Awareness that, through progress reports, individual meetings with the instructor, appraisals by fieldwork supervisors, and class participation, virtually all features of student performance are being closely monitored, with constructive feedback provided, assures high standards of student academic effort. It is expected that the student whose work is being evaluated within the context of a formal course providing unit credits and a letter grade will be more motivated and reliable in fulfilling the academic and fieldwork responsibilities than, for example, a student whose commitment to fieldwork participation is entirely voluntary.

Evaluations of the Course. In addition to the experiential learning associated with the fieldwork itself, this course structure is designed to advance each student's knowledge and academic skills of inquiry, analysis, and communication. Students' course evaluations, written reports, and subsequent achievements suggest that the course has been very effective.

With regard to course evaluations, the University's Office of Instructional Development made available beginning in 1976 a wide array of course evaluation question items from which individual faculty could develop their own questionnaires for each of their courses and have the results computer-analyzed by the Office. Table 1 provides a comparison of anonymous student evaluations of the fieldwork course with evaluations of all other courses using the same evaluation items. The fieldwork course data are based upon the Fall Quarter offerings from 1976 through 1979, and the comparison data are based upon all other campus uses of the same questions during the 1976-79 period. It will be noted that on each of the ten items, the response distribution for the fieldwork course was extremely high relative to the campus average for all other courses (all $p < .001$). Among other things, the student evaluations attest to the perceived efficacy of the course in teaching different methods of inquiry and expression, improving cognitive and problem-solving abilities, promoting professional skill development, and enhancing the student's sense of personal responsibility.

It has also been rather common to find, in students' open-ended written evaluations of the fieldwork course, comments indicating that for many participants the course was one of their most valuable college experiences. For example, the following comments were selected from the (anonymous) responses of five different students during the Fall Quarter, 1980: "This is by far the best course I have ever taken." "I consider this class to be a major life experience." "This is the best psychology course I've ever taken." "This course has been incredible for me as an academic, but especially for me as a person." "This course has been the most worthwhile educational experience I'd had at UCSB." Favorable evaluations for fieldwork courses have also been reported elsewhere (e.g., Barton & Duerfeldt, 1980; Yates, 1980).

Table 1. Response Percent Distributions on Student Course Evaluations: Fieldwork Course Compared to Other Courses on Same Items

Item	Option[a]	Fieldwork Course	Other Courses
1. This course helped me learn different methods of inquiry and expression.	A	80.7	36.0
	B	15.8	53.5
	C	3.5	10.5
	n[b]	57(4)	641(26)
2. This course helped me develop specific skills, competencies, and points of view needed by professionals in this discipline.	A	94.8	41.7
	B	5.2	45.5
	C	0.0	12.8
	n	58(4)	578(22)
3. This course helped me improve my ability to think, to solve problems, and to make decisions.	A	67.9	37.2
	B	30.4	48.9
	C	1.8	13.9
	n	56(4)	583(25)
4. This course helped me develop a sense of personal responsibility (self-reliance, self-discipline).	A	78.9	39.1
	B	19.3	46.2
	C	1.8	14.7
	n	57(4)	409(15)
5. I worked harder in this course than in most courses I have taken.	A	82.5	59.2
	B	17.5	40.8
	n	57(4)	835(23)
6. In rating or evaluating a course, you can consider course material itself OR what the instructor does with the material. PLEASE GRADE ONLY THE COURSE MATERIAL.	A	88.9	36.1
	B	7.4	44.4
	C	3.7	14.9
	D	0.0	3.8
	F	0.0	0.8
	n	54(4)	3319(84)
7. In rating or evaluating a course, you can consider course material itself OR what the instructor does with the material. PLEASE GRADE ONLY THE INSTRUCTOR'S TEACHING.	A	81.5	44.7
	B	16.7	34.3
	C	1.9	14.2
	D	0.0	5.0
	F	0.0	1.8
	n	54(4)	3457(88)
8. Assume this course is not required. Knowing what the course covers, if you had not already taken it, you would:	A	85.7	36.6
	B	10.7	36.3
	C	0.0	13.3
	D	1.8	9.0
	E	1.8	4.8
	n	56(4)	2615(74)
9. How would you rate this course compared to other courses you have taken at this University?	A	89.5	48.8
	B	7.0	20.1
	C	3.5	22.1
	D	0.0	5.4
	E	0.0	3.7
	n	57(4)	2819(46)
10. The overall quality of the course was:	A	77.2	37.5
	B	14.0	27.5
	C	8.8	24.9
	D	0.0	7.2
	E	0.0	2.9
	n	57(4)	2790(44)

Nonparametric statistical tests were employed to compare the response distributions, and the differences were highly significant with $p < .001$ for each item. For all items except # 5, the Kolmogorov-Smirnov two-tailed test for two large independent samples was used; for item # 5, the Chi-Square 2 x 2 contingency table test for two independent samples was used (Siegel, 1956).
[a]Options for items 1-4 were "more, same, or less than other courses"; item 5—"agree, disagree"; items 6-7—familiar letter grades; item 8 from "definitely want to" to "definitely not want to;" 9-10—appropriately worded from strong approval (A) to strong disapproval (E).
[b]The first number represents the number of students responding to the evaluation item, and the second number (in parentheses) denotes the number of courses involved.

It should be noted that the only consistent complaint received from staff at the fieldwork facilities concerns the vacuum left by the departure of our students at the end of the academic year; in several instances, the staff had become so dependent on the contributions of particular students that offers of employment were extended to individuals upon graduation. Cole (in Caffrey, Berger, Cole, Marx, & Senn, 1977) also reported that his practicum in clinical psychology was viewed as mutually advantageous by the agencies, and Boltuck, Peterson, and Murphy (1980) presented data revealing the desirability of undergraduate fieldwork experience to employers in the clinical sector (see also Erdwins & Olivetti, 1978). The vocational implications of fieldwork experience may account in part for the increasing number of colleges which offer practicum courses (Matthews, 1979). The only notable complaint received from students, which does not appear to have discouraged others from seeking enrollment, is that the course requires so much time that more unit credits should be given.

Within this context, it probably should be noted that the course also requires a substantial time commitment from the instructor. Responsibilities include selecting and formulating fieldwork arrangements with psychological-service facilities, organizing student fieldwork assignments and staff supervisory sessions, advising on and monitoring individual readings and fieldwork activities, reviewing and providing written feedback on each student's weekly progress report, meeting with students on an individual basis in addition to weekly sessions with the entire class, helping students deal with the occasional crisis situations which inevitably arise, systematically evaluating student performances along multiple dimensions, and regularly reappraising the suitability of psychological facilities for continuation of fieldwork arrangements in conjunction with the course. Issues and problems related to some of these (and other) factors involved in organizing and conducting a psychology fieldwork course have been discussed elsewhere (e.g., Barton & Duerfeldt, 1980; Hess, Harrison, Shantz, Fink, Zepelin, Lilliston, Aponte, & Korn, 1978; Prerost, 1981; Shiverick, 1977; Vande Creek & Thompson, 1977), though it should be emphasized that difficulties encountered in implementing the present course have been few and minor in comparison with the many benefits. Although more instructor time is required than for the typical lecture course, contributing to and observing the academic progress of the students can make the experience very rewarding for the instructor as well.

Summary and Conclusions. A description of a refined and time-tested fieldwork course in psychology has been presented along with student evaluation data attesting to the academic impact of the course, and a conceptual analysis of some of the factors presumed to be responsible for its apparent success. Within this perspective, the fieldwork experience appears to serve as a catalyst in augmenting the intellectual challenges and academic benefits associated with other course activities. The synergistic effect of the academic and experiential components appears to emerge from their integration in the psychology fieldwork course together with the special features noted above. In certain respects this resembles the approach often taken in psychology research courses where academic and laboratory components are coordinated to provide students with a comprehensive experience in learning about the methods and substance of psychological research.

The purported educational desirability of merging the academic with the experiential is not a novel proposition. In his classic work entitled *Walden*, published in 1854, Henry David Thoreau included the following passage within a discussion of educational philosophy:

> Which would have advanced the most at the end of a month—the boy who had made his own jackknife from the ore which he had dug and smelted, reading as much as would be necessary for this—or the boy who had attended the lectures on metallurgy at the Institute in the meanwhile, and had received a Rogers' penknife from his father? Which would be most likely to cut his fingers? (Krutch, 1962, p. 143)

The basic view expressed here so succinctly by Thoreau, and throughout this paper, is that educational progress in certain domains will be enhanced by integrating real-life experience with academic instruction. It is a reasonable hypothesis worthy of continued exploration.

References

Barton, E. J., & Duerfeldt, P. H. Undergraduate psychology practica pragmatism. *Teaching of Psychology*, 1980, 7, 146-149.
Boltuck, M. A., Peterson, T. L., & Murphy, R. J. Preparing undergraduate psychology majors for employment in the human service delivery system. *Teaching of Psychology*, 1980, 7, 75-78.
Caffrey, B., Berger, L., Cole, S., Marx, D., & Senn, D. Integrating professional programs in a traditional undergraduate psychology program. *Teaching of Psychology*, 1977, 4, 7-13.
Erdwins, C., & Olivetti, L. J. Psychology related employment settings for graduates of submaster's programs in psychology: A bibliography. *Teaching of Psychology*, 1978, 5, 38-39.
Hess, A. K., Harrison, A. O., Shantz, D. W., Fink, R. S., Zepelin, H., Lilliston, L., Aponte, J. F., & Korn, J. H. Critical issues in undergraduate training in various community settings. *Teaching of Psychology*, 1978, 5, 81-86.
Krutch, J. W. (Ed.). *Thoreau: Walden and other writings*. New York: Bantam Books, 1962.
Matthews, J. R. Undergraduate field placement: Survey and issues. *Teaching of Psychology*, 1979, 6, 148-151.
Prerost, F. J. The feasibility of undergraduate field experiences in child psychology: Program factors and suggestions. *Teaching of Psychology*, 1981, 8, 19-22.
Shiverick, D. D. A full-time clinical practicum for undergraduates. *Teaching of Psychology*, 1977, 4, 188-190.
Siegel, S. *Nonparametric statistics for the behavioral sciences*. New York: McGraw-Hill, 1956.
Vande Creek, L., & Thompson, G. Management of undergraduate psychology internships. *Teaching of Psychology*, 1977, 4, 177-180.
Yates, B. T. Benefits and costs of community-academia interaction in a paraprofessional training course. *Teaching of Psychology*, 1980, 7, 8-12.

Notes

1. A brief description of an earlier version of the psychology fieldwork course at the University of California, Santa Barbara was presented by the author in the *Directory of Teaching Innovations in Psychology*, edited by J. B. Maas and D. A. Kleiber, Washington, DC: American Psychological Association, 1975, Pp. 363-364. Portions of the present paper were presented in preliminary form as part of a Symposium on "Conceptual Models of Fieldwork in Psychology" at the national convention of the American Psychological Association, Toronto, Canada, in August, 1978.

b.   Specific Settings and/or Clientele

Gary Stollak described a program at Michigan State University that required students to work as mental health agents with normal and clinic-referred children. Advertisements in a college newspaper and enrollment in a Sensitivity to Children course recruited participants for this 30 week program. Students made video-tapes of their weekly one-half hour play encounters and then received feedback on their performance. This course contained a large classroom component with students attending twice weekly lectures and reading extensively. Stollak's work may be a guideline for those instructors searching for innovative ways to develop an experiential component for a child psychology course.

Frank Prerost's article elucidated the issues and problems encountered by supervisors of child clinical settings. He identified factors that can make the experience in child settings particularly unsatisfying for both the student and professional staff. He noted that most procedures for selecting students are inadequate and that unprepared students are likely to have severe adjustment problems. Drawing on five years experience supervising students at Western Illinois University, he described a four phase program for selecting and training students. Readers who place students in child settings can benefit from his caveats and insights.

Samuel Moore and Andrew Bondy outlined a program sponsored by Rutgers University — Camden College that trained students as behavior assessors in day care centers. Students spent from six to seven hours a week for 15 weeks to gain additional credit in a Clinical Psychology or Behavior Disorders class. After six weeks of training with an assessment instrument, students assessed the cognitive and physical behaviors of day-care children were the sites for these volunteers who worked a minimum of 10 hours. In a posttest evaluation students reported anxiety reduction and more realistic percepeven though it requires substantial work.

Robert Fox and Wanda Lopunch from Marquette University joined with Eve Fisher from Ohio State in a study of 37 students. Eleven agencies serving exceptional children were the sites for these volunteers who worked a minimum of 10 hours. In a post-test evaluation students reported anxiety reduction and more realistic perceptions of exceptional children. The range of novel settings, which included placements from schools for the blind to day-care centers, that these authors used indi-

cates that placement experience can be a strong component to bring "real world experience" to an Exceptional Child course.

Elizabeth Swenson from John Carroll University outlined the field placement component for a course in pediatric psychology. Her students worked 75 hours a semester in a large hospital. They also attended weekly lunch hour seminars and group awareness sessions. It is not surprising that all but one of the 14 students stated that they had learned more in this novel course than they had in most of their other college courses.

Judith Kuppersmith, Rema Blair, and Robert Stolnick, three community psychologists, reported on a closely supervised pilot program that trained students as co-leaders of multi-family counseling groups. Students at Richmond College, CUNY, underwent a rigorous selection procedure and 10 weeks of training before working with families referred by the Department of Probation. Supervision included a large group discussion, and review of video and audio tapes of student's counseling behaviors. The authors have provided us with a detailed guide to develop similar programs. Included is a description of selection criteria, training program models, and supervision methods. The reader will notice that a successful program of this nature is not casually implemented or supervised.

Richard O'Brien and Andrew Goff from Hofstra University collaborated with William Sperduto from B-MOD Associates to discuss a field placement course in industrial behavior modification. The 4 credit-hour course required students to spend 3 hours per week in class as well as 3 hours per week at a placement site. Students selected their own business site and designed a behavior modification intervention to solve an industrial problem. Typical problems were: productivity, sales improvement, waste, customer service, and quality control. Interventions included praise, charting, and providing feedback. Of interest to industrial psychologists is the detailed description of three interventions including charts of actual data. Research indicates that as many as 60 percent of all psychology majors will find work in business settings. Those students can greatly benefit from the kinds of placements described in this article. Instructors will find this article valuable as a guideline for developing their own industrial placements.

Sensitivity to Children: Helping Undergraduates Acquire Child Care Giving and Mental Health Skills

Gary E. Stollak
Michigan State University

A program designed to train and utilize students as mental health agents working with normal and clinic-referred children.

Since 1970 approximately 400 college undergraduates at Michigan State University have been participants in programs I lead which attempt to help them develop communication skills with young children and to utilize these skills in mental health treatment or preventive capacities. Participants in these programs have been recruited through advertisements in the college newspaper and through their enrollment in an academic year-long (30-week) course entitled "Sensitivity to Children."

Play Encounters With Normal Children. Let me first summarize the student's activities in the course as it has been conducted since 1970.

During the first meeting of class, all 100-150 students complete a projective questionnaire. This "Sensitivity to Children" (STC) questionnaire[1] asks respondents to read short descriptions of 16 different problem situations involving six-year-old children and to write down their exact words and/or actions in response to each situation. An example is: "You are having a friendly talk with a friend on the phone. Your son, Carl, rushes in and begins to interrupt your conversation with a story about a friend in school." They are also informed that they are to begin play encounters with a normal 4-8 year old child as quickly as possible and that they will be responsible for finding the child. I give each of them several letters of introduction to parents.[2] Although a few encounter difficulties, typically, within two weeks all students begin weekly one-half hour long individual play sessions in or near the child's home or in one of our Psychology Department playrooms.

I have focused on the free play encounter with children, to provide the basic source of material for training, for several reasons:

1. Free play is often the preferred mode of expression and communication of inner experiences primarily because of a young child's limited cognitive and verbal skills.

2. Through repetitive patterning and sequencing of play and fantasy, we can gain insight into child fears and concerns, areas of strength, competency, and skill (see, for example, the work of Gould, 1972; and Singer and his colleagues, 1973).

3. Through play we can create a situation in which children may become aware of the feelings they have not allowed themselves to recognize. It is probable that almost all children often misperceive their parents' and others' in-

tentions and feel unhappy or insecure or abused for very little apparent reason. Often children may not be aware of their own needs and feelings, and thus adults cannot always help them in their usual ways, such as through conversation or confrontation. An adult's clear communication of awareness, and acceptance of the child's feelings, needs, wishes, and desires as natural and valid human experiences and clear communications helping a child understand how his other social actions derive from such thoughts and feelings, can help children come to a better understanding of how to cope with feelings they experience.

4. Another way a play encounter could provide an opportunity for an adult to help children learn to cope with feelings is by providing them, during those occasions in which they express feelings and needs in an unacceptable manner (such as wanting to hit or throw objects at the adult for limiting the length of the play session), with two or three alternative and constructive ways to express their desires.

5. Through joint participation in play, and especially fantasy play, a child can build up increasing trust and confidence in an adult. It could increase children's feelings that they can communicate more fully and honestly about their experiences. This device should eventually lead to more mature ways of expression of needs, and less fear that being open will cause the loss of an adult's respect or affection.

6. Just as we expect that over time an adult will feel that he or she is trusted and has become an intimate of a child, through play, a child increasingly can feel trusted and respected.

7. One of our goals is for all children to feel more secure in making their own decisions, where that is appropriate. All children need to learn to be less fearful of making mistakes. It is important for them to learn that they have choices and are themselves responsible for much of what befalls them. By allowing them freedom of choice in the play encounters and by allowing them to experience the consequences of free choice, adults can help children build upon their self-confidence.

The weekly play encounters between undergraduates and children are supervised by students in graduate programs in clinical, developmental, and educational psychology, child and family sciences, and social work, whom I supervise (see Stollak, 1973a, for a more detailed description of the graduate student course sequence). Each graduate student is assigned a group of 8-10 undergraduates and these groups meet one and one-half hours weekly throughout the school year.

Although some of the material for supervision is provided through role-playing of possible problems they might experience during the play encounters, and undergraduate notes of their sessions, the major source of discussion material is provided by video-tapes made of each undergraduate and child. Approximately once each month each undergraduate brings his or her child to one of our playrooms equipped with video-taping facilities. The recordings made of these sessions are played back and discussed during the small group meetings. The verbal and non-verbal behaviors of the undergraduate are extensively discussed especially with regard to the possible effects of the undergraduate's actions on the emotions and actions of the child. The participants, including the group leader, also discuss how *they* would respond to a specific child behavior during play and how their response might affect the child. As implied by the above discussion, I believe in "child-centered" play encounters. The undergraduate is asked to minimize questioning, criticism, praise, teaching or initiation of activities with the child and through reflection and interpretations of the content and feelings expressed in the child's play, to maximize their communication of understanding and acceptance of the child's inner experiences. Books such as Virginia Axline's *Dibs*, and her *Play Therapy*, and Clark Moustakas' *Psychotherapy With Children* also provide material for the small group discussions.

I must note here that the small groups meet from the very beginning of the school year. During these first meetings (while the undergraduate searches for and initiates his first play encounters with a young child), there is a discussion of each of the STC items. The group leader attempts to get the group to reach agreement as to how best to respond to each problem situation. This procedure allows the students to get to know each other better by having them struggle to resolve their inevitable and often very significant differences in responding to each problem. The group leader clarifies similarities and differences among the group members' answers but does not provide answers or solutions; the group members being told to struggle among themselves.

Discussion of STC items typically occupies about 5 hours of group time. In the large class meetings, consisting of all undergraduate participants (see below), I discuss child-rearing values and theory and research relating to sensitive and effective communication with children. At the conclusion of these lectures and discussion, I provide what I feel are some basic principles of sensitivity to children and possible solutions to the STC items (see Stollak, 1973b).

Lectures, Discussions, and "One-Scene Dramas." Concurrent with their weekly play encounters and small group meetings, the undergraduates also attend twice weekly lectures and discussions I provide and lead that cover a wide variety of topics[2] including:
1. the goals of child-rearing,
2. principles of sensitive and effective communication with children,
3. the social and personality development of children from birth through eight years of age,
4. problems in living with young children and possible

solutions,
5. child psychopathology and psychotherapy.

Along with very extensive readings in both theory and research, the student is asked to apply this knowledge in his writing of "one-scene dramas" centering around child and adult behavior in such problem areas as lying, stealing and cheating, sibling rivalry, involvement in dangerous activities, childhood fears, child sexual behavior, etc. In each "drama" the student is asked to:

"1. Describe the setting (time of day, location, etc.) and situation leading up to an incident relating to the problem area.
2. Describe what the child said and/or did, then: (a) what you said and/or did then, (b) what the child said and/or did, and then finally, (c) what you said and/or did to their reply.
3. Describe what you should *not* say and/or do (could be as described in 2). Also, describe why such actions are *undesirable* including the child's likely reaction (his or her feelings, thoughts and actions) to your behaviors.
4. Describe what you *should* say and/or do (could be as described in 2). Also describe why such actions are desirable, again including the child's likely reactions to your behavior."

Many of these "dramas" are acted out during our class meetings each week, provoking stimulating and often personally meaningful discussion.

Utilization of Knowledge and Skills. During the course of the school year (and often including the following school year) many of these students further practice and utilize their developing skills in at least one of two ways:

1. After comprehensive assessment of the psychological functioning of 4-8 year old clinic-referred children and their families, we often attempt to help one or both of the parents to learn to encounter and play with their own children in ways similar to our training of undergraduates (and similar to Guerney's, 1964, conduct of filial therapy sessions).

After initial introduction to the theory underlying the benefits of play encounters and observation of a graduate student playing with their child, each week one of the parents has a play session with the child in one of our playrooms. While a graduate student provides feedback and supervision to the parent, as well as providing help as needed with other aspects of both parents' lives, an undergraduate will engage in a half-hour or more of play with the child. Although this could be seen as a "baby-sitting" activity, the undergraduate is being provided with an opportunity to have a relatively lengthy and continuing encounter with a "difficult" child and, further, receive individual supervision for their play sessions. The child's behavior during these sessions, especially in its differences from or elaboration upon previous behavior with the parents is often helpful to the graduate student in understanding family dynamics and communication patterns.

2. We have often also felt that a clinic-referred child could use more individual attention and acknowledgement while at school. After consultation with teachers, several undergraduates are scheduled for blocks of time in the kindergarten or first grade child's classroom. Rather than being

a "teacher aide" or "tutor" or otherwise becoming specifically involved in a teaching function, we envisioned the undergraduate acting as a listener; a person with whom the child could, at any time, talk about anything he or she might wish; a person to whom one could express feelings of frustration, fear, boredom or anger. In our initial work we thought that the undergraduates would be able to spend almost all of their time in the classroom being physically and psychologically close to the clinic-referred child. Instead, we quickly found that almost all of the children in these classrooms appreciated the smile, and touch, and eye, and ear of these "roving goodwill ambassadors." This has resulted in our now having "contracts" with several nursery school, kindergarten, and first grade teachers for such "ambassadors" whether or not the teachers perceive the presence of disturbing or problem children in their classes.

The undergraduate's listening and communication skills, ability to quickly respond to individual crises, and, in many cases, prevention of developing crises, helps teachers fulfill *their* teaching function. I feel that, even in the early elementary school years, the large teacher-student ratio contributes to the fact that so many teachers need help. Not only with their providing information and teaching of cognitive and motor skills, but also help with their attempts to facilitate the development and increase the number of emotional and interpersonal skills of *each* child.

I am also currently working out the details of a program to supervise undergraduates in *their* helping high school students develop communication skills with young children. With the cooperation of local high schools selected college juniors who have completed the year-long "sensitivity to children" course in their sophomore year will be assigned 8-10 volunteering high school students and provide the high school students with a similar experience they, the undergraduates, had in the previous year. I and others will supervise the undergraduates' supervisory activities. I like to believe that, someday, all high school students, as part of their education, and to fulfill societal needs, will be participants in child-rearing and parent education courses and provide service as "good will ambassadors" in elementary school classrooms. A recent issue of *Children Today* (1973) describes several already existing programs along these lines.

Research on the Effects of Training Programs. We have recently completed a project, independent of the programs described above, involving a detailed study of the process and outcome of play encounters between undergraduates and clinic-referred children (see Stollak, Green, Scholom, Schreiber, and Messe', 1973, for a more complete description of this project).

The undergraduates in this study responded to an advertisement in the college newspaper, and from the over 400 students who completed several questionnaires, four groups were formed: a "high potential" trained, a "high potential" untrained, a "low potential" trained, and a "low potential" untrained group.

The trained students received small group supervision of play encounters with normal children similar to that experienced by students in the course sequence, whereas the untrained students received only a booklist and were informed that they would receive neither training nor supervision from us during the course of the project.

After comprehensive psychological assessment of 4-8 year old clinic-referred children and their families, and with parental consent, appropriate cases were randomly assigned to a "therapist in training" from one of the four groups, for fifteen one-half hour "play assessment" sessions. At the conclusion of the fifteenth session, another comprehensive psychological assessment was conducted and further recommendations, if needed, were made. We did not provide any other form of help to the child, parents, or teacher during the course of the fifteen play sessions. All sessions were observed through a one-way window by the graduate student in charge of the case and the first and each ensuing fifth session was video-tape recorded. The trained students received supervision immediately after completion of each session.

Analysis of process and outcome data[3] obtained from almost 30 completed cases indicated that (a) training seemed to "wash out" whatever "potential" differences existed, (b) trained students had significantly higher "communication of acceptance" and "movement toward" scores, especially in response to "neutral" child behaviors (Rutledge, 1974) than untrained students during each of the video-taped play sessions, and (c) although we did not expect significant changes in child behavior in such a short period of time, there were trends in the data suggesting that both parents and teachers observed (as determined from their completion of various problem and behavior checklists) greater changes in children seen by the trained as compared to the untrained undergraduates. Of course, neither the parents, teachers nor coders were informed of the characteristics of the persons the children encountered.

The data also indicated that neither the parents, teachers nor graduate students perceived *increasing* frequency or intensity of disturbing child behavior over the 4-5 months it typically took to complete the fifteen sessions. However, the possibility of "halo" and "expectation" effects and the possibility of "regression to the mean" in child behavior must qualify even the most tentative interpretations of these results.

In another study of twenty one-hour long play encounters between nine trained and nine untrained undergraduates and *normal* children (see Reif and Stollak, 1972), we found that trained undergraduates were significantly less directive, critical and restrictive and displayed significantly greater amounts of behaviors (such as "reflection of content" and "compliance with clarification") indicative of a "child-oriented" orientation than did untrained students. Further, children seen by trained undergraduates engaged in a significantly greater number of more "complex," "clinically rich," fantasy behavior than did children seen by untrained students. The fantasy play of the children seen by trained undergraduates involved the child's emotional life and concerns with identification and the present and future roles they play and might someday play in life; all suggesting a process of "problem solving" and of achieving "ego-mastery." Unfortunately, we did not evaluate whether any of the observed changes or differences affected child behavior outside the play sessions.

In summary, our work indicates both at the impressionistic and quantitative level, that within the framework of continuing play encounters undergraduates *can* significantly alter their behavior with young children, and they *can* be helped to verbally and nonverbally communicate understanding, awareness, and acceptance. We wish we had hard evidence that the undergraduate's behavior positively and significantly affected children's behavior at home with their parents and siblings, and in the school, toward their work and with their peers and teachers. The small sample sizes studied, the relatively few number of encounters between undergraduates and children, and the less than adequate evaluation of child behavior outside the play sessions could all have contributed to our, so far, meager findings.

One of our long-term goals *is* to more definitively demonstrate that undergraduates *can* provide additional manpower to meet our nation's need for child mental health agents. Recent research by Bower (1969), Cowen and his colleagues (Cowen, Izzo, Miles, Telschow, Trost, and Zax, 1963), and Thomas, Chess and Birch (1968), has shown that up to 37% of children in kindergarten and first grade classes could be designated as "high risk" and less than adequately adjusted. Follow-up studies through high school and adulthood indicate continued troubles and the use and need for mental health services (see, e.g., Bower, 1969; Robins, 1966; Westman, Rice and Berman, 1967; Cowen, Pederson, Babigian, Izzo and Trost, 1973). To meet the need for mental health manpower it becomes natural to turn to undergraduates. Their intelligence, their desire to serve, their motivation regarding skill development, their interest in children, and not of least importance, their wide availability, make them a very large, and a relatively untapped source of mental health agents for young children. However, the present and past research has not been as adequate, definitive, or as clear as we all wish (see Gruver, 1971, for a review of the literature in this area). I have no doubt that future work will yield more encouraging results.

A second goal is to demonstrate that trained undergraduates can help non-clinic referred children increase their *positive* adaptation to their environment including childrens' expression of awareness and acceptance of self; considerateness, creativity and imaginativeness, self-confidence, self-control, spontaneity, tolerance, etc. Whether as teachers, or aides to teachers, in day care centers, nursery schools or elementary school classrooms, or whether as consultants to high school students wishing to become more skilled in their encounters with children, I hope that it can be demonstrated that undergraduates can become a significant positive figure and model in the lives of all children they encounter.

Closely related is our hope that our training programs will have positive effects on the *undergraduates'* values and attitudes toward child-rearing, *their* expectations regarding how children should act, and are capable of acting at different ages, *their* perceptions of the meaning of child behavior, and, most important, their behavior toward their own future children.

If our future research indicates that the children of the undergraduates who have and will participate in our programs not only elicit fewer complaints from their parents, peers, and teachers, but also display a wide variety of behaviors indicative of positive mental health, then, at the very least, the null hypothesis that I, as a college teacher, have no effect on student lives will, partially, be disconfirmed.

References

Bower, E. M. *Early identification of emotionally handicapped children in school* (2nd ed.). Springfield, Ill.: Charles C Thomas, 1969.

Children Today. Superintendent of Documents. U.S. Government Printing Office, Washington, D.C., Volume 2, Number 2, March-April, 1973.

Cowen. E. L., Izzo, L. D., Miles, H., Telschow, E. F., Trost, M. A., & Zax, M. A preventive mental health program in the school setting: Description and evaluation. *Journal of Psychology*, 1963, 56, 307-356.

Cowen, E. L., Pederson, A., Babigian, H., Izzo, L. D., & Trost, M. A. Long-term follow-up of early detected vulnerable children. *Journal of Consulting and Clinical Psychology*, 1973, 41, 438-446.

Gould, R. *Child studies through fantasy.* New York: Quadrangle, 1972.

Gruver, G. G. College students as therapeutic agents. *Psychological Bulletin*, 1971, 76, 111-127.

Guerney, B. G., Jr. Filial therapy: Description and rationale. *Journal of Consulting Psychology*, 1964, 28, 303-310.

Kallman, J. R., & Stollak, G. E. Maternal behavior toward children in need arousing situations. Paper presented at the 1974 meeting of the Midwestern Psychological Association, Chicago, Illinois.

Reif, T. R., & Stollak, G. E. *Sensitivity to young children: Training and its effects.* East Lansing: Michigan State University Press, 1972.

Robins, L. *Deviant children grown-up.* Baltimore: Williams and Wilkins, 1966.

Rutledge, T. Sequential analysis of the behavior of undergraduates and clinic-referred children in play encounters. Unpublished Ph.D. dissertation, Michigan State University, 1974.

Singler, J. L. *The child's world of make-believe.* New York: Academic Press, 1973.

Stollak, G. E. An integrated graduate-undergraduate program in the assessment, treatment and prevention of child psychopathology. *Professional Psychology*, 1973a, 4, 158-169.

Stollak, G. E. *What happened today: Stories for parents and children.* Dubuque, Iowa: Kendall/Hunt, 1973b.

Stollak, G. E., Green, L., Scholom, A., Schrieber, J., & Messe', L. The process and outcome of play encounters between undergraduates and clinic-referred children: Preliminary findings. Paper presented at the 1973 meeting of the Society for Psychotherapy Research, Philadelphia, Pennsylvania.

Stollak, G. E., Scholom, A., Kallman, J. R., & Saturansky, C. Insensitivity to children: Responses of undergraduates to children in problem situations. *Journal of Abnormal Child Psychology*, 1973, 1, 169-180.

Thomas, A., Chess, S., & Birch, H. G. *Temperament and behavior disorders in children.* New York: New York University Press, 1968.

Westman, J. C., Rice, D. L., & Bermann, E. Relationships between nursery school behavior and later school adjustment. *American Journal of Ortho-psychiatry*, 1967, 37, 725-731.

Notes

1. See Kallman and Stollak (1974) and Stollak, Scholom, Kallman and Saturansky (1973) for results obtained from administration of the STC to various subject populations. Please write to the author for copies of the STC.
2. Samples of the letter of introduction to parents and the course syllabus may be obtained from the author.
3. The help of Allan Scholom and Lawrence A. Messe' in conducting the data analyses is very greatly appreciated.
4. The development of the program and the research conducted and described was made possible, in part, by Grant MH 16444 from the National Institute of Mental Health, United States Public Health Service.

The Feasibility of Undergraduate Field Experiences in Child Psychology: Program Factors and Suggestions

Frank J. Prerost
Western Illinois University

This paper is an elucidation of the attitudinal, experiential, and training problems inherent in field placement.

The traditional programs in undergraduate psychology have demonstrated a trend in encouraging and providing field experiences for students. The students earn academic credit through volunteered work as milieu staff at human service agencies. Courses for field experience are electives typically selected during the junior or senior years. Student demand for this course option has dramatically increased in both the university (Van de Creek & Thompson, 1977) and community college (Becker, 1978). Interest in relevancy of education among academic psychologists and students has facilitated field experience implementation (Caffrey, Berger, Cole, Marx, & Senn, 1977). Students who wish to expand self-knowledge and develop rudimentary therapeutic skills are particularly attracted to field courses. Agency participation centers around the need to supplement staffs while supporting a mission as a training facility.

The popularity among students for field experience settings has varied, but students consistently report a preference for placement in child psychiatric settings (Becker, 1978). This is reinforced by academic supervisors who rate child facilities as providing particularly beneficial rewards for students (Hess, Harrison, Fink, Lilliston, Aponte, & Korn, 1978; Kuppersmith & Blair, 1977). Increasing numbers of undergraduate practicum students working in psychiatric facilities for children have resulted. Supervisors of advanced graduate students and interns now find they must be increasingly accepting and understanding of undergraduate students.

After supervising field experience students for five years, I have noted the unexpected difficulties that supervising staff from agencies have encountered working with undergraduates. Upon entering the clinical child setting undergraduates usually find themselves poorly equipped and unprepared for the stresses contronting them in day care, residential, or hospital environment. The demands of such settings require trainees to initiate formal and informal communication with unfamiliar and possibly intimidating health care professionals (Drotar, 1975). Exposure to an intensive care facility and the emotional, physical, and developmental disabilities evidenced by clients will be stress evoking. These child care settings can present overwhelming demands even for the graduate student.

Previous educational background of practicum students lacks the specific training in the fields of pediatric, abnormal child, or clinical child psychology. Consequently the undergraduate student is sent into the milieu with little more than his/her own intuitive knowledge to aid adjustment to the stresses faced (Budner, Arnold, & Gooman, 1971). Selection of field experience participants follows general academic procedures. Students must complete prerequisite number of hours in psychology courses, but the courses generally available to undergraduates emphasize the experimental and non-applied areas of psychology. Curricula at this education level are designed for general background in the science of psychology. Selection procedures incorporating grade point average or references are not reflective of student capabilities and potential reactions in an applied setting for children.

The student beginning placement needs a high level of support and direction from supervisor, but agency supervisors are usually unaware and unprepared for the ramifications of this training deficiency. The erroneous belief of adequate student training combines with inherent difficulties facing supervisors in communicating directions in action settings (Trieschman, Whittaker, & Brendtro, 1969). Supervisors must understand the ways undergraduate psychology students differ from trainees in specialized certificate/training programs in child care who receive instruction in applied methods and techniques (Felton, 1975; Felton & Hall, 1976; Obbard & Davia, 1975). This paper is designed to elucidate the problems in offering a clinical child field experience for undergraduates.

Practicum Issues. Because of the difficulties in implementing a child psychology field experience, I surveyed students and supervisors about their previous experiences. Examination of the comments and evaluations of past experiences in child psychology practica has yielded a group of significant issues affecting adjustment and satisfaction with the experience. It is beneficial for field supervisors to be cognizant of the following reported factors while considering the implications they have on the interactions between student, supervisor, and professional staff.

The first factor of significance is that the student must complete field work without monetary reward *or* identity as a formal staff member. Unlike the volunteer worker, the student is paying for academic credit and commits him- or herself for a fixed period of time to the facility. Consequently, a monetary value is placed on the practicum experience, and the student begins the practicum experience with the orientation that because of tuition payments some deferential treatment is expected from the facility's staff. Students quickly feel neglected or "put off" by on-site supervisors. During undergraduate schooling, students develop an expectation that academic professors demonstrate frequent availability and easy access outside of the classroom. This expectation develops from viewing oneself as a consumer paying for services from the university and academic staff. Expectations of this nature are then transferred to the field experience setting as the students perceive the facility as an extension of the academic institution. In initial experiences with the mental health setting, the student does not recognize the impracticality of the expectation being realized in the caregiving milieu.

Grading was a second major factor listed by students and supervisors because grading incorporates an evaluation from the supervisor at the agency. Inasmuch as students view field experiences as beneficial for graduate school aspirations, the evaluation and subsequent grade assumes added importance. If a letter grade is used, supervisors express difficulty in differentially evaluating student performance in these terms. Pass or fail type of grading creates difficulty in determining reasonable criteria for a passing evaluation.

The third factor cited by the supervisors and students as affecting adjustment to the facility is the part-time involvement of students. This role prevents the student from developing an overall view of the facility's treatment goals and care giving strategies. It leads to expressed feelings of being distanced from full-time staff and patients. The supervising staff, constrained by their limited time, allow less time for direct supervision of the students compared to full-time workers. This factor has particular impact on the student because the practicum students typically believe they are required to assume duties and tasks similar to many full-time workers. But the practicum student in completion of these duties lacks the understanding of the overall purpose of his or her duties and believes tasks of least importance are being assigned.

Interwoven in the practicum student's adjustment is the fourth factor of professional identity, which remains tied to his or her academic institution. The student has an identity as student from a particular college or university, and this role contributes negatively to the perceived or real distancing between student, professional staff and field supervisor. This factor is a crucial one which differentiates the undergraduate practicum student from practicum students in graduate, paraprofessional or professional programs such as nursing or social work who complete field practica. In the preprofessional type of programs, the students are involved in academic programs designed to develop specific skills and field practica are carefully designed as an integral part of the program's curricula. The field work is completed at a specified time complementing previous academic course experiences. Undergraduate field experience courses in psychology are usually electives which typically do not follow a systematic program of prerequisites building to the implementation of skill training in field work. Thus, the student completing field work functions with no specific goal or plans concerning the development of competencies as a child care professional or paraprofessional. The field work is not considered by the academic institution or the student as an apprenticeship in learning specific skills. The students lack an identity in the field work and field supervisors question what the students' motives are for completing field experiences in child psychology. The relationships and interactions with professional staff are often negatively affected when staff concludes that these students are seeking "easy"

academic credit or lack the motivation for adequate therapeutic functions. Further friction develops as students expect professional staff to provide training goals, as they assume a passive role waiting for direction. As Harrison (1978) points out, supervisors view this as a sign of unreliability or lack of personal knowledge.

The final factor of particular importance affecting student adjustment to the field experience is the nature of the disabilities and disorders exhibited by the children in the mental health facility. Students are not prepared for the initial encounter with the wide range of emotional, physical, mental, and developmental disabilities found in child facilities. The student reacts with apprehension concerning the nature of the child's afflictions and his/her ability to interact with the child. This apprehension and uncertainty leads the student to evaluate the field work as particularly difficult, thereby enhancing the importance of the factors outlined above. The undergraduate academic course offerings describing disorders of childhood are cursory and of limited value to the student who will be working directly with handicapped and disabled children. Without reassurances during this period of reactions to the children, the psychology student retreats from the clients and the supervisors. Fear of criticism from supervisors and fear of expanded assignments with children may produce avoidance of supervisors. This avoidance can easily be interpreted as irresponsibility or disinterest in field work.

Conclusions. It has become apparent to me that in numerous cases, the undergraduate psychology field experience in settings for children often results in mutually unsatisfying experiences for both student and professional staff. This is not to say that undergraduates have not experienced rewarding and satisfying child psychology practica, nor that cooperating facilities have not experienced conscientious and competent students. But positive outcomes result from extraordinary effort invested by academic and professional staff who assist students in overcoming the shortcomings discussed. In the cases when both student and facility expressed satisfaction with the practicum, the supervisors at the mental health facility worked diligently with the students to overcome their apprehensions and anxieties accruing from their adjustment. This result required an investment of time and energy by the supervisors usually unavailable in most mental health service sites.

Thus one must question the continued feasibility and practicality of assigning one's students to institutions serving children for an undergraduate practicum. Current methods of selecting students for participation in the undergraduate practicum such as grade point average, prerequisite courses, references from classroom professor, and interview with practicum directors are inadequate in predicting the student's on-site behavior while being insensitive to the needs of student and institution. It now may be more beneficial for students and the long term cooperative arrangements between academic and service institutions to carefully limit or restructure the undergraduate psychology practicum until reliable selection procedures are developed, or until academic preparation can be expanded to overcome deficiencies in undergraduate curricula for field experience students.

Practicum Program Suggestions. Attempting to compensate for the real and potential problems of a practicum in applied child psychology, I have used a four phase program to implement field experiences. Use of this program has modified the impact of the problems outlined above on both students and field supervisors. Phase one entails meetings with supervisors and academic adviser at the cooperating agencies. Specific discussion of the students' educational background is made, centering on the generalities of their coursework. A detailed description of the identified factors inhibiting adjustment to field experience is provided together with illustration of the effects felt by students. Less emphasis is placed on potential duty assignments of participants during this phase than in expanding awareness of supervisors' knowledge concerning the educational characteristics and circumstances of the participating students. It has been useful to include in these discussions students who have recently completed field experience. First hand reports from these individuals exemplify the discussion points and demonstrate the genuine concern and desire among students to assist an agency in its therapeutic milieu.

In the second phase, focus is placed on preparing students for the placements by supplementing their completed courses in psychology. The students need greater exposure and description of abnormal child behavior than previously provided in undergraduate psychology courses. A seminar situation has been found useful as a mode of disseminating information to students. Materials, written and video, illustrating childhood disorders are reviewed to increase student familiarity with the myriad of emotional, mental, developmental, and physical conditions exhibited by handicapped children. Increasing student awareness of what they can expect to encounter when working in the field, partially diminishes an anxiety producing situation.

The third part of the program focuses its emphasis on the cooperating agency and the field supervisor. Development of student activity assignments and responsibilities at the agency occurs between supervisor and academic advisor. Creation of a specific goal for each participating student serves as a framework for assignment of appropriate tasks and duties for each student. This task scheduling process can now occur in light of the knowledge garnered about the students during the initial series of informational seminars. At these group meetings, special attention is made to student reactions and comments to the pathology and syndromes discussed and illustrated. Judgments are made concerning the student's ability to relate effectively with different special populations. Goal setting can then be accomplished on an individual basis producing satisfying and worthwhile experiences for patients and students.

The last phase of the practicum program provides a constant opportunity to monitor student adjustment and activities during field experience. Students are required to participate in weekly seminars designed for expression of feelings and the examination of problems the students face in the field. These seminars, attended concurrently with field activities, serve two primary functions. First, they allow for the possible modification of student work goals and activity schedule as his or her field behavior is assessed. And second, students are provided a medium for shared problem solving and expression of personal frustrations in the field experiences. This outlined program permits the student to learn greater flexibility and increased discriminatory dexterity in the clinical use of the self.

References

Becker, J. Curricula of associate degree mental health/human service training programs. *Community Mental Health Journal*, 1978, *14*, 133-146.

Budner, S, Arnold, I., & Gooman, L. The plan and reality: Training and utilization of paraprofessionals for the retarded. *American Journal of Public Health*, 1971, *88*, 297-307.

Caffrey, B., Berger, L., Cole, S., Marx, D., & Senn, D. Integrating professional programs in a traditional undergraduate psychology program. *Teaching of Psychology*, 1977, *4*, 7-13.

Drotar, D. Clinical psychology training in the pediatric hospital. *Journal of Clinical Child Psychology*, 1975, *4*, 46-49.

Felton, G. A new role for the psychologist: Training the pediatric paraprofessional. *Journal of Clinical Child Psychology*, 1975, *4*, 52-55.

Felton, G., & Hall, H. An experimental program for the interdisciplinary training of new professionals as child health care worker. *Journal of Clinical Child Psychology*, 1976, *5*, 62-69.

Harrison, S. Expanding the role of supervision in child psychiatric education. *Child Psychiatry and Human Development*, 1978, *9*, 40-53.

Hess, A., Harrison, A., Fink, R., Lilliston, L., Aponte, J., & Korn, J. Critical issues on undergraduate training in various community settings. *Teaching of Psychology*, 1978, *5*, 81-86.

Kuppersmith, J., & Blair, R. Training undergraduates as co-leader of multi-family counseling groups. *Teaching of Psychology*, 1977, *4*, 3-7.

Obbard, J., & Davia, L. Characteristics of child development and child care training programs: A report of a survey. *Child Care Quarterly*, 1975, *4*, 244-248.

Trieschman, A., Whittaker, J., & Brendtro, I. *The other 23 hours.* Chicago: Aldine, 1969.

Van de Creek, L., & Thompson, G. Management of undergraduate psychology internships. *Teaching of Psychology*, 1977, *4*, 177-180.

Undergraduate Participation as Behavior Assessors In a Day-Care Consultation

Samuel F. Moore and Andrew S. Bondy
Rutgers University-Camden College

Students achieved skill in observation and assessment techniques, but did not fully develop the objectivity hoped for.

Within undergraduate curricula in psychology, structured field interactions and observation are frequently offered as valuable supplements to formal classroom materials in general accordance with the proverb "I hear, I forget; I see, I remember; I do, and I understand." To some extent, the provision of applied experiences at the undergraduate level is also responsive to the needs of those students who are concerned with finding employment immediately upon receipt of the baccalaureate degree. Although meeting such concerns cannot be the principal goal of university departments of psychology, urban universities such as ours serving largely first generation college students must be at least partially responsive to the vocational aspirations of their students.

This article describes a program sponsored by the Rutgers—Camden Psychology Department which enrolled a number of upper level psychology majors in a community consultation project. The program was designed to provide a relatively structured, closely supervised, clinical experience appropriate to the students' level. It was thought that the experience would supplement and enliven the sometimes abstract, theoretically-oriented material of two of the department's advanced courses. Finally, participation in the program was intended as an introduction to a number of skills that might facilitate students' selection and acquisition of psychology-related employment after graduation.

The Consultation. The opportunity to involve undergraduates in a community consultation was provided by a request to the department from two area day care centers. From a number of meetings between the centers and the authors, a program of skills-assessment for application to their children was established to facilitate the centers' efforts. With continued problem-solving interchanges, both centers expressed interest in assessment programs that would lead directly to the design of appropriately enriched learning/socialization environments and the tailoring of center activities to the individual needs of the children they served. Both centers viewed the assessment programs as an on-going evaluation procedure to be repeated at specified intervals for both planning and outcome measure purposes.

Relation of Project to Existing Department Courses. Both authors offer advanced undergraduate courses that

appeared to be particularly relevant to the issues and concerns of the proposed consultation. The first of these, Introduction to Clinical Psychology, is directed at informing those students who have interests in psychology as a human services endeavor about the scientific and professional aspects of clinical psychology. During the second half of the course particular emphasis is placed on clinical psychology's increasing involvement in primary and secondary prevention programming. The second course, Behavioral Disorders of Children, provides an overview of behavior assessment procedures for both normal and pathological behaviors. In addition, a variety of perspectives on etiology is reviewed, especially with regard to their implications for assessment and treatment endeavors.

Both instructors share a behavioral orientation toward assessment and treatment. Consequently, both courses focus on the need for objectively defining problem behaviors, intervention strategies, and response aspects for use in evaluating the outcome of change strategies. Additionally, both courses reflect a bias that promotes preventive strategies as the ideal model in human service endeavors. It was this meshing of what we perceived to be the methods and goals of the day care center consultations and the issues and principles stressed in our two courses that suggested the desirability of involving interested students from the courses in the consultation program. Involvement appropriate to their undergraduate level would allow them to experience firsthand the translation of many of the principles and issues central to the courses into the specific activities involved in the first cycle of a prevention-oriented community consultation.

Selection and Initial Training of Students. From those students in the two courses who expressed interest in the project, we selected only those who had done well in other departmental courses. Participation in the 15-week project entailed a commitment of six to seven hours per week beyond the requirements of either of the two academic courses. Consequently, an additional credit in a departmental fieldwork course was arranged for the project students.

Because the two day-care centers had each decided upon a different assessment instrument as a function of their particular program needs, the students were placed into one of two groups, one with nine members, the other with ten. Each of the course instructors supervised one group for the entire semester. Orientation sessions were arranged by the day-care centers for the students. Training began after attendance at a brief session at the center in which they were to work for the rest of the semester.

For the first six weeks the students spent the majority of their project time in group supervision/training sessions. These sessions focused initially on the background and rationale of a skills-assessment consultation. Many of the issues implicit in early screening and prevention programs were central to these sessions. Particular emphasis was placed on the importance of selecting assessment procedures which could facilitate the goals of the program in which they were utilized. It was pointed out in the case of the day care project that only those assessment instruments that could lead quite directly to the design of skills-development opportunities were suggested to the centers for their consideration. Related issues, reflecting in part the behavioral orientation of the instructors, included the advantages for such a program of criterion vs. normative referenced assessment procedures and the importance of targetting clearly defined, observable behaviors as opposed to inferred internal states and conditions. Most of these issues are typically covered in the two courses in one of which the students were enrolled simultaneously, and in our experience are somewhat counter to many of the "trait as explanation" and dynamic models of assessment and treatment held by many undergraduates. We were, therefore, particularly interested in whether the additional coverage and particularization to the project of these issues would lead to changes in project participants' assumptions about behavior change processes beyond those accomplished for students enrolled in the Clinical or Behavior Disorders course alone.

The second major issue in the initial training period involved general considerations of assessment procedures and an introduction to the particular assessment instruments to be used at the day-care centers. Some of the general issues included: the assessment process as a standardized sampling procedure; the importance of judging and recording actual as opposed to inferred behavior; and the need to prevent pre-conceived assumptions and "intuitive" judgments from biasing individual assessment administrations. Other issues reviewed included time-sampling and frequency count procedures and the computation and maintenance of inter-observer reliability. Finally, emphasis was placed on delineating the nature of assessment processes and their intent from those characterizing therapeutic relationships. This issue was encountered with some resistance, both within the group supervision sessions and during the students' initial test administrations, as described later in the article.

Assessment Instruments and Their Administration. Following the consideration of general assessment issues, training began with the two instruments to be applied in the day care centers: the McCarthy Scales of Children's Abilities (McCarthy, 1972) and the Learning Accomplishments Profile (LAP) (Sanford, 1974). Both measures tap a wide range of cognitive and physical behaviors. Each depends upon a presence/absence methodology in which the assessor evaluates the occurrence (or lack) of a specified behavior. The McCarthy scale is designed to be administered on a one-to-one basis, but the LAP can be used in observing normal ongoing classroom activities. With adequate training and supervision, we were confident that subprofessionals could be trained as proficient administrators of either measure. It should be noted that the purpose of using each assessment device was not to obtain a numerical indicator of a child's rate of development (e.g., IQ score). Rather, the use of each device permitted identification of specific skills within a number of areas to be pinpointed for appropriate enrichment activities programming.

After an introduction to the nature of the assessment instrument which they would be applying, each group began working with their assigned instrument. Extensive modeling and role-playing activities were used in the early, familiarization stages of training. In addition, assignments to be completed between group sessions were outlined in which students practiced various observation techniques. For the LAP group in particular, practicing nonreactivity was stressed since their observations were to be conducted within the classrooms. On the other hand, the McCarthy group spent more time practicing a variety of management procedures because their interactions with the children would proceed in a separate testing room on a one-to-one basis.

All students observed the authors working with day-care age children in both structured and "free" situations. In addition, the McCarthy students observed the direct administration of the device, and a video-taping of this testing session was reviewed periodically. The McCarthy students rehearsed administrating small groups of the test subscales and the video-tapes of these rehearsals were then reviewed and critiqued by the group and the supervisor. The McCarthy students were also taught to observe the children in the classroom in order to tap targetted, objective behaviors in the realm of social skills which the McCarthy scales do not assess. Pairs of LAP students monitored interobserver reliability within their practice observations. Reliability with the supervisor's rating of children was also assessed and discussed on a periodic basis.

By the end of the sixth week, students began individual assessments of the day-care children. During the assessment period, each student spent at least three hours per week in direct assessment. By the end of the twelfth week of the semester, each McCarthy student had completed assessments and classroom observations on no less than three children. During the assessment period, the supervisors observed one or more test administration sessions for each student, and weekly individual or group supervision sessions continued. The LAP students, working in pairs, completed their observations of fifty children in five classrooms by the end of week 14. Reliability with the supervisor's ratings were monitored weekly for each student, and group review sessions were maintained throughout the assessment period.

Assessment results were scored, and the final reports recommending specific, hierarchically arranged skills-development activities for each child were prepared by the supervisors. However, the students' final individual supervision sessions entailed a review of the assessment and observational data with the supervisor who would be preparing the report. The students participated in the translation of the available data into tentative compensatory/enrichment activity recommendations and in the consideration of means of evaluating the outcome of the recommendations. This activity was particularly useful in contrasting the potential outcomes of the more traditional normative-referenced, global assessments with those we hoped to achieve on the basis of the criterion-referenced skills-assessment procedures of the project. The final supervision session (sometimes several) also provided students with the opportunity to experience the degree to which preventive programming depends upon a close match between the assessment information collected and the decisions one hopes to arrive at on the basis of that information. We also believed that participation in the planning of recommendations was important in allowing students to see that the assessment process should not become an end in itself, but rather a beginning and ongoing process in preventive programming.

Project Effects on Student Participants. By way of review, the consultation project was directed at providing student participants with particularized examples of issues central to two academic courses. At one level, then, the project represented an opportunity to reinforce and supplement the students' understanding of behaviorally-oriented skills assessment and preventive programming processes. In addition, we hoped to provide the students with the skills necessary for the competent administration of at least one assessment device.

Support for the accomplishment of these objectives exists at several levels, ranging from subjective impressions on the part of the instructors and the student participants, to observations at various stages of the students' assessment instrument administrations, to the results of two pre- and postproject paper and pencil inventories.

Subjective reactions. At the subjective level, a number of impressions suggest that the project was relatively successful. For example, project students increasingly offered examples and experiences drawn from their assessment activities in the day-care centers in illustration of many of the sometimes abstract classroom discussions of issues and concepts. These experientially-based inputs from the students, beyond demonstrating the degree to which the course materials were becoming increasingly meaningful to them, also facilitated other, non-project students' appreciation for the applicability of the course material. Student reports on their reactions to participation in the project also confirm our impression that project participation was a significant enrichment of the two courses from which they were drawn.

Following is a sampling of statements from the students' final summary reports:

This experience gave me a genuine understanding into the subject matter of the clinical course. I now know, first hand, what it is like to work with a community institution . . . and the importance of considering the vast individual differences existing in (within any grouping of) young children in planning classroom activities.

Probably the most valuable part of the project was learning how to apply principles that I am learning (about) in class

work to an actual situation. Simple cueing and reinforcement techniques that appear quite contrived (when discussed in class) proved to be very effective tools in such a situation (i.e., the assessment).

Many of the behavioral principles discussed in the course seemed terribly abstract at first. Now, they provide a useful framework for me, and they (behavioral techniques) work as demonstrated by testing experiences.

This (the project) was an extremely valuable experience for those of us who had not worked with children before. The importance of "objectively" evaluating a child's behavior in planning future activities suddenly struck me as "fair" rather than cold-blooded for the first time.

I realize, after thought provoked from the course and this project, that my attempts to solve social injustices and problems, might best begin at the individual level. The experience of assessing the children's behavior and planning individualized environments is important in preventing the development of social and learning disabilities.

It should be noted that the project also had some impact on students' perspectives on their future professional roles and preferences in psychology. Several of the students suggested in their summary reports that it had become clear to them that work with children did not match their own characteristics or interests. This outcome was one we had envisioned as an objective for the project. It also parallels results reported by Holzberg (1967) and Klein and Zax (1965) which indicated that many college students serving as companions to mental patients found the experience useful in firming up mental health profession career plans while others found that such careers were not for them.

Changes in assessment skills. The summary statements prepared by the project participants also reflect their increased sophistication as assessment instrument administrators, but perhaps most revealing were the changes which we were able to observe over their test administration sessions. In the case of the McCarthy, many of the students were clearly uncomfortable with the new experience of working in a highly structured, leading fashion with one child. Beyond initial confusions with the assessment materials themselves, student discomfort was evidenced in their leading or cueing statements to the children which were more likely to evoke non-compliance than cooperation on the part of the child. We found that having the students conduct a warm-up period with the child prior to formal assessment, where structure was gradually increased on non-test activities, helped a great deal. With increased experience with assessment materials, the efficiency and accuracy of students' McCarthy administrations increased dramatically. Equally noteworthy were the changes evidenced in the students' management skills. The tentative, sometimes pleading cues and almost random reinforcement of the child's behaviors were pointed out in the supervision sessions. Role-playing, the provision of alternative responses, and the students' increased experience with the children resulted in the development of highly skillful and appropriate management techniques by a majority of the students.

In the case of the LAP students, their greatest difficulty, beyond that of becoming familiar with the LAP procedure, was in learning to be non-reactive observers. Our observations suggest that they accomplished this almost without exception. In addition, the LAP students' observations were found to be uniformly reliable between student pairs and with the supervisor's observations. The students' observations were also found to be consistent with teacher observations of specific skills, and day care personnel were very pleased with the role observers maintained throughout the assessment period. Perhaps the clearest summary we can give of our impressions of the students' assessment skills is that, in our view, the students' application of the two instruments was equal in quality to what would be expected of first or second year graduate students.

Rating scale changes. The final source of evaluation data for the project is provided by two rating scales that we constructed prior to the project. One of the scales was directed at general testing procedures and issues. We anticipated that project students, in comparison with non-project students, would demonstrate an increased understanding of these issues. The second scale was constructed to evaluate the degree to which project and non-project students demonstrated a behavioral orientation toward assessment and treatment prior to and at the conclusion of the project/courses. This orientation was clearly the avowed position both within the academic courses and the project. We sought to determine with this scale whether participation in the project had a greater influence on the adoption of the behavioral perspective relative to the influences of the courses alone.

For the behavioral orientations scale, paired statements relative to assessment information were presented, and students were asked to select the one which would be most useful in understanding a child and/or planning an intervention strategy. In general, the comparisons were between behaviorally-oriented statements and those reflecting either a psychodynamic perspective or global, trait-like statements. The behavioral/dynamic pairings included such pairings as: "knowing how the child's behavior relates to certain times of the day vs. knowing how the child's behavior relates to underlying dynamics"; and "knowing how specific behaviors relate to present events vs. knowing how specific behaviors relate to past events." Behavioral/global pairings included such pairs as: "knowing the child's current behavior vs. knowing the child's personality type"; and "knowing the child's grade record vs. knowing the child's IQ score."

On this measure, both project and non-project students tended to become more behaviorally-oriented (as we defined it). However, a greater proportion of project students changed their orientation on seventeen of the eighteen pairings to a behavioral preference as compared to the number of non-project student changes in the behavioral direction. The exception to this trend involved a somewhat ambiguous pairing in which knowing about the child's "inner feelings" was used as the dynamic member of the pair. A majority of the project students surprisingly maintained their preference for this information while the majority of the non-project students changed their preference to the behavioral statement of this pairing. Overall, however, it would appear that the project was relatively more influential in modifying what we previously discussed as the "trait as explanation" and dynamic model preferences held by the students at the beginning of the semester.

So far as the results for the general assessment procedures scale is concerned, they are rather sobering even given their tentative nature. This scale presented a number of procedural issues that the students were to rate on a seven-point scale from "not at all important" (to the assessment process) to "critically important." Among the items included were: "beyond recording the actual responses, the examiner should understand the reasons behind the child's responses"; "the examiner should set limits on the child's behavior"; "the examiner should be very sympathetic to the child during testing"; and, "the examiner should do everything possible to insure that the examinee perceives him/her as a friend." In essence, the statements posed the assessment process as either a standardized, carefully structured sampling procedure or as a process more akin to a permissive, relatively loosely structured and intuitive therapeutic interaction. We recognize the limits of the scale, especially with regard to its lack of standardization (including comparison norms based on a sample of experienced clinicians' responses). Much supervision time was spent differentiating between assessment and therapeutic processes, as mentioned earlier. Consequently it is surprising (and disappointing) to note that non-project students changed their ratings in the direction we had hoped for to a greater extent than did the project students.

Two interpretations of this result can be offered, which while admittedly speculative, might provide direction for further investigations of this unexpected outcome. The first interpretation refers to resistance on the part of the participants to viewing the assessment situation as different in nature from a helping relationship. This was noted early in the project by a number of reports by students of feeling confined in their role as assessors. Such statements generally indicated dissatisfaction at not being able to somehow "help" the child, to accomplish a more significant relationship. This same dissatisfaction was also expressed in three of the summary reports at the conclusion of the project. It would appear, then, that although project students were able to conduct themselves appropriately as test administrators according to our observations, residual frustrations at not being able to achieve greater closeness with the children—to take the opportunity to more directly intervene—continued to be reflected on the post-administration of the testing procedures scale. On the other hand, non-project students not confronted with an actual child and the opportunity for a close interpersonal relationship, accepted a more abstract viewpoint of assessment procedures by the conclusion of the courses.

A second interpretation suggests that project students began to feel that their direct experiences with children, however limited, could provide a different but equally valid type of information than that provided simply by a standardized assessment device. It has been our experience, and that of many peers, that something of this nature occurs frequently in clinical graduate programs and again after receipt of a clinical degree. With continued experience, many clinicians tend to rely less upon their training and its stress upon empirical approaches and more upon intuitions or phenomenological understandings. This same issue is of course prominent in the continuing statistical vs. clinical prediction debate. Our results would appear to suggest that this insulation process can occur with undergraduates given applied experiences during a single semester.

Reflections and Plans. In summary, our own impressions, reports from the students, and the majority of the quantifiable results suggest that a carefully structured and integrated applied experience such as that provided in the project can make an important contribution to an undergraduate curriculum. It can also provide an introduction to some marketable skills for students concerned with immediate employment. A continuation of the project will enable us to explore in more detail many of the results which have been presented in this article, including the impact of the project on employment and career selection and acquisition by project participants. We will also continue an examination of the unexpected preference of project participants at the conclusion of the project for what we can only identify as intuitive, non-empirical approaches to assessment. Although we are generally optimistic about the potential benefits of carefully structured applied experiences as part of an undergraduate curriculum, we would also like to be assured that such experiences do not insulate students from profiting from didactic materials.

References

Holzberg, J. D., Knapp, R. H., & Turner, J. L. College students as companions to the mentally ill. In E. L. Cowen, E. A. Gardner, and M. Zax (Eds.). *Emergent approaches to mental health problems.* New York; Appleton-Century-Crofts, 1967, pp. 91-109.

Klein, W. L., & Zax, M. The use of a hospital volunteer program in the teaching of abnormal psychology. *Journal of Social Psychology,* 1965, 65, 155-165.

McCarthy D. *McCarthy Scales of Children's Abilities.* New York: The Psychological Corporation, 1972.

Sanford, A. R. *Learning accomplishments profile.* Winston-Salem, NC: Kaplan Press, 1974.

Notes

1. This project was supported for the Spring 1977 semester and is continuing as Project No. 11 for the 1977-78 academic year through a grant to the authors from the Council on Instructional Development, Rutgers University.

Using Volunteer Work To Teach Undergraduates About Exceptional Children

Robert A. Fox and Wanda R. Lopuch
Marquette University
and Eve Fisher
Ohio State University

Most universities and colleges offer a course on the psychology and education of exceptional children. For many undergraduate students, such a course may be their first and possibly only formal exposure to this special population of children. Therefore it is important that instructors structure an experience for these students that will enhance their understanding and appreciation of exceptional children. McCallum (1979) provided classroom activities to foster an "empathetic" rather than a "sympathetic" understanding of the problems of such children. Many instructors teaching a course in this area include a practicum or volunteer experience to provide direct student contact with exceptional children, but the impact of these experiences occurring outside of the classroom had been minimally reported in the literature. For example, Stainback and Stainback (1982) found that undergraduates exposed to severely retarded individuals had more positive attitudes about integrating these handicapped students with their nonhandicapped peers than did a control group of undergraduates. Clearly more studies of this nature are needed.

The purpose of this study was to begin to establish an empirical base concerning the impact of volunteer experiences on the undergraduate student in terms of their understanding and attitudes toward children with special needs.

During a fall quarter at Ohio State University, the first author taught a course entitled the Psychology of Developmental Disabilities. Six male and 32 female undergraduate students agreed to volunteer for a minimum of ten hours with an agency serving exceptional children. The majority of these students were juniors and seniors (N = 34) with a mean age of 21.3 years (SD = 1.3). Students represented a variety of different disciplines including psychology, nursing, social work, physical therapy, speech, home economics, and others. Psychology was the most frequent major (N = 17). Twelve students reported having at least two years of previous experience with exceptional individuals; five students had one to two years of previous experience; nine students had less than one year of experience and twelve students had no previous experience with exceptional people.

Eleven different agencies or programs serving exceptional individuals provided the volunteer experiences. Students were given a choice of settings in which to volunteer. They reported engaging in a variety of experiences that were unique to each volunteer setting. Some students chose to volunteer at a large residential public institution for severely and profoundly retarded children and adults. These students functioned as aides providing routine care (e.g., dressing, feeding, toiletting) and as assistants to a staff psychologist who was developing and implementing programs on the institutional wards. Four of the volunteer settings offered early intervention or day care services for children with developmental disabilities between the ages of two and five. Students reported that these settings served a variety of children including those who were mentally retarded, autistic-like, physically handicapped (cerebral palsy, blind), epileptic and environmentally disadvantaged. They worked as teaching assistants and became involved in implementing various objectives of the childrens' Individual Educational Plan such as developing self-help skills, teaching basic knowledge and improving social interaction. These early childhood settings were very popular among the students. Another group of students also worked as teaching assistants but with older mildly and moderately retarded children in the public schools. A school for the blind also interested some students who functioned primarily as classroom aides. A few students became therapy assistants in an established play therapy program for developmentally disabled children. These students met weekly with a doctoral student for the play therapy session. They also attended a weekly group session with the supervising professor of psychology. The remainder of students volunteered in programs serving the adult retarded. These adult experiences included participation in recreational programs (e.g., dances, bowling), helping out in a group home, and assisting in an obesity research project. Ten hours of volunteer work was required, but the majority of students exceeded this minimum.

Near the end of the quarter students completed an anonymous questionnaire regarding their volunteer experience. In addition to describing the content of their work, they responded to a number of Likert type scale items that assessed their perceptions about various aspects of the experience. Students also retrospectively completed the Adjective Generation Technique (AGT, Allen & Potkay, in press). The AGT required that the students write down five adjectives that would best describe them when they first learned they would be doing volunteer work with exceptional children and again following their volunteer experience. Finally the questionnaire included general questions where the students could provide narrative comments regarding their feelings about exceptional individuals before and after their volunteer experience.

Several of the questionnaire responses that could be quantified were subjected to a simple correlation analysis. Students rated their respective volunteer settings using a one (very negative) to seven point scale (very positive) on a number of characteristics including the general atmosphere of the setting, how well the volunteer experience was organized for them and the helpfulness of the supervision provided. They also rated the degree to which they felt personally involved while volunteering (one = very limited, to seven = highly involved) and how they felt their attitudes had changed toward exceptional children (one = not at all to seven = very significantly). The three ratings for the volunteer setting (i.e., atmosphere, organization and supervision helpfulness) were combined, resulting in one overall rating. This overall rating was found to correlate significantly with the degree that students became involved in the volunteer experience ($r(36) = .45$, $p<.01$); but not with attitude change toward exceptional people. Also a significant correlation was found between years of previous student experience with exceptional individuals and perceived attitude change toward this population ($r(36) = -.70$, $p<.01$). Surprisingly, previous experience did not correlate significantly with the degree of student involvement.

The AGT was scored using available norms (Allen & Potkay, in press) on a favorability and an anxiety dimension. T-tests for related measures for AGT scores prior to and following the volunteer experience, reported retrospectively, showed a significant reduction on the anxiety dimension ($t(37) = 9.48$, $p<.001$) and an increase on the favorability dimension ($t(37) = 5.38$, $p<.001$).

Student responses to the questions requiring narrative comments were categorized according to common themes. Sixty-three percent of them (N=24) felt that the volunteer experience changed their perceptions about exceptional children. Comments such as "I now know how to work with a cerebral palsied child and what kinds of activities can be done to help them." "I was surprised at the wide range of abilities." "I'm more aware of the need for early intervention." "I now know that in most cases the handicapped individuals are very similar to the nonhandicapped person in attitude, emotions, etc." were typical of this theme. Thirteen students also reported personal changes (e.g., "I'm much more sensitive to this population." "The first day I was there I just stared at them and felt so sorry for them; now I know I can work with them and I'm more sure of myself." "I now feel more confortable with myself knowing the problems of others." "It gave me some more confidence"). Fourteen students mentioned that they were encouraged to do more volunteer work and several actually continued to volunteer at their settings during the following quarter. Seventeen students also reported that the experience will help them with some future decisions they will be making (e.g., "Now I know I don't want to work with the mentally retarded and I do want to do more volunteer work with other populations." "It reinforced my desire to work with mentally handicapped people and has helped me to choose a minor in special education." "Confirmed which age range of developmentally delayed population I want to work with—infants and preschoolers").

In summary, most students initially reported being anxious about working with exceptional children. However, with some initial encouragement from the instructor to get involved, students entered the volunteer experience and reported reduced levels of anxiety and increased levels of favorability following volunteering. Many reported wanting to do more volunteer work in the future and some continued volunteering within their chosen setting even after the course was over. Students were more likely to increase their personal involvement in an agency or setting if it was well-organized, had a positive atmosphere and provided good supervision. It also appears that students with little or no previous experience with exceptional populations were likely to change their attitudes in a positive direction as a result of volunteering and taking a course on the topic. Although these findings are preliminary, they do suggest that including some direct contact with exceptional populations as part of a didactic course on the topic may enhance the impact of this experience for undergraduate students.

217

References

Allen. B. P., & Potkay, C. R.   *Adjective Generation Technique (AGT): Research and applications.* New York: Irvington Press, in press.
McCallum, L. W.   Experiences for understanding exceptional children. *Teaching of Psychology,* 1979, 6, 118-119.

Stainback, S., & Stainback, W.   Influencing the attitudes of regular class teachers about the education of severely retarded students. *Education and Training of the Mentally Retarded,* 1982, 17, 88-92.

A Content-Oriented Practicum in Pediatric Psychology

Elizabeth V. Swenson
John Carroll University

This article describes a two-semester course in pediatric psychology which was first offered in the fall of 1979 at John Carroll University. The rationale for the course was that students who had studied human development in the classroom would broaden their understanding of the ecology of development by first-hand experience with chronically ill, emotionally disturbed and abused children and their families within a hospital setting. In addition, they would learn skills in dealing with these individuals and develop an understanding of various aspects of hospitalization. The course has three components: a field placement, reading and writing assignments, and a weekly seminar.

Fourteen junior and senior students (all psychology majors with the exception of one pre-med chemistry major) were placed as supervised child life workers at Rainbow Babies and Children's Hospital in Cleveland, Ohio. Floor assignments, which changed after the first semester, were divided according to chronological age of the patients and medical or surgical problem area. Each student reported to the child life worker responsible for his/her floor. Every student was required to be on the floor for 75 hours a semester, divided into two three-hour time blocks per week. The central task was to provide emotional support to hospitalized children and their families (who are encouraged to be in attendance at this hospital).

Through this field placement it was anticipated that students would gain or increase their knowledge about the effects of hospitalization and physical problems on children and their families, and how this interacts with normal developmental processes. Secondarily, students learned about the hospital as an institution, the roles of professional and nonprofessional staff, specific illnesses, treatments and surgical procedures. They also developed skills in communicating sensitively with children and their parents, preoperative and pre-procedural teaching, selecting appropriate activities for children of varying ages and disabilities, and working with groups of children and of parents.

Students attended weekly lunch-hour seminars either at the hospital or the university. Those at the hospital (about half) were run typically by professional persons who gave informative lectures on topics such as techniques for working with hospitalized children and their families and information on specific disorders and medical procedures. Seminars at the university were group awareness sessions in which students dealt with their feelings about illness, abuse, death, mental retardation and more specific problems with patients and staff. Relating to hospitalized children, and particularly older adolescents, was at times highly stressful for the students, and they needed a neutral place to unload

on fellow classmates and their psychologist-professor. These sessions turned out to be an integral part of the course.

To supplement the practicum learning, students were required to read specific writings on the behavioral aspects of illness and physical disability. These were the textbooks by Magreb (1978) and articles by Blom (1958), A. Freud (1952), Levy (1945), and Lewis (Note 1). The readings, seminars and fieldwork were synthesized by keeping a personal log of experiences and observations and writing two short papers, typically a case study and a specific research.

At the end of the year, all students but one rated the course as one in which their total learning had been more than most of their other college courses. Several felt the excessive time demands would not have been tolerable in a traditional course, but here had contributed to a valuable experience. Some felt strongly that work with chronically ill or disturbed children was a likely career choice after graduation, while others learned that the emotional demands could not be tolerated on a long-term basis. As one student put it "I had to learn to come to grips with my feelings about life . . . . No text can substitute for experiencing other people's problems. The opportunity was priceless."

References

Blom, G. E.   The reactions of hospitalized children to illness. *Pediatrics,* 1958, 22, 590-600.
Freud, A.   The role of bodily illness in the mental health of children. *Psychoanalytic Study of the Child,* 1952, 7, 69-81.
Levy, D. M.   Psychic trauma of operations in children. *American Journal of Diseases of Children,* 1945, 69, 7-25.
Magreb, P. R.   *Psychological management of pediatric problems* (Vol. 1 & 2). Baltimore: University Park Press, 1978.

Notes

1. Lewis, M. The many facets of the care of children in hospitals. Address presented at the Sixth Annual Conference of the American Association for Child Care in Hospitals, November 1971.
2. The author wishes to thank Mrs. Carole Klein, Director of the Child Life Program at Rainbow Babies and Children's Hospital, and Dr. Donald K. Freedheim, Professor of Psychology at Case Western Reserve University, for invaluable assistance with this course.
3. A supplementary bibliography on pediatric psychology is available from the author.

Training Undergraduates as Co-Leaders
of Multifamily Counseling Groups

Judith Kuppersmith, Rima Blair
and Robert Slotnick
Richmond College, City University of New York

From a closely supervised pilot program, the
authors describe a model for a field work/academic
program beneficial to all of the participants.

In the winter of 1973 a probation officer from the Staten
Island Department of Probation approached the community
psychology faculty at Richmond College for help with a
problem. He wanted to create some form of group therapeutic treatment that would enable him to provide a meaningful
service to an enormous caseload which included many
young offenders whose parents had initiated PINS (People in
Need of Supervision) petitions. As community psychologists
in a college setting, we were especially interested in this
problem because it provided us with an opportunity to create
a training model using a treatment modality consistent with
our theoretical orientation. We also could utilize our undergraduate population as providers of service through this
treatment modality. Our theoretical approach is an integration of family process theory and developmental
psychoanalytic ego psychology. From family process theory
we use the differentiation of self formulations of Anonymous
(1972), the structural model of Minuchin (1974) and Haley
(1971), and the communication theory approach of Satir
(1967). We succeeded in combining these approaches with
the cognitive and ego function models of Bellak (1973),
Jacobson (1964), and Erikson (1964). We felt that by integrating these major theoretical orientations we could provide the
broadest educational benefit to students. It is from this
vantage point that we approached problems of family
breakdown and adolescent delinquency. We were especially interested in understanding individual and family
functioning in relation to the broader societal context of
community psychology.

As we developed our training model and plans for
intervention, we chose to teach students to support areas of
successful ego development and to foster positive mental
health in the families they worked with. We felt it imperative to
emphasize solving "real life" problems such as finding jobs
for adolescents, and helping to build social networks for
isolated single parent mothers. Students were also sen-
sitized to recognize and deal with psychological problems,
such as intervening to clarify dysfunctional communications
between family members.

From this theoretical stance we analyzed the probation
officer's proposal as having two components. One, a manpower problem, we felt we could help him with by training
undergraduates as co-leaders of groups. The other problem
was to develop a suitable treatment modality for these
families in crisis. We knew that there was considerable
evidence that undergraduates could undertake mental

health roles successfully (Sanders, 1967; Cowen, 1967;
Holzberg, Knapp & Turner, 1967; Persons, Clark, Persons,
Kadish & Patterson, 1973; Poser, 1966; Freitag, Blechman, &
Berck, 1973), but we had never read of a specialized training
program for undergraduates preparing them to be co-
leaders of multifamily groups working specifically within the
court system. Consistent with our theoretical orientation, we
chose the therapeutic modality of multifamily counseling
groups (Leichter & Schulman, 1974) because we knew it to
be a particularly effective treatment model for families experiencing a breakdown of parental control and family
communication.

The multifamily group setting was useful for several
reasons. Parents looking to the police and courts for rescue
could experience competence by helping one another see
their own children in a new light. Many of these families are
isolated, rigid and/or missing a parent—these are indications that multifamily groups would be especially suitable.
Adult-child relationships across family boundaries within the
multifamily group potentially could develop, and, through
understanding and empathy, lessen alienation between
generations (Leichter & Schulman, 1974). We concluded that
the existing psychological model of multifamily group counseling could provide a meaningful supplement to the handling of individual cases through the courts by probation
officers.

Most Richmond College undergraduates come from
Staten Island's working class ethnic communities; they are
predominantly Italian and Irish Americans. The court cases
we intended to work with came from these same communities. This meant that the selected undergraduate
trainees would be familiar with the complex socio-economic
and cultural family patterns which might have influenced
parents who turn to the court. They would also be aware of the
economic privations experienced by these families.
Moreover, as long-term residents of Staten Island, the
undergraduate trainees would have the knowledge and
neighborhood contacts necessary to aid families in learning
to deal with the community and with the organizational
realities of the Island.

The three faculty members involved in the program
developed a careful student selection process which will be
described below. Then, with the help of the probation officer,
we began planning the training sessions. We anticipated a
10 week training program for 16 undergraduates to be
followed by 8 weeks of closely supervised experience in

leading the multi-family counseling groups. (The under-graduate trainees received 6 college credits. As in any advanced college course, they were required to submit written work based on relevant readings in the psychological literature.)

From the 16 students selected we chose two especially mature students who had already had considerable group work experience. They began at once to conduct a "pilot" group with the probation officer as well as also joining the 14 others in the complete training process. We did this because the Department of Probation had an immediate need and we had two students with a great deal of experience who were capable of leading groups. We also wanted these students to act as peer training models for the other students.

The faculty trainers made a careful evaluation after each training session and spent a great deal of time planning for the subsequent sessions. We kept a careful record of the curriculum as it developed. The next section of the paper describes the selection and training procedure in some detail in the hope that this will be helpful to those interested in undertaking a similar program.

Selection of Students.   Faculty recruited students by describing the course in several advanced psychology classes, requesting interested students to sign up for an interview. We developed the following set of criteria in an attempt to elicit personality qualities and to account for actual life experience.

1. We asked students to describe ways in which studying psychology had influenced their relationship to their families and their communities.
2. We questioned them on their basic knowledge of psychology, especially as it pertained to social definitions of abnormality, treatment techniques they knew of and strategies of intervention in group conflict.
3. We questioned them on their knowledge and ability to negotiate the neighborhood and organizational realities of Staten Island (the community field setting for the course).
4. We reviewed their job and/or voluntary experience in helping roles.
5. We looked for such characteristics as maturity, warmth, flexibility, empathy, initiative, expressive ability, and the ability for self-reflection. Finally, all of the students were interviewed by the participating probation officer who had had no previous contact with them.

Training Procedures.   The training sessions were designed to integrate the formal properties of didactic teaching with experiential learning. We feel we succeeded in enhancing the students' theoretical understanding by utilizing their emotional experiences while also focusing on their acquisition of particular clinical skills. We did this through the *Theme Focused Training Seminars.* At the beginning of each training session we announced the particular theme or topic to be covered. We then provided the students with a concrete, common, unifying group experience through an exercise, an observation, or a video demonstration, which gave them a vivid reference point for discussion of theoretical concepts related to the single theme chosen.

For each of the ten weeks of training, the 16 students were organized into two groups of eight students with two trainers (co-leader model) for each group. Thus they were members

of a group which roughly resembled the ones they were being trained to lead. The following themes were covered, each one in a single training session:

1. Getting to know each other through the "Go-Around" technique.
2. Role Playing.
3. Group Dynamics and Non-Verbal Communication.
4. Verbal Communication Systems.
5. Observation of a Live Multi-Family Group.
6. Interventions for Improving Communication.
7. Simulation of Distressed and Well Families.
8. Leader Skills.
9. Co-Leader Skills.
10. The Family and the Identified Patient.

Each training session related the single theme to the particular problems of court referred clients. A brief description of the content of some of the sessions may help to clarify our training model.

In session two, role playing was used to help students break down stereotypes and to allow them to experience one another's point of view. Playing various familial and sex roles made students aware of the power and constraints of individual family members and helped them to conceptualize alternative role possibilities for family members. An added benefit was the students acquired role playing as a technique to be added to their skill repertoire.

By the middle of the ten week training period the undergraduates were expressing considerable anxiety about the prospect of running their own groups. We thought that this was an opportune time to have them observe an ongoing multifamily counseling group conducted by competent and accessible professionals. We took them to visit Bronx State Hospital where we had developed a consultative relationship with a multifamily therapy team. To the students' surprise they were able to intelligently participate in a post session analysis of the group they observed. The Bronx State team became role models for the students, exemplifying cooperative co-leader relationships and a willingness to observe and criticize one another. Several weeks later in Training Session 7, the Bronx State team visited our training group and led a workshop in which they simulated problem families scapegoating the identified patient.

The Different Supervisory Models.   The students began co-leading their own groups the week following the last training session. The multifamily counseling groups were established through referrals from the Department of Probation in the family court. A student serving as field coordinator for the project organized and scheduled the multifamily groups. Groups ranged from one large, extremely disorganized family, to four families within a single group. Once the groups were underway, our concern was directed toward providing necessary and appropriate supervision of the students. We felt that it was most helpful to employ varied and extremely thorough supervising techniques. This was necessary because of the relative inexperience of the students and our sense of responsibility to the families. These techniques will be distinguished from one another for reasons of presentation; however, they formed a coherent whole experienced by students as "continuous supervision." The techniques were the following:

1. Large group supervision.
2. Co-leader and peer supervision.
3. Continuous observation.
4. Tape recording and videotaping as supervision.

Large Group Supervision.   All 16 students met for supervision one and one-half hours before the meeting with their actual multifamily groups. The supervision group generated energy and enthusiasm among the co-leaders, was particularly reinforcing when any difficulties arose, and generally helped to allay anxiety.

These supervisory sessions were attended by the faculty as well as the participating probation officer. Students could receive community and court information from the probation officer, whereas the three faculty members, differing in their personal and professional styles, provided diverse theoretical and technical information. Thus, students were exposed to various approaches and were free to seek out additional individual supervision.

Students were encouraged to discuss their training critically. Their comments tended to go through three stages. In stage 1, they began by overestimating what they had learned; stage 2 reflected the opposite, a marked underestimation. Finally, in stage 3, the students arrived at a fairly realistic evaluation of their training and skills. In stage 2, their most negative phase, students blamed all their difficulties or failures on the faculty and the "newness" of the course. Faculty encouraged immediate and direct ventilation of student anger so that they could continue to use their energies constructively with their family groups.

The decision not to become involved in lengthy interpretation of the students' feelings was based on reasoning similar to that which persuaded us to call our program counseling and not therapy. We were responding to certain realistic constraints: (a). That the co-leaders would be relatively inexperienced. (b). That the multifamily sessions were limited to 8 weeks. Therefore, students were taught to focus upon solving problems common to all members of the families and to open communications within and across families to encourage a supportive network of ties that could continue functioning outside of the multifamily sessions. This focus meant that co-leaders would not respond to or explore certain sensitive dynamic issues within families. It was felt that avoiding serious intrafamilial pathology would reduce the introduction of specific emotional and life history material. This material might have the effect of isolating the families from one another and would require therapeutic expertise of a level beyond the student's capabilities. Peer supervision was built into the training program by our focusing on the co-leader relationship as a support system and as a system of checks and balances.

Continuous Observation.   The advantages of continuous observation as a form of in-service training were made clear to students and families alike. Students were encouraged to discuss their anxiety on being observed. On the whole there were few objections; the primary feeling seemed to be one of relief that faculty or experienced professionals would be around to help in case of difficulties. Midway through the course students complained if they were *not* observed.

Tape Recording and Videotaping Supervision.   Co-leaders were encouraged to tape-record their sessions. They were told to listen to the tapes both alone and together and

make "supervisory" comments to one another. Following the written consent of the families, video tapes were made of four different multi-family groups. Families were invited to view the tapes either immediately following or during the actual group session, or at another scheduled time.

The Technique of Posting.   Posting consisted of an immediate review of what had occurred during the group session. The first fifteen minutes of the posting enabled the co-leaders to unwind and talk to one another about their session; the last fifteen minutes were opened to observer comments. The observation-posting techniques which were employed with families included: (a) families posting with the co-leaders and the observers and: (b) families observing the co-leaders and observers posting, immediately followed by joint discussion with the families taking the floor. These two techniques were increasingly successful as the families became more engaged in their own group dynamics and as they learned about the purpose and process of the groups. They felt less of a separation between themselves and the co-leaders and observers, and an increased sense of self-esteem.

Benefits of the Project.   There were considerable benefits to all involved; the families, the students, the community, the Department of Probation and the College. We feel that pilot projects are an important and essential step to take before launching a new intervention with a large scale evaluation component. In short, we have found that pilots are less costly, they iron out unforeseen problems, test the feasibility of a curricular innovation, and provide a working basis for applying for additional funding.

Our pilot project was initiated in response to a pressing need. We did not want to sacrifice the opportunity to carry out this project just because, in so short a time period, we could not set up a formal evaluation based on empirical data. Instead, we developed an impressionistic and informal data base. Our informal evaluations include the following: videotaped sessions of the multifamily groups, student logs, verbatim interviews with families who participated, and the subjective appraisal of probation officers.

Benefits to Students.   In February of 1975, we contacted the students who had participated in the program in the spring and summer of 1973. We asked them to describe the impact of their experience in the project on their career development. We were able to identify two areas in which the program was of direct benefit to students: (a) in their personal development and (b) through the acquisition of skills which enabled them to gain immediate employment in community mental health programs and/or helped them to gain admission to graduate schools.

Personal Development.   Students were required to keep logs of their multifamily sessions. They unanimously wrote of their increased self-esteem and reported a more realistic understanding of their ego strengths and weaknesses.

There was some overlap of personal development with the development of skills related to career pursuits. Many of these students intended to become professionals in the helping services. This experience enabled them to define more accurately that professional role for themselves. A most significant aspect of this effect was how quickly the helping role was demystified. Several students reported they no longer felt that they could or should provide total solutions; they had begun to understand that the processes of change and/or development in people's lives was fairly slow, and they understood the meaning of "working through" interpersonal situations.

Even though our screening techniques enabled us to pick very suitable students for this project, inevitably there were a few students whom we later felt should not be encouraged to work intensively with people. It was somewhat difficult to inform these students of our evaluations of their general ability but we felt it was our responsibility to do so. In so doing we were able to point out students' shortcomings honestly and early enough in their potential careers to encourage more appropriate and realistic career choices.

Skill Development. Students were required to conceptualize group and family dynamics in terms of theory. They realized that understanding these conceptualizations was essential to the timing and sequence of successful interventions.

Students were asked to share information about community resources with the families. In some cases students merely described the service and its location, but in other instances the students accompanied family members in order to provide mediation between service providers and the person in need of service. For instance, family members often perceived any initial difficulty with agency personnel as insurmountable and they made a hasty retreat, leaving an impression of disinterest. Students offered role modeling and support in seeking help from agencies, thus encouraging the family to persist in seeking the service.

Benefits to Families. On the impressionistic level the families appeared satisfied with the service since there was regular attendance and they expressed the desire for the project to continue.

The videotapes themselves provide more tangible evidence of family benefits. Over the duration of the project the tapes show evidence of greater communication between parents and children. A number of the children, in getting part-time jobs (something we encouraged when appropriate) took significant steps toward establishing autonomy that was sanctioned by their parents.

Benefits to the College and the Community. The College benefited in several ways. It demonstrated to community agencies, especially the Department of Probation, that the College was willing to make a commitment to provide training that was immediately useful to that agency and to the community. The College, being a small, fairly new senior college, was eager to establish itself as a resource institution within the community. The project required students to have some contact with a wide variety of social agencies and public programs.

Benefits to the Department of Probation. The project provided a much needed referral source for the Department of Probation. It also helped to lighten the heavy caseloads carried by the probation officers. Probation officers who referred their probationers reported that during the duration of the project probationers who ordinarily called them frequently asking for advice in family conflicts stopped doing so. Several probation officers observed the sessions and noted with surprise large differences in the demeanor of their probationers, whom they had seen on a one to one basis and whom they now were seeing within the family context. Therefore, contact with the multifamily project gave probation officers a broader view of their clients. This project became an important source of skilled manpower for the Department of Probation. The Department of Probation eventually hired four undergraduates who had participated in the project.

Although this was a relatively small pilot project, it has led to the development of two video training tapes which have application far beyond the scope of the project.

In short, this project is an excellent example of how a relatively short field training program can provide benefits to all those involved. Particularly at the teaching and training levels we feel that our model is an especially useful prototype for various community psychology and community mental health interventions.

References

Anonymous. Toward the differentiation of a self in one's own family. In J. L. Framo (Ed.). *Family interaction: A dialogue between family therapists and family researchers.* New York: Springer, 1972.

Bellak, L. *Twelve ego functions in schizophrenics, neurotics and normals: A systematic study.* New York: Wiley, 1973.

Cowen, E. L. Emergent approaches to mental health problems: An overview and directions for future work. In E. L. Cowen, E. A. Gardner, & M. Zax (Eds.). *Emergent approaches to mental health problems.* New York: Appleton-Century-Crofts, 1967.

Erickson, E. H. *Childhood and society* (Rev. ed.). New York: Norton, 1964.

Freitag, G., Blechman, E., & Berck, P. College students as companion aides to newly-released psychiatric patients. In G. A. Specter & W. L. Claiborn (Eds.). *Crisis intervention.* New York: Behavioral Publications, 1973.

Haley, J. *Changing families: A family therapy reader.* New York: Grune & Stratton, 1971.

Holzberg, J. D., Knapp, R. H., & Turner, J. L. College students as companions to the mentally ill. In E. L. Cowen, E. A. Gardner, & M. Zax (Eds.). *Emergent approaches to mental health problems.* New York: Appleton-Century-Crofts, 1967.

Jacobson, E. *Self and the object world.* New York: International University Press, 1964.

Leichter, E., & Schulman, G. L. Multi-family group therapy: A multi-dimensional approach. *Family Process,* 1974, *13,* 95-110.

Minuchin, S. *Families and family therapy.* Cambridge: Harvard University Press, 1974.

Persons, R. W., Clark, C., Persons, M., Kadish, M., & Patterson, W. Training and employing undergraduates as therapists in a college counseling service. *Professional Psychology,* 1973, *4,* 170-178.

Poser, E. G. The effect of therapist training on group therapeutic outcome. *Journal of Consulting Psychology,* 1966, *30,* 283-289.

Sanders, R. New manpower for mental hospital service. In E. L. Cowen, E. A. Gardner, & M. Zax (eds.). *Emergent approaches to mental health problems.* New York: Appleton-Century-Crofts, 1967.

Satir, V. *Conjoint family therapy.* Palo Alto, CA: Science and Behavior Books, 1967.

Notes

1. Judith Kuppersmith and Rima Blair are now at the College of Staten Island, St. George Campus, and Robert Slotnick is now at Creedmoor State Hospital.
2. The authors wish to express their appreciation to Helen Brody, Larry Brown, and Carol Butler; and to Ted Gross and Philip Vota of the Staten Island Department of Probation.

An Undergraduate Practicum in Organizational Behavior Management: Course Description and Project Outcomes

Richard M. O'Brien, *Hofstra University*
William A. Sperduto, *B-MOD Associates*
Andrew B. Goff, *Hofstra University*

Students learn behavior analysis and
strategies of experimentation while
they become more marketable in business.

Since the mid-sixties behavior modification has been applied with increasing frequency to industrial/organizational problems (O'Brien & Dickinson, 1982). Using techniques such as feedback and positive reinforcement, psychologists have reported a large number of successful interventions in industry through applied behavior analysis (Frederickson, 1982; O'Brien, Dickinson & Rosow, 1982). Over the same period of time there has been increasing concern about the employment potential of the bachelor's degree in psychology (Caffrey, Berger, Cole, Marx, & Senn, 1977; Korn & Nodine, 1975; Ware & Meyer, 1981). Korn and Nodine (1975) estimate that 50 percent of BA psychology graduates go into business after they obtain their degree. It would seem desirable to provide these students with some real-world experience in applying their psychological training to industry (Caffrey et al., 1977; Harper, 1982).

Application to real world problems has been viewed as a positive addition to the teaching of industrial psychology (Millard, 1983), behavior modification (Barrera & Glasgow, 1976; Bijou, 1970; Moore & Bondy, 1978), and experimental psychology (Glenwick & Burka, 1976). In response to the need to make the psychology degree more relevant to industry and improve student response to learning the techniques of experimental psychology and applied behavior analysis, Hofstra University began to offer a field course in industrial behavior modification five years ago. This course is one of a group of research seminars offered by the psychology department. Each psychology major must take one of these seminars. Enrollment in the course is limited to 25 students with 15 being optimal. It is made up primarily of senior psychology majors, although some juniors and some business majors have also taken it. The course currently has three prerequisites: a four hour course in experimental psychology, a four hour course in statistics, and a three hour survey course introducing industrial psychology. The latter two courses may not be critical, although they provide useful background for the student. Requiring an introductory course in behavior analysis, on the other hand, would allow the instructor to begin the course at a higher level and give the student greater skills at the initial stage of the project. However, this advantage must be weighed against the danger of limiting enrollment by having too many prerequisites. Since the inception of the seminar, students have been responsible for a large number of successful interventions in organizational settings. The purpose of this article is to describe the course and some of the types of projects that students have produced in it, so that other universities can expand the opportunities that they provide for students to learn applied behavior analysis and techniques of experimentation.

This four credit seminar is scheduled for six class hours per week in three hour blocks. Three hours are spent in classroom activities and the other three hours are set aside as the minimum commitment expected of the student at the field placement. These placements are obtained by the students either through personal contacts, existing jobs, or direct requests of local companies, although it is advisable for the instructor to maintain two or three settings for those students who have difficulty finding placements. At a more residential school where the students have fewer local contacts, the instructor may have to take a larger role in placement acquisition. Although any organizational setting is acceptable, students are encouraged to have their field placements in profit-making businesses as opposed to non-profit organizations and are generally prohibited from running projects within the university in order to ensure off-campus experience.

Each student is provided with several copies of a cover letter on University stationary explaining the course to be given to potential project sites. This letter explains that the students are looking for a project in which they can use advanced behavioral techniques to improve productivity or decrease a company problem. Simply observing or becoming involved in a personnel selection program is not an acceptable project. All projects involve the application of behavior analysis. Potential problem areas mentioned to the students in the introductory lecture include absenteeism-tardiness, productivity, safety, sales, incentive systems, equipment maintenance, theft, cost containment, and quality control. The final paper on the project accounts for 40 percent of the student's grade. The students are instructed in various kinds of traditional experimental strategies but the projects are expected to employ a repeated measures approach (Komaki, 1977; Dickinson & O'Brien, 1982), preferably a reversal or multiple baseline design. Given the limitations of a one semester class, comparison designs are also acceptable. It should be noted that incompletes are not uncommon in this course. The instructor should establish a policy to deal with projects that fall through or cannot be completed through no fault of the student. Our course is always offered in the spring semester so that students who run into difficulty can be given an incomplete which they can finish over the summer. Graduating seniors are urged to begin their projects early to avoid an incomplete that would delay graduation, although this has not been a significant problem to date.

The advantage of weekly class meetings while students carry out field projects has long been recognized (Wolfgang, 1976). They are particularly important in this practicum because the lectures and readings cover the actual problems to be dealt with from a behavioral perspective. The second three hours of the week should be used by the instructor to hold individual meetings with students to discuss their project and to visit project sites. The instructor is well advised to show the flag at each site at least once during the semester.

For this reason among others, the presence of a graduate assistant (or perhaps an undergraduate who has already taken the course where no graduate students are available) is highly recommended. In addition to the normal duties of a teaching assistant, the graduate student can mind the store for meetings with some students while the instructor visits others, as well as carry out some of the site visits. Because the assistant will be engaged in problem solving with students and represent the University to the public, careful selection and coaching is recommended. At Hofstra the graduate assistants have carried the major burden of site visits without a single untoward incident in the five years of the program. Since site visits may involve some lengthy automobile trips, the instructor should arrange for the administration to reimburse travel expenses for both the faculty member and the assistant.

Readings. Two textbooks are required in the course but frequent reference is made to several ancillary texts and the *Journal of Organizational Behavior Management*. The primary text is *Industrial Behavior Modification: A Management Handbook* (O'Brien, Dickinson & Rosow, 1982). It provides the student with theoretical background as well as hands-on examples for the kinds of tasks that they will face in their projects. The second text, *Principles of Everyday Behavior Analysis* (Miller, 1980), provides the basic language and skills of applied behavior analysis for the student who is new to this approach. This programmed text has 26 lessons that can be assigned at the rate of approximately two per week.

Several supplementary texts (Brethower, 1972; Frederiksen, 1982; Gilbert, 1978; Luthans & Kreitner, 1975; & Miller, 1978) and two source bibliographies (Brown & Presbie, 1976; Prue, Frederiksen & Bacon, 1978) are put on library reserve for student use.

It is crucial that the lectures in the course serve to both introduce the student to the general behavioral skills to be employed in the projects and provide examples of how these skills can be used to improve specific performance areas in industry. The focus of these lectures ranges from building specific responses through shaping, chaining and coaching (Feeney, Staelin, O'Brien & Dickinson, 1982; Simek & O'Brien, 1981) to system wide applications (Abernathy, Duffy & O'Brien, 1982; Harshbarger & Maley, 1974).

Results. The impact of the course may be judged in a number of ways. One estimate of student learning may be gained from the projects that they have completed. Table 1 presents a summary of the actual projects carried out by the students for the first three years that the course was offered. The table provides breakdown of the settings, problems, types of intervention, and results obtained. To help the reader judge the effects that have been achieved four projects that dealt with different kinds of problems are presented in greater detail.

Project 1: Quality Control—Sherry Milman. This student contacted an electronics company where she knew the owners from informal family contacts. They expressed concern about the product rejection rate among a group of employees manufacturing relays but they had not collected any baseline data to investigate this quality control problem. The student collected baseline data nightly on the percentage of parts rejected for two weeks. Management found the 34% rejection rate that she uncovered quite disturbing. They asked a consultant who was working in other areas of the company to provide these employees with an educational training program on the importance of quality control but they allowed the student to continue to collect data. Two weeks after the consultant's workshop the student began a program of individualized daily feedback for each employee on the number of parts that were rejected. The results for the three phases of the project are presented in Figure 1. Clearly, the consultant's lecture-slide presentation did little to immediately improve quality control while the feedback program produced a considerable gain in acceptable parts.

Table 1. Summary of Student Projects By Site, Problem, Intervention and Performance Improvement[a]

Sites	N	Problem[c]	N	Interventions[c]	N	Percent Performance Improvement[c]	N
Retail Stores	10	Waste	13	Praise	16	> 100	6
Restaurants	7	Productivity	7	Charting	15	50 - 99	4
Manufacturing Plants	5	Sales	7	Feedback	14	20 - 49	10
Human Services	5	Customer Service	3	Prompts	8	10 - 19	4
Professional Offices	4	Attendance	3	Tangible Rewards	7	1 - 10	6
Banks	3	Maintenance	2	Goal Setting	3	0	5
		Theft	2	Activity Rewards	3	Project Terminated	5
Total[b]	34	Total	37	Total	66	Total	40

[a]A case by case summary of these results may be obtained from the authors.
[b]Detail records of six of the first year projects are not available so these are not included in this table.
[c]Since some projects included more than one problem, the intervention and performance improvement column totals differ.

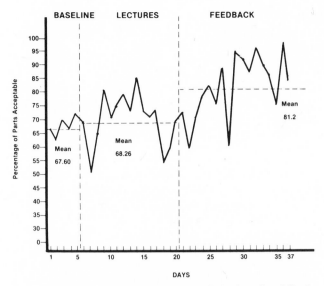

Figure 1. Daily percent of acceptable parts during baseline, following the quality control lecture and during feedback.

Of course it is possible that the lecture program had a delayed effect on performance.

Project 2: Productivity Improvement—Donald Scandell. The setting for this study was a die casting factory which employs, among other workers, four machine operators. The machine operators are responsible for the production of molded metal units called shots which are broken up, after cooling, into the small parts which are the final product at this installation. Although at baseline one of the four workers (Worker 3) produced at a consistently high rate, the other three showed extremely sporadic production. Management indicated that frequent machine breakdown was responsible for the many peaks and valleys in production, however direct observation revealed that many of these breakdowns were under the control of the operators.

The project utilized posted feedback in a comparison design. Baseline data on the number of shots produced by each worker, were collected for ten days. A graph which contained a separate baseline for each worker was then conspicuously posted. During the ten day intervention period, each worker's production was added to the graph on a daily basis.

As can be seen in Figure 2, the intervention had an effect on the production of all four workers. For three of the workers (1, 2 and 4), the increases were marked, ranging from 3.9 percent of baseline to 21.8 percent of baseline. Total production for the department increased 6.5 percent. The lesser effects on worker 3's response rate may reflect a ceiling effect related to his consistently high rate of production. It is interesting that he was the only one of the four workers who was paid on a piece-rate basis. Similar relationships between fixed salary and performance have also been reported in other areas (Howard, Figlerski & O'Brien, 1982). These results suggest that feedback can effectively produce productivity increases that are financially meaningful among salaried manufacturing employees.

Project 3: Equipment Maintenance—Robert LaFroscia. Cleaning and maintenance tasks tend to be neglected in psychological interventions in the workplace. Because of the nonreinforcing nature of these tasks and the delayed nature of the negative consequences that result from their neglect, they tend not to be attended to, especially when workers are primarily responsible for other jobs (Komaki & Collins, 1982). Project 3 was designed to increase cleaning and maintenance behaviors among six teenage employees of an ice cream parlor.

In this study both antecedents and consequences were manipulated in order to increase the rate of cleaning and maintenance behaviors. Efficacy was evaluated within an ABCA, reversal design. Working with the manager of the ice cream parlor, the student constructed a 40 item manager's checklist of cleaning and maintenance activities. This checklist was filled out by the manager twice a day for seven days, it revealed a baseline completion rate of 64 percent for the maintenance tasks. Beginning on day eight, a daily checklist of cleaning and maintenance jobs was handed out to each shift. Workers were asked to check off whether or not each task was completed, to make appropriate comments, and to initial each list upon finishing work. In addition, a notice was posted which explained the purpose of the checklists, provided feedback (baseline data), and set a goal of 90 percent for task completion. During this week of intervention 92 percent of the tasks were completed. On day 15, these posted baseline data were updated to include the previous week's performance and verbal feedback and contingent praise were added to the intervention. Performance remained high, showing a 95 percent completion rate. A reversal phase commenced on day 22, during which the manager collected data with the manager's checklist. A performance decrease occurred during this seven day period, as work completed dropped to 83 percent. Although this project only lasted four weeks, it should be noted, that in

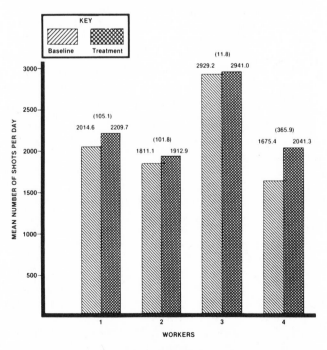

Figure 2. Daily mean number of moulded metal units (shots) produced by each worker during baseline and treatment phases.

this case, as in several others, the manager chose to continue the system designed by the student and attempted to devise similar ones for other work behaviors.

Project 4: Attendance and Tardiness—Joanne Anthony. In contrast to cleaning and maintenance activities, tardiness has received a good deal of attention from industrial psychologists (Carlson & Sperduto, 1982). In this project we sought to decrease tardiness among five female counselors at a sleep-away camp who comprised the waterfront staff. It utilized an ABAB, reversal design to determine the efficacy of feedback and positive reinforcement in increasing punctuality at the dock.

During the 14 day baseline period, the subjects reported for work punctually 36 percent of the time. During the two week intervention phase which followed, the baseline data were presented to the group, a sign-in program was initiated and individual arrival times and group punctuality percentages were posted conspicuously. In addition, contingent praise was utilized and water skiing time was offered as a reward for perfect punctuality during the entire two weeks. Punctuality across subjects increased to 81 percent.

A partial return to baseline was instituted for weeks five and six during which the sign-in procedure, the posting of individual arrival times, and the water skiing reward were no longer in effect and contingent praise was administered sporadically. Punctuality decreased to 66.6 percent. During the following ten days all treatment conditions were reinstated and punctuality increased to 90%. The results of Project 4 illustrate the efficacy of an inexpensive program of feedback, verbal praise and activity reinforcers in improving the punctuality of summer camp staff.

Evaluation. Aside from student projects there is other evidence of the effectiveness of the course. Student enrollment has increased each year the course has been offered, from 12 to 22 over five years. Informal student evaluations have been overwhelmingly positive taking exception only to the brevity of the course (frequently) and the restriction against selection-personnel type projects (twice). Formal student evaluations were conducted during the second year of the course among 13 of the 15 students in the class. The average rating over 13 questions on a 1 (positive) to 5 (negative) scale was 1.49. Eleven of the 13 indicated that they would highly recommend (1) the course to other students. Students routinely list the course project as experience on their resumes and report positive reactions from job interviewers when they describe their experience. At least one student each year has been hired by the company in which they did their project.

Company responses to the program have usually been changed from a cautious and condescending tolerance at the beginning of the semester to considerable enthusiasm when the project is completed. The most common description of the course from managers is that it provides free consultation in which the manager gets the instructor's expertise and the students hands to carry through the program. Three times in the four year history of the course a project started by a student in one setting has been adapted for use throughout a chain of related stores in the area. Since these projects were not designed to be either long lasting or

generalizable to sites other than the one in which they were instituted, this has been an unexpected benefit of the program to the company's involved. Anecdotally, perhaps the most gratifying data on any of the projects came when a student in the first session of the fifth year described the contingent reinforcement system for suggestive selling that was in use in the shoe store in which he worked part-time. It sounded familiar to the instructor who on inquiry discovered that it had been set up as a student project in the first year of the course and was still in operation, although the student has long since left the setting.

Although there has been little attempt to formally evaluate this course, project effects, student responses, and feedback from managers at project settings all suggest that it is meeting its goals. Students are learning behavior analysis and strategies of experimentation while they become more marketable in business at the bachelors degree level. Managers have become more data centered, less punitive, and more reinforcing.

As behavior modification becomes more widely known in industry, the behavioral techniques that the students currently bring to the business world may become less novel and unique. Until that happens however, this blend of applied behavior analysis and on-site business experience would appear to be a potent technique for increasing the expertise and employment potential of undergraduate psychology majors as well as the involvement of the university with its surrounding community.

References

Abernathy, W. B., Duffy, E. M., & O'Brien, R. M. Multi-branch, multi-systems programs in banking: An organization-wide intervention. In R. M. O'Brien, A. M. Dickinson, & M. P. Rosow (Eds.), *Industrial behavior modification: A management handbook.* Elmsford, NY: Pergamon, 1982.

Barrera, M., Jr. & Glasgow, R. E. Design and evaluation of a personalized instruction course in behavioral self-control. *Teaching of Psychology,* 1976, *3,* 81-84.

Bijou, S. J. What psychology has to offer education—now. *Journal of Applied Behavior Analysis,* 1970, 3, 65-71.

Brethower, D. M. *Behavioral analysis in business and industry: A total performance system.* Kalamazoo, MI: Behavioradelia, 1972.

Brown, P. L., & Presbie, R. J. *Behavior modification in business, industry, and government.* New Paltz, NY: Behavior Improvement Associates, 1976.

Caffrey, B., Berger, L., Cole, S., Marx, D., & Senn, D. Integrating professional programs in a traditional undergraduate psychology program. *Teaching of Psychology,* 1977, *4,* 7-13.

Carlson, R. M., & Sperduto, W. A. Improving attendance and punctuality through positive reinforcement within a behavioral consultation model. In R. M. O'Brien, A. M. Dickinson, & M. P. Rosow (Eds.), *Industrial behavior modification: A management handbook.* Elmsford, NY: Pergamon, 1982.

Dickinson, A. M., & O'Brien, R. M. Performance measurement and evaluation. In R. M. O'Brien, A. M. Dickinson, & M. P. Rosow (Eds.), *Industrial behavior modification: A management handbook.* Elmsford, NY: Pergamon, 1982.

Feeney, E. J., Staelin, J. R., O'Brien, R. M., & Dickinson, A. M. Increasing sales performance among airline reservation personnel. In R. M. O'Brien, A. M. Dickinson, & M. P. Rosow (Eds.), *Industrial behavior modification: A management handbook.* Elmsford, NY: Pergamon, 1982.

Frederiksen, L. W. (Ed.). *Handbook of organizational behavior management.* New York: Wiley, 1982.

Gilbert, T. F. *Human competence: Engineering worthy performance.* New York: McGraw-Hill, 1978.

Glenwick, D. S., & Burka, A. A. Relevance rides again: Enhancing the attractiveness of undergraduate research experiences. *Teaching of Psychology*, 1976, 3, 137-138.

Harper, R. S. Our old-fogy curricula. *Teaching of Psychology*, 1982, 9, 33-35.

Harshbarger, D. D., & Maley, R. F. *Behavior analysis and systems analysis: An integrative approach to mental health problems.* Kalamazoo, MI: Behaviordelia, 1974.

Howard, S. R., Figlerski, R. W., & O'Brien, R. M. The negative effects of long-term, guaranteed contracts on the performance of major league pitchers. In R. M. O'Brien, A. M. Dickinson, & M. P. Rosow (Eds.), *Industrial behavior modification: A management handbook.* Elmsford, NY: Pergamon, 1982.

Komaki, J. Alternative evaluation strategies in work settings: Reversal and multiple baseline designs. *Journal of Organizational Behavior Management*, 1977, 1, 53-77.

Komaki, J., & Collins, R. L. Motivation of preventive maintenance performance. In R. M. O'Brien, A. M. Dickinson, & M. P. Rosow (Eds.), *Industrial behavior modification: A management handbook.* Elmsford, NY: Pergamon, 1982.

Korn, J., & Nodine, B. Facts and questions concerning career training for the psychology major. *Teaching of Psychology*, 1975, 2, 117-119.

Luthans, F., & Kreitner, R. *Organizational behavior modification.* Glenview, IL: Scott Foresman, 1975.

Millard, R. J. A morale survey project as a group activity in an industrial/organizational course. *Teaching of Psychology*, 1983, 10, 110-112.

Miller, L. K. *Principles of everyday behavior analysis* (2nd Ed.). Monterey, CA: Brooks/Cole, 1980.

Miller, L. M. *Behavior management: The new science of managing people at work.* New York: Wiley, 1978.

Moore, S. F., & Bondy, A. S. Undergraduate participation as behavior assessor in a day-care consultation. *Teaching of Psychology*, 1978, 5, 135-139.

O'Brien, R. M., & Dickinson, A. M. Introduction to industrial behavior modification. In R. M. O'Brien, A. M. Dickinson, & M. P. Rosow (Eds.), *Industrial behavior modification: A management handbook.* Elmsford, NY: Pergamon, 1982.

O'Brien, R. M., Dickinson, A. M., & Rosow, M. P. (Eds.). *Industrial behavior modification: A management handbook.* Elmsford, NY: Pergamon, 1982.

Prue, D. M., Frederiksen, L. W., & Bacon, A. Organizational behavior management: An annotated bibliography. *Journal of Organizational Behavior Management*, 1978, 1, 216-257.

Simek, T. C., & O'Brien, R. M. *Total golf: A behavioral approach to lowering your score and getting more out of your game.* New York: Doubleday, 1981.

Ware, M. E., & Meyer, A. E. Career versatility of the psychology major: A survey of graduates. *Teaching of Psychology*, 1981, 8, 12-15.

Wolfgang, D. G. The psychology teacher and undergraduate field experience courses: The problem of supervision. *Teaching of Psychology*, 1976, 3, 183-184.

Notes

1. Portions of this paper were presented at the annual meeting of the Association for Behavior Analysis, Milwaukee, May 1981.

c. Using Placements for Training

A psychology technician training program was the subject of an article by William Nish from Georgia College. The author noted that as many as 45 percent of clinical psychology department in state hospitals used bachelor-level technicians as psychologist's assistants. But many of these technicians had majored in sociology, education, and home economics. An average of seven students per year have found employment as parole agents, substance abuse counselors, and halfway house directors. The author shared keen insights into the evaluation and refinement of the program, which other instructors will find very practical. One suggestion was to avoid labeling the course "Technician Training".

Five professors from Clemson University, noted that as many as 80% of psychology students seek employment immediately after graduating from college. Bernard Caffrey, Leonard Berger, Spurgeon Cole, David Marx, and David Senn also reported on their department's efforts to prepare students for employment. They described four undergraduate programs: industrial-applied, community-clinical, pre-college teaching of psychology, and an interdisciplinary option. The common element in each was a heavily-weighted field placement component. Departments that are developing pro-

grams to train students to meet community needs in specific areas will find this article useful.

A full-time clinical field experience is the topic of an article by David Shiverick from State University College at Potsdam. Students worked full time for a semester at a psychiatric facility and obtained 15 hours of credit. The author elaborated on the wide variety of wards and programs where students can be used. Students gained experience in alcohol rehabilitation wards, token economy wards, and geriatric wards. The author gave special attention to a discussion of the planning and operation of the placement; he hoped that the contents of the article would stimulate the growth of other courses in medical settings.

K. Shemberg and S. Kelley from Bowling Green State University conducted an intensive 40 week program to train undergraduates as subprofessional community mental health workers. The placement component of the course began with a field trip, followed by discussions of the experience. More detailed observations of patients preceded 20 weeks of placement in the institution. A detailed description of the program's three phases and goals may be beneficial in helping students' transition into similar placements.

A Psychology Technician Training Program

William W. Nish
Georgia College

This paper is an account of how a small department has met the needs of its region by adding an applied program, but retaining its traditions.

The Psychology Technician Training Program at Georgia College is an optional sequence of courses which the student can complete along with the psychology major requirements for a Bachelor's degree. All majors take general, statistics, and experimental; and technicians add applied, abnormal, testing, testing practicum, personality theory, learning, applied learning, and clinical practicum (a quarter's full-time supervised field experience in a nearby state mental institution). The program is designed to prepare the student with a Bachelor's degree in psychology for work under the supervision of a PhD psychologist in such settings as state institutions, mental health clinics, counseling centers, corrections agencies, testing centers, and possibly personnel departments. It is emphasized to the students that the department does not in any way consider that the program trains clinicians who are qualified to work on their own, but rather that the program trains technicians who will be able to perform certain duties under the supervision of a Doctoral-level psychologist. Students are also advised that they should not get so heavily involved in the applied aspects of the technician program that they neglect a well-rounded background in undergraduate psychology to the extent that it restricts their future options, such as graduate school.

Background.   Georgia College is a four-year state college with approximately 2500 undergraduate and 900 graduate students. The psychology department has five full-time and two part-time professors and about 90 majors. In September, 1978, the department started an MS program designed largely for part-time students who are working in the Middle Georgia area, and about 25 students are expected in that program. In 1972, Dr. Robert Wildman, then Chief Clinical Psychologist at Central State Hospital (a state mental institution near the Georgia College campus), pointed out to us that Central State Hospital was using 30 Bachelor-level psychology technicians with considerable evidence of success (Quattlebaum, Groves, Carroccio, Hendricks, Jones, Lanier, Lanier, & Ressenger, Note 1; Elliott, Smith, Dixon, & Wildman, Note 2; Beissel, Gates, & Ressenger, Note 3). Dr. Wildman also documented that the use of Bachelor-level technicians to help meet the demand for psychological services was a nationwide phenomenon. In a survey of clinical psychology departments in applied clinical settings, conducted in 1971 (Wildman, Wildman, & Elliott, 1972), it was found that 39% of the 242 departments which responded were making use of Bachelor-level technicians. Caffrey,

Berger, Cole, Marx, and Senn (1977) have also provided evidence that subprofessionals can be trained to work effectively in clinical settings. Dr. Wildman suggested that the Georgia College Psychology Department consider the development of an undergraduate program which would better prepare these technicians for the work they were doing in the clinical setting.

The department went through considerable soul searching over the appropriateness of any form of clinical training at the undergraduate level, inasmuch as most of us had been indoctrinated with the belief that clinical services are to be performed by PhD clinical psychologists. We would have been more comfortable if we could have found some inkling from the American Psychological Association that sub-doctoral programs with clinical training are respectable. However, Woods' (1971) review of 25 years of APA debates and conferences about the desirability and respectability of, exact role of, designations for, and professional status of sub-doctoral persons delivering psychological services, rather emphatically led us to abandon the hope that we should seek clear guidelines from the parent professional organization. It seemed to us that, while psychology was arguing with itself about the suitability of sub-doctoral psychological services, other professions such as sociology, education, health, and home economics were rapidly spreading into the psychological areas of the helping professions arena with persons who were performing psychological services. In many cases, these persons were less well trained for offering those services than Bachelor-level psychology majors. Caffrey et al. (1977) have also taken note of this trend toward jobs in psychology-related areas being filled by individuals with less adequate training than psychology majors. We decided that, because the need had been demonstrated and our Bachelor-level students were in fact being employed in clinical psychology departments, we should develop the appropriate training rather than retreat to the safety of the academic tower.

We asked the psychology staff at Central State Hospital to provide us with a description of the characteristics, knowledge, and skills they would like to find in a product of a psychology technician training program, and the following were provided: (a) A good background in learning theory; (b) A knowledge of applied learning theory, especially clinical studies of behavior modification; (c) Practical experience in a clinical setting; (d) Ability to administer basic psychological tests; (e) Experience in report writing; (f) Familiarity with basic statistical techniques for data analysis and presentation; (g) Personality characteristics appropriate to the work of a technician (such as tact, a willingness to accept responsibility, and enthusiasm for one's work). The empirical-behavioral orientation of the staff which provided this list seems clear.

Curriculum. We then began to translate the needs listed in the last paragraph into an undergraduate program. We examined the model of the Mental Health Assistant at the Associate degree level which had been described by Hadley and True (Note 4), but we decided that this model did not provide sufficient depth for the work being done by technicians. It was our aim to produce psychologists' assistants, not mental health generalists. We also did not want to have a program which was so specialized and so separate from the usual undergraduate psychology program that the graduates of the technician program would find their options seriously narrowed for future graduate work or other jobs outside the mental health field.

The importance in career-related programs of keeping the course of study flexible enough that the student does not find his options after graduation too narrow, and of being sure that applied field work is not stressed to the point of detracting from necessary academic background has been stressed by Korn and Nodine (1975), Shiverick (1977), and Hess, Harrison, Fink, Lilliston, Aponte, and Korn (1978). The courses listed in the first paragraph of this paper constitute the Psychology Technician Training Program we devised. All of the courses with the exception of the testing practicum, applied learning, and the clinical practicum were already a part of our undergraduate curriculum. In adding these courses, we were most fortunate to have available qualified psychologists at Central State Hospital who were willing to teach on a part-time basis and to provide supervision for the clinical practicum field experience.

Assessment. Since the first graduation from the program in 1974, 39 students have completed the requirements of the program, for an average of about seven per year. This represents approximately one-fourth of our major graduates during the same period. We have tried to assess the program by having the students make written evaluations at the completion of the practicum, by interviews with seniors, by alumni surveys, and by informal conversations and correspondence. The student response to the program has been very positive, and this has been especially true for the opportunity to have a quarter's field experience for academic credit. Only one student during the six years has been more negative than positive about the program, and that was because of his criticism of the way he was supervised in the clinical practicum. The main theme of the students' positive statements is the chance to apply their classroom learning to an actual job situation in the field experience. The main theme of the students' negative statements has been that they were not adequately prepared for coping with the realities of the everyday work situation in a state mental institution. We have not been certain that there is a way to prepare them for this "cultural shock," because it appears to be something which must be experienced in order to be understood. The students do have early field trips to Central State Hospital in connection with abnormal psychology and the testing practicum.

Keeping up with the job situation of the graduates has been difficult because of the high rate of mobility and the related disappointing rate of return of alumni questionnaires. Our difficulty is apparently not unique, for Korn and Nodine (1975) report similar problems at a number of institutions. Of the first eight graduates of the program in 1974, six were employed as psychology technicians at Central State Hospital. The over-all rate of employment at the Hospital for the six year period has been about one-fourth of the program's graduates. However, this rate of employment is not a direct indication of success, for many of the students in the program do not apply for a technician position. Some of them just find the program an interesting experience, some see the program as a good background for graduate work in an area such as clinical psychology or counseling, and some have preferences about the area in which they live and work which preclude a position as a technician.

Graduates of the program have also been employed as parole agents, employment counselors, court service workers, drug and alcohol abuse workers, corrections counselors, testing program assistants, rehabilitation counselors, vocational counselors, halfway house directors, unit directors in institutions for disturbed children and adolescents, and in a variety of jobs in psycho-education centers and mental health centers. The one main thing that seems to impress employers is that the students have had a full quarter's supervised field experience. Another important variable in the employment situation at Central State Hospital is that budget and grant fluctuations, internal reorganizations, and periodic reassessments of the state merit system classifications and policies make it somewhat unpredictable as to when the hospital will be able to hire technicians. We rather frequently have the situation in which the hospital wants to hire some of the graduates of the program but cannot get the necessary clearance. Employers from whom we have been able to get evaluations of the work of graduates of the program have uniformly expressed satisfaction.

Advantages. In our opinion, the Psychology Technician Training Program at Georgia College has had the following advantages: (a) It has provided mental health institutions and agencies in the area with an increased pool of trained workers at the Bachelor-level. (b) It has increased the level of our interaction with psychologists in the area institutions and agencies and improved our working relationships with them. (c) It has increased the employment potential for the capable psychology graduate who does not have the resources, verbal aptitude, or motivation for graduate school. It is not uncommon for students to be hired by the same unit in which they had their supervised clinical practicum. Korn and Nodine (1975) and Thomas (1975) have pointed out that the majority of undergraduate psychology majors do not go to graduate school and that we have a responsibility of helping this majority find careers that are possible with a Bachelor-level training in psychology.

Furthermore, the program (d) has provided a chance for some students who are planning for graduate school to gain valuable practical experience before entering graduate school. (e) For some students, it has been an avenue for funding of graduate school in that a few agencies have had funds with which to sponsor a technician's graduate educa-

229

tion in return for a specified term of service to the agency. (f) The program has been comprehensive enough to allow students to consider a number of options following graduation. If the student changes his mind about the program part way through or completes the program and then cannot, or does not want to, work as a technician, he still has the psychology major. (g) The courses in the program have been open to all qualified students and hence have provided a greater variety of course offerings in the psychology department. (h) The program has provided to both students and faculty the stimulation of combining application and experience with the usual course work.

Difficulties. The problems associated with the technician program have been the following: (a) The department is small, with a heavy teaching load, and this has made the supervision of the practicum a problem. Until 1978-79 we handled this by appointing a PhD clinical psychologist on the Central State Hospital staff as a part-time professor in our Psychology Department during the quarter of the clinical practicum. This person has arranged for practicum experiences in various areas of the hospital under supervisors who have at least the Master's degree in psychology or a closely related field, and has met with the practicum students as a group once a week for discussion of their work. The great majority of the supervision has been well done. However, Central State Hospital is a very large and diversified institution with periodic changes in staff and organization, and there have been situations in which the supervision was not adequate. The importance of and suggestions for the proper supervision of field work for psychology undergraduates has been discussed by Wolfgang (1976), Creek and Thompson (1977), and Shiverick (1977). In September 1978, our Psychology Department employed its first full-time clinical psychologist, and that person assumed the responsibility of the arrangements for and supervision of all off-campus education experiences for psychology students.

In addition, (b) some of the technicians, after several years in that position, have expressed dissatisfaction with the opportunities for advancement available to them with the Bachelor's degree. The fact that a responsible position as a psychologist will require graduate work is something which we communicate to all of our majors, and especially to our technician students. (c) The identity of the program has presented some problems, because it is not a traditional academic program. We must continually interpret the program to our majors and encourage them to start in the course sequence early enough to get the required courses at the right times if they are interested in the program. It is not unusual to find a student at the end of the junior year who finally faces the realization of job hunting in another year and who, at that point, tries to make special arrangements for the technician program requirements, which take a minimum of two years to complete. The completion of the program is identified on the student's official transcript by the notation "Psychology Technician Training Program Completed," placed beside the notation that the student was a psychology major. Employers at Central State Hospital are aware of the meaning of this notation, and students have found that employers elsewhere accept a verbal explanation from the graduate. We have offered to write a letter of explanation of the program to any potential employer, but neither students nor employers have requested such a letter to date. (d) We have some indications that more students would participate in the program if the requirements were not so demanding. The program requires 20 quarter hours beyond the minimum number of quarter hours required for a psychology major, and it also requires some theoretical courses such as psychology of learning and personality theory.

Reassessment. During 1978-79, we have been taking a close look at the technician program and the level of student participation in it. The addition of a full-time clinical psychologist to our staff has already lessened our problems in the areas of opportunities for and supervision of field experiences for academic credit. With the start of our MS program in the fall of 1978, technicians in the area now have the opportunity for the graduate training they may need for advancement in their jobs.

We have decided that it would be better not to use the word "technician" in the title of the program. The term is apparently giving students the impression that the program is designed to prepare them for only a specific job, such as the appointments which have been available at Central State Hospital. As has been mentioned above, graduates of the program have found employment in a great variety of jobs and settings. Another problem with the title "technician" is that different states and agencies use different terms for persons employed with the Bachelor's degree in psychology, and the terms change periodically with new professional developments and with re-examination of job classifications. This problem of a lack of a match of the skills of students from Bachelor-level training programs with jobs available within the personnel classification systems of local, state, and federal agencies has also been pointed out by Hess, et al. (1978). We have found that in various situations a person working with a Bachelor's degree in psychology might be designated as a technician, or a behavior specialist, a human services worker, a case worker, a psychologist's aide or assistant, a clinical services worker, or as a mental health technician or associate. As a result of these considerations, we are planning to change the name of the program to the Psychological Services Program.

Some students have told us that the main thing which has kept them from participating in the program has been the impossibility of arranging their job, family, or other course responsibilities so as to be able to take the full-time field experience, which has been offered in the spring quarter. Consequently, we are planning to try to arrange it in any quarter for which it is appropriate for a given student, and also to reduce the required hours of field work from fifteen quarter hours (full-time work at the agency) to ten hours (two-thirds time work at the agency). Shiverick (1977) has made a good case for the advantages of a full-time field experience over a part-time field experience. We are in agreement with him and plan to arrange for full-time in every situation in which it is possible. However, so many of our students are now dependent upon jobs to see them through college and/or have family responsibilities which cannot be changed, that we believe that some accommodation is necessary. We are also attempting to make the field work available at a variety of settings in our area which provide psychological services, rather than just at Central State Hospital as in the past.

As a part of our review, we have taken a close look at the courses required. We have decided that the following are essential and should continue to be required: Abnormal Psychology, Tests and Measurements, Testing Practicum, Psychology of Learning and Motivation, Behavior Modification (new course title for Applied Learning), and at least ten quarter hours of supervised field experience. In order to allow flexibilities in students' schedules, we have decided to allow the student to choose any two of the following three courses: Applied Psychology, Clinical Psychology (a new course in 1979-80), and Theories of Personality. As before, the courses required in the Psychological Services Program will be in addition to the courses required of all psychology majors—namely, General Psychology, Statistics, and Experimental Psychology. In re-examining the program, we have had the usual long debates with ourselves about requiring all of the things which we think should be included in an ideal career-oriented concentration as opposed to what it is realistic to expect of diversified students and a small, busy teaching staff.

Overview.   The trend away from terminal Master's programs in clinical psychology may increase the need for technicians at the Bachelor's level. Even with the alleviation of the shortage of PhD clinical psychologists, there will be situations, especially in state institutions and agencies, in which budgetary considerations will prevent the heavy use of PhD's to deliver psychological services. Wildman, Nish, and Wildman (Note 5) have pointed out that the use of sub-doctoral technicians under supervision to do some of the more routine tasks such as interviewing, administering certain tests, making behavioral observations, and running behavior modification programs, can release the PhD clinical psychologist for more involvement in program planning, improvement of services, and research. This will be even more true if the trend away from the psychoanalytic model and toward the behavioral model of treatment continues, as it appears to be doing.

In a follow-up to their 1971 survey, Wildman and Wildman (1977) surveyed again in 1976 clinical psychology departments in applied clinical settings for their use of doctoral and sub-doctoral personnel. They found that, although the average number of PhD's and interns per clinical setting did not increase between 1971 and 1976, the average number of Bachelor-level technicians increased during the same time period by 38%. Their data also show that, whereas in 1971, 38% of the responding departments employed Bachelor-level technicians, by 1976, that percentage had risen to 45%. McConnell (1977, p. 687) estimates that, because of rapid advances in behavioral technology, at least 10% of the US work force will be in jobs for which the title "psychologist" or "behavioral engineer" will be appropriate by the year 2000.

Even if we cut this prediction to a more conservative 5%, we are left with a situation in which it appears that there will be an increasing need for sub-doctoral technicians in the delivery of psychological services.

References

Caffrey, B., Berger, L., Cole, S., Marx, D., & Senn, D.   Integrating professional programs in a traditional undergraduate psychology program. *Teaching of Psychology,* 1977, *4,* 7-13.

Creek, L. V., & Thompson, G.   Management of undergraduate psychology internships. *Teaching of Psychology,* 1977, *4,* 177-180.

Hess, A. K., Harrison, A. O., Fink, R S., Lilliston, L., Aponte, J. F., & Korn, J. H.   Critical issues in undergraduate training in various community settings. *Teaching of Psychology,* 1978, *5,* 81-86.

Korn, J. H., & Nodine, B. F.   Facts and questions concerning career training of the psychology major. *Teaching of Psychology,* 1975, *2,* 117-119.

McConnell, J. V.   *Understanding human behavior* (2nd ed.). New York: Holt, Rinehart, & Winston, 1977.

Shiverick, D. D.   A full-time clinical practicum for undergraduates. *Teaching of Psychology,* 1977, *4,* 188-190.

Thomas, E. R.   An alternate approach to undergraduate training in psychology. *Teaching of Psychology,* 1975, *2,* 80-81.

Wildman. R. W., & Wildman, R. W., II.   Sizes and salary schedules of agency clinical psychology programs, 1976. *The Clinical Psychologist,* 1977, *30,* 8-10.

Wildman, R. W., II, Wildman, R. W., & Elliott, T. N.   Sizes and salary schedules of agency clinical psychology programs. *American Psychologist,* 1972, *27,* 407-411.

Wolfgang, D. G.   The psychology teacher and undergraduate field experience courses: the problem of supervision. *Teaching of Psychology,* 1976, *3,* 183-184.

Woods, P. J.   A history of APA's concerns with the master's degree: Or "discharged with thanks." *American Psychologist,* 1971, *26,* 697-707.

Notes

1. Quattlebaum, L. F., Groves, I. D., Carroccio, D. F., Hendricks, J., Jones, R., Lanier, C. C., Lanier, D., & Ressenger, J. G. *Behavior modification at Central State Hospital.* Paper presented at the meeting of the Georgia Psychological Association, Atlanta, GA, 1970.

2. Elliott, T. N., Smith, R. D., Dixon, G. R., & Wildman, R. W., II. *The psychology program for children and adolescents at Central State Hospital.* Paper presented at the meeting of the Georgia Psychological Association, Augusta, GA, 1971.

3. Beissel, G. F., Gates, J. J., and Ressenger, J. G. *A token economy with chronic psychiatric patients: Systems and subsystems.* Paper presented at the meeting of the Southeastern Psychological Association, Atlanta, GA, 1972.

4. Hadley, J. M., & True, J. E. *The associate degree in mental health technology.* Paper presented at the meeting of the American Psychological Association, Washington, DC, September 1967.

5. Wildman, R. W., Nish, W. W., & Wildman, R. W., II. *The training and use of sub-doctoral personnel in agency clinical psychology departments: A status report.* Paper presented at the meeting of the Georgia Psychological Association, Macon, GA, 1972.

6. Adapted from a paper presented at the American Psychological Meetings, Toronto, 1978.

Integrating Professional Programs in a Traditional Undergraduate Psychology Program

Bernard Caffrey, Leonard Berger, Spurgeon Cole,
David Marx, and David Senn
Clemson University

How this department has attempted to meet
the students' need for job preparation and
still maintain the liberal arts tradition.

The following four papers were presented as a symposium at the 1974 meeting of the American Psychological Association. The symposium centered on discussions of four specific professional areas for which undergraduate psychology majors can be prepared without a marked deviation from a traditional undergraduate psychology program. Because of the emphasis on the need for graduate-level training for performance as a psychologist, undergraduate programs have de-emphasized professional training as such, leaving for those who do not plan to attend graduate school the promise that the "liberal education" in psychology would help them in a "broad variety" of professions. Although a certain proportion of undergraduates do attend graduate school, a larger proportion enter the active job market upon graduation. Many students today express a desire to be prepared for a professional occupation upon graduation from college. Without any drastic revision of our undergraduate program at Clemson University, we have begun to focus on curriculum modules that will prepare the student for specific occupations upon graduation.

In 1968 Boneau reported that only one-fourth of all undergraduate psychology majors ever obtained a master's degree. He expressed serious concerns about the manpower waste implicit in this situation. He projected that 200,000 psychology majors would graduate between 1968 and 1978 who would not obtain advanced degrees (Boneau, 1968). There is more recent evidence that Boneau's estimate is conservative. Cates (1973) reported that bachelor's degrees in psychology are expected to rise to 79,000 *per year* by the end of the 1970's. If this increase becomes a reality, it will represent a growth of 114% during this decade. Obviously, the interest in psychology as an undergraduate major is growing dramatically in all areas of the country. However, many students do not feel that graduate training is appropriate for them. For those seeking advanced training, it is often found that the opportunities for graduate study have not increased proportionately. Thus, the percentage of psychology graduates seeking employment and a vocational identity upon receiving a B.A. degree may reach and surpass 80%. Are undergraduate curricula changing to meet the vocational needs of *all* students, or is the challenge of providing an immediate vocational identity going unheeded? Certainly the mere addition of two or three elective courses to the curriculum does not adequately meet this challenge.

Coupled with these pressures for change has come an increasing awareness among academic psychologists that teaching techniques and methodologies are in drastic need of revision. The traditionally heavy emphasis upon course content and the dispensing of information is shifting from such information *giving* to information *getting*. Rather than trying to provide answers for students, they are taught *how* to go about trying to find answers to meaningful questions. In essence, an attitude or an approach to knowledge is taught rather than specific content. Helping students learn how to learn is generally accompanied by greater personal involvement and participation. It is not surprising that these student-centered techniques and emphases have resulted in a variety of self-paced learning programs (e.g., personalized systems of instruction).

Given these two sources of pressure—the undergraduate who seeks an immediate vocational identity and the need for revised teaching techniques—we must discover and implement alternatives to and modifications of the traditionally structured undergraduate program. Unfortunately, the very discipline which ostensibly is concerned with the study and development of individual differences has lost this perspective in its undergraduate programs. Education for the masses has failed to stimulate individually defined compentencies and, in general, undergraduate curricula have not met changing social and personal needs. Individual differences do indeed exist! A curriculum that forces all students to achieve along a single, linear dimension denies the individuality of each student and lessens his or her sense of competence and self-worth. The 1973 Vail Conference on Levels and Patterns of Professional Training in Psychology concurred with this appraisal. They recommended that some programs be oriented to training students in specific competence areas so that they can meet specific community needs (Korman, 1974).

The four areas discussed in this symposium were (a) The Industrial-Applied Option; (b) The Community-Clinical Option; (c) The Pre-College Teaching of Psychology Option, and (d) The Interdisciplinary Option. Since we have experienced a great deal of student enthusiasm for these programs, and they are still in various stages of development, we would like to share our experiences. Hopefully others who have plans for such programs, or who are themselves engaged in the development of similar programs, will be encouraged to share their insights with us. We feel that academic psychology can answer the need for relevance without sacrificing its basic orientation to an objective understanding of human behavior. It has been our experience that even those students who plan to attend graduate school profit greatly from involvement in professional psychology as an undergraduate; thus the programs we discuss are not to be viewed as directed toward the poor or marginal student. The programs are an integral part of a comprehensive undergraduate education in psychology.

Bernard Caffrey

An Undergraduate Practicum in Industrial Psychology

The pressures upon a BA degree holder to have a skill increase as the job market becomes tighter. In some cases undergraduate practicums might help to provide a means of skill-development. In one institution it was found that about one third of the undergraduate practicum students realized that this area of interest was not for them, another third found that this area of concentration *was* for them, whereas others decided to go on to graduate school in various areas related to the practicum (Fields, 1974). Pinkus and Korn (1973) surveyed potential employers of psychology graduates and found that employers in the social sciences generally considered the BA degree holder a generalist and lower paid than the MA specialist. In the business community, the BA in psychology was not found an asset. It was considered as equal to any Liberal Arts degree. Pinkus and Korn suggest that the preparation of undergraduate majors for careers requires (a) that the students be given enough flexibility so that they gain experience from a field project, (b) some preparation for the field experience be given to them, and (c) their education should include some professional level courses. Even with this preparation the master's degree holder is still valued above the professional bachelors degree, especially in social service locations.

The objective of my Practicum in Industrial Psychology is to give students a chance to apply their coursework and see the relevance of psychology. Although the Industrial Practicum was not designed to be vocationally preparatory in any specific manner, it was hoped that students could get the flavor of applied psychology in an industrial setting.

We wrote to business and government offices to determine their interest in the program two months prior to its beginning. Many locations, including hospitals, industries, and state governmental agencies and commissions, responded positively. No remuneration was asked for the practicum students, but some agencies volunteered to pay student transportation.

Many locations had to be eliminated because of their distance from the University (one disadvantage for a rural university). Some interesting projects therefore were not considered—from affirmative-action reporting to accident-prevention. Five locations were finally selected: including one hospital, one textile industry and one large printing shop.

Ten students were accepted for the course. Each student was to choose a project of interest. The course was set up with a one hour class meeting each week and four hours of practicum. After the first four weeks the one class hour was eliminated and the job requirement was increased to six hours per week and one meeting with me. The course requirement included a written completed project report (approved by the industrial sponsor and by me) as well as a final test based on readings related to the individual practicum area. Two students dropped out after two weeks of the practicum because they could not find the time. The remaining eight finished the course.

The projects included the following:

1. Hospital—Reduction of nurses aide turnover.
2. Printing shop—Improved selection of applicants.
3. Textile Industry—Reduced weaver turnover.
4. Textile Industry—Measure attitude toward female employment in supervisory and managerial positions.
5. Advertising Agency—Discover feasibility of opening a chain-food stand in an area based upon population attitudes.
6. State Agency—Perform job analysis and recommend changes of selection and promotion within the job occupation (3 students).

The practicum was clearly a success from all vantage points: students, university, and industry. The students applied their previously learned skills by completing attitude measurement, sampling techniques, job analysis, and biographical information blanks. As a side benefit, they also learned how to work with computers, industrial managers, and employees; and they learned a bit of self reliance. Their general comment was that they learned more useful information from this course than any other. Indeed, two students stated they got more from this course than all others in their college career.

All of the industries benefited from the program. The students performed projects which agencies did not have the time or resources to perform. In most cases the research pointed out specific directions of actions for the hiring agencies. Finally, the university benefited through its participation in the community and the fulfillment of its service mission.

There *were* problems in the presentation of the practicum. First, the students had to schedule their industrial sessions during their free time and the free time of the sponsors. This proved difficult and at time impossible. Some solutions evolved. Work was set up for two- or three-week periods with frequent telephone contacts between the industrial sponsor and me. Second, the variation in their projects eliminated any normative-based assessment, which put more responsibility on each member to achieve individually. Third, time was a problem. One semester is a short time to plan, execute and write up a project which requires many meetings. Fourth, although it was never mentioned to me personally, some intangible pressure is felt by a faculty of an undergraduate class under ten, with indefinite class meetings. This arrangement of the practicum violated traditional practice and it is a credit to the administration that no mention was made of our departure from usual procedures. The fifth problem is faculty time. Any faculty

233

member supervising a practicum must be available to visit the sponsor and meet with the students separately. The faculty time spent on this course is more than double the usual time spent with a traditional class of forty. Time may be reduced by assigning two or more students to each project and by limiting the number of sites. However, the faculty commitment is required as well as that of the administration and the participating industries. Presently, the practicum session is equal to one traditional course for the faculty load.

There might be some solutions to these problems. Many of them centered around scheduling. Presently, a new plan for practicums is being discussed which may help. The practicum credit could be doubled to equal six semester hours (over one or two semesters) giving the student and faculty advisor more flexibility in meeting their responsibilities. The remainder of the student's semester could be spent in another practicum or special courses set up for complementing the practicum (as a course dealing with research problems in applied settings or a directed studies course), or the student could enroll in PSI type courses which could be completed at the student's convenience.

Student selection is an additional difficulty. While many students see the value of a practicum course and desire it, it may conflict with their curriculum management. Those deciding to apply to graduate school get involved in preparatory courses or research and many students hesitate to enroll in a course which requires so much self reliance in an unknown atmosphere. In agreement with Pinkus and Korn (1973), I believe that undergraduate vocational guidance is a must. In order to use the practicums to the fullest, students entering occupations upon graduation must know and prepare for their future. Therefore the Industrial Practicum will be of optimum use as a vocational tool when used with a program of vocational guidance.

Leonard Berger

Practicum in Clinical Psychology

There's an old story about a young man who, upon receiving his AB degree in psychology went out looking for work. The personnel manager of a rather large industrial plant decided to employ the new graduate and instructed him to get a broom and begin sweeping up offices. The young graduate was rather dismayed by this order and quickly explained that there must be a mistake because he was a college graduate with a degree in psychology. The personnel manager apologized for his thoughtlessness and said, "In that case, I'll get someone to show you how."

Many students who major in psychology have a genuine interest in people and want to work in a psychology-related profession. More often than not, they desire a position dealing with people in a therapy situation. What can one honestly say to a potential psychology major who asks about the opportunities in the area of clinical psychology? The truth is that psychology departments have been turning out graduates in droves but many of them are forced to accept positions in non-psychological areas. These students are being short-changed because they are not receiving the type of training that is necessary for them to obtain psychology-related positions.

There are many jobs available for students who have obtained some experience in the applied field. Because of the lack of training in applied psychology at the undergraduate level, however, our students are no better prepared for these positions than someone majoring in sociology, anthropology, or even history or English. In other words, there are jobs available in psychology-related areas that could best be filled by students who have majored in psychology, but because of the lack of practical and applied orientation in undergraduate programs, these jobs go unfilled or they are filled by individuals with less adequate training.

There is significant evidence that subprofessionals can be trained to work effectively in clinical settings. Projects Re-ed in Tennessee and North Carolina has been successful in training selected teachers to work with disturbed children with the support of mental health and educational specialists. Hallowitz (1974) has obtained comparable success using subprofessionals and believes that the advantages of using such persons far outweigh the disadvantages. Hobbs (Note 1) pointed out that the most promising approach to the problem of delivering mental health services to a large number of persons is to use mental health specialists to guide the work of other carefully selected persons with limited training.

The teaching of undergraduates has changed very little over the past 10 or 15 years, whereas the application of clinical psychology has changed drastically. Undergraduates cannot learn how to give the Rorschach or do psychoanalysis, but they can learn contingency management techniques. Accumulation of knowledge in the area of applied psychology has advanced to such a point that we can teach students on an undergraduate level how to perform many useful functions.

For the past two years I have been conducting an undergraduate practicum in clinical psychology. Many anticipated problems simply never materialized. For example, transportation to the site of the practicum seemed as though it might create a problem with our shrinking travel budget, but the students were quite willing and able to provide their own transportation. The agencies also accepted legal responsibility for the work done by the students.

Although initially it was somewhat difficult to obtain placements for students it did not prove to be an exceedingly difficult task. It became obvious to many agencies very early in the program that the students possessed skills that would be beneficial to the agency. Now that the practicum has been in progress for a few years it is apparent that the agencies believe that the program is mutually advantageous.

In the early stages of the program most students were placed in the local comprehensive mental health center. The students, all senior psychology majors, were carefully screened in order to aid the program's initial success. As our confidence in the program grew, we began to branch out and found other suitable placements. By having students evaluate the quality of their experiences it was possible to eliminate unsatisfactory placements. For example, although a crisis intervention program would appear to be an excellent placement, it did not prove to be satisfactory. As the program has continued to grow, more and more agencies have asked for students to be placed in their agency. At the present time there is no difficulty in placing all students and many requests must be turned down even though the size of the class has almost doubled.

In order to give the readers an idea of the type of experience that the student receives, let me describe the program from last semester in some detail. Four students were placed in the alcohol and drug abuse center. Their duties included working in the alcohol safety activity program with clients who had been arrested for driving while under the influence of drugs. In addition they participated in group therapy sessions with drug abusers and worked with local industry in alcohol prevention clinics. Three students were placed in the developmental centers for exceptional children. Many of the children suffered from multiple handicaps and it was necessary for the students to acquaint themselves with sign language and Braille. Because the program employed a type of token economy, the students were able to employ their behavior modification skills. Three students were placed at the Mental Health Center. Not only were they exposed to a complete Mental Health facility but they were allowed to work in small group therapy sessions with children. Occasionally an autistic child would become the sole responsibility of a student. This meant that the student would spent the entire afternoon with the child. A textbook could not possibly teach the type of things learned in this situation.

One particularly satisfactory placement was the home for youthful offenders. The children, ages 12-16, had been removed from their homes for various reasons and placed in this continuous care center. The four students placed in the center worked in crafts, recreational activities, and in academic pursuits. A halfway house for delinquent girls was another excellent placement facility. The three students working in this facility taught the girls how to use makeup, dress properly and develop other social skills. In addition they were allowed to attend family court and see first hand the detrimental effects of an unhappy family unit.

If an undergraduate student, who has neither the inclination nor the GPA to do graduate work, decides to work in a community mental health center dealing with disorders of children he/she has little hope to realize that goal. If this student is earning a degree from a traditional program the chance of doing meaningful work in the area is very slight. Basic psychology courses should be followed by a series of content courses in the areas of clinical psychology that would include applied, abnormal, and personality. The student would then be prepared for specialty courses in principles of behavior and behavioral techniques. In these specialty courses the student would learn systematic desensitization, assertive training, contingency management procedures and extinction training. Following the specialty courses, the student is usually prepared to reap the benefits of some practical experience. If the student later decides to go to graduate school, the experience is valuable, at least to determine whether this is the area in which the student is interested. Above all, this type of program should enable the student to compete satisfactorily in the present job market.

Spurgeon Cole

Issues and Recommendations in the Precollege Teaching of Psychology

Another area that should be affected by the trend in undergraduate psychology education is the preparation of secondary-school teachers of psychology. One fundamental question that must be answered initially is whether psychology should be offered on the secondary level. On one side, some professionals are opposed because they feel (a) psychology may satiate its audience in a manner similar to that done by other areas; (b) students should be free of prior biases and expectations (MacLeod, 1971); and (c) many high school instructors are not qualified to teach the area (Stahl & Casteel, 1973). On the other hand, people are becoming more interested in human behavior and it is our responsibility to help nurture this curiosity. Further, we must provide those not attending college with the fundamentals so that they may also reap the benefits of our work. Finally, precollege psychology could better prepare students to enter college psychology programs. This would permit departments to upgrade their introductory course and thus improve their entire program.

Assuming, then, that psychology should be taught on the secondary level, what curricula should be developed for prospective teachers to better prepare them for their future task? According to MacLeod (1971), "teaching is an exercise in communication, and successful communication depends on a multitude of factors which the teacher must identify and control. Many of these are rooted in the psychology of motivation, learning, attitude formation, and the like, and every good teacher is, in a practical sense, a good psychologist" (p. 248). Psychology majors anticipating a career as teachers should take certain basic content courses in a variety of areas and several practica or on-the-site training courses. Specifically, these students should take Social Psychology, Developmental, Motivation, Cognitive, Abnormal, Psychometrics, and a course on learning including the principles and application of behavior modification. Benassi and Lanson (1972) in a national survey discovered that most behavior modification classes provide some practicum experience and that many involve behavior modification techniques in the school setting. This trend must continue and such procedures should be incorporated as part of a basic curriculum. We also recommend that the student study such courses as Group Processes, Personality, Attitude Change, or Applied Psychology.

Flanagan (1973) stated that there must be not only individualization of educational outcomes but there must also be an "effective system of individualized instruction that is applied to the program to achieve the common objectives as well" (p. 553). It is our contention that those students striving to be teachers should be familiar with the Personalized System of Instruction (Keller, 1968). This means that they must acquire the ability to construct precise and meaningful behavioral objectives, they must be able to break a complex and comprehensive subject area into manageable units, and they must be able to guide students through a unit-by-unit mastery of the material. Furthermore, they should understand the practical mechanics for organizing this type of system and of integrating the unit blocks into a complete whole. In general, students should be able to establish a PSI course upon leaving an undergraduate program.

One way in which I have accomplished this goal is to have students partake in a practicum on the teaching of psychology through PSI methods. Each student registers for the course at the invitation of the instructor and is then designated as a proctor and placed in charge of five to eight general psychology students. The proctor interviews each student on each unit, tests them on a series of mastery tests, and assists the student whenever requested to do so. All mastery decisions are made by the proctor under the guidance and rules specified by the instructor. In addition, the proctor must construct sample behavioral objectives for units which are then reviewed and critiqued by the instructor. Each student must rewrite those which violate the principles of sound behavioral objectives. Each participant organizes a sample course in general psychology and constructs unit quizzes and more comprehensive mastery tests. The final indicator of mastery is determined by the performance level achieved by the proctor's students and by the proctor's ability to apply the proper mechanics to any type of basic material.

A high school course in psychology should emphasize not only basic concepts and principles but also the application of psychological knowledge. One course I have taught which provides some structure to the area of application is our course entitled *Applied Psychology*. Here, the student learns the relationship between the physical and social environments and human behavior. Three prominent subjects recently stressed are noise and its effect on performance and satisfaction, overcrowding and methods of overcoming its psychological effect, and the meaning of various types of architectural designs. However, more important than these so-called academic areas is the opportunity afforded students to participate in the simulation of an actual community. Each person assumes a community role unlike his/her usual behavior and is responsible for researching and enacting that role to the fullest. The main activity of the simulation centers around meetings of the town council and a full-blown political convention. Students experientially learn about power, opinion change, movement of masses, communication, gender and racial roles, and the acceptance of people for what they are. Thus, students not only learn much in the cognitive domain but, far more importantly, they finally acquire some understanding and empathy in the affective domain.

As noted by Hoetker and Ahlbrand (1969), teaching is still predominantly "telling" with the student being intellectually passive and dependent on the teacher. Prospective instructors should learn how to increase student involvement in their courses. They should gain expertise in leading discussions, conducting laboratory exercises, designing field experiments, and employing games and simulation techniques to permit high school students to discover principles on their own in a manner similar to that mentioned by Mosher and Sprinthall (1970). My course on Group Processes covers much of this material. Students not only study the theoretical aspects of group behavior but they also

learn the practical skills of dealing with groups. They analyze group reactions under stressful circumstances, the meaning and conveyance of nonverbal communication, leadership and the proper usage of leadership in the classroom and in other situations, and techniques to be utilized in promoting the free and uninhibited exchange of ideas.

In conclusion, the problem of training teachers for the classroom is quite complex because of the different orientations of educators and the political and economic barriers encountered in this field. However, training prospective instructors in the area of psychology has an unexpected dividend. It shows that psychology does have some relevance in an area common to all citizens—that of the education of their youth.

David J. Marx

Experientially Based Learning Through Placements in Community Agencies and Recommended Interdisciplinary Curricula

Field training need not come at the expense of other psychology courses nor obstruct the educational process. An undergraduate curriculum does not have to be drastically changed to accommodate these experiences. With some ingenuity and hard work, field experience can be built into many existing courses. The pendulum need not swing from the traditional "basic" courses to a strictly applied curriculum.

In modifying the traditionally structured program, undergraduate psychology instructors should give serious consideration to two readily available sources of experientially based learning: the interdisciplinary preparation of students and experiential learning in regularly established psychology courses.

If we are serious about preparing our students for immediate employment in social and community agencies, we must combine our efforts with other disciplines. At the present time, available training for psychology undergraduates is often inappropriate or inadequate. Students are either overtrained for the available positions or their training is inconsistent with the needs of the community. By combining forces with other disciplines we may better train paraprofessionals with the skills and field experiences required by social and community agencies. Although we have not yet been able to incorporate these into our own program, the following are some examples which we are considering. Several are similar to the curricular modules established by the Department of Psychology at the University of Washington (Lunneborg & Kanda, Note 2).

1. *Architecture Supplement.* Courses in architectural design, urban planning, and health care facilities could prepare the student for public and community-relations specialties or a role in urban and regional planning.

2. *Environmental Engineering Supplement.* Preparation in environmental systems, environmental health, and environmental planning and control could lead to employment in a variety of state agencies (e.g., manpower training, pollution and waste control) or corporate management positions.

3. *Art and/or Music Supplement.* Students interested in these disciplines could prepare for a career using music and/or art as rehabilitation, treatment, or recreation in schools for the handicapped, socially deprived, or mentally retarded child, or in a variety of public or private institutions concerned with "occupational therapy."

4. *Horticulture Supplement.* As surprising as it may seem initially, a new therapeutic area is emerging referred to as "hortitherapy." Students at Clemson can now enroll in a horticultural therapy course which presents aesthetic and physical activities designed to be of value to patients in any type of therapeutic situation. Job opportunities are very similar to those in the art and music areas.

5. *Communications Supplement.* Public speaking, persuasion and public opinion, advertising, and mass media are all supplementary courses for the student seeking a career in public relations, marketing research, advertising research, or other communications related media.

6. *Recreation and Park Administration Supplement.* Numerous courses in recreation leadership, planning, and analysis together with recreation for the ill and handicapped, recreation therapy, etc. could prepare the undergraduate student for work as a recreation manager, planner, or therapist in a variety of commercial, hospital, civic, or other institutional settings.

7. *Industrial Management Supplement.* Courses in personnel management, marketing management, marketing communication, management of human resources, and consumer behavior could qualify the student for managerial positions in business and industry. In addition, positions related to personnel matters, public relations, and consumerism would also be available.

Obviously, these examples are not meant to be exhaustive. However, they illustrate how cooperative paraprofessional training for the psychology undergraduate is possible in areas other than the biological, health and social sciences. These curricular modules can also be implemented without drastically changing one's present curriculum and without incurring large expenditures for new applied programs and staff. Overcoming these two obstacles greatly increases the viability of an undergraduate paraprofessional program. Sharing the responsibility for training paraprofessionals with other departments would produce other benefits for both student and faculty participants. Presumably the cooperative efforts could be extended to include joint supervision and evaluation of field experiences as well as collaboration in interdepartmental seminars and colloquia. Most importantly, the student would be provided with the opportunity for developing a professional work role gaining applied experience as an essential part of his training. The result—an employable undergraduate psychology major with a baccalaureate degree in hand.

Whether or not one is able to implement an interdisciplinary program for the training of paraprofessionals, practically all undergraduate psychology instructors should be able to incorporate experientially based learning into their courses. At present, this vital learning experience is usually denied students with average academic ability. Yet, these students comprise the majority of those seeking employment immediately after graduation.

During the past several years, I have had the opportunity to observe and supervise such students in a number of field settings as part of my courses in Social and Developmental psychology. The personal growth and involvement of many of these students as they interacted with persons of all ages attests to the validity of these field experiences. For example, from one developmental psychology course, few students will forget the dynamic exchanges which resulted from weekly discussions with elderly residents of a nursing home. Others became absorbed in the developmental capabilities of children in a school for the emotionally disturbed and mentally handicapped. In each of these instances, and in others as well, students not only satisfied their individual needs but they also discovered significant work roles. As a result of these experiences, several students revised their undergraduate programs and later sought employment opportunities consonant with their new interests.

Many similar examples can be drawn from the community mental health field. Psychology as a discipline has a great deal to offer the general public in this area. Moreover, not all of our skills and technology need to be dispensed by doctoral level professionals. In 1971, Lanyon identified eight major areas within mental health which were clearly technological in nature. Represented among these areas were automation of psychological assessment and psychiatric diagnoses, machine-aided counseling and therapy, and the various behavior modification procedures. We can now add to this listing the relatively new and critical area of program and treatment evaluation. Most mental health facilities are adding an evaluation and research component to their programs. This appears to be an excellent employment opportunity for the appropriately trained college graduate. This past year one of our senior undergraduate students served as a follow-up worker for a local community mental health center. Working with a professional staff person, this student interviewed former clients of the center to help assess the effectiveness of the center's program. During this next year our department hopes to expand upon this experience and involve several additional students in the evaluation component of two nearby mental health facilities. We expect to find, as others have found (Smith & Spatz, 1974), that such experientially based learning in community agencies will be challenging and rewarding and will result in the student's greater sense of competence and worth.

Through interdepartmental cooperation and commitment and well-supervised practicum experiences, the undergraduate can be trained for meaningful professional work roles. However, let us be alert so as not to permit our own limited, preconceived graduate education models from diminishing the individuality of each student and thereby reducing his or her sense of competence and self-worth.

David J. Senn

References

Benassi, V., & Lanson, R. A survey of the teaching of behavior modification in colleges and universities. *American Psychologist*, 1972, *27*, 1063-1069.

Boneau, C. A. The educational base: Supply for the demand. *American Psychologist*, 1968, *23*, 308-311.

Cates, J. Baccalaureates in psychology: 1969 and 1970. *American Psychologist*, 1973, *28*, 262-264.

Fields, C. M. Five to ten per cent of students major in psychology, but after graduation, what do they do? *Chronicle of Higher Education*, May 20, 1974, *18*, 9.

Flanagan, J. C. Education: How and for what. *American Psychologist*. 1973, *28*, 551-556.

Hallowitz,E. Issues and strategies in the use of nonprofessionals. In B. Kleinmutz (Ed.). *Readings in the essentials of abnormal Psychology*. New York: Harper and Row, 1974.

Hoetker, J., & Ahlbrand, W. P., Jr. The persistence of the recitation. *American Educational Research Journal*, 1969, *6*, 145-167.

Keller, F. S. "Good-bye Teacher..." *Journal of Applied Behavior Analysis*, 1968, *1*, 79-89.

Korman, M. National conference on levels and patterns of professional training in psychology. *American Psychologist*, 1974, *29*, 441-449.

Lanyon, R. I. Mental health technology. *American Psychologist*, 1971, *26*, 1071-1076.

MacLeod, R. B. The teaching of psychology. *American Psychologist*, 1971, *26*, 245-249.

Mosher, R. L., & Sprinthall, N. A. Psychological education in secondary schools: A program to promote individual and human development. *American Psychologist*, 1970, *25*, 911-924.

Pinkus, R. B., & Korn, J. H. The preprofessional option: An alternative to graduate work in Psychology. *American Psychologist*, 1973, *28*, 710-718.

Smith, R. G., & Spatz, B. A review of mental health practica for undergraduates. *Teaching Psychology Newsletter*, 1974 (April, 7-8.

Stahl, R. J., & Casteel, J. D. *The status of precollege psychology in the State of Florida during 1970-71 and 1972-73: A comparative report*. Gainesville, FL: P. K. Yonge Laboratory School: Research Monograph No. 8, 1973.

Notes

1. Hobbs, N. Mental health's third revolution. Regional Conference on Inservice Training in State Mental Health Programs. Detroit, MI, October 1963.

2. Lunneborg, P. W., & Kanda, C. N. Interdepartmental programs to produce bachelor's psychologists. Paper presented at the American Psychological Association meetings, Miami Beach, September 1970.

A Full-Time Clinical Practicum for Undergraduates

David D. Shiverick
State University College at Potsdam

Close faculty supervision, continued student academic responsibilities, and excellent staff cooperation supports a successful program.

The intent of this article is to describe a full-time clinical practicum for undergraduates. At present there are many and varied part-time practicums, but these programs cannot meet the needs of students in offering the depth of experience necessary to decide realistically and prepare for a mental health career. Another purpose of this article is to stimulate the growth of other full-time practicums. Consequently, special attention has been given to a discussion of the planning and operation of such a practicum to assist other instructors in establishing similar programs.

The writer's experience with a full-time practicum for over two years indicates that there are three decided advantages to this type of program in contrast to a part-time practicum. The first, and perhaps most important benefit, is the opportunity provided for complete immersion in and realistic appraisal of the workaday world of an institutional setting. A full-time practicum necessitates the students' involving themselves in the daily frustrations, rewards, uncertainties, administrative difficulties, etc. which are not often mentioned in texts and which are only vaguely appreciated by other students who work at the same institution for only a few hours each week.

The second asset of the program derives from the first.

Students who can realistically evaluate the requirements of professional behavior in a mental health setting are better able to make decisions about future careers and plans for graduate school. Some of our undergraduates at the conclusion of their fifteen week experience have indicated that clinical psychology was not what they had thought and have consequently redirected their vocational goals. The student benefits from this appraisal in not wasting additional time in graduate school or in a mental health setting. Of equal importance, graduate schools and mental health settings are spared the task of eliminating individuals who have misevaluated academic and vocational goals.

The third positive feature of such intensive training is that the student may acquire therapeutic skills which seem to be helpful to patients and to be of benefit to ward staffs. One psychologist at the hospital indicated, "I enjoy working with full-time students because after I have trained them they are no longer students but employees who help me on the unit." In fact, the full-time students on one unit at the hospital, in addition to their regular duties, actually orient and help part-time students from another academic institution prepare treatment plans and implement therapeutic procedures. At first the supervisors of the practicum were apprehensive about the limitations of students in providing therapy for patients. However, these fears were unfounded in most cases. Students who learned to adjust to the hospital quickly and were willing to attempt counselling and behavior therapy have more often than not been rewarded for their efforts. (The literature on undergraduates or paraprofessionals who are used as therapists supports this contention, e.g., Durlak, 1973 and Persons, et al, 1973.)

There are, of course, other benefits (e.g., personal growth) provided by the practicum, but these three features, i.e., intensive involvement, realistic vocational planning, and skills acquisition, are stressed because a full-time experience in a mental health setting seems especially appropriate in providing these benefits.

Planning and Management. The effectiveness of the full-time practicum seems, in retrospect, to be due in part to certain planning and managerial procedures. One of the key ingredients was the cooperation of high level administrators both at the College and the St. Lawrence Psychiatric Center in Ogdensburg. The College President and the Deputy Director of the Center were instrumental in conceiving the possibility of the practicum. Eventually, the Department of Psychology at the College became involved through the efforts of two staff members, Harry Kristiansen and myself, who became joint supervisors. In short, the origins of the program were administrative. Eventually, the responsibility has shifted and now it is managed by the people who actually supervise the program. This procedure for starting a practicum has meant that there has been "official" recognition for its presence at the hospital. This type of recognition has obvious advantages: Contacts with the supervisors and team leaders of various units have been facilitated, possible antagonism to the program both at the college and hospital has been minimal (the program has not encountered the type of "de facto" resistance of ward staff and professionals expressed by Rappaport, et al, 1971), and gradual expansion of the program has been ongoing (with the hospital central administration's supervising its growth to insure that the goals of the practicum coincide with the needs of the hospital).

There are, however, certain limitations which arise as a result of starting a practicum in the offices of a central administration. An unavoidable obstacle was that during the early planning meetings only unit supervisors were present to discuss what students would be able to do on their units. Subsequently, when confronted with the realities of a ward, we occasionally found that there was a discrepancy between the description of a unit given by its supervisor and the actual ward life. On some units where we had anticipated that a psychologist or social worker would work with our students, that particular individual was too busy or simply could not provide a meaningful program for students. The best response to these shortcomings is the continuous evaluation of student participation on a given ward. Feedback from both students and staff who work closely with students, as well as actual observation of students on the wards has been helpful.

In several instances students from other practicums have been observed where academic supervisors make an appearance at the start of a program and again at its termination, leaving full responsibility for a student's training to the ward staff. In several instances this procedure led to a great deal of floundering and lack of purpose on the part of students. Certainly students could still learn in this type of setting, but their negative attitudes and the potential for even greater learning with better supervision suggests that closer attention must be given.

Faculty who depend entirely on what ward staff or students indicate is occurring could also encounter difficulty in administering and evaluating their program. Often a member of a ward staff is not fully aware of the goals of a program and may feel that the mere presence of a student's enthusiastic personality is indicative of progress. Some students have graduated from our program smiling more often than they did at the start, but having acquired very few other skills. Direct observation of students working with patients, when possible, is the primary answer to this problem, but a clear set of behavioral objectives for training students, given to the ward staff at the outset, seems to be of equal importance.

Student Activities. The students spend an entire semester (15 to 16 weeks) at the psychiatric facility working an eight hour day, five days a week. They also spend two hours each day commuting to and from "work" at the Psychiatric Center (located 30 miles from the College). In return, the College gives 15 hours of academic credit. Also a certificate, signed by both the President of the College and the Director of the Hospital, indicating a student's participation in the program and the nature of the practicum, is given to a student at the conclusion of his training. The certificate seems especially helpful in providing prospective employers with important information to consider in hiring practicum students.

The first two days of the practicum are spent orienting students to the hospital by hospital personnel who discuss behavior modification, milieu therapy, chemotherapy, and organization of the hospital. Then two days are provided in which the students tour for one to three hours each one of the units where they might train for the semester. This introductory week also seems helpful in reducing students' anxieties, acquainting them with the Center's physical layout, and giving both students and ward staffs an opportunity to estimate who will work best with whom.

There are at present many different facilities available for student training at the Center. What follows is a brief description of each, with the intent of indicating the scope of opportunities students have in the program.

Students who work in Flower Building serve on several different wards of that unit. The staff has supervised students on an acute admissions ward, a Fairweather program, a token economy ward, and a model geriatric ward. The treatment orientation on most of these units has been primarily behavior therapy in both one-to-one counselling and in group therapy sessions. Students are required to learn how to define problems behaviorally, record baselines, implement treatment programs using the whole spectrum of behavior modification techniques, and evaluate their progress with patients.

Ward 17 of Center Building is distinguished from Flower Building because of the greater stress placed on the medical treatment of patients in the former ward. Thus, although there is opportunity for students to participate in group therapy, psychodrama, and counselling in this setting, students cannot assume as active a role as is permitted in Flower Building. Despite the chemotherapeutic orientation of this unit, students still learn a great deal about how a group of very concerned and caring staff can operate to effect changes in behavior.

Ward 7 in Central Building is a combined forensic psychiatric unit and ward for the more aggressive patients at the Center. This unit has given students further training in behavior modification skills and a great deal of experience in milieu therapy.

Some of the other programs which are available to students include the Alcoholic Rehabilitation Unit, several model geriatric wards in units other than Flower Building, the Vocational Rehabilitation Department, and the Social Services Department. The activities of students in these programs has been varied, ranging from the evaluation of ongoing vocational rehabilitation programs to participation in meetings of Alcoholics Anonymous, visiting families and nursing homes in the community, and finally to simply socializing with the elderly on geriatric units.

It would be difficult to generalize and say with certainty what a student can expect from training in any part of the Center. The programs in Wards 7 and 17 of Center Building and Flower Building are now quite familiar settings because of their frequent use by students in the practicum, and we feel reasonably certain about what a student will encounter. However, even on those units and particularly in other settings where our experience is limited, it is often the student's initiative and tact which will determine how much responsibility is given.

In all of the programs at the Center we limit the number of students working on a unit. Usually only one or two students are permitted on each ward to allow for greater contact with hospital personnel and to preclude the students' hindering the staff's activities. Because of these limits we have admitted a maximum of only eight students to the program each semester. Also, we attempt to provide for diversity in experience by requiring that a student rotate to different settings at least twice during the semester. Students have complained about this practice seemingly because they have become familiar with a ward and are reluctant to make yet another adjustment to new surroundings. These enforced changes are helpful, however, as they seem to make students aware of the heterogeneous nature of the institution and the variety of problems to which it must respond.

One final dimension of the program must be described, as it defines the student's training in academic as well as practical terms. Students are required to read several books and journal articles on behavior modification, client cen-

tered therapy, sensitivity training, and perspectives on abnormal behavior during the course of the semester. In addition they must keep daily logs of their activities at the Center. At a weekly three hour seminar their logs and readings are discussed and criticized to combine theory with practice. These sessions are at times resented by students because they are tired of academic approaches and want only to work with their patients. It is difficult to make some students recognize the need for combining these two approaches, but for those who see the necessity, training on the wards seems to proceed with greater ease; they seem more capable of responding with a variety of approaches to problems rather than being bound by the singular approach taught on a particular unit.

In retrospect, it seems that an academic institution, working with a psychiatric center, can provide a meaningful academic *and* pre-vocational experience for students. In fact, if either the practical or academic features of the practicum were eliminated, students could become too immersed in the concreteness of a daily work world or the theoretical abstractions of an academic orientation. The combination of the two institutions is ideal and should be considered by college faculty for inclusion in their curriculum.

As a member of a college faculty, I would add, on a personal note, that it is a very pleasant opportunity to work both at the college and the psychiatric center. The change of pace from one setting to another adds perspective to my teaching psychology in classes and gives me an entirely different professional community to experience and communicate with.

References

Durlak, J. A. Myths concerning the nonprofessional therapist. *Professional Psychology,* 1973, *4,* 300-304.

Persons, R. W., Clark, C., Persons, M., Kadish, M., & Patterson, W. Training and employing undergraduates as therapists in a college counselling service. *Professional Psychology,* 1973, *4,* 170-178.

Rappaport, J., Chinsky, J. M., & Cowen, E. L. *Innovations in helping chronic patients.* New York: Academic Press, 1971.

Notes

1. I wish to express appreciation to the following persons who have contributed in many ways to the program described: President Thomas Barrington, of the College, Dr. Ian Kerr, Deputy Director of the Center, and various Center staff members, especially Mrs. Georgia Voce, Mrs. Ruth Roach, and Mr. Ted Rahn.

Training Undergraduates as Subprofessional Community Mental Health Workers

K. Shemberg and S. Keeley
Bowling Green State University

An intensive 40-week training program combines the academic and the applied in preparation for graduate work or immediate employment.

Over the years, undergraduate students have asked questions like: "What can I do with my psychology training? Do I have to go to graduate school to be allowed to apply what I've learned? Why has my training been so devoid of the interesting, practical applications of psychology?"

Perhaps in response to these questions and in conjunction with increasing manpower needs in the mental health fields, a variety of subprofessional programs have emerged. Some of these focus primarily on giving students an interesting and meaningful educational experience and provide little in the way of formal, academic/clinical training. Hospital "companion" programs typify this approach (e.g., Umbarger, Dalsimer, Morrison, & Breggin, 1962). Others have focused on providing such experiences while utilizing college students as preventative therapeutic agents for a designated clinical population (e.g., Cowen, Zax, & Laird, 1966). Although these programs provide varying degrees of training, they usually do not represent a major academic investment by the student. A third model focuses primarily upon developing a large training program with major departmental investments in funding and staff time. The goals of this approach are primarily to train a cadre of marketable subprofessional mental health workers, such as associate-degree mental health programs (e.g., Baker, 1972).

Over the past five years, the present authors have been developing a subprofessional training program which we view along many of the above dimensions. We want our undergraduates to become involved in and excited about clinical activities. We want them to be well-trained mental health technicians who can provide a service as they progress through the final stages of this experience. We want our students to obtain marketable skills in an expanding field (e.g., Korman, Note 1). We are not training students as companions. Rather, we have elected to train them in broad-based skills for providing threefold services within community agencies: (a) assessment for intervention programs with children (this includes interview and natural environment observation skills); (b) direct intervention in the natural environment, such as carrying out a behavior management program in a classroom; (c) training mediators (e.g., teachers, parents) in child-management competencies (cf. Tharp & Wetzel, 1969). Training in interpersonal skills (e.g., Carkhuff, 1969) is seen as an important prerequisite for providing the above services, but the emphasis of the program is on behavioral assessment and intervention.

The present paper outlines the teaching approach we have evolved to attain the above goals. In general, we have kept our program relatively small in terms of numbers of students trained per year. This allows us to provide a highly intensive personalized experience and one which has been highly satisfying to our trainees.

The current program is divided into three major phases: (a) a 10-week introductory stage, (b) a 10-week block placement, and (c) a 20-week practicum placement. Each phase includes specific didactic and practical experiences designed to prepare the student for the succeeding phase. The following outline represents the essential features of each phase and indicates the specific goals associated with that step in the sequence.

Phase I. This phase is a general introduction to clinical psychology. Approximately 40 students are selected for this course. Selection criteria are: sophomore or junior status, an accumulative grade point of 2.7 or higher, and enrollment as a psychology major.

The goals of this course are twofold: (a) to provide a broad basic background to the general field of professional clinical psychology with special emphasis on clinical intervention strategies, and (b) to provide some basis for selecting 12 of the students who will continue throughout the remainder of the program.

A general textbook in clinical psychology is assigned (e.g., Sundberg, Tyler, & Taplin, 1973) and as the quarter progresses, additional readings are provided. This 10 weeks includes didactic presentations on topics such as: assessment; intervention at the individual, family, and community level; ethics; etc. The course is also heavily weighted with presentations of actual case materials (at least one per week). Video and audio tapes of the authors or graduate students engaging in assessment or treatment are presented and discussed. Presentations by social workers from community agencies and by psychologists working in settings like half-way homes for delinquents are included.

All students take a one-day field trip to the local school for the mentally retarded. In addition to this experience, each student spends one full day per week for five weeks as an observer in the department's Psychological Services Center. Here they see a broad range of "real life" clinical activities including assessment, treatment planning, treatment, and community consultation.

241

The class meets twice a week for two-hour sessions. Two essay examinations form the basis for evaluating academic progress, and students earn four hours of academic credit.

In the final weeks of the course, each student expressing an interest in continuing in the program completes a personal questionnaire covering social and academic history, interests and activities, and backgrounds in and motivation for mental health work. This questionnaire forms the basis for a personal interview with one or both of the authors. Course grade, classroom participation, motivation and personal qualities as judged from the interview and classroom behavior are the data upon which the selection of 12 trainees is based. It is interesting to note that we have never lost a trainee once selection has been made.

Phase II. This is the "meat" of the training program. This phase entails two training modules—the academic module and the clinical team placement module. To ensure that students receive maximum benefit from this phase, we require that they enroll for 12 hours of academic credit with the authors. Thus, the 10-week concentration represents virtually their entire academic responsibility. The emphasis throughout is upon acquiring specific technical skills which the trainees will later be required to apply.

The curriculum for the academic module in Phase II is designed to achieve nine basic goals. These goals and the methods for attaining them are described below:

Goal I: Mastering the basic principles of operant conditioning and social learning. This goal is implemented via a 3-week, 6 hour per week block. A programmed learning text (Miller, 1975) provides the primary teaching materials. Social learning materials are also utilized (e.g., Bandura, 1969). Students receive frequent written progress checks over the programmed text. Class time is primarily devoted to discussing the programmed text and progress checks.

Goal II: Comprehending the contingency management model and social learning model as they apply to behavioral modification in the natural environment. One 2-hour session is devoted to a discussion of our general approach emphasizing behavioral intervention with parents and teachers of disturbed children. The major reading for this section is Tharp and Wetzel (1969), Chapter 3.

Goal III: Acquiring interview and observational skills for behavioral assessment. That is, they should be capable of assessing: (1) the behavioral repertoire of the target, (2) the stimulus situations under which focal behaviors occur, (3) reinforcers maintaining focal behaviors, (4) reinforcement hierarchies of target children, and (5) the potential for utilizing specific mediators in the natural environment.

This unit is comprised of three 2-hour classroom sessions, multiple practicum observations in classrooms of normal and retarded children, and three practice interviews with volunteer subjects. Classroom activities focus on: (a) practice exercises in pinpointing behaviors and in behavioral coding and recording strategies, and (b) observing and discussing interviews with teachers and parents conducted by the instructors. Readings for this unit are Tharp and Wetzel (1969), Chapter 5; Peterson (1968), Chapter 5; sample case studies from previous clinical cases; and handouts on various observational categories.

Goal IV: Acquiring the skills for developing intervention strategies for a wide variety of problem behaviors across diverse settings. Four 2-hour class periods are devoted to the following: (a) presentations of intervention programs previously carried out by the instructors, and (b) discussion of sample intervention programs written by the students for hypothetical problem behaviors. A minimum of three programs for home problems and three for school problems are written and discussed. During this section, students read widely from journals and books of readings which present various intervention programs. In addition, Tharp and Wetzel (1969), Chapter 6, Becker, Engelman, and Thomas (1971), Chapters 9-17, and Homme and Tosti (1971), Unit 3, are read.

Goal V: Learning to carry out direct intervention, contingency management programs in situations where mediators cannot carry out the intervention. One 2-hour class period is utilized in which various approaches to direct intervention are exemplified. Readings are sample articles from behavioral journals and books.

Goal VI: Acquiring the skills to assist professionals in the process of training mediators to carry out behavioral intervention. Three 2-hour sessions are devoted to role playing the situations that arise as subprofessionals make entry into homes or schools of referred children. Also, various approaches professionals use to train mediators are discussed, modeled, and role played. Students familiarize themselves with readings utilized in such training (e.g., Rettig, 1973; Becker, 1971; Patterson & Gullion, 1968; Buckley & Walker, 1970).

Goal VII: Acquiring an awareness of the practical and interpersonal difficulties associated with intervention in the natural environment and strategies for dealing with such problems. One 2-hour session is devoted to discussion of these issues and one is devoted to role playing. The primary resources for this section are the authors' experiences in engaging in behavioral intervention.

Goal VIII: Acquiring an awareness of professional and ethical problems associated with behavioral intervention and with the role of the subprofessional. One 2-hour period is devoted to a specific discussion of these issues. However, ethical and professional problems are continually referred to and examplified throughout training. Students read the A.P.A. Ethical Standards for Psychologists (1968).

Goal IX: Acquiring skills to write reports on assessment and intervention activities. This skill is taught throughout the 10 weeks. Students are required to write reports on all observational and intervention practicum experiences. This requirement insures that all students write at least one report per week. Each student receives ½ hour individual supervision per week to discuss reports written.

Clearly, the most exciting element in Phase II is the one day a week, 10-week placement on a clinical team in the departmental services center. Clinical teams consist of two Ph.D. clinical psychologists and four to six graduate students at various levels of training. Typically there are five such teams, and at least two undergraduates are assigned to each. In contrast to the students' Phase I experience in the center, they now become integrated team members. That is, they often receive clinical assignments from the supervisors which provide the trainees with actual experience in activities such as school and home observation or intervention.

The students become highly identified with their teams and take the responsibilities attending the placement very seriously.

It should be underlined that despite the fact that a substantial amount of reading is required, the emphasis throughout is upon learning via direct observation, role playing, and/or practicum experience. Formal lecturing is minimized, and every effort is made to turn didactic sessions into group discussions focusing on readings as they apply to "real life" clinical problems.

No formal graded examinations are given during Phase II, and the majority of our students register for the hours on a pass/fail basis. Frequent written progress checks are made to ensure the effectiveness of training.

Phase III. This final phase of the sequence is by far the most exciting and rewarding part of the program. After 20 weeks of intensive training and practicum experience, students are now ready to "try it in the real world." Phase III is a two-quarter (20-week) placement in a mental health setting where our undergraduates continue their learning experience while actually providing clinical services under professional supervision.

Students register for six to eight academic hours per quarter on a pass/fail basis. They spend an average of 15-20 hours per week in their "internship" placement, meeting regularly with the professional staff in that agency as well as with the authors. We have successfully placed students in five community agencies: a large urban family services agency, a county school psychology department, a county school for the mentally retarded, a medical college day school for emotionally disturbed children, and our departmental community-based psychological services center.

The particular training experiences received during this 20 weeks varies with the agency. In general, our students gain significant experience in behavioral assessment; in developing, carrying out, and evaluating a wide range of behavioral intervention techniques; in interviewing teachers and parents of disturbed children, and in training these persons in the application of behavioral operations in the home and school.

The authors believe that this program provides students with a university experience that is meaningful in terms of personal, educational and intellectual growth. We are encouraged in this belief by many things. For example, a large number of the students go on to graduate work in the mental health disciplines. Others take jobs as mental health technicians. Still others return to work for us in subsequent programs even for no financial remuneration. Students consistently report that they enjoy the "hands on" approach

where the academic is integrated with "real world experience." Also, frequent requests for additional practical and academic work demanding much more time than is necessary to fulfill academic hourly requirements indicates how involved students become as they progress through the sequence.

These "outcomes" continually encourage us to refine the program, to expand it relative to the kinds of clinical experiences students receive, and to engage in more and more formal data collection aimed at empirically evaluating the various aspects of the sequence.

References

American Psychological Association. Ethical standards of psychologists. *American Psychologist,* 1968, *23,* 357-361.

Baker, E. J. The mental health associate: A new approach in mental health. *Community Mental Health Journal,* 1972, *8,* 281-291.

Bandura, A. *Principles of behavior modification.* New York: Holt, Rinehart, & Winston, 1969.

Becker, W. C. *Parents are teachers.* Champaign, Ill.: Research Press, 1971.

Becker, W. C., Engelman, S., & Thomas, D. R. *Teaching: A course in applied psychology.* Chicago: Science Research Associates, 1971.

Buckley, N. K., & Walker, H. M. *Modifying classroom behavior.* Champaign, Ill.: Research Press, 1970.

Carkhuff, R. *Helping and human relations* (Vol. I). New York: Holt, Rinehart, & Winston, 1969.

Cowen, E. L., Zax, M., & Laird, J. D. A college student volunteer program in the elementary school setting. *Community Mental Health Journal,* 1966, *2,* 319-328.

Homme, L., & Tosti, D. *Behavior technology: Motivation and contingency management.* San Rafael, California: Individual Learning Systems, 1971.

Miller, L. K. *Principles of everyday behavior analysis.* Monterey, California: Brooks/Cole, 1975.

Patterson, G. R., & Gullion, M. E. *Living with children.* Champaign, Ill.: Research Press, 1968.

Peterson, D. R. *The clinical study of social behavior.* New York: Appleton-Century-Crofts, 1968.

Rettig, E. B. *ABCs for parents.* San Marino, California: Associates for Behavior Change, 1973.

Sundberg, N. D., Tyler, L. E., & Taplin, J. R. *Clinical psychology: Expanding horizons* (2nd ed.). New York: Appleton-Century-Crofts, 1973.

Tharp, R. G., & Wetzel, R. J. *Behavior modification in the natural environment.* New York: Academic Press, 1969.

Umbarger, C. C., Dalsimer, J. S., Morrison, A. P., & Breggin, P. R. *College students in a mental hospital.* New York: Grune & Stratton, 1962.

Notes

1. Korman, M. *National conference on levels and patterns of training in professional psychology.* Unpublished manuscript, September, 1973.

3.   DESCRIBING GRADUATE PLACEMENTS

Placements for graduate students constitute the theme for this collection of articles. Two of the programs used experiential activities in class to teach skills that students could gain for placements. The remaining articles focused on using psychological and psychiatric settings to train medical students and psychology graduate students.

Stewart Ehly, Dick Dustin, and Barry Bratton used role plays in a graduate-level consultation theory and practice course at the University of Iowa. Although their course did not include actual field work, it provided students with feedback to develop client consulting and counseling skills. Simulated consultations can bring an element of "real world experience" into the classroom.

Kathleen Ritter described a 10 week classroom experience for students in a master's program in counseling. The author paired students in the class at California State College, Bakersfield with classmates and directed them to share actual life concerns with their partner who practiced counseling techniques. Results of pre- and post-testing revealed that students with relatively little academic experience benefited as much as students having previous academic experience. The author suggested that those findings demonstrated that highly cognitive training programs do not necessarily produce

skilled helpers. The lesson we learn from this study is that it may not be too late in any student's program to begin systematic skills training.

John Keller and Chris Piotrowski's report on a psychiatric placement for clinical graduate students in psychology left little doubt that the "psychiatrist and the psychologist can be friends". During the last 10 years, these authors placed more than 100 University of West Florida graduate students with psychiatrists in a large city hospital. Students made rounds and attended psychiatric lectures. Over one-third of the 100 students indicated that it was the best graduate course they had ever taken. The results of this article indicated that psychiatrists can make a unique contribution to the training of psychology graduate students.

David Glenwick's article described how medical students in a 6 year BS/MD program at Kent State University and Northeastern Ohio University's College of Medicine participated in a community psychology placement experience at a children's community mental health center. Skills consisted of interviewing, assessment, and counseling. The placement described in this article may serve as a model for developing a broader, psychologically-based perspective for other medical specialties.

Evaluation of a Consultation Training Program Component

Stewart W. Ehly
Dick Dustin
Barry Bratton
University of Iowa

Simulated consultations, used to evaluate a training program for students from three disciplines, yielded promising results.

Attention has recently been given to problems associated with documenting outcomes for consultation training. Conoley (1981) identified a skill continuum during consultation training that includes competencies in theory, interpersonal processes, problem-solving, and evaluation. Conoley points out that attainment of competencies can be documented through written assessment of student knowledge, observation of students in field and laboratory settings, and discussions at the individual or small group level of topics associated with consultation. Sufficient evidence exists to suggest that although many variables may affect the process of consultation, the specific skills

necessary at the entry level to consultation have not been identified (Babigian & Pederson, 1972; Cohen, 1976).

We were responsible for developing a new multidisciplinary course in consultation. Three academic disciplines were represented by the three of us—school psychology, counselor education, and instructional design and technology. We brought to the course a range of theoretical and practical knowledge related to consultation interventions. In planning for the multidisciplinary course, the instructors agreed that alerting students to a variety of perspectives on consultation would be a valuable part of the training. One difficulty that was immediately realized was associated with evaluating students' acquisition of skills considered important for successful consultative practice. A decision was made to experiment with an evaluation of student change that included videotaping each student in a consultative exchange. Videotaping would be conducted at the beginning and at the end of the academic semester. The videotapes would be analyzed to assess specific changes in the behaviors of the students. These specific consultative behaviors we taped will be described below.

Less difficult was the decision to select content for the course. The instructors, housed within a College of Education for a midwestern university, approached the task of selecting consultation theory by reviewing existing literature relevant to the settings represented by the instructors' professional identities. Given the newness of the course, the instructors decided to experiment with a variety of group activities during class sessions to deliver training in consultation practice. As a result of the instructors' agreement, students were exposed to small and large group presentations of facts on consultation practice, participated in discussions of these practices as they affected consultation in a number of work settings, participated in role playing activities which allowed for immediate feedback on specific aspects of the students' behaviors, and were involved in large-scale enactments of consultation interventions as derived from the literature.

The current report represents part of the instructors' documentation of the role playing activities incorporated into the evaluation component of the course. The intent of this documentation is to alert trainers in consultation programs to the potential value of videotape assessments of training effects.

Method. Participants were members of a graduate-level consultation theory and practice course. Twenty-three students completed the course and provided two videotaped examples of their consulting behaviors during a simulation exercise conducted at the beginning and end of the semester. Three students were counseling majors, 5 were school psychology majors, and 15 were instructional design and technology majors. None of the students had received previous training in consultation. School psychology students completed the course as part of their requirements.

Students were given 12 hours of lecture and videotaped examples of each of the following consultation models: mental health (Caplan, 1970); behavioral (Bergan, 1977); and process (Schein, 1969). Role play opportunities were provided for each model, allowing students the opportunity to perform both the consultant and consultee roles. Additional sessions were devoted to developing student skills in initiating communication and problem-solving techniques. Discussions of ethical and legal issues were woven into training activities. The entire program was conducted over a 15-week period. Two take-home exams involved students in integrating their ideas on theory and practice covered in lectures and readings.

During the first and again in the final weeks of the semester, videotaped segments of student consulting behaviors were collected. Each student portrayed a consultant in a ten-minute simulation with another member of the class, then served as a consultee while their partner acted as consultant. Following the session at the end of the semester, students were asked to identify their preference for either mental health, behavioral, or process consultation. Within each dyad, the students were randomly assigned to the order in which they portrayed a consultant.

Details on Simulations. Two written scenarios were developed specifically for the videotaping. Each scenario provided a description of a problem situation and directives for the consultant and consultee. Students were assigned on a randomized basis to a scenario, serving as a consultant while a partner acted within the consultee role. Students had an equal chance of performing either scenario on the pretest as well as on the posttest.

Scenario 1—Consultant: "You will be meeting with a teacher at Mount Union High School who teaches Economics to seniors. The teacher has asked to meet with you about a problem with students."

Scenario 1—Consultee: "This is your third year teaching Economics to seniors at Mount Union High School. You majored in Economics/Education in college, and you've always enjoyed teaching except for a problem which seems to crop up every year. Students inevitably fail to turn in assignments on time. This year the situation is worse than ever. You've scolded, threatened, pleaded, but nothing is working. You are wondering if the problem lies with your teaching style, the students, the subject matter, or what. You would like some help to solve this perpetual problem."

Scenario 2—Consultant: "You will be meeting with a math teacher from Allegheny Community College who wants to talk with you about a problem."

Scenario 2—Consultee: "You are just finishing your first year as a math teacher at Allegheny Community College. You are troubled by the fact that practically no one in the school (students and fellow teachers) seems to like you. At faculty meetings, your ideas are either not taken seriously or are quickly rejected out of hand. Students don't voluntarily come to see you during office hours or linger after class to chat. All of this is quite different from you last teaching job at a community college in another state. There you were popular with students and faculty alike. You are seeking some advice about this problem."

Two hypotheses were investigated in this evaluation: (a) There would be significant differences in consultant interviewing behaviors in the two videotaped simulations; (b) There would be significant differences in the focus of consultant behaviors in the two videotaped simulations. Interviewing and focus behaviors were targeted by instructors as being critical facets of consultative exchanges at the entry level of a relationship. A review of the consultation literature supported the relevance and importance of the interviewing and focus behaviors to initiating problem-solving relationships (e.g., Conoley, 1981).

Data Analysis Procedures. All student interview behaviors were rated on the Index of Counseling Behaviors (ICB) (Dustin, Engen, & Shymansky, 1982). The Index provides coverage of behaviors a consultant emits including silence, interruptions, and listening, during an exchange with a consultee. The Index, with titles, focuses on the following consultant actions or statements:

Approval/Praise—Positive evaluation. "Good."
Silence—No one talking during interval
Disapproval—Negative evaluation.
Encourager—Non-evaluative, non-sentences, "hm-hm."
Accurate Feeling—Reflection of client that is acknowledged.
Inaccurate Feeling—Inaccurate or corrected by client.
Self-disclosure—Information about counselor. "I" statement.
Interpretation—Counselor opinion about client.

Topic Jump—New topic by counselor.
Listen—Client talking in interval.
Perception Check—Question about feeling.
Paraphrase—Repeats client question.
Question—Any definite question.
Interrupt—Cuts off client.
Summary—Rephrase of *earlier* client statement.
Propose Action—Tells client to do one thing.
Unclassifiable—Unable to fit into any category.
Should—Should or ought statement.
Propose Client Alternatives—Tell client to carry out more than one
  activity.
Explanation—Giving factual information.
Slash—Interruption of interview.

The videotapes were also rated according to the focus of the interaction. Using Ivey and Gluckstern's (1976) six category system, the foci of the two interviews were compared to determine the degree of consultant attention given to the problem or the consultee. Ivey's six category system incorporates these foci: (a) Consultee; (b) Consultant; (c) Other people; (d) Mutual (Consultant and Consultee); (e) Topic; (f) Other.

Two raters were trained to code and record the appropriate behavior on the ICB and to note at four-second intervals the focus of the interview. The raters were students who had previously completed the course. The training of raters, requiring approximately 12 hours, included helping trainees to understand the definitions for the 21 behaviors and the six focus categories, to become familiar with the codes for each and finally to practice rating until inter-rater reliability exceeded 90%. Raters viewed and coded tapes without knowledge of the tape's recording status (pre- or posttest).

Results. Based on a repeated measures ANOVA, the results indicated that there were significant differences in the consultants' listening, directiveness, and questioning behaviors by the end of training. The listening behaviors of the consultants increased significantly over the course of the semester [$F(1,20) = 9.96$, $p < .01$]. There was a significant decrease in the number of times that the consultants offered solutions or advice during the course of the simulation [$F(1,20) = 10.64$, $p < .004$]. By the end of the semester, consultants were also more likely to ask questions of their partners during the simulation [$F(1,20) = 5.81$, $p < .03$]. None of the other skills indicated any significant change over the semester.

A change in consultant focus behaviors was observed. Specifically, the amount of time that the consultant focused on the consultee increased significantly by the end of the course [$F(1,20) = 5.06$, $p < .04$]. None of the other focus categories showed any significant change.

Additional analyses indicated no significant differences in either consultant skills or in consultant focus across student majors and preferences voiced by students for consultation models.

Discussion. Changes in student consulting behavior across time were observed. Consultants told the consultees what to do significantly less frequently, and they employed more listening and questioning behaviors. This result indicated that some changes had occurred during the semester's study of consultation. In addition, by focusing on the consultee more after the training, the students indicated they were able to "consult" in a more focused manner by the end of training.

It appears from the data collected that the one-semester graduate course did influence selected student behaviors in a simulated consultation interview. This conclusion, however, is a tentative one. Becuase of the limited number of students, it is difficult to generalize the results to other training settings. In addition, the statistical tests featured so many dependent variables (21 skills and 6 focus areas) that a few results would be expected to show significance by chance. Further research using more powerful statistical methods should be conducted to clarify the effects on outcomes of consultation training.

The results did encourage the instructors to continue the role playing component of their student evaluation and to expand training on interviewing and focus behaviors. Data from a second year of multi-disciplinary training are being gathered.

References

Babigian, H. M., & Pederson, A. M. Training mental health consultants. In J. Zusman & D. L. Davidson (Eds.), *Practical aspects of mental health consultation.* Springfield, IL: C. Thomas, 1972.

Bergan, J. R. *Behavioral consultation.* Columbus, OH: C. E. Merrill, 1977.

Caplan, G. *The theory and practice of mental health consultation.* New York: Basic Books, 1970.

Cohen, H. A. A comparison of two consultation training programs. *Professional Psychology,* 1976, 7, 535-540.

Conoley, J. C. Emergent training issues in consultation. In J. C. Conoley (Ed.), *Consultation in schools.* New York: Academic Press, 1981.

Dustin, D., Engen, H., & Shymansky, J. The ICB: A tool for counselor supervision. *Counselor Education and Supervision,* 1982, 22, 70-74.

Ivey, A., & Gluckstern, N. B. *Basic influencing skills.* North Amherst, MA: Microtraining Associates, 1976.

Schein, E. *Process consultation: Its role in organization development.* Reading, MA: Addison-Wesley, 1969.

A Case for Skills Training

Kathleen Y. Ritter
California State College, Bakersfield

Being an additional empirical demonstration
that supervised practice in counseling
is needed beyond didactic coursework.

Research efforts have demonstrated that counseling psychology or counselor education training programs that focus exclusively upon didactic teaching and the cognitive domain produce students who are unable to offer facilitative levels of the primary conditions for therapeutic change and growth (Carkhuff, 1969; Egan, 1975). The body of evidence that documents the necessity of making higher levels of empathy and warmth a specific focus during training is growing, and the fact that this must be done with foresight and regularity has been established (Carkhuff, 1969; Egan, 1975; Truax, 1970; Truax & Carkhuff, 1967).

In the fall of 1975, the counselor education program at California State College, Bakersfield, was in an ideal position to check on validity of the previous research. The M.A. program in counseling was beginning its third year, but it was only the second year the program had two full-time faculty members. One person, with the help of part-time instructors, managed the program in 1973-74, and from 1971 to 1973 counseling classes were taught out of the Division of Continuing Education with instructors hired from the community on a class-by-class basis. As far as can be determined, all the classes were essentially didactic in nature, with unrestricted enrollments. Consequently, by September of 1975 many of the students in the program had a rather "haphazard" counseling background—i.e., many instructors of various abilities and philosophical persuasions, courses taken over the years at many institutions, and little in the way of a carefully thought-out sequential program of experiences. The faculty felt that the actual skill level of most students was fairly low, but this assumption was not tested until a class in systematic skills training was offered.

Method. Fifteen students with 0-5 quarter units of coursework in counseling were admitted to one section of the systematic skills training course on a first-come-first-served basis (Group I). Another section was composed of 15 advanced students who were admitted on the same basis (Group II). The latter group had from 9 to 37 previous quarter units of course work in counseling (M = 21.46 units). The mean age of the Group I students was 30.87 years and the mean for Group II was 30.73 years. Eleven Group I people were employed full time and four were employed half-time. Eleven in Group II were also employed full-time, two were working half time, and two were unemployed. Thus, on the variables of age and employment, there was little difference between the Groups.

During the first class meeting of each Group, each student was asked to think of a current but relatively minor problem in his or her life. The students were paired randomly and each served as the helper for five minutes and as the helpee for the same period of time. They were rated on two of the core dimensions described by Egan (1975) and Carkhuff (1969): (a) Primary Level Accurate Empathy (Responsive or Facilitative dimension); and (b) Advanced Empathy (Initiative or Action-Oriented dimension). Carkhuff's (1969) five point rating scale was used, with five being high and one being low. Two observers rated each session, and Pearson product-moment coefficients between the ratings were .81 for the Responsive dimension and .83 for the Initiative dimension. The students were again paired randomly at the end of the quarter and the same two raters watched the same kind of a five minute session.

During the 10 week quarter, the classes met weekly for 2½ hours. The course was built around the Carkhuff model of systematic skills training, and Egan's text *The Skilled Helper* (1975) was used. Prehelping skills were studied first and a separate meeting was devoted to each of the following eight skills: empathy, respect, genuineness, concreteness, advanced empathy, self disclosure, confrontation, and immediacy. Each meeting began with the instructor or an advanced student modeling both an inappropriate and an appropriate use of the skill. The sessions were frequently videotaped. The helpee, and then the helper, shared his or her experience during the session followed by reactions from the students. After a general discussion of the skill, the students broke into triads. One acted first as the helper, another as the helpee, and the third as the observer. They rotated until each person had played all three parts. No "role playing" was permitted and only actual life concerns were shared by the helpees. At first a five minute time limit was set, but by the last class meeting, 15 minute sessions were held. The instructor circulated among the triads during the practices.

Results. Pre-test results were as predicted—i.e., there were no significant differences between the Groups on either of the dimensions measured. On the responsive dimension the mean of Group I (new students) was 1.83, compared with 2.13 for Group II (experienced students). The t value of 1.84 indicated no significant difference on this dimension. On the initiative dimension the mean of Group I was 1.77, compared with 2.00 for Group II. The t value of 1.37 was not significant. Thus, although the Group II ratings were slightly higher than were those of the beginning students, tests of significance indicated no true differences between the scores of the Groups.

Raw score correlation (Pearson r's) between course

units taken and ratings on the scales of therapeutic functioning were .28 on the responsive dimension and .25 on the initiative dimension (not significant). Thus, among people with academic coursework in counseling there did not appear to be a relationship between amount of work taken and functional skill level.

Posttest results were similar to the pretest findings. The Group I responsive dimension mean was 2.96 compared with 3.08 for Group II. The t value was -.63 (not significant). Initiative dimension means were 3.04 for Group I and 3.12 for Group II with a t value of -.43. Thus, no true differences between the Groups were detected on either of the outcome measures.

As was true for the pretest, posttest correlations between number of quarter units of counseling coursework taken by the Group II students and performance on the skills tests were nonsignificant. A Pearson coefficient of .03 was found on the responsive dimension and .31 was noted on the initiative dimension.

In spite of the lack of significant differences between the Groups on any pretest or posttest scores, highly significant changes within the Groups were noted on the two skill dimensions measured. For Group I, the beginning students, t values of 6.51 and 7.33 were found on the responsive and initiative dimension respectively. For Group II, the experienced students, t values of 4.98 and 6.44 for the Responsive and Initiative dimensions were detected (see Table 1).

Discussion. Despite previous coursework in counseling, the more experienced students in this study were not rated significantly higher initially than their beginning colleagues on two measures of therapeutic functioning. This does not necessarily mean that their instruction had been poor or their instructors less than competent. What it demonstrates, however, is that highly cognitive training programs do not necessarily produce skilled helpers (Egan, 1975). The skills one wants the students to demonstrate must be taught and modeled by the instructors and practiced by the students. To assume that students will acquire the prescribed skills is not enough. Some of them will, but many will not. "There are many professional helpers with the proper credentials (de-

Table 1
Pretest—Posttest Differences

Dimension	Pretest Mean	Posttest Mean	Diff.	t value
Responsive				
Group I	1.83	2.96	1.13	6.51*
Group II	2.13	3.08	.95	4.98*
Initiative				
Group I	1.77	3.04	1.27	7.33*
Group II	2.00	3.12	1.12	6.44*

*p<.001

grees, licenses, and so on) but without essential skills" (Egan, 1975, p. 18).

Students need time to integrate didactic and experiential modes of learning, and it is the judgment of this researcher that systematic skills training ideally ought to occur early in a program of studies. There appears to be some evidence (Egan, 1975) to support this point, but much empirical data are needed in this critical area. What is known at the present time is that it is not too late in any student's program to begin systematic skills training. In fact, in the present study there was little correlation between amount of previous classroom experience and both beginning and final skills ratings. Further, there was little difference between the more academically experienced group of students and the new people on the final outcome measures. Most students, regardless of prior academic training, gained as a result of the skills training. The gain of both Groups on each of the two dimensions exceeded the .001 level of significance.

References

Carkhuff, R. R. *Helping and human relations* (Volumes 1 & 2). New York: Holt, Rinehart & Winston, 1969.

Egan, G. *The skilled helper.* Monterey, CA: Brooks/Cole, 1975.

Truax, C. B. An approach to counselor education. *Counselor Education and Supervision,* 1970, *10,* 4-15.

Truax, C. B., & Carkhuff, R. R. *Toward effective counseling and psychotherapy.* Chicago: Aldine, 1967.

Psychiatric Psychopathology: A Practicum Approach

John W. Keller and Chris Piotrowski
University of West Florida

A graduate level didactic/experiential course in psychopathology has been offered at the University of West Florida since 1975. The focus of this course (titled "Practicum in Psychiatric Approaches to Psychopathology") is to introduce clinically-oriented psychology students to the applied and practical aspects of the field of psychiatry. The approach is a novel endeavor in light of the professional cleavage between clinical psychology and psychiatry. During the post-war era clinical psychology's identity emerged from the hallmark of psychodiagnostic assessment into the professionally prestigious role of psychotherapy. With the advent of this shift in

professional practice, clinical psychology threatened the long-standing foundation of psychiatry's reign in the diagnosis and treatment of psychological disorders.

To make matters more complicated, clinical psychologists have directed attention toward neo-behavioral approaches (e.g., cognitive-behavior therapy, community psychology) that depart from traditional clinical orientations. Meanwhile, psychiatry has maintained its focus on the psychodynamic/medical model as the basis for assessment of the vast spectrum of emotional, cognitive, and behavioral problems. Of course, the newly revised Diagnostic and

Statistical Manual of the APA (DSM III) has attempted to clarify and differentiate more accurately clinical disorders. Further, the mental health field has today greatly expanded in terms of practitioners (e.g., social workers, nurses, counselors, rehabilitation specialists), client populations (e.g., learning disabled, the aged), and various psychotherapeutic modalities. Thus, the task of clinical educators, to provide a comprehensive approach toward the field of psychopathology, has become more complex over the years. For example, just ten years ago there were but a handful of texts on the subject of psychopathology. This list has now proliferated to include subjects in clinical assessment, behavior analysis, cognitive appraisals, and psychiatric foundations of both psychodynamic and neo-Freudian orientations, not to mention the new advances in neuropsychology and psychopharmacology. It is no surprise, therefore, that the integration of a psychological/psychiatric model as the basis for a "practical" course in psychopathology would be both challenging and nontraditional.

Over the past eight years our course has been modified and improved to foster a unique practical learning experience for students interested in gaining insight into the practice of psychiatry.

Format. The basic practicum course outline is organized as follows: (a) Each student (total N = 10) is assigned to a psychiatrist on the psychiatric unit at a city hospital. Students make "rounds" two mornings each week and observe the interaction between the psychiatrist and patient, while focusing on symptoms as well as therapeutic intervention, including effects of psychotropic medication. (b) Each week a specific psychiatric disorder is assigned to be studied and researched. The student focuses on the designated disorder in observing characteristics and symptoms of patients. (c) The entire class meets every other week as a seminar group for the purpose of exchange of ideas, as well as open discussion based on practical experience and assigned readings. The instructor acts as facilitator. (d) On alternative weeks, each student attends a professional psychiatric lecture in the community. (e) A weekly written report, based on the practical experience on the ward is required. The instructor evaluates and gives feedback on the report. (f) A text on psychiatric theory and practice with a psychodynamic orientation toward various clinical entities is utilized. Also, the DSM III is used as a reference guide and manual. In addition, an extended reference list of texts in the areas of psychopathology, abnormal personality, and psychiatric approaches is available as supplemental reading. (g) Lastly, each student presents a formal presentation to the class on a specific psychiatric disorder; this presentation is based on research data retrieved from the literature.

Course Goals and Benefits. Within the above course context, the following goals are achieved: (a) intense observation of clinical symptoms and psychiatric techniques; (b) familiarity with popular psychotropic drugs administered, and the effects of such drugs on subsequent patient behavior; (c) the ability to differentiate between various organic, psychotic, neurotic, and personality disturbances; (d) the formulation of a dynamic framework for various types of emotional and behavioral disorders, as well as an understanding of psychiatric manifestations of organically based syndromes; (e) an appreciation of the range of professional techniques available in interacting with seriously disturbed individuals; (f) confidence and comfort in interacting with psychiatrists in various mental health settings; (g) a fostering of one's identity as a clinician through interaction with professional role models; and (h) an awareness of the current state of research of psychopathology.

The formal evaluations of the course, as well as the students' spontaneous feedback, indicated that a practicum approach is extremely valuable. Of the 100 students who have completed the course, one third stated that it was the best graduate course they had ever taken; the remaining students consistently ranked the course as outstanding or superior. More specifically, the students were impressed with how much they could learn about psychotropic medication in a relatively short period of time. For the first time the students realized why it is important for counselors and psychologists to be knowledgeable in this area. Further, the students gained an appreciation of the diversity of psychological disturbance. Most of their clinical experience had previously occurred with individuals not seriously disturbed; as a result, the exposure to the psychiatric ward was an "eye-opening experience." Conversely, the psychiatrists were able to gain a more accurate perception of the role of the psychologist. The psychiatrists reported that they were impressed with the students' psychodynamic formulations of mental disorders as well as the comfort the students developed in being around seriously disturbed persons.

Discussion. Positive evaluations of a "practical" teaching framework have been recently reported (Dodendorf, 1981; Halgin, 1982; Sherman, 1982). The benefits gained from the practical experience of interaction with psychiatrists and seriously disturbed individuals are truly noteworthy; particularly because the course format deviates markedly from the traditional didactic approach in teaching psychopathology. The students advance their knowledge while learning the realities of psychiatric care. The experience fosters both professional and personal growth. This novel and nontraditional approach has truly been worth the effort for instructor, psychiatrists, and students alike. Furthermore, attainment of a mutually beneficial relationship between the psychological and psychiatric community has been viewed by many quite skeptically. On the contrary, this was not our experience. Several psychiatrists were initially invited to informal meetings at the University for exchange of ideas. It became evident that the psychiatrists had a unique contribution to offer graduate students in clinical training. This led to the formation of the practicum. Over the years the course has proved so satisfactory that an increasing number of psychiatrists have been participating. As stated by Jay T. Shurley in an Invited Editorial in the *Journal of Clinical Psychology* (1982), "But there is also no doubt that the psychiatrist and the psychologist can be friends, maximizing the gains for the science and art and practice of mental healing and personality growth and development that are the fruit of long years of successful collaborations and friendly competition."

References

Dodendorf, D. M.   A "real-life" developmental psychology course. *Teaching of Psychology*, 1981, *8*, 172-173.
Halgin, R. P.   Using an experiential group to teach a group therapy course. *Teaching of Psychology*, 1982, *9*, 188-189.

Sherman, A. R.   Psychology fieldwork: A catalyst for advancing knowledge and academic skills. *Teaching of Psychology*, 1982, *9*, 82-85.
Shurley, J. T.   "The sheepman and the cowman should be friends": Psychiatrists and psychologists. *Journal of Clinical Psychology*, 1982, *38*, 901-902.

Training in Community Psychology for Medical Students: The Development of a Child-Oriented Community Practicum

David S. Glenwick
Kent State University

Among the salient foci of community psychology, in contradistinction to traditional clinical approaches, are: (a) prevention and early intervention; (b) the impact of supraindividual (e.g., group, organizational, community, and societal) forces upon individual behavior; (c) the value of paraprofessionals and nonmental health professionals as direct mental health care-givers; and (d) the changing role definition of the mental health professional, emphasizing such functions as consultation, supervision, training, and program evaluation, as opposed to the direct service tasks characteristic of the clinical psychologist (Rappaport, 1977).

Training in community psychology for medical personnel is particularly timely for several reasons: (a) recently proposed federal funding increases for training primary care physicians (e.g., pediatricians and family practitioners) in mental health; (b) research demonstrating that front-line medical care-givers are turned to by the public for assistance for many of their emotional and behavioral discomforts (Gurin, Veroff, & Feld, 1960); (c) the effect of psycho-social determinants upon the expression and treatment of health and illness behaviors in a given culture and community; and (d) the broadening of the physician's role to include consultation, administration, and membership in multidisciplinary teams. Concerning the evolution in professional responsibilities, Tourlentes (1978, p. 35) observed that "traditional office practice with individual patients will not be sufficient to meet growing public demands and expectations."

Program Goals.   The community psychology practicum to be described here consisted of a ten-week 1½ day/week summer experience for students completing the second year of a six-year B.S./M.D. program at Kent State University and the Northeastern Ohio Universities College of Medicine. They appeared especially appropriate to focus upon because it was hoped that exposure to a community psychology perspective fairly early in their education would promote the development of desirable attitudes regarding such matters as services for children and adolescents, the influence of non-physical causation upon intra- and interindividual functioning, the importance of community structures and values, and the contributions of psychologists and the behavioral sciences. Such an approach might counterbalance and modulate the already existing predispositions

of beginning medical students toward "a 'somatic' view of illness [and] the accompanying belief that the cure is mostly contingent upon . . . close scrutiny of the patient's biological/chemical status," a view usually intensified by the medical school curriculum (Gay, 1978, p. 7).

The Portage County Children's Services Center (PCCSC)—the county's community mental health center for children—served as home base for the practicum. Such a child facility was considered an advantageous setting because (a) children represent a high priority population for community psychology, and (b) many medical students will, following graduation, have wide contact with child and family problems. Thus even if, as a community psychologist, one works with only a relatively few medical students, one is potentially indirectly affecting hundreds of families, as well as the general health care system.

In line with the community psychology framework, a final broad objective was to transmit to the students intervention skills and knowledge concerning a variety of target levels (individual, group, organization, community, and society) and to foster an awareness of the interrelationships existing among these levels.

Program Description.   The program description is most conveniently organized according to the target levels mentioned in the preceding paragraph.

Individual and group. Students acquired interviewing, assessment, and counseling skills by participating as co-intake workers and co-therapists in counseling and testing sessions involving children, parents, and families seen at PCCSC.

Organizational and interorganizational. Ongoing involvement in several aspects of PCCSC's functioning (e.g., administrative, clinical, training and education)—for example, through observation of PCCSC's daily activities and attendance at staff meetings and case conferences—produced extensive discussion of the community, political, and economic forces affecting PCCSC's operation, as well as the impact of PCCSC upon the structure and functioning of the surrounding community. In addition, the students participated in PCCSC's consultation program to the local school for the trainable mentally retarded, being involved both in providing direct service to multiply handicapped youngsters and consultation to school staff and the youngsters' parents. The experience resulted in a similar analysis by the students of this educational facility's responsiveness to community needs and pressures.

Community and societal. Weekly discussions were held at PCCSC with representatives of child-related community agencies, including the welfare department's protective services division, the county board of education office, the local crisis center, and the Community Action Council. These representatives explored with students practical and ethical aspects of topics such as child abuse, special education, foster care, and anti-poverty programs at both the local and national levels—issues which vitally influence children's and families' health and functioning, but to which physicians (and, unfortunately, psychologists) often devote only minor attention.

Program Evaluation. While students' pre- to posttest scores on broad, formal scales of general community mental health ideology and interest did not change over the course of the practicum, essays written by them indicated that specific attutudinal shifts—generally in accordance with the program's goals and objectives—did occur concerning such subjects as (a) the significance of the environment upon child development and human behavior; (b) the competencies possessed by psychologists, and psychologists' ability to function compatibly in teams with psychiatrists and other physicians; and (c) the role of the community in adopting an activist stance and of government in providing supportive human services.

Suggestions and Recommendations. Although the practicum outlined here proved satisfying to both the medical students and PCCSC's community psychology personnel, two recommendations may be advanced to (a) enhance the value of such practica and (b) broaden students' exposure to a community psychology philosophy:

1. Offering students social psychology, community psychology, and sociology seminars, containing both theory and empirical research, would provide a foundation for the experiential knowledge gained in community practica. As Lipsitt and Spiro (1978, p. 4) observed,

Much of the wispy, "hot air" quality which characterizes these clinical areas—[i.e.,] group therapy, family therapy, community consultation, aspects of prevention, and the understanding of the social context of development, health, and disease—may be related to lack of integration with their basic sciences of social psychology and sociology .... The premedical and preclinical years are largely given over to required preparation in the basic sciences .... No equivalent requirement exists in social psychology and sociology.

2. Rather than be restricted to a one-shot "inoculation" such as a summer practicum, the framework represented by the community model could be made an integral, pervasive component of the entire medical curriculum and philosophy. If the hallmarks of community psychology were seen as valuable in conceptualizing and treating physical, as well as mental, health problems in general, students could be assisted in applying this model to a variety of specialties that are all too often considered from only a narrow clinical perspective. While pediatrics, preventive medicine, family practice, and physical rehabilitation are perhaps among the most obviously relevant specialties, probably any area of medicine would be the beneficiary of such an approach.

References

Gay, R. L.   The clinical psychologist and psychotropic medication. *The Clinical Psychologist,* 1978, *31,* 7.

Gurin, G., Veroff, J., & Feld, S. *Americans view their mental health: A nation-wide interview survey.* New York: Basic Books, 1960.

Lipsitt, D. R., & Spiro, H. R. Major issues in mental health. *Psychiatric Opinion,* 1978, *15,* 4-5.

Rappaport, J. *Community psychology: Values, research, and action.* New York: Holt, Rinehart and Winston, 1977.

Tourlentes, T. T. Psychiatric administration: A unique mental health responsibility. *Psychiatric Opinion,* 1978, *15,* 33-35.

Note

A version of this paper was presented at the American Psychological Association annual convention, Toronto, August 1978. An extended report is available from the author.

4. EVALUATING PROGRAMS

Readers will note wide variability in approaches to program evaluation. Some authors have provided descriptive accounts based on posttests of students' reactions. Others focused on characteristics of the programs. Still others have examined both immediate and delayed affects on career choice and graduate study. The only article that employed a no-treatment comparison group and a pre- and posttest design investigated attitudes toward behavior modification. Many significant questions about the effect of placement activities remain to be answered. Researchers will find that this section is a rich source of ideas.

Stephen Morris and Leonard Haas reported on the evaluation of a field placement course at the University of Utah. They hypothesized that the quality of students' supervision by an agency would be strongly related to goal attainment and satisfaction with the placement. Results from 44 students who completed a post program evaluation form revealed that satisfaction and goal achievement were related to factors present in the placement setting. Implications of the study emphasize the importance of the agency structure in determining satisfaction; placement supervisors may consider responding to this challenge.

Ricki Kantrowitz, Christina Mitchell, and William Davidson II explored two major components of placement courses. They investigated training/supervision content and intensity (size of classes) in a pre- and posttest design. Students from Michigan State University worked with youthful offenders 8 hours per week for 18 weeks. The evaluation questionnaire administered at 10 weeks and then again at 30 weeks revealed that different training/supervision methods and group intensities had varying impact on a number of dependent variables. Students who received highly structured and intense supervision felt that they had more support during the placement. The major implications of this study are that placement directors should provide students in certain programs with extensive training and supervision.

Abraham Jeger from New York Institute of Technology at Old Westbury and Gary McClure from State University of New York at Stony Brook employed a pre- and posttest design and a control group. They sought to determine whether didactic and experiential behavioral training lead to differential attitudes toward behavior modification. Students in a didactic course on behavior modification served as a control and those in a placement course served as the experimental group. The investigators administered an attitude toward behavior modification instrument to both groups. Findings suggested that merely using behavior modification is not sufficient for providing a more favorable attitude toward behavior modification.

Brian Yates reported on field placements' monetary and nonmonetary costs and benefits. He evaluated a gram at Stanford University that trained students to work as paraprofessionals with behaviorally disturbed preadolescents. The dollar costs to academia were based on variables such as meeting room space, advertising, and professors' time. The author reported that the costs/benefits ratio was .89, which showed monetary costs outweighed the benefits. However, the author also reported that if non-monetary benefits, such as research publication and dissertation data were included, the university more than broke even. Moreover, 80% of the students stayed beyond their first quarter and some obtained jobs in the agency. Yate's unique approach to program evaluation provides further evidence that field programs benefit both students and institutions.

Frank Prerost added yet another dimension to program evaluation. Noting that a lack of follow-up research on field placement existed, he examined the following questions: Does the placement experience direct more students to traditional graduate training or to professional schools in psychology? Are participants more successful in securing employment in service areas? Does placement provide students with a better understanding of employment opportunities? Data consisted of responses from five graduating classes at Western Illinois University. The author surveyed psychology majors who either enrolled or did not enroll in a placement course that assigned students to mental health human services agencies. Although the study did not answer all of the questions, it demonstrated many benefits from placement experience. It also lead Prerost to emphasize potential dangers in overemphasizing the practice of psychology as a career choice. Large numbers of students pursuing professional psychology may be detrimental to students and to the profession.

Stuart Keeley and Jeffery Kreutzer documented the follow-up evaluation of a formalized mental health worker training program at Bowling Green State University. The authors surveyed 22 students who completed the program during an eight year period. The survey asked about employment, graduate school status, current professional interests and evaluations of the experience. Readers will find that the results of this article contribute to the extensive literature that supports placement programs.

Evaluating Undergraduate Field Placements: An Empirical Approach

Stephen B. Morris and
Leonard J. Haas
University of Utah

Achievement of personal goals in field placement is not related to supervision quality, but apparently to structuredness.

Courses offering undergraduate field experience in psychology are relatively widespread (Matthews, 1979), but most of the literature about these courses has been concerned with implementation, supervision, costs and benefits, and other pragmatic issues (Barton & Duerfeldt, 1980; Kuppersmith, Blair & Slotnick, 1977; Shiverick, 1977; Vande Creek & Thompson, 1977; Yates, 1980). Although some authors mention the methods they use to evaluate their programs (e.g., Barton & Duerfeldt, 1980; Sherman, 1982), these descriptions are often cursory, focus on the *course* rather than the placement, or present data on satisfaction only. As the authors of one paper stated, it is difficult to find programs that provide useful data to help evaluate their effectiveness (Hess, Harrison, Fink, Lilliston, Aponte, & Korn, 1978).

The purpose of the present paper is to provide information about a method of evaluating students' field placements that takes into account attainment of individual goals and quality of supervision. The method will be described and some results of its use reported. In addition, suggestions about the evaluation process and about the structure of field placements will be made.

At the outset quality of supervision was expected to be a key factor in determining outcome. Specifically, we hypothesized that the quality of supervision students received at the agency should be strongly related to their goal attainment and satisfaction with the placements.

Method. The undergraduate field experience course in psychology at the University of Utah is an upper-division elective that carries variable credit. Students may enroll for up to 6 credits per quarter, up to a total of 21 credits. Six of these credits may apply toward the upper-division credits required for the psychology major. There are four objectives stated on the course syllabus: (a) integrate theory and practice; (b) develop an awareness of the kinds of work that require psychology training; (c) provide experience to help students decide whether to pursue graduate work in psychology; and (d) develop marketable skills.

At the beginning of the quarter students fill out a contract form with their agency supervisor that outlines their goals for the quarter and the specific activities that will lead to the achievement of the goals. Students are required to attend monthly meetings (or write papers in lieu of attendance) and to fill out evaluation forms at the end of the quarter (for evaluating their placement and mechanics of the course).

Supervisors are invited to attend a meeting once each quarter and are also asked to fill out an evaluation of the student at the end of the quarter.

The subjects were 44 undergraduates (45% male, 55% female) primarily psychology majors, who were enrolled in the field experience course during 1981-82. Because some of them repeated the course, the data base comprises 62 evaluations they filled out about their placements (representing a 93% return rate). Fourteen placement settings are represented; number of students per agency per year ranged from 1 to 14 (mdn = 2, mode = 1). The agencies cover a wide variety of settings including medical/psychiatric (36%), mental health treatment (29%), crisis/hot line (21%), and educational (14%).

The evaluation form filled out by the students consists of seven items that cover information about goal achievement, achievement of course objectives (see above), changes the student would have made in his/her placement, overall supervision quality at the agency, relevance of previous psychology courses, reactions to the mechanics of the course and additional comments. For the goal achievement (GA), achievement of course objectives (CO), and overall supervision quality (SQ) items, the student is asked to provide a rating score of 1—high to 5—low, on a Likert scale, as well as detailed verbal explanations of reasons for the ratings. For example, on the GA items, students are asked to describe their goal, give a numerical rating, and describe the factors that contributed to their achievement of that goal.

The analysis of the data provided by the 62 evaluations included several steps:

1. Goals were heterogeneous and idiosyncratic across students, so mean goal achievement (within-student) was computed. These means were then averaged across all students in each agency during the year to yield a mean figure for the agency. Mean GA across all agencies was also computed.

2. Because course objectives were the same for all students, student ratings for each objective were averaged across all students at a given agency. They were averaged across all agencies as well.

3. Overall supervision quality ratings were averaged across all students at a given agency (in nearly all cases there was only one supervisor per agency). These were also averaged across all agencies.

4. Written comments across all students for a given agency were noted on a separate sheet.

5. To test the original hypothesis, all agency ratings in each of the three areas (GA, CO, SQ) were plotted on a single graph. Partial correlations were computed to show the strength of association between all combinations of the three variables.

Results and Discussion. The overall means (across all agencies) for each variable are as follows: GA: $M = 2.058$ (SD = .447); CO: $M = 1.81$ (SD = .297); SQ: $M = 1.89$ (SD = .84). In order to control for interdependencies among the variables, partial correlations for each of the 3 unique pairs of variables were computed. Partial correlations are as follows: GAxCO:.714 (p .01); GAxSQ:.323 (n.s.); COxSQ:.094 (n.s.).

In general, the numerical data do not support the original hypothesis; CO and GA are not related to SQ. Examination of the written comments helps explain this somewhat surprising result. It appears that although supervision quality is important to students, their satisfaction and the degree to which they achieve their goals and objectives seems to be related to the "structuredness" of their experience. Important components of structure seem to include clarity of role, regularity of supervision, working for only one boss, and explicitness of feedback and communication processes. Agencies that receive the highest ratings often provide such structural and procedural information in written form or make it clear in other explicit ways. The agency that received the best overall ratings seems to have the clearest process for training, integrating, supervising, and evaluating students. The structure of field training experience deserves further study. It may be that an approach such as that of Insel & Moos (1974) to assessing the training environment would be fruitful in better understanding the link between structure and outcome. The variable we call structure seems most closely related to the system maintenance dimension of organization climate described by Moos (1974). This aspect of organization has been shown to have effects on staff productivity, morale, and other aspects of individual functioning.

In considering these results it is important to bear in mind the limitations of this study. First, the data are derived from a single source, the students' retrospective self reports. That students' reports may have been biased is suggested by an apparent inflation in the numerical ratings (on all 62 evaluations there is not a single "5-very poorly" rating). It is possible, for example, that students may rate their placements favorably to keep their supervisor happy in the event they want future placements there, or to reduce the dissonance that may result from investing much time and effort in what turned out to be an unpleasant experience, or to appear in a favorable light. Of course, it is also possible that students give favorable ratings because they are generally pleased with their placements.

Second, evaluations of goal achievement are collapsed within students and within agencies. This procedure may mask important qualitative differences in goal achievement, which, if examined, might yield information about specific issues the agency or the University should address.

Conclusions and Recommendations. It seems clear from these results that the most satisfactory placements are those in which there is a well-organized, explicitly structured training program. Students seem to desire clear expectations, explicit communication processes, and clear lines of authority as well as regularly scheduled supervision. Discussion with participants suggests that this is particularly true of inexperienced students. Thus, as students gain more experience in an agency it may be desirable to gradually relax the structure (according to an explicit schedule) to allow them to explore their interests more freely.

It seems that the above description of a desirable placement is not different from descriptions that have been provided of well-functioning organizations in general (Goodstein, 1978). Although students in our program are free to arrange field placements in "untried" agencies, those who do so generally have focused interests and/or personal acquaintance with a potential supervisor. As a rule it may be wise for coordinators of field experience courses to evaluate the organizational health of agencies before students are assigned to them. This could be done through visits to the agency and conversations with employees and volunteers (present and past).

In addition to evaluating the desirability of certain agencies as placements for students, it may be wise to prepare students for their placements by discussing organizational issues with them before they arrive on the job. Discussions of topics such as appropriate assertion, communicating clearly, how to give and receive feedback, how to fit in as a newcomer, and other survival and adjustment issues may be useful.

It seems important to gain quantifiable as well as nonquantifiable information when conducting evaluations of placements. The quantified information obtained in this evaluation is useful in several ways. First, it gives us a way to quickly determine which agencies seem to be providing the best experiences for our students. Second, this information is very helpful in providing feedback to agency supervisors when we meet with them. They seem interested in learning how their agencies are evaluated and appear eager to know what features of a placement contribute to its success. Third, this information provides a basis for making recommendations to students who ask for help in deciding on a placement.

It also seems important to provide agency supervisors with information about their performance. We recommend some sort of personal contact with them, such as a site visit or a meeting, to accomplish this. For our purposes the meeting seems especially useful because it allows supervisors to hear about what is happening in other agencies and to share ideas with each other. The meeting also provides support for the occasional supervisor who is having a difficult time. The numerical information provides a comfortable vehicle for both university and agency personnel to evaluate the quality of students' placements.

In conclusion, we find a structured evaluation helpful. It allows us to study our own performance, as well as that of the agencies, and helps us provide an even more positive experience for our students. The very positive reactions of our students to their field experiences, as well as the employment opportunities that occasionally grow out of them, show us that field experience for students (and the evaluation of that experience) is well worth the effort involved.

References

Barton, E. J., & Duerfeldt, P. H. Undergraduate psychology practica pragmatism. *Teaching of Psychology*, 1980, *7*, 146-149.

Goodstein, L. D. *Consulting with human service systems*. Reading, MA: Addison-Wesley, 1978.

Hess, A., Harrison, A., Fink, R., Lilliston, L., Aponte, J., & Korn, J. Critical issues in undergraduate training in various community settings. *Teaching of Psychology*, 1978, *5*, 81-86.

Insel, P., & Moos, R. Psychological environments: Expanding the scope of human ecology. *American Psychologist*, 1974, *29*, 179-188.

Kuppersmith, J., Blair, R., & Slotnick, R. Training undergraduates as co-leaders of multi-family counseling groups. *Teaching of Psychology*, 1977, *4*, 3-7.

Matthews, J. Undergraduate field placement: Survey and issues. *Teaching of Psychology*, 1979, *6*, 148-151.

Moos, R. *Evaluating treatment environments: A social ecological approach*. New York: Wiley, 1974.

Sherman, A. R. Psychology fieldwork: A catalyst for advancing knowledge and academic skills. *Teaching of Psychology*, 1982, *9*, 82-85.

Shiverick, D. D. A full-time clinical practicum for undergraduates. *Teaching of Psychology*, 1977, *4*, 188-190.

Vande Creek, L. V., & Thompson, G. Management of undergraduate psychology internships. *Teaching of Psychology*, 1977, *4*, 177-180.

Yates, B. T. Benefits and costs of community-academia interaction in a paraprofessional training course. *Teaching of Psychology*, 1980, *7*, 8-12.

Varying Formats of Teaching Undergraduate Field Courses: An Experimental Examination

Ricki Kantrowitz, Christina Mitchell, and William S. Davidson II
Michigan State University

Undergraduate psychology departments have been under fire to move away from the classroom and into the community (Baskin, 1967). Available research indicates that the use of undergraduates in field experiences benefits all concerned—the university, the student and the target individuals (Durlak, 1971; Gruver, 1971). However, the field work supervisor is frequently left with little sound research with which to develop the practicum.

This study began to explore systematically two major components of field courses. One aspect of field experience examined was that of training/supervision content. There are three common approaches used in nonprofessional programs. First, some programs offer no specific training at all, but rather focus on the natural skills and attributes of the nonprofessionals (Durlak, 1971; Korchin, 1976). A second common focus is that of interpersonal communication, based upon principles and practices developed by Rogers (e.g., Danish & Brock, 1974; Truax & Carkhuff, 1967). A third training/supervision content that has increased in popularity focuses on behavioral change skills coupled with community advocacy skills (Davidson, Seidman, Rappaport, Berck, Rapp, Rhodes, & Herring, 1977).

Another major component of field experience examined in this study was intensity. Two aspects of the intensity were varied: (a) the frequency of supervision meetings, and (b) the size of the classes. The focus of this study was the relative impact of varying training/supervision approaches on students' perceptions of and satisfaction with the experience. For pragmatic reasons, the design of the study was a modification of a completely crossed design. A comparison of extremes was made: high intensity training coupled with either behavioral contracting/child advocacy or relationship skills training; low intensity training coupled with the "natural skills" training. In addition, group size was varied within the low intensity condition. Although the results reported only begin to explore the differential outcomes, they do shed light on the effects of some aspects of field experience supervision on undergraduates' perceptions of their experiences.

Method. Students were randomly selected, controlling for sex, from a group of 134 undergraduates who had expressed interest in the field course. Students were juniors and seniors, between the ages of 19 and 22; most were psychology or criminal justice majors, planning careers or graduate study in human service fields. All students in this research worked with youthful offenders diverted to the program by the local juvenile court. Each student worked one-on-one with a youth six to eight hours per week for 18 weeks.

In the *High intensity: Action field experience condition*, seven males and seven females were randomly assigned to the two "Action" classes each led by two graduate students. Training in the Action Condition centered around an eight unit manual on behavioral contracting and child advocacy skills. Following training, each student met in weekly supervision groups and was assigned to a youth referred to the program. Students were expected to assess the youth's situation, implement the behavioral contracting/advocacy strategy, work in conjunction with the supervision group and the significant others of the youth, and monitor the intervention's impact. Weekly supervision sessions (weeks 9-30) were group problem-solving in nature, focused on case-specific information.

In the *High intensity: Relationship field experience condition*, seven males and seven females were randomly assigned to the two "Relationship" classes. (Two females dropped from the group prior to assignment to a youth and are not discussed further.) Relationship training centered on an eight-unit manual on establishing a trusting, helpful relationship and facilitating autonomy in the problem-solving process.

For the *Low intensity: Small group field experience condition,* seven males and seven females were randomly assigned to two "Small" classes. The Small condition included three, two-hour orientation meetings held during the first three weeks. These meetings included a general introduction to the program, lectures on theories of delinquency and the justice system, an overview of what students might do with the youth and the importance of being supportive of their youth. Supervision sessions were two hours in length and held monthly for the remainder of the three terms. The overall philosophy in supervision was that the interest, commitment and high level of motivation and enthusiasm of volunteers could have positive impact on the youth.

For the *Low intensity: Large group field experience condition,* eight males and eight females were randomly assigned to the "Large" condition. (One male dropped prior to assignment to a case.) The Large condition was identical to the Small condition except that this group had 15 students meeting as a group.

An extensive Course Evaluation questionnaire was generated and was given at two time periods—Time 1 (after 10 weeks) and Time 2 (after 30 weeks). Items were generated which attempted to measure the students' attitudes about different aspects of the course: the amount and content of training, the usefulness of the course in future plans, the overall field experience, the structure of the class, case discussions, and so on. All questions were in the form of a five-point Likert-type scale. On the basis of principal components/varimax rotation procedures using Kaiser's criteria (Kaiser & Caffry, 1965), five orthogonal components were extracted: *Evaluation of Academic Course Learning, General Course Evaluation, Evaluation of Didactic Training, Evaluation of Class Discussion of Cases, and Social Support Received.*[2] With these components, it was possible to examine differential impacts of the four conditions.

Results and Discussion.   Because of the orthogonality of the components generated, all five components were analyzed using a 4 x 2 (condition x time) analysis of variance. Effects were found on all five components. When appropriate, planned multiple comparisons were computed using the Scheffé method. It should be noted that only those comparisons which reached a significance level of $p < .05$ are reported here.

A significant main effect for condition on the *Evaluation of Academic Course Learning* component was observed. (See Table 1.) Using the Scheffé criteria, the only significant comparisons indicate the Action group and Small group were more satisfied with the academic course learning than did Large at Time 2. A main effect for time on the *General Course Evaluation* component was significant. No Scheffé comparisons were significant.

For the *Evaluation of Didactic Training* component, a main effect of condition was indicated. Both High Intensity groups scored significantly higher than the Low Intensity groups on how much they liked and how useful they found their training. Main effects for condition and time were significant on the *Evaluation of Class Discussion of Cases* component. Using Scheffé criteria there were no between group differences at

Time 1. By Time 2 only the Relationship group was significantly lower than Action and Small. The Relationship group dropped significantly across time. The *Social Support Received* component exhibited a significant main effect for condition. Using Scheffé tests, the combined Action and Relationship groups perceived more social support than did the combined Low Intensity groups.

Although the results are tentative due to the design, the clearest point to emerge from this study was that it does make

Table 1. Mean Scores for Course Evaluation Scales

	CONDITION							
	Action		Relation-ship		Small		Large	
Scale	T1*	T2*	T1	T2	T1	T2	T1	T2
Evaluation of Academic Course Learning	4.08	4.07	3.92	3.65	3.88	3.92	3.65	3.39
General Course Evaluation	3.87	3.89	3.91	3.58	4.19	3.85	4.18	3.83
Evaluation of Didactic Training	3.66	3.89	3.83	3.50	3.29	3.07	3.00	2.57
Evaluation of Class Discussion	4.75	4.38	4.40	3.92	4.66	4.43	4.38	4.12
Social Support Received	3.16	3.43	2.94	2.81	2.50	2.61	2.06	2.52

*Time one and Time two.

a difference how field experience courses are run. The results are not unequivocal, but different training/supervision contents and different group intensities had varying impact. When specifically evaluating their didactic training, the two groups that received the highly structured, more concrete training felt better about their training. Perhaps the most interesting finding is that students who received highly structured, more concrete and highly intense training/supervision felt they had more support within and outside of class concerning their cases, particularly early in the experience.

Some applications of these findings for undergraduate educators who are arranging community practica for college students can be demonstrated. These results support McKeachie's (1967) statement that in classes where applications of knowledge are important large groups may be a disadvantage. However, more than group size may be involved. Students felt more socially supported and evaluated their didactic learning more positively if they received frequent and intense supervision.

Some authors (e.g., Durlak, 1971 Korchin, 1976) have stated that training of nonprofessionals can "wash out" personal effectiveness—that which is based on natural skills and enthusiasm. From this preliminary study though, it is suggested that in planning such curricula one should consider offering extensive training and supervision in a set of specific skills, in order to facilitate the nonprofessional's identification of a specific role for him/herself with the target and his/her environment. Obviously, further research will need to identify the specific source of such effects.

References

Baskin, S.   Innovations in college teaching. In C. B. T. Lee (Ed.), *Improving college teaching.* Washington, DC: American Council on Education, 1967.

Danish, S. J., & Brock, G. W.   The current status of training for paraprofessionals. *The Personnel and Guidance Journal*, 1974, *53*, 299-303.

Davidson, W. S., Seidman, E. S., Rappaport, J., Berck, P. L., Rapp, N., Rhodes, W., & Herring, J.   Diversion program for juvenile offenders. *Social Work Research and Abstracts*, 1977, *1*, 40-54.

Durlak, J.   The use of nonprofessionals as therapeutic agents: Research, issues, and implications. Unpublished doctoral dissertation, Vanderbilt University, 1971.

Gruver, G. G.   College students as therapeutic agents. *Psychological Bulletin*, 1971, *76*, 111-127.

Kaiser, H. F., & Caffry, J.   Alpha factor analysis. *Psychometrika*, 1965, *30*, 1-14.

Korchin, S. J. *Modern clinical psychology: Principles of intervention in the clinic and community.* New York: Basic Books, 1976.

McKeachie, W. J.   Research in teaching: The gap between theory and practice. In C. B. T. Lee (Ed.), *Improving college teaching.* Washington, DC: American Council on Education, 1967.

Truax, C. B., & Carkhuff, R. R.   *Toward effective counseling and psychotherapy: Training and practice.* Chicago: Aldine, 1967.

Notes

1. Based on a paper presented at the 87th Annual Convention of the American Psychological Association, New York, 1979. This work was completed under a grant from the Center for the Studies of Crime and Delinquency from the National Institutes of Mental Health #MH29160.

2. Details of measure development can be obtained by writing to William S. Davidson.

The Attitudinal Effects of Undergraduate Behavioral Training

Abraham M. Jeger
New York Institute of Technology at Old Westbury
and Gary McClure
State University of New York at Stony Brook

Students in a class, but not those in a practicum, became more accepting of behavior modification. Attitudes toward social learning were unchanged.

In recent years we have witnessed a marked increase in the number of college and universities which offer courses in behavior modification at the undergraduate level (Benassi & Lanson, 1972). However, other than employing traditional grading procedures to measure knowledge there appears to be little emphasis on the evaluation of university-based behavioral training. This is in direct contrast to field (inservice) training in behavior modification where the entire area of "training" nonprofessional behavior modifiers emerged as a distinct area of specialization (Balch & Solomon, 1976; Gardner, 1975).

The present study represents an attempt to begin filling this gap by examining the attitudinal effects of academic and experiential behavioral training among undergraduates. The evaluation criteria are: (a) positive or negative attitude toward behavior modification, and (b) endorsement of the broader "social learning" orientation underlying behavior modification (Krasner & Ullmann, 1973; Ullmann & Krasner, 1975), in contrast to the prevailing "disease" conceptions of human problems.

A review by Mazza and Pumroy (1975) indicates that attitude measures have long been employed in the evaluation of behavior modification training. For example, parents' attitudes toward child rearing and teachers' attitudes toward students were employed as dependent measures to assess the impact of behavioral training. Mazza and Pumroy con-

cluded that attitude measures "did not appear to be sensitive to changes made by trainees" and therefore, "researchers have tended to use them less and less" (p.113). It should be noted, however, that the early studies were generally weak from a methodological standpoint (i.e., control or comparison groups were usually lacking). Further, it is the contention of the present authors that attitudinal changes (as opposed to just knowledge gains or behavioral competence) are worthy of study in their own right and that they can provide a useful short-term outcome measure of training. This is particularly so considering the positive relationship between staff attitudes and their behavior in mental health settings (e.g., Ellsworth, 1965). Inasmuch as the present study is concerned with attitudes toward behavior modification and endorsement of a social learning model, a brief overview of previous attempts to assess these attitudes is presented here.

A notable trend to measure attitudes toward behavior modification is apparent in the area of teacher training. In one-year follow-up studies of teachers who received behavioral training both Vane (1972) and Ryan (1976) found the majority of teachers to report favorable attitudes. Although these studies relied on global ratings to assess attitudes, Musgrove (1974) standardized a 20-item, Likert-type Attitudes Toward Behavior Modification (ABM) scale. Research with this instrument found more positive attitudes among teachers holding MA degrees compared to those with only a BA (Musgrove & Harms, 1975), as well as more positive attitudes among teachers with previous exposure to behavior modification (Throll & Ryan, 1976). Jeger (1977) found the scale sensitive in detecting pre-post changes among psychiatric aides receiving behavioral training. The present study extends the use of this scale in evaluating differential training experiences among undergraduates.

The notion of assessing the impact of training on endorsement of a social learning view of human problems follows from earlier research on attitudes toward "mental illness." Following Gilbert and Levinson's (1956) Custodial Mental Illness Ideology Scale (CMI), measuring one's adoption of a "custodial" versus "humanistic" orientation, Cohen and Struening (1962) developed their multidimensional Opinions About Mental Illness Scale (OMI) tapping five factors—Authoritarianism, Benevolence, Mental Hygiene Ideology, Social Restrictiveness, and Interpersonal Etiology. Although the thrust of training mental health staff was to imbue them with a Mental Hygiene Ideology (i.e., the dominant "disease" model of human problems: "mental illness is an illness like any other"), the advent of alternative conceptions of human problems, i.e., the social learning and sociocultural models, makes it necessary to determine the effects of training in a particular modality on endorsement of its underlying orientation. Toward this end, Morrison (Note 2) developed the Client Attitude Questionnaire (CAQ) to measure one's endorsement of a "disease" versus "social learning" orientation of human problems. The CAQ found psychologists and social workers scoring higher in the social learning direction, relative to psychiatrists and nurses (Morrison, Yablonovitz, Harris & Nevid, 1976) and was sensitive in detecting pre-post changes among staff (Morrison & Becker, 1975) and patients (Morrison, 1976) following "demythologizing" seminars. Using the CAQ, Jeger (1977) found significant changes toward a social learning direction among psychiatric aides receiving behavioral training. The present study extends the use of this scale in evaluating differential training experiences among undergraduates.

Thus, the current study sought to determine whether didactic and experiential behavioral training lead to differential attitudes toward behavior modification and endorsement of the underlying social learning orientation.

Method. Psychology students (N=21) enrolled in an undergraduate course on behavior modification at the State University of New York at Stony Brook served as subjects. Prerequisites for the course included two introductory psychology courses, abnormal psychology, and statistics. The text by Rimm and Masters (1974) was the major source of reading. The class met twice weekly with lectures and discussions being the primary format.

Another group of students (N=12) enrolled in a psychology practicum also served as subjects. Two introductory psychology courses were the only prerequisites. Each of the students worked for six hours per week on a behavior modification ward for autistics at a nearby state psychiatric hospital. Their primary activities consisted of carrying out behavioral interventions with individual clients under supervision of the ward administrator.

A 20-item, 5-point Likert-type scale tapping one bi-polar dimension—"favorable" (high score, based on summed items) versus "unfavorable" attitude toward behavior modification—served as a dependent measure. Originally developed by Musgrove (1974) to assess teacher attitudes toward behavior modification (see previous section of this paper), this instrument was slightly reworded for use with general populations. Some specific items are: "The benefits of behavior modification have been exaggerated"; and, "Behavior modification helps a person to learn how to cope with his/her environment."

Form B of Morrison's (Note 2) Client Attitude Questionnaire (CAQ-B), a 20-item Likert-type scale measuring the extent to which one endorses a "medical" versus "social learning" (high score, based on summed items) view of human problems served as the other dependent measure. Examples of specific items are: "There are some people who clearly suffer from 'schizophrenia' "; and, "There is no such thing as mental illness, just people with problems." Morrison's three-point format was converted to a five point format for the present study to maintain the same "set" as the ABM scale.

The two attitude instruments were administered to both groups of subjects during the first week of the semester and again during the last week of the semester (approximately 13 weeks apart). Completing the questionnaires was voluntary, with no refusals encountered. Students were given individual and group feedback following the semester.

Results. As is depicted in Table 1, on the ABM, both groups held comparably favorable attitudes toward behavior modification at the outset. However, only the "didactic" group showed a significant pre-post change toward the positive direction, $t(20) = 4.32$; $p<.001$. No changes in any direction were found in the "practicum" group. Between-group "change" scores were significant at the .05 level, $t(31) = 2.44$.

Whereas subjects in the "didactic" group scored higher on the CAQ relative to the "practicum" subjects at the outset, $(t(31) = 2.14; p<.05)$, neither group showed any significant pre-post changes (See Table 1). Between-group "change" scores were likewise not significant.

Discussion. The present findings suggest that, at least for college students with already favorable attitudes toward behavior modification, didactic training is sufficent to further

Table 1
Means and Standard Deviations on the Attitude toward Behavior Modification Scale (ABM) and Client Attitude Questionnaire (CAQ)

Measure	Condition	Pretest		Posttest	
		$\overline{X}$	SD	$\overline{X}$	SD
ABM	Didactic	74.19	9.32	80.29*	5.96
	Practicum	73.00	8.47	73.16	9.14
CAQ	Didactic	65.19	7.03	65.95	6.53
	Practicum	59.00	9.51	60.50	9.12

Note. Possible range for scores on both measures is 20-100.
*Pre-post mean difference significant at the .001 level, t test.

enhance such attitudes. Merely working as behavioral engineers and functioning as effective behavior change agents is not sufficient for enhancing attitudes. As such, the finding is consistent with data reported by Marholin, Taylor and Warren (1978), that relative to students who received in-service training in behavior modification, those with didactic training held more positive attitudes. The present study extends the results of Marholin et al. (1978), whose findings are based on "retrospective" data. Broader exposure, similar to that obtained through didactic training, appears warranted to induce more favorable attitudes toward behavior modification. However, this conclusion is limited by the lack of evidence concerning the comparability of the groups on such measures as SAT scores, GPA, etc. (although their pre-test ABM scores were comparable). Further, future research is necessary to determine changes in attitudes toward behavior modification for a comparable group receiving a combination of didactic training coupled with field experience.

Data derived from the CAQ showed that neither training experience was successful in shifting students' attitudes toward a social learning direction. A possible explanation is that behavior modification may still be viewed within a "medical" model context—i.e., that behavioral techniques are just another "bag of tricks" useful for treating "mental illness." In order for students to grasp the underlying social learning orientation, perhaps special emphasis on the broader environmental framework needs to be incorporated into training programs. It appears that such content is beginning to be emphasized in undergraduate programs which conceptualize behavior modification as but one aspect of a larger "environmental design" effort (e.g., Krasner, 1979).

The fact that advanced undergraduates (those in the didactic group) were higher in the social learning direction at the outset is consistent with previous research on the CAQ which found psychology students to score highest relative to other student groups (Morrison et al., 1976). What remains for future research to determine is whether psychology training imbues students with the social learning orientation or whether those endorsing the social learning viewpoint are likely to be attracted to psychology. Further, additional research is necessary to determine the impact of combined didactic and experiential behavioral training on students' endorsement of the underlying social learning orientation.

The present study demonstrates the utility of the Musgrove (1974) Attitudes toward Behavior Modification Scale and the Morrison (Note 2) Client Attitude Questionnaire as dependent measures in the evaluation of behavioral training among undergraduates. The scales are short, easy to administer, and can be incorporated as built-in evaluation tools for academic and/or field training experiences. It is hoped that feedback derived from the continued use of these instruments will lead to the development of optimal training programs geared toward specific "behavioral" objectives.

References

Balch, P., & Solomon, R. The training of paraprofessionals as behavior modifiers: A review. *American Journal of Community Psychology*, 1976, *4*, 167-179.

Bennassi, V., & Lanson, R. A survey of the teaching of behavior modification in colleges and universities. *American Psychologist*, 1972, *27*, 1063-1069.

Cohen, J., & Struening, E. L. Opinion about mental illness in the personnel of two large mental hospitals. *Journal of Abnormal and Social Psychology*, 1962, *64*, 349-360.

Ellsworth, R. B. A behavioral study of staff attitudes toward mental illness. *Journal of Abnormal Psychology*, 1965, *70*, 194-200.

Gardner, J. M. *Training nonprofessionals in behavior modification*. Worthington, OH: Jones Publishing Company, 1975.

Gilbert, D. C., & Levinson, D. J. Ideology, personality, and institutional policy in the mental hospital. *Journal of Abnormal and Social Psychology*, 1956, *53*, 263-271.

Jeger, A. M. The effects of a behavioral consultation program on consultees, clients, and the social environment (Doctoral Dissertation, State University of New York at Stony Brook, 1977). *Dissertation Abstracts International*, 1977, *38*, 1405B. (University Microfilms Number 77-20,019)

Krasner, L. (Ed.). *Environmental design and human behavior: A handbook of theory and application*. Elmsford, NY: Pergamon Press, 1979.

Krasner, L., & Ullmann, L. P. *Behavior influence and personality: The social matrix of human action*. New York: Holt, Rinehart, & Winston, 1973.

Marholin D., II, Taylor, R. L., & Warren, S. A. Learning to apply psychology: Didactic training, experience, and opinion about behavior modification. *Teaching of Psychology*, 1978, *5*, 23-26.

Mazza, J., & Pumroy, D. K. A review of evaluation of behavior modification programs. *The Psychological Record*, 1975, *25*, 111-121.

Morrison, J. K. Demythologizing mental patients' attitudes toward mental illness: An empirical study. *Journal of Community Psychology*, 1976, *4*, 181-185.

Morrison, J. K., & Becker, R. E. Seminar-induced change in a community psychiatric team's reported attitudes toward "mental illness." *Journal of Community Psychology*, 1975, *3*, 281-284.

Morrison, J. K., Yablonovitz, H., Harris, M. R., & Nevid, J. S. The attitudes of nursing students and others about mental illness. *Journal of Psychiatric Nursing and Mental Health Services*, 1976, *14*, 17-19.

Musgrove, W. J. A scale to measure attitudes toward behavior modification. *Psychology in the Schools*, 1974, *2*, 392-396.

Musgrove, W. J., & Harms, R. A. Teachers' attitudes toward behavior modification. *Journal of SPATE*, 1975, *13*, 133-138.

Rimm, D. C., & Masters, J. C. *Behavior therapy: Techniques and empirical findings*. New York: Academic Press, 1974.

Ryan, B. A. Teacher attitudes toward behavior modification one year after an in-service training program. *Behavior Therapy*, 1976, *7*, 264-265.

Throll, D., & Ryan, B. A. Research note: Teacher attitudes toward behavior modification. *New Zealand Journal of Educational Studies*, 1976, *11*, 68-71.

Ullmann, L. P., & Krasner, L. *A psychological approach to abnormal behavior* (2nd Ed.). Englewood Cliffs, NJ: Prentice-Hall, 1975.

Vane, J. R. A school behavior modification program: Teacher attitudes a year later. *Behavior Therapy*, 1972, *3*, 41-44.

Notes

1. Now at Georgia Southern College, Statesboro, Georgia 30458.
2. Morrison, J. K. *The client attitude questionnaire: A brief manual*. Unpublished manual, Department of Psychiatry, Albany Medical College, Albany, NY, 1975.
3. Thanks are due to Judith Lifshitz for her assistance with the study.

Benefits and Costs of Community-Academia Interaction In a Paraprofessional Training Course

Brian T. Yates
Stanford University

Analysis of monetizable and nonmonetizable benefits and costs shows both parties with a favorable ratio in this practicum program.

Academic institutions and communities can help each other in ways that produce tangible benefits for both with few tangible costs. Paraprofessional training programs can play a crucial role in forming these mutually beneficial exchanges of resources between academia and communities. By offering paraprofessional training courses that utilize community facilities and community staff, academic institutions receive tuition dollars without corresponding overhead and personnel costs. Also, the practical, job-oriented nature of paraprofessional training courses can increase enrollments in academic institutions. Communities benefit from the inexpensive student manpower provided by paraprofessional training courses that involve practica in community-based service programs. Communities may benefit further from participating in paraprofessional training systems by hiring the graduates, because paraprofessionals can be as effective as professionals but cost much less (e.g., Brown, 1974; Rioch, 1967).

How is such a mutually beneficial relationship between community and academia initiated and how does it stabilize? What are the actual costs and benefits of such interactions, and how can they be assessed quantitatively? These questions are answered in the following sections; the first with an illustration of how such a relationship developed, the second with monetary and nonmonetary data from the community and academia.

The Evolution of a Mutually Cost-Beneficial Community-Academia Relationship

Observer Stage. The monetary and nonmonetary benefits and costs of community-academia relationships seem related to the nature of the relationships and how they evolve. What developed into a course sequence for paraprofessional training in working with disturbed children began as an effort to collect observational data for evaluation research. A psychology graduate student at an academic institution became interested in working in some capacity at a local residential treatment program for behaviorally disturbed preadolescents. The program used a token economy to shape-up the children's behaviors, and later returned the children to their parents (or to foster parents) after teaching the children cognitive-behavioral self-control techniques (Russell & C. Thoresen, 1976; K. Thoresen, C. Thoresen, Klein, C. Wilbur, Becker-Haven & Haven, 1979; Tobey & C. Thoresen, 1976). Married "teaching parents" acted as children's surrogate father and mother while conducting treat-

ment, counseling the parents of the children, and maintained the house that served as the treatment facility.

The program director suggested that the graduate student collect observational data on how the program affected behavior of the disturbed children in home, school, and treatment environments. Seven observers were recruited from an undergraduate psychology course and an observation system was designed for their use. The undergraduates received academic credit for observing. At this point, the exchange of costs and benefits between academia and community was fairly one-sided. The community program received evaluation data and weekly synopses of the children's behavior in various settings. Academia provided all supervision and labor.

Tutor Stage. The initial investment of resources by academia soon paid off. From the beginning, observers had expressed a desire to become more involved in the treatment program. Involvement as observers, however, was out of the question because this might invalidate observation data.

One type of student involvement in the residential treatment did, however, suggest itself. An observer's schedule changed, preventing her from observing during convenient hours. Because this student had previous experience in tutoring problem children, her position was changed to tutor of a child in the program. This arrangement worked well; the child's school work improved and other children began asking for their own tutor, perhaps to receive the individual attention that the first child had received rather than to improve their scholastic performance. Because of this initial success, leaders of the community program were persuaded to allow five of the observers to become tutors after one academic quarter of observation.

Because the first set of tutors performed satisfactorily, tutoring established itself as a regular component of the community program. Students continued to receive academic credit for their work, with the graduate student serving as their primary supervisor. The community staff also began to work with tutors to coordinate tutoring with treatment procedures. This led the staff to provide supervision and training of tutors in treatment techniques. In turn, regular staff members received respite from their duties during the "tutoring hour" when the children were being taken care of by the tutors. Moreover, staff began to interact with the second-quarter students in a way that had not been possible with non-participant observers. Tutors essentially became junior colleagues of staff, providing admiration and psychological support for harried staff members. Thus, the community began incurring costs, such as tutor supervision, and academia received benefits of the same. The relationship was becoming an exchange of nonmonetary but very real costs and benefits.

The experimental tutoring program developed rapidly into a permanent type of student involvement in the community program. The opportunity to become a supervised adjunct to program staff attracted new students. It was decided jointly by the graduate student and staff that new students should spend one quarter as observers before being considered for a tutor position. This requirement maintained the observational data collection system, provided staff with useful information about the behavior of the children in other environments, and discouraged less motivated students from entering the training program. It also provided a research orientation on which clinical skills could later be built.

Assistant Stage. Although some of the original students left the paraprofessional system after serving as tutors for several quarters, others wished to further intensify their involvement in the community program. Because these students were the self-selected "cream" of the original crop of observers, it was not difficult to convince regular staff to take on these students in additional capacities. It was noted that advanced students could assist staff by performing teaching parent duties, by counseling the parents of the disturbed children, or by assisting the graduate student in his cost-effectiveness analyses of the treatment program.

The first few students who served as teaching parent assistants, assistant parent counselors, or assistant cost-effectiveness analysts demonstrated the benefits that the community could receive by allowing students familiar with program operations and the community context to become assistants to regular staff. The same benefits that had been received by the program from student tutors (e.g., time off from supervision of children, admiration, and support) were produced to an even greater degree by the student assistants. The time "cost" of allowing the students to occupy treatment-related positions (e.g., supervision by staff) increased of course, but so did the benefits. Soon the assistant parent counselors were allowed to counsel parents in the homes, and functioned as teaching parents while the regular staff counseled parents at the treatment facility. Teaching parent assistants also took the disturbed children on outings. The assistant cost-effectiveness analysts collected data on costs of the community program, working with the graduate student on a computer program that eventually generated cost-effectiveness indices for different children (Yates, Haven & C. Thoresen, 1979).

To maintain each of the stages in the context of the community program, a large influx of new students was required at the observer stage so that after attrition and screening by staff there would be several students in each of the third-quarter positions. To improve enrollments, the three-quarter sequence was adopted as an experimental course at the academic institution (before this, students had received credit under "independent study" or "directed research" courses). This formalization benefited both academia and community as it solidified the paraprofessional system and increased the theoretical and methodological background of trainees. The paraprofessional course had four major components at each stage of training: (a) readings, (b) practica, (c) supervision, and (d) written reports. The reading component included a manual explaining the course sequence and other manuals written for each stage by the graduate student, staff, and students who had pioneered the stages. Students at each stage of training also were assigned readings appropriate in sophistication and topic for their stage.

Quantifiable Benefits and Costs

Benefits and Costs to Academia. The formal paraprofessional training program generated $280 per student per academic quarter for the private academic institution, resulting in an average influx of $4760 per quarter and approximately $16,600 per year (lower summer enrollments produced the equivalent of one-half the normal tuition during summers). True, these students might simply have taken other courses at the university had the paraprofessional training system not existed. It is, however, important to note that such enrollments would have required some additional time from professors and other academic staff, and might have prevented other students from taking classes with limited enrollments. At least the tuition values provide a metric of the unique scholastic and training contribution that the paraprofessional program made to the academic institution—a contribution that would not have been possible if the residential program and paraprofessional training program had not existed. Nonmonetizable but quantifiable benefits to academia included more than five publications (e.g., Yates, Haven & C. Thoresen, 1979), a senior honors project, and more than seven student papers presented at regional and national conventions. The latter benefits, although nonmonetizable, seem especially significant because they are more the coin of the realm in academia than are dollars.

In return for the above benefits, academia contributed meeting room space (prorated on the basis of square-foot rental rates for comparable office facilities at $2000/year), office equipment (prorated at $320/year), and advertising for personnel (approximately $80/year). Academia also contributed a substantial amount of labor to the training system, and thus to the community, via student involvement. If the time that graduate and undergraduate personnel put into the program had been paid according to local payscales for mental health workers, it would have cost approximately $5600/quarter or $19,600/year (given lower enrollments during the summer quarter).

Of course, the above costs are estimates and are somewhat subjective. They are, however, based on observable events and services, and provide some quantitative measure of the very real if "intangible" resources exchanged between academia and community.

In economics terminology, these were "opportunity costs"—resources that were valuable simply because they might have been consumed by other organizations—but they were not "cash" costs (cf. Thomas, 1971). Nevertheless, the above estimates allow some nonmonetary costs incurred by academia because of the training course to be quantified and compared to the estimated values of benefits. The opportunity costs total to roughly $22,000/year—about $5400 more than tuition benefits, with a benefit/cost ratio of .89. However, if research, publication, dissertation, and paper-reading benefits could also be expressed in dollar units, the benefit-to-cost ratio would certainly exceed unity. Thus, academia broke more than even in terms of benefit/cost, from *its* perspective. To the extent that these costs were not tangible from the perspective of the academic institution, it received more in benefits than it paid in costs in its relationship with the community.

Benefits and Costs to the Community. It was in the very nature of the community-academia relationship stimulated by the paraprofessional training system that what were *costs* to the academic institution were *benefits* received by the community treatment program, and that benefits received by the academic institution were opportunity, if not cash, costs paid by the community program. Thus, the community received from academia about $22,000/year of manhours, meeting space, and office equipment. As an opportunity cost only, the community provided to academia approximately $19,600/year in tuition. Again, it might be said that these tuition monies would have been received through other courses if the training program had not existed. It also could be said that the training program allowed other students to take better advantage of academic resources, and may even have allowed additional students to take regular courses. These tuition figures provide a measurement of a contribution; the data are not perfect, but they serve the purpose better than any other

data. Also, because the academic institution was attended by students from across the nation, only a small fraction of the actual tuition was paid by the immediate community in which the treatment program was based. Just as the benefit-to-cost ratio was approximately one for academia, so was it close to unity (1.12) for the community.

Of course, organizations, whether "profit" or "nonprofit," rarely engage in activities in which they do not obtain what they *perceive* to be substantially more benefits than costs. Why did the academic institution and the community-based program become involved in the paraprofessional system—an activity in which they apparently lost as much as they gained? The answer is that, *from the perspective of academia,* there were few tangible costs and the relationship was mainly "gravy." The benefits of course instruction, supervision, research, and the other factors listed in Table 1 were tangible to academia, but its costs were not. *From the perspective of the community,* its opportunity costs were also intangible but the manhours, space, and equipment provided by the academic institution were very tangible benefits. In this way, the relationship was cost-beneficial for both academia and community *when viewed from the particular perspectives held by the different organizations.* This phenomenon might be termed "cost-beneficial symbiosis." If benefits had not been perceived as exceeding costs by either party, the relationship probably would have been terminated.

Benefits to Paraprofessional Trainees. This paper has focused primarily on the role played by the community and academia, and on the benefits received and costs incurred

Table 1

Community-Academia Interaction as an Exchange of
Nonmonetary and Monetary Costs and Benefits of a Paraprofessional Training System

Costs		Benefits	
Nonmonetary	Monetary	Nonmonetary	Monetary
Academia			
-Time devoted to nonresearch and noninstructional activities	$22,000 (opportunity cost)	-Instructors -Paraprofessional training -Research opportunities -Publications -Dissertations -Opportunity to test theories -Increased employment opportunities for graduates	$19,600 (tuition)
Community			
-Instruction and training of students -Extra time devoted to research-related activities	$19,600 (opportunity cost)	-Third-party information about parent and child behavior in non-treatment environments -Tutoring of children -Assistance to teaching parents in work with children and parents -Teaching Parent and Program Coordinator Candidates -Innovative treatment techniques -Savings in "break-in" time for staff	$22,000 (labor)

Note.   Monetary costs are per annum. The monetary and nonmonetary costs and benefits are largely independent. The monetary cost and benefit values are not attempts at placing dollar units on the value of the nonmonetary cost and benefit items. Rather, nonmonetary costs and benefits are noted because they are difficult or impossible to monetize, but are nevertheless important in analyzing the community-academia interaction.

by the same. But what about the students who received paraprofessional training and who thus provided the medium for the cost-beneficial relationship between the community and academia? Did they, the third party and principal intermediary of the academia-community relationship, actually benefit in a measurable manner? Certainly the students paid the cost of their time and effort, and the opportunity cost of forsaken employment. Although the training system has not functioned long enough to judge its impact on students' employment potential (or increments in expected lifetime earnings), more immediately available data suggest that the course benefited trainees in several ways.

The most obvious measure of benefit to students is the enrollment of new and continuing students in the training system. Over the several years in which the system was developed, more than 100 student-quarters of participation were produced. About 80% of these students were returning to participate in another stage of the system; some staying as long as five quarters. In addition, several graduate students from another local academic institution participated in the course sequence for several quarters without even receiving academic credit.

Student course ratings also indicated that the course was "worth it." The ratings were anonymous and students were not told that ratings would be used in this article. In response to the question:

> This course has taught me _____ about how to function in applied psychology treatment programs than other courses have.

students gave a mean rating of 7.3 on a 10-point scale that had the anchor points "much less" (1) and "much more" (10). This mean rating was significantly different from the mid-scale rating of 5.5, $t(9) = 2.84$, $p<.01$. Trainees also indicated that the course had increased their interest in applied psychology, giving a mean rating of 7.0 on the same 10-point scale in response to:

> During my participation in this course, I have become _____ interested in administering psychological treatment.

This mean rating was also significantly different from the mid-scale rating, $t(9) = 2.19$, $p<.05$.

Perhaps most significantly, one of the students who married after he graduated from the course sequence was accepted by the community program along with his wife as a full-time, paid teaching parent. The couple later became the coordinators of the entire program, occupying a position only below that of the director of the treatment program. The former trainee continued to work in this capacity; his wife became a graduate student in counseling psychology at the academic institution.

Another student who progressed through the training stages also has become a full-time, paid staff member of the community program. This student also supervises the paraprofessional training system. The fact that the treatment program is paying former trainees is perhaps the strongest indicator that the community perceives the training system to be cost-beneficial, and that students can benefit from the training in terms of employability.

References

Brown, W. F. Effectiveness of paraprofessionals: The evidence. *Personnel and Guidance Journal*, 1974, *53*, 257-263.

Rioch, M. J. Pilot projects in training mental health counselors. In E. L. Cowen, E. A. Gardner, & M. Zax (Eds.), *Emerging approaches to mental health problems*. New York: Appleton-Century-Crofts, 1967.

Russell, M. L., & Thoresen, C. E. Teaching decision-making skills to children. In J. D. Krumboltz & C. E. Thoresen (Eds.), *Counseling methods*. New York: Holt, Rinehart & Winston, 1976.

Thomas, J. A. *The productive school: A systems analysis approach to educational administration*. New York: Wiley, 1971.

Thoresen, K. E., Thoresen, C. E., Klein, S. B., Wilbur, C. S., Becker-Haven, J. F., & Haven, W. G. Learning House: Helping troubled children and their parents change themselves. In J. S. Stumphauzer (Ed.), *Progress in behavior therapy with delinquents* (Vol. 2). Springfield, IL: Charles C Thomas, 1979.

Tobey, T. S., & Thoresen, C. E. Helping Bill reduce aggressive behaviors. In J. D. Krumboltz & C. E. Thoresen (Eds.), *Counseling methods*. New York: Holt, Rinehart & Winston, 1976.

Yates, B. T., Haven, W. G., & Thoresen, C. E. Cost-effectiveness analyses at Learning House: How much change for how much money? In J. S. Stumphauzer (Ed.), *Progress in behavior therapy with delinquents*. Springfield, IL: Charles C Thomas, 1979.

Notes

1. Thanks is given to the many people who helped the course described in this paper become a reality, especially William G. Haven and Stanley Klein, Dr. Carl E. Thoresen, Dr. Steven M. Zifferblatt, the staff and clients of Learning House, and the students of Stanford University. Andy Parnes of the Stanford Workshops on Political and Social Issues was most helpful in obtaining university sponsorship of the course. The American University assisted in final preparation of this manuscript.

Post-Graduation Educational and Occupational Choices of Psychology Undergraduate Practicum Participants: Issues for the Psychology Profession

Frank J. Prerost
Western Illinois University

Participants enter human services in greater proportion and show greater diversity if graduate work is elected.

A significant development in undergraduate curricula for psychology majors has occurred in the past decade. The availability of a field experience course has been instituted at numerous universities (Matthews, 1979) and Community Colleges (Becker, 1978). These applied options for psychology majors have required students to volunteer in human service agencies as a method to earn academic credit. The popularity of field experiences among students has been well documented (Caffrey, Berger, Cole, Marx & Senn, 1977) and appears to be increasing (Boltuck, Peterson & Murphy, 1980). In their participation, students achieve insight into the application of theories and information encountered in the classroom. Support for implementing field experiences has come from academic psychologists who view this endeavor as a means toward personal enhancement while providing a service to the community (Caffrey et al., 1977; Kuppersmith & Blair, 1977). Students' self-confidence and esteem is beneficially affected as they enter the delivery system for human services. A sense of accomplishment and purpose for studying psychology ensues (Hess, Harrison, Fink, Lilliston, Aponte & Korn, 1978).

Agencies involved in the human services have been cooperative partners in the development of field experiences (Becker, 1978; Vande Creek & Thompson, 1977). Mental health care facilities have sought practicum students as a means to supplement staff while augmenting an identity as a training facility. The latter function enhances the community visibility and reputation of the care-giving facility. The result has been a dramatic increase in the number of students working in human services in order to earn academic credit.

The field experience courses are one attempt to respond to the needs of students immediately entering the job market (Nazarro, 1976). The field work trains students for work supervised by doctoral level psychologists in state institutions, mental health clinics, counseling centers, correctional facilities, testing centers, and personnel departments (Nish, 1979). Field experience enables students to learn specific skills in the areas of observation and assessment techniques, report writing, applied learning theory, and personal relationships.

Prior to the increment of field work courses, psychology departments followed curricula primarily designed to prepare students to enter graduate training programs (Thomas, 1975). This situation prevailed despite evidence indicating that many undergraduate psychology majors were seeking employment in the human services directly upon graduation rather than continuing in graduate programs. Cates (1973) found only 29% of those earning a bachelor degree in psychology plan for graduate education and of this number 50% do not find graduate placement. Consequently, Korn and Nodine (1975) pointed to the conclusion that the vast majority, up to 85%, of psychology majors enter the job market with a bachelor's degree as their sole preparation for career work in the human services.

Although the potential goals and benefits of field experiences have been delineated, a lack of follow-up information exists. Prerost (1980a) examined field experience students during their practicum activities. He found a differential pattern of success during the practica depending on coping strategies used by the students in response to stresses encountered. Further research by Prerost (1980b) has indicated that certain field experiences do not lend themselves as beneficial learning situations for practicum students. Keeley and Kreutzer (1981) documented the beneficial effects of a formalized mental health worker program for undergraduates, but the question of how general practical experiences may affect student career/educational choices following graduation remains unclear.

With the increased implementation of practica options, a number of pertinent questions concerning the impact of field experience on students must be addressed. Among the issues currently unanswered include: Does field experience direct more students to traditional graduate training or to the professional schools in psychology? Are participants more successful than regular majors in securing employment in the human service areas? Do participants prefer entry to the human service field? Does field experience provide students a better understanding of the diversity of employment opportunities for the psychology major? These questions are suggested issues of significance for undergraduate training in psychology and need to be addressed by the professional community. Both the practicing and academic psychologist have increasing possibility of encountering field experience students, so they need an understanding and awareness of such experience and its effects on students.

This paper attempts to examine some of the issues outlined above. Students participating in field experiences were surveyed for five graduating classes to determine the type of placement assumed by these graduates. The placement data for five graduating classes of psychology majors who did not complete a field practicum served as a basis of comparison to the former practicum students.

Method. The information reported in this study concerns students who in the past five years were graduates from one medium sized university where they were psychology majors. The field experience program consists of elective courses available to the psychology major in the junior or senior year of study. Students can select this option for one or two semesters. The vast majority of students select the field experience course in their senior year and complete only one of the two courses available. The participating students are required to work in a mental health/human service agency a minimum of nine hours per week during the semester to earn three hours of academic credit.

The university's psychology department provides a traditional selection of courses with degree requirements centered around research and non-applied courses. Students who choose the field experience course must complete the same major requirements as all psychology majors.

In the last five years, a total of 96 students completed the field practica (56 males, 40 females). The average age of the students during participation was 21.2 years. In this period of time, 327 students (171 males, 156 females) were psychology graduates who did not participate in field experience. The average age for this group was 21.7 years. The majority of students shared a middle socioeconomic urban background.

Although all students interested in a field practicum received a screening interview with the program coordinator, no student requesting a field placement was refused. Only one student dropped from the course after placement began.

No typical field practicum can be described because the placements and nature of duties varied greatly in this five year period. New settings were constantly added as others limited or cancelled their involvement. But all students, regardless of placement setting, were provided the following: (a) direct service contact with a clinical group evincing psychological, emotional and/or intellectual handicaps; (b) direct supervision from an agency staff person; (c) a variety of service activities; and (d) weekly seminars at the academic institution allowing for a sharing of information and experience among students.

Results. Of the ninety-six students who completed the field experience in the five year period studied, 92 (96%) of these students entered employment or advanced education related to the human services following graduation. Of the four remaining students, three began law school and the fourth developed a serious illness precluding employment or advanced study. Within this field experience group, a majority of students (59%) found employment at human service agencies, and 41% continued their formal education in graduate or professional schools. On a percentage basis, the field experience students, when compared to the 327 psychology majors who graduated during this period, exhibited a greater orientation toward the human service field. Only 29% of the nonparticipating majors secured employment in the social services or continued their education in graduate programs. The psychology majors without field experience tended to secure employment falling in the categories of sales, management, clerical, and education. This group of employment situations accounted for 60% of the graduates in the five year study period. Occupations not necessarily requiring a college degree; e.g. carpentry, truck driving, accounted for the remaining 11% of the graduating majors.

Examination of the advanced education choices among field experience students demonstrated a diversity in options selected. The field experience group was accepted at and entered a wider range of social/human service related programs than did the other students. The former group enrolled in programs such as school psychology, social work, community mental health, physical therapy and professional schools in psychology in addition to traditional clinical and counseling programs. The non-field practicum students focused on clinical or experimental graduate work predominately at the master's degree level.

Diversity was also found in the applied jobs obtained by individuals who completed field practica, and these graduates showed a wide range of official titles. Vocational counselor, youth/adolescent worker, mental health technician, alcoholism counselor, psychometrician, social worker, intake worker, substance abuse counselor, child care work, mental retardation specialist, evaluator, and rehabilitation specialist are only a sampling of the variety of roles assumed by field experience graduates. Numerous graduates entered employment at the facility or agency where their practicum was completed. The agencies which hired former practicum students reported that the field experience was an opportunity to observe potential staff. The practicum served as a trial period for students to demonstrate competencies and potentials for therapeutic skills. This observational function of the field experience for potential employers is a beneficial arrangement for both agency and students. The students who earned employment began staff functions at a higher salary level than normally offered entry level personnel. Adjustment to the new role of staff member was reported to be facilitated as a result of practicum experience.

Discussion. The results raise significant issues related to the possible effects of practica on student occupational pursuits. Although caution must be observed in the interpretation of results in terms of cause and effect, the outcomes are indicative of the need for further and continued research on field experiences and student occupational plans. This study found large differences between field experience students and other majors in terms of their continued involvement in the human service field following graduation. These findings support many of the rationales utilized in the creation and support of undergraduate field experience course options.

Vital questions that must be examined pertain to the students who participate in field experience. Does a practicum course attract the highly motivated and concerned student? Are field experiences instilling motivation and human concern within those who participate? Does a practicum merely reinforce existing concern and interest in the human services? Depending on how these questions are answered, there may be a significant impact on professional psychology. If field experience courses increase the number of students searching for entry level positions in the human services, can agencies absorb the influx of new applicants? Will this depress salary levels for entry positions as the number of applicants increases? Bachelor level individuals under supervision could begin to replace master's degree students, or compete for existing openings in the human/social services. Increased desire for advanced training could entail the support of new professional schools in psychology. This latter development may eventually lead master's degree programs to obsolescence. Undergraduate programs may begin to emphasize the applied nature of psychology as they respond to the practicum students' success in realizing human service employment. The conjectures suggested above point to potential dangers in overemphasizing the applied fields as viable alternatives for the majority of students in psychology.

The practical benefits students derive from field experiences, a broader understanding of self and the human services, must be evaluated in light of the issues suggested. Continued evaluation of the impact of practical experiences in individuals' career choices is indicated. Clear identification and description of who selects field work is a necessary step in this evaluation process.

References

Becker, H. J. Curricula of associate degree mental health/human service training programs. *Community Mental Health Journal*, 1978, *14*, 133-146.

Boltuck, M. A., Peterson, T. L., & Murphy, R. J. Preparing undergraduate psychology majors for employment in the human service delivery system. *Teaching of Psychology*, 1980, *7*, 75-78.

Caffrey, B., Berger, L., Cole, S., Marx, D., & Senn, D. Integrating professional programs in a traditional undergraduate psychology program. *Teaching of Psychology*, 1977, *4*, 7-13.

Cates, J. Baccalaureates in psychology 1969 and 1970. *American Psychologist*, 1973, *28*, 262-264.

Hess, A., Harrison, A., Fink, R., Lilliston, L., Aponte, J., & Korn, J. Critical issues on undergraduate training of various community settings. *Teaching of Psychology*, 1978, *5*, 81-86.

Keeley, S. M., & Kreutzer, J. S. A follow-up evaluation of an undergraduate community mental health worker training program. *Teaching of Psychology*, 1981, *8*, 28-31.

Korn, J., & Nodine, B. Facts and questions concerning career training of the psychology major. *Teaching of Psychology*, 1975, *2*, 117-119.

Kuppersmith, J., & Blair, R. Training undergraduates as co-leaders of multi-family counseling groups. *Teaching of Psychology*, 1977, *4*, 3-6.

Matthews, J. Undergraduate field placements: Survey and issues. *Teaching of Psychology*, 1979, *6*, 148-151.

Nazarro, J. Identity crisis in psychology. *Change*, 1976, *8*, 44-45.

Nish, W. W. A psychology technician training program. *Teaching of Psychology*, 1979, *6*, 206-209.

Prerost, F. J. Reactive patterns of undergraduate psychology practicum students in residential child care facilities: Implications for supervisors and child care workers. *Child Care Quarterly*, 1980, *9*, 117-123. (a)

Prerost, F. J. Issues in the implementation of a child psychology practicum for undergraduates. *Child Psychiatry and Human Development*, 1980, *11*, 96-104. (b)

Thomas, E. An alternative approach to undergraduate training in psychology. *Teaching of Psychology*, 1975, *2*, 80-81.

VandeCreek, L. B., & Thompson, G. Management of undergraduate psychology internships. *Teaching of Psychology*, 1977, *4*, 177-180.

A Follow-up Evaluation of an Undergraduate Community Mental Health Worker Training Program

Stuart M. Keeley and
Jeffrey S. Kreutzer
Bowling Green State University

Detailed post-graduate data about careers of students having had field experience are supportive.

Presently, a variety of programs are offered to the undergraduate psychology major to provide him/her with "real world" clinical experience as well as useful applied clinical skills (e.g., Danish et al., 1978; Eason, 1979; Lorion, 1979). Whereas many of these programs require a good deal of time commitment on the student's part, little is known about the impact of such training opportunities on the participating student (Titley, 1979). A number of questions remain unanswered. Do the students find the experience beneficial? Are these students attracted to postgraduate applied clinical work? Does program participation result in improved job opportunities? What are students' reactions to the often times frustrating encounters in actual mental health work?

In an effort to answer these questions, we conducted a follow-up evaluation of the formalized mental health worker training program we have been conducting with psychology undergraduates at Bowling Green State University since the Fall of 1973 (see Shemberg & Keeley, 1976, 1979, for a complete program description). Although many details of the program have changed over the years, the major emphasis has remained the same. Students receive one quarter of behaviorally oriented assessment and intervention skills, followed by a two-quarter placement in a community mental health setting, where students function primarily as Behavior Analysts. The general Behavior Analyst program goals have been to: (a) provide undergraduates interested in the mental health field with "relevant" educational and practicum experiences; (b) stimulate undergraduate interest in the mental health profession; (c) provide these undergraduates with marketable skills; and (d) provide services to local mental health agencies as the student progresses through the program.

Traditionally, we have obtained feedback from students immediately following program completion. While this feedback has been consistently positive, its utility is limited. Students just completing the program cannot realistically evaluate the effects of the program on future experience, and it is likely that their immediate feedback about the program's impact is significantly biased by demand characteristics. Post-graduate follow-up evaluation provides the student with a greater opportunity to reflect on the program's utility. Additionally, students can evaluate the impact of the program on their subsequent vocational and professional choices and performance. Thus, to evaluate the long-term impact of the program, follow-up information was obtained by use of a questionnaire.

Method. A list of all individuals who had completed the Behavior Analyst program since its inception in 1973 and who had graduated from the University was obtained from course registration records. This yielded 11, 12, 10, and 6 individuals for the years 1973-1974, 1975-1976, 1976-1977, and 1977-1978, respectively, a total sample of 39. The program was not operative during 1974-1975. The mean overall undergraduate grade point average of these psychology majors was 3.2 on a 4 point scale.

In addition to providing current demographic data, the questionnaire focused on three primary areas: (a) student employment and graduate school status, including relevance of subprofessional training to post-graduate employment experiences; (b) student evaluations of their experiences in the program; and (c) current professional interests. Detailed information on each of these areas is presented below.

Student employment and graduate status. Information was obtained on employment since completing the Behavior Analyst program, including: dates employed, salary, position held, and responsibilities. In addition, graduates were asked whether training had or had not been helpful in the position and to explain their reasons for the belief. Subjects presently holding a mental health position were asked to indicate the percentage of time they spent directed toward: individual focus, family or peer involvement, case consultation, agency program consultation, and other unspecified areas. Respondents who were enrolled in graduate training programs or who had completed advanced degrees were asked to specify the type of degree, the school they were enrolled in, inclusion dates, and when they had completed or expected to complete the degree requirements. Additionally, those individuals who had not taken a position related to the mental health field were asked to indicate the reasons for this outcome.

Student evaluation of Behavior Analyst program. Respondents were asked to list their training program field experiences and inclusive dates. They were required to indicate their two most valuable and two least valuable training

experiences in the program and explain these views. The questionnaire assessed subjects' opinions on the least and most valuable skills provided in the program, and allowed additional comments regarding the training model. Additionally, subjects were asked to indicate content areas that should be eliminated, content that should be included that was not adequately presented, and their reasons for these views. Finally, the following forced choice item was asked: "Indicate which of the following you most agree with: (a) the Behavior Analyst program should continue to be offered as it is with no major changes; (b) the Behavior Analyst program should continue to be offered, but major changes should be made in it; (c) the Behavior Analyst program should be discontinued, and should be replaced by a mental health training program based on an entirely different model; and (d) the Behavior Analyst program should be discontinued, and should not be replaced by any kind of mental health training program.

Current professional interests. Respondents were asked to indicate their current theoretical orientation and their membership in any professional organizations. In an attempt to assess continuing educational experiences, subjects were asked to indicate: (a) conferences, workshops, and special training seminars they had attended; (b) publications related to the mental health profession read monthly; and (c) any other means used to remain abreast of developments in the mental health field. A list of teaching experiences, including conferences and workshops taught, was also obtained. Respondents serving in community agencies on a voluntary basis were asked to specify the name of the organization along with their role and responsibilities. Various aspects of research interests were assessed including publications/ presentations, grants received, and current major research interests. Additionally, respondents were asked to indicate the position or responsibilities they would ideally like to have five years from the present.

Addresses of former graduates were obtained from University alumni listings. Listings were obtained for 32 of the 39 graduates. The questionnaire was mailed with a cover letter explaining its purpose, and emphasizing its importance as a feedback device. Subjects were asked to return the completed questionnaires within a month. Those not complying within two months were sent a follow-up letter.

Results. A total of 22 questionnaires were returned, a return rate of 69%. Return rates for each class were: 1973-1974 (5/8), 1975-1976 (8/10), 1976-1977 (5/8), and 1977-1978 (4/6). A comparison of results obtained from early and late respondents (those responding to the follow-up letter) indicated similar satisfaction regarding the Behavior Analyst program for both groups, suggesting that a delay in returning completed questionnaires was not an indication of lesser satisfaction with the program. Therefore, data for early and late respondents, as well as males (n = 9) and females (n = 13) were analyzed as a whole. The mean GPA of the 22 respondents was 3.3 whereas that of the non-respondents was 3.2, suggesting a high degree of similarity in ability. Results are presented in terms of the three primary questionnaire content areas:

Student employment and graduate school status. A major intent of the survey was to determine how many graduates became directly involved in the mental health profession following graduation. Thus the graduates' listings of positions were categorized as: mental health position; graduate school in mental health related program; graduate school in non-mental health related program; and other. Respondents were classified as having a mental health position if their duties included any of the following: therapy, counseling, assessment, treatment planning, and research or administration directly related to these. Respondents were classified independently by the two authors into one of the four categories with 100% agreement.

At the time of the survey, 45% of the graduates held mental health positions, 27% were enrolled in a mental health related graduate school program, 5% were enrolled in a graduate program not directly related to providing mental health services (experimental psychology), and 23% were neither engaged in mental health positions nor enrolled in graduate school. Fifty-nine percent had held at least one mental health position (excluding university assistantships) since completing the program, and 50% had either completed or were in the process of completing advanced degrees.

Seventeen of the program graduates had held at least one mental health related position since graduating, a total of 24 positions. Seven graduates listed working in residential child/adolescent treatment centers as child care workers (n = 2), hospital aides (n = 2), a social worker, a security youth worker, and a behavior analyst. Three positions had been obtained in children's day treatment centers—as social workers (n = 2) and as an associate teacher (primary function being behavior management). Included among seven positions in community intervention and related programs were: staff therapist, treatment coordinator, psychologist (n = 3), and probation officer (n = 2). Four graduates listed working in adult residential treatment centers, three as alcohol addiction counselors and one as a recreation therapist. Two were working as school psychologists.

The most frequently listed responsibilities for the 24 positions held included: therapy/counseling (n = 7), behavioral assessment (n = 6), social and personal skills training (n = 4), and community consultation (n = 2). Eighty-six percent of the respondents answered affirmatively to the question, "Has behavior analyst training been helpful?" The primary reason offered for this response was that more of the skills acquired in the program were directly relevant to job requirements.

For those 15 persons citing their most recent employment in the mental health field, the average percent of time spent in the following areas were: individual focus (44%), family or peer involvement (9%), agency involvement (7%), case consultation (10%), agency consultation (17%), and other miscellaneous activities (13%).

The salary range for those employed in the mental health field who did not obtain advanced degrees (n = 6) was $4,000-9,000 annually. For those employed with advanced degrees (n = 4), the annual salary range was $10,000-16,500. The advanced degrees earned included two Masters of Education, a Master of Social Work, and a Specialists Degree in Education.

Those who were not employed in the mental health field included seven individuals in the process of completing advanced degrees. These degrees were: clinical psychology (n = 3), behavior analysis, experimental psychology, social work, and school psychology. Of the remaining graduates not employed in the mental health field (n = 5), three indicated they still felt the training program was helpful.

Reasons for employment outside the field included: lack of mental health employment opportunities (n = 3), financial advantage in other fields (n = 2), and greater interest in other careers (n = 1).

Evaluation of experiences while enrolled in Behavior Analyst program. Respondents were asked to state their two most and two least valuable training experiences. Three kinds of experiences were emphasized as most valuable. Eighty-six percent stated that their placement in the field was one of the most valuable experiences. The fall quarter experiences of "sitting-in" on a Psychological Services Center team (41%) and interview practice (27%) were the two other most frequently cited experiences. Sitting in on a Psychological Services Center team involved a weekly, full-day observation of clinical faculty and graduate students engaged in ongoing assessment and treatment planning activities.

Only eight respondents cited least valuable experiences. Two experiences were cited more than once; sitting-in on the Psychological Services Center team (n = 3), and the use of the programmed text in behavior modification. (This text was abandoned after the 1973-1974 training year.)

Respondents were asked to state the least and most valuable *specific skills* acquired in the program. Twenty-one respondents listed 39 skills. Frequently cited valuable skills were: behavior modification program design and management (12/39), interviewing skills (11/39), and assessment/observation techniques (5/39). Also listed were: report writing, counseling, and research skills. Fourteen least valuable skills were listed by 13 respondents, and none were listed more than twice.

Eighteen respondents cited material that was not adequately presented, but there was little consensus. Suggestions for additional material included requests for greater emphasis on report writing (n = 2), training in projective and other forms of personality testing (n = 4), training in Gordon's Parent Effectiveness Training (n = 2), ethical issues, research techniques (n = 3), and career planning for program graduates. When asked to indicate content that should be dropped, eight left the item blank and 11 stated that nothing should be dropped. There was no aspect of the program that more than one individual desired to see dropped.

On the forced choice item reflecting general satisfaction, 91% of program graduates agreed with the statement that the Behavior Analyst program should be continued as is, with no major changes. The remaining 9% indicated that the program should be continued, but with major changes. None indicated that the program should be discontinued.

Current professional interests. A majority of respondents specifically listed their current theoretical orientation as either eclectic (45%, 9/20) or behavioral (40%, 8/20). The remainder (n = 3) considered their orientation client-centered, physiological, or psychoanalytic.

A majority of graduates continued to pursue interests in the mental health field. Ninety-one percent had had continuing education experiences. This included participation in workshops, conferences, and graduate courses. Sixty-four percent reported reading at least one mental health related journal regularly each month. Many graduates were members of mental health organizations at local, state, or national levels. Sixty-seven percent were members of at least one organization, with half of these enrolled in two or more. A number of graduates have either been employed as teaching assistants in university settings (9%), or have served as workshop instructors (63%). Additionally, 32% were serving voluntarily in community mental health organizations.

Seventeen respondents listed research interests. Among these were: behavior analysis/modification, child/developmental psychology, psychophysiology, social psychology, community psychology, drug/alcohol addiction, family therapy, sexual function/dysfunction, and program evaluation. Although none of the program graduates had received a grant, one was awaiting a decision on a submitted grant proposal, and another was in the process of writing a grant. Thirty-two percent of the sample had either published a journal article or had given a presentation.

All respondents indicated their ideal employment position five years in the future. A majority (81%) desired mental health related positions. Frequently cited were positions in community mental health centers (27%) and school settings (18%). Others desired positions in child guidance centers, counseling and family service agencies, universities, and psychiatric hospitals. Three graduates were uncertain of their future goals, and one desired to pursue a career in business.

Discussion.   These follow-up data clearly indicate that graduates of the Behavior Analyst program regard their training as a useful and positive experience which contributes significantly to their career development and upward mobility. Program graduates have remained actively involved in the mental health field at an exceptionally high rate. This rate of participation in mental health related positions seems especially high in comparison to data obtained in other related follow-up studies. Typically, a majority of psychology graduates find employment or advanced education in business, law, and other non-psychology related professions and trades (Davis, 1979; Titley, 1979). However, more than 75% of our graduates are either employed in mental health related positions or are seeking advanced degrees directly related to this area.

Students who enter the Behavior Analyst program are carefully screened prior to their admittance into the program, and their mean overall grade point average, 3.2, is somewhat higher than that reported in other surveys of training programs for undergraduates (Davis, 1979). Also, students tend to enter the program because of a reported interest in "helping others." As such, it is difficult to ascertain to what degree this high rate of involvement in the mental health field is directly affected by their experiences in the program. However, it seems quite clear to us that the program does have a significant effect on students' later involvement in psychology-related activities. For example, many students have taken jobs which have required the skills learned in the program, and a number reported receiving jobs because of their participation. This suggests a direct link between the program and future career activities.

Another major piece of converging evidence to suggest that the program has a substantial impact on the students' careers is the large number of unsolicited letters received by the program directors. Students have written describing how the training has been helpful not only in their professional lives, but in their non-professional lives as well. In the last three years, the program directors have received ten such letters which in our opinion and experience far exceeds the typical rate of such feedback from undergraduate psychology majors.

Graduated behavior analysts unanimously viewed the program as something which should continue to be offered in the psychology department, and only two of 22 saw a need for any major changes. Additionally, the majority of graduated BAs rated a number of specific skills as valuable to them. Student placements, including field experiences, "sitting in" on the Psychological Services Center team, and interview practice were also rated as valuable training experiences. These findings suggest that the placement experiences, and the skills being taught—observation, assessment, intervention, and communication—have true relevance to the student well beyond the year-long training period.

Initially, we had been uncertain as to whether students might see the program orientation as too "narrow" and perhaps would perceive a greater need for training in a psychodynamic or humanistic orientation as a result of working with diverse professionals. The finding that few graduates suggested major program changes, and that 40% listed themselves as behavioristic and 45% as eclectic supports the inference that the program's behavioristic orientation had an enduring influence.

Although there is converging evidence supporting the success of the program in achieving its goals, several reservations remain about inferences drawn from the data. All data are self-reports and not anonymous; such data could be biased. For example, responses could be affected by an effort to please the investigators. However, it is our belief that biases affecting the major conclusions are minimal. Most of the questions required primarily descriptive, rather than evaluative responses. Questions like What is your present occupation? and What are your job responsibilities? are much less subject to bias than a question like, Was Behavior Analyst training helpful on the job?

A sampling bias may also exist in that respondents' attitudes, and post graduate choices from non-respondents may have been different. This is impossible to ascertain, but the high rate of responses and the relatively uniform positive reaction suggests that the missing data would have had to be strikingly different to have a significant impact on the overall pattern of results.

In summary, program graduates look upon their experiences with a favorable eye. Students leave the program with a postive attitude toward the skills they have learned and toward the mental health field in general. Not only does the Behavior Analyst program seem to provide a unique and directly relevant educational experience, but it also appears to be having the impact of directly counteracting the manpower shortage problem in the mental health fields. Those who complete the program continue to participate in the mental health field. Encountering real world problems and frustrations does not turn them off to psychology. In our opinion, if a psychology department is interested in facilitating interest in applied psychology and providing a program that meets the students' needs for "relevance" we highly recommend the implementation of an experiential program similar to that developed at Bowling Green State University.

References

Danish, S. J., D'Augelli, A. R., Brock, G. W., Conter, K. R., & Meyer, R. J.   A symposium on skill dissemination for paraprofessionals: Models of training, supervision, and utilization. *Professional Psychology*, 1978, *9*, 16-37.

Davis, J. R.   Where did they all go? A job survey of BA graduates. In P. J. Woods (Ed.), *The psychology major*. Washington, DC: American Psychological Association, 1979.

Eason, R. G.   A combined degree-certificate program for paraprofessional training. In P. J. Woods (Ed.), *The psychology major*. Washington, DC: American Psychological Association, 1979.

Lorion, R. P.   Undergraduate training in community psychology and community mental health. In P. J. Woods (Ed.), *The psychology major*. Washington, DC: American Psychological Association, 1979.

Shemberg, K., & Keeley, S. M.   Training undergraduates as subprofessional community mental health workers. *Teaching of Psychology*, 1976, *3*, 118-120.

Shemberg, K., & Keeley, S. M.   Undergraduate training in community mental health services. In P. J. Woods (Ed.), *The psychology major*. Washington, DC: American Psychological Association, 1979.

Titley, R. W.   Whatever happened to the class of '67? Psychology baccalaureate holders one, five, and ten years after graduation. In P. J. Woods (Ed.), *The psychology major*. Washington, DC: American Psychological Association, 1979.

Subject Index

Appendix

All articles in this book appeared originally in the journal, *Teaching of Psychology.* This appendix provides the year and volume of original publication, plus page numbers, to facilitate proper citation of these articles.

Section I: Advising

1. Developing Strategies for Advising
   Titley & Titley, 1982, *9,* 45–49.
   Halgin & Halgin, 1984, *11,* 67–70.
   Kremer, 1980, *7,* 177–179.
   Gielen, 1980, *7,* 238–239.
2. Improving Academic Performance
   a. Study Techniques
   O'Connor, Chassie, & Walther, 1980, *7,* 231–233.
   Spiers & Pihl, 1976, *3,* 33–34.
   Aamodt, 1982, *9,* 118–120.
   Aamodt, 1982, *9,* 234–235.
   Dean, Malott, & Fulton, 1983, *10,* 77–81.
   Hindman, 1980, *7,* 166–168.
   b. Note Taking Strategies
   Palkovitz & Lore, 1980, *7,* 159–161.
   Baker, & Lombardi, 1985, *12,* 28–32.
   c. Test Taking Strategies
   Paul & Rosenkoetter, 1980, *7,* 108–109.
   Johnston, 1977, *4,* 148–149.
   McClain, 1983, *10,* 69–71.
   Cirino-Gerena, 1981, *8,* 53–54.
   d. Changing Answers on Multiple Choice Tests
   Benjamin, Jr., Cavell, & Shallenberger, 1984, *11,* 133–141.
   Johnston, 1975, *2,* 178–179.
   Johnston, 1978, *5,* 44–45.
   Skinner, 1983, *10,* 220–222.
   Best, 1979, *6,* 228–230.
   Edwards & Marshall, 1977, *4,* 193–195.
3. Investigating Graduate Education in Psychology
   a. Admissions Variables
   Smith, 1985, *12,* 194–198.
   Couch & Benedict, 1983, *10,* 3–6.
   Nowaczyk & Frey, 1982, *9,* 163–165.
   Littlepage, Bragg, & Rust, 1978, *5,* 16–20.
   Korn & Lewandowski, 1981, *8,* 149–152.
   Wright & Kausler, 1984, *11,* 191.
   b. Professional School Considerations
   Scheirer, 1983, *10,* 11–15.
   Cole, 1979, *6,* 179–180.
   c. Additional Issues
   Henderson, 1982, *9,* 184–185.
   Gottlieb, 1975, *2,* 159–161.
   Lunneborg, 1982, *9,* 140–142.
   Zimbardo, 1976, *3,* 187–188.
4. Promoting Graduate Student Development
   a. Personal Development
   Delfin & Roberts, 1980, *7,* 168–171.
   Bloom & Bell, 1979, *6,* 231–232.
   Perlman & Dehart, 1985, *12,* 67–71.
   b. Teaching Skills
   Strachan, Welch, Barker, Compas, & Ferguson, 1980, *7,* 180–182.
   Lattal, 1978, *5,* 208–209.
   Grosslight, 1979, *6,* 111–112.
   Hettich, Lema-Stern, & Rizzo, 1981, *8,* 156–158.
   c. Scholarly Skills
   Glenwick & Burka, 1978, *5,* 213–214.
   Blanton, 1983, *10,* 74–77.
   Fox, 1983, *10,* 177–178.
   Heesacker, 1984, *11,* 238–239.
   Fox, 1984, *11,* 239–241.

Section II: Career Development

1. Stimulating Career Exploration and Development
   McGovern, 1979, *6,* 183–184.
   Ware, 1981, *8,* 67–71.
   Ware & Beischel, 1979, *6,* 210–213.
   Lattal, 1980, *7,* 243–244.
   Bluestein, 1977, *4,* 146–147.
   Ware & Matthews, 1980, *7,* 36–38.
2. Identifying Occupational Opportunities for Psychology Majors
   Ware & Meyer, 1981, *8,* 12–15.
   Wise, Smith, & Fulkerson, 1983, *10,* 53–54.
   Erdwins & Olivetti, 1978, *5,* 38–39.
3. Developing Occupationally Related Skills
   McGovern & Ellett, 1980, *7,* 237–238.
   Marzano, 1985, *12,* 102–103.
   Korn, 1980, *7,* 153–156.
   Prerost & Reich, 1984, *11,* 218–220.
4. Assessing Job Satisfaction Among Psychology Majors
   Lunneborg & Wilson, 1982, *9,* 199–201.
   Lunneborg, 1985, *12,* 21–22.

Section III: Field Placement

1. Exploring Administrative Issues
   VandeCreek & Fleischer, 1984, *11,* 9–14.
   Matthews, 1979, *6,* 148–151.
   Vande Creek & Thompson, 1977, *4,* 177–180.
   Barton & Duerfeldt, 1980, *7,* 146–149.
   Wolfgang, 1976, *3,* 183–184.
   Anderson & Stein, 1984, *11,* 178–179.
   Keller, 1979, *6,* 240–241.
   Dalton, 1984, *11,* 186–188.
2. Describing Undergraduate Placements
   a. Diversified Settings/Clientele
   Hess, Harrison, Shantz, Fink, Zepelin, Lilliston, Aponte, & Korn, 1978, *5,* 81–86.
   Fernald, Tedeschi, Siegfried, Gilmore, Grimsley, & Chipley, 1982, *9,* 155–160.
   Sherman, 1982, *9,* 82–85.
   b. Specific Settings/Clientele
   Stollak, 1975, *2,* 8–11.
   Prerost, 1981, *8,* 19–22.
   Moore & Bondy, 1978, *5,* 135–139.
   Fox, Lopuch, & Fisher, 1984, *11,* 113–115.
   Swenson, 1981, *8,* 49.
   Kuppersmith, Blair, & Slotnick, 1977, *4,* 3–6.
   O'Brien, Sperduto, & Goff, 1984, *11,* 149–153.
   c. Using Placements for Training
   Nish, 1979, *6,* 206–209.
   Caffrey, Berger, Cole, Marx, & Senn, 1977, *4,* 7–13.
   Shiverick, 1977, *4,* 188–190.
   Shemberg & Keeley, 1976, *3,* 118–121.

3. Describing Graduate Placements
    Ehly, Dustin, & Bratton, 1983, *10,* 222-224.
    Ritter, 1978, *5,* 148-149.
    Keller & Piotrowski, 1984, *11,* 185-186.
    Glenwick, 1980, *7,* 59-61.
4. Evaluating Programs

Morris & Haas, 1984, *11,* 166-168.
Kantrowitz, Mitchell, & Davidson II, 1982, *9,* 186-188.
Jeger & McClure, 1979, *6,* 226-228.
Yates, 1980, *7,* 8-12.
Prerost, 1981, *8,* 221-223.
Keeley & Kreutzer, 1981, *8,* 28-31.